EXCEPTIONAL CHILDREN

EXCEPTIONAL CHILDREN

An Introductory Survey of Special Education

Second Edition

WILLIAM L. HEWARD
MICHAEL D. ORLANSKY
The Ohio State University

Charles E. Merrill Publishing Company
A Bell & Howell Company
Columbus Toronto London Sydney

Published by
Charles E. Merrill Publishing Company
A Bell and Howell Company
Columbus, Ohio 43216

This book was set in Quorum
Text Design: Cynthia Brunk
Production Coordination: Linda Hillis Bayma
Cover Design: Tony Faìola
Cover photo by Bruce Johnson

Photo Credits: Susan Bolton, pp. 222, 223; John Bonvillian, p. 175; Donn Brolin, p.
511; Rich Bucurel, p. 367; Cincinnati Recreation Commission, Division of Therapeutic
Recreation, pp. 103, 319, 516; Paul Conklin, pp. 389, 412; Mike Davis, pp. 14, 434,
514; Jack Dinger, Boy Scouts of America, p. 13; Celia Drake, pp. 56, 181; Carol Egan,
p. 502; Faculty for Exceptional Children, The Ohio State University, p. 380; Mark
Freado, Pressley Ridge School, pp. 154, 161, 191; Susan Hartley, p. 170; Jerry Harvey,
p. 233; Ed Heston, pp. 89, 92; William L. Heward, pp. 59, 60, 117, 138, 242, 243,
251, 452, 490; Tom Hutchinson, pp. 5, 9, 45, 257, 278, 332, 333, 339, 447, 455,
499, 504, 505; Bruce Johnson, pp. 25, 37, 70, 76, 349, 426, 433, 467, 469, 477,
510, 519; Kurzweil Computer Products, A Xerox Company, p. 281; Freda Leinwand, p.
480; Calvin Mason, Lynchburg Training School and Hospital, p. 351; Marjorie
McEachron, Cuyahoga County Board of Mental Retardation, Cleveland, Ohio, pp. 2, 94,
198, 220, 283, 318, 329, 419, 464, 470; Irma D. McNelia, p. 437; Greg Miller, p.
402; Ohio Department of Mental Health and Retardation, p. 74; Michael D. Orlansky, p.
303; Phillips Photo Illustrators, pp. 52, 121, 130, 135, 141, 203, 310, 385; Marjorie
Pizzino, p. 335; Charles Quinlan, p. 266; Andrew Rakoczy, pp. 64, 276, *Resource
Teaching*, Charles E. Merrill, p. 168; Paul M. Schrock Photos, p. 507; Robert
Shrewsberry, p. 353; Marie Skandera, p. 84, Jan Smyth, pp. 215, 230, 241, 248, 253;
Strix Pix, pp. 17, 26, 207, 302, 372, 374, 379, 396; Tom Tondee, pp. 298, 316;
Steven C. Tuttle, p. 315; Luanna Voeltz, p. 408, Martin Wiig, p. 520.

Library of Congress Catalog Card Number: 83–43105
International Standard Book Number: 0–675–20130–6
Printed in the United States of America
        4   5   6   7   8   9   10/89   88   87   86

CONTENTS

CONTENTS

x

PREFACE

While there have been many additions, expansions, and revisions in this second edition of *Exceptional Children*, our goal in writing it remains unchanged: to present special education as the story of *people.* The participants in this story include the disabled child who is attending a regular public school; the young adult who has recently moved from a large institution into a group home in her community; the parents who seek educational services for their child; and the teacher who works with other professionals, with parents, and the child himself in planning and delivering an appropriate program of education. You will meet these people, and many others, in this book. Special education is the story of all of them. Far from being dry, dull, or pedantic, special education is a young, exciting, and rapidly changing field.

Before we prepared this revision, an extensive survey of instructors and students who had used the first edition of *Exceptional Children* was conducted. The results of the survey, along with our own experiences as teachers of an introductory survey course in special education, directed us to maintain the basic concept of our book as one that presents comprehensive, accurate, and professional information about current research and practice in the education of people with special needs. At the same time, we learned that our readers view the book's "human" perspective as equally important. We have thus again incorporated into each chapter several special features that present the firsthand stories of people with disabilities, their parents, and teachers, or that focus on attitudes or innovative, unique, or noteworthy programs. These features, we believe, lend an inviting and significant dimension to the study of exceptional individuals.

Two entirely new chapters have been added to the second edition. Chapter 12, "Multicultural Special Education," explores the ways in which students' diverse ethnic, cultural, and linguistic backgrounds may be of importance in a special education setting. Chapter 13, "Working with Parents," provides an understanding and appreciation of the involvement of parents and families of exceptional children in educational programs. Each of the 13 other chapters has been extensively revised and updated, with special emphasis upon incorporating recent research and theoretical contributions; new educational strategies, materials, and technology; and various other developments that affect the right of the exceptional child to receive an education in the least restrictive and most appropriate environment. Since the appearance of the first edition in 1980, Public Law 94–142 has been fully implemented in the United States, giving educators an opportunity to observe how the public schools, in particular, have responded to the inclusion of many children with special needs. These recent experiences, too, are reflected throughout this book.

We have maintained the book's organization around traditional categories of exceptionality, supplemented by several chapters that are generic or cross-categorical in scope. Our experience leads us to believe that most introductory students of special education find it convenient to organize information along categorical lines and that most instructors prefer to teach their survey courses accordingly. To the extent that is possible in a book of this kind, we have attempted to use terminology that is consistent with the humanity and dignity of children and adults who have special needs. We have de-emphasized such impersonal terms as "the handicapped," "the mentally retarded," and "the deaf"—those labels sometimes tend to minimize the vast differences between individuals in any given category. Instead, the more "human" words—such as "children," "students," or "people"—are used when descriptive terms are needed.

Whether you are a graduate student or an undergraduate, a regular class teacher, a special educator, or a parent, a beginner, or a person with years of experience, we hope that you will find our book informative, readable, and challenging. We would be glad to hear your reactions to the book at any time. We hope that you will continue your study and involvement with exceptional children and adults—and that you will come to know each one of them as an individual person.

ACKNOWLEDGMENTS

Many people contributed ideas, suggestions, and insights during the revision, and we are grateful to all of them. Francie Margolin, who was "present at the creation" of the first edition, continued to work closely with us as a special editor. Her interest in *Exceptional Children*, and her editorial skills, are reflected on every page.

Vicki Knight, education editor at the Charles E. Merrill Publishing Company, was instrumental in bringing about this second edition and in coordinating the constructive review process. For their valuable suggestions we thank James Van Tassell, Ball State University; A. Carol Hartman, Valdosta State College; Anne Golloway, California State University; Sheila Fox, Western Washington University; W. N. Creekmore, Northeast Louisiana University; George Fair, University of Texas; Ann Turnbull, University of Kansas; James Patton, Virginia State University; Al Prieto, Arizona State University; Ann Troutman, Memphis State University; Larry Brendtro, Augustana College; Sam Minner, Murray State University; and Dennis Fahey, Western Oregon State College. We also thank all of the special educators who participated by sharing their evaluations and comments.

Linda Bayma, senior production editor, ably managed each and every detail as the second edition moved closer to reality. Phyllis Chorpenning provided much-needed support at various stages of the book's development. And we reiterate our debt to Tom Hutchinson, who introduced us to each other and was the moving force behind the original conceptualization of this survey text in special education.

We appreciate the efforts of our colleague, Ray Swassing, in contributing Chapter 11, "Gifted and Talented Children." Dave Test has done an "exceptional" job of revising the Instructor's Manual that goes with this book. Beverley Shoemaker, who typed much of the manuscript, was again a valuable member of our team.

We add an affectionate thank you to our wives, Jill Dardig and Janice Zatzman Orlansky (both of whom are special educators), and to our children, Lee and Lynn Heward and Tamar and Robin Orlansky, for putting up with husbands and fathers who were frequently absent or preoccupied with this revision. The support and encouragement of our families helped us complete the task in good shape.

A special thanks is extended to all the people—both named and unnamed in the book—who shared their feelings, experiences, and accomplishments with us, especially in the features within each chapter. Perhaps most of all, our students over the years have taught us a great deal about how to better teach the introductory special education course. We know that their contributions have enriched this book, too.

W. L. H. & M. D. O.

EXCEPTIONAL CHILDREN

I
Introduction

1
Keys to Special Education

Educating exceptional children is an exciting, challenging, and rapidly changing career. In this introductory text, we have tried to capture for you some of the action and excitement of special education. But before we describe facts about and profiles of handicapped and gifted children, specific educational programs and instructional techniques, and some of the joys and accomplishments that can be obtained when professionals and parents work together, we need to present several concepts basic to an understanding of exceptional children and special education.

WHO ARE EXCEPTIONAL CHILDREN?

Before we can list the general characteristics of exceptional children, we must define and differentiate three terms: exceptional, handicap, and disability.

Exceptional is an inclusive term that refers to any child whose performance deviates from the norm, either below or above, to such an extent that special education programming is indicated. Thus, the term **exceptional children** would include both intellectually gifted and severely retarded children.

Terms in **boldface** are defined in the glossary.

Handicap refers to the problems and difficulties a person encounters because a physical disability or a behavioral characteristic marks him or her as different from other individuals. Handicapped is a more restrictive term than *exceptional* and does not include the gifted.

Disability is a physical problem that limits a person's ability to perform certain tasks that most other people can perform. It is basically the same as an impairment. A disabled person is not handicapped, however, unless that physical problem leads to educational, social, vocational, or other difficulties.

Exceptional children can be loosely classified as falling into one or more of the following categories:

1. Mental retardation
2. Learning disabilities

3. Behavior disorders (emotionally disturbed)
4. Communication (speech and language) disorders
5. Hearing impairments
6. Visual impairments
7. Physical and other health impairments
8. Severe handicaps
9. Gifted and talented

We will be looking at children in each of these categories in Part Two of this book. For now, though, you simply need to remember that exceptional children are more like other children than they are different. Each is an individual who needs individual attention, nurturing, and caring.

We are as diverse as the rest of the population. We can't speak with one voice, and no one can speak for us. . . . (Sharyn Duffin, 1981)

How Many Exceptional Children?

Let's take a quick look at some of the major findings of a survey of special education in the United States conducted at the request of Congress (U.S. Comptroller General, 1981).

We will define the terms used in these statistics as they become relevant; right now we simply want to get a broad look at the current picture.

☐ Nearly 4.2 million children received special education during the 1980–81 school year.

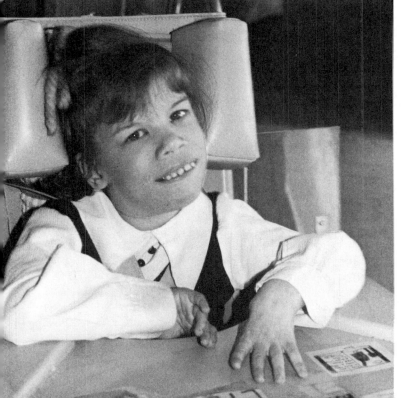

P.L. 94–142 gives first priority to previously unserved children like Lisa, who has severe handicaps.

□ The number of children receiving special education services averages about 8.5% of the school-age population.

□ The "typical" child participating in special education in public schools is 12 years old, male, and mildly handicapped.

□ Children receiving special eduation in the public schools are young—about 67% are 12 years of age or younger.

□ Twice as many males as females receive special education.

□ Of those counted under Public Law 94-142 in school year 1980–81, about 36% were learning disabled, 30% speech impaired, and 19% mentally retarded.

□ Of the children served, 13% have severe handicaps, 36% have moderately severe handicaps, and the majority, at 51%, have mild handicaps.

Stating precisely how many exceptional children live in the United States is very difficult if not impossible. In 1979, the U.S. Department of Education estimated that there were 5.8 million handicapped children age 3 to 21. If the estimates that 3% to 5% of school-age children are gifted are correct, then there are between 1,450,000 and 2,415,000 such children. However, during the 1981–82 school year, only 4.2 million children received special education services. Programs for the gifted and talented served 909,437 children (Mitchell, 1981, pp. 6–7). Table 1.1 shows the actual number of handicapped children identified and receiving services. The category labels reflect the government's classification system.

TABLE 1.1
Handicapped children receiving special education under P.L. 94-142, school year 1981–1982

	Number of Children Served, Ages 3–5	Number of Children Served, Ages 6–17	Number of Children Served, Ages 18–21	Total Number of Children Served, Ages 3–21	Percentage of All U.S. Children, Ages 5–17
Mentally retarded	17,149	610,185	71,096	698,430	1.44
Hard of hearing	2,821	27,973	2,082	32,876	.06
Deaf	2,421	13,978	1,000	17,399	.03
Speech impaired	159,678	958,590	5,941	1,124,209	2.32
Visually handicapped	1,595	16,865	2,442	20,902	.04
Emotionally disturbed	5,602	284,541	13,125	303,268	.62
Orthopedically impaired	6,503	37,031	4,924	48,458	.10
Other health impaired	3,207	68,905	4,062	76,174	.15
Learning disabled	20,287	1,538,284	49,965	1,608,536	3.33
Deaf/blind	188	1,142	80	1,410	—
Multihandicapped	8,161	45,910	4,682	58,753	.12
Total	227,612	3,603,404	159,399	3,990,415	8.26

SOURCE: "Report of Handicapped Children Receiving Special Education and Related Services" (internal report), United States Department of Education, Special Education Programs, June 22, 1982.

THE ABLE DISABLED

"Handicapism" is "Attitudes and practices that lead to unequal and unjust treatment of people with disabilities." The word "handicap," in fact, is thought to come from a time when disabled people had to beg in the streets, with cap in hand ("Avoiding Handicapist Stereotypes," 1977, p. 1). Today, an increasing number of disabled and nondisabled people are trying to overcome handicapism—to change presentations of disabled people as strange, odd, fearsome, helpless, or otherwise stereotyped. These images of the disabled are frequently found in books and TV shows for children. Does every character in the story have a name except "the blind man"? Have you ever seen a villain portrayed as hunchbacked, one-eyed, and limping? What about a dim-witted cartoon animal who constantly stutters? Some people feel that realistic presentations of disabled people are especially important, because they can encourage children to interact with exceptional people on a more "human" basis—rather than mock them, pity them, or be scared. Several organizations interested in the realistic portrayal of disabled people in children's books prepared these guidelines.

Avoiding Handicapist Stereotypes

☐ Shun one-dimensional characterizations of disabled persons. Portray people with disabilities as having individual and complex personalities and capable of a full range of emotions.

☐ Avoid depicting disabled persons only in the role of receiving; show disabled people *interacting* as equals and giving as well as receiving. Too often the handicapped person is presented solely as the recipient of pity.

☐ Avoid presenting physical characteristics of any kind as determining factors of personality. Be especially cautious about implying a correlation between disability and evil.

☐ Refrain from depicting persons with disabilities as objects of curiosity. It is entirely appropriate to show disabled people as members of an average population or cast of characters. Most disabled people are able to participate in all facets of life and should be shown in many situations.

☐ A person's disability should not be ridiculed or made the butt of a joke. (Blind people do not mistake fire hydrants for people or bump into every object in their path.)

☐ Avoid the sensational in depicting disabled people. Be wary of the stereotype of disabled persons as either the victims or perpetrators of violence.

☐ Refrain from endowing disabled characters with superhuman attributes. To do so is to imply that a disabled person must overcompensate and become superhuman to win acceptance.

☐ Avoid a Pollyanna-ish plot that implies a disabled person need only have the "will" and the "right attitude" to succeed. Young readers need insights into the societal barriers that keep disabled people from living full lives—discrimination in employment, education, and housing; inaccessible transportation and buildings; and exorbitant expense for necessities.

☐ Avoid showing disabled people as nonsexual. Show disabled people in loving relationships and expressing the same sexual needs and desires as nondisabled people.

From *Interracial Books for Children Bulletin*, 1977, *8* (6,7), p. 1. Published by Council on Interracial Books for Children, 1841 Broadway, New York, NY 10023. Used with permission.

Historically, society's response toward handicapped people has covered virtually the entire range of human reactions and emotions—from extermination, superstition, ridicule, pity, and exclusion to service, scientific study, and respect as human beings first and handicapped persons second. The history of special education is long and colorful, in itself an intriguing and illuminating study of mankind (Hewett & Forness, 1977; Patton, 1981.) In the chapters that follow, we will trace some of that history as it pertains to the different areas of special education. In this section we will take a look at two important indications of society's response to exceptionality: the ways in which exceptional children are described and classified and the legal rights of handicapped citizens.

Problems of Labeling and Classifying Exceptional Children

Centuries ago, labeling and classifying people was of little importance. Survival was the main concern. Those whose handicaps prevented their full participation in the activities necessary for survival were left on their own to perish, or in some instances, were even exterminated. In later years, derogatory labels like "dunce," "imbecile," and "fool" were applied to mentally retarded and emotionally disturbed people. Other demeaning words were often used to refer to persons with other disabilities or physical deformities. In each instance, however, the purpose of classification was the same—to *exclude* the handicapped person from the activities, privileges, and facilities of normal society.

Some educators argue that even today the classification of exceptional children functions to exclude people from normal society. Others argue that a workable system of classifying exceptional children (or their exceptional learning needs) is a prerequisite to providing the special educational programs that those children require if they are to be integrated into normal society. Some educators, in fact, believe that labeling may actually lead to better adjustment and more positive peer acceptance of the labeled child. No other aspect of special education has been more widely debated during the past several years than the classification and labeling of exceptional children. The classification of children is a complex issue, involving emotional, political, and humane considerations, in addition to scientific and educational interests. Research results shed little light on the problem; those studies which have been conducted to assess the effects of labeling have produced inconclusive, often contradictory evidence and have generally been marked by methodological weakness (MacMillan, 1982).

As with most complex, important questions, there are valid arguments on both sides. Here are some of the reasons that have been given for and against the classification and labeling of exceptional children.

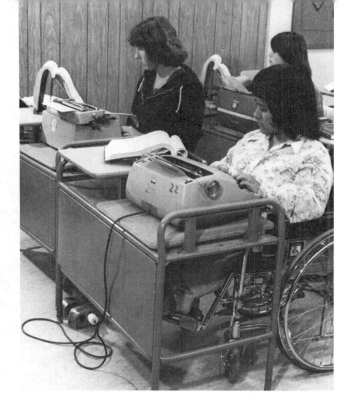

Students with disabilities are no longer excluded from regular public school programs.

Possible Benefits of Labeling

1. Categories can relate diagnosis to specific treatment.
2. Labeling may lead to a "protective" response, in which nonlabeled children accept certain behaviors of their handicapped peers more fully than they would accept those same behaviors in "normal" children (MacMillan, 1982).
3. Labeling helps professionals to communicate with one another and to classify and assess research findings.
4. Funding of special education programs is often based on specific categories of exceptionality.
5. Labels allow special interest groups to promote specific programs and spur legislative action.
6. Labeling helps make the special needs of exceptional children more visible in the public eye.

A "protective" response by nonhandicapped children toward a handicapped peer could be a disadvantage if it decreased the labeled child's chances to develop independence and learn appropriate social skills.

Possible Disadvantages of Labeling

1. Labels usually focus on negative aspects of the child, causing others to think about the child only in terms of inadequacies or defects.
2. Labels may cause others to react to and hold low expectations for a child based on the label, resulting in a self-fulfilling prophecy.

3. A labeled child might develop a poor self-concept.

4. Labels might lead peers to reject or ridicule the labeled child.

5. Special education labels have a certain permanence about them. Once labeled as "retarded" or "learning disabled," it is difficult for a child ever again to achieve the status of being "just like all the other kids."

6. Labels often provide a basis by which children can be kept out of the regular classroom.

For more on culturally diverse children, see chapter 12.

7. A disproportionate number of children from minority culture groups may be inaccurately labeled "handicapped," especially as educably mentally retarded.

As you can easily see, there are strong reasons both for and against the classification and labeling of exceptional children. In the early 1970s, the U.S. government ordered a comprehensive study of the classification of exceptional children. This 2-year project involved 93 psychologists, educators, lawyers, and parents working on 31 different task forces. The results of this extensive and carefully done project can be found in *Issues in the classification of children, Vols. I and II,* under the editorship of the project's director, Nicholas Hobbs (Hobbs, 1976a, 1976b). A third book, *The futures of children* (Hobbs, 1975), summarizes the findings and recommendations of the project. These important works are available for anyone who wants to understand fully all the perspectives surrounding this complex issue. Other sensitive and well-documented reviews of labeling and classification of exceptional children can be found in MacMillan (1977) and Smith, Neisworth, and Hunt (1983). None of these discussions has produced conclusive arguments that could lead to the total acceptance or absolute rejection of the practice of labeling.

What we *can* say about the possible benefits of classifying exceptional children is that most of those benefits are experienced not by individual children, but rather by groups of children, parents, and professionals who are associated with a certain category. On the other hand, the negative aspects of labeling all affect the individual child who has been labeled. Of the possible advantages of labeling we listed, only the first two could be said to benefit an individual child. And the argument that labels associate diagnosis with proper treatment is tenuous at best, particularly when you consider the kinds of labels used in special education today.

> The children are given various labels including deaf, blind, orthopedically handicapped, trainable mentally retarded, educable mentally retarded, autistic, socially maladjusted, perceptually handicapped, brain-injured, emotionally disturbed, disadvantaged, and those with learning disabilities. For the most part the labels are not important. They rarely tell the teacher who can be taught in what way. One could put five or six labels on the same child and still not know what to teach him or how. (Becker, Engelmann, & Thomas, 1971, pp. 435–436)

Alternative Classification Systems for Special Education

Classification is a necessary activity for virtually all disciplines, special education included. Classification helps create order out of a mass of facts and events; it allows communication and research to be more systematic. Traditional classification systems in special education have been based largely on a medical model, a system which focuses on real or assumed physical or psychological *defects* of the child. As a result, most labels used to identify exceptional children are negative and often produce the stigma and other disadvantages we discussed earlier. But an equally strong criticism of these classification systems is that they are not educationally relevant. Knowing that a child is classified as "mentally retarded" does not indicate what specific skills he needs to learn nor how he can best be taught those skills.

Recently, some efforts have been made to devise and use special education classification systems that are based on educationally relevant variables (Iscoe & Payne, 1972; Quay, 1968; Stevens, 1962). For example, in Iscoe and Payne's (1972) system, children are assessed and classified along three basic dimensions, each of which is further broken down into three subcomponents:

1. Physical status
   a. Visibility of physical deviation
   b. **Locomotion** capabilities and limitations
   c. Communication capabilities and problems
2. Adjustment status
   a. Peer acceptance
   b. Family interaction
   c. Self-esteem
3. Educational status
   a. Motivation
   b. Academic achievement
   c. Educational potential

Using this system, a child's status is assessed and recorded in each of these nine areas. Each area is educationally relevant; that is, each suggests, or leads to, educational strategies tailored to that child's individual needs. There is an important difference between a classification scheme like this one and traditional systems. Traditional classification systems are based on either how a child deviates from normal or on some (actual or presumed) cause of the child's problem. Iscoe and Payne's system is based instead on an objective assessment of the child's current performance on educationally meaningful characteristics.

While none of the proposed alternative classification systems has been widely adopted yet, the development of educationally based classification systems for exceptional children promises to suggest appropriate education programs for children and to promote objective communication and research efforts by professionals without resulting in the negative labeling of children.

LEGISLATION AFFECTING EXCEPTIONAL CHILDREN

The 14th Amendment to the United States Constitution guarantees equal protection under the law for all citizens. Yet it has required a long series of court cases and federal legislation to make "equal protection" with respect to education a reality for the almost 6,000,000 handicapped children in this country. Closely related to the civil rights movement of the 1950s and 1960s, a "civil rights movement for the handicapped" has resulted in legislation guaranteeing that exceptional children can no longer be denied appropriate educational services.

A discussion of the many court cases and laws pertaining to exceptional children is far beyond the scope and intent of this book. (LaVor, 1976, reports that 36 federal bills which affected the handicapped and gifted were passed by Congress in 1974 alone. See Table 2.1, page 28, for an outline of some of the major court cases and legislation that have affected the education of exceptional children.) Instead, we will focus our attention on Public Law 94–142, the Education for All Handicapped Children Act, which became law in 1975. P.L. 94–142 has been called landmark legislation. It is the culmination of the efforts of a great many educators, parents, and legislators to bring together in one comprehensive bill this country's laws regarding the education of handicapped children. The law reflects our current concern with treating handicapped people—including children—as full citizens with the same rights and privileges as all other citizens.

A basic understanding of P.L. 94–142 is central to understanding many of the changes and trends in special education today. The major features of the law are: (1) a free, appropriate public education must be provided for all handicapped children; (2) school systems must provide protective safeguards to protect the rights of handicapped children and their parents; (3) handicapped children must be educated with nonhandicapped children to the maximum extent possible; (4) an individualized education program (IEP) must be developed and implemented for each handicapped child; and (5) parents of handicapped children are to play an active role in the process used to make any educational decision about their handicapped children.

We will discuss each of these features of P.L. 94–142 in chapter 2.

We will look at the relationship between educators and parents in depth in chapter 13.

INTERVENTION

Intervention is a general name for all of the efforts we make on behalf of handicapped people. The overall goal of intervention is to eliminate, or at least reduce, the obstacles that keep a handicapped person from full and active participation in society.

There are three basic kinds of intervention efforts: *preventive* (keeping possible problems from becoming serious handicaps), *remedial* (overcoming handicaps through training or education), and *compensatory* (giving the handicapped person new ways of dealing with his or her disability).

Preventive efforts are most promising when they begin early in life—even before birth in many cases. In later chapters, we will explore some of the exciting new methods available for preventing handicaps—methods such as genetic counseling, amniocentesis, and screening early in infancy for metabolic disorders and other conditions that produce disabilities. We'll explore, too, the efforts being made in social and educational programs to stimulate infants and very

SCOUTING FOR HANDICAPPED YOUTH

Ever since its founding in 1910, the Boy Scouts of America (BSA) has had fully participating handicapped members. Since 1970, however, the BSA has conducted a major campaign to include handicapped youth in Scouting programs. Today, close to 60,000 handicapped boys are members of special Scout units, and an additional 125,000 handicapped youth are full members of regular Scout units.

Advancement

The basic premise is that the boy with a handicap wants most to be like other boys—and Scouting gives him that chance. Thus, we work to encourage the inclusion of handicapped boys into the regular Cub pack, Scout troop, or Explorer post. Scouts with handicaps participate in exactly the same program as do their peers. They must meet the same requirements as others, with one exception—there is a special advancement track

Scouting provides opportunities for learning and friendship.

Quotations and photographs courtesy of Boy Scouts of America.

and a series of badges for moderately mentally retarded Boy Scouts that takes them to a special award equivalent to First Class. The purpose is to keep the handicapped Scout as much in the mainstream as possible. Thus, a Scout in a wheelchair can meet a hiking requirement by propelling himself or a camping requirement that he carry his pack by transporting that pack when he goes in his wheelchair. Giving more time and permitting the use of special aids are other ways leaders can help handicapped Scouts in their efforts to advance. All age restrictions on advancement by severely handicapped Scouts have been removed. Thus, Cub Scouts over 11, Boy Scouts over 18, and Explorers over 21 may continue to advance at their own pace.

Functional Skills in the Classroom

The BSA also has a program of Skill Awards that can be used in the classroom. There are Skill Awards for First Aid, Cooking, Physical Fitness, Family Living, Community Living, and Communications. Requirements for each Skill Award are described in 32-page, high interest, low reading level student booklets. A leader's manual provides teachers with activities for helping children learn the skills. Both boys and girls can participate, though only boys are registered as members of BSA. A colorful metal belt loop is awarded to each student who masters the required skills.

Many special education teachers have found that the Scouting materials match their desire to teach functional daily living skills and that the Skill Awards are effective incentives for students. Information on Scouting programs and materials for handicapped children can be obtained from:

Education Relationships
Boy Scouts of America
1325 Walnut Hill Lane
Irving, Texas 75062

Graduation day!

See chapter 14, which focuses on these and other early intervention efforts.

young children to acquire skills that most children learn normally, without special help.

Unfortunately, prevention programs have only just begun to affect the number and severity of handicaps in this country. And some researchers estimate that it will take well into the 21st century before we are able to reduce handicaps by even a small percentage (Hayden & Pious, 1979). In the meantime, we must count on remedial and compensatory efforts to help handicapped people achieve fuller and more independent lives.

Remedial programs are supported largely by educational institutions and social agencies. In fact, the word **remediation** is primarily an educational term; the word **rehabilitation** is used more often by social service agencies. Both have a common purpose—to teach the handicapped person basic skills needed for independence. In school, those skills may be academic (reading, writing, speaking, computing), social (getting along with other children, following instructions, schedules, and other daily routines), or even personal (feeding, dressing, using the toilet without assistance). More and more, schools are also teaching career and job skills, to prepare exceptional youngsters for jobs as adults in the community. In so doing, they are sharing more of the responsibilities that social service agencies have historically accepted. Vocational training, or **vocational rehabilitation,** includes preparation to develop work habits and work attitudes, as well as specific training at a particular skill like auto mechanics, carpentry, or assembly-line work (Flexer & Martin, 1978).

The underlying assumption of both remedial and habilitative programs is that handicapped people need special help if they are to succeed in the "normal" world. Whenever possible, this special help is designed to teach handicapped people the same skills that nonhandicapped people have, only through different or more intensive methods than nonhandicapped people use.

Still another approach, however, is to compensate for a handicapped person's loss or disability by giving him a kind of substitute skill, device, or setting on which to rely. An example of this kind of compensatory effort can be seen

INTRODUCTION

with physically disabled children. A child with cerebral palsy can still be trained to make maximum use of her hands, but the use of a headstick and a template placed over a regular typewriter may effectively compensate for lack of muscle control by letting her type instead of writing lessons by hand. (Of course, the device itself implies that training is also needed—she will have to learn to type with the headstick). The point here is that compensatory efforts aim to give the handicapped person some kind of asset that normal individuals do not need, whether it be a device like a headstick or special training like mobility instruction for a blind child.

The Professional's Role

Something else is evident when we look at the ways we work with handicapped students. To be successful, intervention must involve specialists from many professional disciplines. Without the physician and medical researcher, most of our current knowledge about the causes and prevention of many handicaps would not exist. Moreover, the physician is the one professional who has early and continued contact with the handicapped infant and the family. It is often the family doctor who must be relied on to recognize early enough the conditions or symptoms that indicate a handicap. In addition to the family doctor, hospitals house a wide variety of professionals who serve handicapped clients. Physical therapists, occupational therapists, speech-language pathologists, psychiatrists, and psychologists are among these.

In later chapters, we will discuss some of the serious effects that a deprived or impoverished environment can have on how children grow and learn. Thus, the social worker who visits the home of a handicapped child may play a critical role in identifying the child as handicapped, in referring the parents to places where they can get special help for their child, and in making certain that a lack of money does not prevent the parents from getting that help. In the same way, others who may observe children before school age—day-care workers, preschool teachers, nurses—can be watchful for the child who may have special needs.

Beyond the contributions that social welfare professionals can make, social service agencies offer their handicapped clients both vocational training and, in many cases, job placement. In addition, social service agencies often help support special job settings called **sheltered workshops,** where severely handicapped adults can work in less demanding but still productive settings. Moreover, state vocational rehabilitation agencies generally provide funds to support handicapped adults' living expenses while they are training, to provide tools needed for certain jobs, to give support for medical expenses, and to provide continued counseling and guidance after the individual begins a job.

Sheltered workshops and other life-style options for handicapped adults are discussed in chapter 15.

The Educator's Role

A major goal of this book, in addition to introducing you to exceptional children and their special needs, is to focus on the educational programs and classroom strategies that are available for those children. At no other time in the life of a handicapped person do more people have more opportunities and resources with which to intervene than during the school years. Regular classroom and special teachers—supported by administrators, school psychologists, speech and language specialists, classroom aides, and other school personnel—bear the primary responsibility for helping exceptional children learn in spite of their differences and special needs. To the children they work with, these teachers may seem no different than any of the other students' teachers. But to the parents and the other people in the school, professionals who work with exceptional children are indeed "special educators."

WHAT IS SPECIAL EDUCATION?

For many years, the notion of special education usually held at least one common meaning from one school to the next. Regardless of the child's handicap, *special* meant "separate." The early history of special education is largely a history of separate schools, especially for children who were blind, deaf, or mentally retarded. In the public schools, children who could not succeed—or more to the point, children who failed miserably—were taken out of one classroom and put in another. Perhaps the child's schoolwork was clearly much poorer than that of his classmates, or possibly he was so "naughty" that his disruptions interfered with the orderly progress of the class activities. Whatever the problem, the solution was to put him (and more often the pupils were, in fact, boys) in a class with other children who were having similar troubles in school.

This is not to suggest that the only reason for separating these children was that they disrupted the class or frustrated their teachers. It was also obvious that something significantly different had to be done for them if their school years were to be at all productive. Sometimes, the teachers in these "special" classes were no more experienced or no more capable than the teachers in the classrooms the children had left. But if they did not give up in frustration, these teachers developed a strong sense of themselves as professionals with special methods for helping children learn.

Looking back, it seems easy enough to see that this separation of exceptional children was part of a larger social response to exclude handicapped people from the mainstream of society. But it was not without its advantages as well. First of all, most people in the school recognized the added challenge of teaching these children, and classes were generally kept smaller. Instead of 25 or 30 children, a separate special education class might have only half that many children. Second (and certainly related to the smaller class size), instruction in the special class tended to be more individualized. Children from several different grades usually were collected in a single room; though none of them may have been successful in their previous rooms, some were clearly at more advanced levels than others. These differences, plus the very individual problems of the children, meant that instruction had to be more or less tailored to fit each child's current level of performance and estimated potential.

And so "separate" became only one of the meanings associated with special education. In fact, what came to be as significant as the placement of the

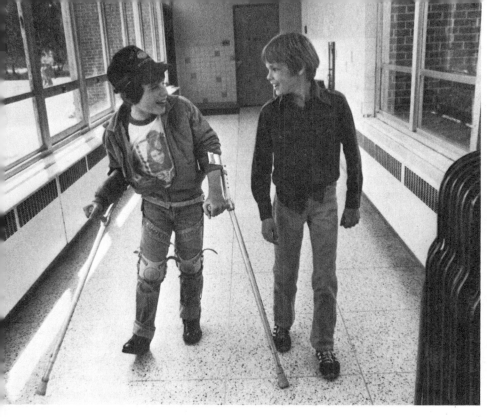

Mainstreaming affords the opportunity for new friendships.

child in a given room was the idea that in that room he could receive a specially arranged and individually planned series of learning activities (sometimes alone, sometimes with other children). Those activities would allow him to improve more rapidly than he had in the classroom where he had been before. This became a kind of ideal for special education, if not necessarily the reality in every special classroom.

But as society's response to handicapped people gradually began to shift away from exclusion and more toward acceptance and integration, critics of special classes began to express doubt that separation offered any particular merits (Connor, 1968; Dunn, 1968; Johnson, 1969).

> The overwhelming evidence is that our present and past practices (of creating separate special classes) have their major justification in removing pressures on regular teachers and pupils at the expense of the . . . slow learning pupils themselves. (Dunn, 1968)

As we shall note in chapter 2 when we examine school practices more closely, this shift in attitude evolved into the belief that children in separate classes should again be integrated with their nonhandicapped peers in the regular classroom. This reintegration, or **mainstreaming** as it has been called, took on some of the force of a popular movement, and many of the more vocal backers of the mainstreaming effort read Public Law 94–142 to mean that mainstreaming had become the law of the land. Of course, the law's provision for placing handicapped children in the "least restrictive environment" was never meant as an order to relocate every handicapped child in a regular classroom, but it clearly supports the idea that handicapped children should not be kept out of the mainstream of normal school life simply because of their disabilities.

What then, is special education? In one sense, it is a profession, with its own tools, techniques, and research efforts, all focused on improving instructional arrangements and procedures for evaluating and meeting the learning needs of exceptional children and adults. At a more practical level, special education is the individually planned and systematically monitored arrangement of physical settings, special equipment and materials, teaching procedures and the other interventions designed to help exceptional children achieve the greatest possible personal self-sufficiency and academic success.

OUR PERSONAL VIEW OF SPECIAL EDUCATION

We have tried throughout this chapter to give you a clear and objective explanation of some of the basic concepts that combine to make up special education. We recognize, of course, that our own views of the field and of exceptional children are surely implicit in our words—between the lines, as they say. But we believe we owe you an even clearer statement of what we have already implied. Though we do not necessarily expect you to agree with us, we want you to know that our views affect both the substance and the tone of the remaining chapters.

1. We believe that handicapped people have the right to live and participate in settings that are as normal as possible, that they have the right to as much independence as we can help them to achieve, and that our society's current support and development of services for handicapped people ought to continue to grow.

2. We believe that education and the other helping professions must recognize the needs of all handicapped people, including the very young and the adult, as well as the school-aged child. And so we have included chapters on each of these age ranges and have tried to outline ways the profession is beginning to meet the needs of the handicapped members of these groups.

3. We believe that effective intervention for handicapped people can progress only if efforts cut across all of the disciplines in the helping professions— and into the community as well. As educators, we see our primary responsibility in improving instruction in all areas—personal, social, and vocational as well as academic. But we consider it foolish to argue over territorial rights when we can accomplish more by working with other professionals in medicine, psychology, the social services, and vocational rehabilitation.

4. We believe that professionals have for too long ignored the needs of the parents and families of exceptional children, treating them more as patients

or adversaries than as clients, consumers of services, or co-workers. We believe that we have too often given the impression that parents were there to serve professionals, when in fact the opposite is more correct. We believe that we have long neglected to recognize parents as a child's first—and in many ways best—teachers. We believe that no really successful intervention program can fail to involve parents who want to take part in their child's education.

5. We believe that teachers must demand effectiveness from their instructional approaches and that the best way to evaluate instructional effectivenss is through direct observation and measurement of each child's performance of the skills being taught.

6. Finally, we are essentially optimistic about the futures of handicapped children. That is to say, we have enough confidence in their potentials to affirm that they can succeed in building fuller and more independent lives in the community. We believe that we have only begun to discover the ways to improve teaching, to increase learning, to prevent handicapping conditions, to encourage acceptance, and to develop technology to compensate for disabilities. And while we make no predictions for the future, we are certain that we have not come as far as we can in helping exceptional individuals to help themselves.

WHAT SHOULD WE CALL THEM?

In this article, Tom Lovitt, a Professor of special education at the University of Washington, offers his views about how to refer to the exceptional children who will be entering regular classes because of new federal and state laws.

"What should we call the special children who are sent to our classes?" This question might be asked by regular education teachers who are about to have special education children mainstreamed in their classes. Should they carefully study the dossiers of the children to figure out what others have called them? Should a regular teacher, for instance, try to remember that Roy, who will soon be sent to his regular class, was called *emotionally disturbed* by two school psychologists, a social worker, and a reading teacher (even though he was referred to as *learning disabled* by another school psychologist)? Should he hang onto the fact that Amy was called *mentally retarded* by most of the people who wrote reports for her folder? Likewise, should he make every effort to recall that Tim was most often referred to as *learning disabled*?

No. Those labels do not help teachers design effective programs for the special children they will teach. They won't help teachers decide where to seat the children; they certainly won't help them to design educational and management strategies.

But if regular teachers shouldn't call them mentally retarded, etc., why did the special teachers and others do so? Good question. I'm not certain how the labeling business as we know it today got started, but even special education teachers will admit (most of them at least) that the labels have not helped them to teach children to read, write, or cipher, or to behave more appropriately.

But if we shouldn't refer to these special children by using those old labels, then how should we refer to them? What should we call them? For openers, call them Roy, Amy, and Tim. Beyond that, refer to them on the basis of what you're trying to teach them. For example, if a teacher wants to teach Roy to compute, read, and comprehend, he might call him a student of computation, reading, and comprehension. We do this all the time with older students. Sam, who attends Juilliard, is referred to as "the trumpet student"; Jane, who attends Harvard, is called "the law student."

But categories can be useful to regular teachers with special children; we shouldn't do away with all categories simply because the current system doesn't help. It seems to me that most of these children fall into one of five categories or have characteristics of more than one of the categories. Many children share doses of several of the various types, but there are some "purees." Let me elaborate a bit.

What to Call Them?

Slow Academically

A great majority of the first wave of children to be sent back into the mainstream are having problems in the basic skills, more often than not in reading. Many of them are good citizens and highly motivated, but for some reason or other they can't read, spell, or write as well as some people think they should.

Poorly Motivated

These are the children who could do certain things but they don't want to. On one day a child of this type can finish his arithmetic assignment, but he won't do it the next. He's the one who never gets a thrill out of learning, the one who moans and groans each time he is asked to do something. Not that they don't have enough of these children already, but with the advent of mainstreaming, regular teachers will receive dozens of these youngsters.

Naughty Behaviors

Perhaps the main reason for evicting youngsters from regular classes in the past was because of their naughty behaviors—professionally referred to as "inappropriate behaviors." Hundreds of children were sent from regular to special classes because they talked out of turn too often or popped out of their chairs more times than they should. Other children, of course, were dismissed from regular classes because of more irksome behaviors: they hit, lied, stole, threatened, or defiled.

Poor Endurance

Some children who could perform many academic tasks, were good citizens, and were reasonably well motivated were still sent to special classes. They are the youngsters who can't sit still and don't finish their tasks. They shift from one activity to another very rapidly. Although they might do well on their arithmetic or spelling assignments as long as they work, they seem to be distracted by almost any object and sound. If someone comes into the room or simply passes by outside, they drop everything and focus on the visitor. Or if they hear a paper or pencil rustle to the floor, they attend to the noise.

Special Equipment

Many children have been sent to special classes because they need special equipment or a special type of instruction. In fact, the first children who were sent from regular classes were dismissed for these reasons. They were the youngsters classified as deaf, blind, and orthopedically handicapped.

Conclusion

Regular teachers cannot take their responsibilities lightly now that many special children will be returning to their classes. And I'm certain they won't. Neither should they be overly concerned about their new pupils, for in the past many regular teachers have dealt with pupils a lot like the ones they will receive. The difference is that now those pupils are returning with labels like *mentally retarded* and *emotionally disturbed* and *learning disabled*. When they left, they were referred to as *naughty* and *slow*.

Teachers must forget about these labels and go about the business of designing individualized programs. To do so, they should continue using the practices that have been successful in the past and be prepared to add to their repertoires when they need to.

Excerpted from T. Lovitt, What should we call them? *Exceptional Teacher,* 1979, 1(1), 5–7 Reprinted with permission of Special Press.

SUMMARY

1. Special education serves exceptional children, whose early development or school performance indicate a need for special programming.
   a. This includes both gifted and talented children and those who have difficulties because of their delays or differences from other people.
   b. The number of exceptional children is hard to determine, but it has been estimated to be 12% of all children from birth to 19 years old.
   c. A little more than 8% of the school-age population is currently receiving special education services.
2. Society's response toward handicapped persons has ranged from extermination to respect. Our current response is reflected in our labeling and classification systems.
   a. Current labeling practices may have administrative and political benefits, but seem to have a negative effect on the individual child who is labeled.
   b. Classification systems are generally based on deviation from "normal" or on supposed "causes" of handicapping conditions.
   c. New proposed classification systems are based on educational characteristics of individual children.
3. A relatively new federal law, P.L. 94–142, the Education for All Handicapped Children Act, reflects today's concern with treating handicapped children as full citizens with all the rights of other citizens.
4. There are three kinds of intervention efforts: preventive, remedial, and compensatory.
   a. Most educational programs are either remedial, to teach basic necessary skills that everyone needs, or compensatory, to teach a substitute skill needed to overcome a specific disability.
   b. Effective intervention requires the cooperation of many different professionals, including educators, medical professionals, social welfare workers, and vocational rehabilitation professionals.
5. Special education is a profession focused on improving instructional arrangements and procedures for teaching exceptional children and adults.
6. To be successful, special education programs must involve parents as much as possible.
7. The best way to evaluate instructional effectiveness is through direct observation and measurement of the child's performance of the skill being taught.
8. Handicapped people are people first, children and adults who happen to have special needs. They have the same rights as the rest of us, and deserve to have as much independence as we can help them to achieve. To do so, we must work along with other professionals and with parents.

Books

Orlansky, M. D., & Heward, W. L. *Voices: Interviews with handicapped people.* Columbus, Ohio: Charles E. Merrill, 1981.

Payne, J. S., Patton, J. R., Kauffman, J. M., Brown, G. B., & Payne, R. A. *Exceptional children in focus,* 3rd ed. Columbus, Ohio: Charles E. Merrill, 1983.

Organizations

The Council for Exceptional Children, 1920 Association Drive, Reston, VA 22091. Includes over 70,000 teachers, teacher educators, administrators, and other professionals involved in educating exceptional children and adults.

2

The Promise and the Challenge

Special education is a new and exciting field. There have always been handicapped and gifted children, but attention has not always been given to their special needs. The inclusion of exceptional children into regular public schools is a relatively recent phenomenon; for many years, special education simply did not exist. It has been written that "societies can be judged by the way in which they treat those who are different"—and according to this criterion, our society has usually not distinguished itself (Fiske, 1976).

In the past, many handicapped children were entirely excluded from any publicly supported program of education. Some children were totally neglected and hidden away; others were abused and exploited. On the other hand, some children were educated by devoted parents or teachers. In many communities, there were no facilities or services whatsoever to help exceptional children and their families.

Children with mild to moderate learning and behavior problems and children with special gifts and talents, were usually treated like all other children—in the regular classrooms. They were often labeled "disciplinary problems" and suspended from school or called "ineducable" or "slow learners" if they did not make satisfactory academic progress. Children with severe and profound disabilities and many with visual, hearing, physical, and health impairments were generally placed in institutions or kept at home. Many of them—if they survived—received no education at all. Gifted and talented children, it was felt, would be able to "make it on their own" without special help.

As Reynolds and Rosen (1976) observe, exceptional children have come a long way: from silent neglect to participation in local schools. This progress reflects the expansion of the concepts of equality, freedom, and justice. The fact that a child is "different from the norm" is no longer regarded as a valid reason to deprive that child of the opportunity to grow, learn, and develop as much as he or she is able to.

The full extension of educational services to exceptional children has involved immense changes—for "special" educators, "regular" educators, parents, and many other people. Earlier in this century, when local public schools began to accept a measure of responsibility for the education of certain exceptional students, a philosophy of segregation usually prevailed, a philosophy that continued unchanged until recently. Children received labels, such as *mentally retarded, crippled,* or *emotionally disturbed* and were mainly confined to isolated "special classrooms." One special education teacher describes the sense of isolation she felt, and the crude facilities in which her special class operated:

> In the 1960s I accepted my first teaching position, a special education class in a basement room next door to the furnace. Of the 15 "educable mentally retarded" children assigned to work with me, most were simply nonreaders from poor families. One child had been banished to my room because she posed a behavior problem to her fourth-grade teacher.
>
> My class and I were assigned a recess spot on the opposite side of the play yard, far away from the "normal" children. I was the only teacher who did not have a lunch break. I was required to eat with my "retarded" children while other teachers were permitted to leave their students. . . . Isolated from my colleagues, I closed my door and did my thing, oblivious to the larger educational circles in which I was immersed. Although it was the basement room, with all the negative perceptions that arrangement implies, I was secure in the knowledge that despite the ignominy of it all I did good things for children who were previously unloved and untaught. (Aiello, 1976)

Sebine enjoys reading in her free time.

We will be looking at these concepts in depth later in this chapter.

A "quiet revolution" is occurring in our schools today (Weintraub & Abeson, 1974). We can no longer regard exceptional children as beyond the responsibility of their local public schools. Recent legislation and court decisions have confirmed that the exceptional child, no less than any other citizen, has the right to a *free, appropriate program of public education in the "least restrictive" learning environment possible*. This means that most handicapped students will spend at least part of their school day in regular classrooms, alongside their nonhandicapped peers. Other students will receive an appropriate education in special classes within regular public schools and will have some contact with nonhandicapped students. Still other students, who may not be able to attend regular public schools, will receive a specially designed program of education within a special school, institution, hospital, or perhaps at home.

Whatever the setting, each handicapped child must have an **individualized education program (IEP)** that is developed especially to suit his or her abilities and needs. Special educators, regular educators, and parents need no longer be in an "us" and "them" relationship, but can work together to individualize instruction, manage behavior, and plan cooperatively to meet the needs of their students. For the schools, this quiet revolution has enormous consequences, many of which we will examine in this chapter.

LEGAL BACKGROUND: SPECIAL EDUCATION AS CIVIL RIGHTS

The recent provision of educational opportunities to handicapped children in the public schools did not come about by chance. Many laws and court cases, reflecting the issues and conflicts of our times, have had important effects on the education of exceptional children. Table 2.1 summarizes important laws and judicial cases that have influenced special education.

"I'll read this part to you . . ."

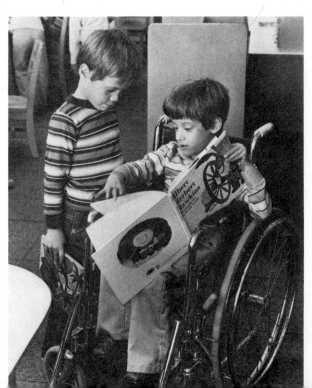

The concept of educating handicapped children in regular public schools can be considered an outgrowth of the civil rights movement. It was strongly influenced by social developments and court decisions in the 1950s and 1960s especially by the landmark case of *Brown* v. *Board of Education of Topeka* (1954). This case challenged the then-existing practice of segregating schools according to the race of the children. The U.S. Supreme Court declared that education must be made available to *all* children on equal terms, noting that:

> Today, education is perhaps the most important function of state and local governments. Compulsory school attendance laws and the great expenditure for education both demonstrate our recognition of the importance of education to our democratic society. It is required in the performance of our most basic responsibilities. . . . *In these days, it is doubtful that any child may reasonably be expected to succeed in life if he is denied the opportunity of an education.*

The *Brown* decision, and the ensuing extension of public school education to black and white children on equal terms, began a period of intense concern and questioning among parents of handicapped children. Did not the same principles of equal access to education apply to their children as well? Many cases brought by parents and other advocates of handicapped children expressed their growing dissatisfaction with school procedures that resulted in the segregation of handicapped students, or the denial of educational programs to them. Generally, the parents based their arguments on the 14th Amendment to the Constitution, which provides that no state shall deny any person within its jurisdiction the equal protection of the law, and that no state shall deprive any person of life, liberty, or property without **due process** of law. The concepts of equal protection and due process are of such fundamental importance in special education today that it is worthwhile to examine them in some detail.

Equal Protection

In the past, children with disabilities usually received "differential treatment." That is, they were excluded from certain educational programs or were given "special" education in segregated settings. Basically, the courts have examined whether or not such treatment is *rational* and whether or not it is *necessary* (Williams, 1977). One of the most important cases to examine these questions in regard to handicapped children is the *Pennsylvania Association for Retarded Children* v. *Commonwealth of Pennsylvania* (1972). The association (PARC) challenged a state law which denied public school education to certain children who were then considered "unable to profit from public school attendance."

The lawyers and parents supporting PARC argued that, though the children had intellectual disabilities, it was neither rational nor necessary to assume that they were ineducable and untrainable. And the state was not able to prove that the children were, in fact, ineducable and untrainable, or to demonstrate a rational basis for excluding them from public school programs. The court decided that the children were entitled to receive a free, public education. In ad-

TABLE 2.1

Court cases and legislation affecting education of exceptional children

Court cases

1954 — *Brown* v. *Topeka Board of Education* (Kansas)
Established the right of all children to an equal opportunity to an education.

1967 — *Hobson* v. *Hansen* (Washington, D.C.)
Declared the track system, which used standardized tests as a basis for special education placement, unconstitutional because it discriminated against black and poor children.

1970 — *Diana* v. *State Board of Education* (California)
Declared that children cannot be placed in special education on the basis of culturally biased tests or tests given in other than the child's native language.

1972 — *Mills* v. *Board of Education of the District of Columbia*
Established the right of every child to an equal opportunity for education; declared that lack of funds was not an acceptable excuse for lack of educational opportunity.

1972 — *Pennsylvania Association for Retarded Citizens* v. *the Commonwealth of Pennsylvania*
Class action suit to establish the right to free public education for all retarded children.

1972 *Wyatt* v. *Stickney* (Alabama)
Declared that individuals in state institutions have the right to appropriate treatment within those institutions.

1979 — *Central York District* v. *Commonwealth of Pennsylvania Department of Education*
Ruled that school districts must provide services for gifted and talented children whether or not advance guarantee of reimbursement from the state has been received.

1979 — *Larry P.* v. *Riles* (California) (first brought to court in 1972)
Ruled that IQ tests cannot be used as the sole basis for placing children in special classes.

1979 *Armstrong* v. *Kline* (Pennsylvania)
Established right of some severely handicapped children to an extension of the 180-day public school year.

1982 *Rowley* v. *Hendrik Hudson School District* (New York)
First case based on P.L. 94–142 to reach the U.S. Supreme Court. While denying plaintiff's specific request, upheld each handicapped child's right to a personalized program of instruction and necessary supportive services.

Legislation

1958 P.L. 85–926 *National Defense Education Act*
Provided funds for training professionals to train teachers of mentally retarded children.

1961 P.L. 87–276 *Special Education Act*
Provided funds for training professionals to train teachers of deaf children.

1963 P.L. 88–164 *Mental Retardation Facility and Community Center Construction Act*
Extended support given in P.L. 85–926 to training teachers of other handicapped children, as well as mentally retarded children.

1965 P.L. 89–10 *The Elementary and Secondary Education Act*
Provided money to states and local districts for developing programs for economically disadvantaged and handicapped children.

1966 P.L. 89–313 *Amendment to Title I of The Elementary and Secondary Education Act*
Provided funding for state-supported programs in institutions and other settings for handicapped children.

1966 P.L. 89–750 *Amendments to the Elementary and Secondary Education Act*
Created the Bureau of Education for the Handicapped.

1969 P.L. 91–320 *The Learning Disabilities Act*
Defined learning disabilities; provided funds for state-level programs for children with learning disabilities.

1970 P.L. 91–230 *Amendments to the Elementary and Secondary Education Act*
Recognized handicapped and exceptional children as a single population with special needs.

1973 P.L. 93–112, Section 504 *Rehabilitation Act* (actually adopted in 1977)
Declared that handicapped people cannot be excluded from any program or activity receiving federal funds on the basis of the handicap alone.

1974 P.L. 93–380 *Education Amendments*
Extended previous legislation; provided money to state and local districts for programs

INTRODUCTION

TABLE 2.1 (continued)

	for gifted and talented students for the first time. Also protected rights of handicapped children and parents in placement decisions.
1975	P.L. 94–103 *Developmental Disabilities Assistance and Bill of Rights Act*
	Affirmed rights of mentally retarded citizens and cited areas where services must be provided for retarded and other developmentally disabled people.
1975	P.L. 94–142 *Education for All Handicapped Children Act*
	Mandated free, appropriate public education for all handicapped children regardless of degree of severity of handicap; protected rights of handicapped children and parents in educational decision making; required that an individualized education program (IEP) be developed for each handicapped child, and that handicapped students receive educational services in the least restrictive environment.
1978	P.L. 95–561 *Gifted and Talented Children's Education Act*
	Provided financial incentives for states and local education agencies to identify and educate gifted and talented students, for in-service training, and for research.

dition, the court maintained that the children's parents had the right to be notified before any change was made in their child's educational program, and that certain procedures known as *due process* of law must be followed to ensure that parents are fully and fairly informed.

The wording of the PARC decision is particularly interesting, not only for its influence on subsequent federal legislation, but also for its recognition of the particular learning needs of exceptional children:

> It is the Commonwealth's obligation to place each mentally retarded child in a free, public program of education and training appropriate to the child's capacity. . . . [P]lacement in a regular public school class is preferable to placement in a special public school class and placement in a special public school is preferable to placement in any other type of program of education and training. An assignment to homebound instruction shall be re-evaluated not less than every 3 months, and notice of the evaluation and an opportunity for a hearing thereon shall be accorded to the parent or guardian.

Due Process

In the past, handicapped students (and some nonhandicapped students as well) were not always considered "people" in the eyes of the law. Several recent laws and court decisions, however, have clearly established that students are, indeed, people, entitled to exercise such rights as privacy, freedom of travel, the practice of religion, and "personal rights," such as choosing their own clothing and hair styles. While school officials may enforce reasonable regulations, they may *not* operate unfairly or arbitrarily, and they do not have absolute authority over their students.

The extension of due process of law to exceptional students is a broad concept that cannot be reduced to a simple step-by-step procedure. It is constantly changing as the values and priorities of our society change. An important element of due process is the acknowledgment of a student as a person, with important rights and responsibilities. Some people have questioned why highly specific legal safeguards are necessary to protect the rights of handicapped children—aren't they protected by the same laws and due process procedures that apply to all citizens? But a review of how handicapped children were treated by schools (and by society in general) in the past shows that our laws and legal procedures were often not equally applied to handicapped people. Meyen (1978) cited five reasons why specific legal safeguards for handicapped children are necessary:

1. Once placed in a special education program, many handicapped children remained there for the rest of their educational careers. Such a system permanently excludes many children from regular classrooms once they are placed elsewhere.
2. Decisions to place students in special education programs were often made primarily on the basis of teacher recommendation or the results of a single test.
3. Severely and profoundly handicapped children have routinely been excluded from public school programs. If they received any education at all, their parents usually had to pay for it.
4. A disproportionate number of children from minority cultural groups have been placed in special education programs.
5. The level of educational services provided to residents of institutions has often been very low or even nonexistent.

These circumstances led to increased activism by parents of exceptional children, and by lawyers, educators, and other "advocates" who were concerned that these children were not being treated fairly. Many legislators and judges agreed. The concept of due process for handicapped students is now embodied in our legal and educational systems. Several elements of this concept, as Williams (1977) points out, have particularly important implications for special education in the schools today.

1. Notice. The person (or parents) must be told about a decision, or change in educational program, that is about to take place. This gives the affected people the information necessary to respond to those issues or charges. Notice of providing or removing services must be given, because the child's status may be substantially altered by decisions regarding his or her educational program.
2. A hearing before an impartial party. Parents and students have the right to challenge or examine the case before an impartial party. "Impartial," is generally interpreted to mean a person who is not employed by the school district that has made the decision affecting the child.
3. The right to present a defense. This includes the right to present evidence, answer charges, and in general, "give your best effort at convincing that decision maker in the way that you want to convince him." The school must

THREE STUDENTS—THREE TEACHERS—THREE SCHOOLS

A Resource Room

Vincent is 9 years old. He attends a regular elementary school near his home in San Jose, California. Although Vincent performs well in some academic areas, his teachers became concerned over his slow progress in reading. He was not able to keep up with his classmates last year and frequently displayed behavior problems in the regular third grade classroom, apparently because of frustration with his reading difficulties.

Vincent now goes to a *resource room* for 2 hours each day. During this time, Ms. Roberts, the resource room teacher, provides individual and small-group instruction for Vincent and five other children who have similar reading and language problems. The resource room has tables at which students can work independently and some quiet screened-off areas for individual tutoring and testing. There are many instructional and audiovisual aids, including tape recorders, overhead projectors, a Language Master which reads words and sentences aloud, and a personal computer on which students follow individualized programs.

"Some people think I function simply as a tutor," Ms. Roberts explains, "but there's a lot more to a good resource room program than that. I look for ways of finding out *how* children learn. I work with the child's regular teacher in providing instruction that is appropriate to his or her special needs."

So far, the resource room placement appears to have helped Vincent. The flexible schedule enables him to be with his peers in the regular classroom for most of the school day. His behavior seems to have improved as a result of the additional instruction he now receives in reading and language arts. Ms. Roberts also feels that Vincent is benefiting from extra attention and encouragement. At the end of this school year Vincent's progress will be reviewed by his teachers and parents. He may be assigned to a resource room again next year, or he may spend virtually all of his time in the regular classroom, with a special education teacher providing consultation to his regular teacher.

A Self-Contained Special Class

Teresa, 15, is considered to have moderate to severe mental retardation as a result of Down syndrome. She previously lived in a large residential institution in another state, where little education or training were provided. Recently, Teresa left the institution and was placed in a foster home in Houston, Texas. She now attends a *self-contained special class,* which is located in a regular high school building.

Teresa spends most of the day in her special classroom, with nine other students who have moderate, severe, and multiple disabilities. A teacher, Mr. Simmons, and two paraprofessional aides are assigned to the class. Teresa interacts with nonhandicapped students on the school bus, at recess, and in the cafeteria. In addition, a peer tutoring program brings students from the regular high school classes into Teresa's room to provide individual help under the teacher's supervision. Mr. Simmons seeks to provide a mixture of group and individualized instruction, emphasizing practical tasks for living and working in the community. He frequently teaches outside the school building. For example, Teresa has learned how to ride a city bus from her home to a shopping center.

"At first I didn't know how well we'd be accepted in a regular high school," reports Mr. Simmons. "We've had a bit of a problem with kids calling our students 'retards' or 'dummies,' and imitating some of their less desirable behaviors. But most of the high school students are friendly and helpful, and Teresa has made some new friends. Our principal is supportive; she considers our class a part of this school in every way. We have our pictures in the yearbook, and we go to dances and basketball games just like anyone else."

Teresa will probably remain in a self-contained special class next year, with additional attention being given to exploring vocational placements and independent living opportunities in the community. Her foster parents have visited the class several times and are pleased with Teresa's progress.

A Special School

Nadine, who is 11 years old, has severe spastic cerebral palsy. She usually uses a wheelchair for mobility, though she is learning to use a walker for short periods. She has occasional seizures and has considerable difficulty articulating clearly. Nadine requires a special diet, regular medication, and assistance in dressing and toileting.

Nadine lives in a large suburban school district on Long Island, New York. She attends Bayview School, a public *special school* exclusively for children who have physical, orthopedic, neurological, and health-related disabilities. Nadine's parents had the option of sending her to a public school closer to home, but preferred that she attend Bayview. They feel that Nadine benefits from the smaller class size and greater concentration

of teachers and therapists that Bayview offers. They also have become involved in the school's parent-teacher organization and have assisted with numerous field trips and recreational outings.

Bayview looks much like any other public school, except that most of the children use adaptive devices such as wheelchairs, walkers, protective helmets, and communication boards. The school is completely barrier-free. There are no stairs; all doorways and restroom stalls are wider than usual. Nadine enjoys swimming in the school's therapeutic pool. In the cafeteria, staff members bring food to those children who cannot go through the serving line and help them eat if necessary. Nadine rides to school on a specially equipped bus, with a driver and aide who have received training in positioning, seizure management, communication, and other procedures.

The students at Bayview range in age from 5 to 21. "We have ten children in our class this year," says Ms. Hamner, Nadine's teacher, "and most of them are functioning pretty close to grade level. We basically follow an academic program with extra instruction and therapy to meet each student's needs. We have a hard-working staff that cares. I think it's good for the kids to be exposed to other youngsters with disabilities."

Nadine's placement will be reviewed at the end of each school year. In the future, she may attend a regular public school for all or part of the day, if it is considered appropriate by her parents and teachers—and by Nadine herself.

give parents or students adequate time and information to prepare a defense, and must allow them to be represented by lawyers or other advocates if they so desire.

4. Written decision. Following any hearing, parents, students, and the school district must have a written statement that specifies the facts that were considered and the conclusions that were drawn.

5. Right to appeal. If the parents, students, or school district are not satisfied with the results of the impartial hearing, they may appeal the decision to the state department of education and to the courts.

Further guidelines on due process, written especially for parents of exceptional children, are provided in Figure 2.1. Teachers, administrators, and other school personnel should be familiar with these guidelines.

Other Court Cases

In addition to the PARC case, several other judicial decisions have had a major effect on special education and are regarded as forerunners to Public Law 94–142, the Education for All Handicapped Children Act. We will discuss several of the most important of these cases.

Hobson v. *Hansen* (1967)

In this case, a court ruled against the so-called "tracking system," in which children were placed into either regular or special classes according to their scores on intelligence tests. Most of these tests had been standardized on a population of white middle-class children. This case involved black working-class children, who comprise most of the population of the Washington, D.C., public schools. Thus these children, it was decided, were not being classified according to their ability to learn, but rather according to environmental and social factors that were irrelevant to their learning ability and potential.

Standardized intelligence tests are examined in more detail on pages 71 and 73–75.

Diana v. *State Board of Education* (1970)

A Spanish-speaking student in California had been placed in a special class for mentally retarded children on the basis of intelligence tests that were given in English. The court ruled that this placement was inappropriate and that the child must be given another evaluation in her native language.

Mills v. *Board of Education* (1972)

Seven children had been excluded from the public schools in Washington, D.C., because of learning and behavior problems. The school district contended that it did not have enough money to provide special education programs for them. The court held that lack of funds is no excuse for failing to educate the children and ordered the schools to readmit and serve them appropriately. Even if funds are limited (as is often the case today), handicapped children must not be denied access to the public schools.

IN A NUTSHELL

Here's a quick review to keep in mind the main steps involved in due process. Each of these steps reinforces your right to stay on top of decisions about your child.

1. You must receive notice in writing before the school system takes (or recommends) any action that may change your child's school program. Notice in writing is also required if a school refuses to take action to change your child's program.

2. You have the right to give—or withhold—permission for your child to be: tested to determine whether or not he requires special education services (identification); evaluated by specialists to determine what his educational needs are (evaluation); placed in a specific school program to meet his needs (placement).

3. You have the right to see and examine all school records related to the identification, evaluation and placement of your child. If you find that certain records are inaccurate or misleading, you have the right to ask that they be removed from your child's file. Once removed, they may *not* be used in planning for your child's placement.

4. If you do not agree with the school's course of action at *any* point along the way, you have the right to request an impartial due process hearing. This means that you can initiate a hearing to protest any decision related to identification, evaluation or placement of your child.

5. If you fail to win your case, you have the right to appeal the results of the due process hearing to the State Department of Education; you can appeal to the courts if you lose your case at the state level.

Calling for a due process hearing is your right, but remember that it can be an exhausting process. Before going this route, be sure you have tried to settle differences through every other means—by being as persuasive as possible in meetings with teachers, the principal, special education administrators. If you know that you're up against a brick wall, and you're sure that a due process hearing must be held to resolve conflicting points of view, then you must prepare your case as thoroughly as possible. Be sure to get help from an advocacy group or a lawyer who is familiar with education law and procedures in your state, or an experienced parent. (According to law, the school system must tell you about sources of free legal aid. Ask for this information.)

Know your rights at a hearing:

☐ The hearing officer must be impartial, may not be employed by the school district or involved in the education of your child.

☐ You have the right to legal counsel (which includes the advice and support of any advocate, not necessarily a lawyer); to examine witnesses; present evidence; ask questions of school spokespeople; obtain a record of the hearing and all of its findings.

NOTE: Write directly to the superintendent of schools in your district to request a hearing. Hearings must be held not later than 45 days after requested. State Departments of Education must review appeals within 30 days.

SOURCE: From *Closer Look.* Washington, D.C.: Department of Health, Education and Welfare, Fall 1977, p. 4.

FIGURE 2.1
Guidelines on due process for parents

Larry P. v. Riles (1979)

This case considered the placement of black children in special classes because of inappropriate testing and labeling to be unfair. The IQ tests that were used, said the court, failed to recognize the children's cultural background and the learning that took place in their homes and communities. When different tests were used, it was found that the children were not mentally retarded. The court ordered that IQ tests not be used as the *sole* basis for placing children into special classes.

These important decisions, and many others, have helped establish the schools' responsibility to provide education for handicapped children and to treat them fairly. Exceptional children, who have suffered from exclusion and segregation in the past, are today moving toward greater inclusion and integration into the schools. Gilhool (1976), an attorney who was instrumental in the PARC case, aptly summarizes recent judicial and social developments: "Integration is a central constitutional value. Not integration that *denies* differences, but rather integration that *accommodates* difference."

LEGISLATION: P.L. 94–142

The trend toward inclusion and integration of handicapped children culminated in Public Law 94–142, the Education for All Handicapped Children Act. This law was passed by the U.S. Congress in 1975, but was not fully implemented until 1980. It has been described as "blockbuster legislation" (Goodman, 1976) and hailed as the law that "will probably become known as having the greatest impact on education in history" (Stowell & Terry, 1977). In our view, the law has clearly had a great deal of impact, but its long-range effects on special education and regular education have yet to be determined.

In this section, we will present and discuss several of the major features of P.L. 94–142 to indicate important current trends in the field of special education. These trends have affected virtually every school in the country, and have changed the roles of regular and special educators, school administrators, and many others who are involved in the educational process.

What Does the Law Say?

Public Law (P.L.) 94–142 states that all handicapped children between the ages of 3 and 21, regardless of the type or severity of their disability, shall receive a "free, appropriate public education which emphasizes special education and related services designed to meet their unique needs." This education must be provided at public expense—that is, without cost to the child's parents.

Note that P.L. 94–142 does not refer to gifted and talented children.

Education of exceptional students is expensive. The law was designed to back up its mandate for free, appropriate public education by providing federal funds to help state education departments and local school districts meet the additional costs of educating handicapped children (many of whom had not previously been served by public schools). States and local school districts are required to pay at least the amount of money that is spent to educate a nonhandicapped child, and Congress intended that approximately 40% of the total cost of educating each handicapped child would be covered by federal funds. Many state and local educational administrators, however, contend that the federal financial assistance to provide education for handicapped students has not been sufficient and that their schools are hard-pressed to meet the costs of educating exceptional children. This problem is particularly serious today when many school districts are experiencing severe financial difficulties.

P.L. 94–142 is directed primarily at the states, which are responsible for providing education to their citizens. To receive financial assistance from the federal government to aid in educating handicapped students, each state must ensure that its local school districts comply with the law and:

- ☐ Locate and identify all children who have handicaps, evaluate their educational needs, and determine whether those needs are being met.
- ☐ Develop an Individualized Education Program (IEP) for every handicapped child in the state.
- ☐ Submit to the federal government a state plan for the education of handicapped children, and revise the state plan yearly.
- ☐ Describe the means by which handicapped children will be identified and referred for diagnosis.
- ☐ Avoid using racially or culturally discriminatory testing and evaluation procedures in placing handicapped children; administer tests in the child's native language.
- ☐ Protect the rights of handicapped children and their parents by ensuring due process, confidentiality of records, and parental involvement in educational planning and placement decisions.
- ☐ Provide a comprehensive system for personnel development, including in-service training programs for regular education teachers, special education teachers, school administrators, and other support personnel.
- ☐ Educate handicapped and nonhandicapped children together to the maximum extent which is appropriate. Handicapped children are to be placed in special classes or separate schools only when education cannot be achieved satisfactorily in the regular classroom, even with special aids and services.

Least Restrictive Environment

P.L. 94–142 also mandated each handicapped child's right to be educated in the **least restrictive environment** (LRE). The least restrictive environment is one in which the child's special educational needs can be met and at the same time most closely parallels a regular school program—the "normal" placement. Conversely, the "most restrictive environment" might be the setting that is farthest removed from a regular public school program, such as the home or a hospital.

This concept had been articulated in the earlier *PARC* court case.

INTRODUCTION

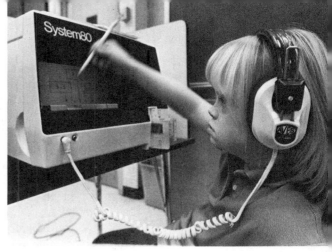

Sebine divides her time between a regular third grade class and a resource room program. For more about Sebine, who is featured on the cover, see the peer tutoring insert at the end of this chapter and photos on pages 467 and 469.

A child educated at home, for instance, would have little or no opportunity to interact with nonhandicapped children.

"Least restrictive environment" is a relative concept; what is the LRE for one child may not be for another. A variety of options or choices must be available to meet the individual needs of exceptional children. There have been many differences of opinion regarding which type of setting is "least restrictive" and "most appropriate" for handicapped students. While some educators, lawyers, and parents consider *any* decision to place a handicapped child in a special class or school to be overly restrictive, most realize that a regular class placement in which a child's instructional needs are not adequately met, is also restrictive. It is generally accepted that there is more than one "best" way of providing educational services to a handicapped child, and that there are wide individual differences, even among children who share the same categorical classification.

Current interpretation of the least restrictive environment, based on recent court cases, is that a child should be removed from the regular school program only to the extent that there is clear evidence that this removal is necessary for that child to receive appropriate educational services. The child's parents must be properly informed if removal from the regular classroom is being considered, so they can either consent or object to the removal and can present additional information if they wish. No removal from the regular school program should be regarded as permanent; there should be a plan for returning the child to as "normal" a setting as possible, as soon as certain needs or conditions are met. Each handicapped child, then, must have access to educational experiences as close as possible to those that a nonhandicapped child would have, as long as the education is appropriate to that child's special needs.

Other Provisions of P.L. 94–142

Two priorities are set forth in P.L. 94–142 for the expenditure of funds to educate handicapped children. The first priority is given to those handicapped children currently *unserved* by an educational program of any kind. The second priority is given to those children who are currently *inadequately served.* Many previously unserved and inadequately served children are those with severe and multiple handicaps; many have been kept at home or in institutions. An especially high priority is given to unserved and inadequately served children with severe disabilities.

P.L. 94–142 also requires that, in cases where appropriate education cannot be provided in the public schools, handicapped children may be placed in private school programs at no cost to their parents, if they are placed in private schools or referred to them by state or local education officials. This has proven to be a particularly controversial aspect of the law. Parents and school officials have frequently disagreed over whether private school placement, at public expense, is the most appropriate way of meeting the needs of an exceptional child.

Handicapped children are sometimes prevented from attending regular schools by circumstances other than their educational performance. A child who uses a wheelchair, for example, may require a specially equipped school bus. A child with special health problems may need to be given medication several times a day. The law calls for schools to provide any *related services,* such as special transportation, counseling, physical therapy, and other supportive assistance, that a handicapped child may need in order to benefit from special education. This provision has also been highly controversial, with much disagreement over what kind of related services are necessary and reasonable for the schools to provide and what services should be the responsibility of the child's parents.

What Effects Has the Law Had?

Since P.L. 94–142 was enacted, there has been a steady increase in the number of exceptional children identified and served in public educational programs. In one recent year, an estimated 2 million individual evaluations of handicapped children were conducted, and over 99% of these evaluations were "for the most part satisfactory to the children's parents" (U.S. Department of Education, 1982a, p. I). As the law intended, most handicapped students are currently being educated in regular school buildings with their nonhandicapped peers. In fact, the Department of Education reports that less than 7% of handicapped children now receive their education outside of regular school buildings. There has been especially rapid growth in the number of handicapped adolescents and young adults (ages 18 through 21) who have recently been provided special education services.

Legal Challenges Based on P.L. 94–142

Thousands of due process hearings and numerous court cases have been brought by parents and other advocates of handicapped children, citing the provisions of P.L. 94–142. The assumption of responsibility for educating handicapped children in the public schools has led to widely differing interpretations of just what is meant by the phrase "appropriate public education." The law uses this term repeatedly but, in the view of many parents, educators, and judges, does not clearly define it. Many cases have required a judge, court, or hearing officer to determine what is, or is not, "appropriate" for a certain handicapped child, and whether or not a public school district should be compelled to provide a particular kind of service.

Some cases have resulted from parents protesting the suspension or expulsion of their handicapped child. The case of *Stuart* v. *Nappi* (1978), for example, concerned a high school student who spend much of her time wandering in the halls, even though she was assigned to special classes. The school sought to have the student expelled on disciplinary grounds, since her conduct was considered detrimental to order in the school. The court agreed with the student's mother that expulsion would deny the student a free, appropriate public education, as called for in P.L. 94–142. In other cases, however, the expulsion or suspension of handicapped students has been upheld if the school could show that the grounds for expulsion were not related to the student's disability.

Most public school programs operate for approximately 180 school days per year. Parents and educators have argued that for some handicapped children, particularly those with severe and multiple disabilities, a 180-day school year is not sufficient to meet their needs. In the case of *Armstrong* v. *Kline* (1979), the parents of five severely handicapped students claimed that their children tended to regress during the usual breaks in the school year and called upon the schools to provide a period of instruction longer than 180 days. The court agreed and ordered the schools to extend the school year for these students. Several states and local districts now provide year-round educational programs for some handicapped students, but there are no clear and universally accepted guidelines regarding which students are entitled to free public education for a longer-than-usual school year.

The first case based on P.L. 94–142 to reach the U.S. Supreme Court was *Rowley* v. *Hendrick Hudson School District* (1982). The parents of a fourth-grade deaf student who attended regular classes requested that the school provide a sign-language interpreter to accompany the child in all of her classes. The school had provided several special services for this student, but contended that she did not require a full-time interpreter. They felt, in fact, that an interpreter might hinder the child's interactions with her teacher and peers. It was also noted that this service would cost the school district as much as $25,000 per year. The Supreme Court ruled that the child, who was doing well in school without an interpreter, was receiving an adequate education, and that the school district could not be compelled to hire a full-time interpreter.

No clear direction has emerged from these and other recent court cases. Challenges and differing views on whether or not a certain program or procedure is "appropriate" are sure to continue. The high cost of providing special education services, while clearly not a valid basis for excluding handicapped students, will likely be considered by many courts in determining what schools may reasonably be expected to do. As Flygare (1982) observes, the *Rowley* case does not bode well for the further expansion of related services for handicapped students. However, even though the parents' request for an interpreter was denied, the court's opinion established that each handicapped student is entitled to a personalized program of instruction and supportive services that will enable him or her to benefit from an education.

> Incidentally, the *Rowley* case marked the first time a deaf attorney had ever argued a case before the U.S. Supreme Court.

Possible Changes to P.L. 94–142

In 1982, the federal government proposed several important changes in P.L. 94–142. These changes were generally viewed, by both supporters and opponents, as consistent with President Reagan's "New Federalism" policy, in which state and local agencies are encouraged to make decisions that affect them directly and in which the federal government's role in regulation and direction is reduced. The revisions would have cut back or eliminated many of the current requirements for the states to report data on their special education plans and programs. The proposed changes would have reduced the "related services" that schools were required to provide, and "reasonable" time limits would have been acceptable. There would have been less emphasis on the requirement to educate handicapped children with nonhandicapped children "to the maximum extent appropriate," as long as each child's placement was individually determined. There also would have been a procedure for placing handicapped children in more restrictive settings, if it could be shown that they "disrupted" regular classes or took up too much of the teacher's time. The proposed changes aroused a great deal of controversy and were viewed by many parents, educators, and professional organizations as detrimental to the interests of handicapped children. In late 1982, the Department of Education withdrew several of the most controversial proposed changes. However, it is quite possible that additional changes to P.L. 94–142 will be proposed in the future.

Section 504

Another relatively recent and very important law that extends civil rights to handicapped people is Section 504 of the Rehabilitation Act of 1973 (actually adopted in 1977). This regulation states that:

> No otherwise qualified handicapped individual shall, solely by reason of his handicap, be excluded from the participation in, be denied the benefits of, or be subjected to discrimination in any program or activity receiving federal financial assistance.

This law, worded in language almost identical to that of the Civil Rights Act of 1964, which prohibited discrimination based on race, color, or national origin, promises to expand opportunities to handicapped children and adults in education, employment, and various other settings. It calls for the provision of "auxiliary aids for students with impaired sensory, manual, or speaking skills," such as readers for blind students, interpreters for deaf students, and people to assist physically disabled students in moving from place to place. This requirement does not mean that schools, colleges, and employers must have *all* such aids available at *all* times; it simply demands that no handicapped person may be excluded from a program because of the lack of an appropriate aid. Section 504 is also expected to increase the number of handicapped people employed as teachers in public schools.

Architectural accessibility is an important facet of Section 504. However, a completely "barrier-free" environment is not called for. The emphasis is upon accessibility to *programs*, not on the physical modification of all existing structures. If a chemistry class, for example, is required for a premedical program of study, a college might make this program accessible to a physically disabled student by reassigning the class to an accessible location or by providing assistance to the student in traveling to an otherwise inaccessible location. All sections of all courses need not be made accessible, but a college should not segregate handicapped students by assigning them all to a particular section regardless of disability. Like Public Law 94–142, Section 504 calls for nondiscriminatory placement in the "most integrated setting appropriate" and has served as the basis for many court cases over alleged discrimination against disabled individuals, particularly in the right to employment.

Gifted and Talented Children

Although P.L. 94–142 and Section 504 do not specifically apply to gifted and talented children, the specialized needs of this population have also been addressed in recent legislation. Public Law 95–561, the Gifted and Talented Children's Education Act of 1978, provides financial incentives for state and local education agencies to develop programs for their gifted and talented students. P.L. 95–561 provides for the identification of gifted and talented children, including special procedures for identifying and educating those from disadvantaged backgrounds. There is also funding available for in-service training programs, research and other projects meeting the needs of gifted and talented students.

SPECIAL EDUCATION IN THE SCHOOLS TODAY: BEYOND COMPLIANCE

Maynard Reynolds, an experienced and articulate special educator, offers the following observation of the implementation of P.L. 94–142:

> Without even trying, I have been shown at least six sets of transparencies, listened to endless audio cassettes on the requirements of Public Law 94–142, and I have been guided through several versions of "sure-fire" forms to satisfy all of the new regulations.
> What I see and hear seems well designed to keep teachers out of jail—to comply with the law, that is—but usually I sense little vision of how people might come together creatively to design environments for better learning and living by handicapped students. (Reynolds, 1978)

Indeed, the creation of effective learning environments for exceptional students and their peers must involve far more than filling out forms and "staying out of jail." Regular educators and special educators now find themselves confronted with countless new challenges and responsibilities; in effect, they are defining a new relationship with each other, and with their students. Where children were formerly given a label (such as "mentally retarded" or "emotionally disturbed") and removed from the regular classroom, it is now increasingly recognized that exceptional children have special needs in (for example) reading, arithmetic, or controlling their behavior, and *the services are moving to the child.*

Special education services are often provided in the form of training and support for the regular teacher. In fact, special education in the schools today may rightly be viewed as a *system* for the delivery of services to children, rather than as a separate, specialized content area apart from regular education (Nelson, 1978; Reynolds & Birch, 1982). The regular teacher who works with Susan in her classroom, the physical therapist who sees Susan and consults with her teacher twice a week, and the resource room teacher who works with Susan and communicates with the regular teacher are all participating in the system that delivers special education services to Susan.

"Mainstreaming"

The word *mainstreaming* has been popularized to describe the process of integrating handicapped children into regular schools and classes. Much discussion, and many misconceptions, have arisen regarding whether all handicapped children must now attend regular classes—the so-called "mainstream" of our public school system. Some people seem to view mainstreaming as placing all exceptional children into regular classrooms with no additional supportive services, while others have the idea that mainstreaming can mean completely segregated placement of handicapped children, as long as they interact with nonhandicapped peers in a few activities (perhaps at lunch or on the playground). Many parents have strongly supported the placement of their exceptional children in regular classes, while others have resisted it just as strongly, feeling that the regular classroom does not offer the intense, individualized education that their children need.

Interestingly, nowhere in P.L. 94–142, which has sparked most of the debate, is the word "mainstreaming" even used. What the law does call for is that each child is to be educated in the least restrictive appropriate educational setting, not removed any farther than necessary from the regular public school program. As Heron and Skinner note, the least restrictive environment is:

> That educational setting which maximizes the . . . student's opportunity to respond and achieve, permits the regular education teacher to interact proportionally with all the students in the classroom, and fosters acceptable social relations between nonhandicapped and [handicapped] students. (1981, p. 116)

P.L. 94–142 does not advocate the placement of all handicapped children in regular classes, call for handicapped children to remain in regular classes without the supportive services they need, or suggest that regular teachers educate all handicapped students without help from special educators and other specialists. It does, however, specifically call for regular and special educators to cooperate in providing an equal educational opportunity to exceptional students.

As Gresham (1982) points out, simply placing a handicapped child into a regular classroom does not mean that the child will learn and behave appropriately or that he or she will be socially accepted by nonhandicapped children. It is important for special educators to teach appropriate social skills and behavior to the handicapped child and to educate nonhandicapped children about the differences in their new handicapped classmates. But these challenges should not mean that handicapped children are denied the right to participate in a regular classroom for all or part of the school day. Becky's main educational handicap, for example, is that she has very limited vision. It would be overly restrictive to send Becky to a residential school 200 miles from her home, where she could interact only with other visually impaired children (though this would probably have been done not too long ago). Her needs might well be met in the regular public school, if the school can provide special materials and tutoring for Becky and consultation for her regular teacher.

Sapon-Shevin suggests that we should conceive of mainstreaming "not as changing the special child so that he will fit back into the unchanged regular classroom, but rather as changing the nature of the regular classroom so that it is more accommodating to all children" (1978, p. 120).

PREPARING FOR MAINSTREAMING: A SPECIAL TEACHER'S CHECKLIST

Teachers and parents must be committed to carrying out the least restrictive alternative concept for handicapped children. If handicapped individuals are ever to be fully accepted in our society, this integration should occur as early and widely as possible. Educators should be willing to put forth their best efforts to make a regular class experience rewarding and enriching for handicapped students. Special class teachers can do much to make these mainstreaming successes happen.

The key to a successful mainstreaming experience is preparation. The checklist below can serve as a guide for the special class teacher in preparing not only the handicapped student, but also the other people who must support the mainstreaming effort. Before placing each handicapped student in a mainstreamed setting, the teacher should examine and work on each element of the checklist, until most, if not all, of the "yes" boxes can be checked.

1. Handicapped student:

Yes No

☐ ☐ Is familiar with rules and routine of the regular classroom?

☐ ☐ Follows verbal and written directions used in the regular classroom?

☐ ☐ Remains on-task for adequate time periods?

☐ ☐ Has expressed a desire to participate in the regular class setting?

☐ ☐ Reacts appropriately to teasing, questions, criticism, etc.?

☐ ☐ Student's IEP objectives match instructional objectives in regular class?

2. Regular class teacher:

Yes No

☐ ☐ Has been given rationale for mainstreaming activities and asked to cooperate?

☐ ☐ Has information about handicapped student's needs, present skills, and current learning objectives?

☐ ☐ Has been provided with special materials and/or support services as needed?

☐ ☐ Has prepared class for mainstreaming?

☐ ☐ Has acquired special helping skills if necessary?

☐ ☐ Will be monitored regularly to identify any problems that arise?

3. Nonhandicapped peers:

Yes No

☐ ☐ Have been informed about handicapped student's participation and about handicapping condition (if appropriate) with the opportunity to ask questions?

☐ ☐ Have been asked for their cooperation and friendship toward handicapped student?

☐ ☐ Have learned helping skills and praising behaviors?

4. Handicapped student's parents:

Yes No

☐ ☐ Have received verbal or written information about mainstreaming situation?

☐ ☐ Have been asked to praise and encourage child's progress in regular and special class?

5. Nonhandicapped students' parents:

Yes No

☐ ☐ Have been informed about mainstreaming activities at PTA meeting, conferences, or through other vehicle, and asked for their cooperation?

6. School administrator:

Yes No

☐ ☐ Has been informed about specifics of mainstreaming activities?

☐ ☐ Has indicated specific steps she or he will take to encourage and support these activities?

Adapted from J. C. Dardig, Helping teachers integrate handicapped students into the regular classroom, *Educational Horizons*, 1981, *59*, 124–130. Used with permission.

Matt tells Ronni, his resource room teacher, how things went this morning in the regular classroom.

Heron (1978) has proposed a decision-making model for analyzing problems and adapting the regular classroom environment to allow handicapped children to participate.

This model would be used when a problem involving an exceptional child develops within the regular classroom in which he or she has been placed.

Figure 2.2 shows the sequence of alternatives. The first step is to define the problem. For example, is the student having difficulty in academic or social skills? Is he having difficulty with his normal peers? Is the classroom teacher having problems interacting with the exceptional student?

Given that the problem can be reasonably determined, the second step is to determine whether the primary focus of intervention should be directed toward child behavior or teacher behavior. If the focus is determined to be the child's behavior, then the strategies listed under Exceptional Child (2.1) would be used. Or, if an intervention were needed with the normal children in the classroom, then those options listed under Normal Child (2.2) would be considered. The same procedure would apply if the focus of the intervention were directed toward teacher behavior.

The alternatives recommended under each category (e.g., child behavior, teacher behavior) are arranged in a hierarchy. That is, those options requiring the least amount of teacher time or effort are listed first, while those requiring more teacher time or effort follow. In addition, the alternatives are based on three criteria: (1) their demonstrated effectiveness in previous studies, (2) their applicability to a wide range of behaviors, and (3) the likelihood that their effects will endure over time.

Finally, these strategies are familiar to many regular education teachers, supervisors, and principals. In short, the implementation of this model would

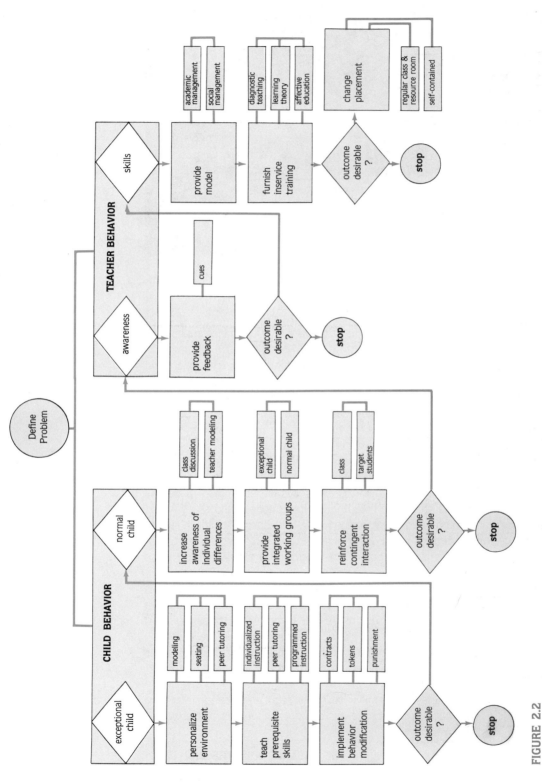

FIGURE 2.2

A decision-making process for maintaining a mainstreamed child in the regular classroom.

Source: From T. E. Heron, Maintaining the mainstreamed child in the regular classroom: The decision-making process. *Journal of Learning Disabilities*, 1978, *11*(4), p. 213. Copyright 1978 by Professional Press, Inc. Reprinted by special permission of Professional Press, Inc.

not require extensive retraining of these professionals. In the final analysis what Heron is suggesting is that school personnel at all levels use current teaching and management skills more efficiently and systematically.

A Continuum of Services

There is a wide variety of special assistance that may, from time to time, be needed by exceptional children and their teachers. Today, most schools make a genuine effort to provide a *continuum of services*—a range of educational placement options that can be provided to serve children appropriately.

The continuum may be viewed as a pyramid, with placements ranging from "least restrictive" (regular classrooms) at the bottom to "most restrictive" (special residential school facilities) at the top. The fact that the pyramid is widest at the bottom indicates that the greatest number of exceptional children can be accommodated in regular classrooms, and the number of children who require more restrictive, intensive, and specialized placements gets smaller as we move up. As we have already noted, most children who are considered handicapped have mild and moderate disabilities. The number of mildly mentally retarded children, for example, is far greater than those who are severely retarded. Children with mild and moderate behavior disorders greatly outnumber those with severe behavior disorders. As the severity of problems increases, the need for more specialized services also increases, but the number of students decreases.

It is worth noting that, of the seven levels of service depicted in Figure 2.3, the first five are generally available in regular public school buildings. Children at levels 1 through 4 attend regular classes with their nonhandicapped peers; supportive help is given by special teachers who provide consultation to the child's regular teachers or in special **resource rooms.** A resource room usually has a specially trained teacher who provides instruction to exceptional students for part of the school day, either individually or in small groups. Children at level 5, who require full-time placement in a special **self-contained class,** are with other exceptional children for all or most of the school day. But they may still have the opportunity to interact with nonhandicapped children at certain times, such as during recess or on the bus to school. While this alternative provides less integration than the regular classroom, it provides much more opportunity for interaction than placement in a residential institution or a special school for handicapped children. Self-contained classes in regular school buildings are gaining acceptance as an appropriate placement for many children with severe and multiple disabilities (Kenowitz, Zweibel, & Edgar, 1978).

The placement of an exceptional child at any level on the continuum of services should not be regarded as permanent. The child's specific goals and objectives should be periodically reviewed, in consultation with teachers, parents, and administrators. New placement decisions can be made; in fact, the continuum concept is intended to be flexible, with children moving from one placement to another as dictated by their current educational needs. A child may be placed into a less integrated setting for a limited time. When a review of his or her performance shows that certain goals have been achieved, then the child

Again, recall that each child must be placed in the least restrictive environment *in which he or she can succeed.*

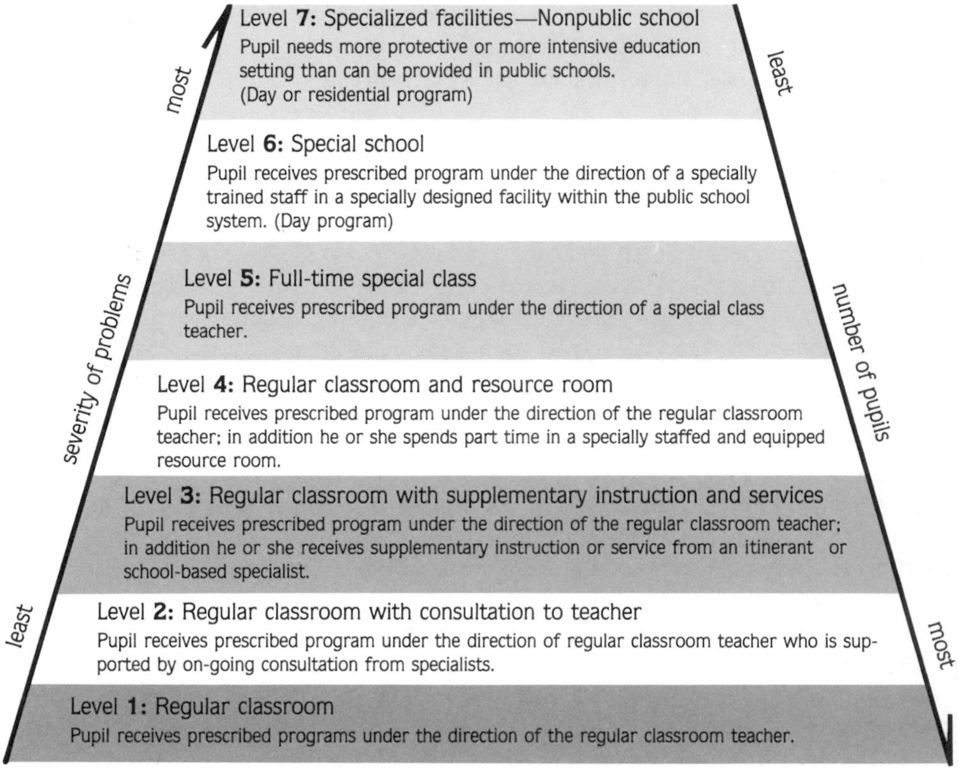

Level **7:** Specialized facilities—Nonpublic school
Pupil needs more protective or more intensive education setting than can be provided in public schools. (Day or residential program)

Level **6:** Special school
Pupil receives prescribed program under the direction of a specially trained staff in a specially designed facility within the public school system. (Day program)

Level **5:** Full-time special class
Pupil receives prescribed program under the direction of a special class teacher.

Level **4:** Regular classroom and resource room
Pupil receives prescribed program under the direction of the regular classroom teacher; in addition he or she spends part time in a specially staffed and equipped resource room.

Level **3:** Regular classroom with supplementary instruction and services
Pupil receives prescribed program under the direction of the regular classroom teacher; in addition he or she receives supplementary instruction or service from an itinerant or school-based specialist.

Level **2:** Regular classroom with consultation to teacher
Pupil receives prescribed program under the direction of regular classroom teacher who is supported by on-going consultation from specialists.

Level **1:** Regular classroom
Pupil receives prescribed programs under the direction of the regular classroom teacher.

FIGURE 2.3
Continuum of educational services.
Source: Montgomery County Public Schools, Rockville, Md. Used with permission.

should return to a more normalized setting as soon as possible. The continuum concept requires that several options be available to handicapped children in order to meet their current needs.

The Team Approach

Many students need services from several different disciplines. One survey of handicapped preschool children in a noncategorical public school program found that, of the 81 children receiving services, 56 were served by four or more professionals, 16 were served by three professionals, and 9 were served by two professionals. No child was served by only one professional (Northcott & Erickson, 1977). Today there is a clear trend toward involving several professional and paraprofessional personnel, working together as a "team," to assess children and plan cooperatively to meet their diverse needs. In this approach, each member of the team assumes certain responsibilities for providing services to students, and recognizes the importance of teaching, learning from, and working with other members of the team. It is widely felt that group decisions provide a form of insurance against erroneous or arbitrary decisions in the complex issues that face educators of exceptional students.

One study by Pfeiffer (1982) concluded that team decision making was generally consistent and effective, superior to individual decision making in the placement of exceptional children. "A cooperative work group brings to bear on a complex task differing values as well as unique professional perspectives. This enhances the problem-solving effectiveness that is required" when determining the most appropriate educational program for an exceptional child (p. 69).

Other potential advantages of the team approach have been summarized by Williamson (1978).

☐ The child need no longer be "splintered" into segments along disciplinary lines. An old saying pictured the handicapped child as giving "his hands to the occupational therapist, his legs to the physical therapist, and his brain to the teacher."

☐ There is opportunity for increased communication among team members.

☐ The child is encouraged to develop a trusting relationship with the professionals on the team. Usually, the child sees the same specialists over an extended period of time.

☐ The team approach is thought to be more cost-effective, since professionals can share their expertise with each other and serve a greater number of children through consultation.

An effective interdisciplinary team, with all members sharing their information and skills, can do much to provide an appropriate and consistent educational program to exceptional children and to increase the individual effectiveness of each of its members. Of course, all of these advantages are not necessarily realized in practice in all cases. Dardig and Heward (1981b) have developed a six-step procedure that can be used by an IEP-planning team to help set priorities for a child's learning goals while giving equal consideration to each member's input. Team members must learn to put aside professional rivalries and work for the benefit of each handicapped child.

Assessment and Educational Planning

For many years, handicapped students were tested largely to *exclude* them from public school programs. Charles might have been denied entrance into his local school if, for example, he obtained a score below 50 on an IQ test, or if he was unable to follow verbal directions, or if he required assistance in using the toilet. Assessment was typically done in a special "testing" room, often by an examiner who was unfamiliar with the child and who had had little or no contact with the child's parents or teachers. The examiner then "interpreted" the results of the tests, applied a label to the child (for example, *trainable mentally retarded*), and ruled the child eligible or ineligible for educational services.

Today, assessment is a process of *including* a person on the basis of what he or she *can* do, rather than *excluding* a person because of what he or she *cannot* do. As Hammer (1978) observes, we must not limit assessment to the defining of *disability* (we probably already know that the child is "different" before assessment even begins), but should instead focus on finding *ability*. What can the child do? How and in what situation does he learn most effectively? What are some materials and techniques that appear to be appropriate? The answers to these and other questions can, of course, be of great value in planning a child's educational program. Assessment is virtually useless unless it leads to action, in the form of specific instruction, treatment, or other intervention given to the child.

Chapter 4 discusses specific types of assessment instruments often used with handicapped children.

Assessment is thus coming to be seen not as an isolated discipline, but as an inseparable part of the child's ongoing educational program. Today, assessment is often accomplished in natural settings, such as the child's regular classroom or home. There is generally less reliance on standardized tests that give numerical scores and "predictions" of children's potential, and more reliance on precise, structured observations of children's behavior. A teacher might, for example, count how many times Greg is out of his seat during a 10-minute period. A parent might observe that Jill is able to pick up small pieces of meat with a spoon, but has difficulty using a fork. Observations like these, made over a period of time by people who are familiar with the child, can readily be translated into educational goals and objectives.

Public Law 94–142 reflects current concern for fair, appropriate, multifaceted assessment. The law specifically calls for certain "safeguards," including:

☐ Evaluation that assesses the child's specific areas of educational need, not merely provides a single general intelligence quotient.

☐ Assessment to be made by a multidisciplinary team or group of persons.

☐ Assessment of *all* areas in which disability may be suspected (including vision, hearing, motor abilities, health, communication, and other appropriate areas).

☐ Tests to be administered by trained personnel.

☐ Evaluation that does not discriminate against the child because of racial or cultural background, or because the child speaks a language other than English.

☐ A wide range of evaluation procedures; *no single assessment may be used as the sole criterion* for determining the child's placement.

Parents have the right to obtain an independent evaluation of their child by examiners of their choice, from outside the school system. The results of any such independent evaluations must be considered along with the school's assessment in determining the child's program and placement.

The outcome of any evaluation process should be to obtain information that will be useful to the student, the teachers, and the parents in planning activities that will enhance the child's learning and future development.

INTRODUCTION

The Individualized Education Program (IEP)

Perhaps the most significant component of P.L. 94–142 (and certainly one of the most controversial) is the requirement that an individualized education program (IEP) must be developed and maintained for every handicapped child. The law is specific in stating what an IEP must include and who is to take part in its formulation. Each IEP must be the product of the joint efforts of the members of a child study team, which must include at least: (1) the child's teacher or teachers, (2) a representative of the local school district other than the child's teacher, (3) the child's parents or guardian, and (4) whenever appropriate, the child himself. Support staff such as physical educators or speech-language pathologists may also be involved in the IEP conference.

Although the actual formats used by different school districts vary, most IEPs include:

1. A statement of the child's present levels of educational performance, including academic achievement, social adaptation, prevocational and vocational skills, psychomotor skills and self-help skills;
2. A statement of annual goals that describes the educational performance to be achieved by the end of the school year under the child's program;
3. A statement of short-term instructional objectives, presented in measurable, intermediate steps between the present level of educational performance and the annual goals;
4. A statement of specific educational services needed by the child (determined without regard to the availability of services), including a description of:
   a. All special education and related services needed to meet the unique needs of the child, including the physical education program, and
   b. Any special instructional media and materials that are needed;
5. The date when those services will begin and length of time the services will be given;
6. A description of the extent to which the child will participate in regular education programs;
7. Objective criteria, evaluation procedures, and schedules of determining, at least annually, whether the short-term instructional objectives are being achieved;
8. A justification for the type of educational placement that the child will have; and
9. A list of the individuals who are responsible for implementing the individualized education program.

Ideally, the child's IEP is a system for spelling out where the child is, where he should be going, how he will get there, how long it will take, and how to tell when he has arrived (Bierly, 1978). The legal requirement of an IEP is

Students should participate in planning their own IEPs whenever possible.

new, but the principles of sound planning and systematic teaching are not. For many years, regular and special education teachers have been using assessment, short-range objectives leading to long-range goals, and evaluation procedures in working with their students. "In reality," state Hayden and Edgar (1978), "almost everything required for the IEP is currently being done by competent teachers" (p. 67).

Figure 2.4 shows one format for IEPs, but the format will vary according to the needs of each child and the services provided. Some school districts now use computerized systems to keep track of a child's performance, goals, and evaluations (Brown, 1982). Although written forms are required, the IEP is not a legally binding contract. That is, a child's teacher and school cannot be prosecuted in the courts if the child does not achieve all the goals set forth in the IEP. Nevertheless, the teacher should be able to document that a conscientious and systematic effort was made to achieve those goals.

Each child's IEP must be reviewed, and revised if necessary, at least once per year. The child's parent or guardian must consent to the IEP and must

Date ___11-28-81___

(1) Student	(2) Committee

Name: Joe S.
School: Adams
Grade: 5
Current Placement: Regular Class/Resource Room

Date of Birth: 10-1-70   Age: 11-1

		Initial
Mr. Havlichak	Principal	CH
Mrs. Snow	Regular Teacher	ES
Mr. Bigelow	Counselor	C-B
Mr. Sheets	Resource Teacher	RS
Mrs. S.	Parent	aS

IEP from ___12-1-81___ to ___12-1-82___

(3) Present Level of Educational Functioning	(4) Annual Goal Statements	(5) Instructional Objectives	(6) Objective Criteria and Evaluation
MATH Strengths 1. Can successfully compute addition and subtraction problems to two places with regrouping and zeros. 2. Knows 100 basic multiplication facts. Weaknesses 1. Frequently makes computational errors on problems with which he has had experience. 2. Does not complete seatwork. Key Math total score of 2.1 Grade Equivalent.	Joe will apply knowledge of regrouping in addition and renaming in subtraction to four-digit numbers.	1. When presented with addition problems of 3-digit numbers requiring two renamings the student will compute the answer at a rate of one problem per minute and an accuracy of 90%. 2. When presented with subtraction problems of 3-digit numbers requiring two renamings the student will compute the answer at a rate of one problem per minute with 90% accuracy. 3. When presented with addition problems of 4-digit numbers requiring three renamings the student will compute the answer at a rate of one problem per minute and an accuracy of 90%. 4. When presented with subtraction problems of 4-digit numbers requiring three renamings the student will compute the answer at a rate of one problem per minute with 90% accuracy.	Key Math (after 4 mos.) Teacher made tests (weekly) Key Math (after 4 mos.) Teacher made tests (weekly) Key Math (after 4 mos.) Teacher made tests (weekly)

READING
 	
Woodcock Reading Mastery Tests
 	
              Grade
            Equivalent
Letter identification 3.0
Word identification 1.8
Word Attack 2.0
Word comprehension 4.3
	The student's oral reading rate for reading material at his comfortable reading level will increase from 30 words per minute to 36 words per minute.
	
	Student will improve his reading fluency.
		1. When presented with a list of 250 basic sight vocabulary words listed in order of difficulty and/or commonly taught, the student will correctly pronounce 200 of them by the end of the year.
		
		2. When presented with a list of 37 direction words listed in order of difficulty and/or commonly taught, the student will correctly pronounce 24 of them.
		
		3. When presented with a list of 40 words and phrases frequently seen on signs listed in order of difficulty the student will correctly pronounce 30 of them.
			Brigance Diagnostic Inventory of Basic Skill (after 4 and 9 mos.) Teacher observation (daily)
			
			Brigance Diagnostic Inventory of Basic Skill (after 4 and 9 mos.) Teacher observation (daily)
			
			Brigance Diagnostic Inventory of Basic Skill (after 4 and 9 mos.) Teacher observation (daily)

SOCIAL EMOTIONAL Strengths 1. Joe cooperates in group activities. 2. Attentive and cooperative in class. Weaknesses 1. Reluctant participant on playground. 2. Makes derogatory comments about himself frequently during the school day. 3. Has few friends, is ignored by peers.	Joe will speak about himself in a positive manner. Joe will participate with peers in small groups on the playground and in class.	1. In a one-to-one situation with the teacher Joe will talk about his strengths as a person for five min. a day. 2. In a one-to-one situation with the teacher Joe will state 5 strengths he possesses for 3 days in a row. 3. After a small group activity (3-4 students), Joe will tell the teacher 3 things he did well in the group. 4. After a small group activity Joe will tell the teacher 6 things he did well in the group. 5. In a small group activity Joe will ask a peer for help instead of asking an adult: a) With verbal reminders from an adult 70% of the time. b) With nonverbal reminders 60% of the time. c) With no signals 60% of the time. 6. In a small group activity Joe will offer assistance to a peer: a) With verbal reminders from an adult 60% of the time. b) With nonverbal reminders 50% of the time. c) With no signals 50% of the time.	Teacher observation (daily) for 15 days. Anecdotal records (daily) Anecdotal records (daily) 3 consecutive days Anecdotal records (daily) 5 consecutive days Anecdotal records (daily) 5 consecutive days Teacher observation. Data collected 30 min. a day, 3 days a week Teacher observation. Data collected 30 min. a day, 3 days a week

FIGURE 2.4
Portions of a completed IEP (continued on page 54).

(7) Educational Services to be Provided

Services Required	Date Initiated	Duration of Service	Individual Responsible for the Service
Regular Reading-Adapted	12-1-81	12-1-82	Mrs. Jones
Resource Room	12-1-81	12-1-82	Mrs. Green
Counselor Consultant	12-1-81	12-1-82	Mr. Baskin
Monitoring diet and general health	12-1-81	12-1-82	Health Dept.-Mrs. Winger/ School Nurse-Ms. Allen
Dental examination	1-10-82	1-17-82	Health Dept.-Mrs. Winger
Counseling family	12-1-81	6-1-82	Mental Health Center — Mr. Sanford

Extent of time in the regular education program: 60% increasing to 80%
Justification of the educational placement:
It is felt that the structure of the resource room can best meet the goals stated for Joe; especially coordinated with the regular classroom.

It is also felt that Joe could profit enormously from talking with a counselor. He needs someone with whom to talk and with whom he can share his feelings.

(8) I have had the opportunity to participate in the development of the Individual Education Program.
  I agree with the Individual Education Program   (✔)
  I disagree with the Individual Education Program   ( )

Mrs J.

Parent's Signature

FIGURE 2.4 (continued)

SOURCE: A. P. Turnbull, B. B. Strickland, and J. C. Brantley, *Developing and implementing individualized education programs.* Columbus, Ohio: Charles E. Merrill, 1982, pp. 195, 198, 200, 203. Reprinted with permission.

For a detailed explanation of the development and implementation of IEPs, see Turnbull, Strickland, and Brantley (1982).

receive a copy of the document. Figure 2.5 illustrates a format that one school district uses for its annual review of exceptional children's IEPs.

Some observers have asked, "If handicapped children must have IEPs, then why not extend this requirement to *all* children in the public schools?" Indeed, some states and local school districts now use individual educational planning with both handicapped and nonhandicapped students. Utah, for example, has adopted the requirement that an "individual education plan for the projected education program to be pursued by each student during membership in the school" be developed cooperatively by teachers, parents, and the student himself or herself. It has reportedly led to increased conferences, improved career planning, and greater parental involvement (Robinson, 1982). Although some teachers view IEPs as an added burden of paperwork and some parents do not wish to become involved in the planning process, the IEP seems to be gaining acceptance. All children can benefit from the accurate specification of individual goals, periodic evaluation, parent involvement, and contributions from various disciplines that the IEP offers to exceptional children.

The IEP is an inescapable measure of accountability for teachers and schools. Whether or not a particular school or educational program is effective will be judged, to some extent, by how well it is able to help children meet the goals and objectives set forth in their IEPs. Like other professionals, teachers

INTRODUCTION

ANNUAL REVIEW OF IEP AND PLACEMENT

Student _____ Birth Date _____ Date of Review _____

Description of student's current educational placement:

Annual Goals Met:	Annual Goals Not Met:

Recommendations of Review Team:
A. Related Services Currently Provided
   Services to be continued: _____
   Services to be discontinued: _____
B. New Related Services to be Implemented: _____

C. Placement
   □ Continue in same placement next year, without modification.
   □ Continue in same placement next year, with the following modifications _____
   □ Change to different special education placement, as follows: _____
   □ Discontinue special education services.
   □ Other placement recommendations (specify): _____

Additional comments and recommendations:

Members of Review Team _____
                             _____
                             _____
                             _____
                             _____

Parent or Guardian _____

FIGURE 2.5
Annual placement review.

IEPs for older students should include career-related goals and objectives.

are increasingly being called upon to demonstrate competent performance, and the IEP provides one way for them to do so. However, the IEP is much more than an accountability device. Its real benefits are improved planning, consistent implementation, regular evaluation, and clearer communication of each child's educational program.

In-Service Training

Although not all handicapped children attend regular public school classes, it is generally true that "regular" teachers are being expected to deal with a wider variety of learning, behavioral, and physical problems among their students than they did even a few years ago. The provision of **in-service training** for regular educators is an important (and sometimes neglected) aspect of Public Law 94–142. Regular educators are understandably wary of having exceptional children placed into their classes when little or no training or support is provided. They do not want their classrooms to become large catch-all groups. Regular classroom teachers are entitled to be involved in decisions about children who are placed in their classes and to be offered continuous consultation and other supportive services from special educators.

Today, special educators are often called upon to provide training to regular educators, school administrators, and others in the specialized techniques and materials that are used with exceptional children. Many school districts have set up cooperative relationships with universities, special education schools, and other facilities, so that their regular teachers can become more familiar with the needs of exceptional students. Some states now require all regular elementary or secondary teachers to take certain courses in special education before they can be certified; this requirement is likely to be more widely adopted in the future.

As Rauth (1980) points out in a report to the American Federation of Teachers, the most typical attitude of regular teachers is one of "a cautious acceptance of mainstreaming across the country." Most teachers want to see each exceptional child educated in the most suitable, least restrictive environment. But, with justification, regular teachers tend to resent administrators who seem to view "mainstreaming" as a way to cut costs and who increase problems of class size, paperwork, and discipline by placing exceptional students in regular classes without adequate support.

Administrators of general education programs—school principals and superintendents—are often the most influential people in establishing the climate for including exceptional students in their schools. Some administrators set a positive climate for mainstreaming, while others are neutral or even negative in tone. The administrator is clearly in a position to make important decisions about the quality of education offered to handicapped children in the regular school. In a recent study, Joiner and Sabatino (1981) found that general education administrators demonstrated a relatively low level of "consciousness" toward important provisions of P.L. 94–142, such as due process, parent involvement, and student assessment. The authors suggest that special educators devote increased attention to making general education administrators more aware of the key principles involved in providing an appropriate education to exceptional students in the least restrictive environment.

PROMISE AND PROBLEMS

The promise of a free, appropriate public education for all handicapped children has been described as a new "Bill of Rights" for the exceptional (Goodman, 1976). Many people—both within and outside of education—have welcomed the recognition of handicapped children's rights, the increased involvement of parents in the educational process, and the financial assistance offered to schools in the education of exceptional children, all of which are inherent in recent legislation and court decisions. Many other people, however, have detected significant problems in the implementation of these laws and decisions; indeed, when President Ford signed Public Law 94–142, he was quoted as saying, "This bill promises more than the federal government can deliver" (Bierly, 1978). School administrators have expressed concerns over excessive paperwork and unclear guidelines. Regular class teachers have expressed dissatisfaction over the placement of handicapped children into their classes without adequate preparation or support. Special education teachers have frequently felt inadequately prepared for their new responsibilities. Some parents of handicapped and nonhandicapped children are opposed to the integration of exceptional students into regular classes. There are many other problems, real and perceived, and no simple solutions can be offered.

The challenge of special education in the schools today is great. Whether or not the promise of a "free, appropriate public education" can be fulfilled will depend largely upon the readiness of professionals to work together, to assume new roles, and to communicate with each other. We do not know what the long-range outcome of our current efforts will be. Caution, at times, appears well advised; Hechinger (1976) suggests that we "slow down the bandwagon of instant change and the confusion between civil rights and the right kind of education for every child." Yet the quiet revolution continues. "At the minimum," write Weintraub and Abeson (1974), "it will make educational opportunity a reality for all handicapped children. At the maximum, it will make our schools healthier learning environments for *all* our children."

CLASSWIDE PEER TUTORING: INTEGRATING HANDICAPPED CHILDREN INTO THE REGULAR CLASSROOM

Including a handicapped child in classwide academic activities can present a difficult challenge. The regular classroom teacher is expected to deliver individualized instruction to the handicapped student, maintain effective programming for the rest of the class, and help the mainstreamed child become socially integrated into the classroom. One method that has been used successfully to individualize instruction for handicapped students without requiring them to leave the regular classroom is in-class tutoring. Certified tutors, classroom aides, parent and grandparent volunteers, and older students have all served as effective in-class tutors for handicapped children. However, obtaining extra adult help or out-of-class students as tutors on a regular basis is often a problem.

An often untapped and always available source of tutoring help exists in every classroom—the students themselves. While the idea of peer tutoring (same-age classmates teaching one another) is not new (Lancaster, 1806), it has recently become the focus of renewed interest and research. As peer tutoring is typically implemented, a few high-achieving students are assigned to tutor students who have not mastered a particular skill, and the handicapped or low-achieving student is singled out for special help. By contrast, a *classwide* peer tutoring system allows the handicapped student to become a full participant in an ongoing whole-class activity. Direct, individualized instruction is provided to *every* student in the class and social interactions between handicapped and non-handicapped classmates are encouraged. One classwide peer tutoring program that has been developed for teaching basic sight word vocabulary in the primary grades is described here.

Every student in the class has a tutoring folder containing 10 flash cards in a "GO" pocket (page 60). Each card has one word to be taught to the child's partner. Thus, children serve as both tutor and student each day. When in the role of student, each child practices words from an individualized list of new words that the teacher has chosen after giving a pretest.

Tutor Huddle

The daily peer tutoring session begins with the students getting their folders and participating in a 5-minute "Tutor Huddle" with two or three other tutors. (See the photo below.) The children take turns presenting and orally reading the sight words they will shortly be responsible for teaching to their partners. (Meanwhile, their partners are in other Tutor Huddles working on the words they will soon be teaching.) Fellow tutors confirm correct responses by saying "yes,"

Tutor Huddle.

and try to help identify words a tutor doesn't know. The teacher circulates around the room, helping Tutor Huddles who cannot identify or agree upon a given word.

Practice

After Tutor Huddle, partners join one another to practice their words. One child begins in the role of tutor and presents the word cards as many times as possible during the 5-minute practice period. Tutors are trained to praise their students from time to time for correct responses. When a student makes an error, the tutor says "try again." If the student still does not read the word correctly, the tutor says "The word is 'tree', say 'tree'." A timer signals the end of the first practice period and the partners switch roles. The child who was in the role of student now becomes tutor, and vice versa.

Testing

After the second practice period, roles are again reversed and the first tutor tests his partner by presenting each sight word once,

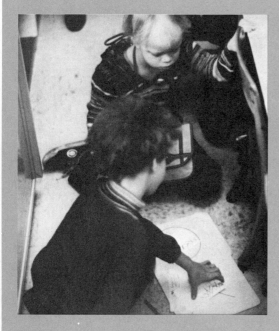

Testing.

providing no prompts or cues. (See the photo on page 60.) Words the student reads correctly are placed in one pile and words missed in another. Roles are switched again, and the first tutor is now tested on the words he practiced. The peer tutoring session ends with the tutors charting on the "animal graph" the number of words said correctly by their partners during the test and praising one another for their good work. ("We learned a lot today!") When a child correctly reads a word on the test for three consecutive sessions, that word is considered learned and is moved to the folder's "STOP" pocket. When all 10 words have been learned, a new set of words is placed in the "GO" pocket.

Results

This peer tutoring system was originally developed and evaluated over a 5-month period in a first grade classroom of 28 children. The class included one learning disabled boy and one mentally retarded girl, both of whom attended a special education resource room for part of the school day. Results showed that all children in the classroom learned sight words at a rapid, consistent pace (Heward, Heron, & Cooke, 1982). The children also retained the words they had taught one another. The class average on 10-word review tests given 1 week after each set of words was learned was 8.9 words correct. Of particular interest was the performance of the two handicapped children in the class. The learning disabled boy functioned successfully both as a student and as a tutor. While the mentally retarded child did not serve as a tutor, she participated as a student, learning at the rate of almost one

new word each day. Her sight word vocabulary increased from a pretest score of 4 to a total of 51 words by the end of the study. (See the bar graph below.) She, too, remembered the words she had learned, averaging 8.7 words correct out of a possible 10 on the 1-week review tests. Both tutor and student enjoyed the daily sessions. When the long program ended, her tutor wrote, "I like peer tutoring. I liked my student vary [sic] much." The positive social interactions of a classwide peer tutoring program such as this one may, in the long run, prove an equal or even greater benefit to the children involved than the actual learning gains themselves.

This classwide peer tutoring system has been replicated in many primary classrooms with both sight words and math facts. Interested readers may obtain a detailed description of the peer tutoring system by writing William L. Heward, College of Education, The Ohio State University, Columbus, OH 43210.

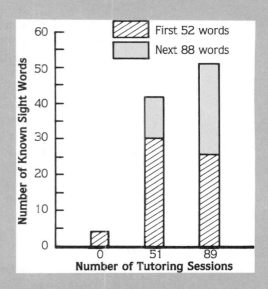

SUMMARY

1. Public school programs for exceptional children are a relatively recent development in American education.
   a. For many years, special education simply did not exist.
   b. Early special education programs were segregated from the rest of the educational world, in separate buildings or classrooms.
   c. Today, most handicapped children will spend all or at least part of the school day in regular classrooms with nonhandicapped peers. Others will attend special classes in regular schools, and a few others will be educated in other special settings.

2. The current movement to extend educational opportunities to handicapped children is an outgrowth of the civil rights movement.
   a. All children are now recognized to have the right to equal protection under the law, which has been interpreted to mean the right to a free public education in the least restrictive, appropriate setting.
   b. All children and their parents also have the right to due process under the law, which includes the rights to be notified of any decision affecting the child's educational placement, to have a hearing and present a defense, to see a written decision, and to appeal any decision.
   c. Court cases have also established the rights of handicapped children to fair assessment in their native language and to education at public expense regardless of the school district's financial constraints.

3. Recent legislation has extended and clarified the legal rights of exceptional children.
   a. P.L. 94–142 made many trends in special education part of the law. It extends public education to all handicapped children between ages 3 and 21, with special priority to those currently unserved and underserved. It also sets out requirements for diagnosis, nondiscriminatory assessment, individualization of programming, and personnel development.
   b. A number of court cases have challenged the way particular school districts implement specific provisions of P. L. 94–142. No trend has yet emerged from these cases.
   c. Section 504 of the Rehabilitation Act forbids discrimination in all federally funded programs—including educational and vocational programs—on the basis of handicap alone.
   d. The Gifted and Talented Children Act addresses the educational needs of this special group.

4. Special education today is a system of delivering services to exceptional students.
   a. The concept of mainstreaming remains controversial. However, it does not mean the movement of all handicapped children into regular classrooms overnight. Rather, each student should be placed into the most integrated setting in which he or she can succeed.

b. There should be a range of service options available to all exceptional students, so that each student can receive the necessary help for as long as it is indicated and can then move to a less restrictive setting as soon as possible. The less integrated the setting, the fewer students it should serve.

c. A team approach, where teachers, other professionals, and paraprofessionals share information and skills, can help make each student's education as effective and consistent as possible.

d. Assessment is now seen as an ongoing part of a child's program, where a teacher (or other member of the team) finds out what the child currently can do in a specific situation.

e. The Individualized Education Program (IEP), which many teachers have been using in one form or another for years, is simply a way of ensuring that each child is assessed, that long-range goals and short-term objectives are set, and that the child's progress is evaluated regularly.

f. Special educators will be called upon to provide more support and in-service training for regular educators in the future.

5. While the new laws and court decisions promise many welcome advances in special education, they also present a tremendous challenge to the field.

FOR MORE INFORMATION

Journals

Exceptional Children. Published eight times a year by the Council for Exceptional Children. Designed to assist all professionals who work in exceptional child education.

Journal of Special Education. Published quarterly. Publishes articles from all disciplines dealing with research, theory, opinion, and review in special education and areas of particular concern to general education.

Teaching Exceptional Children. Published quarterly by the Council for Exceptional Children. Publishes classroom hints, reports of materials and techniques, teacher ideas, and other information for the teacher of exceptional children.

Books

Gardner, W. I. *Learning and behavior characteristics of exceptional children and youth.* Boston: Allyn & Bacon, 1977.

Haring, N. G., & Schiefelbusch, R. L. (eds.). *Teaching special children.* New York: McGraw-Hill, 1976.

Howell, K. *Inside special education.* Columbus, Ohio: Charles E. Merrill, 1983.

Soderbergh, P. A. *Special education USA: A socio-professional almanac.* Columbus, Ohio: Special Press, 1982.

Turnbull, A. P., Strickland, B. B., & Brantley, J., *Developing and implementing Individualized Education Programs,* Columbus, Ohio: Charles E. Merrill, 1982.

White, O. R., & Haring, N.G. *Exceptional teaching,* 2d ed. Columbus, Ohio: Charles E. Merrill, 1980.

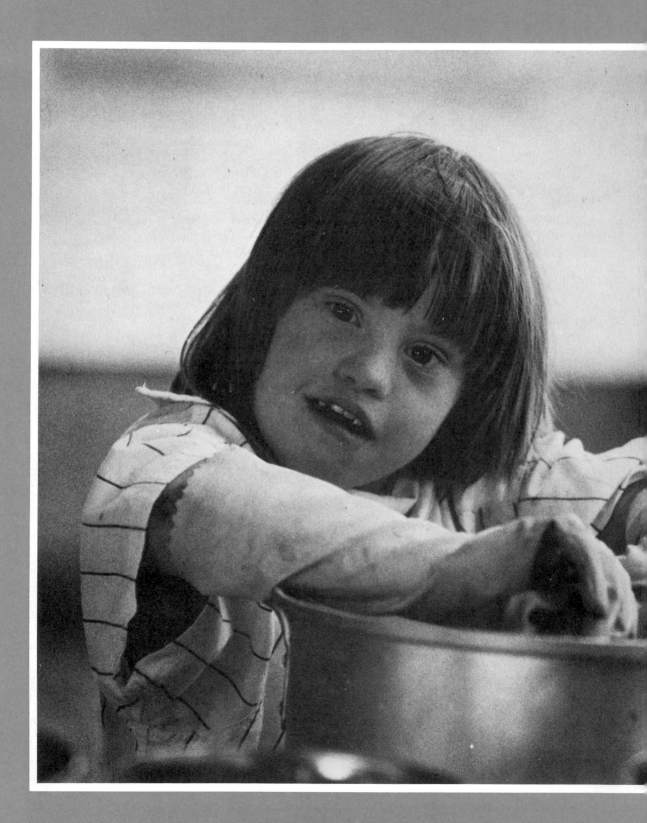

II
Exceptional Children

3 Mental Retardation

Most people have some ideas of what mental retardation is and what mentally retarded people are like. When they hear the words "special education," they think of mental retardation. The first public school special education classes, in 1896, were held for mentally retarded children. Of course, things have changed since then. The past 25 years especially have witnessed significant improvements in the education, care, and treatment of children and adults with retarded development. At the same time, public awareness of mental retardation has been increasing. Unfortunately, even today much of that awareness consists of superstition, half-truths, and oversimplifications. This chapter presents some key concepts in understanding the very complex concept called mental retardation. We will also look at some contemporary educational practices that have helped improve the outlook for mentally retarded children—one of the largest categories of exceptionality.

HISTORY OF TREATMENT AND SERVICES FOR MENTALLY RETARDED INDIVIDUALS

The history of mental retardation is long. In all probability, some people have been slower to learn than others as long as people have populated the earth. The Greeks in 1552 B.C. and the Romans in 449 B.C. were among the first to recognize people officially as mentally retarded. There are also passages in the Bible referring to slow learners (Barr, 1913; Lindman & McIntyre, 1961).

Several special educators and historians have written detailed and interesting accounts of the changing philosophies, beliefs, and treatment of mentally retarded people over the years. For example, Hewett and Forness (1977) describe the role and importance of survival, superstition, science, and service in treatment of mentally retarded people during different historical periods. Kolstoe and Frey (1965) describe five chronological eras of treatment: extermination, ridicule, asylum, education, and occupational adequacy. Gearheart and Litton (1975) characterize the early history of mental retardation (prior to the 1800s) as consisting primarily of superstition and extermination; the 19th century as the era that produced institutions for the mentally retarded; the 20th century as the era of public school classes; the 1950s and 1960s as the era of legislation and national support; and the 1970s as the era of normalization, child advocacy, and litigation. In this chapter we will only very briefly cover some of the changing attitudes and significant events that have affected the care and treatment of mentally retarded people.

The primary goal of human beings in primitive societies was survival. The sick, physically handicapped, and elderly were often abandoned or even killed to increase the chance of survival by others. The Greeks and Romans often sent mentally and physically defective children to places far away from the community, where they would perish on their own. Later, as survival became less of a 24-hour concern and society separated into levels, ridicule of mentally retarded people was common. Superstitions and myths developed. Words like *idiot, imbecile,* and *dunce* were used, and some kings and queens and other wealthy people kept "fools" or "imbeciles" as clowns or court jesters.

During the Middle Ages, as religion became a dominant force, a more humanitarian view was taken. Asylums and monasteries were erected to care for mentally retarded people. However, no one thought their behavior could be altered.

Around the turn of the 19th century, the first attempt to educate a retarded person was recorded. In 1798 three hunters found and captured an 11- or 12-year-old boy in the woods of Aveyron, France. The boy, later called Victor, the Wild Boy of Aveyron (Itard, 1894/1962), was completely unsocialized and had no language. He was pronounced an "uncurable idiot." Jean Marc Gaspard Itard, a physician who was working at an institution for the deaf, refused to believe that Victor was uneducable. Itard began an intensive training program with Victor. After almost 5 years he concluded his work, deeming it a miserable failure because he did not reach his original goals for Victor. However, the changes that did occur with Victor were significant: He was much more socialized and could read and write a few words. For the first time it was recognized that intensive training could produce important gains.

Edward Seguin, a student of Itard's, founded a school for retarded children in Paris in 1837. He later came to the United States, where he helped to establish the Pennsylvania Training School, an early educational facility. The first person to advocate educational programs for mentally retarded children in the United States was Samuel Gridley Howe, who had already devoted much of his life to the education of blind, deaf, and other disadvantaged children. In 1848, thanks to his powerful letter arguing for the rights of mentally retarded people in a democratic society, the Massachusetts legislature overrode a governor's

Itard may have been the first "special educator."

veto and provided Howe with $2,500 for the first institution for the mentally retarded in this country. For the remainder of the 19th century, large state institutions for the mentally retarded and the mentally ill (they were often viewed as the same) became the primary means of service delivery. As the institutions became overcrowded and understaffed, the optimism sparked by the educational gains produced by Itard, Seguin, and Howe began to wane. State institutions came to be viewed as "custodial" rather than "educational," a view that has taken years of effort to change, extending to the present.

The first public school class for mentally retarded children was formed in 1896 in Providence, Rhode Island. Thus began the special class movement, which saw 87,030 children enrolled in special classes in 1948, 703,800 in 1969, and 1,305,000 in 1974. The great increases in children being served by the public schools paralleled increases in federal aid to education, particularly to special education, in the 1950s and 1960s.

Those interested in a more in-depth history of mental retardation are encouraged to read MacMillan (1982), Payne and Patton (1981), or Scheerenberger (1982).

Today, we are witnessing a move away from total reliance on the large state institution and the self-contained special class in the education and care of mentally retarded children. The trend today is toward more normalized community-based facilities and education in the least restrictive environment, which for a significant number of mentally retarded children includes the regular classroom.

DEFINING MENTAL RETARDATION

Mental retardation describes performance; it is not a "thing" children are born with inside their heads.

Mental retardation is, above all, a label; it is a term used to identify an observed performance deficit—failure to demonstrate age-appropriate intellectual and social behavior. Definitions of mental retardation have been proposed, debated, revised, and counterproposed over many years. And still the debate goes on.

Since mental retardation is a concept that affects and is affected by people in many different disciplines, it has been defined from many different perspectives. A definition offered by a professional within a given discipline may be functional only if you are using that particular perspective. For example, a definition of mental retardation based solely on biological or medical criteria, while useful to doctors and nurses, would not be functional for a teacher or a psychologist.

But, as MacMillan (1982) points out, disagreements among professionals over what constitutes mental retardation are "not merely academic exercises in semantics." A subtle difference between two definitions can determine whether or not the label of mental retardation will be affixed to a particular child. The critical importance of definition was noted as early as 1924 by Kuhlman, who recognized that definitions of mental deficiency can be used to "decide the fate of thousands every year."

You might reasonably ask why it is so important whether or not a person is classified as mentally retarded or not mentally retarded. There are some children and adults so clearly deficient in academic and social skills that it is obvious to anyone who interacts with them that they require special services and educational programming. How mental retardation is defined is not much of an issue for these individuals; they are severely retarded in all areas of development. But this group comprises only a small segment of the total population identified as mentally retarded. The largest segment of the mentally retarded population consists of school-age children who are mildly retarded. The way that mental retardation is defined determines whether or not thousands of children are classified as mentally retarded and, consequently, what special educational services they may be eligible to receive.

In early times, only the severely retarded were identified; the term *idiocy* was used (derived from a Greek word meaning "people who did not hold public office" [MacMillan, 1982]). In the 19th century, the label *imbecile* (derived from the Latin word for weak and feeble) was applied to not so severely retarded people. The term *simpleton* was eventually added to identify those cases less severe than imbeciles (Clausen, 1967). As defined by Ireland in 1900,

> Idiocy is mental deficiency, or extreme stupidity, depending upon malnutrition or disease of the nervous centers, occurring either before birth or before the evolution of mental faculties in childhood. The word *imbecility* is generally used to denote a less decided degree of mental incapacity. (p. 1)

Most of the early definitions emphasized the biological or medical aspects of mental retardation, since physicians were the first professional group to work with mentally retarded people.

The two definitions referred to most often during the first half of this century were written by Tredgold and Doll. Tredgold's (1937) reads:

> A state of incomplete mental development of such a kind and degree that the individual is incapable of adapting himself to the normal environment of his fellows in such a way to maintain existence independently of supervision, control, or external support. (p. 4)

In 1941, Doll wrote that six criteria were essential to the definition and concept of mental retardation.

> These are (1) social incompetence, (2) due to mental subnormality, (3) which has been developmentally arrested, (4) which obtains at maturity, (5) is of constitutional origin, and (6) is essentially incurable. (p. 215)

The AAMD Definitions

In 1959, the American Association on Mental Deficiency (AAMD) published a manual of terminology and classification on mental retardation which included a definition. That definition was revised in 1961 to read:

> Mental retardation refers to subaverage general intellectual functioning which originates during the developmental period and is associated with impairment in adaptive behavior. (Heber, 1961, p. 3)

AAMD is a national organization comprised of professionals—in education, medicine, psychology, social work, speech pathology, etc.—as well as students, parents, and others concerned about the study, treatment, and prevention of mental retardation.

Twelve years later, the AAMD definition was revised to read:

Mental retardation refers to significantly subaverage general intellectual functioning existing concurrently with deficits in adaptive behavior, and manifested during the developmental period. (Grossman, 1973, p. 5)

At first glance, the two definitions seem almost the same; they use the same terminology and similar word order. However, there are important differences between the two. First, according to the 1961 definition, mental retardation was equated with "subaverage general intellectual functioning," *associated with* adaptive behavior impairments. According to the revised definition, an individual must be well below average in *both* intellectual functioning *and* adaptive behavior. That is, intellectual functioning is no longer the sole defining criterion. A second important change is the *degree* of subaverage intellectual functioning that must be demonstrated before a person is called mentally retarded. The word "significantly" in the 1973 definition refers to a score of two or more standard deviations below the mean on a standardized intelligence test (we will explain this below); the 1961 definition required a score of only one standard deviation below the mean. Furthermore, this change eliminated the category of "borderline" mental retardation. A third change, although not as important as the first two, was also included in the revised definition. The developmental period was extended from birth through 16 years to birth through 18 years to coincide with the usual period of public schooling. The definition specifies that the deficits in intellectual functioning and adaptive behavior occur during the developmental period in order to help distinguish mental retardation from other disorders (for instance, an adult whose performance is suddenly impaired as the result of a severe physical injury).

"C'mon in, the water's fine!"

Measuring Intellectual Functioning

Intellectual functioning, as used in special education, is most often measured by a score on a standardized intelligence (IQ) test. An IQ test consists of a series of questions and problem-solving tasks that are assumed to require certain amounts of intelligence to answer or solve correctly. Thus, an IQ test samples a small portion of the full range of an individual's skills and abilities. That observed performance sample is used to derive a score that is taken to represent the test taker's overall intelligence.

When we say that an IQ test is "standardized," we mean that the same questions and tasks are to be presented in a certain, specified way, and that each test taker's responses are to be scored using the same procedures each time the test is administered. A standardized test has also been "normed"; that is, it has been administered to a large sample of people, selected at random from the population for whom the test is intended. The test scores of the people in the random sample are then used as "norms," or averages of how people perform on the test. On the two most widely used intelligence tests, the Stanford-Binet (Terman & Merrill, 1973) and the Revised Wechsler Intelligence Scale for Children (WISC-R) (Wechsler, 1974), the norm or average score is 100.

Standard deviation is a mathematical concept. It refers to the amount by which a particular score varies from the mean, or average score, on a given test, with respect to all the scores in the norm sample. (See Figure 3.1 for further information about standard deviation.) One standard deviation on the Stanford-Binet is 16 points; on the WISC-R, 15 points. (The difference stems from the difference in the distribution of scores obtained by the samples of children used to derive the norms for the two tests.) Thus, according to the 1961 AAMD definition of mental retardation, a child could be labeled mentally retarded on the basis of an IQ score as high as 84 or 85, depending upon the test used. The 1973 AAMD definition of mental retardation requires an IQ score *two* standard deviations below the mean (as well as deficits in adaptive behavior), which would be 68 or 70 on the two tests.

As you might guess, the change in the definition of mental retardation by 15 IQ points affected many children. In California, a state law was passed saying that a child must fall two full standard deviations or below on both the verbal and performance subtests of the WISC-R in order to be classified mentally retarded. Virtually overnight 20,000 school children who had been considered mentally retarded no longer were. Of course, even though children whose IQ scores had placed them in the category of "borderline" mental retardation, which was eliminated by the revised definition, are no longer labeled mentally retarded, some of them may still need special education services in order to succeed in school.

There are a number of reasons why educators and other professionals in mental retardation advocated the 1973 AAMD definition, which is much more conservative (than the earlier definition) in terms of who shall be called mentally retarded. Four of those reasons are summarized here:

The test taker's age is considered when computing an IQ. To obtain a score of 100, a 5-year-old child must respond correctly to those questions and tasks most 5-year-olds get right. A 16-year-old who responded correctly to only those test items the average 5-year-old got right would receive a score much lower than 100.

Stanford Binet — 16 pts.
WISC-R — 15 pts.

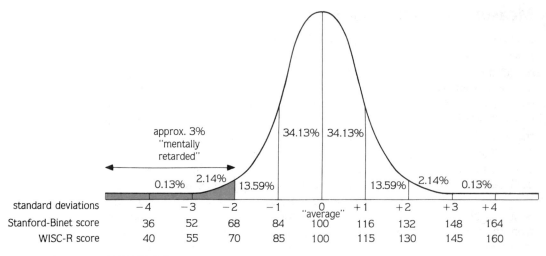

standard deviations	−4	−3	−2	−1	0 "average"	+1	+2	+3	+4
Stanford-Binet score	36	52	68	84	100	116	132	148	164
WISC-R score	40	55	70	85	100	115	130	145	160

FIGURE 3.1

IQ scores seem to be distributed throughout the population according to a phenomenon called the **normal curve,** shown here. To describe how one particular score varies from the mean (average score), the population is broken into units called *standard deviations.* Each standard deviation includes a fixed portion of the population. For example, we know that 34.13% of the population will fall within 1 standard deviation above the mean, and another 34.13% will be within 1 standard deviation below "normal." By applying an algebraic formula to the scores achieved by the norm sample on a test, we can tell what value equals 1 standard deviation for that test. We can then take a person's IQ test score and describe it in terms of how many standard deviations above or below the mean it is.

Looking at the graph, we can see that just under 3% of the population falls 2 or more standard deviations below the mean, which the AAMD calls "significantly subaverage." That means that if we used IQ scores as the sole criterion, about 3% of the population would be considered "mentally retarded."

1. Possible negative effects of labeling a child retarded. Some educators feel that when a child is "officially" labeled mentally retarded, the damage done by the label itself outweighs any positive effects of special education and treatment that follow as one of the consequences of being labeled (Kugel & Wolfensberger, 1969; Smith & Neisworth, 1975).

2. Cultural bias of intelligence tests. Both the Binet and Wechsler IQ tests have been heavily criticized for being culturally biased. That is, the tests tend to favor children from the population on which they were normed—primarily white, middle-class children. Some of the questions on an IQ test might tap learning that only a middle-class child is likely to have experienced. The tests, which are highly verbal, are especially inappropriate for children for whom English is a second language. Mercer (1973a) points out that when an IQ test is used to identify children for special class placement, many more black,

EXCEPTIONAL CHILDREN

Mexican-American, and poor children "earn" the label mentally retarded than do white, middle-class children.

3. IQ scores can change significantly. Several studies have shown that IQ scores can change, particularly in the range that used to constitute "borderline" retardation (MacMillan, 1982). And since mental retardation tends to be used as a permanent label for the child, even though it only is supposed to describe present performance, educators were concerned that many children were being identified as mentally retarded because of a test score that might be increased by as many as 15 to 20 points after a period of effective instruction (Bruening & Davis, 1981).

4. Intelligence testing is not an exact science. While the major intelligence tests are among the most carefully standardized and developed psychological tests, they are still far from perfect. Among the variables that can affect a child's final score on an IQ test are motivation, when and where the test is administered, and bias on the test giver's part, which may affect how he or she scores any of the child's responses that are not exactly covered by the test manual. Even the choice of which test to use can be critical. For example, Wechsler (1974) reports that the WISC-R and the revised Stanford-Binet correlate with each other at about the .70 level. This means that it is possible for a child to be identified as mentally retarded by one test but not the other.

Robinson and Robinson (1976), in their excellent discussion of intelligence testing, summarize some potential values and pitfalls of IQ tests:

> The development and popular utilization of the IQ as a single, simple, objective index of the rate of intellectual growth has been a mixed blessing. When properly understood and carefully used, an IQ test can be valuable in assessing a child's rate of progress, but it refers to only those aspects of mental ability tapped by a particular test. Its measurement is subject to error from a number of sources, some of them capable of drastically affecting scores. There is little doubt that IQs have been seriously misused because of persistent and erroneous notions about their supposed permanence or their magical power to predict future performance. Such a simple index of present behavior as the IQ cannot possibly reflect all the many aspects of the complex developmental phenomenon known as intelligence.
>
> Nowhere has the IQ proved to be a more mixed blessing than in matters concerning the welfare of mentally retarded children. To be sure, the development of intelligence tests provided a means for more objective assessment. Tests have been very useful in helping to identify children who need special training and in establishing more orderly methods for admissions procedures in institutions. Many retarded children have been helped to lead more productive lives because of the early identification of their problems. Other children whose school failures were not due to overall intellectual deficits have also been identified and treated accordingly.
>
> On the other hand, the apparent simplicity of the IQ led to an enthusiastic but largely misguided movement to label or classify children primarily on the basis of their scores on intelligence tests. Accurate classification of intellectual defi-

SPECIAL OLYMPICS: A REWARDING EXPERIENCE

Special Olympics is an international program of physical fitness, sports training, and athletic competition for over 1 million mentally retarded participants in 40 countries. Created and sponsored by the Joseph P. Kennedy Foundation, the Special Olympics offers 16 official sports, including track and field, swimming, diving, gymnastics, basketball, softball, soccer, bowling, Alpine and Nordic skiing, and wheelchair events. Mentally retarded individuals 8 years and older are eligible to participate; there is no upper age limit. Olympic-type events with all the pageantry and excitement of opening and closing ceremonies, spectators, and awards presentations are held annually at the state and national levels. International Games are held every 4 years. More than 4,000 Special Olympians participated in the 1983 International Summer Games, held in Baton Rouge.

On the local level, Special Olympics is a year-round program. Rick McCune, director of the Special Olympics program in Franklin County, Ohio, explained, "We have 10 full-time coaches who, along with dozens of volunteers, offer Wednesday evening practice sessions throughout the year for about 500 mentally retarded individuals in the county. In addition to the 'official' Special Olympics events, we also offer wrestling and cross country. Just like other athletes, the Special Olympians are always in training, preparing themselves for the next meet or event held at the county and regional level throughout the year.

"They are given the chance to extend themselves, strive for new goals, wear a uniform, hear cheers, and win and lose. In addition, the organized competitions give participants the chance to travel, meet new people, and use self-help and social skills in meaningful ways. The complaint is sometimes heard that Special Olympics programs aren't nor-

Team sports encourage cooperation.

malized because they bring together only handicapped participants. But the athletes are grouped together for competition according to age and skill levels, just as in any other organized sports program. In the sense of the 'typical person' being able to participate, how normalized is the NBA, the NFL, or a high school track and field team? In fact, one of our principal objectives is the 'graduation' of Special Olympians into a regular school or community-sponsored team or sports program. But realistically, such opportunities are seldom available for our athletes. Without Special Olympics few, if any, of the individuals in our program would have the opportunity to participate in organized sporting events."

Special Olympics is primarily a volunteer-run program, using the skills, resources, and efforts of thousands of volunteers each year. You can help out with the Special Olympics program in your area. You'll find it a rewarding experience. For more information, contact:

Eunice Kennedy Shriver, President
Special Olympics, Inc.
1701 K Street NW, Suite 203
Washington, DC 20006

cit was thought to be all that was required to achieve understanding of retarded children, individual characteristics being grossly underestimated. Furthermore, undue belief in IQ constancy led to a diminution in research and treatment. Professional interest in many complex problems declined over a long period, not to be rejuvenated until the mid-1960s. Fortunately, a more realistic view now prevails. (p. 343)

Clearly, intelligence tests have both advantages and disadvantages. Here are several more important considerations to keep in mind.

☐ The concept of intelligence is a hypothetical construct. No one has ever seen a thing called "intelligence"; it is not a precise entity, but rather something that we infer from observed performance. We assume it takes more intelligence to learn to perform certain tasks than others.

☐ There is nothing mysterious or powerful about an IQ test. An IQ test is simply a series of questions and problem-solving tasks.

☐ An IQ test only measures how a child performs at one point in time on the items included in one test. We *infer* from that performance how a child might perform in other situations.

☐ IQ tests have proven to be the best single predictor of school achievement. Since IQ tests are composed largely of verbal and academic tasks—the same things that a child must master in order to succeed in school—they correlate with school achievement more highly than any other single testing device.

☐ In the hands of a competent school psychologist, an IQ test can provide useful information, particularly in objectively identifying an overall performance deficit.

☐ Results from an IQ test are generally *not* useful in planning individualized educational objectives and teaching strategies for a child. Direct, teacher-administered, criterion-referenced assessment of a child's performance on the specific skills he needs to learn is more useful for planning instruction.

☐ Results from an IQ test should *never* be used as the only criterion to label, classify, or place a child in a special program.

Measuring Adaptive Behavior

. . . To be classified as mentally retarded, a person must be *clearly* subnormal in adaptive behavior. It would be pointless to identify and classify as mentally retarded a person who faces no unusual problems or whose needs are met without professional attention. Some people with an IQ below 70 do well in school and society. Such people are not mentally retarded, and should not be labeled as such. (MacMillan, 1982, p. 42)

Many children who used to be called "retarded" were anything but retarded outside of school; they coped very well indeed with the requirements of their home, their neighborhood, and their friends. In 1969, the President's Committee on Mental Retardation described the "6-hour retarded child." They were referring to the fact that many children are only considered mentally re-

For example, a criterion-referenced test for single-digit addition might be to give the child 10 such problems. Rather than judging the child's performance by comparing it to other children's (i.e., norm-referenced), the child's performance is compared to a standard criterion. If he gets 9 or 10 correct, instruction will not be necessary on that skill; if he gets less than 9 correct, a teaching program for single-digit addition problems will be implemented.

Adaptive behavior includes self-care skills such a toothbrushing.

tarded during the 6 hours of each day they spend in school, but that they function normally and are not considered retarded by the people they interact with during the other 18 hours of the day. In this sense, the demands of school could be actually said to "cause" mental retardation. To counteract this problem and other criticisms of the use of an IQ test as the sole criterion for mental retardation, the definition was revised to require that a child show deficits in adaptive behavior as well as intellectual functioning.

Grossman (1973) defined adaptive behavior as "the effectiveness or degree with which the individual meets the standards of personal independence and social responsibility expected of his age and social group." AAMD further defines the areas where deficits in adaptive behavior can be found within different age groups.

   During infancy and early childhood:
   1. Sensory-motor skills
   2. Communication skills (speech and language)
   3. Self-help skills
   4. Socialization skills (interacting and getting along with others)

   During childhood and early adolescence:
   5. Application of basic academic skills in daily life activities
   6. Application of appropriate reasoning and judgment in mastery of the environment
   7. Social skills (participation in group activities and interpersonal relationships)

   During late adolescence and adulthood:
   8. Vocational and social responsibility and performance. (Grossman, 1973, p. 11-12)

The AAMD manual mentions two scales that are used to measure adaptive behavior—the AAMD Adaptive Behavior Scale (Nihira, Foster, Shellhaas, & Leland, 1974) and the Vineland Social Maturity Scale (Doll, 1965). Other adaptive behavior scales have been and are being developed. All of these scales list many behaviors that would be expected of people of different ages. The behaviors are classified into areas such as those listed above. To measure adaptive behavior, the tester must directly observe how an individual performs the behaviors on the scale in the settings where they would normally occur. Thus, measuring adaptive behavior can take quite a long time and many resources. (Certainly one of the attractions of IQ tests is that they can be given in the psychologist's office in about an hour's time.)

The instrument most widely used to measure the adaptive behavior of individuals thought to be retarded is the AAMD Adaptive Behavior Scale (ABS). The ABS consists of two parts. Part I consists of 10 domains related to independent functioning and daily living skills. It is further broken down into 21 subdomains. Part II of the ABS assesses the individual's level of maladaptive (inappropriate) behavior. Another version of the ABS has been developed for use in public schools to measure the adaptive behavior of children with suspected mild retardation (Lambert, Windmiller, Cole, & Figueroa, 1975).

Table 3.1 lists the parts of the ABS. Figure 3.2 shows one page of the ABS.

The ABS can be administered in several ways. Sometimes it is completed by someone familiar with the person being assessed, such as direct care worker, teacher, or parent; sometimes an examiner completes the ABS by interviewing a direct care worker or parent; and sometimes direct observation is conducted.

While including the concept of adaptive behavior in the definition of mental retardation is beneficial, its measurement has proven troublesome. Nowhere is there a list that everyone would agree describes exactly those adaptive behaviors that all of us should exhibit. As with IQ tests, cultural bias is also inherent in adaptive behavior scales. For instance, one item on some scales requires a child to tie a laced shoe, but some children have never had a shoe with laces. Research being conducted today on the measurement of adaptive behavior may help resolve these problems.

The Still Unresolved Issue of Definition

The 1973 AAMD definition was incorporated into P.L. 94–142 as the federal definition of mental retardation and is the definition most frequently cited in the special education literature. Since 1973, the AAMD definition has been slightly revised two times (Grossman, 1977, 1983) in efforts to clarify the importance of clinical judgment in the diagnosis of mental retardation. When the 1973 AAMD definition reduced the upper IQ limit from 85 to 70, the largest group of children previously considered mentally retarded could no longer be classified as such and, in some cases, were denied needed special education services. Kidd (1979) felt that many children who desperately needed the specialized instruction offered in programs for the mildly retarded were "now being drowned in the mainstream" (p. 75). The newest AAMD manual (Grossman, 1983) emphasizes that the IQ cutoff score of 70 is intended only as a guideline and should not be interpreted as a hard and fast requirement. The IQ score of

TABLE 3.1
Areas covered by the AAMD Adaptive Behavior Scale.

Part One	Part Two

I. Independent Functioning
  A. Eating
  B. Toilet Use
  C. Cleanliness
  D. Appearance
  E. Care of Clothing
  F. Dressing and Undressing
  G. Travel
  H. General Independent Functioning	

II. Physical Development
  A. Sensory Development
  B. Motor Development
	I. Violent and Destructive Behavior
	II. Antisocial Behavior
	III. Rebellious Behavior
	IV. Untrustworthy Behavior
	V. Withdrawal

III. Economic Activity
  A. Money Handling and Budgeting
  B. Shopping Skills
	VI. Stereotyped Behavior and Odd Mannerisms
	VII. Inappropriate Interpersonal Manners

IV. Language Development
  A. Expression
  B. Comprehension
  C. Social Language Development
	VIII. Unacceptable Vocal Habits
	IX. Unacceptable or Eccentric Habits

V. Numbers and Time	X. Self-abusive Behavior XI. Hyperactive Tendencies

VI. Domestic Activity
  A. Cleaning
  B. Kitchen Duties
  C. Other Domestic Activities
	XII. Sexually Aberrant Behavior
	XIII. Psychological Disturbances
	XIV. Use of Medications

VII. Vocational Activity	

VIII. Self-Direction
  A. Initiative
  B. Perseverance
  C. Leisure Time	

IX. Responsibility	
X. Socialization	

SOURCE: *AAMD Adaptive Behavior Scale*, pp. 6–7, 1975. Copyright, 1975, the American Association on Mental Deficiency.

EXCEPTIONAL CHILDREN

PART ONE
I. INDEPENDENT FUNCTIONING

A. Eating

(1) Use of Table Utensils (Circle only <u>ONE</u>)

Uses knife and fork correctly and neatly	6
Uses table knife for cutting or spreading	5
Feeds self with spoon and fork—neatly	4
Feeds self with spoon and fork—considerable spilling	3
Feeds self with spoon—neatly	2
Feeds self with spoon—considerable spilling	1
Feeds self with fingers or must be fed	0

(2) Eating in Public (Circle only <u>ONE</u>)

Orders complete meals in restaurants	3
Orders simple meals like hamburgers or hot dogs	2
Orders soft drinks at soda fountain or canteen	1
Does not order at public eating places	0

(3) Drinking (Circle only <u>ONE</u>)

Drinks without spilling, holding glass in one hand	3
Drinks from cup or glass unassisted—neatly	2
Drinks from cup or glass unassisted considerable spilling	1
Does not drink from cup or glass unassisted	0

(4) Table Manners (Check <u>ALL</u> statements which apply)

Swallows food without chewing	_____
Chews food with mouth open	_____
Drops food on table or floor	_____
Uses napkin incorrectly or not at all	_____
Talks with mouth full	_____
Takes food off others' plates	_____
Eats too fast or too slow	_____
Plays in food with fingers	_____

8-number checked =

None of the above _____
Does not apply, e.g., because he or she is _____ bedfast, and/or has liquid food only. (If checked, enter "0" in the circle to the right.)

A. Eating ──────── ADD 1-4 △

B. Toilet Use

(5) Toilet Training (Circle only <u>ONE</u>)

Never has toilet accidents	4
Never has toilet accidents during the day	3
Occasionally has toilet accidents during the day	2
Frequently has toilet accidents during the day	1
Is not toilet trained at all	0

(6) Self-Care at Toilet
(Check <u>ALL</u> statements which apply)

Lowers pants at the toilet without help	_____
Sits on toilet seat without help	_____
Uses toilet tissue appropriately	_____
Flushes toilet after use	_____
Puts on clothes without help	_____
Washes hands, without help	_____

None of the above _____

B. Toilet Use ──────── ADD 5-6 △

C. Cleanliness

(7) Washing Hands and Face
(Check <u>ALL</u> statements which apply)

Washes hands with soap	_____
Washes face with soap	_____
Washes hands and face with water	_____
Dries hands and face	_____

None of the above _____

(8) Bathing (Circle only <u>ONE</u>)

Prepares and completes bathing unaided	6
Washes and dries self completely without prompting or helping	5
Washes and dries self reasonably well with prompting	4
Washes and dries self with help	3
Attempts to soap and wash self	2
Cooperates when being washed and dried by others	1
Makes no attempt to wash or dry self	0

(9) Personal Hygiene
(Check <u>ALL</u> statements which apply)

Has strong underarm odor	_____
Does not change underwear regularly by self	_____
Skin is often dirty if not assisted	_____
Does not keep nails clean by self	_____

4-number checked =

None of the above _____
Does not apply, e.g., because he or she is completely dependent on others. (If checked enter "0" in the circle to the right.)

(10) Tooth Brushing (Circle only <u>ONE</u>)

Applies toothpaste and brushes teeth with up and down motion	5
Applies toothpaste and brushes teeth	4
Brushes teeth without help but cannot apply toothpaste	3
Brushes teeth with supervision	2
Cooperates in having teeth brushed	1
Makes no attempt to brush teeth	0

FIGURE 3.2
AAMD Adaptive Behavior Scale

SOURCE: From K. Nihira, R. Foster, M. Shellhaas, H. Leland. *AAMD Adaptive Behavior Scale.* Washington, D.C.: American Association on Mental Deficiency, 1974, p. 3. Reprinted with permission.

a retarded child can be extended upward to 75 if, according to a clinician's judgment, the child exhibits deficits in adaptive behavior felt to be caused by impaired intellectual functioning.

However, while the 1973 AAMD definition of mental retardation dominates the field, not everyone is happy with it. Sidney Bijou (1966) prefers a strictly behavioral definition that states that "a retarded individual is one who has a limited repertoire of behavior shaped by events that constitute his history" (p. 2). Bijou and Dunitz-Johnson (1981) have described an "interbehavior analysis" view of mental retardation that attributes a limited (retarded) behavioral repertoire to the hampering effects of biomedical impairment, handicapping sociocultural conditions, or both. Biomedical impairment can retard an individual's development through injury to the response equipment or the internal or external sources of stimulation. Handicapping sociocultural conditions may include an impoverished home environment, limited educational opportunities, and negative parental practices such as indifference or abuse. This view maintains that if the environment were properly arranged, the individual might no longer act retarded. And, in fact, research is beginning to show that much of the "retarded behavior" of many mentally retarded persons can, in fact, be replaced with more normal behavior.

Jane Mercer, a sociologist, believes the concept of mental retardation is a sociological phenomenon and that the label *mentally retarded* is "an achieved social status in a social system" (Mercer, 1973a, p. 3). Mercer's research (1973a, 1973b) shows that many children identified as mildly retarded by the school system, especially children from cultural minorities, get labeled mentally retarded because their behavior does not meet the norms of the white, middle-class social system. She has developed a system for diagnosing mental retardation in children from minority groups. Called SOMPA (System of Multicultural Pluristic Assessment), it is designed to eliminate cultural bias in intelligence testing. Using SOMPA, the examiner converts the WISC-R IQ scores into what is called an estimated learning potential (ELP) score. The ELP score is affected by such variables as ethnic group membership and family size and structure. While many school districts have begun using SOMPA, its validity and ultimate usefulness must await further research. Oakland (1980) found that WISC-R IQ scores correlated more highly with achievement than did ELP scores. As MacMillan points out, it is yet to be determined precisely how SOMPA can be used in education.

> At present, the SOMPA system might reduce the number of minority children eligible for EMR [educable mentally retarded] programs, but whether this is in their best interest remains to be seen; it will probably depend on the availability of alternative programs to meet their learning needs when they are no longer eligible for EMR-related services. (1982, p. 234)

Another alternative definition of mental retardation was proposed by Marc Gold (1980a). According to Gold, mental retardation should be viewed as failure

"Response equipment" refers to parts of the body that produce movement or responses. It includes the brain, the eyes, the speech organs, and so forth.

For more on special education and the student from a culturally diverse subgroup, see chapter 12.

by society to provide sufficient training and education, rather than as a deficit within the individual.

M. Gold

> Mental retardation refers to a level of functioning which requires from society significantly above average training procedures and superior assets in adaptive behavior, manifested throughout life. The mentally retarded person is characterized by the level of power needed in the training process for [the person] to learn, and not by limitations on what [the person] can learn. The height of a retarded person's level of functioning is determined by the availability of training technology and the amount of resources society is willing to allocate and not by significant limitations in biological potential. (1980a, p. 148)

Gold's "social responsibility" perspective is a highly optimistic one, stating that the ultimate level of functioning of a mentally retarded person is determined by the technology available for training and the amount of resources we are willing to devote to the task.

The alternate definitions of mental retardation offered by Bijou, Mercer, and Gold are important ones. All three emphasize the fundamental notion that mental retardation represents a current level of performance; it is not something a person *has*, the way you "have" the measles or red hair. Second, performance can often be altered significantly by manipulating certain aspects of the environment (teaching nonretarded behavior, or, in Mercer's view, altering one's own culturally biased perspective of what constitutes retarded behavior). All of these approaches agree that mental retardation is a relative phenomenon and need not be a permanent condition.

The debate over the definition of mental retardation is likely to continue. In the meantime, all of the major professional organizations who work with mentally retarded children and adults use the AAMD definition and advocate its continued use because it promotes universal standards and communication to a greater degree than other definitions.

CLASSIFICATION OF MENTAL RETARDATION

Many systems have been proposed for the classification of mentally retarded persons. In 1963, Gelof reported that 23 different classification systems were in use in English-speaking countries. As we discussed in chapter 1, classification of exceptional children is a difficult but necessary task. Various systems have been developed that classify mental retardation according to **etiology** (cause) or clinical type (for example, **Down syndrome**). While these classification systems are useful to physicians, they have little utility for educators. For example, two children might be classified correctly as having Down syndrome, but one might be able to function well in a regular second grade classroom for part of the day, while the other is unable to perform even the most basic self-help tasks. The AAMD classifies mental retardation by degree or level of severity, as measured by an IQ test. Table 3.2 lists the levels of mental retardation according to AAMD, and the corresponding IQ scores for each level on the two most widely used intelligence tests.

TABLE 3.2
Levels of mental retardation

Level	Intelligence Test	
	Stanford-Binet	Wechsler
Mild	68–52	70–55
Moderate	51–36	54–40
Severe	35–20	39–25
Profound	19 and below	24 and below

(EMR) — Mild; (TMR) — Moderate; (S & PR) — Severe, Profound — handwritten annotations)

The AAMD classification system is the most widely used by diagnosticians. But because the skills and abilities of mentally retarded children vary so widely, particular care must be devoted to classification. Classifying a child as "severely retarded" solely on the basis of IQ score could limit that child's access to potentially useful programming designated for "higher functioning" children. Because of this, a system of classification that parallels the AAMD system has developed in education (Smith, 1971). While IQ scores play an important role in educational classification, the specific skill levels and educational needs of a given child are the primary determinants of which of the three groups he or she is placed in. The three phrases used most by educators to classify mentally retarded children are *educable mentally retarded* (EMR), *trainable mentally retarded* (TMR), and *severely/profoundly retarded*.

Mild Retardation

Mildly retarded children are often referred to by educators as educable mentally retarded (EMR). These children have traditionally been educated in self-contained classrooms in the public schools. Today, many mildly retarded elementary school children are being educated in regular classrooms, with a special educator helping the classroom teacher with individualized instruction for the child and providing extra tutoring in a resource room as needed. Most mildly retarded children are not identified as retarded until they enter school and often not until the second or third grade, when more difficult academic work is required.

A self-contained classroom is a class made up only of handicapped children. It may have only EMR children, or it may include children with physical handicaps or sensory impairments.

School programs for mildly retarded students usually stress the basic academic subjects—reading, writing, and arithmetic—during the elementary years. The emphasis shifts to vocational training and work-study programs in junior high and high school. Most mildly retarded children master academic skills up to about the sixth grade level and are likely to be able to handle semiskilled jobs well enough to support themselves independently or semi-independently. Mildly retarded adults usually develop social and communication skills similar to those of their nonretarded peers; many are not recognized as retarded outside of school or after they finish school.

Moderate Retardation

Moderately retarded children are sometimes referred to by educators as train-able mentally retarded (TMR). The word "trainable" is used because of the belief that most moderately retarded children will not benefit from a traditional school curriculum featuring academics and that they need a specialized training program that concentrates on self-care, communication, and social skills. Unlike mildly retarded children, who are usually not identified as needing special education until they reach school, most moderately retarded children show significant delays in development during their preschool years. As they grow older, discrepancies between moderately retarded children and their nonhandicapped age-mates in overall intellectual, social, and motor development generally grow wider. Of those classified as moderately retarded, approximately 30% are children with Down syndrome. About 50% of all moderately retarded persons have some form of brain damage (Neisworth & Smith, 1978). Other handicapping conditions and physical abnormalities are more common in moderately retarded people than in the mildly retarded population.

During their school years, moderately retarded children are usually taught in self-contained classrooms with highly structured instructional programs designed to teach daily living skills. Academics are usually limited to development of a basic sight-word vocabulary (for example, "survival" words such as "exit," "don't walk," "stop"), perhaps some functional reading skills (such as simple recipes), and some basic number concepts. Some moderately retarded adults hold unskilled jobs in the community, but most who work do so in sheltered workshops. While in the past many moderately retarded persons were removed from society and placed in institutions, where they had little opportunity to develop and learn how to get along in the world, the trend today is away from institutional placement for moderately retarded children. While it is likely that moderately retarded people will require some supervision throughout their lives, small community-based residences and neighborhood group homes are proving to be a workable alternative to large institutions.

See chapter 15 for more information on how retarded adults live and work.

Severe and Profound Retardation

Severely and profoundly retarded individuals are almost always identified at birth or shortly afterwards. Most of these infants have significant central nervous system damage, and many have other handicapping conditions. While the AAMD distinguishes between the severely and profoundly retarded on the basis of IQ scores, the difference is primarily one of functional impairment. Training for the severely retarded typically consists of self-care skills—toileting, dressing, and eating and drinking—and language development. A profoundly retarded person may not be able to care for his or her personal needs, may be confined to a bed or wheelchair, and may require 24-hour nursing care. However, recent developments in instructional technology are showing that many severely and profoundly retarded persons can learn skills previously thought beyond their

DANIEL

"Hey, hey, hey, Fact Track!" The 11-year-old boy chose one of his favorite programs from the table next to the computer in his parents' dining room. He inserted the floppy disc, booted the system, and waited for the program to load. "What is your name?" appeared on the monitor. "Daniel Skandera," he typed. A menu scrolled up listing the program's possibilities. Daniel chose multiplication facts, Level 1. "How many problems do you want to do?" the computer asked. "20." "Do you want to set a goal for yourself, Daniel?" "Yes, 80 sec." "Get ready!"

Daniel Skandera, Jr., was born with Down syndrome, a chromosomal abnormality that usually causes moderate to severe mental retardation. "A psychologist tested Daniel at 12 months and told us he was three standard deviations below normal, untestable. That assessment was the basis for Daniel being denied enrollment in an infant stimulation program. We knew the tests were invalid and accepted the challenge of teaching Daniel ourselves," explained Daniel's father, himself a clinical neuropsychologist at a children's mental health center. "Between Marie and myself, we spent about 10,000 hours working with Daniel by the time he was 5. It's paid off a million times over. He's an inspiration and joy."

"We believed that we had learned enough about how Daniel learns to work with him confidently," says his mother, Marie, a former IBM systems instructor. "If something doesn't work, if he becomes frustrated, we are challenged to try another approach. Daniel is an only child and we were older when he was born. When we're gone, we want him to be able to take care of himself, to be a taxpayer instead of a tax burden."

Randomly generated multiplication facts flashed on the screen: 4 × 6, 2 × 9, 3 × 3, 7 × 6. Daniel responded, deftly punching in his answers on the computer's numeric keypad. Twice he recognized errors and corrected them before inputting his answers.

Daniel attends a regular fourth grade classroom at Robinwood Elementary School in Whitehall, Ohio. Academically he performs at grade level except for two subjects. For math and spelling, his best subjects ("Hooray, I love spellin' "), he leaves the fourth grade classroom each day—for the fifth grade. Daniel is not a special education student; he has no IEP. His extracurricular activities are those of his classmates and neighborhood friends—riding his bicycle, working out on his regulation-size trampoline, playing along with tape recorded rock' n 'roll on his professional, six-piece drum set, rough-housing, spending the night at a buddy's.

"Positive expectations are the key words," agreed Daniel's parents. "With Daniel it might take a little longer, but we get there."

The computer tallied the results. "You completed 20 problems in 66 seconds. You beat your goal. Problems correct = 20. Congratulations Daniel!" Demonstration over, the 11-year-old paid a hasty "Nice to meet you" and "Come over again" to the visitors and asked to be excused to the TV room. The Lakers and 76ers were about to tip-off for an NBA championship game. Daniel wanted to see the first half before bedtime.

Daniel brought his computer to school for a demonstration.

capability—even to the point of becoming semi-independent adults able to live and work in the community.

Until very recently, the severely and profoundly retarded were virtually ignored by the American educational system. Fortunately, this is changing. Litigation and legislation assuring the rights of handicapped children, regardless of the type or degree of handicap, and advances in educational methods have both contributed to this change. P.L. 94–142 mandates that all children must receive an appropriate education, and furthermore that the first priority for use of federal special education monies is to be those children currently not receiving educational services. The "unserved" are mostly severely and profoundly retarded children. The outlook for severely and profoundly retarded individuals is improving. A growing organization, The Association for the Severely Handicapped (TASH), consisting of researchers, teachers, parents, and other interested individuals, is working to help that future.

Chapter 10 is devoted to the special characteristics, programming, and educational issues related to severely and profoundly handicapped students.

Problems in Classifying Mentally Retarded Individuals

As with the definition of mental retardation, there have been numerous suggestions and schemes for the classification of mentally retarded people. And, also as with definitions, most classification schemes are designed to meet the needs of their developers. Unfortunately, educators have not yet developed a functional classification system for those children whose development is retarded. Salvia describes the situation like this:

> Education has borrowed definitions and classifications from biology, psychology, and sociology; unfortunately, these definitions have only limited utility in the education of children. In the past, the label of mental retardation could be used to exclude individuals from the public schools. Today, according to various state and federal laws (e.g., P.L. 94–142), all handicapped children are entitled to a free and appropriate education at public expense—as are all other children. The classification of mental retardation, as well as its many subclassifications, has less, really, to do with the task of educating people than alternative classifications which denote a child's level of achievement and anticipated progress under various educational plans. Knowing that a person reads at the second-grade level and has the social maturity of an adolescent has more to do with planning and implementing an educational program than the fact he or she earns a score of 70 on the Stanford-Binet. The schools must teach individuals, regardless of whether they are retarded. Now, perhaps educators will develop a functional classification system that is related to educational treatment. (1978, p. 46)

PREVALENCE

Changing definitions of mental retardation, the lack of a nationwide, systematic reporting system, and the relatively uncertain status of mildly retarded school children (are they still retarded after they have left school?) contribute to the difficulty of estimating the number of mentally retarded people. When prevalence figures are based upon IQ scores alone, 3% of the population would theoretically score in the retarded range—two standard deviations below the mean (see Figure 3.1). This 3% prevalence figure is still widely quoted.

However, basing prevalence estimates only on IQ scores ignores the other necessary criterion for mental retardation—adaptive behavior. Since there are, as of yet, no universally accepted measures of adaptive behavior, no major prevalence studies have been based on it. Some professionals feel that if adaptive behavior were included with intellectual ability when estimating prevalence, the figure would drop to about 1% (Baroff, 1982; Mercer, 1973b; Tarjan, Wright, Eyman, & Keeran, 1973).

MacMillan (1982) and Neisworth and Smith (1978) suggest that the 3% probably more accurately reflects **incidence**—the percentage of people who, at some time in their lives, will be diagnosed as mentally retarded—and that the number of retarded persons at any one time, or the **prevalence**, is probably closer to 1%. Two factors causing the discrepancy between incidence and prevalence are the high mortality rate of severely and profoundly retarded infants and the fact that many mildly retarded school children are independent and self-sufficient as adults (Edgerton & Bercovici, 1976; Richardson, 1978).

Baroff (1982) has developed a formula for estimating the number of persons needing services for the mentally retarded. He suggests there are 4 people per 1,000 population in the moderate-severe-profound ranges and 5 people per 1,000 who are mildly retarded. This .9% is about one-third the traditional 3% estimate. Using IQ score only as a basis for classification, Haywood estimates that:

> On a population base of 222 million persons (which the United States Bureau of the Census estimates will be our population in 1980) we shall have 110,000 persons with IQs less than 20, and 444,000 with IQs between 20 and 50, but we shall have 6,693,940 individuals with IQs between 50 and 70. Thus in 1980 there will be more than 12 times as many mentally retarded persons in the IQ 50 to 70 range as there will be with IQs less than 50. (1979, pp. 430–41)

CAUSES OF MENTAL RETARDATION

Mildly retarded individuals make up 80 to 85% of the people identified as retarded, and in the vast majority of those cases the etiology (cause) is unknown. These people have no demonstrable organic pathology—no brain damage or other physical problem. In general, when no actual organic damage can be found, we say the cause of the retardation is **cultural-familial.**

The term *cultural-familial* suggests that the combination of a poor social and cultural environment early in the child's life leads to retarded development. While there is no direct proof that social and familial interactions cause mental retardation, it is generally believed that these influences cause most mild cases of retardation.

While over 250 known causes have been identified, the actual cause is determined in only about 10 to 20% of all cases of mental retardation—usually in the less prevalent ranges, the moderate, severe, and profound cases (Dunn, 1973; Kolstoe, 1972). All of the known causes of retardation are biological or medical. They are referred to as *clinical* or *pathological* (brain damage) retardation. There are many known causes of moderate, severe, and profound retardation. These causes have been categorized by AAMD as:

1. Infections and intoxication (for example, **rubella,** syphilis, encephalitis, meningitis)
2. Trauma and physical agent (for example, accidents before, during and after birth; **anoxia**)
3. Metabolism and nutrition (for example, **phenylketonuria** or PKU)
4. Gross brain disease (such as tumors)
5. Prenatal influence (for example, **hydrocephalus, microcephalus**)
6. Chromosomal abnormality (such as Down syndrome)
7. Gestational disorders (for example, premature births)
8. Psychiatric disorders (seldom cited as a cause today)

RESIDENTIAL ALTERNATIVES FOR MENTALLY RETARDED INDIVIDUALS

Institutions

Approximately 200,000 individuals in the United States reside in over 150 public institutions for the mentally retarded. Scheerenberger (1976) estimates that 90% of the retarded people in institutions are severely and profoundly retarded. Most of our nation's public institutions were set up in the 19th or early 20th century, when it was generally felt that people with mental retardation could not be educated or trained. The large custodial institutions have helped keep retarded people segregated from the rest of society, and they were never designed to train people to live in normal society. Institutions have come under severe criticism in recent years for their general inability to provide individualized services in a comfortable, humane, and normalized environment. The complaints are not leveled against the concept of residential facilities; there will always be severely and profoundly handicapped persons who need the 24-hour care and supervision that only residential facilities can offer. The problem lies with the level of humane treatment large institutions can offer and with the concept of **normalization.**

See, for example, Blatt, 1976; Blatt and Kaplan, 1966; Kugel and Wolfensberger, 1969; Wolfensberger, 1969.

In recent years, much effort has been expended to improve the quality of life and services provided by institutions for mentally retarded children and adults. The United States Department of Health, Education and Welfare (1974) and the Joint Commission on the Accreditation of Hospitals (JCAH, 1971) have both developed extensive, and almost identical, standards for residential facilities for the mentally retarded. These standards cover a wide range of topics, from building construction to staffing to habilitative and educational programming. Residential units meeting the government or JCAH standards are called "licensed" facilities. Licensed units are usually eligible for additional funding not available to units that do not meet the accreditation standards.

Repp and Barton (1980) compared the interactions (verbal instruction, custodial guidance, no interaction, and so on) between residents and staff and the behaviors of residents (on-task, no programming, self-stimulatory, and so on) that took place in two licensed and six unlicensed cottages at a large state institution. Each of the eight cottages had from 12 to 40 severely and profoundly mentally retarded residents, some with additional handicaps (hearing or visually impaired, physically handicapped). The licensed cottages had resident to staff ratios of 4 to 1, while in the unlicensed cottages the resident to staff ratios ranged from 4 to 1 to 10 to 1. Thus, the licensed units had an advantage of more staff available to provide programming. For 16 days four observers each recorded staff and resident behavior for more than 4 hours per day, yielding almost 160,000 individual 6-second observations.

Figures 3.3 and 3.4 display the study's results. The most striking finding is the "overwhelming number of the observations" in which no interactions between residents and staff (Figure 3.3) and no programming (Figure 3.4) occurred. Whether licensed or not, there were few instances of praise or encouragement (see "social behavior" in Figure 3.3) directed by staff toward the residents. Figure 3.4 shows that, on the average, every resident, whether in a licensed or unlicensed cottage, spent more time engaging in self-stimulatory behaviors than in programming. In discussing the results of their study, Repp and Barton write:

> These data, quite objective and reliable, show that despite all the excitement over the Education for All Handicapped Children Act, 1975, that despite all the promises of court cases . . . , we still do not provide sufficient educational opportunities for many retarded citizens, even in our licensed facilities. These data cannot be interpreted too strongly, for they were recorded with the complete awareness of the administration and of the staff being observed, and they were recorded during the hours one would expect most of the educational opportunities in a resident's life to be made available. If they are biased, they are biased in a direction *favorable* to the facility. . . .
>
> In summary, these results are extremely discouraging. They indicate that: (1) facilities can be licensed and still not provide habilitation for their clients; (2) despite the technology we have developed for teaching adaptive and reducing maladaptive behaviors, many people remain unaffected; and (3) we still do not provide habilitative opportunities for all retarded citizens, despite all that the recent judicial decisions and governmental regulations seem to promise. (pp. 339–41)

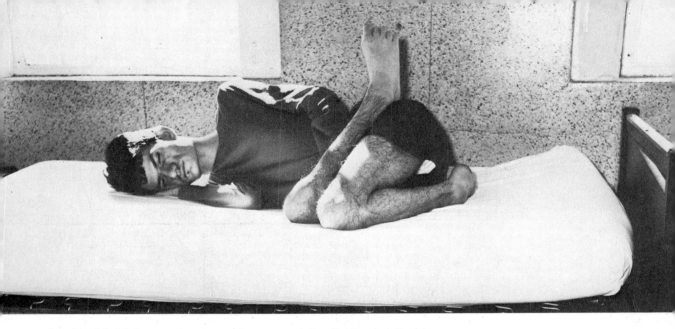

In spite of legislation, court cases, and improvements in educational methodology, some severely and profoundly mentally retarded persons experience long periods of inactivity in our nation's institutions. We still have a long way to go.

Fortunately, no new large state institutions for the retarded are presently on the drawing boards, and a variety of alternative residential placements are coming into reality. We will briefly describe some of these below.

Before moving on, however, it is important to make one point. There are many caring and competent professionals working in institutions who have dedicated their careers to providing the best possible education and living conditions for the retarded people who reside there. Many of these professionals themselves do not think large institutions are the best way to care for our severely and profoundly retarded citizens. Yet they are trying to do the best job possible under the prevailing conditions. Happily, the movement toward deinstitutionalization has decreased the population of some institutions to a more manageable number, so that some programs are now able to provide more appropriate services for their residents.

See pages 104–105 for more on deinstitutionalization.

Regional Facilities

Regional facilities offer total-care, 24-hour residential programs like the large state institutions, but on a much smaller basis, serving only those persons in a given geographical area within the state. The reduced distance to family and community allows for more normalized and individualized treatment programs. Hemming, Lavender, and Pill (1981) compared the quality of life of 51 retarded adults who were transferred from a large institution to smaller living units with a matched control group of 50 adults who remained in the large

For a look at how one regional facility operates, see pages 352–353.

FIGURE 3.3

The mean percentage of 6-second observations in which each type of staff interaction with residents occurred. Cottages A and B were licensed, but none of the other cottages was licensed.

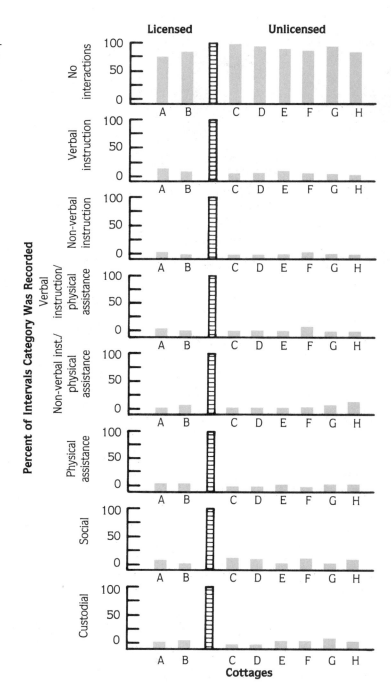

EXCEPTIONAL CHILDREN

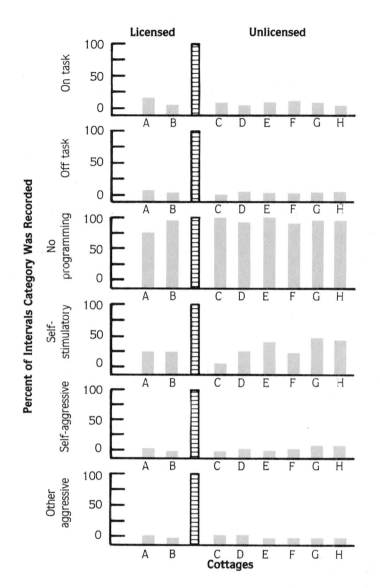

FIGURE 3.4

The mean percentage of 6-second observations in which each type of resident activity was recorded. After each observation, either no programming, on task, or off task was recorded. If self-stimulation, self-aggressive, or other aggressive occurred, it was marked during the same interval. Cottages A and B were licensed, while none of the other cottages was licensed.

SOURCE: A. C. Repp and L. E. Barton, Naturalistic observation of institutionalized retarded persons: A comparison of licensure decisions and behavioral observations, *Journal of Applied Behavior Analysis*, 1980, *13*, 333–41. Copyright 1980 by the Society for the Experimental Analysis of Behavior, Inc. Used with permission.

institution. Residents who had been transferred to the smaller units from the more "restricted" wards showed significant improvement in adaptive behavior (as measured by the Adaptive Behavior Scale) and increased participation in culturally normative activities.

Group Homes

A group home usually consists of between 6 and 12 retarded adolescents or adults living in a large, family-type dwelling in a residential neighborhood. Professional staff are responsible for supervision and overall programming for the residents. The residents often work at sheltered workshops and participate in social and recreational activities in the community.

In recent years, we have witnessed tremendous growth in the establishment of group homes and other community-based residential alternatives for the mentally retarded. A 1982 survey found 7,669 community-based residential facilities operating throughout the country, a significant increase over the 4,290 community-based residences operating in 1977 (Center for Residential and Community Services, 1983; Conroy, 1977).

For an idea of how two people feel about living in a group home, see pages 504–505.

Apartment Living

A variety of residential alternatives involve apartment living for retarded adults. Alternatives include independent apartments with minimal supervision, to apartment clusters, to coresidence arrangements (a retarded resident and a nonretarded roommate). A follow-up study of 69 mentally retarded adults 5 years after they had been placed into independent living arrangements found 80% of the group still in their original independent housing placement (Schalock, Harper, & Carver, 1981). These adults reported they were proud of their apartments and that they felt good about "doing their own thing."

Sheltered Workshops

While not a residential alternative, sheltered workshops provide supervised employment for many mentally retarded teenagers and adults. Employees generally perform piecework labor and are paid on either an hourly or performance-output basis. Some sheltered workshops, referred to as *transitional workshops*, provide short-term training for those individuals who can move on to a job in the community. Competitive employment should always be the goal for retarded adults who can acquire the necessary job skills and work habits.

Chapter 15 covers sheltered workshops in more detail.

A group home provides meaningful opportunities to practice daily living skills.

Special Schools

Many states, counties, and large school districts operate special schools for retarded students. These special schools offer an education and training curriculum specially designed for their students, usually moderately (trainable) mentally retarded children. These children usually live at home with their families. While in the past many of these programs were completely administered by state Departments of Mental Health and Mental Retardation, P.L. 94–142 requires that state Departments of Education are now responsible for the education of all children. Sometimes a number of small neighboring school districts will pool their resources to offer a special school program for the moderately and severely mentally retarded students in their area. More and more special school programs for severely and profoundly retarded children are being implemented.

Regular Public Schools

The regular public schools, which are now responsible for the education of all handicapped children, are changing their ways of providing services to retarded students. Traditionally, the mildly retarded (EMR) student was educated in a self-contained classroom with 12 to 18 other EMR students. Children whose retardation was more severe were usually placed in special schools or institutions. Today, P.L. 94–142 mandates that handicapped children are to be educated with their nonhandicapped peers to the greatest extent possible. Thus, many EMR students are now spending all or part of the school day in the regular classroom, with supplemental instruction provided by a resource teacher. Some school districts that, in the past, offered no educational programming for moderately retarded children are now beginning to provide classrooms and teachers for these retarded learners.

But, as we saw in chapter 2, simply putting a handicapped child in a regular classroom does not necessarily mean he or she will be accepted socially or receive the instructional programming most needed (Gottlieb, 1981). Research shows that many regular classroom teachers still hold a generally negative attitude toward mainstreamed EMR students (Childs, 1981). Nevertheless, many special and regular educators are developing programs and methods for integrating the instruction of mentally retarded students with their nonhandicapped peers. Systematically planning for the integration of retarded students into the classroom through team games, group investigation projects, and directly training handicapped and nonhandicapped students in specific skills for interacting with one another are just some of the methods for increasing the chances of a successful regular class placement (Gottlieb & Leyser, 1981; Stainback, Stainback, Raschke, & Anderson, 1981). Cooke, Heron, Heward, and Test (1982) describe a classwide peer tutoring system implemented in a first grade classroom in which a Down syndrome student participated. Over the course of

A student in this special classroom checks to see what his job is today.

See pages 59–61 for a description of this peer tutoring program.

this 5-month study, the retarded child not only interacted directly and positively with her peer tutor, but was taught more than 40 sight words by her nonhandicapped classmate.

Educational Methodology

Research on specific educational techniques for mentally retarded children began when Itard started his work with Victor, the Wild Boy of Aveyron. But not until the last two decades has the scientific method been employed systematically in an attempt to discover effective and reliable teaching methods for retarded students. While this research is far from finished—indeed, we must continually search for better teaching methods—one approach has been demonstrated to be effective. As a result, it is the most popular and widely used method for teaching mentally retarded students. This method is the behavioral approach, usually referred to as **behavior modification** or **applied behavior analysis.**

Applied behavior analysis can be defined as systematically arranging environmental events to produce desired changes in behavior. Behavior analysts verify the effects of their instruction by directly measuring student performance (Cooper, 1981). Behavior analysis is not a single technique, but an entire approach to education based on scientifically proven principles that describe how the environment affects learning. Applied behavior analysis has been used effectively with mentally retarded students, and with many other groups, to increase the rate with which they perform desirable behaviors, to decrease the rate with which they perform inappropriate, or maladaptive behaviors, and to teach new, complex behaviors (Kazdin, 1978).

The first step in the behavioral approach to instruction is to specify exactly what skills, or behaviors, the learner is to acquire. *Task analysis,* a method

EXCEPTIONAL CHILDREN

where large skills are broken down and sequenced into a series of subskills, lets a teacher break a task into small, easy-to-teach subtasks. These subtasks are then sequenced from easiest to most difficult (Gold, 1976; Moyer & Dardig, 1978), or in the natural order in which they must be performed (for example, in many dressing skills). Assessing a child's performance on a sequence of task-analyzed subskills helps pinpoint exactly where instruction should begin.

See pages 106–107 for more on task analysis.

Another hallmark of the behavioral approach is *direct and continuous measurement*. Academic achievement tests have traditionally been the major source of data used in evaluating educational programs. While these data have some use, they are not useful for daily instructional planning. Achievement tests are usually only given once or twice a year, and the information they provide is too general. Systematic instruction requires direct and continuous measurement.

> When the purpose of measurement is to facilitate daily instructional planning, measurement tactics that are both direct and continuous must be selected. Measurement must be direct by providing data on student responses to materials used during the instructional process. Measurement must be continuous by providing frequent samples of performance throughout the instructional process. (Cooper & Johnson, 1979, p. 10)

Only through diligent direct and continuous measurement of student performance will teachers be able to provide the individualized instruction so vital to the growth and progress of mentally retarded children.

In addition, most behaviorally based teaching techniques hold the following in common:

1. They can be replicated by people other than the originator.
2. They require the student to perform the target behavior repeatedly during each session.
3. Immediate feedback, usually in the form of **positive reinforcement,** is provided to the student.
4. Cues and prompts that help the student respond correctly from the very beginning of the lesson are systematically withdrawn.
5. Efforts are included to help the student generalize the newly learned skill to different, nontraining environments.

Teaching Mentally Retarded Students to Eat in Fast-Food Restaurants

An instructional program that was developed to teach mentally retarded secondary students to eat in fast-food restaurants (van den Pol, Iwata, Ivancic, Page, Neef, & Whitely, 1981) is an excellent example of how applied behavior analysis is used to design and evaluate educational programs. While successful programs have been developed to teach basic survival skills such as money handling (Cuvo, Veitch, Trace, & Konke, 1978) and telephone use (Leff, 1975) to mentally retarded students, it is not clear whether these skills will continue to be used unless they are part of more complex, functional activities (such as going to the store and purchasing a needed item).

Van den Pol and his colleagues designed and evaluated a program to teach restaurant skills to three mentally retarded students. The students, all males, were 17 to 22 years of age, and their handicaps included mental retardation (IQ scores 46 to 75) and at least one other disability, including emotional impairment, epilepsy, and deafness. The students' math and reading abilities had been assessed at the first to second grade level. All three students had previously eaten in restaurants but could not order or pay for a meal without assistance. The first step in developing the teaching program was to construct a task analysis of the skills needed to order and eat at a fast-food restaurant. The experimenters accomplished this by eating at several fast-food restaurants and recording each step of the process. Four major components were identified: Locating, Ordering, Paying, and Eating and Exiting. Table 3.3 shows the list of steps generated and definitions of appropriate and inappropriate responses at each step.

TABLE 3.3

Task analysis of skills required to eat in a fast-food restaurant.

Skill	Appropriate Response	Inappropriate Response
1.1	Does not initiate social interaction. Does not self-stimulate.	Talks/makes manual sign to customer or trainer. Engages in motor/vocal self-stimulation so that customers differentially attend to him.
1.2	Enters double door within 2 min of start.	Uses wrong door. Does not enter within 2 min.
1.3	Goes directly to counter. Does not leave line except to get into shorter line.	Not in line or at counter within 30 sec. Gets out of line.
2.1	Makes ordering response within 10 sec of cue. If written, finishes within 2 min.	Does not respond within 10 sec. Responds before cue. Makes inappropriate (i.e., nonordering-related) verbalization. Not finished writing within 2 min.
2.2	Says "How much for . . .? when giving order.	Does not inquire "How much for . . .?"
2.3	Orders food that he can afford, appropriate item combination (i.e., minimum order—sandwich & drink; maximum—sandwich, drink, side order, & any other item).	Orders more food than he can pay for. Uses inappropriate item combination.
2.4	Says "Eat here" when asked.	Does not say order is to dine in. Says "To go."
3.1	Begins to get money within 10 sec of cue. Does not let go of money on counter before cashier cue.	Does not get money within 10 sec. Releases money before cue.
3.2	Hands cashier appropriate combination of bills.	Does not give enough money. Gives too much money so that same bill is returned.

TABLE 3.3 (continued)

Skill	Appropriate Response	Inappropriate Response
3.3	Displays fingers on at least one hand.	Does not display fingers.
3.4	Inquires "Mistake?" if short billed.	Does not inquire if short billed. Inquires "Mistake?" when change is accurate.
3.5	Puts money in pocket.	Does not take change. Puts money on tray instead of pocket.
3.6	Requests salt, pepper, or catsup.	Does not request any condiments.
3.7	Takes a napkin from dispenser.	Does not take napkin from dispenser.
3.8	Says "Thank you."	Does not say "Thank you."
4.1	Sits at unoccupied, trashfree table within 1 min of availability.	Sits with other customer. Sits at a table with trash present. Does not sit down within 1 min.
4.2	Eats food placed only on paper.	Eats food off tray, table, etc.
4.3	Puts napkin in lap *and* wipes mouth or hands.	Does not put napkin in lap. Does not wipe hands or mouth on it.
4.4	Does not spill food or drink.	Drops food off tray or spills drink.
4.5	If spills occur, picks up every one, does not eat any spilled item.	Does not pick up or blot. Eats spilled food.
4.6	Puts trash in container, tray on top, within 2 min of finishing eating.	Does not put trash in container within 2 min. Uses inappropriate container. Throws tray in container.
4.7	Exits within 1 min of trash or 3 min of finishing eating.	Does not exit within time limits.

SOURCE: From R. A. van den Pol, B. A. Iwata, M. T. Ivancic, T. J. Page, N. A. Neef, and F. P. Whitley, Teaching the handicapped to eat in public places: Acquisition, generalization, and maintenance of restaurant skills, *Journal of Applied Behavior Analysis*, 1981, *14*, 61–69. Copyright 1981 by the Society for the Experimental Analysis of Behavior, Inc. Used with permission.

The students were trained on each of the four components, in sequence, in the classroom. Instruction consisted of students role-playing with the teacher the various steps in simulated customer-cashier interactions and responding to questions about slides showing customers at a fast-food restaurant performing various steps in the sequence. Correct student responses during instruction were followed by social reinforcement (for example, "Good job! You remembered to ask for your change.") Incorrect responses were followed by feedback describing why the response was incorrect and a remedial trial. If the student response on a remedial trial was incorrect, the teacher modeled the correct response and gave another remedial trial. This sequence was followed until a correct response was made. Each training session consisted of 10 trials, not counting remedial trials. Only one component skill was taught each session. The next skill was not taught until the student performed at 100% accuracy on the previous skill for two consecutive sessions. When a student mastered the final skill of a component, a review consisting of 10 trials covering all previously learned skills was conducted.

The program's effects were evaluated by giving each student a randomly determined amount of money between $2.00 and $5.00 and instructing him to go to lunch. These restaurant "probes" were conducted before training, several times during the instructional program, and after training. Observers inside the restaurant recorded the students' performance of the various steps but offered no assistance.

Figure 3.5 shows the results of the program. Before instruction, the three students correctly performed an average of 48%, 30%, and 39% of the 22 steps. Their scores on the final training probe were 86%, 80%, and 95%. Follow-up data collected in a different restaurant showed the students were able to generalize skills to another fast-food restaurant. One-year follow-up observations showed a drop in performance for two of the students, but all three followed the restaurant sequence more accurately than a sample of 10 randomly chosen regular customers observed as a normative sample. Discussing their study, the authors wrote:

Results indicate that following approximately 10 hours of classroom instruction, students' restaurant skills generalized to several different natural environment

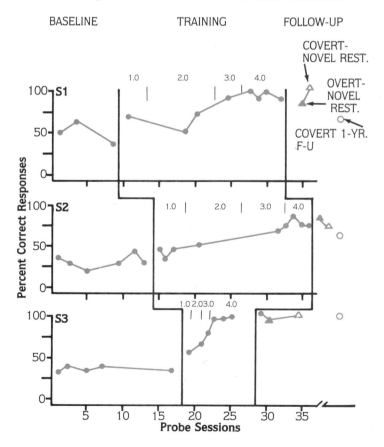

FIGURE 3.5

Percent correct responses during restaurant probes for Students 1, 2, and 3 across experimental conditions. During followup, closed triangles represent probes conducted at a Burger King restaurant using typical observation procedures, open triangles represent Burger King probes during which students did not know that their performance was being observed, and open circles represent covert probes conducted in a different McDonald's one year following the termination of training.

SOURCE: R. A. van den Pol, B. A. Iwata, M. T. Ivancic, T. J. Page, N. A. Neef, and F. P. Whitley, Teaching the handicapped to eat in public places: Acquisition, generalization, and maintenance of restaurant skills," *Journal of Applied Behavior Analysis*, 1981, *14*, 61–69. Copyright 1981 by the Society for the Experimental Analysis of Behavior, Inc. Used with permission.

settings, and that their posttraining performance was not dependent upon either the assistance or even the presence of known trainers/observers in the restaurant. Additional probe data collected one year following the termination of training suggested that restaurant skills maintained at high levels or were at least comparable to those exhibited by a nonretarded sample of persons. (van den Pol et al., 1981, p. 68)

This instructional program offers an excellent example of how applied behavior analysis is advancing an effective technology of teaching mentally retarded students.

CURRENT ISSUES/FUTURE TRENDS

In 1961, the first President's Committee on Mental Retardation was created by John F. Kennedy. The committee was charged with conducting an intensive study of mental retardation and making recommendations for national policy, based on their findings. A year later, results of the many task forces, public hearings, visits to facilities for retarded people, and extensive interviews with professionals, parents, and retarded persons were compiled into the committee's report, *A Proposed Program for National Action to Combat Mental Retardation* (Mayo, 1962). The report contained specific recommendations related to human and legal rights, prevention, research, education, and medical and other services for the mentally retarded. Many of the committee's recommendations set the stage for much of what took place in the 1960s and early 1970s, particularly in the area of research and legislation confirming the rights of retarded citizens.

Subsequent presidents have reconvened the Committee on Mental Retardation in order to track the accomplishment of earlier goals and to attempt to predict future needs of retarded citizens. In their 1975 report to the president, the committee attempted to outline the country's major objectives in the field of mental retardation, through the year 2000. Seven major goals were stated:

Goal I: The attainment of citizenship status in law and in fact for all mentally retarded individuals in the United States, exercised to the fullest degree possible under the conditions of disability.

Goal II: Reduction of the incidence of mental retardation from biomedical causes by at least 50% by the year 2000.

Goal III: Reduction of the incidence and prevalence of mental retardation associated with social disadvantage to the lowest level possible by the end of this century.

Goal IV: Adequate and humane service systems for all retarded persons in need of them.

Goal V: The attainment of a high and stable level of international relations in the cooperative resolution of the universal human problems of preventing and ameliorating mental retardation.

Goal VI: Achievement of a firm and deep public acceptance of mentally retarded persons as members in common of the social community and as citizens in their own right.

Goal VII: Equitable, coordinated, efficient, and effective use of public resources in all mental retardation programs.

The Committee went on to list specific objectives by which they thought the major goals could be obtained. Although a great deal remains to be done if these goals are to be realized, some accomplishments have been made in each of the seven areas. We will briefly describe some recent accomplishments and current activities in three related areas: human and legal rights, prevention, and the concepts of normalization and deinstitutionalization.

Rights of Mentally Retarded Citizens

We have come a long way since the time when mentally retarded people were exterminated, ridiculed, or employed as court jesters—but we still have a long way to go. Of all the goals of the first President's Committee on Mental Retardation, we have the most concrete evidence of accomplishment of the goal of legal rights for retarded persons.

Friedman (1976, 1977) has detailed the history of the legal rights movement on behalf of mentally retarded people. Numerous court cases in recent years have advanced the position that a mentally retarded person has and should be able to exercise, with assistance from society if necessary, the same rights and freedoms as a nonhandicapped citizen. Following are rights of mentally retarded persons as advocated by the AAMD.

> Mentally retarded citizens are entitled to enjoy and to exercise the same rights as are available to nonretarded citizens, to the limits of their ability to do so. As handicapped citizens, they are also entitled to specific extensions of, and additions to, these basic rights, in order to allow their free exercise and enjoyment. When an individual retarded citizen is unable to enjoy and exercise his or her rights, it is the obligation of the society to intervene so as to safeguard these rights, and to act humanely and conscientiously on that person's behalf.

> Basic Rights

> I. The basic rights that a retarded person shares with his or her nonretarded peers include, but are not limited to, those implied in "life, liberty, and the pursuit of happiness," and those specified in detail in the various documents that provide the basis for governing democratic nations. Specific rights of mentally retarded persons include, but are not limited to:

> A. The right to freedom of choice within the individual's capacity to make decisions and within the limitations imposed on all persons.

> B. The right to live in the least restrictive individually appropriate environment.

> C. The right to gainful employment, and to a fair day's pay for a fair day's labor.

> D. The right to be part of a family.

> E. The right to marry and have a family of his or her own.

F. The right to freedom of movement, hence not to be interned without just cause and due process of law, including the right not to be permanently deprived of liberty by institutionalization in lieu of imprisonment.

G. The rights to speak openly and fully without fear of undue punishment, to privacy, to the practice of a religion (or the practice of no religion), and to interaction with peers.

Specific Extensions

II. Specific extensions of, and additions to, these basic rights, which are due mentally handicapped persons because of their special needs, include, but are not limited to:

A. The right to a publicly supported and administered comprehensive and integrated set of rehabilitative programs and services designed to minimize handicap or handicaps.

B. The right to a publicly supported and administered program of training and education including, but not restricted to, basic academic and interpersonal skills.

C. The right, beyond those implicit in the right to education described above, to a publicly administered and supported program of training toward the goal of maximum gainful employment, insofar as the individual is capable.

D. The right to protection against exploitation, demeaning treatment, or abuse.

E. The right, when participating in research, to be safeguarded from violations of human dignity and to be protected from physical and psychological harm.

F. The right, for a retarded individual who may not be able to act effectively in his or her own behalf, to have a responsible impartial guardian or advocate appointed by the society to protect and effect the exercise and enjoyment of these foregoing rights, insofar as this guardian, in accordance with responsible professional opinion, determines that the retarded citizen is able to enjoy and exercise these rights. (From *Rights of Mentally Retarded Persons: An Official Policy Statement of the American Association on Mental Deficiency*, 1973)

Many states have organized "citizen advocacy" programs for the mentally retarded. **Advocates** are volunteers who commit themselves to become personally involved with the welfare of a mentally retarded person and to become knowledgeable about the services that are available for that person. In a sense, an advocate is an informed friend who can legally take a stand to see that his client's rights are not abused and that the educational and other services he or she should be receiving are in fact delivered. Being an advocate is an excellent way to serve a retarded citizen and learn much about the field in the process.

Prevention of Mental Retardation

Each week in this country about 2,100 babies are born who are either mentally retarded or will, at some point in their life, become retarded. As scientific research—both medical and psychological—has generated new knowledge about the causes of mental retardation, procedures and programs designed to prevent its occurrence have increased.

Probably the biggest single preventive strike against mental retardation (and many other handicapping conditions, including blindness and deafness) was the development of an effective rubella vaccine in 1962. When rubella (German measles) is contracted by mothers during the first three months of pregnancy, it will cause severe damage in 10 to 40% of the unborn children (Krim, 1969). Fortunately, this cause of mental retardation can be eliminated if women are vaccinated for rubella before becoming pregnant.

Phenylketonuria (PKU) is a genetically inherited condition in which the child is born without an important enzyme needed to break down the amino acid phenylalanine, which is found in many common foods. Failure to break down this amino acid causes brain damage that results in severe mental retardation. By analyzing the concentration of phenylalanine in a newborn's blood plasma, doctors can diagnose PKU, and it can be treated with a special diet. Most PKU children who receive a phenylalanine-restricted diet early enough have normal intellectual development (Berman & Ford, 1970).

Advances in medical science have enabled doctors to identify certain genetic influences strongly associated with mental retardation. **Genetic counseling,** a discussion between a specially trained medical counselor and prospective parents about the possibilities that they may give birth to a handicapped child, based upon the parents' genetic backgrounds, is one approach to prevention that is being offered by many health service organizations.

Amniocentesis is a procedure in which a sample of fluid is withdrawn from the amniotic sac surrounding the fetus during the second trimester of pregnancy. A chromosomal analysis of the amniotic fluid allows doctors to identify the presence of 29 specific genetic disorders prior to birth. Many of these disorders, such as Down syndrome (O'Brien, 1971), are associated with mental retardation.

Medical advances such as these have noticeably reduced the incidence of mental retardation caused by some of the known biological causes, but much more research is needed if the goal of reducing the incidence of biomedical mental retardation by 50% by the year 2000 is to be reached.

As we saw earlier, the great majority of those children labeled mentally retarded fall in the mild range and have no clear-cut etiology. These are the children whose developmental delays are thought to be primarily the result of a poor environment during their early years. The poor environment may be a result of culture, parental neglect, poverty, disease, lack of parental interest in education, diet, and other factors—many of which are completely out of the hands of the child's parents. During the last 10 years or so, the number of research projects aimed at serving "high-risk" preschoolers and their parents has increased. While measuring the effects of a preventive program is much more difficult than measuring the decreased number of children suffering from a disease like PKU, the preliminary results of these projects are encouraging.

See chapter 13 for more on intervention programs for young handicapped children.

Normalization

The principle of normalization refers to the use of progressively more normal settings and procedures "to establish and/or maintain personal behaviors which are as culturally normal as possible" (Wolfensberger, 1972, p. 28). Normalization is not a single technique or set of procedures that is done to people, but rather an overriding philosophy. That philosophy says that mentally retarded persons should be both physically and socially integrated into the mainstream of society to the greatest extent possible, regardless of the degree or type of disability. Madle states that

> Such integration is maximized when all people live in a culturally normative setting in ordinary community housing, can move and communicate in age-appropriate ways and are able to use typical community services such as schools, stores, churches, and physicians. (1978, p. 469)

Menolascino (1977) makes the following recommendations for normalizing the delivery of educational, residential, and community services to mentally retarded people.

1. Programs and facilities for mentally retarded persons should be physically and socially integrated into the community.
2. No more mentally retarded people should be congregated in one service facility than the surrounding neighborhood can readily integrate into its resources, community social life, and so on.
3. Integration—and, therefore, normalization—can best be attained if the location of services follows population density and distribution patterns.
4. Services and facilities for the retarded, if they are to be normalizing in their intent, must meet the same standards as other comparable services and facilities for nonretarded people, not be stricter nor more lenient.
5. Staff personnel working with retarded persons must meet at least the same standards as those working with comparable nonretarded individuals.

Outdoor camping can be part of a program of normalization.

6. In order to accomplish maximum normalization, mentally retarded persons must have maximum exposure to the nonretarded population in the community.

7. Daily routines should be comparable to those of nonretarded persons of the same age.

8. Services for children and adults should be physically separated, both because the probability that children will imitate the deviant behavior of their elders will be less and because services to adults and children tend to be separated in the mainstream of our society.

9. Mentally retarded individuals should be taught to dress and groom themselves like other persons their age; they should be taught a normal gait, normal movements, and normal expressive behavior patterns; their diet should be adjusted to assure normal weight.

10. As much as possible, the mentally retarded adult, even if severely handicapped, should be provided the opportunity to engage in work that is culturally normal in type, quantity, and setting. (Adapted from Menolascino, 1977, pp. 79–83)

As belief in normalization grows among both professionals and the public, the time gets nearer when all mentally retarded people can have humane and effective treatment and education.

Deinstitutionalization

While *mainstreaming* is a word often used to describe putting normalization into effect in school settings, **deinstitutionalization**—the movement of mentally retarded people from large, impersonal institutions to smaller, community-based living environments such as foster or group homes—further increases the degree of normalization of mentally retarded people who have previously resided in institutions. Deinstitutionalization is more than a philosophy or goal of concerned individuals; it is, and has been, an active movement over the past 20 years. As Telford and Sawrey (1977) report, despite a 40% increase in the population of the United States between 1955 and 1973, the number of persons in our public mental hospitals decreased by half (from 500,000 to 250,000) during that same time period.

Our nation's residential institutions for the mentally retarded and severely disturbed have come under attack both by professionals (see, for example, Blatt, 1976; Blatt & Kaplan, 1966) and by the courts (for example, *Wyatt* v. *Stickney*, 1972) as being unable to provide the care and educational services needed by the persons living in them. Given the principle of normalization, large residential institutions are inherently inappropriate places in which to place retarded citizens, even if all of the institutions were providing humanistic care and good educational programming.

However, deinstitutionalization must be carried out thoughtfully. As Scharr points out,

Deinstitutionalization has all too often meant the unceremonious dumping of former patients into hostile communities, where they roam the streets aimlessly or live in the degradation of welfare hotels or flophouses—with no semblance of follow-up care or treatment. (1976, p. 1)

As we begin to provide more community-based living alternatives for handicapped people, and learn more about preparing institutionalized residents for the transition to those facilities, deinstitutionalization can help result in a more normalized existence for many of our retarded citizens.

PRACTICAL TASK ANALYSIS

Task analysis helps teachers pinpoint their students' specific functioning levels on targeted skills and provides the basis for sequential instructional programs that move the learner toward mastery of a goal at an appropriate pace.

No one method of analysis is equally well suited to all tasks. To become skilled in selecting the right method of analysis for each task, teachers must be aware of each of the available methods.

Guidelines for Task Analysis

There are several general guidelines that teachers should follow to conduct task analyses.

First, the scope of the main task should be *limited*.

Second, subtasks should be written in *observable* terms.

Third, terminology should be at a *level* understood by potential users of the analysis—the teachers.

Fourth, the task should be written in terms of what the *learner* will do.

Finally, the *task* should be the focus of attention, not the learner.

Methods of Task Analysis

Method 1. The "watch a master perform" method is especially well suited to psychomotor tasks. The analyst watches a person proficient in the performance of a task and writes down in correct order all the steps the master performs. Every step should be recorded, except those judged to have no relevance to the major task. The steps should be written as accurately and concisely as possible.

Practice exercises:
Alphabetizing a list of words
Making a telephone call
Using correct table manners

Method 2. A variation is for the analyst to perform the task himself. This method is useful but sometimes becomes awkward. Some of the problems are removed when an analyst starts with a behavioral objective, gathers the props necessary, and then verbalizes each step while performing it. Using a tape recorder removes the necessity of stopping to record subtasks. To check the adequacy of the breakdown, the analyst should perform the task a second time following the steps outlined, adding or deleting steps as necessary.

Practice exercises:
Tying a shoe
Writing a business letter
Multiplying by two digit numbers

Method 3. A third method of task analysis is performed by working backward from the terminal objective. It results in a pyramid of tasks leading to successful completion of the major goal.

Practice exercises:
Computing overtime pay
Polishing a pair of shoes
Identifying members of a concept class (e.g., community helpers)

Method 4. A method identified as brainstorming (Frank, 1973) is somewhat less systematic than other methods, but is useful for analyzing complex tasks that do not conform to any strict sequence. The analyst simply writes down all the subtasks involved in a particular goal without regard to any order. Then, the tasks are rearranged in as logical an order as possible.

Practice exercises:
Finding the correct definition
of a word
Making change for sums less
than a dollar
Using a washing machine

Method 5. The fifth method requires the analyst to focus on and break down the conditions specified in the terminal objective. The conditions are modified to make it easier for the learner to perform the behavior. As the learner gains proficiency the simplified conditions are slowly changed to approach the conditions in the original objective. The following objective represents one that might require task analysis in a special class:

> Given a 4 × 6 inch piece of paper with a 3 inch pencil line drawn on it, the pupil will use primary scissors to cut the paper on the line without deviating more than ½ inch from the line at any time. She will stop cutting within ½ inch of the end of the line.

Any of the methods outlined thus far could be used to delineate the steps involved in the actual process. The objective could be further analyzed by simplifying the conditions under which the task must take place. The analyst seeks ways of adding to, deleting from, or otherwise changing the conditions to make the task easier for the learner. One of the most obvious changes that could be made in the paper cutting objective is to shorten the line. It would probably be easier to cut a 1 inch line to criterion than a 3 inch line. The line could be gradually lengthened as the learner's proficiency in cutting increased. Any changes made in the conditions must be systematically eliminated before the learner

can be said to have mastered the terminal objective.

Practice exercises:
Following a sequence of three
oral directions
Shooting foul shots in basketball
Finding the main thought in a
story

Method 6. The final method of task analysis is used most successfully with goals. Mager (1972) described a process of goal analysis for breaking down complex goals. It is particulary useful with affective goals.

1. Write the goal on paper.
2. List the observable behaviors a person would exhibit to show that he or she has attained the goal.
3. Review the list, discarding those behaviors that should not be included and identifying those in need of clarification.
4. Describe what is intended for each goal on the list by determining how frequently or how well the behavior must be performed.
5. Test the statements for adequacy and completeness by determining whether the behaviors in the final list represent comprehensive attainment of the goal.

Practice exercises:
Accepts criticism well
Is a good worker
Has leadership qualities

When the task has been analyzed, the teacher must choose the method that will be used in instruction.

Discussion adapted from J. Moyer and J. C. Dardig, Practical task analysis for special educators, *Teaching Exceptional Children*, Fall 1978, pp. 16–18. Reprinted by permission.

SUMMARY

1. Society's attitude toward mentally retarded people has gone through many stages.
   a. Primitive people left retarded and other handicapped people to die. Later, superstitions about retarded people became common; they were often ridiculed.
   b. In the Middle Ages, a more humanitarian view led to the development of asylums.
   c. The first attempts to educate retarded children came during the early 19th century, beginning in Europe and spreading to the United States. Later in that century, however, large state institutions—seen as custodial rather than educational—became the primary means of service.
   d. Around the turn of the century, separate public school classes for retarded students began to be popular.
   e. The movement today is away from institutions and segregation and toward normalized education in the least restrictive environment.

2. Mental retardation is a complex concept which is difficult to define and measure.
   a. The current AAMD definition, used in P.L. 94–142, states that mental retardation involves both "significantly subaverage general intellectual functioning" and "deficits in adaptive behavior," manifested between birth and 18 years of age.
   b. Intellectual functioning is usually measured by a score on a normed, standardized intelligence test.
   c. An observation scale is usually used in evaluating adaptive behavior.
   d. Both intelligence tests and adaptive behavior scales can be culturally biased and scored subjectively. However, IQ tests are the best single predictor of school achievement.
   e. Important alternate definitions stress that mental retardation denotes a level of performance that can be altered.
   f. The trend today is toward using a more conservative approach to labeling children *retarded* because of the negative effects of labeling and the limitations of the tests.

3. Mental retardation is classified by degree of severity, as measured by IQ scores.
   a. Mildly, or educable, retarded children are often "retarded" only in school. Their social and communication skills are frequently "normal" or nearly so. They are likely to become independent or semi-independent adults.
   b. Many mildly retarded children are educated in regular classrooms with extra help provided as needed. They can generally master standard academic skills up to about sixth grade level.

c. Moderately, or trainable, retarded children usually show significant early delays. Most will require some lifelong supervision, but they can live in community-based residences and work in supervised settings.

d. In school, moderately retarded students are usually taught communication, self-help and daily living skills, and vocational skills, along with limited academics. Most moderately retarded children are educated in self-contained classrooms.

e. Most severely and profoundly retarded people are identified in infancy. Many have physical damage and multiple handicaps. While some severely and profoundly retarded adults can be semi-independent and live in the community, others will need 24-hour care throughout their lives.

f. In spite of their severe handicaps, severely and profoundly retarded people *can* learn. Curricula stress communication and self-help skills.

4. It is difficult to estimate the number of mentally retarded people. Theoretically, 3% of the population would score in the retarded range on IQ tests, but this does not account for adaptive behavior, the other criterion.

5. It is difficult to determine the cause of most cases of retardation.

a. About 80 to 85% of all retarded people are mildly retarded. In most of these cases, there is no known cause, and the retardation is said to be cultural-familial.

b. The cause is known in 10 to 20% of the cases, usually in the moderate, severe, and profound ranges. All the known causes are biological.

6. Today there are many different options available for residential and educational placement of mentally retarded children and adults.

a. Institutions are seen as necessary for fewer and fewer people, and thus, some are able to provide more humane and more appropriate services for their residents.

b. Small regional residential programs help retarded people live more normal lives within their own communities.

c. Some retarded adults live in supervised apartments, some with nonretarded roommates; others live in group homes with houseparents.

d. Many retarded adults work in sheltered, supervised workshops.

e. While some retarded children attend special public schools, more and more are being educated in their neighborhood schools—either in special classes or in regular classes where they receive special help or attend a resource room for part of the day.

7. Behavior modification is widely used in teaching retarded students. Effective techniques include:

a. Task analysis,

b. Direct and continuous measurement, and

c. Positive reinforcement.

8. Recent laws, including P.L. 94–103 and P.L. 94–142, have extended and affirmed the rights of the mentally retarded as citizens. Advocates can help protect the rights of individual retarded people.

9. Recent scientific advances, including genetic counseling, amniocentesis, virus vaccines, and early screening tests, are helping reduce the incidence of clinical retardation. However, there is still no widely used technique to decrease the incidence of cultural-familial retardation, although early identification and intensive services to "high-risk" infants show promise.

10. Our current goal is to make the lives of retarded people—at home, in school, and at work—as normal as possible. With this in mind, institutions are necessarily inappropriate. Thus, we must develop training and transition programs and community services for the retarded and work to change public attitudes.

FOR MORE INFORMATION

Journals

American Journal of Mental Deficiency. Published bimonthly by the American Association on Mental Deficiency. Publishes studies and discussions of original material dealing with the behavioral and biological aspects of retardation, as well as theoretical articles.

Analysis and Intervention of Developmental Disabilities. Published quarterly by Pergamon Press, Elmsford, New York. Publishes original behavioral research and theory on severe and pervasive developmental disabilities.

Applied Research in Mental Retardation. Published quarterly by Pergamon Press, Elmsford, New York. Publishes descriptions of effective methods of treatment and assessment as well as coverage of the legal and ethical aspects of applying treatment procedures to mentally retarded children and adults.

Education and Training of the Mentally Retarded. Published four times per school year by the Division on Mental Retardation of the Council for Exceptional Children. Publishes experimental studies and discussion articles dealing with the education of the mentally retarded.

Mental Retardation. Published bimonthly by the American Association on Mental Deficiency. Concerned with new approaches to methodology, critical summaries, essays, program descriptions, and research studies dealing with mental retardation.

Books

Cegelka, P. T., & Prehm, H. J. (eds.) *Mental retardation: From categories to people,* Columbus, Ohio: Charles E. Merrill, 1982.

Kauffman, J. M., & Payne, J. S. (eds.). *Mental retardation: Introduction and personal perspectives.* Columbus, Ohio: Charles E. Merrill, 1975.

MacMillan, D. L., *Mental retardation in school and society,* 2d ed. Boston: Little, Brown, 1982.

Neisworth, J. T., & Smith, R. M. *Modifying retarded behavior*. Boston: Houghton-Mifflin, 1973.

Neisworth, J. T., & Smith, R. M. *Retardation: Issues, assessment, and intervention*. New York: McGraw-Hill, 1978.

Payne, J. S., & Patton, J. R. *Mental retardation*. Columbus, Ohio: Charles E. Merrill, 1981.

Robinson, N. M., & Robinson, H. B. *The mentally retarded child*, 2c ed. New York: McGraw-Hill, 1976.

Organizations

American Association on Mental Deficiency. 5201 Connecticut Avenue, NW, Washington, DC 20015. Primarily includes researchers, teacher educators, and psychologists interested in mental retardation.

Association for Retarded Citizens. 2709 Avenue E. East, Arlington, TX 76011. An advocacy organization including parents and professionals, with active local chapters in most states.

Division on Mental Retardation, The Council for Exceptional Children. 1920 Association Drive, Reston, VA 22091. Includes teachers, teacher educators, and other members of CEC working with mentally retarded persons from preschool on.

4
Learning Disabilities

No field of special education—or probably all of education, for that matter—has experienced as much rapid growth, extreme interest, and frantic activity as learning disabilities. Learning disabilities has been the center of public attention and interest, as demonstrated in countless newspaper stories, magazine articles, and television documentaries on topics like "Does Your Child Have a Learning Disability?" The field has become a breeding ground for fads and "miracle cures." Learning disabilities, more than any other field of special education, seems to create misunderstandings and generate controversy. There is considerable confusion and disagreement not just on the part of the general public, but by professionals and parents as well, on such basic issues as "What is a learning disability?" and "How do you teach a learning disabled child?" But as we will also see in this chapter, the field of learning disabilities has been the birthplace of educational techniques and developments that have benefited all of special education.

HISTORY OF THE FIELD OF LEARNING DISABILITIES

By the 1950s, most public schools had established special education programs (or at least offered some type of special service) for mentally retarded, blind, deaf, physically handicapped, and emotionally disturbed students. But there remained a group of children who were having serious learning problems at school, yet didn't fit into any of the existing categories of exceptionality. They didn't "appear" to be handicapped. That is, the children seemed physically intact; yet, they were unable to learn certain basic skills and subjects at school. In searching for help in identifying the source of their children's problems and trying to find someone who could help them (remember the public schools had no programs for these children), parents turned to other professionals—most notably doctors, psychologists, and speech and language specialists. Understandably, these professionals viewed the children from the vantage points of their respective disciplines. As a result, terms such as *brain damage*, **minimal brain dysfunction, neurological impairment, perceptual handicap, dyslexia**, and **aphasia** were often used to describe or account for the various problems of the children. Many of these terms are still used today, as a variety of disciplines have been, and continue to be, influential in the field of learning disabilities.

Most historians of special education place the "official" beginning of the learning disabilities movement in 1963, when Dr. Samuel Kirk delivered an address to a group of parents. The children of these parents were experiencing serious difficulties in learning to read, they were **hyperactive,** or they could not solve math problems. These parents did not consider their children's learning problems to be the result of mental retardation or emotional disturbance, nor did they like the labels that were often applied to their children. Kirk said, "Recently, I have used the term 'learning disabilities' to describe a group of children who have disorders in development in language, speech, reading, and associated communication skills" (Kirk, 1963). The parents liked the term and that very evening voted to form the Association for Children with Learning Disabilities (ACLD). The ACLD, which today has chapters in nearly all 50 states, is a powerful advocacy group dedicated to the support of services and programs for learning disabled children. Most ACLD members are parents, though many teachers and other professionals are also members.

In 1968, two more milestones were reached. First, the National Advisory Committee on Handicapped Children drafted and presented to Congress a definition of *learning disabilities,* one that still stands as the basic definition used to govern dispersal of federal funds for support of services to learning disabled children. Second, the Council for Exceptional Children (CEC), the largest organization of educators and other professionals serving exceptional children, established the Division for Children with Learning Disabilities, which is now called the Council for Learning Disabilities (CLD). Today with over 7,000 members, CLD is an independent organization, having left CEC in 1983. Second, 1968 was the year in which Dunn published his article "Special education for the mildly retarded—Is much of it justifiable?" (Dunn, 1968). Dunn argued that the proliferation of self-contained classrooms at that time was not supported by efficacy studies and that the evaluation and placement procedures typically used were questionable on many grounds. This article led many special educators to a much closer self-examination of all their practices, including those involving learning disabilities.

Largely because of the efforts of the ACLD and CLD, legislators were made aware of learning disabled children, who were not covered under any previous legislation providing educational support for handicapped students. As a result of intense lobbying (particularly by the ACLD), the Children with Learning Disabilities Act was presented to Congress in 1969 and signed into law (P.L. 91–230) in early 1970. This legislation authorized a 5-year program of federal funds for teacher training and the establishment of model demonstration programs for learning disabled students. In 1977 five federally funded research

Our discussion of the history of learning disabilities is very limited. While the term *learning disabilities* itself and the rapid growth of the field were phenomena of the 1960s, the field is closely related to research conducted with mentally retarded and brain-injured children in the 1940s and 1950s by Werner, Strauss, Lehtinen, and Kephart. For more detail on the development of the field, see Hallahan and Cruickshank (1973), Kass (1970), Schmid (1979), and Wiederholt (1974a).

See page 150 for more on the learning disabilities research institutes.

institutes were begun at universities to develop empirical data on a wide range of issues related to the education of learning disabled students. Today, learning disabilities is one of the handicapping conditions included in P.L. 94–142 as eligible for federal special education funds.

DEFINING LEARNING DISABILITIES

A major controversy in the field of learning disabilities has been, and continues to be, over definition. Of the many definitions of learning disabilities that have been proposed during the field's relatively short history, none has been universally accepted. However, the definition most widely accepted today was first written in 1968. In that year, the National Advisory Committee on Handicapped Children of the U.S. Office of Education drafted a definition of learning disabilities which was eventually included, with only minor changes in wording, in P.L. 94–142, the Education for All Handicapped Children Act of 1975. It reads:

> "Specific learning disability" means a disorder in one or more of the basic psychological processes involved in understanding or in using language, spoken or written, which may manifest itself in an imperfect ability to listen, think, speak, read, write, spell, or to do mathematical calculations. The term includes such conditions as perceptual handicaps, brain injury, minimal brain dysfunction, dyslexia, and developmental aphasia. The term does not include children who have learning problems which are primarily the result of visual, hearing or motor handicaps, of mental retardation, or of environmental, cultural, or economic disadvantages. (Section 5(b)(4) of P.L. 94–142).

Kirk and Gallagher (1979) suggest that three criteria must be met before a child is considered learning disabled. Each of these three factors are either stated or implied in most definitions of learning disabilities. These three criteria are: (1) a discrepancy between the child's potential and actual achievement, (2) an exclusion criterion, and (3) the need for special education services.

Discrepancy

The term *learning disability* is not meant to be used for children who are having minor or temporary difficulties in learning. The term is meant to identify children with a *severe* discrepancy between ability and achievement. While this is a fairly well-agreed-upon criterion, there is considerable disagreement and confusion about what constitutes a "severe discrepancy." Johnson and Myklebust (1967) found 1 or 2 years below the expected level of achievement to be the most commonly used measure of discrepancy. But they pointed out a serious problem with that practice because "One year below expectancy at eight years of age is not comparable to one year below expectancy at sixteen years of age or, for that matter, at three or four years of age." (p. 18)

McLoughlin and Netick 1983 point out that "Efforts to develop a formula by which to establish the existence of a learning disability have occupied many individuals since the early days of the field." Various mathematical formulas have been proposed for determining whether or not a severe discrepancy exists between a student's ability and achievement. One formula offered by federal agencies involved the child's chronological age (CA), IQ, and several predetermined constants. The result of calculating the formula was supposed to be the academic achievement (grade) level at or below which the child must be functioning in order for a severe discrepancy to exist. The formula was rejected for two main reasons. First, it did not take into account preschool children. Second, the decision as to whether or not a child is eligible for special educational services should not be based only on general measures like IQ and grade level that would not be responsive to the individual needs of children.

The proposed federal formula was [CA(IQ/300 + 0.17) − 2.5 = Severe Discrepancy Level.] Clearly, it was difficult to use and implied more meaningful precision in measurement of the variables included than is practical or realistic.

Still, lack of a specific definition of a "severe discrepancy between achievement and intellectual ability" in the criteria for identifying learning disabled students published by the federal government (see *Federal Register,* Thursday, December 29, 1977, p. 65083) has forced state and local educators to find some means of objectively identifying those children who are to receive special services. For example, the Ohio Department of Education has issued the following rules for determining if the "severe discrepancy" criterion is met:

> Each child shall have a severe discrepancy between achievement and ability which adversely affects his or her educational performance to such a degree that special education and related services are required. The basis for making the determination shall be:
>
> (i) Evidence of a discrepancy score of two or greater than two between intellectual ability and achievement in one or more of the following seven areas:
>   (a) Oral expression,
>   (b) Listening comprehension,
>   (c) Written expression,
>   (d) Basic reading skills,
>   (e) Reading comprehension,
>   (f) Mathematics calculation, or
>   (g) Mathematics reasoning.
> (ii) The following formula shall be used in computing the discrepancy score:
>   (a) From:
>   *(i)* The score obtained for the measure of intellectual ability,
>   *(ii)* Minus the mean of the measure of intellectual ability;
>   *(iii)* Divided by the standard deviation of the measure of intellectual ability.
>   (b) Subtract:
>   *(i)* Score obtained for the measure of achievement,
>   *(ii)* Minus the mean of the measure of achievement,
>   *(iii)* Divided by the standard deviation of the measure of achievement.
>   (c) The result of this computation equals the discrepancy score. If the discrepancy score is two or greater than two, a severe discrepancy exists. (Rules for the Education of Handicapped Children, effective July 1, 1982, p. 69)

The questionable validity and reliability of the tests we have available and problems of applying discrepancy techniques consistently across different age and grade levels are major concerns expressed over the use of discrepancy formulas (Lloyd, Sabtino, Miller, & Miller, 1977; McLoughlin & Netick, 1983). While the concept of discrepancy seems to be logically valid, it remains to be seen whether or not any given practice will be widely accepted as an objective and reliable means to identify and measure it.

Exclusion

The concept of learning disabilities is meant to identify children with significant learning problems that cannot be explained by mental retardation, sensory impairment, emotional disturbance, or lack of opportunity to learn. Kirk (1978b) uses the term *specific learning disabilities* to differentiate the truly learning disabled from the larger group of children with various learning problems.

Several noted special educators have criticized the exclusion clause in the federal definition of learning disabilities because it says that children with other handicapping conditions cannot be considered learning disabled as well. For example, some children whose primary diagnosis is mental retardation do not achieve up to their expected potential (Wallace & McLoughlin, 1979). Hammill (1976) challenges the notion that only children with IQ scores in the normal range can be identified as learning disabled. He rests his criticism on two arguments. First, most IQ tests are made up of items that measure past learning. If a child with a learning disability has not learned enough of the information included on the IQ test, he will score in the retarded range. Second, there are too many sources of measurement error involved in intelligence testing to make clear-cut differential diagnosis statements such as "this child is mildly retarded, and this one is learning disabled."

Special Education

A learning disabled student will need special education that "should involve practices that are unique, uncommon, of unusual quality and that, in particular, supplement the organizational and instructional procedures used with the majority of children" (Ames, 1977). This criterion is meant to keep children who have not had the opportunity to learn from being identified as learning disabled. Those children should progress normally once they are placed in a developmentally appropriate regular education program. Learning disabled children are those who show specific and severe learning problems in spite of normal educational efforts. Therefore, special educational services are needed to help remediate their achievement deficiencies.

The NJCLD-Proposed Definition

The National Joint Committee for Learning Disabilities (NJCLD) is a group comprised of official representatives from six professional organizations involved with learning disabled students. The NJCLD believed that the federal definition of learning disabilities had served the educational community reasonably well but had several inherent weaknesses (Hammill, Larsen, Leigh, & McNutt, 1981). Myers and Hammill (1982) state that the NJCLD was not satisfied with certain elements of the P.L. 94–142 definition.

116

SMALL SUCCESSES

Special education began for me with an incident during the third grade. I was having trouble with the work. I remember staying in from recess on my own to work on spelling, my least efficient subject. The teacher came over to me, took my book, and said, "You can't work with the spelling group. It's too hard for you." From then on she had me go play with blocks during spelling period. I can remember being really frustrated and upset.

There wasn't any such thing as an LD program then, so I wound up in a private school by the middle of fourth grade. My first teacher there started me in the right direction. I'll never forget it. She handed me this great big math workbook and said, "You're going to finish this by the end of the year." I couldn't believe it. By then math was right up there with spelling as my worst subject. When I told her I couldn't do math, she said, "How do you know you can't do it? You haven't even opened the book yet." She took it as a personal insult when her students didn't learn. She expected a lot. But she gave a lot. She broke everything down into small steps or tasks that could be accomplished.

Then she rewarded those small successes. She never put me down; she instilled the confidence in me that I could learn.

In junior high school I was back in the public school, which by then had established an LD program. Again I was fortunate to have a good teacher. He taught me study skills—how to think and how to discipline myself to complete a task. I couldn't say more than 3 or 4 words at a time then. I'd get stuck, couldn't think of the word I wanted to say. He'd make me write down 10 other words that could express that thought. It took a long time, but then I got better at it, then real good at it. Now I hardly ever get stuck.

I took classes every summer during high school and graduated a year early. Six months later I flunked out of a junior college and found myself hating school with a passion. I realize now that I needed the special education support I had received all through high school. But I'm back in school and it's working out well. Wright State has excellent support services for LD students.

If I could give teachers of LD children any advice, what would I say? That's easy. For LD children motivation is the first order of business. They must have confidence in themselves that they can learn. The best way to inspire that confidence is to break down each subject so that small successes can be realized. Say to the students, "I *know* you can do this." Then make sure they do.

Bill Haase was in an LD program from fourth grade through high school. At the time we talked with him, Bill was a sophomore at Wright State University majoring in computer science. He had made the Dean's List the previous quarter.

1. Exclusion of adults. Major interest in understanding the special needs of and developing programs for learning disabled adolescents and adults has emerged recently (Alley & Deschler, 1979; Marsh, Gearheart, & Gearheart, 1978). In keeping with this trend, the ACLD has recently changed its official name to the Association for Children and Adults with Learning Disabilities. Because it deals with public school education, the P.L. 94–142 definition refers only to school-age children, thereby eliminating adults from consideration.

2. Reference to basic psychological processes. Members of the NJCLD maintain that use of the phrase "basic psychological processes" has allowed much debate over how to teach learning disabled students, but that "how to teach" is a curricular issue, not a definitional one. The NJCLD believes the intent of the original phrase was only to show that a learning disability is intrinsic to the person affected.

3. Inclusion of spelling as a learning disability. Since spelling can be integrated with other areas of functioning, namely written expression, it is redundant and should be eliminated from the definition.

4. Inclusion of obsolete terms. The NJCLD believes that inclusion of terms such as *dyslexia, minimal brain dysfunction, perceptual handicaps,* and *developmental aphasia,* which historically have proven difficult to define, only adds confusion to the definition of learning disability.

5. The "exclusion" clause. The wording of the final clause in the P.L. 94–142 definition has led to the belief that learning disabilities cannot occur along with other handicapping conditions. A more accurate statement, according to the NJCLD, is that a person may have a learning disability *along with* another handicap but not *because of* another handicap. In other words, a learning disability is to be considered a handicap in its own right.

In response to these problems with the federal definition, the NJCLD has proposed the following definition of learning disabilities:

> Learning disabilities is a generic term that refers to a heterogeneous group of disorders manifested by significant difficulties in the acquisition and use of listening, speaking, reading, writing, reasoning, or mathematical abilities. These disorders are intrinsic to the individual and presumed to be due to central nervous system dysfunction. Even though a learning disability may occur concomitantly with other handicapping conditions (e.g., sensory impairment, mental retardation, social and emotional disturbance) or environmental influences (e.g., cultural differences, insufficient/inappropriate instruction, psychogenic factors), it is not the direct result of those conditions or influences. (National Joint Council for Learning Disabilities, 1981)

McLoughlin and Netick 1983 have discussed some of the practical implications the proposed definition may hold for assessment and identification of learning disabled students. Commenting on the newly proposed definition, NJCLD members Hammill, Leigh, McNutt, and Larsen (1981) write:

See the "Ability Training" and "Skill Training" sections of this chapter.

The NJCLD consists of representatives from the American Speech-Language-Hearing Association (ASHA), the Association for Children and Adults with Learning Disabilities (ACLD), the Council for Learning Disabilities (CLD), the Division for Children with Communication Disorders (DCCD), the International Reading Association (IRA), and the Orton-Dyslexia Society.

For further rationale and detailed exploration of the NJCLD defintion, see Hammill et al. (1981), Myers and Hammill (1982), and the National Joint Committee on Handicapped Children (1981).

The NJCLD members are the first to acknowledge that the proposed definition is not perfect. Yet, they are convinced that the definition is a substantial improvement over existing ones. They never intended to write the ultimate definition, only a better one; and, doubtlessly, in the years to come, their effort will also be discarded in favor of a newer, improved version. Until then, the Committee believes that the proposed definition is the best one available and recommends that it be considered as a theoretical statement about the nature of learning disabilities. (p. 341)

It is too early to tell what impact the NJCLD definition will have on the field. On one level, the NJCLD definition can be seen as an effort to limit the term *learning disabilities* to the "hard-core" or "truly" handicapped (Myers & Hammill, 1982) with its requirement that the disorder is "intrinsic to the individual and presumed to be due to central nervous system dysfunction."

Other special educators have proposed broader definitions of learning disabilities that do not involve causal explanations. Hallahan and Kauffman (1976, 1977) suggest that a learning disabled child is simply one who is not achieving up to potential. The child may be at any intelligence level, and his learning difficulties may be caused by any number of reasons. Many more children—perhaps up to half the population of some school districts—might be considered learning disabled with this broad definition.

We believe the most important issue, from the educator's standpoint, should not be whether or not a student *has* a learning disability, but how to assess and remediate the specific *skill deficiencies* in each child's repertoire.

CHARACTERISTICS OF LEARNING DISABLED CHILDREN

In describing the various categories of exceptionality, it is often useful to list the physical and psychological characteristics commonly found in the children who make up that group. The inherent danger in these lists of characteristics is the tendency to assume, or at least look for, all of those characteristics in *all* of the children considered to be in the category. This danger is especially acute in the case of learning disabilities. To give you some idea of the extent of this problem—just how different from one another learning disabled children are—consider this: A national task force found 99 separate "characteristics of learning disabled children" described in the literature (Clements, 1966).

From a physical standpoint, learning disabilities is a "hidden handicap." A learning disability:

is not apparent in the physical appearance of the young person. He may have a robust body, good eyes, sound ears, and a normal intelligence. He has a disability of function, however, which is just as real as a crippled leg. (Anderson, 1970, p. 1)

According to Tarver and Hallahan (1976), the following 10 characteristics of learning disabled children are most often cited in the literature:

1. Hyperactivity
2. Perceptual-motor impairments
3. Emotional lability (ups and downs, moodiness, anxiety)
4. General coordination deficits
5. Disorders of attention (distractibility, perseveration)
6. Impulsivity
7. Disorders of memory and thinking
8. Specific academic problems in reading, writing, spelling, and/or arithmetic
9. Disorders of speech and hearing (language problems)
10. Equivocal neurological signs (for example, abnormal brain wave patterns that are difficult to explain or interpret)

One observational study of learning disabled children in regular second and fourth grade classrooms found that task orientation was the primary dimension in which the behavior of the learning disabled students differed from that of their non–learning disabled peers (McKinney, McClure, & Feagans, 1982). The learning disabled children were "on-task" less often and showed more nonconstructive, "off-task" behavior during instructional periods than their non–learning disabled peers.

In reviewing any list of characteristics, we must remember that the single, common characteristic of children with learning disabilities is a specific and significant achievement deficiency in the presence of adequate overall intelligence. Some learning disabled children will also be hyperactive (or show any of the other cited characteristics), and some will not be. You should also note that children with any of these characteristics who do not have deficits in achievement would not be considered learning disabled.

PREVALENCE

Because of the many ways in which the definition of learning disabilities can be interpreted, the different means of diagnosing and identifying learning disabled children from one part of the country to the next, and the unreliable assessment instruments used to diagnose learning disabilities, it is impossible to state how many learning disabled children there really are. Estimates have ranged anywhere from 1 to 30% of the school-age population. In reviewing 21 different surveys of school populations, Bryant (1972) found that learning disabled children were cited as comprising anywhere from 3 to 28% of a school's total enrollment. Statistics from the U.S. Department of Education (1982b) show that 1,538,284 children, or 3.33% of the school-age population, were identified and served as learning disabled during the 1981–82 school year. Learning disabled children comprise approximately 35% of the school-age handicapped population, constituting the largest subgroup of handicapped children.

There are more identified learning disabled boys than girls, but the incidence among girls may be on the rise. In 1976, Lerner claimed a ratio of 4.6

learning disabled boys for every girl. But a more recent survey by Norman and Zigmond (1980) reports a boy-girl ratio of only 3.7 to 1. Lovitt (1982) suggests that more uniform child-rearing practices for boys and girls and more sensitive diagnostic tests may be responsible for the increase in girls labeled *learning disabled.*

CAUSES OF LEARNING DISABILITIES

In almost every case, exactly how a child comes to have a learning problem is unknown. However, a variety of causes of learning disabilities have been proposed. These etiological factors generally fall into three categories—brain damage, biochemical imbalance, and environmental factors.

Brain Damage

Some professionals believe that all learning disabled children suffer from some form of brain injury. The suspected brain damage is not considered extensive enough to cause a generalized and severe learning problem across all kinds of intellectual development (that is, mental retardation), so the children are often referred to as *minimally brain damaged.* In cases where actual evidence of brain damage cannot be shown (and, as we shall see in a moment, this is the situation with the majority of learning disabled children), the term *minimal brain dysfunction* is often used. This phrase implies brain damage by asserting that the child's brain doesn't function very well. The term is still widely used in the field of learning disabilities, especially by physicians.

The exact causes of learning disabilities are unknown.

There are two major problems with current etiological theories of learning disabilities based on brain damage. The first problem is lack of evidence. All learning disabled children do not display clinical (medical) evidence of brain damage. And not all brain-damaged children are learning disabled. Boshes and Myklebust (1964) reported the results of EEG readings given to 200 normal and 200 learning disabled children. Results showed 29% of the normal children and 42% of the learning disabled children displayed abnormal brain wave patterns. While more learning disabled than normal children were rated abnormal, certainly these results prove that there is not a direct, one-to-one relationship between brain injury and learning disability.

The second problem with the brain-damage assumption is that it serves as a powerful, built-in excuse for failure to teach the child. ("Well, it's no wonder I couldn't teach him very much. He's brain-damaged.") If the child doesn't learn, it is thought to be no one's fault; he has a brain injury that "prevents" him from learning. Unfortunately, given the traditional association of the term *learning disability* with the idea of brain damage, some teachers react the same way. ("No wonder I couldn't teach him; he's got a learning disability.")

Nevertheless, some learning disabled children do show definite signs of brain damage which may very well be the cause of their learning problems.

Biochemical Imbalance

Some researchers claim that biochemical disturbances within a child's body are the cause of learning disabilities. Dr. Benjamin Feingold (1975a, 1975b, 1976) has received much publicity over his claims that artificial colorings and flavorings in many of the foods children eat can cause learning disabilities and hyperactivity. He recommends a treatment for learning disabilities consisting of a diet with no foods containing synthetic colors or flavors.

In 1965, Feingold, a San Francisco allergist, treated a woman with an acute case of hives. The woman was put on a diet that removed all salicylates—a group of natural compounds found in certain fruits and vegetables. In less than two weeks the hives had disappeared, and the woman reported she did not feel as aggressive or hostile as before (Feingold, 1975b). He then tried the elimination diet on 25 hyperactive children in one school system and claimed that 16 of the children responded favorably. On the basis of this and several other uncontrolled studies, Feingold held a news conference and announced that "hyperactivity can be greatly reduced by the elimination of artificial food coloring and flavoring" from children's diets and that the diet "brings hope to thousands of parents who have been distressed by the need to cope with the problem of hyperactivity by giving their children prescribed drugs" (Spring & Sandoval, 1976). Appearances on television talk shows, newspaper and magazine articles, more press conferences, and a popular book (Feingold, 1975b) followed. In an article in the *Journal of Learning Disabilities,* Feingold wrote:

> Artificial food colors and flavors have the capacity to induce adverse reactions affecting every system of the body. Of all these adverse reactions, the nervous

system involvement, as evidenced by behavioral disturbances and learning disabilities, is the most frequently encountered and most critical, affecting millions of individuals in this country alone.

The K-P diet, which eliminates all artificial food colors and flavors as well as foods with a natural salicylate radical, will control the behavioral disturbance in 30 to 50% (depending on the sample) of both normal and neurologically damaged children. (1976, p. 558)

The "K-P diet" is Feingold's name for his diet.

Public response to Feingold's claims has been intense. As Divoky writes, "Along comes Feingold. Not only is he going to get hyperactive kids off drugs, but he's going to do it with a wonderfully appealing treatment: additive-free, healthful food" (1978, p. 56). Today the Feingold Association has a membership of over 10,000 people (mainly parents) in 120 local groups.

A number of research studies have been conducted to test the Feingold diet, some claiming positive results (Connors, Goyette, Southwick, Lees, & Andrulonis, 1976; Cook & Woodhill, 1976). However, in a comprehensive review of diet-related studies, Spring and Sancoval (1976) concluded that there is very little evidence in support of Feingold's theory. Many of the studies were poorly conducted, and the few experiments that were scientifically sound concluded that only a small portion of hyperactive children might be helped by the special diet.

But in a more recent, well-controlled study employing "double-blind" procedures, Rose (1978) found that two 8-year-old girls who had been on the Feingold diet for at least 11 months spent less time on-task and more time out of their seats when they had eaten cookies that contained a yellow artificial food coloring just before going to school.

The girls ate a yellow cookie each day, but neither they nor the observers knew whether the cookies contained artificial coloring on any certain day. Thus, the girls' responses and the observers' measurements were not affected by their expectations. This is a "double-blind" procedure.

The controversy over the theory and diet treatment continues, with a great need for continued research (Adler, 1978). The American Council on Science and Health, in a 1979 publication, issued the following statement:

Hyperactivity will continue to be a frustrating problem until research resolves the questions of its cause, or causes, and develops an effective treatment. The reality is that we still have a great deal to learn about this condition. We do know now, however, that diet is not the answer. It is clear that the symptoms of the vast majority of the children labeled "hyperactive" are not related to salicylates, artificial food colors, or artificial flavors. The Feingold diet creates extra work for the homemakers and changes the family lifestyle . . . but it doesn't cure hyperactivity. (p. 5)

Cott (1972) hypothesizes that learning disabilities can be caused by the inability of a child's bloodstream to synthesize a normal amount of vitamins. Based on his contention, some physicians began "megavitamin therapy" with learning disabled children. Megavitamin treatment consists of massive daily doses of vitamins in an effort to overcome the suspected vitamin deficiencies. Kershner, Hawks, and Grekin (1977) performed an experiment to test the effects of megavitamin therapy with learning disabled children. Their results show that huge doses of vitamins did not improve the performance of learning disabled children.

One study has even suggested that trace metals, such as lead and calcium, found in hair samples of learning disabled children may be a causal factor (Pihl & Parke, 1978). These experimenters claim to be able to identify with 98% accuracy whether or not a child is learning disabled by analyzing chemical elements found in the child's hair. However, the scientific rigor employed in this study is highly questionable. For example, 2½ months passed between the time hair samples were taken from the experimental (learning disabled) group and the time they were taken from the control (non–learning disabled) group, which leaves open the possibility that other variables (season, air pollution, and others) might be involved.

Environmental Factors

Lovitt (1978) cites three types of environmental influences that he feels are related to children's learning problems: emotional disturbance, lack of motivation, and poor instruction. Many children with learning problems have behavior disorders as well. Whether one causes the other or whether both are caused by some other factor(s) is uncertain at this time. In addition, it is difficult to identify reinforcing activities for some learning disabled students; they may not be interested in many of the things "normal" children like. Some research studies have shown that finding a key to the child's motivational problem can sometimes solve the learning problem as well (Lovitt, 1977).

One variable that is very likely to be a major contributor to children's learning problems is the quality of instruction they receive. Lovitt states it this way:

> [A] condition which might contribute to a learning disability is poor instruction. Although many children are able to learn in spite of poor teachers and inadequate techniques, others are less fortunate. Some youngsters who have experienced poor instruction in the early grades never catch up with their peers. (1978, p. 169)

Engelmann is even more direct:

> Perhaps 90 percent or more of the children who are labeled "learning disabled" exhibit a disability not because of anything wrong with their perception, synapses, or memory, but because they have been seriously mistaught. Learning disabilities are made, not born. (1977, pp. 46–47)

Lovitt and Engelmann are among a growing number of educators who feel that the best way to help children with learning problems is to emphasize the assessment and training of those specific behaviors (for example, reading and arithmetic skills) that are troublesome for that particular child. Mounting evidence indicates that many students' learning problems can be remediated by direct, systematic instruction. However, it would probably be naive to think that the learning problems of all children stem from inadequate instruction. Perhaps Engelmann's other 10% are those children whose learning disability is caused by a malfunctioning central nervous system. In any event, from an educational perspective, good, systematic instruction should still be the treatment of first choice.

At present there is much more speculation than hard evidence. The search for the real causes of children's learning problems must go on. Only through positive identification of the causes of learning disabilities can prevention become a realistic alternative.

ASSESSMENT

In education, the word *assessment* is synonymous with *testing*. Literally hundreds of tests have been developed to measure virtually every motor, social, or academic response children make (Buros, 1978). Unfortunately, much of the testing in education has been conducted primarily for the purpose of identifying children for certain special education categories and placement. Certainly, assessment for identification is important. As Myers and Hammill point out,

> At some point along the continuum of services provided by the school, there must be a cutoff that dictates which children will be served by special education and which will remain totally the responsibility of the general education program. Obviously, the vast majority of children who have trouble in school will have to stay in regular classes. In any event, the type of assessment that deals with identification is of the utmost importance in states where laws, policies, or traditions make it mandatory that children be classified according to type of handicap before they can qualify for special services. (1982, p. 44)

Because of the complex way learning disabilities is defined, the task of identifying the "true LD child" guarantees that a battery of tests be administered. As a result, learning disabled children have been called the "most diagnosed" of all types of exceptional children (Lovitt, 1982). While identification and placement are appropriate and important functions of educational testing, there is a much more important purpose of assessment: to provide information to use in planning and implementing an instructional program for the child.

Assessment is an area in which the field of learning disabilities has had great impact for all of special education and more and more for regular education as well. This stems from the belief, widely held in the learning disabilities field, in a *diagnostic-prescriptive* approach to assessment. That is, learning disabilities professionals, regardless of their differing ideas about exactly how assessment and instruction should be carried out, agree that the results of any assessment should lead directly to a plan, or "prescription," for classroom instruction. We believe that this is leading to a greater awareness and concern that all educational assessment should be relevant to the classroom.

A variety of tests and procedures are used in the assessment of learning disabilities. At least five different types of tests are commonly used in the assessment of learning disabilities: norm-referenced tests, process tests, informal reading inventories, criterion-referenced tests, and direct, daily measurement. Of the five types, norm-referenced tests and process tests are *indirect* assessment devices. That is, the child's general ability along various dimensions is measured. Informal reading inventories, criterion-referenced tests, and direct daily measurement can all be classified as *direct* assessment techniques. In direct assessment the specific skills and behaviors a child is to be taught are measured. As we shall see in the next section, the choice between direct and indirect assessment is largely determined by the approach to instructional remediation taken by a given school program.

Norm-Referenced Tests

Norm-referenced tests are designed so that one child's score can be compared with that of other children of the same age who have taken the same test. Because deficits in academic achievement are the major characteristic of learning disabled children, standardized achievement tests are commonly used. Some standardized achievement tests, like the Iowa Tests of Basic Skills (Hieronymus & Lindquist, 1978), the Peabody Individual Achievement Test (Dunn & Markwardt, 1970), or the Wide Range Achievement Test (Jastak & Jastak, 1965), are designed to measure children's overall academic achievement. Scores on these tests are reported by grade level; a score of 3.5, for example, means a child is performing at the level of the average child halfway through the third grade. Other norm-referenced tests measure a child's achievement in certain academic areas. Some of the frequently administered reading achievement tests are the Durrell Analysis of Reading Difficulty (Durrell, 1955), the Gates-McKillop Reading Diagnostic Test (Gates & McKillop, 1962), the Gray Oral Reading Tests (Gray, 1963), the Spache Diagnostic Reading Scales (Spache, 1963), and the Woodcock Reading Mastery Tests (Woodcock, 1974). The KeyMath Diagnostic Arithmetic Test (Connolly, Natchman, & Pritchett, 1973) and the Stanford Diagnostic Arithmetic Test (Beatty, Madden, & Gardner, 1966) are often used to test arithmetic achievement.

Process Tests

The concept of process, or ability testing, was created by the field of learning disabilities. It grew out of the belief that learning disabilities are caused by a basic, underlying difficulty of the child to process, or use, environmental stimuli in the same way that normal children do. These general "abilities" are categorized under headings such as visual perception, auditory perception, and eye-motor coordination. The developers and users of these tests believe that if the specific perceptual problems of the child can be identified, treatment programs can then be designed to improve those problems, and the child's learning problem will be remediated.

In the next section, we will further discuss this approach to the treatment of learning disabilities.

A number of process tests have been developed. We will briefly discuss the two process tests most widely used in the diagnosis and assessment of learning disabilities: the Illinois Test of Psycholinguistic Abilities (ITPA) (Kirk, McCarthy, & Kirk, 1968) and the Marianne Frostig Developmental Test of Visual Perception (Frostig, Lefever, & Whittlesey, 1964).

No other test has been as strongly associated with the assessment of learning disabilities as the Illinois Test of Psycholinguistic Abilities (Kirk et al., 1968). First published in 1961 and later revised in 1968, the ITPA consists of 12 subtests, each designed to measure some aspect of psycholinguistic ability considered by Kirk and his colleagues to be central to learning. Results of the test are depicted on a profile (see Figure 4.1) showing in which of the 12 areas the child demonstrates weaknesses.

Many remedial education programs and activities for learning disabled children have been based on the psycholinguistic or "information-processing" model. While research on the effectiveness of these training programs has not

PROFILE OF ABILITIES

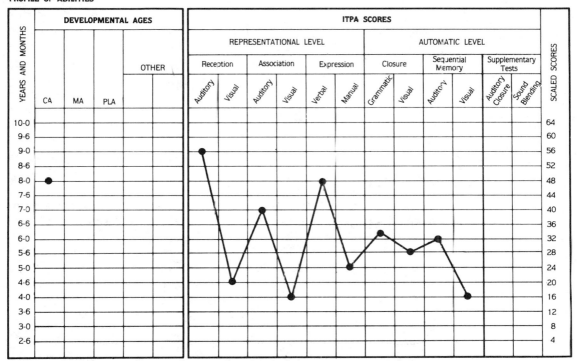

FIGURE 4.1

ITPA profile of abilities. Notice that the child is evaluated on 10 measures involving levels of organization (representational and automatic), psycholinguistic processes (reception, association, etc.), and channels of communication (auditory, visual, etc.). In addition, some children are tested on two supplementary subtests.

SOURCE:1 From S. A. Kirk, J. J. McCarthy, & W. D. Kirk, The Illinois Test of Psycholinguistic Abilities (rev. ed.). Urbana, Ill.: University of Illinois Press, 1968. ©1968 by the Board of Trustees of the University of Illinois. Used with permission.

For a review of this research see Hammill and Larsen, 1974, 1978.

validated their effectiveness, one major contribution of the ITPA to educational assessment cannot be denied. The ITPA was developed and has been used for the primary purpose of gathering data that could be translated directly into an educational program designed to meet the individual needs of a specific child.

The Marianne Frostig Developmental Test of Visual Perception (Frostig et al., 1964) was developed by Dr. Frostig and her colleagues in order to measure certain dimensions of visual perception they considered crucial to a child's ability to learn to read. The Frostig test is comprised of five subtests designed to pinpoint the kinds of perceptual difficulties the child has. These five areas are eye-motor coordination, figure-ground discrimination, constancy of shape, position of objects in space, and spatial relationships.

Informal Reading Inventories

Teachers' growing awareness of the inability of formal achievement tests and process tests to provide truly useful information for planning instruction has led to an increased use of teacher-developed and administered informal tests, particularly in the area of reading. An informal reading inventory usually consists of a series of progressively more difficult sentences and paragraphs that the child is asked to read aloud. By directly observing and recording aspects of the child's reading skills, such as mispronounced vowels or consonants, omissions, reversals, substitutions, and comprehension, the teacher can determine the level of reading material that is best suited for the child and the specific reading skills that require remediation.

Criterion-Referenced Tests

Criterion-referenced tests differ from norm-referenced tests in that a child's score on a criterion-referenced test is compared to a predetermined criterion, or mastery level, rather than to normed scores of other students. The value of criterion-referenced tests is that they identify the specific skills the child has already learned and the skills that require instruction. Some commercially distributed curricula now include criterion-referenced test items used both as a pretest and as a posttest. The pretest assesses the student's entry level, in order to determine what aspects of the program he or she is ready to learn, and the posttest evaluates the effectiveness of the program. Of course, criterion-referenced tests can be, and often are, informally developed by classroom teachers. A sample criterion-referenced test developed to determine a child's "knowledge of the eight basic colors" is shown in Figure 4.2.

Direct, Daily Measurement

Direct, daily measurement means observing and recording, every day, the child's performance on the specific skill that is being taught (Lovitt, 1975a, 1975b). For example, in a program teaching multiplication facts, the student's performance of multiplication facts would be assessed every day. Measures such as

Task: Names each of the eight basic colors when shown

Materials: One box of crayons (to include eight basic colors). One scoring sheet.

Directions (to student): "Say the name of each crayon as I hold it up. You have only three seconds to give me your answer, so pay close attention. (Pick up the first crayon.) What color is this?" Repeat procedure for each of the eight colors. Do not tell the subject if she is correct or incorrect. Do not let the student see what you are marking. Use a stopwatch or a sweep second hand out of the subject's field of vision. Timing should begin immediately following the word *this* in the directions.

Scoring: Wait 3 seconds for response. If the response is incorrect, put the crayon back in the box and mark "incorrect" on the scoring sheet. If the response is correct, put the crayon back in the box and mark "correct" on the scoring sheet. If the child hesitates, wait the full 3 seconds before putting the crayon back in the box and mark "incorrect."

CAP: 100% accuracy

Skill: Knowledge of the eight basic colors
Task: Names each of the eight basic colors when shown

Subject _____ Age _____

Examiner _____ Date _____

Stimulus	*Response* (check one)	
	(correct)	(incorrect)
1. red	1_____	1_____
2. blue	2_____	2_____
3. yellow	3_____	3_____
4. green	4_____	4_____
5. black	5_____	5_____
6. orange	6_____	6_____
7. brown	7_____	7_____
8. purple	8_____	8_____

FIGURE 4.2

Sample criterion-referenced test and scoring sheet.

SOURCE: K. W. Howell, J. S. Kaplan, and C. Y. O'Connell, *Evaluating exceptional children: A task analysis approach.* Columbus, Ohio: Charles E. Merrill, 1979, pp. 97–98. Used with permission.

correct rate (number of facts stated correctly per minute), error rate, and percentage correct are often recorded. The advantages of direct, daily measurement are clear. First, it gives information about the child's performance on the *skill being taught.* Second, this information is available on a *continuous* basis, so that the teacher can change the child's program because of changing (or perhaps not changing) performance, not because of intuition, guesswork, or the results of a test that measures something else. Direct, daily measurement is the cornerstone of the behavioral approach to education introduced in chapter 3. It is becoming an increasingly popular assessment and evaluation technique in all areas of special education (Howell, Kaplan, & O'Connell, 1979). One teaching approach used by many learning disabilities teachers that is based entirely on direct, daily measurement is called **precision teaching.**

Precision Teaching

Precision teaching is a system of direct and daily measurement of children's performances originated by Dr. Ogden R. Lindsley. It is now being used with children at all levels—from regular classes to centers for the severely handicapped.

Lindsley, who had worked with B. F. Skinner at Harvard, sought to translate much of the traditional operant (behavioral) terminology into language that sounded more natural in the schools. Thus, precision teachers look at *behavior* as *movement*, at *antecedent and consequent events* as *events before and after* the child's movement, at *reinforcement schedules* as *arrangements of the events* that follow a movement, and so on. Next, he sought to develop a set of simple but effective procedures that teachers could follow to identify, monitor, and make decisions about critical movements children need to succeed in school. Finally, based on extensive data that indicated that children take bigger and bigger steps as they become more proficient at a movement, Lindsley devised the "Standard Behavior Chart" to show graphically how the child progresses from day to day.

Since its inception, precision teaching has been refined and improved by many teachers and researchers. As it is presently practiced, precision teaching consists of these steps (summarized on page 132 and illustrated in Figure 4.3).

Precise assessment of a student's performance is essential to planning an appropriate instructional program.

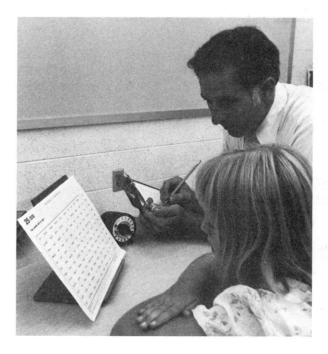

EXCEPTIONAL CHILDREN

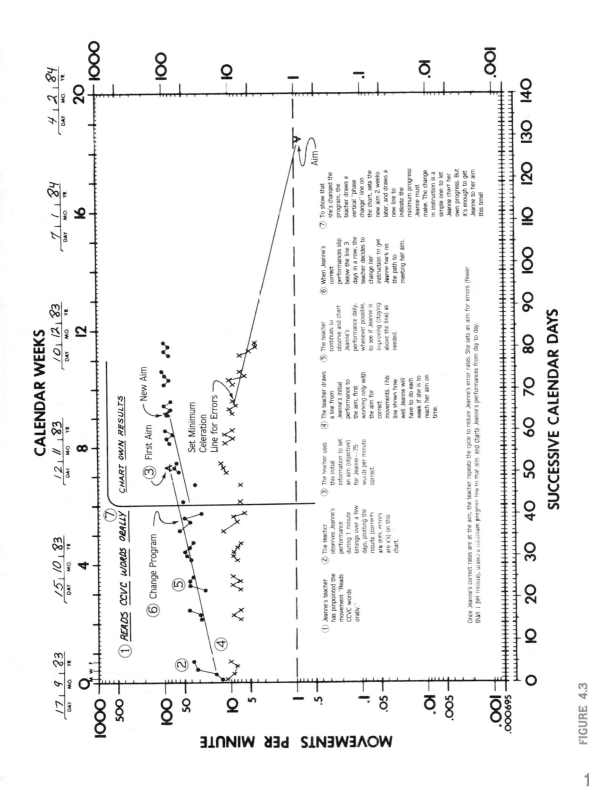

FIGURE 4.3

Using a standard behavior chart in precision teaching.

SOURCE: Adapted from O. White and N. Haring, *Exceptional teaching.* Columbus: Charles E. Merrill, 1976, p. 276. Reprinted by permission.

1. Precisely pinpoint the movement the child must make to learn the skill required—writing digits, saying words, etc.
2. Next, observe the child's performance of the movement, noting both accuracy and fluency (speed), and chart the results.
3. Using the information from a few days' observation, set an aim (objective) for the child—in terms of both accuracy and fluency—and note it on the chart.
4. Connect the average performance from the first few days with this aim, producing a line on the chart that represents the minimum progress the child must make each day to reach the aim in the time available.
5. As the days and weeks pass, continue to measure the child's performances *every day,* charting the information *every day.*
6. Paying careful attention to the chart, follow certain decision rules which tell when the program should be changed—to prevent the child from slipping below the line of minimum progress.
7. Whenever a program change (phase change) is needed, note the change on the chart, draw a new aim and a new minimum progress line, and begin again—*before the child has had a chance to fail.*

See Haring, Lovitt, Eaton, and Hansen (1978) and White and Haring (1980) for descriptions and applications of precision teaching.

EDUCATIONAL APPROACHES

As we mentioned, most learning disabilities specialists believe in a diagnostic-prescriptive approach, where the results of diagnosis (assessment) lead directly to a prescription (plan) for teaching. However, there is still great disagreement over what is to be diagnosed, and there are many approaches to *how* the problem is to be treated.

In an excellent article, Ysseldyke and Salvia (1974) outline two major models of instructional remediation within the overall framework of the diagnostic-prescriptive approach. These two models are the *ability training* (or process) model and the *skill training* (or task-analysis) model. While there is not complete agreement among practitioners within either of the two models as to what constitutes the single, best approach, there are fundamental differences between the two. We will describe the basic assumptions and some of the teaching strategies, and present some of the research on the effectiveness of each model.

Ability Training

Ability trainers believe that a child's observed performance deficit (learning problem) is due to weakness in a particular ability thought necessary to perform a given task. That is, this child cannot read because of a visual-perceptual disorder. These "abilities" are usually classified as perceptual-motor, sensory, or psycholinguistic disorders. Educational remediation involves testing the child (for example, with the ITPA or Frostig tests) to determine disabilities, and then prescribing instructional activities designed to remediate those disabilities. If deficits in these "basic" abilities cause the child's learning problem, remediating those deficits should result in improved achievement. The logic is sound.

A number of distinct approaches can be identified with n the ability-training model. The most popular of these approaches are *psycholinguistic training*, based on the ITPA; the *visual-perceptual approach* (Frostig & Horne, 1973); and the perceptual-motor approach (Kephart, 1971). According to Kephart, motor development precedes visual development; lack of proper perceptual-motor development, such as eye-hand coordination, is often caused by a child's inability to use vision alone, and thus a cause of reading difficulty. In Kephart's program, four areas of motor development are taught: balance and posture, locomotion, contact, and receipt and propulsion.

Another approach to teaching children with learning disabilities is the *multisensory approach*. Although in this approach teachers are more likely to work directly on academic skills than in other ability-training methods, it is still based primarily on an information-processing model. As its name suggests, the multisensory approach employs as many of the child's senses as possible in an effort to help him learn. The most notable multisensory programs are those developed by Fernald (1943) and Slingerland (1971). Fernald's method is known as the VAKT technique. In learning a new letter, for example, the child would see the letter (visual), hear the letter (auditory), and trace the letter (kinesthetic and tactile). Little scientific research has been conducted on the multisensory method.

There is not much research to support the effectiveness of ability training. Hammill, Goodman, and Wiederholt (1974) reviewed the results of studies conducted on the Kephart and Frostig approaches. They concluded that 13 of the 14 studies evaluating the Frostig reading materials produced unimpressive results. Of 15 studies using Kephart's perceptual-motor training program, only 6 reported significant improvements (intelligence, school achievement, and language functioning were measured in these studies). In addition, only 4 of 11 studies reported that the training significantly improved visual-motor performance. In another review, Myers and Hammill (1976) found that, in general, the Frostig materials improved children's scores on the Frostig Developmental Test of Visual Perception (Frostig et al., 1964), but whether or not their reading achievement improved is still in question.

Two more recent comprehensive reviews have also found the effectiveness of the perceptual-motor approach wanting. Kavale and Mattison (1983) reanalyzed 180 studies that investigated the effectiveness of the perceptual-motor approach and concluded that it is "not effective and should be questioned as a feasible intervention technique for exceptional children" (p. 165). After reviewing the results of 85 perceptual-motor training studies, Myers and Hammill state:

> As a consequence of our reviews of these systems, we would recommend that perceptual-motor training in the schools be carefully reevaluated. Unlike a decade ago, when research on the topic was sparse, one can no longer assume that these kinds of activities will be beneficial to the children who engage in them. In

fact, in the long run they may even be somewhat harmful because (1) they may waste valuable time and money and (2) they may provide a child with a placebo program when the child's problems require a real remedial effort. We would suggest that when these programs are implemented in the schools, they be considered as highly experimental, nonvalidated services that require very careful scrutiny and monitoring. (1982, p. 416)

In a major review of 38 studies of ITPA-based psycholinguistic training, Hammill and Larsen (1974, 1978) conclude that "the overwhelming consensus of research evidence concerning the effectiveness of psycholinguistic training is that it remains essentially nonvalidated" (1978, p. 412). Critics of Hammill and Larsen's ITPA review (e.g., Lund, Foster, & McCall-Perez, 1978), claim they were not justified in their conclusions because many of the original studies were poorly controlled. Kavale (1981) reanalyzed the Hammill and Larsen studies and concluded that his investigation "appears to answer affirmatively" that psycholinguistic training is effective.

Minskoff (1975), in responding to the Hammill and Larsen (1974) review, suggested that the earlier psycholinguistic research was not a good basis on which to evaluate the approach because it tended to be "incomplete" and methodologically inadequate. She went on to specify criteria for future psycholinguistic research, presumably so that its effectiveness would be more clearly understood. Sowell, Packer, Poplin, and Larsen (1979) followed Minskoff's criteria in a study designed to evaluate the effectiveness of psycholinguistic training with 63 first graders. They found the psycholinguistic training program to be unsuccessful and concluded their study with this comment:

In summary, the amount of time, effort, and monies currently devoted in the schools to improving psycholinguistic abilities needs to be reevaluated. At best, psycholinguistic training should be viewed as experimental and not be employed extensively until its usefulness can be effectively demonstrated. In reality, the onus of documenting the value of psycholinguistic training procedures falls primarily to those individuals who produce and/or advocate them. Until such time as experimental validation for this approach is forthcoming, educators are well advised to utilize other strategies in attempting to stimulate academic and/or language skills in children under their care. (1979, p. 76)

Skill Training

Skill trainers believe that a child's demonstrated performance deficit *is* the problem; it is not the sign of an underlying disability, but the result of the child not having had an appropriate opportunity to learn. For example, if a child cannot master a complex behavior (such as reading a sentence) *and* he has had sufficient opportunity *and* he wants to succeed, a skill trainer would conclude that he hasn't learned the necessary prerequisite skills (such as letter identification, reading single words, and so on).

Skill trainers use: (1) precise, operational definitions of the specific behaviors they intend to teach, (2) task analysis to break down complex skills into smaller units, or subskills, requiring the learner to master only one component of the task at a time, (3) direct teaching methods that require the learner to practice the new skill many times, and (4) direct, daily measurement to monitor the child's progress and evaluate instruction. Applied behavior analysis, behavior modification, precision teaching, and directive teaching are some of the skill-training approaches. All are closely related to one another, and all systematically manipulate aspects of the child's environment (materials, instructions, cues, rewards, and so on) in an attempt to facilitate the child's acquisition and retention of the new skill.

Task analysis is discussed on pages 106–107 and 342.

One skill-training teaching program is the Direct Instructional System for Teaching Arithmetic and Reading (DISTAR), developed by Siegfried Engelmann and his colleagues. DISTAR programs are available for arithmetic, reading, and language. Each DISTAR program consists of a highly sequenced series of skills, materials, and activities designed to help children practice those skills, and precise instructions for the teacher. The teacher works with a small group of children (4 to 10) who respond both individually and in unison to a fast-paced series of teacher-generated prompts and cues. Sometimes the teacher uses hand signals to direct and guide the children's responses. Corrective feedback for incorrect responses and praise for correct responses are also used. Unlike the ability-training instructional approaches, DISTAR has an impressive body of research demonstrating its effectiveness. A nationwide evaluation of the DISTAR program conducted by Follow Through, involving more than 8,000 children in 20 communities, showed that children made significant gains in academic achievement (Becker & Englemann, 1976). These children caught up to or even surpassed the national norms on several arithmetic, reading, and language skills, as measured by the Wide Range Achievement Test (Jastak & Jastak, 1976) and the Metropolitan Achievement Test (Balow, Farr, Hogan, & Prescott, 1978). On other skills, such as spelling, the DISTAR students finished a little below the

Follow Through is a nationwide comprehensive educational program for economically disadvantaged children, kindergarten through third grade. Many Head Start children enter Follow Through programs. See chapter 13.

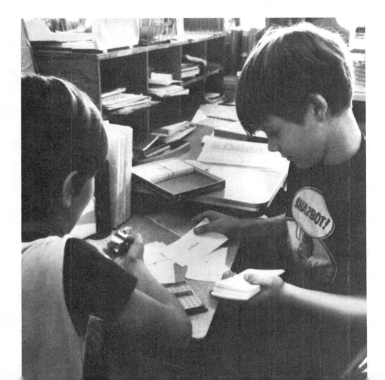

These learning disabled students help each other practice new skills. For more on peer tutoring see the insert at the end of chapter 2.

national norm but still showed significant gains. None of the other educational approaches evaluated by the Follow Through program were as effective as DISTAR.

Detailed accounts of applied behavior analysis and precision teaching procedures, as well as research demonstrating the effectiveness of the skill-training model, can be found in Haring et al. (1978), Haring and Schiefelbusch (1976), D. D. Smith (1981), and the *Journal of Applied Behavior Analysis.*

For a description of the DISTAR method and a review of the research conducted on it, see Haring, Bateman, and Carnine (1977).

SCHOOL SERVICES

Most public schools offer a range of service delivery and placement alternatives for learning disabled students. The most common arrangements are the regular classroom, the consultant teacher model, the itinerant teacher model, the resource room, and the self-contained special class.

The Regular Classroom

One peer tutoring program is described on pages 59–61.

Current legislation requires that handicapped children are to be educated with their nonhandicapped peers to the maximum extent possible, and that they should only be removed from normal settings to the extent that their disability necessitates. This means that some learning disabled children are remaining in the regular classroom, and others are placed there for some time each day. Several factors combine to help make the regular classroom an effective learning environment for many learning disabled children today. These factors include the increased use of individualized instruction, teacher aides, and peer-tutoring programs in many regular classrooms. In addition, school districts are providing more in-service teacher-training programs, many of which focus on the identification, assessment, and remediation of children's learning problems. However, it is probably unrealistic to think that the regular classroom is the best educational environment for children with severe learning disabilities (Reger, 1974). But, as Wallace and McLoughlin point out,

> The practice of considering the regular classroom as a realistic service delivery system is also one aspect of the intention to *prevent* learning disabilities. As we have discussed previously, instructional factors may cause or at least compound the learning difficulties of some children. By including the regular classroom setting as one of the key delivery systems, we may be channeling the necessary information and skills where they are most needed. (1979, p. 365)

In two other service delivery models, the consultant teacher and the itinerant teacher models, the learning disabled student stays in the regular classroom but he and/or his teacher receive additional help.

The Consultant Teacher

A consultant teacher provides support to regular classroom teachers and other school staff who work directly with learning disabled children. The consultant teacher helps the regular teacher select assessment devices, curriculum materials, and instructional activities for the learning disabled children in the regular teacher's classroom. The consultant may even demonstrate new teaching methods or behavior management strategies. The major advantage of this model is that the consultant teacher can work with several teachers, and thus indirectly provide special services to many children. The major drawback is that the consultant has no, or very little, direct contact with the children. Heron and Harris (1982) have described procedures consultant teachers can use to increase their effectiveness in supporting the mainstreamed child.

The Itinerant Teacher

The itinerant teacher is a combination consultant teacher and learning disabilities tutor "on wheels." An itinerant teacher serves several schools in a given district or geographical area. He or she acts as a consultant to the regular teachers on the "route," and also serves as a tutor, providing direct assessment and instruction for some children. The itinerant teacher model attempts to combine the consultant teacher model and the resource room concept in areas where one school does not have enough learning disabled children to warrant its own program. In some rural areas, where learning disabled children are spread over a large area, this may be the only realistic way to provide special education services and allow learning disabled children to remain in the regular classroom.

The Resource Room

The resource room has become the most popular service delivery model for educating children with learning disabilities. A resource room is a specially staffed and equipped classroom where learning disabled children come for one or several periods during the school day to receive individualized instruction (Wiederholt, 1974b).

The resource teacher is a specially trained and certified learning disabilities specialist whose primary role is to teach needed skills to those children who are referred to the resource room. Most of the children are in their regular classrooms for most of the school day, and they come to the resource room only for specialized instruction in the academic skills—usually reading or mathematics—or social skills they need to smooth their integration into the regular classroom. Other children may receive all of their academic instruction in the resource room and attend the regular classroom only for such periods as art, music, and social studies. In addition to the role as a teacher of learning disabled children, the resource teacher also works closely with each student's regular teacher to suggest and help plan the child's program in the regular classroom.

Ronni Hochman, an elementary learning disabilities resource room teacher, offers suggestions for placing a learning disabled child in the regular classroom:

> I think a key to a resource room is identifying where the child's successes are
> and initially putting him back into the regular classroom only in the areas in

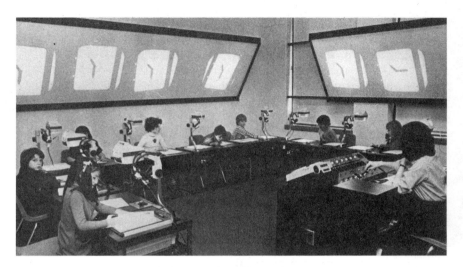

VISUAL RESPONSE SYSTEM - BUCKEYE YOUTH CENTER

The Visual Response System is a resource room specially designed for small group instruction. The teacher can easily see each student's response, enabling her to give direct and immediate feedback (Heward, 1978).

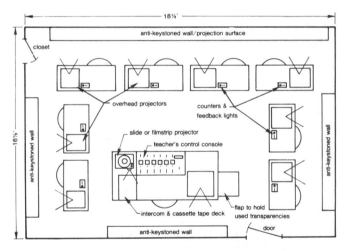

which he can experience a great amount of success. I use the child's time in the resource room to build those skills he needs to learn to be completely integrated into the regular classroom—whether it's learning to read better or simply learning to complete a task.

Some advantages of the resource room model are: (1) the children do not lose their identity with their peer group, so there is a smaller chance they will be stigmatized as "special"; (2) the children can receive the intense, individualized instruction they need every day, which might be impossible for the regular teacher (with 29 other students) to provide; and (3) flexible scheduling allows the resource room to serve a fairly large number of learning disabled students (Mayhall & Jenkins, 1977; Wiederholt, Hammill, & Brown, 1982). A survey of resource room teachers found their biggest concerns were over unclear role descriptions, variable expectations of administrators and regular classroom teachers, and insufficient time for planning, consulting, and observing students (McLoughlin & Kelly, 1982). While the resource room concept is increasingly popular, its success depends on the skills of the resource teacher and the administrative practices used by the school. In particular, procedures must be determined that will help the learning disabled child generalize the skills learned in the resource room.

The Self-Contained Classroom

In a self-contained classroom, the learning disabilities teacher is responsible for all the educational programming for a group of 6 to 12 learning disabled children. The academic achievement deficiencies of some learning disabled children are so severe that they need to be in a full-time learning setting with a specially trained teacher. In addition, their poor work habits and inappropriate social behaviors make some learning disabled children candidates for the self-contained classroom, where distractions can be minimized and individual attention stressed. However, it is important that placement in a self-contained class not be considered permanent. Children should be placed in a self-contained class only after attempts to serve them adequately with other less restrictive alternatives. As Wallace and McLoughlin suggest,

> It is preferable that the basis for placing a child in a special class be diagnostic and instructional experience in the resource room model. In this way, the special class system can be used only for the child who needs the most support. Hopefully, after a period in a highly structured environment and under a consistent intervention program, the child can develop communication and social skills to a satisfactory level and be moved back into a less isolated setting. (1979, pp. 369–70)

A follow-up study of 10 high school students 5 to 6 years after they had been enrolled for a year in a self-contained learning disabilities program showed them to be performing as well as comparison, nonhandicapped students (Leone, Lovitt, & Hansen, 1981). While the students' performances varied considerably, their oral reading ability, free-time and occupational interests, and general success in high school were within the normal range. The results of the follow-up study suggest that placement in a self-contained special class because of significant academic deficits in the elementary grades does not preclude success in high school.

Secondary Programs

During the first 10 years of the learning disabilities "movement," programs and services expanded greatly, but almost exclusively at the elementary level. In 1975, a survey across 37 states found that only 9% of the districts offered educational programming for secondary-level learning disabled students (Scranton & Downs, 1975). Many reasons have been cited for the lack of secondary programs, among them the fact that in many states students can drop out of school after completing the eighth grade or after reaching the age of 16. In

NOTHING SUCCEEDS LIKE SUCCESS

Ronni Hochman is a learning disabilities resource room teacher in a suburban elementary school. Ms. Hochman had taught in a self-contained classroom for EMR students before starting her school's LD resource room program 8 years ago. Ronni talked with us about her resource room program.

Prior to even meeting with the child, I like to meet informally with the regular classroom teacher to identify her expectations for all the children in her room. Once I can identify this, I know exactly what kinds of behaviors the child needs to learn before returning to the classroom. I never lose sight of the fact that my final objective is working my students back into the regular classroom for as long a period of time as they can handle. I think a key to a resource room is identifying where the child's successes are and initially putting him back into the regular classroom only in the areas in which he can experience a great amount of success. Then I use the child's time in the resource room to build those skills he needs to learn to be completely integrated into the regular classroom—whether it's learning to read better or simply learning to complete a task.

What happens in the resource room is based on each child's individual need. If a child has difficulty in quietly walking into the room, getting his assignment out, and going back to his desk, he is praised constantly for doing that kind of thing. Once that behavior is learned, the child is then rewarded for completing the task, and then finally he is rewarded for accuracy on the assignment. Eventually the child is being reinforced for doing the very same kinds of skills he needs to do in the regular classroom. But it is a gradual thing, beginning where the child's skills currently are. If rewards were only available for achieving 90% accuracy, the child who hasn't learned how to complete a task would be left out. And that's what has happened with some of these kids.

One of the tricks many learning disabled children have learned is that they can sit for days at a time and look extremely busy, but they're accomplishing virtually nothing. As a resource room teacher, I've got to help them get over that, help them learn to finish what they start. So you really need to be in 10 places at once, constantly moving around making sure everyone is on task, giving the praise here, the hug there. If you don't do that, the whole system falls apart.

Another thing that helps the children learn what is appropriate is not just hearing it from me, but also from the other kids. After spending time with me and hearing all the positive statements, the kids begin to do it too. Very often I'll hear one child saying to another, "That's great writing, Mel." I also set up situations where kids are allowed to exhibit this even more. Peer tutoring is a good way to get that negative child who is always pouting and has a hard time being nice to the other kids to praise and look for the positives in another child. Often I will set a negative child with a younger child who needs practice on math facts and will show him exactly how I want it done. The tutor displays the cards to his student, and after each correct answer says "Very good," "Super!" and so on. I tell them to try to change the praise each time, and they've come up with some phenomenal ones. "Nanu Nanu" was popular this year. So they praise each other and nothing succeeds like success. If these kids can see it in each other, they can begin to see it in themselves. And that's half the battle.

addition, some feel that elementary learning disabilities programs are successful in remediating the achievement deficits of some students so that they can succeed in high school without special help. In spite of these factors, each year thousands of young men and women leave our nation's high schools with few, if any, marketable skills. Some learning disabled teenagers, who might have been able to attend college had they been given the help they needed in high school, are unable to find jobs of any consequence. Marsh, Gearheart, and Gearheart (1978) feel that the increasing awareness of the need for good secondary programs will result in much more activity in secondary schools by learning disabilities professionals in the next decade.

Fortunately, this "activity" is already beginning. In 1978, McNutt and Heller surveyed 301 school districts and found that only 22.5% did *not* provide any programming for learning disabled adolescents. This is a significant improvement over the survey just 3 years earlier.

Deschler, Lowrey, and Alley (1979) conducted a nationwide survey of junior and senior high school learning disabilities teachers and found five different models or program options were predominant. Alley and Deschler (1979) have described the five models as:

1. Basic skills remediation model. Provides developmental or remedial instruction for basic academic skill deficits. Reading and mathematics deficits receive the most attention.
2. Functional curriculum model. Emphasizes equipping students to function in society. The focus of instruction is on consumer information, completion of

The need for special education programs for learning disabled high school students is gradually being recognized

application forms, banking and money skills, and life-care skills such as grooming. In addition, this approach often attempts to relate academic content to career concepts.

3. Tutorial model. Emphasizes instruction in academic content areas. Areas of instruction are usually those in which the student is experiencing difficulty or failure. The teacher's major responsibility is to help keep the LD student in the regular curriculum.

4. Work-study model. Emphasizes instruction in job- and career-related skills and on-the-job experience. Students typically spend half the day on the job and the remainder of the day in school studying compatible material.

5. Learning strategies model. Instruction is designed to teach students how to learn rather than to teach specific content. For example, the teacher would present techniques for organizing material that has to be memorized for a history test, rather than teaching the actual history content.

In their study, Deschler and colleagues (1979) found that 51% of the existing secondary learning disabilities programs followed the basic skills remediation model. The other models, in order of their presentation above, were used by 17%, 24%, 5%, and 3% of the programs. Since programming for secondary learning disabled students is such a new phenomenon, it remains to be seen which of the above models, or combination of approaches, will prove the most useful. Each of the five models has specific advantages and disadvantages (Alley & Deschler, 1979), and no one approach is probably best for all learning disabled students.

CURRENT ISSUES/FUTURE TRENDS

Learning disabilities is such a dynamic and relatively young field that an entire book could be devoted to a discussion of "current issues." Some of these issues are the question of terminology (is a "reading disability" the same as a "learning disability"?), where learning disabled children should be taught (least restrictive environment), what kind of training learning disabilities teachers should receive, how federal and state funds should be appropriated, and the proliferation of controversial "cures" for learning disabilities (megavitamins and diets free of food additives). We have chosen to discuss only a few of these—the continuing debate over the definition of learning disabilities and the question of who should teach the learning disabled child.

Who Are the Learning Disabled?

The widely differing findings of prevalence studies (from 5 to 30% of the school-age population) indicate that there is no one standard, operational definition of learning disabilities. Some prominent special educators feel that the trend toward expanding the learning disabilities classification to include more and more children indicates a misunderstanding of the concept and only detracts from and weakens services to children who have severe learning problems (Larsen, 1978; Myers & Hammill, 1982; Wallace & McLoughlin, 1979).

Hamill, in an address to the Council for Learning Disabilities, said,

> I know some people in our field who say the incidence of learning disabilities is 35 to 40%, depending on whether you want to throw in delinquents. I know people that see dyslexics under every bed; dysgraphics at every desk. Some people see all children who don't read too well as being learning disabled. And I know a few people who bounce back and forth on the incidence-definition question depending on how much federal and state funding is available. Eventually, we will have to decide just who and what LD is. (1980, p. 4)

Clearly, there is no consensus regarding who is learning disabled. Two recent studies have shown that educators will identify certain children as learning disabled even when all of their evaluative data are in the normal range, and that the single most reliable variable predicting whether or not a child will be identified is the *amount* of information presented on the child—(the more information the more likely the student will be identified—rather than the type of information or how it relates to usual identification criteria (Algozzine & Ysseldyke, 1981; Ysseldyke, Algozzine, Richey, & Graden, 1982).

While all agree that children who have any learning difficulty, major or minor, should receive help, services for the learning disabled should be reserved for those children with *severe* and *specific* learning difficulties (Wallace & McLoughlin, 1979). Kirk (1978a) suggests one solution to this problem. He says that all regular classroom teachers should have access to consultants for assistance with the 10% of all children in any classroom that need some degree of additional help. These professionals might serve between 20 and 40 children at a given time. A second group of special educators would consist of highly trained learning disabilities specialists who would work only with those children who require more intensive, direct help. These teachers might serve only 5 or 6 students per day.

The discussion of what constitutes a "true" learning disability is likely to go on for some time. We believe that what a child's learning problem is called is not so important, but that schools provide a special education system that is responsive to the individual needs of all children who have difficulty in learning.

Who Should Teach the Learning Disabled?

While all areas of special education are interdisciplinary to some degree, only in the field of learning disabilities has there been heated controversy over who should be primarily responsible for teaching the children. Learning disabilities teachers have been vigorously challenged by reading specialists (through their organization, the International Reading Association) and speech-language pathologists (through their organization, the American Speech-Language-Hearing Association) for the right to serve learning disabled children. In their view, learning disabilities specialists can only optimally serve a small proportion of children with learning problems; reading (or speech and language) is the problem most of these children have; and reading teachers (or speech teachers) are the ones best qualified to serve them. The controversy is a genuine one. For many years before there was a group of children known as *learning disabled,* reading and speech teachers worked with children with problems in those areas. Since underachievement in reading and language problems are primary characteristics of learning disabled children, it is only natural for those professionals to feel they should continue to provide remedial services. In 1976, the *Journal of Learning Disabilities* devoted an entire issue to the question of the respective roles of reading specialists, speech-language pathologists, and learning disabilities teachers in the education and management of learning disabled children. In that issue, Larsen (1976) contended that learning disabilities specialists should have primary responsibility for the management of learning disabled children, but that reading and speech-language specialists should be active in educational programs as dictated by the children's individual needs. But, again, we feel that *who* teaches the child is not as important as whether or not the skills of that teacher (whether he be a learning disabilities specialist, a reading teacher, a speech pathologist, or the basketball coach) match the learning needs of the child.

JUST LIKE WE LEARNED IN CLASS

In most states a temporary learner's permit is a prerequisite to a driver's license. Obtaining the permit involves passing a test on road signs and traffic laws. Driver education courses usually focus on teaching how to operate the car. Students are expected to read the state motor vehicle digest and pass the test for the learner's permit. This poses a serious handicap to learning disabled students with poor reading skills.

Cheryl Hoagland, a high school learning disabilities teacher in Hilliard, Ohio, decided to teach the six students in her eighth period class the road signs and traffic laws included in the Ohio Department of Motor Vehicles (ODMV) Digest. Several of her students were hoping to get temporary permits in the coming months. "The reading ability of most of my ninth grade students is closer to that of a fifth grader. We always talk about teaching relevant skills. Here was one, and an important rite of passage as well that LD students should have an opportunity to achieve. But the wording, the vocabulary, and the sentence structure of the Digest make it automatically intimidating for my students."

Cheryl began with a road signs and traffic laws instructional program that had already been established as effective (Test & He-

Students identify the correct road sign by holding up response cards.

ward, 1983). The program had been developed for use in a special classroom called the Visual Response System (see photo and illustration on p. 138), where students respond on overhead projectors built into their desks (Heward, 1978). Cheryl modified the instructional program for use in a conventional classroom setting.

Cheryl needed to create a means for every student to respond to every question in a manner that would enable her to provide immediate feedback. "In the Visual Response System, students respond by placing transparency response slides or writing directly on the stage of their overhead projectors. Every student responds and the teacher can easily see each student's answer. But there is only one overhead projector in my classroom, the teacher's. I made each student a set of response cards, small squares of cardboard with traffic signs on them, "true" or "false," "yes" or "no," and so forth. I projected the instructional transparencies from the original program and had each student hold up a response card to every question. They also traced the movement of their cars through traffic situations and held them up for me to see. By wiping off their marks, we could use the same street scene over and over." Cheryl gave each student a small hand-held counter to keep track of their correct answers. After each class session, they recorded their numbers in a folder.

Throughout the 4-week unit, an average of .8 responses per minute per student were made during each 40-minute period. That translates into a total of 192 individual learning trials each period. The students answered correctly an average of 92% of all questions during those instructional sessions.

To evaluate her program, Cheryl gave a series of tests designed to simulate the actual ODMV test as closely as possible. Criterion for passing the ODMV test is 15 correct on each of the two 20-question parts. On the simulation tests Cheryl's students averaged 90% correct. "I knew they would do well. They really loved the program. They would finish their math early during seventh period and set up the classroom for the driver ed unit so we could start right on time. I know they were motivated by the content of the unit in the beginning, but it was the active pace and immediate feedback that kept them going for a month. It wouldn't be hard to teach this material in a boring, ineffective way."

Shortly after the unit was completed, one of the students turned 15 and took the ODMV test. She scored a passing 85% on each part. Returning to school the next day, she said, "It was a cinch, Ms. Hoagland. Everything was just like we learned in class."

1. Learning disabilities is a relatively new, rapidly growing field in special education.
   a. The term *learning disabilities* was first used in 1963 by Dr. Samuel Kirk to describe children who have serious learning problems in school but no other obvious "handicap."
   b. During the late 1960s, two growing organizations—ACLD and DCLD—helped bring about federal legislation providing funds for learning disabilities programs.
   c. Today, learning disabilities is widely and legally recognized as a separate handicapping condition.

2. There is no one, universally agreed-upon definition of *learning disabilities*. However, most definitions incorporate three criteria that must be met for a child to be labeled *learning disabled*.
   a. Learning disabled children must have a severe discrepancy between potential or ability and actual achievement.
   b. Learning disabled children must have learning problems that cannot be attributed to other handicapping conditions, such as blindness or mental retardation.
   c. Learning disabled children must need special educational services to succeed, services that are not needed by their nonhandicapped peers.
   d. No matter what definition is used, educators should focus on each child's specific skill deficiencies for assessment and instruction.

3. Characteristics of learning disabled children vary widely.
   a. Learning disabilities are not physically apparent. These children look like all other children.
   b. The single, common characteristic is a specific and significant achievement deficiency in the presence of adequate overall intelligence.

4. Because definitions of learning disabilities and assessment and diagnosis procedures vary so widely, there are no reliable prevalence figures. Estimates range from 1 to 30% of the school-age population. In 1981–82, the Department of Education identified 3.33% of the children from age 5 to 17 as learning disabled.

5. Although the actual cause of a specific learning disability can almost never be known, the suspected causes can be grouped into three categories.
   a. Learning disabilities may be caused by brain damage. However, research has not shown a direct cause-effect relationship between the two.
   b. Other researchers feel that various types of biochemical imbalances cause learning disabilities. While research has failed to prove this contention, it is still a matter of considerable debate.

(handwritten margin notes:)
- discrepancy
- exclusion
- spec. educ. need

c. Many professionals believe that environment—including quality of instruction—is a major cause of learning problems. They stress direct instruction in problem skill areas as the best approach to remediation.

6. Most learning disabilities professionals take a diagnostic-prescriptive approach to assessment. That is, results of assessment on any of a variety of types of tests lead directly to a plan for classroom instruction.
   a. Norm-referenced tests compare a child's score with the scores of other age-mates who have taken the same test.
   b. Process tests are designed to measure a child's ability in different perceptual or psycholinguistic areas. The two most widely used process tests are:
      (1) The Illinois Test of Psycholinguistic Abilities;   ITPA
      (2) The Marianne Frostig Developmental Test of Visual Perception.
   c. Teachers use informal reading inventories to observe directly and record the child's reading skills.
   d. Criterion-referenced tests compare a child's score to a predetermined mastery level.
   e. Direct, daily measurement involves regularly assessing the child on the specific skill being taught. One useful system is precision teaching.

7. There are two basic approaches to educating learning disabled children.
   a. Ability training involves prescribing instructional activities designed to remediate a child's weakness in underlying basic "abilities."
   b. Psycholinguistic training, the visual-perceptual approach, the perceptual-motor approach, and the multisensory approach are all types of ability training.
   c. There is not much research to support the effectiveness of ability training. However, this approach is still widely advocated and used in the field.
   d. Skill training, the second approach, is based on the belief that the performance deficit is the problem, not a sign of an underlying disability.
   e. In skill training, remediation is based on direct instruction of precisely defined skills, many opportunities to practice, and direct measurement of the child's progress.
   f. Research has shown the skill training approach—including DISTAR, applied behavior analysis, and precision teaching—to be effective.

8. There are several different arrangements used in educating learning disabled children.
   a. Some learning disabled children are educated in the regular classroom.
   b. In some schools, a consultant teacher helps regular classroom teachers deal with learning disabled children.
   c. In other districts, an itinerant teacher serves as consultant to teachers in several schools and also acts as a tutor for some children.

d. In the resource room, which is the most popular service delivery model for educating learning disabled children, a specially trained teacher works with the children for one or more periods a day on particular skill deficits. The children remain in the regular classroom for the rest of the day.

e. A few learning disabled children attend separate self-contained classes. However, this placement should be used only after attempts to serve the child in a less restrictive setting have failed, and it should not be considered permanent.

9. Learning disabilities programs in the secondary schools are rapidly expanding. We do not yet know which of several current models will prove most useful.

10. While it may be difficult, if not impossible, to determine what is a "true" learning disability, the important point is that schools must respond to the needs of any child who has learning problems.

11. Learning disabilities specialists, reading teachers, speech-language pathologists, and other teachers may all be appropriate teachers for certain children.

FOR MORE INFORMATION

Journals

Journal of Learning Disabilities. Published ten times a year by Professional Press. Publishes research and theoretical articles relating to learning disabilities.

Learning Disability Quarterly. Published four times a year by the Council for Learning Disabilities. Emphasizes practical implications of research and applied research dealing with learning disability populations and settings.

Books

Alley, G. & Deschler, D. *Teaching the learning disabled adolescent: Strategies and methods.* Denver: Love Publishing, 1979.

Kauffman, J. M., & Hallahan, D. P. (eds.). *Teaching children with learning disabilities: Personal perspectives.* Columbus, Ohio: Charles E. Merrill, 1976.

Marsh, G. E., Gearheart, C. K., & Gearheart, B. R. *The learning disabled adolescent: Program alternatives in the secondary school.* St. Louis: C. V. Mosby, 1978.

Mercer, C. D. *Students with learning disabilities,* 2d ed. Columbus, Ohio: Charles E. Merrill, 1983.

Myers, P. I., & Hammill, D. D. *Learning disabilities: Basic concepts, assessment practices, and instructional strategies.* Austin, Tex.: Pro-Ed, 1982.

Smith, D. D. *Teaching the learning disabled.* Englewood Cliffs, N.J.: Prentice-Hall, 1981.

Stephens, T. M. *Teaching skills to children with learning and behavior disorders.* Columbus, Ohio: Charles E. Merrill, 1977.

Wallace, G., & Kauffman, J. M. *Teaching children with learning problems,* 2d ed. Columbus, Ohio: Charles E. Merrill, 1978.

Wallace, G., & McLoughlin, J. A. *Learning disabilities: Concepts and characteristics,* 2d ed. Columbus, Ohio: Charles E. Merrill, 1979.

Organizations

Association for Children and Adults with Learning Disabilities. 5255 Grace Street, Pittsburgh, PA 15236. An active organization of parents and educators which serves as an advocate for learning disabled children.

Council for Learning Disabilities. Department of Special Education, University of Louisville, Louisville, Ky 40292. An organization for professionals who work with learning disabled individuals. Publishes *Learning Disabilities Quarterly,* holds an annual conference to disseminate research and information, and promotes standards for learning disabilities professionals.

Division for Children with Learning Disabilities. 850 Hungerford Drive, Rockville, MD 20850. Includes teachers, teacher educators, and other members of CEC working with learning disabled students.

Learning Disability Research Institutes

Addresses for the five federally-funded learning disabilities research institutes and their primary area(s) of research interest follow:

- Research Institute for the Study of Learning Disabilities (language comprehension)
  Box 118
  Teachers College, Columbia University
  New York, NY 10027

- Chicago Institute for Learning Disabilities (social adjustment, language)
  University of Illinois at Chicago Circle
  Box 4348
  Chicago, IL 60680

- Research Institute in Learning Disabilities (LD adolescents)
  University of Kansas
  Room 313 Carruth-O'Leary
  Lawrence, KS 66045

- Institute for Research on Learning Disabilities (identification, assessment, and placement)
  350 Elliot Hall
  75 East River Road
  University of Minnesota
  Minneapolis, MN 55455

- Learning Disabilities Research Institute (attentional deficits, self-activated learning strategies)
  The University of Virginia, Department of Special Education
  152 Ruffner Hall
  Charlottesville, VA 22903

5

Behavior Disorders

C hildhood is supposed to be a happy time—a time for playing, growing, learning, and making friends—and for most children it is. But for some children, life seems to be a constant turmoil. They are in conflict, often serious, with others and themselves. Or they are so shy and withdrawn that they seem to be in their own worlds. In either case, playing with others, making friends, and learning all the things a child must learn are extremely difficult for these children. They are children with behavior disorders. They are referred to by a variety of terms—*emotionally disturbed, socially maladjusted, psychologically disordered, emotionally handicapped,* or even *psychotic* or *autistic,* if their behavior is extremely abnormal or bizarre.

Behavior disordered children are seldom really liked by anyone—their peers, teachers, brothers or sisters, parents. Even sadder, they often don't even like themselves. They are difficult to be around, and attempts to befriend them may lead only to rejection, verbal abuse, or even physical attack. With some emotionally withdrawn children, any overtures seem to fall on deaf ears; and yet these children are not deaf.

While behavior disordered children are not physically handicapped, their noxious or withdrawn behavior can be as serious a handicap to their development and learning as the mentally retarded child's slowness to learn. Behavior disordered children make up a significant portion of those needing special education services.

Many nonhandicapped children act in the same ways as children with behavior disorders—but not as often or not as extreme. And, of course, behavior disordered children can be likable.

DEFINING BEHAVIOR DISORDERS

In spite of controversy and disagreement, the fields of mental retardation and learning disabilities each use standard definitions that serve as a basis for communication and research. This is not so in the area of behavior disorders. Cur-

151

rently there is no definition of *behavior disorders* that is generally agreed upon. There are several reasons for the lack of a clear definition. First, there are measurement problems. Second, there is no clear agreement about what constitutes good mental health. Third, different theories of emotional disturbance each use their own terminology and definitions. Cultural influence is another problem. The expectations and norms for appropriate behavior are often quite different across ethnic and cultural groups. Next, frequency is a concern. All children behave inappropriately at certain times. Finally, disordered behavior sometimes occurs in conjunction with other handicapping conditions (most notably mental retardation and learning disabilities), making it difficult to tell if one condition is the result or the cause of the other.

In spite of, or perhaps because of, these problems, many efforts to define emotional disturbance in children have been made. According to Hewett and Taylor (1980), a definition of emotional disturbance should ideally (1) help us accurately identify the type of child we are concerned with so the problem can be diagnosed, (2) permit communication with individuals and agencies who determine educational, administrative, and funding policies for behavior disordered children, and (3) help in research by enabling precise specification of the characteristics of disturbed children serving as subjects so that studies can be replicated and findings generalized. Let's review some of the definitions of behavior disorders that have been proposed.

One definition, written by Ross, states:

> A psychological disorder is said to be present when a child emits behavior that deviates from a discretionary and relative social norm in that it occurs with a frequency or intensity that authoritative adults in the child's environment judge, under the circumstances, to be either too high or too low. (1974, p. 14)

This definition stresses the judgment of adults in deciding whether or not the way a child acts deviates too much from the usual.

Bower (1969) wrote a definition of emotional disturbance more closely related to the school environment. With very minor changes, Bower's definition has been adopted by the U.S. Department of Education as the definition of "seriously emotionally disturbed" children, one of the seven categories of handicapping conditions covered by P.L. 94–142.

> Seriously emotionally disturbed is defined as follows:
> (i) The term means a condition exhibiting one or more of the following characteristics over a long period of time and to a marked degree, which adversely affects educational performance.
>   (a) An inability to learn which cannot be explained by intellectual, sensory, and health factors;
>   (b) An inability to build or maintain satisfactory interpersonal relationships with peers and teachers;
>   (c) Inappropriate types of behavior or feelings under normal circumstances;
>   (d) A general pervasive mood of unhappiness or depression; or

(e) A tendency to develop physical symptoms or fears associated with personal or school problems.

(ii) The term includes children who are schizophrenic or autistic. The term does not include children who are socially maladjusted unless it is determined that they are seriously emotionally disturbed. (*Federal Register*, vol. 42, no. 163, August 23, 1977, p. 42478).

See pages 172–181 for more on autism.

Since that time, the federal definition has been amended to move autism from this category to "other health impaired." Regardless of whether autism is included as a behavior disorder, the federal definition is vague and leaves much to the subjective opinion of the authorities (usually teachers) around the child. The inability of this definition to identify a specific group of children precisely is perhaps best illustrated by the widely different prevalence estimates found in the literature. Kauffman defined children with behavior disorders as:

> those who chronically and markedly respond to their environment in socially unacceptable and/or personally unsatisfying ways but who can be taught more socially acceptable and personally gratifying behavior. (1977, p. 23)

This definition adds two concepts: The child's own expectations for his behavior can be taken into account; and importantly, disordered behavior is learned, and the child can learn new, more appropriate ways to act.

While each definition is somewhat different, all agree that a child's behavior must differ markedly (extremely) and chronically (over time) from current social or cultural norms for the child to be considered behavior disordered.

The Role of Teacher Tolerance in Defining Children's Behavior Disorders

While none of the definitions of emotional disturbance proposed so far have provided a consistent, universally agreed-upon standard for identification, diagnosis, communication, and research, they all place the concept of behavior disorders in a "conceptual ballpark" (Hewett & Taylor, 1980). And the key player in that ballpark seems to be teacher tolerance. A number of studies have shown that whether or not a student will be identified as emotionally disturbed is largely a function of the teacher's notion of the expected or acceptable behavior of children. In a **longitudinal study,** Rubin and Balow (1978) found that 59% of all children who had received three or more annual ratings had been identified as behavior disordered by at least one teacher at some time from kindergarten through sixth grade. Of course, this study suggests another important conclusion as well—that a great many children do experience some type of behavioral problem during their early school years. Although they do go away, these problems are identified by teachers at the time as an indication of "emotional disturbance."

A longitudinal study is one that studies the same subjects over an extended time.

Nevertheless, the role of teacher tolerance in identifying children as emotionally disturbed is significant. Algozzine (1980) found that, as a group, regular

In this special behavior disorders program, students play an active role in determining and enforcing classroom rules.

classroom teachers rated certain behaviors as more disturbing than did a comparison group of special education teachers. In a subsequent study, Curran and Algozzine (1980) found teachers with varying levels of tolerance for "immature or defiant" behaviors differentially rated a hypothetical child's likelihood of success in the regular classroom. These studies suggest that "emotional disturbance is a function of the perceiver. . . .What is disturbance to one teacher may not be to another" (Whelan, 1981, p. 4–5).

Defining Disordered Behavior

Perhaps the most functional way to look at behavior disorders is to describe how children who are called *emotionally disturbed* actually act. What aspects of their behavior are different from their normal peers? We can analyze or measure several dimensions of children's behavior—its **rate, duration, topography,** and **magnitude.**

Rate refers to how often a particular behavior is performed. Almost all children cry, get into fights with other children, and sulk from time to time; yet we are not apt to label them *emotionally disturbed*. The primary difference between behavior disordered children and normal children is the rate at which these kinds of undesirable activities occur. While the disturbed child often doesn't do anything that a normal child doesn't, he does certain undesirable things much more often.

Closely related to rate is duration. Duration is a measure of how long a child engages in a given activity. Again, while normal and behavior disordered children might do the same things, the amount of time the behavior disordered child spends in certain activities is often markedly different from that of the normal child—either longer or shorter. For example, many young children have temper tantrums, but they generally last no more than 5 or 10 minutes. A behavior disordered child might have a tantrum for an hour or more. Sometimes the problem is one of too short a duration, perhaps with paying attention or working independently. Some behavior disordered children cannot stick to one task for more than several *seconds* at a time.

Topography refers to the physical shape or form of an action. For instance, throwing a baseball and rolling a bowling ball involve different topographies. While both involve the arm, each activity requires a different movement. Some behavior disordered children make movements seldom seen in normal children. These responses are often pointless or harmful to the child.

Finally, behavior is sometimes characterized by its magnitude or force. It may be either too soft (for example, talking at a volume so low you can't be heard) or too hard (such as slamming the door).

Disturbed children also have difficulty discriminating when and where certain behaviors are appropriate. Learning that kind of control is a major task of growing up, which most children master naturally through socialization. They pick it up from their friends, siblings, parents, and other adults. However, some behavior disordered children often appear unaware of their surroundings. They do not learn the proper time and place for many actions without being carefully instructed.

There are two other important aspects of children's behavior disorders. First, these children usually exhibit a variety of problems across several different areas of functioning. Hewett and Taylor (1980) refer to this as "clustering," the exhibition of two or more types of problem behaviors that increases the chance that the child's behavior will exceed the teacher's range of tolerance. They illustrated "clustering" by the case of Bobby, a child who, in one "infamous morning," destroyed school property, stole a classmate's lunch money and punched her in the stomach, defied the teacher, and used obscene language. Second, behavior disordered children have long-standing problems that require extensive treatment rather than brief intervention.

The advantage of defining behavior disorders in terms of these behavioral dimensions is that identification, assessment, treatment strategies, and evaluation of the effects of the treatment can all revolve around the objective measurement of those dimensions. This approach leads to a direct focus on the child's problem—on the inappropriate behavior—and ways of dealing with it, as opposed to concentrating on some problem ("disturbance" or "mental illness") within the child. If the child can learn new, socially acceptable ways to behave, he or she need no longer be called behavior disordered.

CLASSIFICATION OF CHILDREN'S BEHAVIOR DISORDERS

As we mentioned in chapter 1, classifying observed phenomena within a given field into different categories is an important scientific task. In the area of behavior disorders, a reliable and valid classification system would foster accurate communication among researchers, diagnosticians, and teachers. Better communication could result, most importantly, in a child receiving the educational placement and treatment that have been proven most effective for his or her specific behavior problem. Unfortunately, as yet we are far from having such a workable classification system, which is understandable in light of the problems of developing a widely accepted definition of behavior disorders.

One system of classifying behavior disorders is the Diagnostic and Statistical Manual for Mental Disorders (DSM-III), developed by the American Psychiatric Association (1980). The DSM-III is an elaborate and vast classification system consisting of 230 separate diagnostic categories, or labels, used to identify the various "types" of disordered behavior noted in clinical practice. Because of its more precise language, its use of more examples, and the greater amount of information it requires about the person being diagnosed, the DSM-III represents an improvement in clinical classification over earlier versions (the DSM-I, 1952, and the DSM-II, 1968). While the DSM-III classification system is used quite regularly in the mental health professions, it is not very useful for educational purposes. One problem with the DSM-III is its lack of reliability. That is, even with the latest version's more precise language, it is not uncommon for one psychiatrist or psychologist to classify a child in one category, and a second examiner to place the same child in a completely different category.

But an even greater problem is that putting a child in a given category provides no guidelines for treatment. Knowing that a child has been diagnosed as fitting a certain category in the DSM-III provides a teacher with virtually no useful information on what intervention or therapy is needed.

Another well-known classification system was developed by Quay and his co-workers (Quay, 1972, 1975). Quay collected a wide range of data on hundreds of behavior disordered children, including behavior ratings by parents and teachers, life histories, and responses on questionnaires by the children themselves. By statistically analyzing all of this information, they found that children's behavior disorders tend to appear in groups, or clusters. Children who showed some of the behaviors in a given cluster had a high likelihood of also showing the other traits and behaviors in that cluster. Quay calls the four types **conduct disorder, personality disorder, immaturity,** and **socialized delinquency.**

Children described as having a conduct disorder are likely to be disobedient, disruptive, get into fights, be bossy, and have temper tantrums. A personality disorder in children is identified by social withdrawal, anxiety, depression, feelings of inferiority, guilt, shyness, and unhappiness. Immaturity is characterized by a short attention span, extreme passivity, daydreaming, preferring playmates younger than oneself, and clumsiness. The fourth dimension, socialized delinquency, is marked by truancy, gang membership, theft, and a feeling of pride in belonging to a delinquent subculture. While Quay's system has proven quite reliable—the same four clusters of behavior and personality traits have been found in many samples of behavior disordered children (Quay, 1975)—it does not provide treatment information. Therefore, its usefulness is limited primarily to *describing* the major types of children's behavior disorders.

Hewett and his colleagues have developed a classification scheme based on "levels of learning competence" (Hewett, 1964, 1968; Hewett & Forness, 1977; Hewett & Taylor, 1980). Hewett and Taylor (1980) describe an actual episode that led them to seek better ways of classifying behavior disorders. Donald, an 11-year-old boy, was completely immobilized—he would not walk, talk, eat, or care for himself. He was fed with a stomach tube at first, but later began to swallow juice, his only observable response. At this point Donald's psychiatrist felt that going to school might help him. He introduced him to the teacher by saying:

> "This is Donald. He is in a catatonic schizophrenic stupor with severe psychomotor retardation. Good luck."
>
> Such a description was a bit unsettling for the teacher and is an excellent example of the alien and essentially useless contribution such labels and diagnostic terms have to make in educational settings. As long as the teacher was intimidated by this pathetic little boy in a "catatonic schizophrenic stupor," it was doubtful that any worthwhile program could be provided by the school. But once she set aside the psychiatric jargon and took a long, hard look at Donald, things got better. Here was this immobilized student. We had heard what his psychiatric problem was. Now, what was his educational problem? Simple. Donald *was a severe response problem* in educational and learning terms. He did not move. To learn you must respond. Donald was a candidate for a response curriculum. He was no longer a mysterious alien with catatonic schizophrenia. He was now a learner, and it would be the role of the school to teach him to respond as the initial educational task. (1980, p. 96)

Hewett's classification system includes six levels of learning competence. The *attention* level has to do with children making contact with their environment, the *response* level with active motor and verbal participation, the *order* level is concerned with teaching children to follow instructions and routines, the *exploratory* level has children accurately and thoroughly investigate their environment, the *social* level focuses on interactions with others, and the *mastery* level involves skills related to self-care, academics, and vocational interests. Table 5.1 shows how the classification scheme views behavior problems along a continuum of "too little" through "too much" in respect to the six levels of learning competence.

Hewett and Taylor contend that this classification system is both descriptive and functional; that classifying a child's behavior problem within the system "provides a direct link to the setting of curriculum goals" (1980, p. 99). In the case of Donald, for instance, his nearly total lack of response was the first order of business for the teacher. Hewett's classification system is a considerable advance over systems that provide descriptive labels that only serve to label the child without relating to useful educational strategies.

It is much easier, and procedurally more feasible, to classify *behaviors* objectively than to classify children. In addition, there is an ever-growing body of research literature indicating that certain strategies are often successful in changing certain types of behaviors. Thus, objectively pinpointing the specific

See journals such as *Behavior Therapy* and *Journal of Applied Behavior Analysis.*

TABLE 5.1
Classification of disturbed children by negative variants of six levels of learning competence.

Too Little		Optimal		Too Much
Disturbances in sensory perception	Excessive daydreaming Poor memory Short attention span In a world all his or her own	Attention	Selective attention	Fixation on particu stimuli
Immobilization	Sluggishness Passivity Drowsiness Clumsiness Depression	Response	Hyperactivity Restlessness	Self-stimulation
Failure to develop speech	Failure to use language for communication	Response	Extremely talkative	Uses profanity Verbally abusive
Self-injurious Lawlessness Destructiveness	Disruptiveness Attention seeking Irresponsibility Disobedience	Order	Overly conforming	Resistance to chan Compulsive
Bizarre or stereotyped behavior Bizarre interests	Anxiety Preoccupation Doesn't know how to have fun Behaves like an adult Shyness	Exploratory	Plunges into activities	Tries to do everytl at once
Preoccupation with inan-imate objects Extreme self-isolation Inability to relate to peo-ple	Social withdrawal Alienates others Aloofness Prefers younger playmates Acts bossy Secretiveness Fighting Temper tantrums	Social	Hypersensitivity Jealousy Overly dependent	Inability to functio alone
Blunted, uneven or fragmented intellectual development	Lacks self-care skills Lacks basic school skills Laziness in school Dislike for school Lacks vocational skills	Mastery	Preoccupation with academics	Overintellectualizin

SOURCE: From F. M. Hewett and F. D. Taylor, *The emotionally disturbed child in the classroom: The orches-tration of success,* 2d ed. Copyright © 1980 by Allyn and Bacon, Inc. Reprinted with permission.

inappropriate things a disturbed child does can lead to treatment strategies. Finally, labeling behaviors rather than children is optimistic; it implies that the child will be "normal" once he learns more socially adaptive actions to replace his disordered behavior. This attitude might help to alleviate some of the permanent stigma that often comes from labeling children.

Another method of classifying behavior disordered children is by degree of severity. While emotionally disturbed children have sometimes been referred to as displaying mild, moderate, and severe behavior problems, at least one study suggests that this three-level distinction is not supported in practice. Olson, Algozzine, and Schmid (1980) found that teachers of emotionally handicapped children regularly identified only two levels, or degrees, of behavioral disturbance: mild and severe. Mildly emotionally disturbed children were seen as those children who can respond to interventions provided in regular classrooms by regular class teachers, with the support of guidance counselors or consulting teachers. Severely disturbed children were viewed as those needing intense treatment programs and residential placement.

Most behavior disordered children have mild or moderate problems that are often fairly short lived and can be treated effectively in the regular classroom and at home by knowledgeable teachers and parents. Children who are severely disturbed—often called **psychotic, schizophrenic,** or **autistic**—require intensive, specially designed programming, usually in a highly supervised environment such as a special class or residential treatment center. However, classification by degree of severity is primarily after the fact. Important decisions as to the type of programming a child needs and the environment it should be delivered in should be made on an objective assessment of the individual needs of the child, rather than on someone's opinion that the child is either "moderately" or "severely" disturbed.

PREVALENCE

As we have seen, there is no one operational definition of *behavior disorders* that can be applied uniformly in all instances. As a result, estimates of how many children have behavior disorders vary tremendously. Morse (1975) reviewed a number of surveys and found that anywhere from .1 to 30% of the school-age population were considered behavior disordered. With such widely varying estimates, it is obvious that people are using different criteria for deciding whether or not a child is behavior disordered. Kelly, Bullock, and Dykes (1977) report that teachers identified about 20% of their students as suffering from some kind of emotional disturbance. Based on his survey of California schools, Bower (1969) concluded that two or three children in the average classroom (about 10%) can be expected to show signs of emotional disturbance. The U.S. Department of Education uses the figure of 2% in its estimates for funding and personnel needs for behavior disordered children. The federal government reported that 303,268 children, or 7.6% of the total number of handicapped children age 3–21, received special education services for the emotionally disturbed during the 1981–82 school year.

Wood and Zabel (1978) suggest that the difference in prevalence figures stems as much from the manner in which they are collected as it does from the use of different definitions. Most surveys ask teachers to identify students in their class who are behavior problems at that point in time. Many children display inappropriate behavior for short periods of time, and such "one-shot" screening procedures will identify them, as in the Rubin and Balow (1978) study in which more than half of all students were identified as behavior problems by at least one teacher some time during their elementary school careers. As Hewitt and Taylor observe,

> In our experience, when you walk into any elementary classroom, you can usually pick out two or three children who are "not with it" and who are visible enough to stand out from other members of the class in terms of their problem behavior. And if you stay long enough, you can usually determine if they "fit" within the teacher's range of tolerance for behavioral differences. Whether they would be the same children a week or semester later is debatable. Thus, we get almost no meaning from incidence figures. The U.S. Office of Education's 2 percent is undoubtedly very conservative and may be most accurate in relation to the moderately and severely emotionally disturbed. In general, the more severe the problem behavior the child exhibits, the more likely we are to obtain accurate, stable, and reliable estimates. (1980, p. 42)

Sex

Boys are much more likely to be identified as behavior disordered than girls (Morse, Cutler, & Fink, 1964). Boys labeled disturbed are likely to be aggressive and act out, while behavior disordered girls are typically shy, anxious, and withdrawn. Among the severely disturbed (that is, autistic and schizophrenic), boys outnumber girls anywhere from 2 to 1 to 5 to 1 (Hingtgen & Bryson, 1972; Morse, 1975).

Age

There is relatively little emotional disturbance reported in the early grades, with a sharp increase and peak during the middle grades, and a decline in prevalence beginning in junior high school and continuing through high school (Morse et al., 1964). However, arrest rates for juvenile delinquency, one type of behavior disorder, increase sharply during the junior high years. This probably reflects both the greater harm to society adolescents can cause as a result of their inappropriate behavior and the fact that younger children are often not arrested (and therefore do not show up on the records) for committing the same acts that would lead to arrest for an older child. However, younger children are now committing more serious and violent crimes than in years past (Cavan & Ferdinand, 1975).

Juvenile Delinquency

Each year approximately 3% of all children in this country are referred to juvenile courts (Achenbach, 1974; Cavan & Ferdinand, 1975). In 1979, over 500,000 youth were admitted to juvenile detention and correctional facilities (Heim et al., 1980). While the word *delinquent* is a legal term, the offenses an adolescent commits to be labeled *delinquent* constitute a behavior disorder. The rate and seriousness of crimes committed by juveniles have been increasing significantly (Cohen, 1973). While boys have generally committed crimes involving aggression (such as assault and burglary) and girls have been associated with sex-related offenses (such as prostitution), more and more violent offenses are being committed by girls (Cavan & Ferdinand, 1975). Offenses involving the use of illegal drugs have also increased tremendously over the past two decades.

Severely Disturbed Children

The National Association for Mental Health has estimated that more than 500,000 children in the United States are severely emotionally disturbed. These children are commonly diagnosed and referred to as *autistic, psychotic,* or *schizophrenic.* The National Society for Autistic Children (1977) has estimated that autism occurs in approximately 5 of every 10,000 children. This figure might lead one to conclude that autism is very rare, and yet it is actually more common than blindness in children (Lotter, 1966; Rutter, 1965). Kauffman (1980) suggests that .5% of all children (or 1 in 200) are being served as severely disturbed.

CHARACTERISTICS OF CHILDREN WITH BEHAVIOR DISORDERS

We have already described some of the characteristics of behavior disordered children. In this section we will discuss their intellectual ability and academic

One-to-one counseling plays an important role in working with juvenile offenders.

A HOME TOKEN SYSTEM FOR TERRY

Terry, a 6-year-old boy in a regular first-grade classroom, was brought to a university-operated education clinic because his parents were having extreme difficulty managing him at home. They identified three behaviors as targets for change: Terry would not stay in his bed at night, did not follow their directions, and only ate certain foods at dinnertime. It was decided that a home behavior change program would be developed for the three targeted problems.

After precisely defining the three behaviors, Terry's parents agreed to take baseline measures for a week. With 7 days of data, Terry's parents met with the clinic staff to plan an intervention strategy. They were praised for faithfully observing and recording their son's behavior and were encouraged to continue to do so. They were then told that it would probably be best to work initially on just one behavior, so Terry could adjust to new contingencies and they could implement

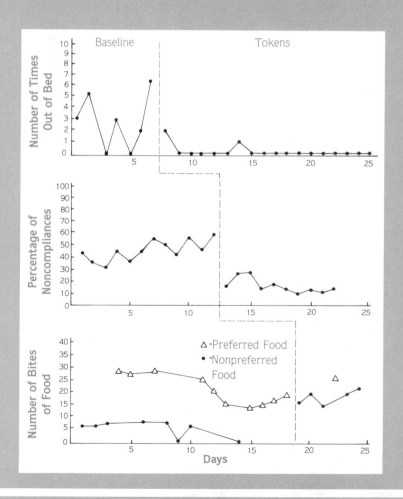

the intervention strategy consistently. Terry's parents agreed; both felt his getting out of bed at night was the most troublesome behavior and should be dealt with first.

After discussing several possible strategies, a simple token system was designed. A token system was selected for two reasons. First, Terry's parents liked the idea and felt confident they could implement it consistently. Second, if the token system was successful with the bedtime behavior, it would be simple to expand it to include noncompliance and limited food preference.

Terry was shown a chart and told that if he stayed in his bed when tucked in at night until the next morning, he would get a star to paste on it. Stars 2 days in a row would earn his choice of activities from a menu his parents compiled. Five stars in a row and he could select from another section of the reward menu that included small toys. In addition, his parents gave him lots of praise in the morning whenever he stayed in his bedroom the night before.

Five days after the program was initiated for the bedtime behavior, noncompliance was added as a target. Each day Terry complied with five requests, he would receive a star. Verbal praise was given each time Terry followed a request. Stars on 2 consecutive days for both bedtime and compliance behaviors were now needed to earn a preferred activity.

Six days later, food preference was added to the system. Terry earned a star for every five bites of nonpreferred food at dinnertime. He was required to earn stars on 2 consecutive days for all three target behaviors to exchange for an item on the reward menu.

During baseline, Terry left his bedroom an average of 2.7 times per night. When the system was put into effect, the number of times Terry left his room after being put to bed dropped to zero in 2 days and remained there for all but 1 day over the next 17 days.

Noncompliance averaged 42% with a range of 34% to 64% during 12 days of baseline. For the 10 days during which data were collected on noncompliance when the token system was in effect, noncompliance dropped to an average of 19%.

During the 18 days of baseline of food preference, Terry ate an average of 22.2 bites of his favorite foods but only 4.8 bites of meats and vegetables. When the token system was implemented, Terry's consumption of nonpreferred food rose to a mean of 17.8 bites.

This case demonstrates the behavioral approach to identify and treat a child's behavior problems and emphasizes the important and effective role parents can play as partners with professionals.

Adapted from R. D. Shrewsberry, A home token system for Terry. In W. L. Heward, J. C. Cardig, & A. Rossett, *Working with parents of handicapped children.* Columbus, Ohio: Charles E. Merrill, 1979. Used with permission.

achievement, as well as the two general types of behavior these children display—aggression and social withdrawal. We will also describe the dominant characteristics of childhood autism.

Intelligence and Achievement

Review chapter 3 for a discussion of IQ tests.

Contrary to one popular myth, most emotionally disturbed children are not bright, intellectually above-average children who are bored with their surroundings. Many more behavior disordered children than normal children score in the "slow learner" or "mildly retarded" range on IQ tests. A score of about 90 is average for behavior disordered children. Many severely disturbed children are untestable, and the average IQ score for those who can be tested is about 50. Occasionally, a severely disturbed child scores very high on an IQ test, but this is a rare exception.

Whether or not behavior disordered children actually have any less "real" intelligence than normal children is difficult to say. Remember, an IQ test measures only how well a child performs certain tasks. It is possible that the disturbed child's inappropriate behavior has interfered with past opportunities to learn the tasks included on the test, but that he or she really has the necessary "intelligence" to learn them. However, IQ tests are good indicators of school achievement, and behavior disordered children are noted for their problems with learning and academic achievement.

Based on his review of research related to the intelligence of emotionally disturbed children, Kauffman (1981a) has hypothesized that, as a group, their IQ scores are distributed as shown in Figure 5.1.

Even when IQ scores are taken into account, behavior disordered children achieve less than their scores indicate they should. Glavin and Annesley (1971), in a study of 130 behavior disordered children, found that 81% were underachieving in reading and 72% were achieving less than would be expected in math.

Data obtained by the state of Florida on a total of 193 eleventh-grade students classified as "emotionally disturbed" or "socially maladjusted" indicated that almost 50% of those students could not read well enough to pass a functional literacy test. Approximately 75% of the sample did not have the mathematics skills necessary for a high school diploma (reported in Cawley & Webster, 1981). A survey of correctional institutions found 34% of incarcerated delinquents to be functionally illiterate (Clearinghouse for Offender Literacy, 1975). Oliver (1974), in a national survey of 12- to 17-year-old public school students, found that over 80% of those who needed "frequent discipline" were behind in their academic achievement.

Usually, the behavior disordered child is an acting-out child in the classroom, constantly defying the teacher's instructions and classroom rules and procedures. Walker and Buckley (1974) have suggested that the behavior disordered child's academic deficits can, at least in part, be explained in terms of the large amount of time the child spends on nonacademic matters (such as running around the room or fighting) at the expense of learning. Hops, Beickel, and

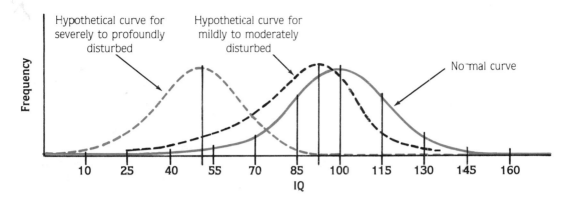

FIGURE 5.1
Hypothetical frequency distributions of IQ for mildly to moderately, and severely to profoundly disturbed compared to a normal frequency distribution.

SOURCE: From J. M. Kauffman, *Characteristics of children's behavior disorders*, 2d ed. Columbus, Ohio: Charles E. Merrill, 1981, p. 127. Reprinted with permission.

Walker (1976) listed the following behaviors as characteristic of the acting-out child in the classroom.

1. Is out of seat
2. Yells out
3. Runs around room
4. Disturbs peers
5. Hits or fights
6. Ignores teacher
7. Complains
8. Fights excessively
9. Steals
10. Destroys property
11. Does not comply with adult commands or directions
12. Argues (talks back)
13. Ignores other teachers
14. Distorts the truth
15. Has temper tantrums
16. Is excluded from activities by peers
17. Doesn't follow directions
18. Doesn't complete assignments

Many educators have noted the close association of learning disabilities and behavior disorders (see, for instance, Stephens, 1977; Wallace & McLoughlin, 1979). Many children with behavior disorders also have the problems in learning described in chapter 4.

Aggressive Behavior

The most common characteristics of behavior disordered children are aggression and acting out. While all children sometimes cry, hit others, and refuse to comply with the requests of their parents and teachers, disturbed children do so frequently. Also, the aggressive behavior of behavior disordered children often occurs with little or no provocation. Aggression takes many forms—verbal abuse toward adults and other children, destructiveness and vandalism, physical attacks on others. These children seem to be in continuous conflict with those

Aggression is the major characteristic of Quay's *conduct disorder* and *socialized delinquent* categories.

around them. Their own aggressive outbursts often cause others to strike back in attempts to punish them. It is no wonder that these children are not liked by others or that they establish few friendships.

Patterson and his co-workers have conducted considerable research on childhood aggression (Patterson, Reid, Jones, & Conger, 1975). Through intensive observations of many aggressive children at home and in school, they have identified 14 different classes of noxious behaviors often shown by behavior disordered children. Table 5.2 shows the different rates at which behavior disordered and normal children perform these inappropriate activities. The data in the table were taken from observations in the homes of aggressive and nonaggressive children. Observations in the classroom indicate similar patterns (Patterson, Cobb, & Ray, 1972).

TABLE 5.2
Noxious behaviors in aggressive and nonagressive children.

Noxious Behavior	Description	Average No. of Mins. between Occurrences*	
		Aggressive Children	Nonaggressive Children
Disapproval	Disapproving of another's behavior by words or gestures	7	12
Negativism	Stating something neutral in content but saying it in a negative tone of voice	9	41
Noncompliance	Not doing what is requested	11	20
Yell	Shouting, yelling or talking loudly; if carried on for sufficient time it becomes extremely unpleasant	18	54
Tease	Teasing that produces displeasure, disapproval, or disruption of current activity of the person being teased	20	51
High Rate Activity	Activity that is aversive to others if carried on for a long period of time, e.g., running in the house or jumping up and down	23	71
Negative Physical Act	Attacking or attempting to attack another with enough intensity to potentially inflict pain (e.g., biting, kicking, slapping, hitting, spanking, throwing, grabbing)	24	108
Whine	Saying something in a slurring, nasal, high-pitched, or falsetto voice	28	26
Destructive	Destroying, damaging, or trying to damage or destroy any object	33	156
Humiliation	Making fun of, shaming, or embarrassing another intentionally	50	100

EXCEPTIONAL CHILDREN

TABLE 5.2 (continued)

Noxious Behavior	Description	Average No. of Mins. between Occurrences*	
		Aggressive Children	Nonaggressive Children
Cry	Any type of crying	52	455
Negative Command	Commanding another to do something and demanding immediate compliance, plus threatening aversive consequences (explicitly or implicitly) if compliance is not immediate; also directing sarcasm or humiliation at another	120	500
Dependent	Requesting help with a task the child is capable of doing himself; e.g., a 16-year-old boy asking his mother to comb his hair	149	370
Ignore	The child appears to recognize that another has directed behavior toward him but does not respond in an active fashion	185	244

*Minutes between occurrences are expressed as approximations of reported average rates per minute (e.g., for aggressive children's "whine," reported rate per minute equals 0.0360, or approximately once every 28 minutes.

SOURCE: From J. M. Kauffman, *Characteristics of children with behavior disorders,* Columbus, Ohio: Charles E. Merrill, 1977, pp. 188–189, adapted from G. R. Patterson, J. B. Reid, R. R. Jones, & R. E. Conger, *A social learning approach to family intervention, Vol. 1: Families with aggressive children.* Eugene, Ore.: Castilia, 1975, p. 5. Copyright © 1975 by Castilia Publishing Company. Used with permission.

As many behavior disordered children grow older, their aggressive behavior causes conflict in the community, leading to run-ins with law enforcement officials and arrests for criminal offenses. Teenage delinquency is a serious problem in the United States today. Youth under the age of 18 are responsible for a large part of each year's criminal arrest statistics. During the period from 1972 through 1981, arrests of children under age 18 increased by 16.9% (U.S. Department of Justice, 1982).

To add to the problem, as we mentioned earlier, the incidence of serious and violent crimes committed by juveniles is also increasing (Cavan & Ferdinand, 1975). For example, in 1981, 9% of all people arrested for murder and nonnegligent manslaughter were under 18. And younger children are being arrested; in 1981 over 600,000 arrests were made of children under 15. A total of 205 of those arrests were for murder and nonnegligent manslaughter (U.S. Department of Justice, 1982).

The total number of criminal offenses committed by youth against others and property is, of course, impossible to determine. Many crimes go unreported or unsolved, leaving identification of the perpetrator unknown. However, the information in Table 5.3 indicates the possible extent of the problem and the many crimes often committed by individual juvenile offenders. Originally intended to show the ability of "positive peer culture" counseling groups to provide confidentiality and to generate a feeling of trust among the youths and their adult leader, this table gives further information on the characteristics of juvenile offenders.

Another popular belief that research has demonstrated to be untrue is the idea that while aggressive, acting-out children cause considerable problems and concern as youngsters, they usually "grow out of" their immature behavior and become normal adults. Robbins (1966) conducted a follow-up study of over 500 adults who as children had been seen by a clinic because of behavior problems. Robbins used structured interviews to gather such information as work history, alcohol and drug use, performance in the armed services, arrest, social relationships, and marital history. A control group of 100 adults who grew up in the same community as the subjects was used for comparison. The results were significant. Of those adults who had been referred to a clinic for behavior problems as children, 45% had 5 or more "antisocial" traits. Only 4% of those in the control group showed that many antisocial characteristics. In analyzing the results further, Robbins found that those children who had been referred to the clinic for antisocial behavior—theft, fighting, discipline problems in school, truancy, and the like—had the most difficulty adjusting as adults. Furthermore, these adults tended to raise children who had a higher incidence of problem behaviors than normal, thus continuing the cycle.

Withdrawn Behavior

These children make up Quay's *personality disorder* and *immaturity* dimensions.

Some behavior disordered children are anything but aggressive. Their problem is the opposite—too little social interaction with others. While children who consistently act immature and withdrawn do not present the threat to others

Aggression and "acting out" are frequently displayed by children with behavior disorders.

that aggressive children do, their behavior still creates a serious impediment to their development. These children seldom play with other children their own age. They usually do not have the social skills necessary to make friends and have fun, and often retreat into their own daydreams and fantasies. Some are fearful of things without reason, frequently complain of being sick or hurt, and go into deep bouts of depression. Obviously, these behavior patterns limit the

TABLE 5.3
Criminal offenses of juvenile delinquents known to court and offenses not known to court but admitted to in a group counseling program.

Offenses Known to Court	Offenses Not Known to Court, Discussed in Group
Student A Petty larceny; brutality (holding 9-year-old boy over burning trash barrel).	Auto theft; breaking and entering.
Student B Beyond control of parent; sexual intercourse with 12-year-old sister.	Auto theft; attempted rape; stealing; shoplifting; breaking and entering; vandalism; sexual acts with animals; incest with mother.
Student C Shoplifting; disorderly conduct; grand larceny; petty larceny; breaking and entering; destroying private property; truancy.	Habituation to drugs; grand larceny; petty larceny; arson; auto theft; carrying concealed weapons.
Student D Curfew violation; auto theft; breaking and entering; public drunk; operating motor vehicle without license.	Carrying deadly weapon; robbery; arson; auto theft; multiple breaking and entering; three instances assault and battery.
Student E Truancy; runaway; obtaining merchandise under false pretenses.	Habituation to drugs; shoplifting; auto theft; vandalism; "rolling queers" for money (assault, battery, robbery).
Student F Petty larceny; contempt of court; curfew violation; breaking and entering.	Malicious cutting and wounding; housebreaking; stealing; forgery; shoplifting.
Student G Breaking and entering; attempted safe burglary; safe burglary.	Carrying a deadly weapon; malicious cutting and wounding; burglary; concealing stolen property; fraud; stealing from automobiles.
Student H Shoplifting; runaway; violation of probation.	Breaking and entering; stealing.
Student I Public intoxication; petty larceny; carrying concealed deadly weapon; burglary; attempted safe-cracking.	Shoplifting; driving without license; breaking and entering.

SOURCE: From H. H. Vorrath and L. K. Brendtro, *Positive peer culture.* Hawthorne, N.Y.: Aldine Publishing, 1974, p. 94. Courtesy of Aldine Publishing.

Positive communication and encouragement can be helpful to a withdrawn child.

child's chances to take part in and learn from the school and leisure activities that normal children participate in.

Happily, for the mildly or moderately disturbed child who is withdrawn and immature and who is fortunate enough to have competent teachers and other school professionals responsible for her development, the outlook is fairly good. Carefully outlining the social skills the child should learn and gradually and systematically arranging opportunities for and rewarding those behaviors often proves successful.

Working with Denise—An Elective Mute

Some children become so shy and withdrawn that they refuse to speak at school, even though they use normal speech in other places or in the presence of other people. The clinical term for this behavior disorder, speaking normally in one setting and not speaking in another, is *elective mutism*. Denise was a 5-year-old kindergarten student who spoke only to her parents and brother when at home (Heward, Eachus, & Christopher, 1974).

Throughout her first 6 months at school no one there had heard Denise talk, laugh, cry, or make any vocalizations whatsoever. Yet her speech at home was reportedly fluent. Denise was described by her mother to be generally "happy and helpful" around the house.

Denise would complete some school assignments at home, but she never attempted any work in school. She rarely took part in any group activities and would sometimes stand in one spot for long periods of time unless she was coaxed to do otherwise.

Since Denise spoke freely at home and was mute at school, it was decided to use a treatment program which united the two environments. A **token economy** was chosen for this purpose.

Since any treatment program bridging the home and school would require full cooperation from Denise's parents, a meeting was arranged. The teacher explained to Denise's parents that when she did certain things at school, she would be given gold stars to take home and "buy" things with, provided that she had enough stars to cover the "cost" of the desired item. Denise's parents then made a list of items and activities their daughter liked. In addition to vocalizations, behaviors that would increase the likelihood of speech were also listed to be rewarded. Those behaviors requiring Denise to speak earned her the most stars.

A chart illustrating the available rewards and their relative "cost" in stars was constructed and taped to the refrigerator door in Denise's house. She also got a folder in which she could save and carry home the gummed stick-on stars.

Denise's teacher explained to her classmates (in Denise's absence) that they were going to play a game, the object of which would be to get Denise to talk at school. Even the promise of the possibility of Denise talking to them was a strong incentive for her peers to cooperate. The teacher then asked Denise's classmates to "try to pay more attention to Denise when she is doing one of these things," and read the list of desired behaviors to them. They were also told to "ignore her at other times."

Denise made rapid progress with this program. Where she earned only one star on the first day, for joining story time, by day 30 she took part in all group activities, said "Hi," and answered seven questions from the teacher. She had accumulated the 40 stars she needed for a new doll.

It is important to note that behaviors other than those which involve speech were rewarded. To get the token economy started, some behaviors Denise was already doing were included for reinforcement. In Denise's case, simply waiting for her to speak would probably have been futile and frustrating. By increasing the frequency of behaviors that required her to confront other people (such as joining group activities), Denise had many more occasions for speaking.

Another important factor in this study was the behavior of Denise's classmates. Before the program, her classmates would answer questions for her, frequently ask her if she was all right, and get things for her. She received a lot of attention for *not* talking. During the program, however, this attention was withheld; Denise's classmates were very good at paying attention to her only when she was participating.

In Denise's case, the "ice was broken" just before the end of the school year. It was feared that her muteness might return again in the fall. To help prevent that, Denise was enrolled in a 6-week summer school session with the same classroom teacher. During the summer session, social praise and special privileges (such as wiping the blackboard, feeding the class turtle) were substituted for the home reward menu and were given at school for doing the same list of behaviors. Gold stars were again used as token reinforcers until the last

A token economy is a system of rewarding desired behaviors with some tangible item (for instance, poker chips, points, stamps, stars) which can be accumulated and traded in for a wide range of back-up reinforcers. The token, which becomes a reward in its own right, bridges the time and space interval between the desired behavior and the presentation of the back-up reward.

week and a half of the summer session. Denise's rate of speech and social activity in general continued to increase during the summer.

A year after Denise's original program, she was described by her teacher as a child who talks "a mile a minute." She had been retained in kindergarten because her extreme withdrawal during the first 7 months of school had prevented her from acquiring most of the prerequisite skills for the first grade. At the end of her first kindergarten year, Denise could not identify any shapes, colors, or numbers, and knew only a few letters of the alphabet.

At the beginning of her second year, Denise would not answer a question unless she felt "sure of the right answer." Her teacher immediately dealt with this temporary muteness by walking away and ignoring her. After 2 days, Denise began to answer "I don't know" to questions she did not understand. She now answers in complete sentences in front of the class, begins conversations, initiates play with other children, and is learning in school.

Autism

Autism refers to a set of behavioral characteristics common to many profoundly disturbed children. Mildly and moderately behavior disordered children usually are not labeled as having a problem during their preschool years; many are not considered behavior disordered by anyone until they reach their middle elementary years at school. This is not true for autistic children. An autistic child often seems different from normal children during the first 2 years. Lovaas and Newsom have described six common characteristics of autistic children:*

Professionals disagree about whether autism is a severe behavior disorder, a severe language disorder, or a health impairment. We include it here because children with autism display a variety of unusual behaviors in addition to language problems; they are most often treated with procedures similar to those used with other behavior disorders.

1. *Apparent sensory deficit.* We may move directly in front of the child, smile, and talk to him, yet he will act as if no one is there. We may not feel that the child is avoiding or ignoring us, but rather that he simply does not seem to see or hear. The mother also reports that she did, in fact, incorrectly suspect the child to be blind or deaf. . . . As we get to know the child better, we become aware of the great variability in this obliviousness to stimulation. For example, although the child may give no visible reaction to a loud noise, such as a clapping of hands directly behind his ears, he may orient to the crinkle of a candy wrapper or respond fearfully to a distant and barely audible siren.
2. *Severe affect isolation.* Another characteristic that we frequently notice is that attempts to love and cuddle and show affection to the child encounter a profound lack of interest on the child's part. Again, the parents relate that the child seems not to know or care whether he is alone or in the company of others.
3. *Self-stimulation.* A most striking kind of behavior in these children centers on very repetitive **stereotyped** acts, such as rocking their bodies when in a sitting position, twirling around, flapping their hands at the wrists, or humming a set of three or four notes over and over again. The parents often report that their child has spent entire days gazing at his cupped hands, staring at lights, spinning objects, etc.

*O. Ivar Lovaas, Crighton D. Newsom, "Behavior modification with psychotic children." in *Handbook of Behavior Modification and Behavior Therapy,* edited by Harold Leitenberg, ©1976, pp. 308–309. Reprinted by permission of Prentice-Hall, Inc., Englewood Cliffs, New Jersey.

EXCEPTIONAL CHILDREN

4. *Tantrums and self-mutilatory behavior.* Although the child may not engage in self-mutilation when we first meet him, often the parents report that the child sometimes bites himself so severely that he bleeds, or that he beats his head against walls or sharp pieces of furniture so forcefully that large lumps rise and his skin turns black and blue. He may beat his face with his fists. . . . Sometimes the child's aggression will be directed outward against his parents or teachers in the most primitive form of biting, scratching, and kicking. Some of these children absolutely tyrannize their parents by staying awake and making noises all night, tearing curtains off the window, spilling flour in the kitchen, etc., and the parents are often at a complete loss as to how to cope with these behaviors.

5. *Echolalic and psychotic speech.* Most of these children are mute; they do not speak, but they may hum or occasionally utter simple sounds. The speech of those who do talk may be echoes of other people's attempts to talk to them. For example, if we address a child with the question, "What is your name?" the child is likely to answer "What is your name?" (preserving, perhaps, the exact intonation of the one who spoke to him). At other times the **echolalia** is not immediate but delayed; the child may repeat statements he has heard that morning or on the preceding day, or he may repeat TV commercials or other such announcements.

6. *Behavior deficiencies.* Although the presence of the behaviors sketched above is rather striking, it is equally striking to take note of many behaviors that the autistic child does *not* have. At the age of 5 or 10, he may, in many ways, show the behavioral repertoire of a 1-year-old child. He has few if any self-help skills but needs to be fed and dressed by others. He may not play with toys, but put them in his mouth, or tap them repetitively with his fingers. He shows no understanding of common dangers.

Clearly, children who act as Lovaas and Newsom describe are profoundly disturbed. Their management and treatment often require intensive, around-the-clock programming. While behavior modification techniques have been effective in controlling some of the self-injurious and self-stimulatory actions of many autistic children, the overall prognosis at present remains poor. Many autistic children are likely to function at a retarded level and to be institutionalized as adults, even after years of extensive intervention, unless systematic programming is provided aimed at maintaining gains (Lovaas, Koegel, Simmons, & Long, 1973).

On the brighter side, however, a great deal of exciting and promising recent research may help lead to better futures for autistic children. Researchers are discovering successful procedures for using sensory stimulation (for example, movement, visual and/or auditory feedback, vibration) to reduce self-stimulation and as a reinforcer for desired responses (Ferrari & Harris, 1981; Rincover, Cook, Peoples, & Packard, 1979). More effective methods of programming important aspects of instruction for autistic children, such as scheduling learning tasks and varying reinforcers, are being experimentally demonstrated (Dunlap & Koegel, 1980; Egel, 1981). Still other researchers are teaching autistic children to communicate through sign language (Bonvillian & Nelson, 1976).

SIGN LANGUAGE WITH AN AUTISTIC CHILD

John Bonvillian.

Children who are diagnosed as autistic often have difficulty producing and understanding language. Their problems may be mild—as in occasional trouble with certain sounds—or severe, even a total inability to produce spoken language. In recent years, educators and psychologists have explored a variety of communication strategies with autistic children, to help them overcome their isolation.

In most cases, the hearing of autistic children is not impaired. But sign language, which has been used by deaf people for many years, is helping some autistic children begin to communicate with other people. John Bonvillian, a psychologist at the University of Virginia with a special interest in sign language and autism, recalls for us his involvement with Ted, a 9-year-old autistic boy who was considered "mute" and uncommunicative.

Ted's parents began noticing something different about him in early infancy. He didn't enjoy being held and cuddled as his older siblings had. He often did not cry in response to pain. As Ted grew, he failed to develop speech, though audiological tests showed that he had hearing within the normal range. Various procedures were tried over the years: individual speech therapy, group play sessions, a computer-assisted language program. But at age 9, when I first met him, Ted had *never* produced any meaningful speech. He made a few apparently meaningless vocalizations, such as "etta." He didn't respond to language or interact socially with other people. He had frequent temper tantrums at home and school, was not fully toilet trained, and displayed bizarre stereotyped gestures and movements.

With the consent and involvement of his parents, a special sign language program was designed for Ted. He received training for a half-hour each day at the special education center he attended. In introducing a new sign, Ted's teacher would follow this procedure:

1. Show Ted a picture of the object or action for which he will learn a sign.
2. Mold and shape Ted's hands into the appropriate gesture, and guide them through the proper motion.
3. Model the correct sign, and ask Ted to imitate it.
4. Show Ted the picture, and ask him to produce the sign in response to it.

We used a token reinforcement system. Ted received a card each time he successfully produced a sign. At the end of the half-hour session, Ted could redeem his cards for a toy or for the privilege of playing outside. Verbal praise and encouragement were also given, of course. Ted's teacher was careful to use speech, too, saying each sign aloud as it was presented. Ted's family learned signs and used them with him at home.

Ted made steady progress. He acquired new signs at the rate of about two per week: *yes, no, ball, Ted, eat, Daddy, book, sleep, Mother, drink.* So you might say this was rather slow. On the other hand, Ted was remarkably consistent. Once he learned a sign, he would almost always use it correctly.

You can imagine our delight when (after about 3 months of training on individual signs) Ted began to combine signs to express more complicated ideas. Some of his earliest two-sign combinations were *boy drink, swim school, no food,* and *more cookie.* After a few more months, he produced combinations of up to five signs—such as *eat turkey tomorrow* and *no mother car play school* (Ted was going to play at school, and his mother was not coming to pick him up in the car).

Over a 2-year period, Ted's useful vocabulary grew to include about 400 signs. He gradually learned to engage in sign language conversations with other people. His tantrums practically disappeared, the bizarre gestures were sharply reduced, and he developed control over his bowel and bladder functions.

Ted is still a handicapped child. He is probably going to need special education and support throughout his life. Yet the sign language program can be viewed as nothing less than a dramatic success story. Ted's experience suggests that other autistic and nonverbal children may be able to learn meaningful communication and appropriate behavior. Their true abilities may not be fully tapped if speech is the *only* method we use to communicate with them.

"Eat" was one of the first signs Ted learned.

For more on main-streaming autistic children, see Knoblock, 1982.

Baseline is the level or amount of a target behavior before beginning an intervention program to be evaluated.

Russo and Koegel (1977) carried out an impressive case study that showed that an autistic child could be successfully mainstreamed in a regular classroom. A 5-year-old girl with a primary diagnosis of autism was placed in a regular public school kindergarten with 20 to 30 normal children and one teacher. For the first 12 weeks (after a 3-week **baseline** period), a therapist was also in the classroom to provide a treatment program of token reinforcement, verbal praise, and prompts for desired behaviors. For the remaining 10 weeks of the school year, the kindergarten teacher, who had been trained by the therapist, carried out the treatment program alone and kept the autistic child in the classroom. Figure 5.2 shows the number of desirable social interactions, amount of stereotypic self-stimulatory behavior (such as rocking and rhythmic manipulation of small objects), and percentage of appropriate responses to questions (such as "What color is this?") asked by the therapist or teacher.

Figure 5.3 shows the same behaviors of the child during the next school year in a regular first grade classroom with another teacher. Comparison of the two graphs shows that at the beginning of first grade, the number of social behaviors had decreased and the amount of self-stimulatory behavior had increased over the levels obtained by the end of kindergarten. However, in-class retreatment by the therapist and training of the first grade teacher resulted in improvements similar to those of the kindergarten year. Russo and Koegel state that no further problems were reported by the school throughout the remainder of the first grade nor during the child's second and third grade years. The researchers reported that four other autistic children were also successfully placed in regular classrooms (three in kindergarten and one in the fifth grade) using the same procedures.

Russo and Koegel's (1977) research is critically important for two reasons. First, they discovered at least some of the variables that can be controlled to help an autistic child function in a regular classroom. Second, their successful results offer real hope and encouragement for the many teachers and parents who are working to learn more about helping autistic children.

CAUSES OF BEHAVIOR DISORDERS

Several theories and conceptual models have been proposed to explain abnormal behavior. Each theory attempts to describe relationships and create order out of the information gathered in the observation of the experimentation with disordered behavior. Each model identifies different causes of disordered behavior, as well as suggesting treatment methods designed to combat those causes. Regardless of the conceptual model from which behavior disorders are viewed, the suggested causes of disordered behavior can be grouped into two major categories—biophysical and psychological.

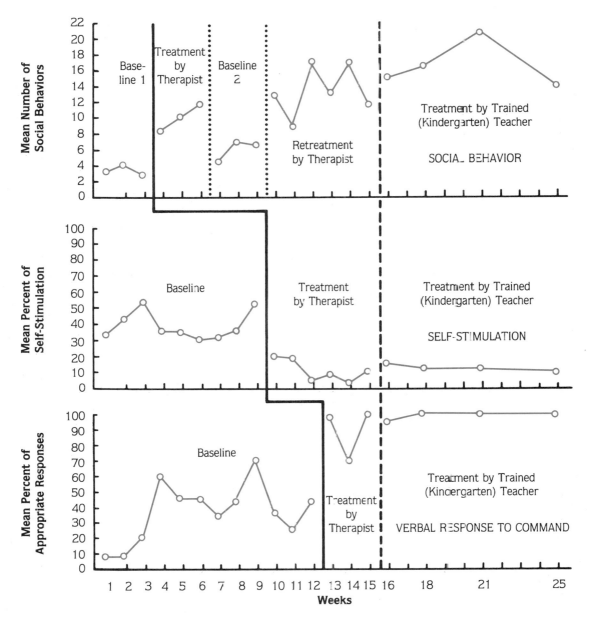

FIGURE 5.2

Social behavior, self-stimulation, and verbal response to command in the normal kindergarten classroom during baseline, treatment by the therapist, and treatment by the
trained kindergarten teacher. All three behaviors were measured simultaneously.

SOURCE: From D. C. Russo and R. L. Koegel. "A Method for integrating an autistic child in a
normal public-school classroom," *Journal of Applied Behavior Analysis,* 1977, *10,* p. 585. Copyright 1977 by the Society for the Experimental Analysis of Behavior, Inc. Used with permission.

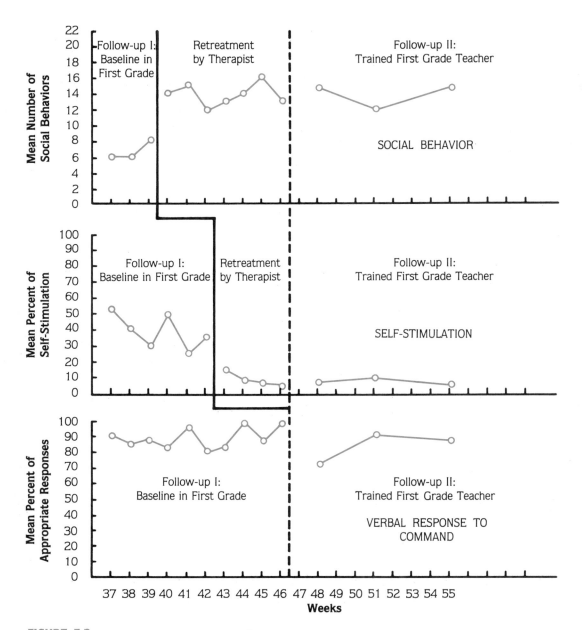

FIGURE 5.3

Follow-up data in the normal first-grade classroom during baseline, retreatment by the therapist on social behavior and self-stimulation, and treatment by the trained first-grade teacher. All three behaviors were measured simultaneously.

SOURCE: From D. C. Russo and R. L. Koegel, "A method for integrating an autistic child in a normal public-school classroom," *Journal of Applied Behavior Analysis*, 1977, *10*, p. 587. Copyright 1977 by the Society for the Experimental Analysis of Behavior, Inc. Used with permission.

Biophysical Factors

For the vast majority of behavior disordered children, there is no evidence of organic injury or disease. That is, they appear to be biologically healthy and sound. Some experts believe that all children are born with a biologically determined "temperament." While a child's inborn temperament might not in itself cause a behavior problem, it may predispose the child to problems. Thus certain events that might not produce abnormal behavior in a child with an "easygoing" temperament would result in disordered behavior by the child with a "difficult" temperament (Thomas, Chess, & Birch, 1968).

Possible biological causes are more clearly evident in severely and profoundly disturbed children. Many autistic children show signs of neurochemical imbalance (Rimland, 1964, 1971), and other biophysical causes of autism (including pre- and postnatal infections, chromosomal disorders, and auditory impairments) have been suspected (Menolascino & Eyde, 1979). Genetics have been shown to play a role in childhood schizophrenia (Buss, 1966; Heston, 1970; Meehl, 1969). However, even when there is a clear biological impairment, no one has been able to say with certainty whether the physiological abnormality actually *causes* the behavior problem or is just associated with it in some unknown way.

Psychological Factors

Psychological factors involve events in the child's life that affect the way he or she acts. Psychological factors are considered important in the development of behavior disorders in all conceptual models (except a strict biophysical stance, which few adhere to). However, the *kinds* of events seen as important and the way in which they are analyzed are viewed differently by professionals with different approaches (for example, by a psychoanalyst and a behaviorist). The two major settings in which these events take place are the child's home and the school.

We know that the relationship children have with their parents is critical to the way they learn to act, particularly during their early years. Observation and analysis of parent-child interaction patterns shows that parents who treat their children with love, are sensitive to the child's needs, and provide praise and attention for desired behaviors tend to have normal children with positive behavioral characteristics. On the other hand, aggressive, behavior-problem children often come from homes in which their parents are inconsistent disciplinarians, use harsh and excessive punishment, and show little love and affection for good behavior (Becker, 1964; Martin, 1975).

Because of the research on the relationship between parental child-rearing practices and behavior problems, many mental health professionals have been quick to pin all of the blame for children's behavior problems on parents. But the relationship between parent and child is a dynamic, *reciprocal* one. In other words, the behavior of the child may affect the behavior of his parents just as

See chapter 14 for an in-depth discussion of working with parents.

much as their actions affect him (Sameroff & Chandler, 1975). Therefore, it is at the least not practical and at most wrong to place all blame for abnormal behavior in young children on their parents. Instead, professionals must work with the parents to help them systematically change certain aspects of the parent-child relationship in an effort to prevent and modify these problems (Heward, Dardig, & Rossett, 1979).

School is the place where children spend the largest portion of their time outside the home. Therefore, it makes sense to observe carefully what takes place in schools in an effort to identify other events that may cause problem behavior. Also, because most behavior disordered children are not identified as such until they are in school, it would seem reasonable to question whether or not the school actually contributes to the incidence of behavior disorders. Some professionals have gone further than simply questioning; they feel that school is the major cause of behavior disorders in children. However, there is no evidence to support this contention. As with physiological or family causes, we cannot say for sure whether or not a child's school experiences are the lone *cause* of the behavior problems, but we can identify ways in which school can influence or contribute to the child's emotional disturbance (for example, inappropriate expectations, inconsistent management).

Several studies have demonstrated that what takes place in the classroom can maintain and actually strengthen deviant behavior patterns, even though the teacher is "trying" to help the child (Bostow & Bailey, 1969; Thomas, Becker, & Armstrong, 1968; Walker & Buckley, 1973). Walker concludes that:

> It is apparent that a child's behavior pattern at school is the result of a complex interaction of: (1) the behavior pattern the child has been taught at home, including attitudes toward school, (2) the experiences the child has had with different teachers in the school setting, and (3) the relationship between the child and his/her current teacher(s). Trying to determine in what proportion the child's behavior pattern is attributable to each of these learning sources is an impossible and unnecessary task. Deviant child behavior can be changed very effectively without knowing the original causes for its acquisition and development. (1979, p. 7)

Kauffman (1981) suggests five ways in which schools should treat children in order to help *prevent* the development of behavior problems.

1. Have a fair attitude for individual differences in interests and abilities; do not force every child to fit a narrow mold.
2. Have appropriately average expectations for behavior and academic achievement. If too low, expectations become self-fulfilling prophecies; if too high, expectations frustrate a child.
3. Manage a child's behavior consistently; just as the parent's being too lax or too rigid encourages disordered behavior, inconsistent school discipline can have the same negative result.

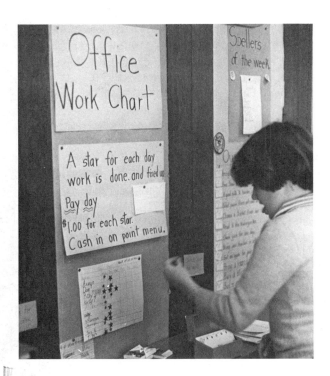

Rewarding desired behaviors in the classroom.

4. Include areas of study which have relevance to the child; not to do so invites truancy or misbehavior.
5. Reward desired behaviors and do not reinforce inappropriate behaviors; from the viewpoint of behavioral psychology, failure to do this contributes to disturbance.

IDENTIFICATION AND ASSESSMENT

Very few school districts use any systematic method for identifying disturbed children. Morse and his colleagues (1964) believe one reason that systematic screening and identification methods are not used is that schools would identify many more children than they could provide special education services for. In 1975, the U.S. Office of Education estimated that only 18% of the emotionally disturbed children in our schools were being served by special education. Given this figure, another reason systematic identification methods are seldom used may be because they are not needed. If only a portion of the children with behavior problems can be served, those children with the more obvious and severe disturbances will receive the services, and they are clearly identifiable without formal methods.

In fact, *most* behavior disordered children are readily identifiable. They stand out. This does not mean, however, that identification is always a sure thing. With younger children, identification of emotional disturbance is more difficult because behavior of all young children changes quickly and often. Also, some withdrawn children go undetected because their problem does not draw the attention of parents and teachers. Aggressive children, on the other hand, seldom go unnoticed. Research has shown that informal teacher ratings are relatively reliable and valid in selecting behavior disordered children (Bolstad, 1974; Bower, 1969; Nelson, 1971).

While there are no reliable tests for determining emotional disturbance, several **screening** devices have been developed. Children identified in the screening are then either watched closely for further signs or given a more intensive examination. The most widely used screening test for behavior disorders is A Process for In-School Screening of Children with Emotional Handicaps (Bower & Lambert, 1962). This device employs ratings of the child's behavior by his teacher, his peers, and himself. If the child is rated very negatively by the teacher and his classmates or by himself, it is suggested he be evaluated further. The instrument has three different forms, one with rating scales and questions appropriate for kindergarten through third grade, one for fourth through seventh grade, and one for eighth through twelfth grade.

Simpson (1981) suggests that a thorough screening/identification process for behavior disordered students should include (1) an interview with the parent(s) or guardian, (2) at least one behavior rating scale, (3) direct classroom observation, (4) peer evaluation, and (5) self-evaluation.

Traditionally, assessment of behavior disordered children has relied heavily on the results of psychological tests and interviews. However, the results of **projective tests** [e.g., Rorshach Ink Blot, (Rorschach, 1942) Draw-A-Man Test (Goodenough & Harris, 1963)] have proven to be of minimal value in prescribing an appropriate intervention. Children often do not respond in a testing or interview situation the same way they do in the classroom or at home. Also, results of these assessment procedures test only a limited sample of the child's behavior and, importantly, do not assess how the child *typically* acts over a period of time. One-time measures are not sufficient to use as a basis for planning treatment.

In recent years, direct and continuous measurement has become more and more popular as a method for assessing children with behavior disorders. With this method, the actual behaviors that cause a child to be considered disturbed in the first place are clearly *specified* and *observed* in the setting where they normally occur (for example, the classroom) every day. In this way, precise statements can be made about what problem behaviors must be weakened and what adaptive behaviors the child needs to learn to perform with greater frequency. In addition to providing specific information on the frequency of occurrence of the problem, direct and continuous measurement also enables the teacher to observe systematically and note what events normally surround the behavior(s) of concern—both before and after it. As we stressed in the chapter on learning disabilities, the *primary purpose of assessment* is not to determine if the child has something called a behavior disorder, but to see if the child's behavior is special enough to warrant special services, and if so, to indicate what

Screening is a procedure where groups of children are examined and/or tested in an effort to identify "high-risk" children, who have a higher than normal probability of either having or getting whatever condition is being screened for.

those services should consist of. Kauffman makes a strong case for direct and continuous measurement with behavior disordered children.

> Disturbed children are considered to need help *primarily because they exhibit behavioral excesses or deficiencies.* Not to define precisely and measure these behavioral excesses and deficiencies, then, is a fundamental error: it is akin to the malpractice of a nurse who decides not to measure vital signs (heart rate, respiration rate, temperature, and blood pressure), perhaps arguing that he/she is too busy, that subjective estimates of vital signs are quite adequate, that vital signs are only superficial estimates of the patient's health, or that vital signs do not signify the nature of the underlying pathology. The teaching profession is dedicated to the task of changing behavior—changing behavior demonstrably for the better. What can one say, then, of educational practice that does not include reliable and forthright measurement of the behavior change induced by the teacher's methodology? I believe this: *It is indefensible.* (1981a, p. 284)

Behaviorally oriented educators are concerned with the social significance of behavior change (Baer, Wolf, & Risley, 1968). It is not enough just to demonstrate that one can alter a child's behavior; teachers must show that the changes they bring about have **social validity** (Van Houten, 1979; Wolf, 1978). One measure of social validity is whether or not newly acquired behaviors are really worthwhile for the child; that is, whether or not the "new" behavior will be viewed as significant by others, people who deal with the child. Walker and Hops (1976) describe one approach for evaluating the effects of treatment on the classroom behavior of elementary school students referred to an experimental class because of inappropriate behavior. Instead of merely demonstrating that the children's behavior could improve in the special class, Walker and Hops compared the behavior of their special students with the actual classroom behavior of their peers in the regular classroom. Figure 5.4 shows the results for one of the three groups in the study.

The special students received a treatment program consisting of systematic social and token reinforcement in the classroom. It produced behavior that was actually better than that of their peers during the same period back in the regular classroom. Continued observation of the students during a 12-week follow-up period after their return to the regular classroom revealed that they maintained appropriate behavior within the "normal" limits defined by their peers' behavior. Walker and Hops not only demonstrated that their treatment program improved the disruptive students' behavior, but that the improvements were socially valid (that is, they now acted as well as their "normal" classmates) and were maintained during a 3-month follow-up.

EDUCATIONAL APPROACHES FOR BEHAVIOR DISORDERED CHILDREN

There are several different approaches to educating emotionally disturbed children, each with its own definitions, purposes of treatment, and types of inter-

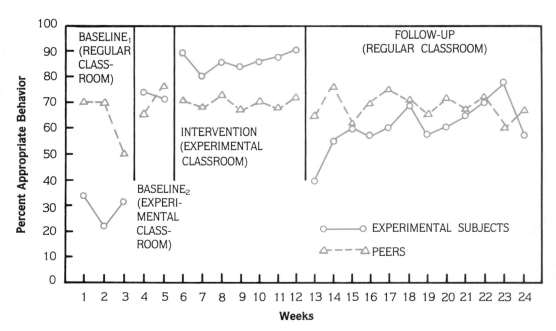

FIGURE 5.4

Appropriate behavior of disruptive students compared to their "normal" peers before, during, and after treatment.

SOURCE: From H. M. Walker and H. Hops, "Use of normative peer data as a standard for evaluating classroom treatment effects," *Journal of Applied Behavior Analysis,* 1976, *9,* p. 165. Copyright 1976 by the Society for the Experimental Analysis of Behavior, Inc. Used with permission.

vention. Based on the work of Rhodes and his colleagues (Rhodes & Head, 1974; Rhodes & Tracy, 1972a, 1972b), Kauffman (1981a) lists six basic models:

1. Psychodynamic. Based on the idea that disordered personality develops out of the interaction of experience and internal mental processes (ego, id, and superego) that are out of balance. This model relies on psychotherapy and creative "projects" for the child (and often the parents) rather than academic remediation.

2. Biological. This model suggests that deviant behavior is a physical disorder with genetic or medical causes. This implies that these causes must be "cured" to treat the emotional disturbance. Treatment might be medical or nutritional.

3. Psychoeducational. This model is concerned with "unconscious motivations and underlying conflicts yet stresses the realistic demands of everyday functioning in school and home" (p. 27). Intervention focuses on therapeutic discussions to allow the children to understand their behavior rationally and plan to change it.

4. **Behavioral.** This model assumes that the child has learned disordered behavior and has not learned appropriate responses. To treat the behavior disorder, a teacher uses behavior modification techniques to teach the child appropriate responses and eliminate inappropriate ones.

5. **Ecological.** This model stresses the interaction of the child with the people around him and with social institutions. Treatment involves teaching the child to function within the family, school, neighborhood, and larger community.

6. **Humanistic.** This model suggests that the disturbed child is not in touch with his or her own feelings and can't find self-fulfillment in traditional educational settings. Treatment takes place in an open, personalized setting, where the teacher serves as "resource and catalyst" (p. 27).

Few programs or teachers use only the techniques suggested by one of the theoretical models. Most programs employ methods from several of the approaches. And the models themselves are not entirely discrete; they overlap in certain areas. Sometimes the difference is primarily a matter of wording; the actual classroom practices may be quite similar.

Our main purpose here is to make you aware of these different approaches. It is beyond the scope of this text to do justice to a description of each model and to compare and contrast them. We will say, however, that there is little empirical evidence to attest to the effectiveness of treatment approaches that are based on searching for underlying subconscious causes of children's problems (Levitt, 1957, 1963). On the other hand, a growing body of research literature supports the effectiveness of the ecological and behavioral models, which analyze and modify the ways in which a child interacts with the environment.

For reviews of some of this research, see Burchard and Harig, 1976; Hobbs, 1982; Lovaas and Newsom, 1976; Montgomery and Van Fleet, 1978; and Walker, 1979.

Teaching Self-Management Skills

Recently an increasing amount of research has been conducted on teaching self-control or self-management skills to children, and the results of much of this work is encouraging (O'Leary & Dubey, 1979; Rosenbaum & Drabman, 1979). Self-management, when taught as a social skill in its own right, includes five elements: (1) self-selection and definition of the target behavior to be managed, (2) self-observation and recording of the target behavior, (3) specification of the procedures to be used to change the behavior, (4) implementation of those procedures, and (5) evaluation of the self-control effort (Heward, 1979; Sulzer-Azaroff & Mayer, 1977).

Many behavior disordered children feel they have little control over their lives. Things just seem to happen to them, and being disruptive is their means of reacting to a world that is inconsistent and frustrating. Children who learn self-management skills find out that they can have some control over their own behaviors and, as a result, over their environment.

When children learn to observe and record their own behavior, they can see for themselves the effects of various events on their performance. They can also be taught to influence certain events themselves. In one study, Drabman, Spitalnik, and O'Leary (1973) taught a group of eight 9- and 10-year-old emotionally disturbed children to evaluate and record their own social and academic "work" behaviors. Initially, they were rewarded with tokens when their own evaluations matched those of the teacher; then just teacher praise was given for accurate evaluations; finally, the students rated themselves and decided how many tokens they had earned during the day. A classroom token economy was operating during this study. Spot checks showed that the children evaluated themselves accurately and honestly. Disruptive behavior decreased, and academic achievement increased.

In another study, Marshall and Heward (1979) taught self-management skills to a group of eight boys in an institution for juvenile delinquents. The boys met as a group for one period each school day in a specially designed resource room. During this class period, the students were taught basic principles of behavior modification, such as defining a target behavior, recording behavior, graphing behavior, positive reinforcement, setting personal goals, and standards for behavior. During the program, each student selected a behavior he wanted to change and designed and conducted a self-management program to accomplish that goal. Students displayed their data and discussed and modified their projects as needed during the 4-week program. At the end of the study, seven of the eight students felt they had successfully changed their behavior with the methods they had learned.

Figure 5.5 shows the results of one student's self-management project. This student had trouble interacting with others. He felt that one reason for his problem was a tendency to "dip," or interrupt, other people's conversations (this apparently had been brought to his attention on numerous occasions). When he simply counted the target behavior during the baseline phase of the project, he "dipped" others an average of 15.9 times per day. When he started his intervention program, he decided to reward himself with a box of raisins at the end of each day in which he had eight or fewer "dips." During the project, he lowered this criterion twice, to six and then to four or fewer "dips" per day. His average number of dips throughout his self-management program was 4.6 per day. At the end of the 8 weeks, he felt his self-management project had been very successful and that he could use the skills learned in the program to change other behaviors.

Another student in the program stated that he wanted to take more responsibility for his life, especially in financial matters. The target behavior he chose was writing and mailing letters to potential employers to request employment applications and to arrange possible interview times. (He was scheduled to be released from the institution 6 weeks after the study.) Figure 5.6 shows the results of his self-management program. During a 15-day baseline he wrote no letters. He chose two candy bars as his reward for meeting the initial criterion he picked—one letter per day. On the eighth day of intervention, he decided to raise the criterion to two letters per day. The student wrote and mailed (as confirmed by a staff member who picked up the mail each day) a total of 21 letters during the 15 days of intervention.

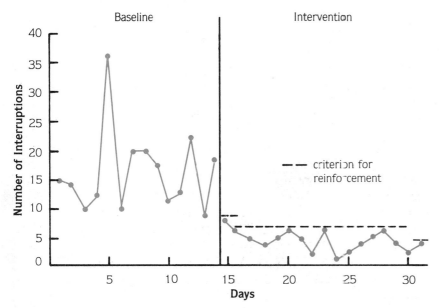

FIGURE 5.5

Sample self-management project: number of verbal interruptions during baseline and self-administered reward.

SOURCE: A. E. Marshall and W. L. Heward, "Teaching self-management to incarcerated youth," *Behavioral Disorders*, 1979, *4*, p. 222.

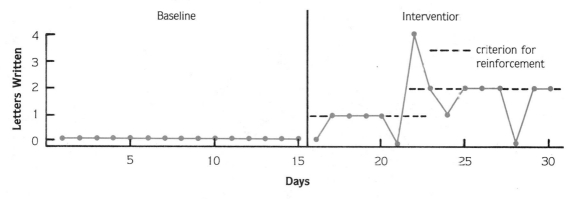

FIGURE 5.6

Self-management project: number of letters of application written during baseline and self-administered reward.

SOURCE: A. E Marshall & W. L. Heward, "Teaching self-management to incarcerated youth," *Behavioral Disorders*, 1979, *4*, p. 222.

Although a great deal more research is needed, teaching behavior disordered children and adolescents to have some control over their own lives by giving them the skills to make changes in their behavior seems to be a promising approach.

Teacher Skills

A continuing concern in the field of behavior disorders is teacher skills—the combination of professional competencies and personal characteristics that make the best teacher of emotionally disturbed children. It goes without saying that a teacher of disturbed children must be effective and creative, able to adapt curriculum materials and activities to the individual needs of the students. While behavior disordered children require the help of a specially trained teacher because of their behavior, the teaching of academic skills cannot be neglected. Most behavior disordered children are already achieving at a rate below their age-mates. Ignoring the three R's would only put them at a bigger disadvantage. Reading, writing, and arithmetic are as important to behavior disordered children as they are to any child who hopes to function normally in our society.

However, the primary task of the teacher of behavior disordered children is to teach improved social skills—helping the students replace their maladaptive behaviors with more socially appropriate responses. This is often a difficult and demanding task, particularly when the teacher seldom, if ever, knows all of the factors that affect the child's behavior. On top of this, there are sometimes a host of contributing factors over which the teacher can exert little or no control (for instance, the delinquent friends with whom the child associates after school). In spite of these limitations, it does little good to bemoan the child's past (which no one can alter), or to use all of the things in the child's environment that cannot be changed as an excuse for failing to help the child in the classroom. Special educators should focus attention and efforts on those aspects of the child's life that they can effectively control. Kauffman says it like this:

> The *focus* of the special educator's concern should be on those contributing factors *which can be altered by the teacher.* Factors over which the teacher has no control may indeed come into the picture in that they may determine how the child is approached initially. However, the teacher of disturbed children is called upon to begin working with children *after* behavior disorders have appeared. The special educator has two primary responsibilities: first, to make sure that he or she does no *further* disservice to the child; and second, to manipulate the child's present environment in order to cause more appropriate behavior to develop *in spite of* past and present circumstances that cannot be changed. The emphasis must be on the present and future, not the past, and on the classroom environment. It is certainly true that it may be profitable for teachers to extend their influence beyond the classroom, perhaps working with parents to improve the home environment or using community resources for the child's benefit. But talk of influence beyond the classroom, including such high-sounding phrases as *ecological management,* is patent nonsense until the teacher has demonstrated that

he or she can make the *classroom* environment productive of improved behavior. (1981a, p. 286)

Managing the classroom environment to change the behavior patterns of disturbed children successfully requires a teacher to be highly skilled in techniques used to change behavior. Procedures such as contingency contracting; ignoring disruptive behavior **(extinction)**; reinforcing any behavior the child does *except* the undesirable response, which must be weakened **(differential reinforcement of other behavior, or DRO)**; removing the child from all chances for reward for a brief time following an inappropriate behavior **(time-out)**; and requiring the child to make restitution beyond the damaging effects of his behavior, like making the child who takes another child's cookie return it plus one of his own (called **overcorrection**) are just some of the many behavior management skills that a competent teacher of behavior disordered children needs. And we have already stressed the importance of direct and daily measurement as the means to monitor and evaluate the effects of the teacher's efforts.

But the effective teacher of behavior disordered children must have skills that go beyond arranging environmental variables and measuring behavior. With behavior disordered children, the way in which assignments, expectations, and consequences for behavior are communicated to the child can be as important as the consequences themselves. Rothman (1977) stresses the importance of not arranging consequences that pit teacher against child in a "win-lose" situation, where the teacher gains status by dominating the child. Rather, a "win-win" arrangement should be strived for—when the child wins, the teacher wins. The teacher of behavior disordered children must, in addition to having instructional and behavior management skills, be able to establish healthy child-teacher relationships. Morse (1976) believes teachers must have two important affective characteristics in order to relate effectively and positively to emotionally disturbed children. He calls these traits *differential acceptance* and *empathetic relationship.*

Differential acceptance means the teacher can receive and witness frequent and often extreme acts of anger, hate, and aggression from children without responding similarly in return. This is much easier said than done. But the teacher of emotionally disturbed children must view disruptive behavior for what it is—behavior that reflects the child's past frustrations and conflict with himself and those around him—and try to help the child learn better ways of behaving. This concept should not be confused with approving of or condoning disturbed behavior—the child *must* learn that he is responding inappropriately. Instead, it means understanding without condemning.

Having an empathetic relationship with a child refers to a teacher's ability to recognize and understand the many nonverbal cues that often are the keys to understanding the individual needs of emotionally disturbed children.

Kauffman (1981a) stresses the importance of teachers communicating directly and honestly with behaviorally troubled children. Many of these children

Explanation of these behavior management techniques is beyond the scope of this book. For more information, see any of the following excellent works on the topic: Alberto and Troutman, 1982; Martin and Pear, 1983; Sulzer-Azaroff and Mayer, 1977; Walker, 1979.

have already had experience with supposedly "helpful" adults who have not been completely honest with them. Emotionally disturbed children can quickly detect someone who is not genuinely interested in their welfare.

The teacher of behavior disordered children must also realize that his or her actions serve as a powerful model for the children. Therefore, it is critical that the teacher's actions and attitudes be mature and demonstrate self-control. Hobbs (1966) describes the kind of person he feels would make a good teacher and model for disturbed children. In his view, and ours, the effective teacher is:

A decent adult; educated, well trained; able to give and receive affection, to live relaxed, and to be firm; a person with private resources for the nourishment and refreshment of his own life; not an itinerant worker but a professional through and through; a person with a sense of the significance of time; of the usefulness of today and the promise of tomorrow; a person of hope, quiet confidence, and joy; one who has committed himself to children and to the proposition that children who are emotionally disturbed can be helped by the process of re-education. (pp. 1106–7)

RE-EDUCATING TROUBLED CHILDREN

Pressley Ridge School in Pittsburgh is a private school licensed by the Pennsylvania Departments of Education and Mental Health to provide special education and treatment services for 120 emotionally disturbed children and youth. Students are referred to Pressley Ridge by local school districts following a determination that they cannot provide appropriate educational services. The most common referral problems include hyperactivity, lack of impulse control, verbal and physical aggression, social withdrawal, depression, truancy/runaway, and poor social interaction skills. In addition, though the students typically have normal or near normal intelligence, they are generally 3 to 4 years below grade level academically. A large number of students also come from multiproblem families where other children or parents are receiving, or in need of, special social, psychological, or educational services. Students range in age from 6 to 18, with a mean age of 14. Approximately 80% of the students are male and about 40% are black. Students typically attend the program for 1½ to 2 years. Upon discharge, the majority of students return to the public schools, with smaller percentages moving into vocational training programs, competitive employment, or other treatment programs.

The school's professional staff is composed of 20 teacher/counselors, assigned to 10 classrooms of 12 students each; 7 family and community liaison workers; specialists in the areas of speech and language, physical education, career education, and educational diagnostics; psychological and psychiatric consultants; 4 supervisors; and the program director.

The program's treatment model is based on a combination of Re-education philosophy (Hobbs, 1982) and behavior analysis principles (Sulzer-Azaroff & Mayer, 1977). Both approaches emphasize that behavior, both positive and negative, is learned. The program does not look within the child (that is, for personality disorders, disabilities, or other pathologies) for the causes of negative, troubling behaviors. Instead the focus is on the child's ecological system, which is seen as supporting the maladaptive behaviors. Treatment, then, focuses less on traditional psy-

Discussing progress toward each individual's goals.

chotherapy and medical intervention and more on restructuring the child's environment to teach and support new, more adaptive behavior. Specific treatment interventions are the result of carefully pinpointing the child's problem areas (academic, personal, and social), analyzing the relevant antecedent and consequent conditions that are maintaining the problem behaviors, and then restructuring the environment to facilitate the development of more adaptive, functional behaviors. In addition to each child's individual academic and treatment programs, the daily operation of every classroom consists of two major components designed to promote successful adjustment in the school, home, and community. The first is group process, which consists of frequent group interactions between students and teachers designed to teach students to (1) set reasonable goals for themselves and structure their environment to help achieve those goals, (2) identify and resolve interpersonal conflict, (3) realistically evaluate their own and others' behavior, and (4) cooperate and actively assist each other in goal achievement. The second component is a behavior management system that enables students to earn daily privileges by following a set of rules regarding appropriate personal and interpersonal behavior.

The following comments about the program were made by a teacher/counselor and a recent graduate from the program.

Our kids are lost, with no sense of direction. They believe that if a person cares about them, they will set no boundaries or limits. But after a few months here, they see that limits and boundaries are set to help them. We give the kids the sense that we really care about them and their development. Even if they leave under less than happy circumstances, we continue to care about them and they are always welcome to return. We use all the parts of our system—individualized academics, group process, point systems, individualized treatment interventions—to try to help meet each student's needs. One of the real strengths of Pressley Ridge is the cohesiveness of all the staff, the way we work together and support each other. This is what keeps us going even when the job seems just too hard to manage.

My name is Wendy and I am almost 19 years old. I came to Pressley Ridge School at the beginning of my junior year in high school. No other school would accept me because of my behavioral problems. I was kicked out of high school twice and no one seemed able to help me. I was sent to several schools and hospitals but instead of getting better I just got worse. I rebelled against all authority, was filled with hatred and depression, and even tried to kill myself. In September of 1981 I came to Pressley Ridge. The first 6 months I rebelled and caused a lot of trouble. I didn't like myself and in my mind they didn't like me either, so I wouldn't listen to them. But they didn't stop trying; they cared and wanted to help me. Finally I stopped fighting. I started listening and working to better myself. I made straight A's in all my subjects, including English, geometry, biology, and Spanish. I also talked and tried to work out some of my problems. I still had some setbacks, but I didn't stay down like I used to. I got up and tried again. Pressley Ridge has taught me not to give up but to keep on trying. They gave me self-confidence and courage to go out and make something of myself, with the understanding that they will always be there if I need them. I left Pressley Ridge in February 1983, with the hope that I'll be somebody important. I have just finished a course in college for emergency medical technicians and work full-time with an ambulance company as crew chief. My future goal is to be a physician's assistant. I only hope that future kids at Pressley Ridge will benefit from their help like I did.

1. There is no single, widely used definition of behavior disorders.

   a. However, most definitions agree that a child's behavior must differ significantly and over time from current social or cultural norms to be considered disordered.

   b. Teacher tolerance of children's behavior has a definite effect on whether a particular child will be identified as behavior disordered.

   c. We can describe behavior disorders in terms of their rate, duration, topography, and magnitude. A child's disordered behavior may differ from his peers' behavior on one or more of these four dimensions.

   d. Most behavior disordered children have a variety of problems in more than one area.

   e. Describing behavior disorders in terms of objective dimensions implies that we can deal with a specific, measurable problem rather than a "disturbance" or "illness." We can teach the child to act more appropriately.

2. As of yet, there is no widely accepted system for classifying behavior disorders.

   a. One system describes four clusters of behavior problems: conduct disorders, personality disorders, immaturity, and socialized delinquency.

   b. A second classification system describes six levels of learning competence, ranging from the attention level to the mastery level.

   c. Behavior disorders can also be described in terms of severity.

   d. Most behavior disordered children have mild to moderate problems that can be treated effectively in the regular classroom and at home.

   e. Severely disturbed children—often called *psychotic, schizophrenic,* or *autistic*—require intensive programming, usually in a more restrictive setting.

   f. Any system for classification should be based on classifying behaviors rather than children, so that the label can lead to specific strategies to replace the disordered behavior with an appropriate one.

3. Estimates of the number of children with behavior disorders range from .1% to 30%. The U.S. Office of Education estimates that 2% of all children are behavior disordered.

   a. Boys are much more likely to be labeled as behavior disordered than girls. Disturbed boys are likely to be aggressive and act out; girls are likely to be shy, anxious, and withdrawn.

   b. Most behavior disorders seem to appear in the middle grades and fall off beginning in junior high school.

   c. However, juvenile delinquency seems to increase sharply during the junior high years and after, although more younger children are committing more serious crimes than in the past.

   d. Only approximately .5% of all children are being served as severely disturbed.

4. On the average, behavior disordered children score somewhat below normal on IQ tests. Their school achievement is even lower than their scores would predict, and many have learning problems.

5. There are two general types of disordered behavior.
   a. Some children are overly aggressive and frequently act out. They seem to be in constant conflict.
   b. Many of these children become delinquents as adolescents.
   c. They also seem to have difficulty adjusting as adults, and may have children with problem behaviors.
   d. Other behavior disordered children are overly withdrawn. They do not have the social skills they need.
   e. For these children, the outlook if fairly good. They can often be taught the needed social skills and learn to be comfortable with other people.

6. Autistic children, who are often identified as toddlers, show six common characteristics: apparent sensory deficit, severe affect isolation, self-stimulation, tantrums and self-mutilation, muteness or psychotic speech, and behavior deficiencies.
   a. Although behavior modification techniques have helped control the destructive actions of many autistic children, even with intensive programs most autistic children remain functionally retarded.
   b. Although most autistic children will require a supervised environment throughout their lives, some autistic children are being successfully mainstreamed in regular classes. The outlook for autistic children is gradually getting better.

7. There are two groups of causes suggested for behavior disorders.
   a. Physiological factors, including inborn temperament, may predispose some children to have problems.
   b. Psychological factors, including parent-child interactions and specific events, are clearly important in the development of behavior disorders.
   c. Because of its central role in a child's life, the school can also be an important contributing factor to a behavior problem.
   d. We can never pinpoint an exact, lone cause of a child's behavior problems, so we must try to identify ways in which physiological factors, the family, and the school influence or contribute to a problem.

8. There are no reliable methods for sure identification of emotional disturbance.
   a. While aggressive children stand out, withdrawn children may go unnoticed.
   b. Several screening tests for emotional disturbance have been developed.
   c. Although they have been widely used for assessment of behavior problems, psychological tests and interviews have limited practical value.
   d. Direct and continuous observation and measurement of specific problem-behaviors, within the classroom, is becoming more and more pop-

ular. It is an assessment technique that indicates directly what intervention is needed.

9. There are at least six approaches to educating emotionally disturbed children: psychodynamic, biological, psychoeducational, behavioral, ecological, and humanistic.
   a. Although each approach has a distinct theoretical basis and suggests types of treatment, many teachers use techniques from more than one of the models.
   b. Research supports approaches that analyze and modify the ways a child interacts with his environment.

10. Teaching behavior disordered children to control their own behavior with self-management skills is one new, promising approach.

11. The primary goal of the teacher of behavior disordered children is to help the children replace inappropriate behaviors with more socially acceptable ones, by modifying those factors in the teacher's control.
    a. To be successful, the teacher must be skilled in changing behavior.
    b. The teacher must also be able to interact with these demanding children, to understand and accept them without condoning disturbed behavior.

FOR MORE INFORMATION

Journals

Behavioral Disorders. Published quarterly by the Council for Children with Behavior Disorders, the Council for Exceptional Children. Publishes research and discussion articles dealing with behavior disorders in children.

Behavior Therapy. Published five times a year by Academic Press for the Association for the Advancement of Behavior Therapy. Publishes research studies with emphasis on statistical results.

Journal of Applied Behavior Analysis. Published quarterly by the Society for the Experimental Analysis of Behavior, Lawrence, Kansas. Publishes original experimental studies demonstrating improvement of socially significant behaviors. Many studies involve behavior disordered children as subjects.

Books

Brown, G., McDowell, R. L., & Smith, J. (eds.). *Educating adolescents with behavior disorders.* Columbus, Ohio: Charles E. Merrill, 1981.

Hewett, F. M., & Taylor, F. D. *The emotionally disturbed child in the classroom: The orchestration of success,* 2d ed. Boston: Allyn & Bacon, 1980.

Hobbs, N. *The troubled and troubling child.* San Francisco: Jossey-Bass, 1982.

Kauffman, J. M. *Characteristics of children's behavior disorders,* 2d ed. Columbus, Ohio: Charles E. Merrill, 1981.

Kauffman, J. M., & Lewis, C. D. (eds.). *Teaching children with behavior disorders: Personal perspectives.* Columbus, Ohio: Charles E. Merrill, 1974.

McDowell, R. L., Adamson, G. W., & Wood, F. H. *Teaching emotionally disturbed children.* Boston: Little, Brown and Company, 1982.

Stephens, T. M. *Teaching social skills in the classroom.* Columbus, Ohio: Cedars Press, 1978.

Walker, H. M. *The acting-out child: Coping with classroom disruption.* Boston: Allyn & Bacon, 1979.

Organizations

American Association for the Advancement of Behavior Therapy, 420 Lexington Avenue, New York, N.Y. 10017. Includes psychologists, educational researchers, and educators (primarily at the university level).

Council for Children with Behavior Disorders, the Council for Exceptional Children, 1920 Association Drive, Reston, VA 22091. Includes teachers and teacher educators interested in behavior disorders.

6

Communication Disorders

I f you ever tried to go through an entire day without speaking, you surely would have a great deal of difficulty communicating with other people. You would probably feel frustrated when trying to express your own needs and feelings. By the end of the day, you might well feel exhausted and incapable of performing your typical daily routines.

Although relatively few people with communication disorders are completely unable to express themselves, an experience like that described above is helpful in highlighting some of the problems and frustrations faced by people who cannot communicate effectively or acceptably. Communication is central to human existence. Children who cannot express their thoughts and feelings in words or who cannot absorb information through listening and reading are virtually certain to encounter difficulties in school and the community. If communication disorders persist, it may be very hard for children to learn and to form satisfactory relationships with other people. But before proceeding to our discussion of specific communication disorders, we need to present a few brief definitions.

COMMUNICATION, LANGUAGE, AND SPEECH

Communication, in its broadest sense, is any interaction that transmits information. Both the sender and the receiver of information must participate in an exchange in order for true communication to exist. An infant cries, and her mother responds by giving her food. A dog barks, and its owner responds by opening the door to the house. A teacher smiles, and his student knows that an assignment has been done well. In each of these instances of communication, there is a *message,* a *sender,* and a *receiver.* It is not necessary for spoken or written words to be used in order for communication to take place.

Communication is not limited to spoken or written language. By pointing to the pictures taped to his tray, Charlie can communicate his wishes during mealtime.

Language is a system used by a group of people for giving meaning to sounds, words, gestures, and other symbols to enable them to communicate with each other. Bloom and Lahey (1978) have defined language as the "knowledge of a code for representing ideas about the world through a conventional system of arbitrary signals for communication" (p. 4). A child may learn to identify a familiar object, for example, by hearing the spoken word *tree,* by seeing the printed word *tree,* by viewing the sign language gesture for *tree,* or by a combination of these signals. When we hear, speak, read, or write with language, we transmit information.

The rules of all languages are essentially *arbitrary,* and spoken English is no exception. The arbitrariness of language means that there is usually no logical, natural, or required relationship between a set of sounds and the object, concept, or action it represents. The word *whale,* for example, brings to mind a large mammal that lives in the sea, but the sound of the word has no apparent connection with the creature. *Whale* is merely a symbol we use to symbolize this particular mammal. A small number of *onomatopoetic* words—such as *tinkle, buzz,* and *hiss*—are considered to "sound like" what they represent, but most English words have no such relationship with what they represent.

There are several different kinds of elements used to convey meaning in language. The English language uses 36 different sound elements, called **phonemes.** Only the initial phoneme prevents the words *pear* and *bear* from being identical, for example; yet in one case we think of a fruit and in the other a large animal. The smallest elements of language that carry meaning are called **morphemes.** The word *baseball,* for example, consists of two morphemes, "base" and "ball." The "-s" added to make *baseballs* would be a third morpheme, because it changes the meaning.

There are also several kinds of language rules. Phonological rules describe how sounds in a language can be combined. Morphological rules are concerned with how morphemes can be strung together. Morphology is part of **syntax**, the system or rules governing the meaningful arrangement of words. For example, *help my chicken eat* conveys a meaning much different from *help eat my chicken*. Finally, rules of **semantics** relate phonology and syntax to meaning; that is, semantics describes how people use language to convey meaning.

One model of language, developed by Bloom and Lahey (1978), describes three components of language—form, content, and use—which make up an integrated system. The form of the language connects sound and meaning. The content is based on knowledge of the world and our feelings about it. Thus the form of language allows us to express content. The use of language refers to the ways that language functions in communication. It includes both our purposes in communicating and the way in which we choose a specific form to express a particular message.

This model can be helpful in understanding and treating a child's communication disorder.

Speech is a complex motor behavior that is the vocal response mode of language (Schiefelbusch & McCormick, 1981). Human beings have the unique ability to talk to each other, as they are able to use their breath, muscles, larynx, lips, tongue, teeth, and other body parts to make sounds in very precise patterns. Other people hear these sounds and interpret them as words. Most languages start out in oral form, developed by people speaking to each other. When we read and write, we are simply using oral language in a different form.

It is possible that certain species of animals have languages, but we do not yet know that.

Despite the complexity of our language system, with its phonemes, morphemes, and syntax, most children learn to understand language and then to speak during the first few years of life, without any formal instruction. They integrate form, content, and use to communicate. The process of learning language is a remarkable one, one that is not fully understood. As Leonard (1982) points out, an understanding of how young, normally developing children acquire language is helpful to the teacher or specialist who works with children who have delayed or disordered communication. A knowledge of normal language development can help the specialist determine whether a particular child is simply developing language at a slower-than-normal rate, or whether the child shows an abnormal pattern of language development.

Figure 6.1 shows the normal speech organs.

Language Development

We will present, in some detail, a summary of normal language development. However, the ages at which a "normal" child acquires certain speech and language skills are not rigid and inflexible. Children's abilities and early environments vary widely, and all these factors affect communication. Nevertheless, most investigators agree that most children follow a relatively predictable sequence in their development of speech and language.

Children who cannot hear have a special set of problems in learning language. See chapter 7.

Birth to 6 Months

The infant first communicates by crying, which involves breath, muscles, and vocal chords. She soon learns that her crying leads to her getting the attention that she needs. Within a few months, the baby develops different types of

Phonemes are represented by letters or other symbols between slashes. For example, the phoneme /ŋ/ represents the "ng" sound in "sing"; /i/ represents the "long e" as in "see."

crying—a parent can usually tell from the baby's cry whether the child is wet, tired, or hungry. Babies also make *comfort sounds*—coos, gurgles, and sighs—which contain some vowels and consonants. The comfort sounds develop into *babbling,* sounds that in the beginning are apparently made for the enjoyment of feeling and hearing them. Vowel sounds, such as /i/(ee) and /ə/(uh) are produced earlier than consonants, such as /m/, /b/, and /f/. At this stage the infant does not attach meaning to the words she hears from others, but she may react differently to loud and soft voices. She turns her eyes and head in the direction of a sound.

6 to 12 Months

Before the first year, baby develops **inflection;** her voice rises and falls. She may seem to be giving you a command, asking a question, or expressing surprise. She appears to understand certain words at this stage. She may respond appropriately to "no," "bye-bye," or her own name, and may perform an action, such as "clap your hands," when told to. When parents say simple sounds and words, such as "mama," the baby will repeat them.

12 to 18 Months

By age 1½, most children have learned to say several words with appropriate meaning (although their pronunciation is far from perfect). The baby may say "tup" when you point to a cup, or "goggie" when she sees a dog. She will probably be able to tell you what she wants by pointing, and perhaps saying a word or two. She will respond to simple commands such as "give me the cup" and "open your mouth."

18 to 24 Months

Most children go through a stage of echolalia, in which they simply repeat, or echo, the speech they hear. If father says, "Do you want some milk?" the baby will repeat "Want some milk?" Echolalia is a normal phase of language development, and most children outgrow it by about age 2½. There is a great spurt in the acquisition and use of speech during this stage. They usually begin to combine words into short sentences, such as "Daddy bye-bye" and "Want cookie." The child's receptive vocabulary—the words she understands—grows even more rapidly. By age 2 she may understand over 1,000 words. She will understand such concepts as "soon" and "later," and will make more subtle differences between objects, such as cats and dogs, and knives, forks, and spoons.

2 to 3 Years

The 2-year-old child *talks.* She can say sentences like "I won't tell you," and can ask questions like "Where my daddy go?" She may have a vocabulary of up to

900 different words, averaging three to four words per sentence (Weiss & Lillywhite, 1976). She is learning how to participate in conversations with the people around her. She can identify colors, use plurals, and tell simple stories about her experiences. She is able to follow compound commands such as "Pick up the doll and bring it to me." The 2-year-old child uses most of the vowel sounds and some consonant sounds correctly. The earliest consonant sounds learned are generally /p/, /b/, and /m/.

3 to 4 Years

The normal 3-year-old has lots to say, speaks rapidly, and asks many questions to obtain information. Her sentences are longer and more varied: "Cindy's playing in water"; "Mommy went to work"; "The cat is hungry." She is able to use speech to request, protest, agree, and make jokes. The 3- to 4-year-old child can understand children's stories, grasp such concepts as *funny, bigger,* and *secret,* and complete simple analogies, such as "In the daytime it is light; at night it is _____." She typically substitutes certain sounds, such as saying "baf" for "bath," or "yike" for "like." Many 3-year-olds repeat sounds or words ("b-b-ball," "l-l-little"). Their repetitions and hesitations are normal and do not indicate that the child will develop a habit of stuttering.

We will discuss true stuttering later in this chapter.

4 to 5 Years

By age 4, children have an average vocabulary of over 1,500 words and use sentences averaging five words in length (Leonard, 1982). They are generally able to make themselves understood, even to strangers. The 4-year-old begins to show the ability to modify her speech according to the listener; for example, she will use longer and more complex sentences when talking to her mother than when she is addressing a baby or a doll. She can define words like *hat, stove,* and *policeman* and can ask questions like "How did you do that?" or "Who made this?" She uses conjunctions such as *if, when,* and *because.* She can recite poems and sing songs from memory. Children at this age may say "I almost fell" or "Let's do something else." They may still have difficulty with such consonant sounds as /r/, /s/, and /z/, or with blends like "tr," "gl," "sk," and "str."

After 5 Years

Language continues to develop steadily, though less dramatically, after age 5. The child acquires more vocabulary and is able to use more sophisticated grammatical forms. A 6-year-old child, in fact, normally uses most of the complex forms of adult English. Some of the consonant sounds and blends, however, are not mastered until age 7 or 8. By the time a child enters first grade, his grammar and speech patterns usually match those of his family, neighborhood, and region. A 6-year-old from rural Alabama will have different pronunciation and rhythms from a 6-year-old who lives in Boston.

DEFINING COMMUNICATION DISORDERS: SPEECH AND LANGUAGE

Specific speech and language disorders are discussed later in this chapter.

As we have said, the development of speech and language is a highly individual process. No child conforms exactly to precise developmental norms; some are advanced, some are delayed, and some acquire language in an unusual sequence. Unfortunately, some children deviate from the normal to such an extent that they have serious difficulties in learning and in interpersonal relations. People who are not able to make themselves understood, or who cannot comprehend ideas that are spoken to them by others, are likely to be greatly handicapped in virtually all aspects of education and adjustment. They will need specialized help. These kinds of problems, called *communication disorders*, occur frequently among children in regular and special education classes.

Most specialists in the field of communication disorders make a distinction between *speech impairments* and *language disorders*. Children with impaired *speech* have difficulty producing sounds properly, maintaining an appropriate flow or rhythm in speech, or using the voice effectively. Thus speech impairments are impairments in language form. Children with impaired language have problems in understanding or expressing the symbols and rules people use to communicate with each other. A specific child can have difficulty with language form, content, and/or use. Some people find it helpful to view speech as the means by which language is most often conveyed. Speech and language are obviously closely related to each other. A child may have either a speech impairment or a language disorder, or both.

Speech Impairments

A child's speech is considered to be impaired if it is unintelligible, abuses the speech mechanism, or is culturally or personally unsatisfactory (Perkins, 1977). If a child's speech deviates so greatly from the speech of other people that it:

1. Draws unfavorable attention to itself;
2. Interferes with communication; or
3. Causes the speaker to have difficulty in social relationships,

then the child is considered to have a speech impairment and will require professional help to improve his or her communication (Van Riper, 1978). A general goal is to have the child speak clearly and pleasantly, so that the listener's attention will be drawn to *what* the child is saying, rather than *how* it is being said.

It is always important to keep the speaker's age, education, and cultural background in mind when determining whether or not "impaired speech" is present. A 4-year-old girl who says "Pwease weave the woom" would not be considered to have a speech impairment, but a 40-year-old woman would surely draw attention to herself by using that pronunciation, since it differs markedly

EXCEPTIONAL CHILDREN

These children receive daily practice on difficult consonant sounds and blends.

from the speech of most adults. A traveler unable to articulate the /l/ sound would not be clearly understood in trying to buy a bus ticket to Lake Charles, Louisiana. A male high school student with an extremely high-pitched voice might be reluctant to speak in class for fear of being mimicked and ridiculed by his classmates.

Language Disorders

Some children have serious difficulties in understanding language or in expressing themselves through language. A child with a *receptive* language disorder may be unable to learn the days of the week in proper order, or may find it impossible to follow a sequence of commands, such as "Pick up the paint brushes, wash them in the sink, and then put them on a paper towel to dry." A child with an *expressive* language disorder may have a limited vocabulary for her age, be confused about the order of sounds or words ("hostipal," "aminal," "wipe shield winders"), and use tenses and plurals incorrectly ("Them throwed a balls"). Children with difficulty in expressive language may or may not also have difficulty in receptive language. For instance, a child may be able to count out six pennies when asked and shown the symbol "6" but may not be able to say the word "six" when shown the symbol. In that case, the child has an expressive difficulty while her receptive language is adequate. She may or may not have other disorders of speech or hearing.

Children with serious language disorders are likely to have problems in school and social development. It is often difficult to detect children with language disorders; their performance may lead people to mistakenly label them as mentally retarded, hearing impaired, or emotionally disturbed, when in fact these descriptions are not appropriate.

Language is so important in academic performance that it can be impossible to differentiate a learning disability from a language disorder. Again, emphasis should be placed on remediating children's skill deficits rather than on labeling them.

A child may also be markedly *delayed* in language development. Even though a relatively wide range of language patterns and age milestones is considered "normal," some children do not acquire speech or the ability to understand language until much later than would be normally expected. A 6-year-old child who cannot tell you what a key is used for or who is not able to use such pronouns as *I, you,* and *me* would be regarded as having a serious delay in language development. In rare cases, children who have no other impairment may even fail to speak at all.

Speech and Language Differences

The way children speak reflects their culture. Before entering school, children have learned patterns of speech and language appropriate to their families and neighborhoods. Sometimes, children's speech and language differs significantly from the standard English used by their teachers. A **dialect** such as black English or a Hispanic accent should *not* be considered a communication disorder. A child should be referred to a communication disorders specialist only if he or she is suspected of having impaired speech or language in addition to any "natural" variations which are appropriate to the cultural group. Problems can arise in the classroom if the teacher does not accept the natural communication differences among children and mistakenly assumes that a speech or language impairment is present (Bankson, 1982; Liebergott, Favors, von Hippel, & Needleman, 1978).

For additional information on improving communication with children from culturally diverse backgrounds, see chapter 12.

PREVALENCE

Estimates of the prevalence of communication disorders in children vary widely. As Matthews (1982) points out, reliable figures are hard to come by, since investigators often use different definitions of communication disorders and study different populations. One frequently cited effort to determine the prevalence of communication disorders estimated that 5% of school-age children in the United States have speech impairments severe enough to warrant special attention (ASHA Committee, 1952). Working with the most recent estimate from the National Health Interview Survey (HIS), Fein has said that "it may be reasonable to conclude that speech impairment is present in 4.2% of the [school-aged] population" (1983, p. 37). This represents a very large population when compared to other categories of exceptional children. It would mean that between 2 and 3 million American children have communication disorders. The federal government reported that 958,590 children, or 2.3% of the school-age population received special education services for speech impairments during the 1981–82 school year.

The major types of communication disorders will be discussed in the next section of this chapter.

Some figures are available on the incidence and prevalence of specific types of communication disorders. In the recent past, **articulation** disorders, which involve difficulties in producing speech sounds accurately, were by far the most common type of communication problem found in children. In 1961 the

American Speech-Language-Hearing Association estimated that 80% of the school-age population with communication disorders had articulation disorders. However, changing emphasis and improved assessment techniques have led to changes in the relative number of children treated for speech and language disorders. A 1982 ASHA survey indicated that "54% of speech-language pathologists' clients were primarily exhibiting language impairments" (cited in Fein, 1983, p. 37). The speech problems of hearing impaired persons are also significant; the 1971 HIS found that 15.2% of the speech impaired population also had hearing impairments (National Center for Health Statistics, 1975).

A study of public school students in the 1968–69 school year showed estimated prevalence rates of 3% for voice disorders, 1.9% for articulation disorders, and .8% for stuttering (Hull, Mielke, Willeford, & Timmons, 1976). We also know that approximately twice as many boys as girls have speech impairments (National Center for Health Statistics, 1981).

While the prevalence of communication disorders appears rather high, the percentage of children with speech and language disorders decreases significantly from the earlier to the later school grades. For example, a study cited by Kirk and Gallagher (1983) found that about 7% of all first-grade boys were reported as having "extreme articulation deviations," but only 1% of third-grade boys and .5% of twelfth-grade boys fell into that category. The prevalence of stuttering and voice disorders also declines as children mature. The largest part of the speech/language impaired population is composed of young children with articulation problems. Many of these disorders, while significant enough to merit professional attention, are apparently not severe enough to persist into adulthood. They respond favorably to intervention or maturation.

TYPES AND CAUSES OF COMMUNICATION DISORDERS

There are many recognized types of communication disorders and numerous possible causes. Speech disorders may be *organic,* indicating that they are caused by physical factors or abnormalities, such as **cleft palate**, absence of teeth, paralysis of the speech muscles, or enlarged adenoids. Organic speech disorders may occur along with other handicapping conditions. For example, children with **cerebral palsy,** impaired hearing, and delayed mental development frequently have speech problems as well.

Most communication disorders, however, are not considered organic, but are classified as *functional.* They cannot be ascribed to a specific physical condition; their origin is not clearly known. As Winitz (1977) points out, decades of research on the causes of many speech and language impairments have produced only uncertainty. A child's surroundings provide many opportunities for him to learn appropriate and inappropriate communication skills; some specialists believe that functional communication disorders derive mainly from environmental influences. It is also possible that some speech impairments are caused by disturbances in the motor control system that we do not fully understand.

Regardless of whether a communication disorder is considered organic or functional, a child who has speech or language which is substantially different from that of others in his or her age and cultural group will require special training procedures to correct or improve the impairment.

Articulation Disorders

Figure 6.1 shows the normal speech organs.

As we have noted, articulation disorders are the type of speech impairment most prevalent among school-age children. The correct articulation, or utterance, of speech sounds, requires us to activate a complicated system of muscles, nerves, and organs. Haycock (1933), who compiled a classic manual on teaching speech, describes how the speech organs are manipulated into a variety of shapes and patterns, how the breath and voice must be "molded to form words." For example, here is Haycock's description of how the /v/ sound is correctly produced:

> The lower lip must be drawn upwards and slightly inwards, so that the upper front teeth rest lightly on the lip. Breath must be freely emitted between the teeth and over the lower lip, and voice must be added to the breath.

Should any part of this process function imperfectly, the child will have difficulty articulating the /v/. Clearly, in such a complicated process, there are many different types of possible errors.

Children may *omit* certain sounds, as in saying "cool" for "school" or "pos" for "post." Consonants are frequently dropped from the ends of words. Most of us leave out sounds at times, but an extensive omission problem can make speech impossible to understand.

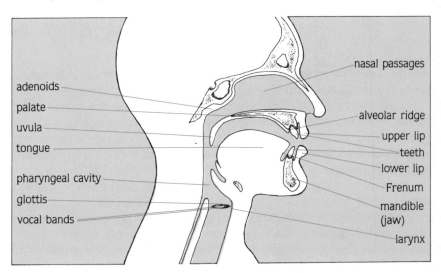

FIGURE 6.1
The normal speech organs.

EXCEPTIONAL CHILDREN

Correct articulation of each sound requires precise movement and coordination of numerous body parts.

Children may *substitute* one sound for another, as in saying "train" for "crane" or "doze" for "those." Children with this problem are often certain they have said the correct word and may resist correction. Substitution of sounds can cause considerable confusion for the listener.

Children may *distort* certain speech sounds, while attempting to produce them accurately. The /s/ sound, for example, is relatively difficult to produce; children may produce the word "sleep" as "schleep," "zleep," or "thleep." Some speakers have a lisp; others a whistling /s/. Distortions can cause misunderstanding, though parents and teachers often become accustomed to a child's use of them.

Children may also *add* extra sounds, making comprehension difficult. They may say "buhrown" for "brown," or "hamber" for "hammer."

Like all communication disorders, articulation problems vary in the degree of severity. Many children have *mild* or *moderate* articulation disorders. It is usually possible to understand their speech, but they may mispronounce certain sounds or use immature speech, like that of younger children. These problems often disappear as the child matures. If a mild or moderate articulation problem does not seem to be improving over an extended period, or if it appears to have a negative effect on the child's interaction with others, referral to a communication disorders specialist may be indicated.

A *severe* articulation disorder is present when a child pronounces many sounds so poorly that his or her speech is unintelligible most of the time. Even the child's parents, teachers, and peers cannot easily understand him. As Liebergott and colleagues (1978) point out, the child with a severe articulation disorder may "chatter away and sound as though he or she is talking gibberish" (p. 17). He may say, "Yeh me yuh a wido" instead of "Let me look out the window," or perhaps "Do foop i dood" for "That soup is good." It is easy to appreciate that articulation disorders, particularly if severe, can cause serious problems in a child's learning and adjustment.

Voice Disorders

Voice disorders occur when the quality, loudness, or pitch of the voice is inappropriate or abnormal. They are far less common in children than in adults. Considering how often some children shout and yell without any apparent harm to their voices, it is evident that the vocal cords can withstand heavy use (Renfrew, 1972). In some cases, however, a child's voice may be difficult to understand or may be considered unpleasant. As Moore (1982) observes, a person's voice may be considered disordered if it differs markedly from what is customary in the voices of others of the same age, sex, or cultural background. Moore uses the term *dysphonia* to describe any condition of poor or unpleasant voice quality, and notes that a voice—whether good, poor, or in between—is closely identified with the person who uses it.

The voice disorders most frequently found among children of school age are *hoarseness*, *breathiness*, and *nasality*. An unusually *hoarse* voice sounds husky and strained most of the time. It can have organic causes, such as growths or irritations on the vocal cords, but hoarseness is most frequently due to chronic "vocal abuse" such as yelling, imitating noises, or habitually talking while under tension. A *breathy* voice is unpleasant because it is low in volume and fails to make adequate use of the vocal cords. *Nasality* results if too many sounds come out through the air passages of the nose (hypernasality), or if there is not enough resonance of the nasal passages *(denasality)*. The hypernasal speaker may be perceived as "talking through her nose" or having an unpleasant "twang," while the denasal speaker may sound as though he constantly has a "cold" or a "stuffed nose," even when he does not. The causes of nasality, like other voice disorders, may be either organic (cleft palate, swollen nasal tissues) or functional (perhaps resulting from learned behaviors or behavior problems).

Fluency Disorders

Normal speech makes use of rhythm and timing. Words and phrases flow easily, with certain variations in speed, stress, and appropriate pauses. **Fluency** disorders interrupt the natural, smooth flow of speech with inappropriate pauses, hesitations, or repetitions. One type of fluency disorder is known as *cluttering*, a condition in which speech is very rapid and clipped, to the point of unintelligibility. The best known—and probably least understood—fluency disorder, however, is **stuttering.** This condition is marked by "rapid-fire repetitions of consonant or vowel sounds, especially at the beginning of words; and complete verbal blocks" (Jonas, 1976). The cause of stuttering remains unknown, though the condition has been studied extensively, with some interesting results. Stuttering is far more common among males than among females. It occurs more frequently among twins. The prevalence of stuttering is the same in all Western countries: no matter what language is spoken, about 1% of the population has a stuttering problem. Jonas (1976) observes that stuttering typically first appears between the ages of 3 and 5, "*after* the child has already made great strides toward fluency. . . . The trouble comes later, just as speech is becoming less of a feat and more of a habit."

All children experience some *disfluencies*—repetitions and interruptions—in the course of developing normal speech patterns. It is important not to over-react to children's disfluencies and insist upon "perfect" speech; some specialists believe that stuttering can be caused by pressures placed on the child when parents and teachers react to normal hesitations and repetitions by labeling the child a "stutterer." Lingwell (1982) explains that stuttering is not just one specific disorder, but many, which may be why there are several conflicting theories about its cause. According to Lingwell, stuttering may be caused by neurological, psychological, or allergic factors, or may result from rhythmic control or faulty learning patterns.

Stuttering is situational; that is, it appears to be related to the setting or circumstances of speech. A child may be likely to stutter when talking to the people whose opinions matter most to him—such as parents and teachers—in situations like being called upon to speak in front of the class. Most people who stutter are fluent about 95% of the time; a child with a fluency disorder may not stutter at all when singing, talking to his pet dog, or reciting a poem in unison with others. The reactions and expectations of parents, teachers, and peers clearly have an important effect upon any child's personal and communicative development.

Several researchers and clinicians have explored the effects of social pressures on stuttering, by examining its incidence in cultures other than our own. Jonas (1976) derives insights from a comparison of American Indian tribes. He observes that certain tribes, such as the Utes and the Bannocks of the Rocky Mountain region, have an unusually permissive attitude toward children's speech and have virtually no stuttering problems. Other tribes, such as the Cowichans of the Pacific Northwest, are highly competitive, expecting children to take part in complicated rituals at a young age, and have a high incidence of stuttering. Jonas suggests that the reason that Ute and Bannock children do not stutter may be that no one ever tries to "make them speak correctly." But he acknowledges that this theory fails to explain "why in so many other cultures some children of nagging parents turn into stutterers while others do not" (Jonas, 1976, p. 14). Van Riper (1972) reflects upon the importance of cultural attitudes toward stuttering in the following passage:

Once, on Fiji in the South Pacific, we found a whole family of stutterers. As our guide and translator phrased it: "Mama kaka; papa kaka; and kaka, kaka, kaka, kaka." All six persons in that family showed marked repetitions and prolongations in their speech; but they were happy people, not at all troubled by their stuttering. It was just the way they talked. We could not help but contrast their attitudes and the simplicity of their stuttering with those which would have been shown by a similar family in our own land, where the pace of living is so much faster, where defective communication is rejected, where stutterers get penalized all their lives. To possess a marked speech disorder in our society is almost as handicapping as to be a physical cripple in a nomadic tribe that exists by hunting. (p. 4)

Language Disorders

Language disorders are usually classified as either *receptive* or *expressive*. A receptive language disorder interferes with the understanding of language. The child, for example, may be unable to comprehend spoken sentences or to follow a sequence of directions. An expressive language disorder interferes with the production of language. The child may have a very limited vocabulary, may use incorrect words and phrases, or may not even speak at all, but communicate through gestures. A child may have good receptive language when an expressive disorder is present, or may have both expressive and receptive disorders in combination.

Chaney and Frodyma (1982) list several factors that can contribute to language disorders in children, including:

1. Cognitive limitations or retardation
2. Environmental deprivation
3. Hearing impairments
4. Emotional deprivation or behavior disorders
5. Structural abnormalities of the speech mechanism

Some professionals feel that autism (discussed in chapter 5 on behavior disorders) is best understood as an extreme language disorder.

Environmental influences are thought to play an important part in delayed, disordered, or absent language. Some children are rewarded for their efforts at communication, while others, unfortunately, are punished for talking, gesturing, or otherwise attempting to communicate. A child who has little stimulation at home and has few chances to speak, listen, explore, and interact with others will probably have little motivation for communication and may well develop disordered patterns of language. Children who have had little exposure to words and experiences may need the teacher's help in encouraging communication. Active participation in experiences gives children the opportunity to learn and use appropriate vocabulary.

Some severe disorders in expressive and receptive language result from brain damage. The term *aphasia* is frequently used to describe a "breakdown in the ability to formulate, or to retrieve, and to decode the arbitrary symbols of language" (Holland & Reinmuth, 1982, p. 428). Aphasia is one of the most prevalent causes of language disorders in adults, most often occurring suddenly, following a stroke. However, aphasia may also be **congenital** or caused by a head injury and occur in children. Most people with aphasia have expressive difficulties, and may be partially or totally unable to produce speech, writing, or other forms of communication. Receptive aphasia, which affects a person's comprehension of language, can also occur.

A congenital disorder is one that is present at birth.

DEVELOPMENT OF THE FIELD OF COMMUNICATION DISORDERS

Although there have always been people with speech and language disorders, special education and treatment for this population are relatively recent developments. Hewett and Forness (1977) report that the first special class for "speech defective" children in the U.S. was established in New York in 1908. Special education for other groups of children, including the deaf, the blind, and the mentally retarded, was begun much earlier, which suggests that communication disorders have historically been considered less severe and less easily recognized than other disabilities.

During the 19th century, some treatment was provided for people with communication disorders at clinics and hospitals. The earliest specialists were college and university professors who, in the course of their study of normal speech processes, became interested in people who had irregular patterns of speech, particularly stuttering and articulation disorders. While American therapists concentrated primarily on the "correction" of speech defects, European specialists (largely physicians) had developed a considerable body of scientific knowledge about communication disorders prior to World War II (Boone, 1977).

The postwar years saw a proliferation of clinical services and research efforts. Many speech pathologists became especially interested in the rehabilitation of military personnel who had developed communication disorders because of damage to the brain or to the physical speech mechanisms. Speech and hearing clinics and centers were established in many cities, often operating in cooperation with hospitals or universities.

In recent years, there has been a notable expansion of services to children with speech and language disorders in the regular public schools. Professionals who provide remedial services to children with communication disorders are today usually called *speech-language pathologists* or *communication disorders specialists*, rather than "speech therapists." In 1978, the name of the major professional organization involved with communication disorders was changed to the "American Speech-Language-Hearing Association" (though it is still abbreviated as ASHA). These changes in terminology reflect a current awareness of the interrelationships among speech, language, and other aspects of learning, communication, and behavior. Speech is no longer viewed as a narrow specialty concerned with disorders to be "corrected" in isolation. Increasingly, speech-language pathologists who work in school settings now function as team members who are concerned with the overall education and development of children. As Matthews (1982) observes, there is a trend for remedial procedures to be carried out in the regular classroom, rather than in a special "speech room," and the speech-language pathologist often provides training and consultation for the child's regular teacher, who may do much of the direct work with a child who has communication disorders.

ASSESSMENT AND EVALUATION

In assessing or diagnosing a child who is suspected of having a communication disorder, the specialist seeks to determine whether or not the communication behaviors are abnormal; the ways, if any, in which these behaviors are abnormal; and whether the abnormalities can be treated (Dickson, 1974). Information obtained during the assessment process is used in planning the treatment or remediation program.

Most professional speech and language assessments begin with the collection of "case history" information from the child and the parent. This typically involves completing a biographical form which includes such diverse information as the child's birth and developmental history, illnesses, medications taken, scores on achievement and intelligence tests, and adjustment to school. The parent may be asked when the child first crawled, walked, and uttered words. Social skills, such as whether the child plays readily with other children, may also be considered.

The specialist examines the child's mouth carefully, noting whether there are any irregularities in the tongue, lips, teeth, palate, or other structures that may affect speech production. If the child has an organic speech problem, the specialist refers the child for possible medical intervention. Testing procedures will vary according to the type of functional disorder suspected. Often the specialist conducts broad screenings to detect areas of concern and then moves to more detailed testing in those areas. Bryant (1970) suggests the following general components of an evaluation to detect communication disorders.

1. Articulation test. The speech errors the child is making are assessed. A record will be kept of the sounds that are defective, how they are being mispronounced, and the number of errors made. Examples of published tests include the Templin-Darley Test of Articulation (Templin & Darley, 1969) and the Test of Minimal Articulation Competence (Secord, 1981).
2. Hearing test. Hearing is generally tested to determine if a hearing problem is the cause of the speech disorder.
3. Auditory discrimination test. This test is given to determine if the child is hearing sounds correctly. If he is unable to recognize the specific characteristics of a given sound, he will not have a good model to imitate. The Wepman Auditory Discrimination Test (Wepman, 1958) and the Templin Speech Sound Discrimination Test (Templin, 1957) are two examples.

EXCEPTIONAL CHILDREN

ASSESSING ARTICULATION

Picture a charming youngster, probably missing some teeth, who's bright and alert but speaks so poorly that only his parents can understand him. The child's problem is articulation. His parents and teachers have a different problem—determining whether his poor articulation requires treatment or is simply something he will outgrow.

To assess articulation, speech-language pathologists administer articulation inventories, such as the Test of Minimal Articulation Competence (T-MAC). T-MAC comes in versions for different age groups and for screening as well as detailed assessment. The T-MAC inventory assesses production of 24 consonants, 21 consonant blends, 12 vowels, and 8 diphthongs (vowel combinations). Because consonants appear before, after, or between vowels, each is assessed in each position in which it appears.

To administer the picture test (used with young children), the clinician sits across from a child and sets up the T-MAC easel, with pictures facing the child and words facing the clinician. The clinician says, "I'm going to show you some pictures, and I want you to tell me what you see." Sometimes prompts are given. For example, to evoke "television," the clinician may ask, "What's the long name?" As the child says each word, the clinician scores the response on the T-MAC record form. They go through all the sounds.

After the picture test, the clinician determines whether the child can produce those phonemes on which he made errors in all positions after hearing those sounds. That is, the clinician says the word and asks the child to repeat it. If the child cannot produce the phoneme, the clinician says the sound alone and asks the child to repeat that. Again, results are recorded on the record form.

Now the clinician knows which sounds the child can produce under what conditions. But the question of intervention is still not answered. The responses must be evaluated in terms of the importance of the error phonemes and the child's age. That is, we cannot simply say. "Anyone who misses six or more sounds needs treatment." Some sounds are used much more frequently than others, so a child who misarticulates five of those may be much less intelligible than one who errs on seven infrequent phonemes. Furthermore, some sounds develop earlier than others. For instance, 90% of children can produce 11 vowel sounds by age 3, but we do not find the 12th in 90% of children until age 6.

To bring all this information together, T-MAC uses a Developmental Articulation Index. The clinician scores each phoneme, based on the child's specific response and a frequency weight that is provided. She then adds the scores of only those phonemes a child that age should be able to produce. The clinician locates the total score on an age-level chart that indicates the child's articulation level, which can range from a profound problem to normal development.

The clinician now knows where the child stands in terms of *minimal* developmental expectations. What's more, by looking at the responses, the clinician can create a plan for treating the errors according to their severity and the importance of the sound. An inventory like T-MAC should not be used alone, however. Instead, it should be part of a multifactored assessment, usually the first step in evaluating a child's speech.

Drawn from Wayne Secord, *T-MAC: Test of minimal articulation competence.* Columbus, Ohio: Charles E. Merrill Publishing Company, 1981. Used with permission.

4. Language development test. This is administered to help determine the amount of vocabulary the child has acquired, because vocabulary is generally a good indication of intelligence. Frequently used tests include the Peabody Picture Vocabulary Test (Dunn, 1965) and the Carrow Elicited Language Inventory (Carrow, 1974).

A fifth evaluation used more and more frequently is an overall *language test,* which assesses the child's understanding and production of language structures (such as important syntactical elements like conjunctions showing causal relationships). An example is the Clinical Evaluation of Language Functions (Semel & Wiig, 1980).

An important part of any evaluation procedure is obtaining a *language sample,* an accurate example of the quantity and quality of the child's expressive speech and language. Some speech-language pathologists use structured tasks to elicit language samples; they may, for example, ask a child to describe pictures or objects, to tell a story, or to answer "who, what, where, and when" questions. According to a recent survey of specialists who work with children, however, *informal conversation* is the procedure most often used to obtain language samples (Atkins & Cartwright, 1982). It is felt that the child's language sample will be more representative if the examiner uses natural conversation rather than using structured activities.

Behavioral observation is becoming increasingly important in the assessment of communication disorders. As Schiefelbusch and McCormick (1981) observe, objective recording of children's language competence in social contexts has added much to our knowledge of language acquisition. It is imperative that the observer have experience in reliably recording speech and language and that the child's behavior be sampled across various settings.

After the assessment procedures have been completed, the speech-language pathologist reviews the results of the case history, formal and informal tests, language samples, and behavioral observations. Recommendations are then made to teachers or parents about the most effective approaches to the speech or language impairment. Today, communication disorders specialists in many school districts conduct regular speech and language screening programs, so that children who have communication disorders can be identified and served as early as possible.

TREATMENT AND REMEDIATION OF COMMUNICATION DISORDERS

In dealing with children with organic speech problems, such as the nasality of a cleft palate, the specialist uses procedures similar to those used with children with functional disorders. In some cases, special devices are used to help compensate for physical disabilities. If the child's communication problem is related to another handicapping condition, such as deafness or cerebral palsy, the specialist must evaluate the child's individual combination of skills and physical disabilities and create a personalized communication program. We will be looking at the communication difficulties of hearing impaired, physically disabled, and severely handicapped students in the chapters that follow.

Articulation Disorders

There are several approaches to the treatment of articulation disorders. The speech-language pathologist usually concentrates on developing the child's ability to listen carefully and discriminate between similar sounds, such as *take* and *cake*. Research appears to support an emphasis on awareness and discrimination of sounds, as there is a generally clear relationship between children's ability to recognize sounds and to articulate them correctly (Winitz, 1977). The specialist may have the child carefully watch how sounds are produced and perhaps use a mirror to monitor his or her own speech production. Children produce problematic sounds in syllables, words, sentences, and stories. They may tape-record their own speech and listen carefully for errors. It is sometimes helpful for children to learn to recognize the difference between the way they produce a sound and the way other people produce it. As in all communication training, it is important for the teacher, parent, or specialist to provide a good language model, to reward the child's positive performance, and to encourage the child to talk. A large percentage of functional articulation disorders are either successfully treated or simply fade away as the child matures.

Voice Disorders

In the case of a child with voice disorders, a medical examination should always be sought. If there are organic causes, they often respond to surgery or medical treatment. Communication disorders specialists sometimes recommend environmental modifications; a person who is consistently required to speak in a noisy setting, for example, may benefit from the use of a small microphone to reduce vocal straining and shouting (Moore, 1982). Most remedial techniques, however, offer direct *vocal rehabilitation,* which helps the child with a voice disorder gradually learn to produce more acceptable and efficient speech. Depending on the type of voice disorder and the child's overall circumstances, vocal rehabilitation

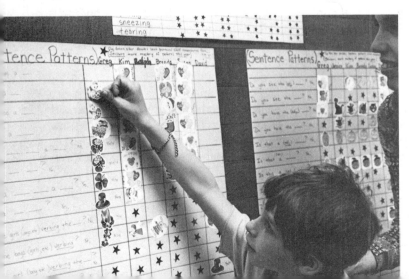

Using varied and more complex sentence patterns is an important goal for children with language disorders.

might include such activities as exercises to increase breathing capacity, relaxation techniques to reduce tension, procedures to increase the loudness of speech, or training in breaking patterns of vocal abuse. Here again, the child's ability to monitor his or her own speech and to develop auditory discrimination skills can help the child with a voice disorder speak more easily and naturally.

Fluency Disorders

The treatment of stuttering and other fluency disorders varies widely, according to the orientation of the specialist. In general, treatment emphasizes either counseling or behavior modification; most speech-language pathologists today combine these approaches to some extent (Kelly, 1982). Children may learn to "manage" their stuttering by deliberately prolonging certain sounds or by speaking slowly to help them get through a "block." They may increase their confidence and fluency by speaking in groups, where pressure is minimized and successful speech is rewarded. They may learn to monitor their own speech and reward themselves for periods of fluency. They may learn to speak to a rhythmic beat or with the aid of devices that mask or delay their ability to hear themselves speak. Tape recorders are often used for drills, simulated conversations, and documenting progress.

For more on self-monitoring of stuttering, see Shames and Florance, 1980.

Teachers, parents, and others who interact with children who stutter can help them develop a positive attitude toward communication by paying attention to *what* they say, rather than to difficulties in saying it. When the child has a verbal block, the listener should be patient and should not "help" the dysfluent speaker by saying something for him. Instead, the listener should keep calm, say nothing, and maintain eye-to-eye contact with the child until he finishes what he wants to say. In many cases, children learn to control their stuttering and to produce increasingly fluent speech as they mature. No single method of treatment has been recognized as most effective. Stuttering frequently decreases when children enter adolescence irrespective of which method of treatment has been used, and even in some cases in which the child has received no treatment at all.

Language Disorders

Treatments for language disorders are also extremely varied. Some programs center around *precommunication* activities, which encourage the child to explore and which make the environment conducive to the development of receptive and expressive language. Clearly, children must have something they want to communicate. Since children learn through imitation, it is important for the teacher or specialist to talk clearly, use correct inflections, and provide a rich variety of words and sentences. The presence of other children in the classroom or clinical setting appears to play a useful role in language development. Lowenthal (1981) found that preschool children with language impairments learned most effectively when they were taught in groups of three or four children.

EXCEPTIONAL CHILDREN

Larger groups, with 10 children, were less effective in encouraging the development of vocabulary and comprehension skills.

Chaney and Frodyma (1982) describe two different methods used to encourage language development in preschool children with various handicapping conditions: the *precision* method and the *experiential* method. In the precision method, children are placed in groups according to their ability levels in each of several areas, such as language, cognition, motor skills, self-help skills, and social skills. Group lessons and activities about 20 minutes long emphasize the teaching of language through performing tasks that a child has not yet learned, and extensive data on each child's performance are maintained. The experiential method uses groups consisting of children with varying levels of language ability; children with higher language skills serve as models for those whose language is not as well developed. Different demands and expectations are placed on each child, and each day's activities are presented around a unified theme or experience. Activities for one day, for example, might revolve around clothing. The children would discuss what clothes they are wearing, paste clothes on paper dolls, wash clothes, and learn concepts of size and color using articles of clothing.

Some specialists in language disorders do a great deal of written and verbal labeling, to help the child develop language content; that is, attach meaning to important objects in the environment. In many instances, children's language skills improve when they become better able to pay attention. The specialist may reinforce the child for imitating facial expressions or body movements or simply for maintaining eye contact. Some speech-language pathologists emphasize the pairing of actions with words, teaching the natural gestures that go along with such expressions as "up," "look," and "goodbye." D'Angelo (1981) recommends the use of wordless picture books as a means of building vocabulary, conversational skills, and positive attitudes with language disordered children. Questions such as "What is happening in the picture?" and "What things do you see?" can be used by a parent or teacher in initiating conversations with a child.

Programs for children with language disorders, while acknowledging the importance of oral speech, are currently moving away from an *exclusive* emphasis on spoken communication. Sign language has been successfully used to develop communicative skills in several children who, though their hearing was not impaired, were apparently unable to develop expressive or receptive language through normal channels. For example, Bonvillian and Nelson (1976) were able to teach sign language to an autistic child who had previously been considered mute and nonresponsive. Sign language, gestures, and symbol systems have also been successfully taught to children whose language disorders are attributed to mental retardation, aphasia, or behavior disorders. These approaches should, however, be viewed as supplements to speech rather than as replacements for speech. Children who are able to initiate communication through signs, gestures, or symbols may be able to transfer to speech as they learn and develop their communicative abilities. Speech is always a desirable goal for children whose cognitive and physical abilities will enable them to achieve it.

No matter what approach to treatment is used, it is clear that children with language disorders need to be around children and adults who have something interesting to talk about. Many children have benefited from being placed in groups of nonhandicapped peers who are communicating actively and effectively. Other children may respond best to individual treatment sessions. Whatever format their program follows, effective speech-language pathologists keep precise records of their students' behaviors, establish realistic goals and objectives, and structure the teaching situation so that the child's efforts at communication will be rewarded and enjoyable.

General Guidelines

All good teachers—whether they are specifically trained as language specialists or not—are also good communication facilitators. The effective teacher can do much to encourage children's communication skills and motivation. The effective teacher speaks with feeling and animation. He or she listens to children with genuine interest. When a child makes an error, the teacher can correct it by naturally rephrasing it:

> Child: "Them boys has football helmets."
> Teacher: "Yes, those boys have football helmets."

Interactions like this may be considered a form of "behavior shaping," and over a period of time, the child is expected to use patterns of speech and language which more closely approximate the appropriate usage. A child's attempts at communication should *never* be punished.

When the teacher is unable to understand a child's speech, he or she may say "Show me what you mean," or attempt to draw more information from the child by asking "who?" "what?" "when?" or "where?" questions. The good teacher creates a classroom atmosphere that offers lots of chances for relaxed communication and makes each child feel that he or she has an important contribution to make. The teacher is a person of primary importance in the development of children's speech and language skills. And effective communication in the classroom enriches the learning situation for all students.

In Chapter 14 we discuss several strategies used by teachers of preschool handicapped children to increase speech and language skills.

Patterns of Service

Although there are some self-contained special classes specifically designed for children with speech or language impairments, the regular classroom is by far the most prevalent setting for school-age children with communication disorders. There is an increasing tendency for communication disorders specialists to serve as consultants for regular and special education teachers (and parents), rather than spending most of their time providing direct services to individual children. All these people are important in the development and practice of

EXCEPTIONAL CHILDREN

speech and language skills. The specialist thus concentrates his or her efforts on assessing communication disorders, evaluating progress, and providing materials and techniques. Teachers and parents are encouraged to follow the guidelines suggested by the communication disorders specialist.

A recent survey conducted by the American Speech-Language-Hearing Association (cited in Matthews, 1982) found that speech-language pathologists are employed in a wide variety of settings. The largest single group—about 45%—work in elementary or secondary schools; the remainder work in clinics, hospitals, rehabilitation centers, universities, and other settings. The majority of speech-language pathologists—over 70%—spend the greatest amount of their time in helping children and adults who have communication disorders. Others are involved in the profession as administrators, supervisors, and researchers. A small percentage teach handicapped children directly in classroom settings.

In some programs, the specialist visits schools according to a regular schedule and gives individual or group therapy to the children. This approach is becoming somewhat less common today. Communication is seen as occurring most appropriately in the natural environment rather than in the clinical setting. Some professionals feel that it is impossible to serve the child adequately with a speech or language disorder if the only "program" consists of one or two 30-minute sessions each week with a specialist. In fact, this method has been described as a futile attempt to "sweep back a river with a broom" (Hatten & Hatten, 1975).

The speech and language specialist may also act as a resource room teacher. Based in a regular school, he or she may then serve a variety of children on a regular basis, maintaining contact with their other teachers. When not scheduled for the resource room, the children are in regular classes.

Children with communication disorders are seldom placed in special self-contained classrooms or schools unless the disorder is extremely severe (as in the case of a completely nonverbal child) or the child has multiple handicapping conditions.

ASHA can provide further information about the training, qualifications, and responsibilities of speech-language pathologists. The address of ASHA is given in the listing of resources at the end of this chapter.

CURRENT ISSUES/FUTURE TRENDS

The future will probably find specialists in communication disorders functioning even more indirectly than they do today. They will continue to work as professional team members, assisting teachers, parents, physicians, and other specialists in recognizing potential communication disorders and in facilitating communication skills. In-service training will become an ever more important aspect of the specialist's responsibilities.

Speech-language pathologists who work in schools are likely to find themselves working with an increasing percentage of children with severe and multiple handicaps, who previously did not receive specialized services from communication disorders specialists. In some school districts, increasing caseloads are coupled with financial restrictions, making it virtually impossible for all students with communication disorders to receive adequate services from the relatively few specialists who are employed. Even though all handicapped students are supposed to receive all special services they need, the schools' financial bind may necessitate difficult decisions at the local level. Some programs may choose to provide special services only to those students with the most severe speech and language impairments. Others may concentrate their professional resources on higher functioning students who are considered to have the best potential for developing communication skills. Parents, advocates, and professional organizations will play an instrumental role in determining which children are to receive specialized speech and language services.

Paraprofessional personnel may, in the future, be more widely trained to work directly with children who have speech and language disorders, while professionals concentrate their efforts on diagnosis, prescriptive programming, evaluation, and the use of technology. Peer tutoring or therapy approaches, using nonhandicapped students as language "models," are likely to become more prevalent. These approaches may allow more students to receive specialized help.

Advances in technology will bring about the widespread use of communicative devices to assist individuals with speech and language disorders of all levels of severity. These devices include computers, which can be programmed with synthetic speech to allow some previously nonspeaking children to express themselves, communication boards with speech output for the severely handicapped, devices that "understand" vocal commands, and electronic aids to enable specialists to obtain more precise assessment of speech impairments.

Currently, speech and language intervention programs are heavily oriented toward the young preschool and school-aged population. While early detection and intervention will continue to have a high priority among communication disorders specialists, professionals are gradually becoming aware of the needs of adolescents and adults, "a huge segment of our population with untreated speech and hearing problems" (Boone, 1977, p. 6). These individuals should have greater access to appropriate services in the future.

A head stick and communication board enables this young man to "talk" to family and friends for the first time.

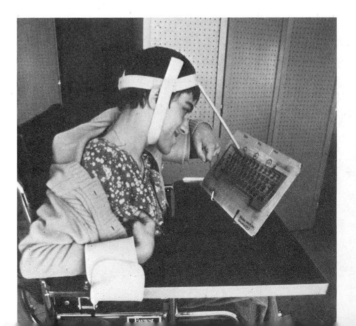

"I HAVE A LOT OF THINGS TO SAY. . . ."

Susan M. Bolton is a speech-language pathologist in the Fountain Valley School District, Fountain Valley, California. Much of Sue's work has been in an innovative project to use new communication technology with non-oral students at Plavan School, where students with and without disabilities are educated together. Sue agreed to discuss some recent developments in augmentative communication—and several of her students also had some things to tell us about!

The ability to communicate through speech is something that most of us take for granted. Yet many children and adults either fail to acquire or lose the ability to use this most precious of human communicative skills.

Widespread use of sign language among deaf people is evidence of the success of augmentative (supplemental to speech) systems for individuals with speech handicaps. The severely physically handicapped, however, often find their ability to use sign language is limited by the same disabilities that prevent them from acquiring oral speech.

Fortunately, modern technology has enabled these individuals to communicate without speech in a variety of ways. Some of the systems, such as communication boards (also known as language or conversation boards) have been widely used with this population. These boards are often customized for the person's needs and are usually inexpensive to develop. In some cases, such as with individuals with low cognitive functioning, the boards adequately meet the needs of the person. But many people require more extensive vocabulary in a personal, portable system.

The answer to these problems came as a result of the microchip revolution. These tiny units of information storage provide the capability of almost limitless vocabulary compacted into systems that can be transported right along with the speech-impaired person.

For the past 6 years, I have worked with children of all ages who require augmentative communication systems in various forms. A "look of the eye" or a facial expression often told us that these children had much to say. Yet, as a speech-language pathologist, I had experienced many frustrating moments because I could not develop the kind of oral speech in these children that I knew society would demand. Once appropriate systems were developed and fitted to these children, I obtained some interesting comments from them which I would like to share with you.

Although these children use a variety of systems (small minitypewriters, scanners, personal computers, and so on), the common thread is strong: before acquiring their systems, limited speech also limited their ability to interact with people, to express feelings, to show humor, or to do many other things we normally expect of children (and ourselves).

Six students, ranging in age from 11 to 19, were asked to address the topic "What my communication aid means to me." Here are their responses:

Jay H. is 11 years old. About all he can say is a resemblance to "yes/no." After 2 years of working on his personal computer, Jay wanted us to know some of his feelings:

> I was sad. Mom and I are happy [to get my computer].

Jay with a Canon Communicator.

Jim T., age 14, reminded us that his oral speech was not very understandable outside of family and friends:

It was hard to get the words out but when I got the [communicator] it got eseer [easier].

Of course, Jim still has to improve his spelling so that the community will understand him, but it's remarkably better than having people guess at his intentions!

Jim and his Canon Communicator.

One student, Monica S., age 14, acknowledges that her small minitypewriter now allows her the freedom to be quite verbal:

One day my father brought me a [communicator]. It opened my life because I can talk with it to anyone who can't intertian [understand] me. I have CP [cerebral palsy] and it infecks [affects] my vocter code [vocal cords].

I am in gril [girl] scout [s]. I stop all of my talking and tell you my name. My name is Monica. I have alot of things to say and I love my [communicator]. I hope I helped you with my grabing [gabbing].

Monica and her Porta-Tel.

A high school student, John M., age 19, was a little reluctant to share his recent successes in communicating with girls, but he was willing to tell us that:

Before I got my [communicator] it was hard for me to talk to people who were not my family and my teachers. I got a [communicator] when I started high school. At first was hard for me to use it. Now it is easy. I think the [communicator] is a great machine. It help me talk to people.

John producing synthetic speech.

In addition to communication, another student, Ivan K., age 18, told me that his system was versatile enough to allow him to demonstrate skills in other ways:

> Since the summer of 1982 I have had . . . [a] computer. Since I got it, I have been able to express myself more than ever. I can draw to show how I feel. The computer has been a great help to me.

Personal computer-based communication systems, like any custom-fitted aids, may not be appropriate for everyone with limited oral speech. Some factors, such as language delay or cognitive impairment, may prevent the acquisition of necessary prerequisite skills. In some cases, language boards are more appropriate and can be considered precursors to the use of more sophisticated systems. The best decision, however, rests in the com-bined agreement of an interdisciplinary team comprised of parents, educators, speech-language pathologists, and appropriate allied health professionals such as doctors and physical and occupational therapists. Often the child can contribute ideas that determine the "best fit."

No matter what the system, the desired outcome is the same: to produce an individual capable of communicating to the best of his or her potential with the greatest number of those in society willing to take time to "listen." Granted these are strange and new ways compared to the familiarity of speech. One unknown author showed considerable foresight in commenting:

> Communicate—from me to you
> Is socially the thing to do
> And as the means to do it changed
> Society was re-arranged![1]

Ivan with an experimental computer.

[1]Displayed at the National Museum of Science and Industry, Washington, D.C., 1980.

SUMMARY

1. Communication is any interaction that transmits information.
   a. A language is an arbitrary symbol system used to enable a group of people to communicate.
   b. Each language has rules of phonology, morphology, syntax, and semantics that describe how users put sounds together to convey meaning.
   c. Language can also be described in terms of form, content, and use.
   d. Speech is the vocal response mode of language. It is the basis on which language develops.

2. Most children learn to use language without direct instruction.
   a. Infants soon learn to make sounds to communicate and to react to people's voices.
   b. They learn to babble, develop inflection, and can respond to familiar words and commands by age 1.
   c. By age 1½, most babies can say several words; they use words and gestures to communicate certain needs.
   d. During the next 6 months, many children go through a stage of echolalia. They learn to use short sentences, and their receptive vocabulary grows rapidly.
   e. After age 2, vocabulary use increases greatly. Most preschool children learn to use progressively longer and more complex sentences. Correct pronunciation, however, takes longer to develop.
   f. By the time most children enter first grade, their grammar and speech patterns match those of the adults around them.

3. Difficulties with speech and language can cause learning and interpersonal problems.
   a. A child has a speech disorder when his or her speech draws unfavorable attention to itself, interferes with the ability to communicate, or causes social or interpersonal problems.
   b. Some children have trouble understanding language (receptive language disorders); others, using language to communicate (expressive language disorders). Still other children have language delays.
   c. Speech or language differences based on cultural dialects should not be considered communication disorders.

4. Children with communication disorders make up a large group of handicapped children. However, the number of these children decreases significantly as they get older. In particular, many articulation disorders disappear as the child matures.

5. Although some speech disorders have physical (organic) causes, most are considered functional disorders.

6. There are several types of communication disorders.
   a. Articulation disorders, a very common type of communication disorder,

involve repeated incorrect utterances of speech sounds. They include omissions, substitutions, distortions, and additions of sounds.

b. Voice disorders involve inappropriate or abnormal quality, loudness, or pitch of the voice. The most common are hoarseness breathiness, and nasality.

c. Fluency disorders, including stuttering, interrupt the normal rhythm or flow of speech.

d. Language disorders include both receptive and expressive difficulties. A child may have either or both types.

7. Treatment of communication disorders is a relatively new field.

a. The professionals who work with communication disorders are called *communication disorders specialists* or *speech-language pathologists,* reflecting awareness of the interrelationships among speech, language, and learning.

b. Today, intervention is increasingly being carried out in the regular classroom. The specialist works with the teacher rather than directly with the child.

8. Assessment of a child who is suspected of having a communication disorder may include some or all of the following components, depending on the problem area:

a. Case history,

b. Physical examination of the child's mouth,

c. Articulation test,

d. Hearing test,

e. Auditory discrimination test,

f. Language development test,

g. Language test,

h. Conversation with the child,

i. Behavioral observation.

9. The different types of communication disorders call for different approaches to remediation.

a. A child with an articulation disorder is taught to discriminate between sounds and practice making them correctly.

b. Some voice disorders are treated medically; others through educational programs involving auditory discrimination, self-monitoring, and modeling.

c. Stuttering can be treated in several different ways, but it is clearly important to help children feel comfortable and relaxed when speaking.

d. Language disorders can also be treated in more than one way, but again it is important to reward children for any attempt at communication, to help them feel relaxed, and to encourage them to converse with other children.

e. Effective teachers of children with communication disorders should encourage them to communicate by being genuinely interested in them, correcting errors unobtrusively, and making the children feel comfortable and important.

10. Most children with speech and language problems attend regular classes.
    a. Some receive special help from their regular teacher, special education teacher, and/or parents, who work with the communication disorders specialist. The specialist concentrates on assessment, evaluation, and providing guidelines for teachers and parents.
    b. In other programs, the communication disorders specialist travels from school to school and gives direct individual or group therapy to the children. However, because this means that therapy is delivered in a clinical (rather than natural) setting and only at certain times each week, this method is becoming less common.
    c. The speech and language specialist may also serve as a resource room teacher.

11. In the future, communication disorders specialists will probably provide services even more indirectly than today. They will help train parents, teachers, and paraprofessionals to work with most children, while they concentrate on diagnosis, programming, and direct intensive services to a few children with special needs.

12. Advances in technology will spread the use of special devices to help individuals with communication disorders.

13. Hopefully, older youths and adults with untreated speech and language problems will receive more services in the coming years.

FOR MORE INFORMATION

Journals

Journal of Speech and Hearing Disorders. Published quarterly by the American Speech-Language-Hearing Association (ASHA). Includes articles dealing with the nature, assessment, and treatment of communication disorders.

Language, Speech, and Hearing Services in the Schools. Also published quarterly by ASHA, this journal focuses on practical applications of speech and language training, and provides activities for teachers and specialists consistent with current research and theory.

Books

Brooks, M., Engman, D., & Johnson, M. *Your child's speech and language.* Lawrence, Kans.: H&H Enterprises, 1978.

Dickson, S. (ed.). *Communication disorders: Remedial principles and practices.* Glenview, Ill.: Scott, Foresman, & Co., 1974.

Eisenson, J. *Is your child's speech normal?* Reading, Mass.: Addison-Wesley, 1976.

Freeman, G. G. *Speech and language services and the classroom teacher.* Reston, Va.: Council for Exceptional Children, 1977.

Jonas, G. *Stuttering: The disorder of many theories.* New York: Farrar, Straus and Giroux, 1976.

Leitch, S. M. *A child learns to speak: A guide for parents and teachers of preschool children.* Springfield, Ill.: Charles C. Thomas, 1977.

Lloyd, L. L. (ed.). *Communication assessment and intervention strategies.* Baltimore: University Park Press, 1976.

McCartan, K. W. *The communicatively disordered child: Management procedures for the classroom.* Hingham, Mass.: Teaching Resources, 1977.

McDonald, E. T., & Berlin, A. J. *Bright promise for your child with cleft lip and cleft palate.* Chicago: National Easter Seal Society, 1979 (also available in Spanish).

Shames, G. H., & Florance, C. L. *Stutter-free speech: A goal for therapy.* Columbus, Ohio: Charles E. Merrill, 1980.

Shames, G. H., & Wiig, E. H. *Human communication disorders: An introduction.* Columbus, Ohio: Charles E. Merrill, 1982.

Van Riper, C. *Speech correction: Principles and methods,* 6th ed. Englewood Cliffs, N.J.: Prentice-Hall, 1978.

Weiss, C. E., & Lillywhite, H. S. *Communicative disorders: A handbook for prevention and early intervention.* St. Louis: C. V. Mosby, 1976.

Organizations

American Speech-Language-Hearing Association. 10801 Rockville Pike, Rockville, MD 20852. The major professional organization concerned with speech and language. ASHA also serves as a certifying agency for professionals who provide speech, language, and hearing services. It publishes several journals, sponsors research in communication disorders, and provides a comprehensive *Guide to Professional Services,* which also includes information on accredited training programs.

Division for Children with Communication Disorders, Council for Exceptional Children, 1920 Association Drive, Reston, VA 22091. Includes teachers and communication disorders specialists who work with exceptional children. Sponsors sessions at state, provincial, and national conferences. Publishes the twice yearly *Journal of Childhood Communication Disorders.*

7

Hearing Impairment

People with normal hearing usually find it difficult to appreciate fully the enormous importance of the auditory sense in human development and learning. Many of us have simulated blindness by closing our eyes or putting on a blindfold, but it is virtually impossible to "switch off" your hearing voluntarily.

Children learn a great deal by using their hearing, starting at birth. Newborn infants are able to respond to sounds by startling or blinking. At a few weeks of age, infants with normal hearing can listen to quiet sounds, recognize their parents' voices, and pay attention to their own gurgling and cooing sounds. During the first year of life, infants acquire much information by listening. They can recognize sounds of familiar people and objects, discriminate meaningful sound from background noise, and localize and imitate sounds (Lowell & Pollack, 1974).

As hearing children grow, they develop language by constantly hearing language used and by associating these sounds with innumerable activities and events. They learn that people convey information and exchange their thoughts and feelings by speaking and hearing. They attach meaning to sound. By the time hearing children reach school age, they are likely to have a vocabulary of over 5,000 words. They have already had perhaps 100 million meaningful contacts with language (Napierkowski, 1981).

As we saw in the last chapter, the process of language acquisition and development, though complex, occurs naturally and spontaneously in most children with normal hearing. Children with a hearing impairment, however, are not able to participate in this process without special help. They may acquire a good deal of information about the world, but have few symbols or patterns available to help them in sending and receiving messages. They miss out on many early, critical opportunities for developing communication skills. Furth (1973) suggests that if you wish to capture something of the experience of a child who is deaf from birth or early childhood, you should try to watch a television program with the sound turned off, in which a foreign language is being spoken. You would be faced with the double problem of reading lips and comprehending an unfamiliar language.

Hearing is vital in every aspect of our daily existence. If you were unable to hear, you would, at best, find it difficult to participate in your school or college, your job, your community, and your family, unless some special adaptations were made. At worst, you might find that our society's great reliance on hearing and speech as avenues of communication made it virtually impossible for you to function effectively.

As Hoemann and Briga (1981) point out, a child's educational, vocational, and social development is influenced by many factors in addition to the type and degree of hearing loss. These include the age at which the hearing impairment began, the attitudes of the child's parents and siblings, the opportunities available for the child to develop oral and manual communication skills, and the presence or absence of other disabilities. A child's potential can certainly not be predicted from a hearing test alone.

Today, many children with impaired hearing are identified in early childhood. They are often helped through surgery or the use of hearing aids. They may learn to communicate with their families and friends by using speech, speech reading, sign language, or other techniques. Many hearing impaired people achieve high levels of educational, professional, and personal success. But it is impossible really to compensate or make up for the loss of hearing. The information and understanding that come through the auditory channel can never be fully replaced.

DEFINITIONS, TYPES, AND MEASUREMENT OF HEARING LOSS

There is no legal definition of the "hearing impaired" population. When we speak of a person with *normal hearing*, we generally mean that he or she has enough hearing to understand speech. Assuming that the listening conditions are adequate, a person with normal hearing will not need to rely on any special device or technique to interpret speech in everyday situations.

Deafness is defined as a sensory deficiency which prevents a person from receiving the stimulus of sound in all or most of its forms (Katz, Mathis, & Merrill, 1978). A deaf person is not able to use his or her hearing to understand speech, though other sounds may be perceived. Even with a hearing aid, the hearing loss is too great to allow a deaf person to understand speech through the ears alone.

A **hard-of-hearing** person has a significant hearing loss that makes some special adaptations necessary. As Ross and Nober (1981) point out, a hard-of-hearing child can respond to speech and other auditory stimuli. His or her speech and language skills, though they may be delayed or deficient, are devel-

Born with a severe hearing loss, this child faces an enormous challenge—learning to communicate in a language he cannot hear.

oped mainly through the auditory channel. Hard-of-hearing children are able to use their hearing to understand speech, generally with the help of a hearing aid.

Both deaf and hard-of-hearing children are said to be **hearing impaired.** This term, used mainly in education, indicates a child who needs special services because of a hearing loss. Most children in classes for the hearing impaired do have some degree of **residual hearing.**

Residual hearing refers to the remaining ability to hear—however slight—by a hearing impaired person.

A hearing impairment may also be described in terms of its *age of onset.* It is important to consider whether a hearing loss is congenital (present at birth) or **adventitious** (acquired later in life). A child who, from birth, is unable to hear the speech of other people will not be able to learn speech and language spontaneously, as do children with normal hearing. A child who acquires a hearing impairment at age 6, after speech and language are well established, will need help in adjusting to the hearing loss and in maintaining the ability to speak clearly.

Educators often use the term **prelingual** to refer to a hearing impairment that is present at birth or occurs before the development of speech and language, as opposed to a **postlingual** hearing impairment, which occurs after speech and language skills have been acquired through the sense of hearing. The educational program of a prelingually deaf child usually focuses upon the acquisition of language and communication, while that of a postlingually deaf child usually emphasizes the maintenance of intelligible speech and appropriate language patterns.

Types of Hearing Impairment

There are two main types of hearing impairments, **conductive** and **sensorineural.** A conductive hearing loss results from obstructions or interference in

EXCEPTIONAL CHILDREN

the transmission of sound from the outer or middle ear into the inner ear. A buildup of excessive wax in the auditory canal can cause a conductive hearing loss, as can a disease which leaves fluid or debris. Some children are born with incomplete or malformed auditory canals. As its name implies, a conductive hearing impairment involves a problem with conducting, or transmitting, sound vibrations to the inner ear. Since the rest of the auditory system is generally intact, conductive hearing losses can often be corrected through surgical or medical treatment. Hearing aids are usually helpful.

A sensorineural hearing loss results from damage to the auditory nerve fibers or other sensitive mechanisms in the inner ear. Because of the impairment in the inner ear, sound may not be delivered to the brain at all, or it may be highly distorted. Amplification—making the source of sound louder—may or may not help the person with a sensorineural hearing impairment. Most sensorineural hearing impairments, unfortunately, cannot be corrected by surgery or medication.

It is also possible for a child to have a *mixed* hearing loss, including both conductive and sensorineural impairments. Diagnosis of a mixed hearing loss is especially difficult, as there are problems with both the conduction and the processing of sound. Treatment will focus on both types of hearing loss.

Figure 7.1 shows the parts of the human ear.

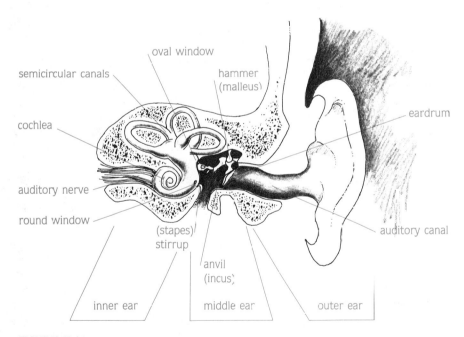

FIGURE 7.1
Parts of the human ear. The external part of the ear and the auditory canal make up the outer ear. The middle ear includes the eardrum, hammer, anvil, and stirrup. The inner ear includes the round window, the oval window, the semicircular canals, and the cochlea. Damage to any part can cause a hearing loss.

Hearing impairment is also described in terms of whether it is *unilateral* (present in one ear only) or *bilateral* (present in both ears). Most children in special programs for the hearing impaired have bilateral losses, though the degree of impairment may not be the same in both ears. Children with unilateral hearing impairments generally learn speech and language without major difficulties, though they tend to have problems localizing sounds and listening in noisy or distracting settings. There is some recent evidence to suggest that children with unilateral hearing impairments may be at a disadvantage in acquiring certain academic skills (Keller & Bundy, 1980).

Measuring Hearing Loss

Table 7.1 shows how degree of hearing loss affects students in the classroom.

Sound is measured in units which describe its *intensity* and *frequency*. Both are important in considering the needs of the child with impaired hearing. The intensity or loudness of sound is measured in **decibels** (dB). "Zero dB" represents the smallest sound the person with "normal" hearing can perceive. Larger dB numbers represent increasingly louder sounds. A low whisper 5 feet away registers about 10 dB, an automobile about 65 dB, and Niagara Falls about 90 dB. Conversational speech 10 to 20 feet away registers about 30 to 65 dB. A sound of about 125 dB or louder will cause pain to the average person. A person may have a loss of up to 25 dB (that is, not be able to hear any sound of less than 25 dB) and still be considered to have hearing within the normal range (Davis & Silverman, 1970).

It is always important to consider the listening environment, as background noise may cause additional problems for the child with a hearing impairment. Northern and Lemme (1982) observe that, for normally hearing adults, speech needs only to be 10 to 15 dB louder than background noise for them to listen and understand comfortably. For children with impaired hearing, it is likely that speech must be significantly louder than background noise, or they will not be able to attend to the message being transmitted.

The frequency, or pitch, of sounds is measured in cycles per second, or **hertz** units (Hz). One hertz is equal to one cycle per second. The lowest note on a piano has a frequency of about 30 Hz, middle C about 250 Hz, and the highest note about 4,000 Hz. Human beings are able to hear frequencies ranging from about 20 to 20,000 Hz (Davis & Silverman, 1970), but many of these audible sounds are outside the *speech range*, the frequency range where ordinary conversation takes place. A person who could not hear very low sounds (such as a foghorn) or very high sounds (such as a piccolo) would perhaps suffer some inconvenience, but would not be significantly handicapped in education and everyday life. A person with a serious hearing loss in the speech range, however, is at a great disadvantage in communication. The frequency range generally considered most important for hearing conversational speech is from 500 to 2,000 Hz. The sounds of English speech vary in their frequency level. For example, the /s/ phoneme (as in the word *sat*) is a high frequency sound, typically occurring between 4,000 and 8,000 Hz (Northern & Lemme, 1982). A child whose hearing loss was more severe in the higher frequencies would thus have particular difficulty in discriminating the /s/ sound. Conversely, phonemes such as /dʒ/ (as in jump) and /m/ occur at low frequencies and would be more problematic for a person with a low frequency hearing impairment.

IDENTIFICATION AND ASSESSMENT

The science of **audiology** has made many advances in recent years. The development of sophisticated instruments and techniques has enabled audiologists to detect and describe hearing impairments with increasing accuracy, even in infants and very young children. The earlier a hearing impairment is identified, the better are a child's chances for receiving treatment and thus developing good communication skills, appropriate behaviors, and satisfying social relationships. If a child's hearing impairment goes undetected until age 5 or 6—the age at which children typically enter school—a great many valuable learning opportunities will have been irretrievably lost. In some regions, infants are routinely tested for possible hearing impairment; it is possible to do this with the aid of electrical or **evoked-response audiometry,** which does not require a voluntary response from the person being tested (Hoemann & Briga, 1981).

Despite modern audiological techniques, hearing impairment still goes undetected in many children. All infants, hearing and deaf alike, babble, coo, and smile. Later on, deaf children tend to stop babbling and vocalizing, since they cannot hear themselves or their parents, but the baby's silence may be mistakenly attributed to other causes. Unfortunately, many hearing impaired children have been erroneously labeled mentally retarded or emotionally disturbed. Some have even spent years inappropriately placed in institutions, because nobody realized that their problem was deafness, rather than mental retardation or emotional disturbance. To avoid such misplacements in the future, efforts are continually made to conduct screening tests for hearing impairment, and to educate doctors, teachers, and parents to recognize the signs of hearing loss in children.

An audiologist can detect the level of hearing loss in each ear with considerable accuracy.

Audiology is the branch of science dealing with hearing.

Evoked-response audiometry and **operant audiometry** are two techniques for measuring hearing that do not call for a verbal response. Thus they can be used with all types of nonverbal people.

Degrees of Hearing Impairment

When hearing is formally tested, the examiner exposes the child to sounds at different levels of intensity and frequency. The device which generates these sounds is called an **audiometer,** and the child's responses are recorded on a chart called an **audiogram.** The test seeks to determine how loud each sound must be before the child is able to hear it. A child with a hearing impairment does not begin to detect sounds until a high level of loudness—measured in decibels—is reached. For example, a child who has a 60 dB hearing loss cannot begin to detect a sound until it is at least 60 dB loud, in contrast to a child with normal hearing, who would detect the same sound at a level between 0 and 10 dB. To obtain a hearing level on an audiogram, the child must be able to detect a sound at that level at least 50% of the time.

Figures 7.2 through 7.5 show audiograms of children with varying degrees of hearing loss.

An individual's hearing impairment is usually described by the terms *mild, moderate, severe,* and *profound,* depending upon the average hearing level, in decibels, throughout those frequencies most important for understanding speech (500 to 2,000 Hz). Table 7.1 presents the decibel levels associated with these degrees of hearing impairment, and lists some likely effects of the hearing impairment upon children's speech and language development and considerations for educational programs.

No two children have exactly the same pattern of hearing, even if their responses on a hearing test are similar. Just as a single intelligence test does not provide sufficient information to plan a child's educational program, a child's

TABLE 7.1
Effects of hearing impairments

Faintest Sound Heard	Effect on the Understanding of Language and Speech	Probable Educational Needs and Programs
Slight 27 to 40 dB	• May have difficulty hearing faint or distant speech. • Will not usually have difficulty in school situations.	• May benefit from a hearing aid as loss approaches 40 dB. • Attention to vocabulary development. • Needs favorable seating and lighting. • May need speechreading instruction. • May need speech correction.
Mild 41 to 55 dB	• Understands conversational speech at a distance of 3 to 5 feet (face to face). • May miss as much as 50% of class discussions if voices are faint or not in line of vision. • May have limited vocabulary and speech anomalies.	• Should be referred to special education for educational follow-up. • May benefit from individual hearing aid by evaluation and training in its use. • Favorable seating and possible special class placement, especially for primary age children. • Attention to vocabulary and reading. • May need speechreading instruction. • Speech conservation and correction, if indicated.

TABLE 7.1 (continued)

Faintest Sound Heard	Effect on the Understanding of Language and Speech	Probable Educational Needs and Programs
Moderate 56 to 70 dB	• Conversation must be loud to be understood. • Will have increasing difficulty with school group discussions. • Is likely to have defective speech. • Is likely to be deficient in language use and comprehension. • Will have limited vocabulary.	• Will need resource teacher or special class. • Should have special help in language skills, vocabulary development, usage, reading, writing, grammar, etc. • Can benefit from individual hearing aid by evaluation and auditory training. • Speechreading instruction. • Speech conservation and speech correction.
Severe 71 to 90 dB	• May hear loud voices about 1 foot from the ear. • May be able to identify environmental sounds. • May be able to discriminate vowels but not all consonants. • Speech and language defective and likely to deteriorate. • Speech and language will not develop spontaneously if loss is present before 1 year of age.	• Will need full-time special program for deaf children, with emphasis on all language skills, concept development, speechreading, and speech. • Program needs specialized supervision and comprehensive supporting services. • Can benefit from individual hearing aid by evaluation. • Auditory training on individual and group aids. • Part-time in regular classes as profitable.
Profound 91 dB or more	• May hear some loud sounds but is aware of vibrations more than tonal pattern. • Relies on vision rather than hearing as primary avenue for communication. • Speech and language defective and likely to deteriorate. • Speech and language will not develop spontaneously if loss is prelingual.	• Will need full-time special program for deaf children, with emphasis on all language skills, concept development, speechreading, and speech. • Program needs specialized supervision and comprehensive supporting services. • Continuous appraisal of needs in regard to oral or manual communication. • Auditory training on individual and group aids. • Part-time in regular classes only for carefully selected children.

needs cannot be determined from an audiometric test alone. Success in communication and school achievement cannot be predicted simply by looking at an audiogram. Children hear sounds with differing degrees of clarity, and the same child's hearing ability may vary from day to day. Some children with very low levels of measurable hearing are able to benefit from hearing aids and can learn

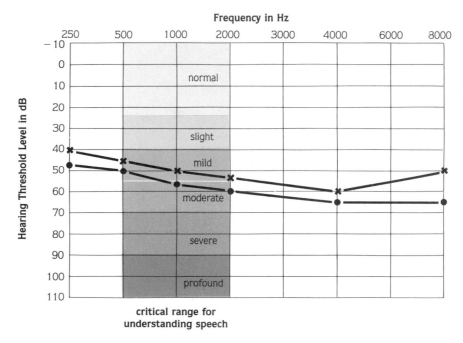

Frequency in Hz

FIGURE 7.2

Audiogram for Vicki (mild hearing impairment).

x = left ear   o = right ear.

to speak. On the other hand, some children with less apparent hearing loss are not able to function well through the auditory channel and need to rely on vision as their primary means of communication.

Figure 7.2 shows the audiogram of Vicki, a child with a mild hearing impairment. Vicki is able to understand face-to-face conversation with little difficulty, but misses much of the discussion that goes on in her classroom—particularly if several children are speaking at once or if she cannot see the speaker clearly. Most of her friends are unaware that she has a hearing impairment. Vicki benefits from wearing a hearing aid and receives occasional speech and language assistance from a speech-language pathologist.

Figure 7.3 shows the audiogram of Raymond, a child with a moderate hearing impairment. Without his hearing aid, Raymond can hear conversation only if it is loud and clear. He finds male voices easier to hear than female voices, because his loss is less severe in lower frequencies. Raymond's teacher attempts to arrange favorable seating for him, but most class discussions are impossible for him to follow. Raymond attends a part-time special class for hearing impaired children and is in a regular classroom for part of the day.

Figure 7.4 shows the audiogram of Brenda, a child with a severe hearing impairment. Brenda can hear voices only if they are very loud and a foot or less from her ear. She wears a hearing aid, but it is uncertain how much she is

EXCEPTIONAL CHILDREN

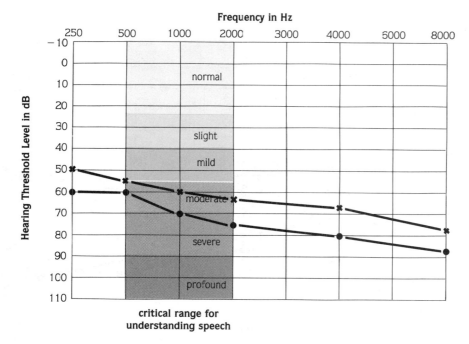

FIGURE 7.3

Audiogram for Raymond (moderate hearing impairment).

x = left ear   o = right ear

gaining from it. She can distinguish most vowel sounds, but hears only a few consonants. She can hear a door slamming, a vacuum cleaner, and an airplane flying overhead. She must always pay close visual attention to a person speaking with her. Brenda attends a full-time special class for hearing impaired children in a regular public school and interacts with nonhandicapped children in several activities.

Figure 7.5 shows the audiogram for Steve, a child with a profound hearing impairment. Steve cannot hear conversational speech at all. His hearing aid seems to help him be aware of certain loud sounds, such as a fire alarm or a bass drum. Steve's hearing impairment is congenital, and he has not developed intelligible speech. He attends a residential school for deaf children and uses sign language as his principal means of communication.

PREVALENCE

Several authorities have concluded that approximately 5% of all school-age children have hearing impairments (Bensberg & Sigelman, 1976; Davis & Silverman, 1970). However, many of these are not considered severe enough to require special education services. Hoemann and Briga (1981) estimate that only about

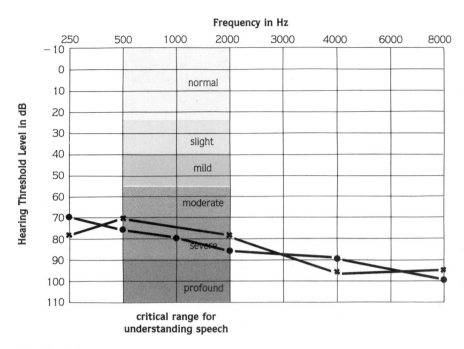

FIGURE 7.4

Audiogram for Brenda (severe hearing impairment).

x = left ear   o = right ear

.2% of the school-age population (1 child in 500) has a severe or profound bilateral hearing impairment.

For every child identified as deaf, there are probably six or seven who are hard of hearing and who may need certain special education services. Recent figures indicate that over 90% of the children in the United States identified as deaf are receiving special services, but only about 20% of the hard-of-hearing population are receiving such services (Moores, 1981). These figures suggest that a significant number of hearing impaired students in regular classes may not be receiving the special assistance they need for effective learning and adjustment. One educator describes the hard-of-hearing child as "the most neglected exceptional child in our public day school system other than the gifted" (Gonzales, 1980, p. 20). Most school districts do not have many hearing impaired students among their population. They may find it difficult to provide a wide range of supportive services, personnel, and materials.

CAUSES

There are many causes of hearing impairment. These vary somewhat from region to region and have changed over the years. According to Moores (1981),

EXCEPTIONAL CHILDREN

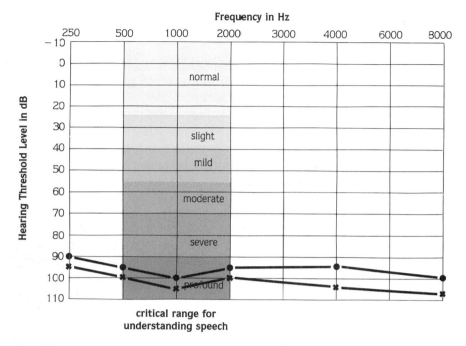

FIGURE 7.5

Audiogram for Steve (profound hearing impairment).

x = left ear   o = right ear

there are five major identified causes of childhood deafness in the United States today.

1. Heredity. There is strong evidence that congenital hearing impairment runs in some families. A tendency toward certain causes of adventitious hearing loss may also be inherited. Various surveys have noted that a high percentage of deaf students have relatives who are also deaf; Moores places this proportion at about 30% of the deaf school-age population.

2. Maternal rubella. Rubella (German measles) can cause deafness and a variety of other disabilities when it affects a woman during her pregnancy, particularly during the first trimester. A high percentage of cases of deafness and deaf-blindness result from this cause. Rubella is the major nongenetic cause of childhood deafness. A major epidemic of rubella took place in North America in 1964 and 1965; the children who were born with disabilities at that time are now young adults who need special educational and vocational services. Although an effective vaccination for rubella is now available, many women of childbearing age still fail to receive it.

3. Prematurity. Premature birth appears to increase the risk of deafness and other disabling conditions. It is difficult to evaluate precisely the effects of

prematurity on hearing impairment, but it appears that early delivery and lower birthweight are more common among deaf children than in the general population.

4. Meningitis. A declining but still important cause of adventitious hearing impairment is **meningitis,** a bacterial or viral infection which can, among its other effects, destroy the sensitive acoustic apparatus of the inner ear. Other severe disabilities and difficulties in balance may also result from meningitis.

5. Blood incompatibility. Damage to cells and nerve tissue can occur if a pregnant woman with Rh negative blood is carrying a fetus with Rh positive blood. Deafness and other disabilities may be caused if antibodies in the mother's system destroy cells in the developing fetus. Good prenatal care can greatly reduce the incidence of handicaps arising from blood incompatibility.

Another significant cause of hearing impairment is **otitis media,** an infection or inflammation of the middle ear. If untreated, otitis media may result in a buildup of fluid and a ruptured eardrum, causing a conductive hearing impairment. Certain viral diseases, such as mumps, measles, influenza, and herpes simplex can also cause permanent hearing loss. Repeated exposure to very loud sounds ("noise pollution") is a growing cause of hearing impairment, which may be either temporary or permanent.

See chapter 10 for more information on children with multiple handicaps.

Hearing impairment occurs more often than would be expected among certain other populations of handicapped children. Down syndrome often involves irregularities in the auditory canal and a tendency for fluid to accumulate in the middle ear; as many as 75% of children with Down syndrome may also have significant hearing impairments (Northern & Lemme, 1982). Among children with cerebral palsy, there is also a substantially higher-than-normal incidence of hearing impairment. It is always advisable to test the hearing of a child who is referred for special education of any kind.

BACKGROUND OF THE FIELD

Deaf children and adults have long been a source of fascination and interest. One of the earliest educational programs for exceptional children was the school for the deaf established around 1578 by Pablo Ponce de León, a Spanish monk. He tutored children in reading, writing, arithmetic, history, and foreign languages, and apparently was successful in teaching speech (Hewett & Forness, 1977). During the 18th century, schools for the deaf were established in England, France, Germany, and Scotland. Both oral and manual methods of instruction were used during this period.

The deaf were among the first groups of handicapped children to receive special education in the United States. The American Asylum for the Education of the Deaf and Dumb opened in Hartford, Connecticut, in 1817. The original name of this institution (which is now known as the American School for the Deaf) indicates the prevailing philosophy of the early 19th century, when deaf persons were viewed as "dumb" or "mute," not capable of benefiting from oral

EXCEPTIONAL CHILDREN

Approximately 40% of school-age deaf children in the United States are served by residential programs.

instruction, and when deaf students were considered most appropriately served in "asylums," special sanctuaries removed from "normal" society. Many of the private, public, and parochial schools for the deaf founded in the 19th century were, in fact, located in small towns away from major centers of population. For the most part, these were residential institutions.

During the second half of the 19th century, instruction in speech and speechreading became widely available to deaf students throughout the United States. Some educators combined both oral and manual methods, while others established "pure" oral schools, in which manual communication was not used. An early oral teacher was Alexander Graham Bell, the inventor of the telephone. Bell's lifelong interest in the deaf was influenced by the fact that his mother had been deaf and that his father and grandfather had both been teachers of speech and articulation. Bell himself married Mabel Hubbard, a deaf student whom he tutored. Several day schools for the deaf were established before the end of the 19th century.

Decibels are named for
A. G. Bell.

Educational opportunities for deaf children in regular public schools have become widespread only in recent years. In most states, parents of deaf children have the option of choosing between day classes and residential school placement. Today, approximately 60% of deaf children in the United States attend day classes and about 40% are served in residential settings (Moores, 1981). Some children attend residential schools during the day only, and most others make regular visits to their homes.

There is increasing emphasis today on the needs of hearing impaired students with additional handicapping conditions, such as mental retardation, learning disabilities, behavior disorders, and physical and health impairments. More than 20% of children currently enrolled in schools and classes for the deaf are considered multihandicapped (Moores, 1981). There is also a good deal of attention currently being paid to the needs of hearing impaired children from

TIPS FOR FACILITATING COMMUNICATION

Hearing impaired people are increasingly participating in community life. It is no longer unusual for a businessperson, bank teller, police officer, or anyone else to need to communicate with a deaf person. Yet many people with normal hearing are still unsure of themselves. They may try to avoid communicating with deaf people altogether or may use ineffective and frustrating strategies.

The following "tips" for facilitating communication with deaf people were suggested by the Community Services for the Deaf program in Akron, Ohio. These tips provide basic information about three common ways in which deaf people communicate: through speechreading, written communication, and with the assistance of a sign language interpreter. Usually, a deaf person will indicate the approach he or she is most comfortable with. If the deaf person relies mainly on *speechreading* (lipreading), here are some things you can do to help:

☐ Face the deaf person, and stand or sit no more than 4 feet away.

☐ The room should have adequate illumination—but don't seat yourself in front of a strong or glaring light.

☐ Try to keep your whole face visible.

☐ Speak clearly, naturally, and not too fast. Don't exaggerate your mouth movements.

☐ Don't raise the level of your voice.

☐ Some words are more easily "read" on the lips than others. If you are having a problem being understood, try substituting different words.

☐ It may take a while to become used to the deaf person's speech. If at first you can't understand what he or she is saying, don't give up.

☐ Don't hesitate to write any important words that are missed.

If the deaf person communicates best through *sign language* (and you do not), it will probably be necessary to use an *interpreter*. Here are some considerations to keep in mind:

- [ ] The role of the interpreter is to facilitate communication between you and the deaf person. He or she should not be asked to give opinions, advice, or personal feeling.
- [ ] Maintain eye contact with the deaf person, and speak directly to him or her. The deaf person should not be made to take a "back seat" in the conversation.
- [ ] Speak directly to the deaf individual. For example, say "How are you today?" instead of "Ask her how she is today."
- [ ] Sit face-to-face with the deaf person. The best place for the interpreter is behind you and a little to the side of your chair. Again, avoid strong or glaring light.
- [ ] Remember, it is the interpreter's job to communicate *everything* that is said by you and the deaf person. Don't say anything that you don't want interpreted for the deaf person.

Written messages can be helpful in exchanging information. Consider the following:

- [ ] Avoid the temptation to abbreviate your communication.
- [ ] It is best to write in simple, direct language.
- [ ] The deaf person's written English may not be grammatically correct, but you will probably be able to understand it. One deaf person, for example, wrote "Pay off yesterday, finish me" to convey the message, "I paid that loan off yesterday."
- [ ] Make use of visual aids, such as pictures, diagrams, and business cards.
- [ ] Don't be afraid to supplement your written messages with gestures and facial expressions.
- [ ] Written communication has limitations— but it is often more effective than no communication at all.

Remember that the language of many deaf people may be quite different from standard English. They are also deprived of a great deal of information because they cannot hear. These factors are not an accurate reflection of a person's intelligence or of the ability to function independently.

"Where's the nearest bank?"

Adapted from materials supplied by Community Services for the Deaf, Akron, Ohio.

See chapter 12.

culturally diverse backgrounds. For most teachers, the challenge of teaching language to a deaf child is particularly complex when a language other than English is spoken in that child's home.

Over the years, many special methods and materials have been developed and used with hearing impaired children, and much research has been conducted. Techniques, theories, and controversies have proliferated, often with passionate proponents. Today, interest in deaf people is as high as ever. Yet we still do not fully understand the effects of hearing impairment upon learning, communication, and personality, nor have we solved the most difficult problem inherent in educating the deaf: *teaching language to children who cannot hear.*

The present state of special education for the hearing impaired is not a happy one. Many deaf students leave school unable to read and write English even at a fifth grade level (Moores, 1981). Others are not able to communicate meaningfully, perhaps not even with schoolmates or members of their own families. Many parents are given confusing, contradictory information and advice when it is discovered that their child has a hearing impairment; the realization that they have a deaf child is often devastating. The rate of unemployment and underemployment among deaf adults is shockingly high, and their wages are often lower than those of the hearing population. Many questions remain unanswered, and many challenges remain to be faced in the education of children with hearing impairments.

AMPLIFICATION AND AUDITORY TRAINING

"Deafness" is often mistakenly interpreted as a total lack of hearing. In years past, it was assumed that deaf children simply did not hear at all; that they were "stone deaf." This view was and is incorrect. As we have seen, we now know that hearing loss occurs in different degrees and configurations. Almost all children who are considered *deaf* have some amount of residual hearing. With help, they need not grow up in a totally silent world.

Modern methods of testing hearing and improved electronic technology for the amplification of sound today enable many hearing impaired children to use their residual hearing productively. Even children with severe and profound hearing impairments can benefit from hearing aids in the classroom, home, and community, regardless of whether they communicate primarily in an oral or a manual mode. As Ross and Nober (1981) suggest, strategies for the acquisition, use, and evaluation of hearing aids should be part of the IEP process for virtually all hearing impaired students.

While recent advances in hearing aid design have been remarkable, it is important to keep in mind that they have certain limitations. No hearing aid can "cure" hearing loss or by itself enable a deaf child to function normally in a regular classroom. Some deaf students, even with the best available hearing aids, will be unable to hear speech because of the kind and degree of their hearing loss. Learning to use residual hearing effectively is a difficult and demanding process, but one that pays worthwhile dividends for the many hearing impaired students who are able to develop an awareness of sound through good amplification, training, and practice. These procedures can also enable many hearing impaired students to improve the quality of their own speech.

A hearing aid is an instrument that amplifies sound; it functions to make sounds louder. There are dozens of different types of hearing aids; they may be worn on the chest, behind the ear, completely within the ear, or in eyeglasses. Today's hearing aids are generally smaller, lighter in weight, and more powerful than older models. They may be worn in one or both ears. Whatever its shape, power, or size, a hearing aid picks up sound, magnifies its energy, and delivers this louder sound to the user's ear. The hearing aid is, in many ways, like a miniature public address system, with a microphone, an amplifier, and controls to adjust the volume and tone (Clarke & Leslie, 1980).

Group hearing aids are also available. Usually the teacher wears a small microphone, and the hearing impaired student or students wear receivers through which they hear the amplified sound of the teacher's voice. Most systems today use an FM radio frequency that does not require wires, so the teacher and students can move freely around the classroom area.

Hearing aids can be helpful to many children in increasing their awareness of sound. They make sounds *louder,* but not necessarily *clearer.* Children who hear sounds with distortion will still experience distortion when hearing aids are used. The effect is similar to turning up the volume on a cheap transistor radio—you can make music louder, but you may not be able to understand the words any better. Even the most powerful hearing aids generally cannot enable children with severe and profound hearing losses to hear speech sounds beyond a distance of a few feet. In all cases, it is the wearer of the hearing aid—not the aid itself—who does most of the work in interpreting conversation.

To derive the maximum benefit from a hearing aid, a child should wear it throughout the day. Residual hearing cannot be effectively developed if the aid is removed or turned off outside the classroom. It is important for the child to hear sounds while eating breakfast, shopping in the supermarket, or riding the school bus. Financial assistance from local or state agencies is often available for the purchase and maintenance of hearing aids.

The earlier in life a child can be fitted with an appropriate hearing aid, the more effectively he or she will learn to use hearing for communication and awareness. Today it is not at all unusual to see hearing aids worn by infants and preschool children; the improved listening conditions become an important part of the young child's speech and language development. It is a worthwhile goal to have a sense of hearing that is "integrated into the personality" (Lowell & Pollack, 1974).

Auditory training helps children make better use of their residual hearing. All hearing impaired children, whatever their preferred method of communication, should participate in lessons and activities which help them to improve their listening ability, and especially to recognize speech sounds. As Ross (1981) observes, many hearing impaired children have much more "auditory potential" than they actually use, and their residual hearing can be most effectively developed in the context of actual communication and daily experiences. An auditory training program should not be limited to artificial "exercises" in the classroom.

An auditory training program for a young hearing impaired child would be likely to emphasize the *awareness* of sound. Parents might direct the child's attention to such sounds as a doorbell ringing or water running. They might then focus on the *localization* of sound, for example, by hiding a radio somewhere in the room and encouraging the child to look for it. *Discrimination* of sounds is another important concept; a child might learn to notice the differences between a man's voice and a woman's voice, a fast song and a slow song, or between the words "rack" and "rug." *Recognition* of sounds comes when a child is able to identify a sound, word, or sentence through listening.

Some teachers find it helpful to conduct formal auditory training sessions, in which a child is required to use *only* hearing—he or she would have to recognize sounds and words without looking at the speaker. In actual practice, however, the student will gain useful information from vision and the other senses, to supplement the information received from hearing. All senses should be effectively developed and constantly used.

Speechreading

Hearing impaired children, whether they have much or little residual hearing, and whether they communicate primarily through oral or manual means, use their vision to help them understand speech. Some sounds are readily distinguished by watching the lips of the speaker. For example, the word "pail" begins with the lips in a shut position, while in the word "rail" the lips are somewhat drawn together and puckered at the corners. Paying careful attention to a speaker's lips may help a hearing impaired person derive important clues—particularly if he or she is also able to gain some information through residual hearing, signs or gestures, facial expressions, and familiarity with the context or situation.

However, speechreading, or lipreading, is difficult and has many limitations. Only about 30% of the sounds in the English language can be detected through speechreading alone (Davis & Silverman, 1970). To make matters worse, about half of all English words have some other word or words **homophonous** to them. That is, they may sound quite different, but they look alike on the lips. Words such as "pear," "bear," and "mare," for example, look exactly alike and simply cannot be discriminated by watching the lips.

The frustrations of lipreading are graphically described in this passage by Shanny Mow, a teacher who is deaf:

> Like the whorls on his fingertips, each person's lips are different and move in a peculiar way of their own. When young, you build confidence as you guess correctly "ball," "fish," "top," and "shoe" on your teacher's lips. This confidence doesn't last. As soon as you discover there are more than four words in the dictionary, it evaporates. Seventy percent of the words when appearing on the lips are no more than blurs. Lipreading is a precarious and cruel art which re-

wards a few who have mastered it and tortures the many who have tried and failed. (1973, pp. 21–22)

Many speakers are virtually unintelligible through speechreading; they may seem not to move their lips at all. It is extremely tiring to watch lips for a long period of time, and it may be impossible to do so at a distance, such as during a lecture.

Despite the problems inherent in speechreading, it can be a valuable adjunct in the communication of a hearing impaired person. According to Moores (1981), few new techniques have recently been developed and little research has been done into the most effective ways of teaching speechreading. Although speechreading cannot take the place of hearing, improved methods might well enable many hearing impaired people to make better use of their vision in decoding messages.

EDUCATIONAL APPROACHES

Teaching hearing impaired children is considered among the most "special" areas of special education. As Kirk (1981) observes,

> Special education has been defined as that education which is unique, uncommon, or of unusual quality and is in addition to the procedures used with the majority of children. The special techniques that have been developed over the years to assist deaf children in processing information without the sense of hearing are certainly unique, ingenious, and highly specialized. (p. xi)

Effects of Hearing Impairment on Language and Education

The effects of hearing impairment—especially if severe and present from birth—are so complex and pervasive that special techniques, materials, and people are indeed called for. It is perhaps impossible for a person with normal hearing to comprehend fully the immense difficulties of a deaf child trying to learn language. Hearing children typically acquire a large vocabulary and a knowledge of grammar, word order, idiomatic expressions, fine shades of meaning, and infinite other aspects of verbal expression by listening to others and to their own speech from early infancy. A child with a hearing impairment, however, is exposed to verbal communication only partially or not at all.

Hearing impaired children—even those with superior intelligence and abilities—are at a great disadvantage in acquiring language skills. When standard measures of achievement in reading and writing are used with deaf students, we typically find that their vocabularies are smaller and their sentence structures are simpler and more rigid than those of hearing children of the same age or grade level (Meadow, 1980).

Deaf children must undergo intensive instruction and drill in order to master language concepts learned "spontaneously" by their hearing peers.

As Norris (1975) points out, the grammar and structure of English often do not follow logical rules, and a prelingually hearing impaired person must put forth a great deal of effort to read and write with acceptable form and meaning. For example, if the past tense of "talk" is "talked," then why doesn't "go" become "goed"? If the plural of "man" is "men," then shouldn't the plural of "pan" be "pen"? It is far from easy to explain the difference between the expressions "He's in" and "He's all in" to a person who has never had normal hearing.

Many deaf students tend to write sentences that are short, incomplete, or improperly arranged. They may omit endings of words, such as the plural *-s, -ed,* or *-ing.* They may have difficulty in differentiating questions from statements. The following excerpts from papers written by deaf high school students (Fusfeld, 1958, cited in Meadow, 1980, p. 33) illustrate some language problems directly attributable to impaired hearing:

> She is good at sewing than she is at cooking.
> Many things find in Arkansas.
> To his disappointed, his wife disgusted of what he made.
> I was happy to kiss my parents because they letted my playing football.

Since language development is closely related to reading and to achievement in all academic areas, many investigators have found that hearing impaired children are, as a group, significantly behind normally hearing children on standardized tests of reading and academic achievement. As Napierkowski (1981) observes, few deaf children progress beyond a fourth grade reading level. Reading is clearly central to educational achievement and to obtaining information throughout one's life; we must continue to seek more effective ways of teaching reading and writing to hearing impaired students. However, it is important that we not equate verbal performance with intelligence. Most deaf children have normal intellectual capacity, and it has been repeatedly demonstrated that their scores on nonverbal intelligence tests are approximately the same as those of the general population. Deafness "imposes no limitations on the cognitive capabilities of individuals" (Moores, 1981, p. 162).

The problems that deaf students often experience in their education and adjustment may be largely attributable to a "bad fit" between their perceptual abilities and the demands of spoken and written English (Hoemann & Briga, 1981). Command of English is only one indicator of a person's intelligence and ability.

Hearing impairment can also influence a child's behavior and social-emotional development. Research has not provided clear insights into the effects of hearing impairment upon behavior; it appears that the extent to which a child successfully interacts with family members, friends, and people in the community depends largely on the attitudes of others and the child's ability to communicate in some acceptable way. Feelings of loneliness and isolation are frequently expressed by deaf persons. Some observers have noted that deaf people often tend to associate largely with other deaf people; this may mistakenly be interpreted as clannishness. It is certain that communication plays a major role in any person's adjustment. Most hearing impaired people are fully capable of developing satisfying relationships with their hearing peers when they can develop a mutually acceptable means of communication. There may well be a significant number of hearing impaired students who have behavior disorders that require treatment, but unfortunately few special programs have been designed specifically to address the needs of this population.

Special Methods

Educational programs and techniques for hearing impaired students are "special" primarily because of the many challenges involved in teaching communication to children who cannot hear normally. Educators, scientists, philosophers, and parents—both hearing and deaf—have for many years debated over the most appropriate instructional methods for deaf children. Today, this controversy is as lively as ever.

The fundamental disagreement concerns the extent to which deaf children should express themselves through speech and perceive the communication of others through speechreading and residual hearing. Some educators insist that a "purely oral" method is best for helping deaf students develop speech and language-related skills. These "oralists" often discourage the use of sign language and gestures. Other educators believe that sign language, gestures, cues, fingerspelling, and other "manual" means used along with speech are a more natural way of communicating, and enable hearing impaired children to express themselves more fully and to understand other people.

Virtually no responsible educator today would argue that speech is unimportant or that manual communication should be used in place of speech. Speech is, of course, the principal way that people communicate; it can be of great value to a deaf person in moving into a less restrictive educational and living environment. It is generally recognized that speech is important and that it should be developed to the greatest extent possible. Rather than viewing the controversy over instructional methods as a simple debate between "oralists" on one side and "manualists" on the other, it is better to say that there are differences of opinion over the degree to which speech should be emphasized in the education of hearing impaired children.

The Oral Approach

Educational programs with an **oral** emphasis view speech as essential for the deaf person's "integration into the hearing world." Training in speech and language is incorporated into virtually all aspects of the child's learning; it is important to keep in mind that speech is a means of communication, not an educational program in and of itself.

A hearing impaired child who attends a program with an oral emphasis typically uses several means to develop residual hearing and the ability to speak as intelligibly as possible. Much attention is given to amplification, auditory training, speechreading, and above all, *talking*. Some schools and classes are "purely oral," and may even prohibit children from pointing, using gestures, or spelling words out to communicate: the children *must* express themselves, and learn to understand others, through speech alone. Other programs also emphasize speech but are less rigid. They may use a variety of approaches to help the student produce and understand spoken language.

Cued speech is one method of supplementing oral communication. It is considered a "visual/oral methodology," rather than a manual system, since it carries no meaning without an accompanying speech signal (Clarke & Leslie, 1980). The "cues" consist of hand signals used near the lips; the hand serves to identify sounds that cannot be distinguished through speechreading alone. There are eight different hand shapes, used in four different positions; these cues are neither signs nor fingerspelling. According to Cornett (1974), who developed the system, cued speech can clarify the patterns of spoken English, allowing young deaf children to acquire verbal language more readily than if oral methods were used alone. Of course, the cues must be learned by the child's parents and teachers, and preferably by his or her peers as well. While the use of cued speech appears to be growing, it has not yet found wide acceptance in North America.

This system is widely used by hearing impaired people in Australia.

Oral educators acknowledge that teaching speech to hearing impaired children is difficult, time-consuming, and painstaking for the teacher, the parents, and—most of all—for the child. The rewards of successful oral communication, however, are thought to be worth all the effort. Many hearing impaired children and adults are able to learn speech well enough to communicate effectively with hearing people.

AROUND THE WORLD IN SIGN LANGUAGE

Is sign language universal? Students frequently ask, "When deaf people from other countries get together, can they understand each other?"

Sign language is not universal. Dictionaries of sign languages have been published in several countries, and there appears to be little uniformity of signs. The photos we have here, for example, show how the sign for "mother" is made quite differently in six different countries.

Just as there are different dialects among hearing people in different parts of the United States, so there are regional differences in sign language. However, a deaf traveler does have certain advantages in communicating with deaf people in other regions or countries. If the traveler is accustomed to using signs, gestures, and "body language," he will probably be able to work out some ways of communicating with a foreign deaf person. Indeed, hearing travelers often devise their own "sign language" to convey information and ask questions when they do not know the oral language of the country they are visiting.

United States

Denmark

England

Brazil

Finland

China

Total Communication

Programs with emphasis on **total communication** use a variety of methods to assist the deaf child in expression and language development. Speech is supplemented by one or more manual communication techniques, and meaningful communication is encouraged between teacher and student and among students. In most cases, however, these manual techniques are not understood by the general public.

Sign language uses gestures to represent words, ideas, and concepts. Many signs convey meaning by motions which appear to imitate or "act out" their message. In making the "cat" sign, for example, the signer seems to be stroking feline whiskers on his or her face; in the sign for "eat," the hand moves back and forth into an open mouth (see figure 7.6). Many other signs, however, have little or no resemblance to the objects or actions they represent. If sign language were simply a form of pantomime, then most nonsigners would be able to understand it with relatively little effort. But several studies have shown that the majority of signs cannot be guessed by people who are unfamiliar with the sign language (Klima & Bellugi, 1979).

American Sign Language (often referred to as ASL or Ameslan) is a language widely used by hearing impaired people in the United States and Canada. There has been a great deal of recent interest in the study of ASL; psychologists, linguists, and educators now generally view ASL as a complex and legitimate language in its own right, rather than an imperfect variation of spoken English. In ASL, the hands' shape, location, and movement, the intensity with which motions are made, and the signer's facial expressions all communicate meaning and content.

Since ASL has its own syntax, vocabulary, and grammatical rules, it does not correspond exactly to spoken or written English. Articles, prepositions, tenses, and plurals may be left out, and word order may be different from that in standard English. It would be difficult to make precise word-for-word translations between ASL and English, just as it is difficult to translate French or German directly into English.

FIGURE 7.6
Sign language for "cat" (left) and "eat" (right).

Total communication combines speech, sign language, and fingerspelling to produce meaningful communication between student and teacher.

Teachers who use sign language generally speak as they sign and make a special effort to follow the form and structure of spoken English as closely as possible, to help hearing impaired students acquire reading and writing skills. Several sign language systems have been designed primarily for educational purposes; they incorporate many features of ASL and also seek to reproduce "correct" English through word-for-word signing. These systems include Seeing Essential English (Anthony, 1971), Signing Exact English (Gustason, Pfetzing, & Zawolkow, 1980), and Signed English (Bornstein, 1974). Hearing impaired students often use two or more sign language systems, depending upon the person with whom they are communicating.

Fingerspelling, or the *manual alphabet*, consists of 26 distinct hand positions, one for each English letter. A one-hand manual alphabet is used in the United States and Canada (see Figure 7.7). Some manual letters, such as *C, L,* and *W,* resemble the shape of printed English letters, while others, such as *A, E,* and *S,* have no apparent similarity. As in typewriting, each word is spelled out letter-by-letter. To fingerspell the word "tiger," for example, the hand must be made into five different shapes.

Fingerspelling is often used in conjunction with other methods of communication. A user of sign language relies on fingerspelling to spell out proper names for which no sign exists and to clarify meanings which may be unclear. The Rochester Method uses a combination of oral communication and fingerspelling, but does not use sign language. The teacher fingerspells every letter of every word as he or she speaks, and the hearing impaired student learns to use the same means of expression. The Rochester Method also emphasizes reading and writing; its advocates believe that this approach facilitates the acquisition of correct language patterns. Fingerspelling is also used by many people who are both deaf and visually impaired; the manual alphabet can be used at very close distances or felt with the hand if the person is totally blind.

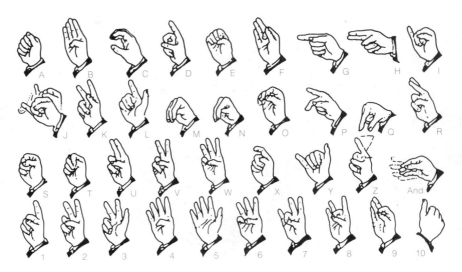

FIGURE 7.7
The manual alphabet.

Supporters of total communication methods believe that it is the best way to provide a "reliable receptive-expressive symbol system," especially in the preschool years when communication between parent and child is vitally important (Denton, 1972). Several recent studies have found that very young children are able to make and understand signs effectively (Bonvillian, Orlansky, & Novack, 1983; Maestas y Moores & Moores, 1980; Prinz & Prinz, 1979). Some educators feel that the use of sign language will interfere with the child's ability to develop oral language skills, but this view is not supported by research evidence (Meadow, 1980; Moores, 1981; Rooney, 1982). Total communication is currently gaining wide acceptance in educational programs for hearing impaired students.

Language Instruction

Many techniques and materials have been developed for the purpose of helping hearing impaired children acquire and use written language. The relationship between written and spoken expression is obviously a close one, but there is no exact correspondence between the type of communication method a child uses (oral only or total communication) and the method of language instruction that a particular school or class employs.

Instructional programs in language for the hearing impaired are generally classified as either *structured* or *natural*. A well-known structured method, developed more than 50 years ago but still widely used, is the Fitzgerald Key (Fitzgerald, 1929). This method provides several labeled categories, such as *who, what, where,* and *when*. The child learns to generate "correct" sentences by placing words into the proper categories. An example of a natural method is Natural Language for Deaf Children (Groht, 1958). This method emphasizes

EXCEPTIONAL CHILDREN

language development through modeling and conversation; games and activities are preferred to formal drills and exercises. Moores and Maestas y Moores (1981) provide a helpful review of methods of language instruction, noting that virtually no research has been conducted to evaluate the advantages of one approach over the other and that most educational programs today tend to use a combination of structured and natural methods.

Controversy and Choices

The controversies over communication and instructional methods for hearing impaired students are likely to continue well into the future. Research has not provided—and will probably never provide—a definitive answer to the question of which communication method is "best." There is general agreement, however, that our educational programs leave much room for improvement.

Different children communicate in different ways. Some hearing impaired children, unfortunately, have experienced deep frustration and failure because of rigid adherence to an "oral only" program. They have left their programs without having developed a usable avenue of communication; they are unable to participate in meaningful conversations with other people. Equally unfortunately, other hearing impaired children have not been given an adequate opportunity to develop their auditory and oral skills, because they were placed in educational programs that did not provide good oral instruction. Their potential for learning speech was not fully developed. In both cases, children have been unfairly penalized. Every hearing impaired child should have access to an educational program that uses a communication method appropriate to his or her unique abilities and needs.

EDUCATIONAL SERVICE ALTERNATIVES

Early detection of hearing loss and early intervention with the hearing impaired child and the family are generally recognized to be critical. Many schools, speech and hearing clinics, and other agencies provide educational programs for preschool children. Usually the child's hearing is tested, an amplification aid is provided, and the program emphasizes communication with adults and other children. Parent groups and home visits are an important part of a preschool program; through these efforts parents may be helped to communicate with their child more effectively. A hearing impaired child who receives no specialized assessment, amplification, or training until age 5 or 6 will surely be at a great disadvantage in his or her communication and general development.

School programs for hearing impaired children are available in residential schools, special day schools, and regular public schools. Hearing impaired children in regular schools may attend self-contained classes specifically for hearing impaired students or may be integrated with nonhandicapped children for part or all of the school day. The specialized needs of children with severe hearing impairments make some special services necessary in virtually all cases. In an integrated setting, special services for a hearing impaired child might include:

- [ ] Smaller class size;
- [ ] Regular speech, language, and auditory training instruction from a specialist;
- [ ] Amplification systems;
- [ ] Services of an interpreter, if the child uses manual communication;
- [ ] Special seating in the classroom to promote speechreading;
- [ ] Captioned films;
- [ ] Good acoustics and reduction of background noise;
- [ ] Special tutoring or review sessions;
- [ ] Someone to take notes in class, so the hearing impaired student can pay more constant attention;
- [ ] Instruction for teachers and nonhandicapped students in sign language or other communication methods used by the hearing impaired.

Several recent publications (Bishop, 1979; Froehlinger, 1981; La Porta, McGee, Simmons-Martin, Voce, von Hippel, & Conovan, 1978; Mollick & Etra, 1981; Orlansky, 1979) provide helpful guidelines and practical suggestions to encourage the successful integration of hearing impaired students into regular classes.

Postsecondary Education

A growing number of educational opportunities are available to hearing impaired students after completion of a high school-level program. The oldest and best known of these is Gallaudet College, an institution of higher education in Washington, D.C., which offers a wide range of undergraduate and graduate programs in the liberal arts, sciences, education, and other fields. Hearing impaired students from throughout the United States, Canada, and other countries compete for admission into Gallaudet. The National Technical Institute for the Deaf, located at the Rochester (New York) Institute of Technology, provides wide-ranging programs in technical, vocational, and business-related fields. More than 50 other institutions of higher education, which do not serve hearing impaired students exclusively, have developed special programs of supportive services for them. Among these are California State University at Northridge, Delgado Vocational Technical Junior College (New Orleans), St. Paul Technical Vocational Institute, Seattle Central Community College, Western Oregon State College (Monmouth), Western Maryland College (Westminster, Maryland), and Columbus Technical Institute (Columbus, Ohio).

CURRENT ISSUES/FUTURE TRENDS

As more hearing impaired children come to be educated in regular public school settings, it appears likely that oral methods of instruction will hold a position of great importance. Speech, after all, is the most widely used form of communication among teachers and students in regular classes. Concurrently, however, manual communication will probably become more familiar to the general public. Training in sign language is already offered to children with normal hearing in some schools, and an increasing number of people who contact the public in the course of their jobs—such as police officers, firefighters, flight attendants, and bank tellers—will learn to communicate manually with deaf individuals. Television programs, films, and other media using interpreters or printed captions are becoming more widely available. It's no longer unusual to see a sign language interpreter standing next to a public speaker.

Despite the recent expansion of postsecondary programs of education and training, many hearing impaired adults still find limited opportunities for appropriate employment and economic advancement. Recent court decisions regarding the rights of hearing impaired students have had mixed results. In one case (*Barnes* v. *Converse College,* 1977), a court ordered a private college to provide, at its own expense, an interpreter for a deaf student. In another case (*Southeastern Community College* v. *Davis,* 1979), the U.S. Supreme Court decided that a college could not be compelled to admit a hearing impaired student into its nursing program. A widely publicized Supreme Court case (*Rowley* v. *Hendrick Hudson School District,* 1982) resulted in the ruling that a local school district was not required to provide, at its expense, a sign language interpreter for a deaf child who was succeeding without one in the regular classroom. Similar cases are certain to arise in the future, as hearing impaired people become increasingly aware of their civil rights and seek access to education, employment, and other rights.

The Rowley case was also discussed in chapter 2.

Future technological developments will undoubtedly result in more sophisticated techniques to detect hearing impairment—particularly in infants and young children—and to make effective use of even the slightest amount of residual hearing. It is hoped that new and improved methods of teaching expressive and receptive language will follow.

TTY systems enable a deaf person to send and receive typewritten messages by telephone.

Through advances in electronics and computer technology, the telephone and television are rapidly becoming available to people with hearing impairments. The telephone has long served as a barrier to deaf people in employment and social interaction, but Teletypewriter Assistance for the Deaf (often called TTY) now enables many people to send and receive immediate written messages over telephone lines. Closed captioning is being used on more and more television programs; a hearing impaired person who has a special decoding device is able to read captions or subtitles on the television screen. Although such aids as the TTY and the caption decoder are relatively expensive, they are gradually making a broader range of educational, vocational, and recreational opportunities available to people with impaired hearing.

A PARENT REMINISCES

This story was shared with us by the mother of Jennifer, who has a severe congenital hearing impairment. Jennifer (not her real name) is now in her mid-twenties, successfully employed as a clerk with a government agency. In this account, Jennifer's mother recalls some of her early experiences.

Jennifer was my first child. Just as many people learn parenting with their first child, I was flying blind all the way with her. Parents' initial reactions vary only in the ways we declare our ignorance. I remember another mother who said that, when they learned of their child's hearing loss, her husband's first remark was, "Where will we ever find a deaf Jewish boy for her?" I thought a hearing aid and school for the deaf would be the answer.

My daughter was born 9 weeks early, so the fact that she was late developing in many ways didn't alarm me or the doctor. When she had no speech at age 2½, I began taking her to specialists, and I was always told to return in 6 months.

When Jennifer was 3½, I took her to a medical center in Toronto, expecting at best a cure and at worst an accurate diagnosis. She was seen by a neurologist, a speech therapist, and an ophthalmologist. They told me her main problem was receptive aphasia, complicated by a high-frequency hearing loss. They recommended speech therapy and assured me she was not mentally retarded.

So Jennifer began having speech therapy—half an hour a week. It was about as significant as putting a pail of water on an acre of potatoes, but she enjoyed it and seemed to try very hard.

At age 5 Jennifer really had no speech, so we arranged with a nursery school teacher to have her in her class. She wasn't accepted by the other children, but she loved going. The next year she still wasn't ready for public school, and we couldn't get her back into the nursery school, so we appealed to the parochial school system. With perhaps a 25-word vocabulary she certainly wasn't ready for first grade, but they took her.

By the time Jennifer was 10 years old, she was struggling unsuccessfully with fourth grade work. At this point, I had 6 younger children and no time to give her much help. I was quite devastated by this; I didn't realize that what she missed from me, she gained from her constant exposure to other children. She became a very good lipreader by being continually exposed to oral speech.

We had never considered the school for the deaf for Jennifer, because the speech therapists advised strongly against sending her there. And we still were thinking of her main problem as brain damage (aphasia). At about this time, she was seen by a specialist who said her problem was hearing loss only and not aphasia. He told us to send her to the school for the deaf. It was called an "oral" school, but signing was used almost exclusively. The pupils—most of whom had been there since age 5—did not communicate orally.

Jennifer was at the school for the deaf for 4 months. There she learned to sign, which was good for her, since most people in the deaf community are not oral. She was very unhappy at the school for the deaf, though. She couldn't relate to the silent atmosphere. She wasn't accepted by the other pupils because she could speak and they couldn't. If we had left her there, she would have lost her speech from lack of use.

We next heard that special classes for hearing impaired children were starting in our home town. My husband made several inquiries but was unable to find anything concrete. At the beginning of the following school year, we kept Jennifer home as a form of protest. She was so upset that she made herself ill. She always wanted to go to school, and we couldn't communicate with her well enough to explain the situation. We tried tutoring and various private schools.

When Jennifer was 13, we learned through a friend that "outreach classes" for hearing impaired children had been started in the public schools. That September, my husband delivered her to school, prepared to insist that she be admitted. They took her in, just as though they had been expecting her. So at 13 years old, Jennifer began her first meaningful schooling.

Jennifer's first teacher was an outstanding middle-aged woman who knew, from hard experience, how to reach her pupils. Most of the other teachers were younger women, and Jennifer related to them very well. She was the oldest pupil there, and she enjoyed helping with the young children.

Jennifer received a ninth grade equivalency certificate, but she was not encouraged to go to high school, as no resource help was available. The vocational teacher thought a course in child care might be beneficial, so she took one the next year. She worked at a day-care center, but felt she was being exploited—cleaning pet cages, bathrooms, and so on. She then had a series of simple jobs. Finally she took a course to become a clerktypist. But she was unable to obtain a job, because most offices demand that employees use the telephone. She spent months at home, pursuing her job placement officer. Eventually she took a temporary job with the Civil Service Commission which got extended. Now, a year later, she is on the permanent staff and has received a couple of promotions.

I think my daughter is well adjusted. She enjoys her work and the people at her office. She is the first hearing impaired person to be employed by the local Civil Service Commission and is very proud to be able to do the work. She feels she is accepted by the staff and not labeled specially.

Today's educational opportunities seem quite wonderful to me, compared to what was available back then. And it is a delight for me to see the changes in educators' attitudes, compared with the uninformed people I dealt with a decade or two ago. Then I was afraid of being at all forceful, for fear of jeopardizing my child's situation or being classed as overprotective and biased. The situation today is healthier and allows a beneficial mutual exchange of information.

If I were my daughter, I'd be asking, "Why was I born too soon, to miss all these advantages?" Jennifer is aware of what is happening, as she keeps in touch with her former teachers and the young students she helped with. She is only happy for them.

The hearing impaired people I have known have more empathy for our problems than we have for theirs. They are warm, caring people. I think these exceptional children become exceptional adults when we give them a chance. If we could walk in their shoes, they would have an easier time living in our world.

1. Hearing is a critical part of everyday life and communication, and its loss can never be fully compensated for.

2. There is a wide range of hearing ability.
   a. A person with normal hearing can understand speech in everyday situations.
   b. A hard-of-hearing person needs special adaptations to understand speech.
   c. A deaf person cannot use his or her hearing alone—even with amplification—to understand speech.

3. There is more than one way to classify hearing impairment.
   a. A hearing impairment may be either congenital or adventitious, depending on whether or not it is present at birth.
   b. It may be prelingual or postlingual, depending on when it is acquired.
   c. It may be conductive or sensorineural, depending on the location of the damage. It may also be a combination of the two.
   d. Hearing impairment may be unilateral or bilateral.

4. Both the intensity and the frequency of a sound are measured.
   a. Intensity is measured in decibels. A person can have a loss of up to 25dB and still be considered to have "normal" hearing.
   b. Frequency is measured in hertz. The frequency range of most speech is 500 to 2,000 Hz.

5. Hearing impairments can now be detected in infants and young children, allowing early intervention.
   a. Some children's hearing impairments are not detected until they reach school.
   b. A formal hearing test generates an audiogram, which shows graphically the faintest sound a child can hear at each of several frequencies.
   c. Based on the faintest sounds a person can hear, hearing impairment may be classified as mild, moderate, severe, or profound.
   d. The audiogram is only one source of information about a hearing loss. Watching how a child acts at home and at school can also give useful information about hearing impairment.

6. Hearing impairment is a low-incidence handicap.
   a. About 5% of all school-age children have hearing impairments, but many do not require special education.
   b. Only about 1 child in 500 (.2%) has a severe or profound bilateral hearing impairment.
   c. While most deaf children do participate in special education programs, only about 20% of the hard-of-hearing receive those services.

7. There are five major causes of deafness in children:
   a. Heredity.
   b. Maternal rubella.

c. Prematurity.

d. Meningitis.

e. Blood incompatibility.

f. Other, less frequent causes include otitis media, various childhood diseases, and repeated exposure to loud sounds.

8. Education of the deaf has a long history.

a. Schools for the deaf were first established in 18th-century Europe.

b. Early American programs for the deaf during the 19th century considered deaf people to be permanently mute and best served in isolated, residential settings.

c. Speech and speechreading instruction became popular during the last half of the 19th century.

d. Regular public school classes for the deaf are a recent innovation. Today most states offer both residential and day classes.

e. We still do not know how to teach language effectively to children who cannot hear. Many deaf children never develop adequate language skills; they remain unemployed and underemployed as adults.

9. Most deaf children have some residual hearing which they can use.

a. Hearing aids can amplify the sounds a child hears, but will not eliminate distortion.

b. Children who need hearing aids should be fitted as young as possible, and should wear the aids all day long.

c. All deaf children should receive auditory training to help them learn to use their residual hearing, even though the process is difficult and demanding.

d. Hearing impaired children use their vision to help them understand speech, but speechreading is difficult and of limited use.

10. Because of the widespread effects of deafness, special educational techniques and materials are called for.

a. Deaf children have tremendous difficulties learning all aspects of language—including word order, vocabulary, and grammar.

b. Their difficulty with language contributes to problems in reading and other academic areas.

c. Deafness can also affect a child's behavior and personal adjustment.

d. One group of educators believes in a purely oral approach to educating deaf children. They stress speech as an ability which is essential for integration into the hearing world.

e. The oral approach emphasizes amplification, auditory training, speechreading, and talking. Cued speech may also be used.

f. Other educators advocate a total communication approach, which supplements speech with manual communication techniques that are not understood by the general public. This approach is said to facilitate language use.

g. Manual communication techniques include sign language and finger-spelling.

h. Language instruction may be either structured or natural, or a combination of both.

i. It is not clear which communication and instructional methods are better. Therefore we must consider the individual child and choose the program best suited to that child's needs.

11. There are several different options for educating hearing impaired children.

a. Special services, including amplification and parent training, should begin before the child reaches school age.

b. In school, the hearing impaired can be educated in residential schools, special day schools, special classes for the hearing impaired, or regular classes with nonhandicapped children. Within a regular class, a deaf child may require other special services, including instruction from a specialist and the aid of an interpreter.

c. There are several special postsecondary programs for deaf students, spread throughout the country.

12. At the same time that more deaf children are learning to speak more intelligibly, more hearing people are learning to use manual communication systems.

13. As deaf persons become more aware of their civil rights, their employment and economic opportunities should expand.

14. Advances in electronics and computer technology promise to make a broader range of experiences possible for deaf individuals.

FOR MORE INFORMATION

Journals

American Annals of the Deaf, published bimonthly by the Convention of American Instructors of the Deaf and the Conference of Executives of American Schools for the Deaf. Publishes articles dealing with education of deaf and hearing impaired students.

Journal of Rehabilitation of the Deaf, published by the Professional Rehabilitation Workers with the Adult Deaf. Focuses on research, innovations, patterns of service, and other topics related to deaf adults.

Sign Language Studies, published quarterly by Linstok Press, Silver Spring, Md. Contains research and practical articles related to sign language and manual communication.

The Volta Review, published nine times a year by the Alexander Graham Bell Association for the Deaf. Encourages teaching of speech, speechreading, and use of residual hearing to deaf persons. Advocates oral approach.

Books

Griffin, B. F. (ed.). *Family to family.* Washington, D.C.: A. G. Bell Association for the Deaf, 1980.

Katz, L., Mathis, S. L., & Merrill, E. C. *The deaf child in the public schools,* 2d ed. Danville, Ill.: Interstate Printers and Publishers, 1978.

Meadow, K. P. *Deafness and child development.* Berkeley: University of California Press, 1980.

Methods of communication currently used in the education of deaf children. London: Royal National Institute for the Deaf, 1976.

Moores, D. F. *Educating the deaf: Psychology, principles, and practices,* 2d ed. Boston: Houghton Mifflin, 1981.

Orlansky, J. Z. *Mainstreaming the hearing impaired child.* Hingham, Mass.: Teaching Resources, 1979.

O'Rourke, T. J. *A basic course in manual communication.* Silver Spring, Md.: National Association of the Deaf, 1975.

Organizations

Alexander Graham Bell Association for the Deaf, Inc., 3417 Volta Place, N.W. Washington, DC 20007. Provides information about hearing impairment and education, with an oral emphasis. Sponsors organizations for parents, teachers, and oral deaf adults.

Gallaudet College, 7th and Florida Ave., N.E., Washington, DC 20002. Includes a bookstore with one of the most complete collections of professional and popular literature about hearing impairment, education of the deaf, and related topics. Children's sign language books appeal to many readers. A free book list is available.

John Tracy Clinic, 806 West Adams Boulevard, Los Angeles, CA 90007. Provides free correspondence courses for parents of young deaf and deaf-blind children throughout the world. Emphasizes assessment, communication, and support to parents and teachers.

National Association of the Deaf, 814 Thayer Ave., Silver Spring, MD 20910. A clearinghouse for information about education, communication, employment, and other topics. Offers material on manual communication and activities for deaf adults and parents of deaf children.

8

Visual Impairment

Sixteen-year-old Maria is a bright, college-bound student who has been totally blind since birth. She recently took a series of intellectual and psychological tests. Maria generally performed well, scoring at about her expected age and grade level. Something unusual, however, happened on one test. The examiner handed Maria an unpeeled banana and asked, "What is this?" Maria held the banana for several minutes and took several guesses, but could not answer correctly. The examiner was astonished, as were Maria's teachers and parents. After all, this section of the test was intended for very young children.

Maria had eaten bananas many times but had missed out on one important aspect of the "banana experience": she simply had never held and peeled a banana by herself. This true story (adapted from Swallow, 1978) illustrates the tremendous importance of *vision* in obtaining accurate and thorough information about the world in which we live. Teachers find it necessary to plan and present many, many firsthand experiences when working with children who are visually impaired. Much of the information and understanding that children with normal vision seem to acquire almost effortlessly may not be learned at all by visually impaired children—or may be learned incorrectly—unless someone deliberately teaches it to them.

Even when information *is* deliberately presented to visually impaired children, they may not learn it in exactly the same way as children with normal vision would. They may learn to make good use of their other senses. Hearing, touch, smell, and taste can be very useful channels of sensory input, but they do not totally compensate for the loss of vision. Touch and taste cannot tell children very much about things that are far away from them—or even just beyond the length of their own arms. Hearing can tell them a good deal about the near and distant environment, but it seldom provides information which is as *complete*, as *continuous*, or as *exact* as the information people obtain from being constantly able to see their surroundings.

The classroom is one important setting in which vision is critical for successful learning and development. In school, normally sighted children are routinely expected to exercise several important visual skills. They must be able to see clearly. They must focus on different objects, changing easily from near to far as needed. They must have good eye-hand coordination and must be able to remember what they have seen. They must discriminate colors accurately. They must be able to see, and interpret, many things simultaneously. They must be able to maintain visual concentration. Should they not have any of these skills, children will find it difficult to learn. They will need special procedures or materials to let them function effectively in school.

DEFINING VISUAL IMPAIRMENT

There are both legal and educational definitions of visual impairment. The *legal* definition of blindness relies heavily on measurements of **visual acuity.** Visual acuity is the ability to clearly distinguish forms or discriminate details at a specified distance. Most frequently, visual acuity is measured by having children read letters, numbers, or other symbols from a chart 20 feet away. The familiar phrase "20/20 vision" simply indicates that, at a distance of 20 feet, the eye can see what a "normally seeing eye" *should* be able to see at that distance. As the bottom number increases, visual acuity decreases.

If a person's visual acuity is 20/200 or less in the better eye, even after the best possible correction with glasses or contact lenses, then he or she is considered **legally blind.** If Jane has 20/200 vision while wearing her glasses, she needs to stand at a distance of *20* feet in order to see what most people can see from *200* feet away. In other words, Jane must get much closer than normal in order to see things clearly. Her legal blindness means that Jane will likely find it difficult to use her vision in many everyday situations, but there is a good chance that a child with 20/200, or even 20/400, vision will be able to succeed in a regular classroom with special help. Some students are unable to

Blindness does not prevent participation in a vigorous sport like wrestling.

perceive fine details at any distance, even while wearing glasses or contact lenses.

A person may also be considered legally blind if his **field of vision** is extremely restricted. When gazing straight ahead, a normal eye is able to see objects within a range of approximately 180 degrees. If David's field of vision is only 10 degrees, he is able to see only a very limited area at any one time (even though his visual acuity in that small area may be quite good). Some people with limited field of vision describe it as being like viewing the world through a narrow tube or tunnel; they have good *central* vision, but poor *peripheral* vision at the outer limits of the visual field. Other people may have relatively good peripheral vision, but be unable to see things clearly in the central visual field.

See Figure 8.2 for a diagram depicting normal field of vision.

Whether the visual field impairment is central or peripheral, a person can be considered legally blind if he or she is restricted to an area of 20 degrees or less out of the normal 180-degree field. It is common for the visual field to decrease slowly and for the decrease to go undetected in children and adults. A thorough visual examination should always include measurement of the visual field, as well as visual acuity.

Legally blind children are eligible to receive a wide variety of educational services, materials, and benefits from governmental agencies. They may, for example, obtain records, tapes, and record players (known as "Talking Books") from the Library of Congress. Their school may receive an allotment of money to buy books and educational materials from the American Printing House for the Blind. A legally blind person is entitled to vocational and mobility training, free U.S. mail service, and an additional income tax exemption. While all these services and benefits are important to know about, the legal definition of blindness is not especially useful to teachers. Some children, though they are not legally blind, have visual impairments severe enough to require special educational techniques and materials. Other students, whose vision would qualify them as legally blind, find little or no use for many of these specialized services.

The *educational* definition of visual impairment considers the extent to which a child's vision affects learning and makes special methods or materials necessary. Educators often differentiate between **blind** and **low vision** students. This distinction does not rely on precise measurements of visual acuity or visual field.

A blind child is totally without sight or has so little vision that he or she learns primarily through the other senses. Most blind children, for example, use their sense of touch to learn to read **braille.** A low vision child, on the other hand, *is* able to learn through the visual channel and generally learns to read print. Today, the great majority of children who are enrolled in educational programs for the visually impaired have useful vision: low vision students comprise between 75% and 80% of the school-age visually impaired population (Bryan & Jeffrey, 1982).

Braille is a system of representing letters, numbers, and other symbols with combinations (patterns) of six raised dots. It also uses special abbreviations for certain common words. See page 277.

Barraga (1980) uses the phrase *visual efficiency* to denote how well a person can *use* whatever vision he or she has. Visual efficiency cannot be determined by measuring a child's visual acuity or visual field. Some children have severe visual impairments, but are able to use their vision very capably. Other children have relatively minor visual impairments, but are unable to function as visual learners; they may even behave as though they were blind. Barraga and her colleagues have shown that systematic training in visual recognition and discrimination can help many visually impaired children to use their remaining vision more efficiently.

Although the most frequently mentioned visual impairments are in visual acuity and field of vision, there are several other significant ways in which a person's vision may be impaired.

Ocular motility, or the eye's ability to move, may be impaired. This can cause problems in **binocular vision;** that is, getting both eyes to look at the same object at the same time so that a single image is perceived. As Miller (1979) points out, binocular vision is actually a complicated process, requiring good vision in each eye, normal eye muscles, and smooth functioning of the coordinating centers of the brain.

Several conditions make it difficult or impossible for a child to use his or her eyes together effectively. **Strabismus** is a term that describes an inability to focus on the same object with both eyes, due to an inward or outward deviation of one or both of the eyes. The colloquial terms "squint," "cross-eyed," and "wall-eyed" have been applied to children with strabismus.

If left untreated, strabismus and other disorders of ocular motility can lead to permanent loss of vision. When the two eyes cannot focus simultaneously, the brain avoids a "double image" by suppressing the visual input from one eye. Thus the "weaker eye"—usually the one that turns inward or outward—can actually lose its ability to see from lack of use. **Amblyopia** refers to this reduction or loss of vision in the weaker eye. The usual treatment for amblyopia is to place a patch over the stronger eye, so that the weaker eye is forced to develop better vision through training and experience. This treatment is most effective if started in early childhood. Eye muscle surgery may also help to correct the muscle imbalance and prevent further loss of vision in the weaker eye (Batshaw & Perret, 1981).

Other kinds of visual impairments include problems in *accommodation,* in which the eye cannot adjust properly for seeing at different distances. A child with difficulty in accommodation might have trouble in shifting from reading a book to looking at the chalkboard, and back again. Some visually impaired children have a condition known as **nystagmus,** in which there is a rapid, involuntary back-and-forth movement of the eyes. Nystagmus may make it difficult for a child to focus on objects or to read smoothly.

Some children's eyes are unusually sensitive to light. This condition is known as **photophobia.** The child may need to wear tinted glasses and avoid sitting in areas of strong light or glare. Children with **albinism** almost always have photophobia, since their eyes (and skin and hair) lack normal pigmentation.

Color vision may also be impaired. A child with deficient color vision is not "color-blind"; that is, he does not see only in black and white. However, he may

SEE IT MY WAY

Marilyn Swieringa lost her vision completely at age 38, due to diabetes. A booklet she wrote, See It My Way, *describes the "bumps and bruises" she experienced, and the ways in which sighted people did not always respond to her positively and helpfully.*

The Perplexed

One afternoon in Grand Rapids, I met Mr. Perplexed at the corner of a busy intersection. He nearly sent me to the hospital!

"Do you want to cross this street, Miss?"

"Yes, but I can do it myself."

"O.K. You can start across now." Then he shouted, "No, don't go!"

I heard car tires screech. If I had listened to him and stepped off the curb, I might have been killed.

Then he went into the street and stopped all the cars until I had used my cane to go across. When I reached the other side, I suddenly realized that in the confusion I had crossed the wrong way.

First Mr. Perplexed nearly scared me out of my wits. Then he got me so turned around that I was lost. What a hectic day that was!

Rule: Please see it *my* way. Do no "good deeds" for me, unless, of course, you ask me first.

The Preoccupied

We were in a large department store in Grand Rapids. I paid the clerk for my purchase and turned to my friend to say, "Let's go home now, Marge, I'm tired."

Marge wasn't there. I waited and waited at that counter. Where could she have gone? Why did she abandon me?

Suddenly she was back—breathless. "I thought you wouldn't mind, Marilyn. I just had to go over to look at those new bikinis they have on sale today."

Rule: Please see it *my* way. Help me avoid the panicky feeling of being separated or lost. Tell me about your plans before you decide to leave me. Who knows—maybe I would like to have a bikini, too.

Under no circumstance should you ever leave a blind friend without telling her.

From M. Swieringa, *See It My Way*. Grand Rapids, Mich.: The Institute for the Development of Creative Child Care, 1972.

find it difficult to distinguish between certain colors, especially between red and green. Color deficiency is one of the most common types of visual problems, occurring in about 8.4% of the population (Batshaw & Perret, 1981). Deficient color vision is almost always found in males rather than females and does not get better or worse as the child grows older. It is usually not considered an educationally significant visual impairment.

Age at Onset

Again, a congenital disorder is present at birth, while an adventitious disability is acquired later in life.

Like other disabilities, visual impairment may be congenital or adventitious. It is useful for a teacher to know the age at which a student acquired a visual impairment. A child who has been blind since birth naturally has quite a different view of the world from a child who became blind at, for example, 12 years of age. The first child has a background of learning through hearing, touch, and the other nonvisual senses, while the second child has a background of visual experiences to draw upon. Many adventitiously blind people retain a "visual memory" of things they formerly saw. This can be helpful in a child's education; an adventitiously blind child may, for instance, remember the appearance of colors, maps, and printed letters. At the same time, however, his or her need for emotional support and acceptance may be greater than that of the congenitally blind child, who does not have to make a sudden adjustment to the visual impairment.

TYPES AND CAUSES OF VISUAL IMPAIRMENT

A simplified diagram of the eye appears in Figure 8.1.

The basic function of the eye is to collect visual information from the environment and transmit it to the brain. The eye is stimulated by light rays, reflected from objects in the visual field. In the normal eye, these light rays come to a clear focus on the central part of the **retina.** This multilayered sheet of nerve tissue at the back of the eye has been likened to the film in a camera: For a clear image to be transmitted to the brain, the light rays must come to a precise focus on the retina. The **optic nerve** is connected to the retina. It conducts visual images to the brain.

In the process of vision, light rays must pass through several structures and substances in the eye itself. Each of these bends the light a little bit in order to produce the ideal clear image on the retina. The light first hits the **cornea,** the curved transparent membrane that protects the eye (much as an outer crystal protects a wristwatch). It then passes through the **aqueous humor,** a watery liquid that fills the front chamber of the eye. Next, light passes through the **pupil,** a circular hole in the center of the colored **iris,** which contracts or expands to regulate the amount of light entering the eye. The light next passes through the **lens,** a nearly transparent structure that has an elastic quality to adjust when focusing on near and far objects, and finally through the **vitreous humor,** a jelly-like substance that fills most of the interior of the eye. Disturbances in any of these structures can prevent the clear focusing of an image on the retina.

EXCEPTIONAL CHILDREN

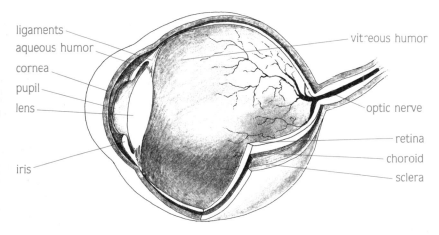

FIGURE 8.1
The human eye

Refractive Errors

Refraction is the process of "bending" light rays to produce a clear image on the retina. The normal eye refracts light rays in the manner described above; no special help is needed. For many people, perhaps half of the general population (Miller, 1979), the size and shape of the eye prevents refraction from being perfect. That is, the light rays do not focus clearly on the retina. Refractive errors can usually be corrected by glasses or contact lenses, but if severe enough they can cause permanent visual impairment.

In **myopia,** or nearsightedness, the eye is larger than normal from front to back. The image conducted to the retina is thus somewhat out of focus. A child with myopia can see near objects clearly, but more distant objects—such as a blackboard or a movie—are blurred or not seen at all. The opposite of myopia is **hyperopia,** commonly called farsightedness. The hyperopic eye is shorter than normal, preventing the light rays from converging on the retina. A child with hyperopia has difficulty in seeing near objects clearly, but is able to focus well on more distant objects. **Astigmatism** refers to distorted or blurred vision caused by irregularities in the cornea or other surfaces of the eye; both near and distant objects may be out of focus. Glasses and contact lenses "correct" refractive errors by changing the course of light rays to produce as clear a focus as possible.

Other Causes of Visual Impairment

Blindness or impaired vision can result from many causes. Only a few specific causes will be discussed here.

A **cataract** is a cloudiness in the lens of the eye, which blocks the light necessary for seeing clearly. Vision may be blurred, distorted, or incomplete. Some people with cataracts liken their vision to looking through a dirty wind-

Figure 8.2 shows how the world may look to people with cataracts or glaucoma.

shield. Cataracts are common in elderly people, but may also occur in children. Surgical treatment involves removal of the lens. Special postcataract glasses or contact lenses must be worn to compensate for the removed natural lens. A permanent lens is sometimes implanted into the eye following cataract surgery, but this procedure is not yet universally accepted by ophthalmologists.

Glaucoma is a prevalent disease marked by abnormally high pressure within the eye. There are various types of glaucoma, all related to disturbances or blockages of the fluids which normally circulate within the eye. Central and peripheral vision are impaired—or lost entirely—when the increased pressure damages the optic nerve. Glaucoma is especially painful, but can usually be treated successfully with medication or surgery if it is detected in its early stages.

We discussed the importance of the retina in the visual process earlier. Several important causes of visual impairment and blindness involve damage to the retina. Children and adults with diabetes frequently have impaired vision due

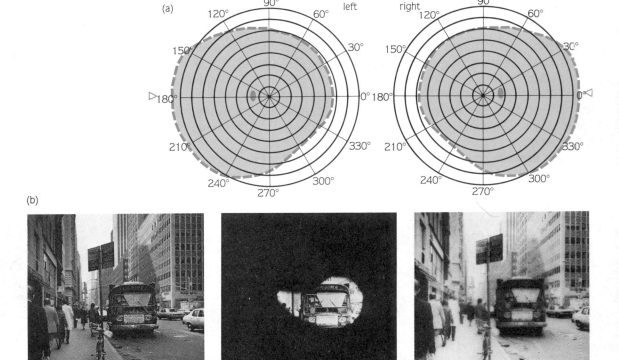

FIGURE 8.2

(a) Charts used to record field of vision; (b) How a person with normal vision, advanced glaucoma, and cataract would see the same street scene.

Source: The Lighthouse, The New York Association for the Blind, New York. Used with permission.

EXCEPTIONAL CHILDREN

to hemorrhages and the growth of new blood vessels in the area of the retina. This condition is known as **diabetic retinopathy.** Surgery with lasers has been helpful in some instances, but there is no effective treatment as yet for most people with diabetic retinopathy.

Retinitis pigmentosa is an inherited disease that causes a gradual degeneration of the retina. The first symptom is usually difficulty in seeing at night, followed by loss of peripheral vision. A small amount of central vision may be maintained. In most cases, retinitis pigmentosa is not treatable. This condition sometimes occurs in congenitally deaf people; the unfortunate combination of congenital deafness and retinitis pigmentosa is known as **Usher's syndrome.**

Macular degeneration is a fairly common condition in which the central area of the retina (the macular area) gradually deteriorates. In contrast to retinitis pigmentosa, the child with macular degeneration usually retains peripheral vision but loses the ability to see clearly in the center of the visual field.

Detached retinas result when the retina becomes partially or totally separated from the outer layers of tissue in the eye. They may occur along with several diseases of the eye or as a result of trauma. Detached or torn retinas can frequently be repaired by surgery.

Retrolental fibroplasia (RLF) affected thousands of children in the 1940s and 1950s. These children were actually born prematurely with normal vision. Because they were premature, they were routinely placed in incubators and given oxygen. The infants survived, but when they were removed from the oxygen-rich incubators, the change in oxygen levels resulted in abnormally dense growth of blood vessels and scar tissue in the eye, often leading to retinal detachment and total blindness. Today, the amount of oxygen given to premature infants is much more carefully regulated, and RLF is no longer a leading cause of visual impairment. However, it still occurs in cases where infants are born at extreme risk and need massive doses of oxygen in order to survive.

A familiarity with the student's visual impairment can be an asset to the teacher. It is useful to know, for example, that Linda has difficulty reading under strong lights, that Richard has only a small amount of central vision in his right eye, or that Ella sometimes experiences eye pain. Basic knowledge of these conditions can help the teacher understand some aspects of a child's learning and behavior and decide when to refer a child for professional vision care.

PREVALENCE

Visually impaired children constitute a very small portion of the school-age population and of the group of children who require special education services. Recent advances in medical care, surgical procedures, and optical correction have enabled many students who formerly would have been visually impaired to function in regular classes without special help.

The American Printing House for the Blind conducts a detailed annual census of the population of legally blind students in the United States. In a recent year, nearly 35,000 visually impaired students were enrolled in formal educational programs. About 74% of these students received their education in regular public schools (Nolan, 1982). Surveys of the reading materials of visually impaired students indicate that an increasing percentage of them use print as their preferred form of reading. Also, a growing number of students are reported as reading "neither" braille nor print. This group apparently includes students who do most of their reading through listening (i.e., to tapes, records, and human readers) and multihandicapped students who are unable to read using any medium.

The actual number of visually impaired students is probably somewhat higher than the figures contained in the American Printing House census, since not all schools and agencies report their students to this organization. A 1976 report of the National Advisory Committee on the Handicapped estimated the national population of visually impaired children, from birth through age 19, to be 66,000. However, this higher figure would still represent less than .1% of the entire school-age population.

Visual impairment is thus considered a **low incidence disability.** There are comparatively few visually impaired students, even relative to other populations of exceptional children. Many educators of the visually impaired are concerned about their low incidence status. In particular, some fear that, in times of limited financial resources, visually impaired students may not receive adequate services because of their relatively low numbers.

BACKGROUND OF THE FIELD

Blind and visually impaired people, while not a large population, have been a conspicuous group throughout history. In most countries, education of blind children is viewed as a high priority; schools and other special programs for blind children have historically been established before those for other groups of disabled children. Today, over 1,000 separate organizations exist to provide special services to visually impaired people in the United States. There are so many resources, in fact, that it is advisable for a blind person to take a special course in how to identify and use the most appropriate services, products, and information available (Winer, 1978).

There are several possible explanations for the special attention given to blind and visually impaired people. Blindness is usually readily apparent to the observer and evokes feelings of pity and sympathy in many people. It is perhaps the most feared of any disability. There are many widely held stereotypes and misconceptions about blind people. One study found that sighted people considered the blind to have "nice," "sweet," and "charming" personalities (Klinghammer, 1964). Other old but persistent assumptions are that blind children are naturally gifted at music, that they have a "sixth sense" enabling them to detect obstacles, that they have better than normal hearing, and that they have superior memory skills.

Valentin Hauy (1745–1822) is generally recognized as the founder of the first school for blind children. Hauy, who was appalled by the humiliating sight of blind children begging on the streets of Paris, opened his school in 1784. It had a workshop for teaching vocational skills and used embossed print to teach reading and writing. Hauy's school was later taken over by the French government. By the early 19th century, residential schools for blind children were established in several other European countries.

American educators, influenced by the European institutions, established private residential schools for blind children in Boston, New York, and Philadelphia around 1830. Within the next few decades, most states had opened public residential schools for visually impaired children. Residential schools continued to educate the great majority of visually impaired children until the mid-20th century (Koestler, 1976).

The first American public school class for totally blind children opened in Chicago in 1900, the first class for low vision children began in Boston in 1913, and the first itinerant teaching program for visually impaired children attending regular classes was implemented in Oakland, California, in 1938 (Ward, 1979). The "mainstreaming" of visually impaired children thus has a relatively long and successful history.

"Sight-Saving" Classes

For a good part of this century, many children with low vision were educated in special "sight-saving" classes, both in regular public schools and residential schools for the blind. It was generally believed that a child's remaining vision should be "conserved" by not using it too much. In extreme instances, children with impaired but useful vision were even blindfolded or educated in dark rooms, so that their precious vision would not be "lost." Today, a dramatically different approach prevails. Eye specialists agree that vision, even if imperfect, *benefits* from being used; educational programs for visually impaired children concentrate on helping them to develop and use their visual abilities as much as possible.

This trend parallels the emphasis on teaching hearing impaired children to use their residual hearing as much as possible.

The "Retrolental Fibroplasia Wave"

In the 1940s and 1950s, thousands of infants became blind or severely visually impaired because of retrolental fibroplasia (RLF), described earlier in this chapter. This tragic medical occurrence, however, had a beneficial "side effect" in expanding the educational opportunities available to visually impaired children. Since the residential schools then in existence were unable to accommodate the large, sudden influx of children affected by RLF and since many parents did not wish their children to attend distant residential schools, educational programs and services for visually impaired students became much more widely available in the regular public schools during the 1950s and 1960s.

Although the majority of children blinded by RLF are now adults, public school programs for visually impaired children have continued to develop and diversify. Today, in most regions of the United States and Canada, parents may choose between public school and residential school education for their visually impaired children.

EDUCATIONAL APPROACHES

Teachers of visually impaired children are often associated with specialized equipment and materials, such as braille, canes, tape recorders, and magnifying devices. Media and materials do play an important role in the education of children with impaired vision. But the effective teacher must know a great deal more than how to use these special techniques.

Since they are frequently called upon to teach skills and concepts that most children acquire through vision, teachers of visually impaired students must be knowledgeable, competent, and creative. They must plan and carry out activities that will help their students gain as much information as possible, by using the nonvisual senses and by participating in active, practical experiences.

Many educators and psychologists have described the obstacles to learning imposed by blindness or severe visual impairment. Lowenfeld (1973), for example, observes that a blind child may hear a bird singing, but gets no "concrete idea of the bird itself" from this sound alone. A teacher interested in teaching that student about birds—to follow up on Lowenfeld's example—might plan a series of activities that would have the student touch birds of various sizes and

A blind teacher instructs a blind student to read braille.

	1	2	3	4	5	6	7	8	9	0
	a	b	c	d	e	f	g	h	i	j

The six dots of the Braille cell are arranged and numbered thus:

```
1 ● ● 4
2 ● ● 5
3 ● ● 6
```

The capital sign, dot 6, placed before a letter makes it a capital. The number sign, dots 3, 4, 5, 6, placed before a character, makes it a figure and not a letter.

k	l	m	n	o	p	q	r	s	t

u	v	w	x	y	z	Capital Sign	Number Sign	Period	Comma

FIGURE 8.3

The braille system for representing numbers and letters.

Source: The Division for the Blind and Physically Handicapped, The Library of Congress, Washington, D.C. 20542

species and manipulate related objects (such as eggs, nests, and feathers). The student might assume the responsibility for feeding a pet bird at home or in the classroom. Perhaps a field trip to a poultry farm could be arranged. Through experiences such as these, visually impaired children will gradually obtain a more thorough and accurate knowledge of birds than they could if their education were limited to reading books about birds, memorizing vocabulary, or feeling plastic models.

Of course, while opportunities for firsthand discovery and exploration are particularly vital for visually impaired children, they are also useful and appropriate for children with normal vision.

There are virtually no limits on the extent to which a visually impaired child may participate in a full, well-rounded school program. As Scholl observes, the "guiding principle for curriculum planning should be to permit the visually handicapped pupil to try out his skills in all regular subject areas and expect as much as reasonable given the visual limitation" (1979, p. 190).

Special Adaptations for Blind Students

Braille is a system of reading and writing, in which letters, words, numbers, and other symbols are made from arrangements of raised dots. It was developed around 1830 by Louis Braille, a young Frenchman who was blind. Although the braille system is over 150 years old, it is by far the most efficient approach to reading by touch and is still an essential skill for people who have too little vision to read print. Blind students can read braille much more rapidly than they could by feeling raised letters of the standard alphabet.

Figure 8.3 shows the braille alphabet and numerals.

The braille system is complex. In many ways, it is like the shorthand used by secretaries. Abbreviations, called *contractions,* help save space and permit faster reading and writing. For example, when the letter *r* stands by itself, it means *rather.* The word *myself* in braille is written *myf.* Frequently used words, such as *the, and, with,* and *for,* have their own special contractions. For example, note how the *and* symbol (⠿) appears four times in the following sentence:

Andrew's hands and feet are sandy.

Many similar abbreviations assist in the more efficient reading and writing of braille. Mathematics, music, foreign languages, and scientific formulas can all be put into braille. When blind children attend regular public school classes, a specially trained teacher provides individual instruction in braille reading and writing. Cooperative planning with the regular classroom teacher is critical, so that books can be ordered or prepared in advance. It is usually not expected that the regular classroom teacher will learn braille, but some teachers find it helpful and interesting to do so. The braille system is not as difficult to learn as it first appears to be.

Most blind children are introduced to braille when they are at about the first grade level. The majority of teachers introduce contractions early in the program, rather than having the child learn to write out every word letter by letter and later have to "unlearn" this. Of course, it is important for the blind child to know the full and correct spelling of words, even if every letter does not appear separately in braille. It usually takes several years for children to become thoroughly familiar with the system and its rules. The speed of braille reading varies a great deal from student to student, but it is almost always much slower than the speed of print reading.

Young children generally learn to write braille using a brailler, a six-keyed device that somewhat resembles a typewriter. Older students are usually introduced to the slate and stylus, in which the braille dots are punched out one at a time by hand, from right to left. The slate and stylus method has certain advantages in notetaking, as it is much smaller and quieter than the brailler.

Several recent devices have applied technology to make braille more efficient. Typically, braille books are large, expensive, and cumbersome. It can be

The Perkins Brailler, which is used somewhat like a typewriter to produce the raised braille dots, enables blind students to write in braille.

EXCEPTIONAL CHILDREN

difficult for blind students to retrieve information quickly when they must tactually review many pages of braille books or notes. One system, known as VersaBraille, is "paperless." Braille is recorded onto small cassette tapes and can be efficiently retrieved when the tape is placed into a special device. This system is similar to a word processor; texts can readily be reviewed or altered without reading or rewriting entire pages in braille.

Typewriting is an important means of communication between blind children and their sighted classmates and teachers and is also a useful skill for further education and employment. Instruction in typing should begin as early as feasible in the child's school program. Today, handwriting is less widely taught to totally blind students. One noteworthy exception is that it is necessary for children to learn to sign their own names, so that they can assume such responsibilities as maintaining a bank account, registering to vote, and applying for a job.

A wide range of specialized materials and devices have been specially developed or modified for the instruction of blind students. Most of these educational materials are available from state instructional materials centers for the visually impaired or from the American Printing House for the Blind.

Mathematical aids for blind students include the Cranmer Abacus. The abacus, long used in Japan, has been adapted to assist blind students in learning number concepts and making calculations. Manipulation of the abacus beads is particularly useful in counting, adding, and subtracting. For more advanced mathematical functions, the student is likely to use the Speech Plus Talking Calculator, a small electronic instrument that performs most operations of any standard calculator. It "talks" by voicing entries and results aloud, as well as presenting them in digital form visually. This is only one of many instances in which the recent development of synthetic speech technology has helpful implications for blind people. "Talking" clocks and spelling aids are also available.

In the sciences and social studies, several adaptations have been designed to encourage blind students to use their tactile and auditory senses for firsthand manipulation and discovery. Examples include embossed relief maps and diagrams, three-dimensional models, and electronic probes that give an audible signal in response to light. Curriculum modification projects such as MAVIS (Materials Adaptation for Visually Impaired Students in the Social Studies) and SAVI (Science Activities for the Visually Impaired) emphasize how visually impaired students can, with some modifications, participate in learning activities along with normally sighted students.

Further information about these programs is available from the organizations listed at the end of this chapter.

The Optacon (optical-to-tactile converter) is a small electronic device that converts regular print into a readable vibrating form for blind people. When its tiny camera is held over a printed "E," for example, the user feels on the tip of one finger a vertical line and then three horizontal lines. The Optacon does not convert print into braille, but instead into a configuration of raised "pins" representing the letter being viewed by the camera. Although extensive training and practice are required, many blind children and adults are able to read regular print effectively with the aid of the Optacon. It can be used along with typewriters, calculators, or computer terminals.

The Optacon uses a tiny camera that "reads" print letter by letter, transforming it into a series of raised "pins" that can be felt with the fingertip.

The Kurzweil Reading Machine is another recent technological development with exciting implications for visually impaired and other disabled students. This sophisticated computer actually reads books and other printed matter aloud, using synthetic speech. The reader can regulate the speed and tone of the voice and can even have the machine spell out words letter by letter if desired. The "intelligence" of the Kurzweil Reading Machine is constantly being improved, and the machines are already in use in many public and residential school programs for visually impaired students.

Special Adaptations for Students with Low Vision

As previously noted, the great majority of children enrolled in educational programs for the visually impaired have some potentially useful vision. Their learning need not be restricted to touch, hearing, and other nonvisual senses. Currently, there is a great emphasis upon developing children's ability to use their residual vision as effectively as possible. This trend is largely attributable to the influential work of Natalie Barraga (1964, 1970, 1976, 1980). She demonstrated that children—even those with extremely limited visual acuity or visual field—can dramatically improve their visual efficiency through a structured program of assessment, training, and evaluation.

Visual efficiency, as defined by Barraga, includes such skills as controlling eye movements, adapting to the visual environment, paying attention to visual stimuli, and processing visual information rapidly. The fundamental premise in developing visual efficiency is that children *learn to see* and must be actively involved in using their own vision. Merely furnishing a classroom with attractive things for children to see is not sufficient. A low vision child may, without training, be unable to derive much meaningful information through vision. Forms may be perceived as vague masses and shapeless, indistinct blobs. Training has

The Kurzweil Reading Machine is a sophisticated device that actually reads printed material aloud with a synthetic voice.

helped many children learn to use their visual impressions intelligently and effectively, to "make sense" out of what they see. Barraga's Program to Develop Efficiency in Visual Functioning, including a helpful *Source Book on Low Vision* (which may be purchased separately), is available from the American Printing House for the Blind.

Many children with low vision are able to benefit from special optical aids. These may include glasses and contact lenses that are worn on or in the eyes, small telescopes that are held in the hand, or magnifiers placed on top of books. These aids cannot give "normal" vision to visually impaired children, but may help them to perform better at certain tasks, such as reading small print or seeing distant objects.

Optical aids are usually specialized, rather than "all-purpose." Juanita might, for example, use her glasses for reading large print, a magnifier stand for reading smaller print, and a monocular (one-eye) telescope for viewing the blackboard. A usual disadvantage of corrective lenses and magnifiers is that the more powerful they are, the more they tend to distort or restrict the peripheral field of vision. Some visual field widening lenses and devices are now available for students with limited visual fields. These include prisms and fish-eye lenses, designed to make objects appear smaller, so that a greater area can be perceived on the unimpaired portions of the student's visual field.

These materials may also be useful with other children who, though not visually impaired, require instruction on basic pre-reading and visual discrimination skills.

Today, a large number of ophthalmologists, optometrists, and clinical facilities specialize in the assessment and treatment of low vision. A professional examination can help determine which types of optical aids, if any, are appropriate for a student with low vision. It is usually a good idea to furnish optical aids on a trial or loan basis, so that the student may gradually learn to use and evaluate them in natural settings. A follow-up session should then be scheduled.

Many books and other materials are available in large print for children with low vision. Although these are helpful in many cases, large print materials have certain disadvantages. When print is made very large, the number of letters and words that can be seen at any one time is sharply reduced; it thus becomes more difficult for the student to read smoothly with a natural "sweep" of eye movements. It is generally agreed that a visually impaired child should use the *smallest* print size that he or she can comfortably read. A child may be able to transfer from large print to smaller print as reading efficiency increases, just as most normally sighted children do.

A significant number of children with low vision are able to learn to read using regular-sized print, with or without the use of optical aids. This makes a much wider variety of materials available and eliminates the added cost of obtaining large print books or enlarging texts through special duplicating machines. The size of print is an important variable, but other equally important factors to consider with low vision students are the quality of the printed material, the contrast between print and page, the spacing between lines, and the illumination of the setting in which the child reads.

Some educational programs use closed circuit television systems to enable low vision students to read regular-sized printed materials. These systems usually include a sliding table on which a book is placed, a television camera with a zoom lens mounted above the book, and a television monitor nearby. The student is able to adjust the size, brightness, and contrast of the material, and may select either an ordinary black-on-white image, or a negative white-on-black image, which is preferred by many students. The teacher may also have a television monitor that lets him or her see the student's work without making repeated trips to the student's desk. A disadvantage of closed circuit television systems—in addition to their cost—is that they are usually not portable, so that the student who uses television as a main reading medium is largely restricted to the specially equipped classroom.

Other classroom adaptations for low vision students are often minor, but can be very important. Many students benefit from desks with adjustable or tilting tops, so they can read and write at close range without constantly bending over and casting a shadow. Most regular classrooms today have adequate lighting, but special lamps may still be helpful for some children. Writing paper should have a dull finish to reduce glare; an off-white color such as buff or ivory is generally better than white paper. Some teachers have found it helpful to give low vision students chairs with wheels, so that they can easily move around the blackboard area or other sections where instruction is taking place, without constantly getting up and down. Dittoed worksheets in light purple or other

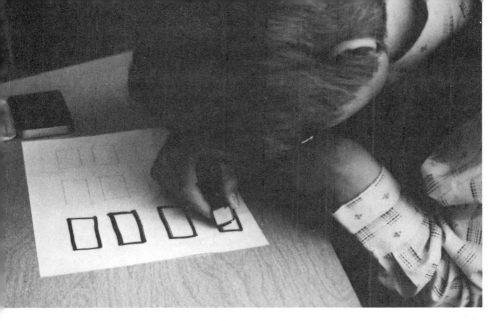

With relatively minor environmental and material modifications, many students with low vision can participate fully in regular classroom programs.

poorly contrasting colors are difficult for most low vision students to use; an aide or classmate may first go over the worksheet with a dark pen or marker. Many other modifications can be made by the teacher, using common sense and considering the needs of the individual student with low vision.

Listening

Visually impaired children—both totally blind and those with low vision—must obtain and retain an enormous amount of information through the sense of hearing. A great deal of time in school is devoted to speaking and listening to others. Visually impaired students also make frequent use of recorded materials particularly in high school. Recorded books and magazines and the equipment to use them can be obtained through the Library of Congress, the American Printing House for the Blind, the Canadian National Institute for the Blind, Recording for the Blind, and various other organizations, usually on a free-loan basis.

Since many visually impaired students are able to process auditory information at a rate faster than average conversational speech, devices are available to increase the rate at which tapes are played back without significantly distorting the quality of the speech. The ever-increasing use of synthetic speech equipment probably means that listening skills will become even more important to visually impaired students in the future. The ability of blind students to comprehend synthetic speech was investigated by Rhyne (1982) who found that the aural (listening) mode was a generally efficient way to learn, and that the students' comprehension increased as they gained more experience in listening to synthetic speech.

Since there are so many useful opportunities for learning through listening, an important component of the educational program for virtually every visually impaired child is the systematic development of listening skills. Children do not automatically develop the ability to listen effectively simply by being placed into a regular classroom, nor are visually impaired students necessarily better listeners than normally sighted students.

Learning to listen activities can take an almost unlimited variety of forms. Young children, for example, may learn to discriminate between sounds that are near and far, loud and soft, high-pitched and low-pitched. A teacher may introduce a new word into a sentence, and ask the child to identify it. Older students might learn to listen for important details while there are distracting background noises, to differentiate between factual and fictional material, or to respond to verbal analogy questions.

Some structured programs for developing listening skills have been developed (Alber, 1974; Stocker, 1973). Instruction in this area can be among the most worthwhile parts of a visually impaired child's curriculum.

Practical Living Skills

Some educators of the visually impaired suggest that academic achievement has traditionally been overemphasized at the expense of important basic living skills. Hatlen (1976) argues that "the most urgent attention" be given to such topics as cooking, grooming, financial management, recreational activities, personal hygiene, and social behavior. Specific instruction in these skills can facilitate the student's eventual independence as an adult.

Hatlen (1978) further recommends that, if necessary, the visually impaired student be taught how to deal with strangers, how to interpret and explain the visual impairment to other people, and how to make socially acceptable gestures in conversation. It is also important for students to be aware of the range of career opportunities available to them and to be informed about services, resources, and responsibilities in their communities.

Another area of some concern to educators is special mannerisms, repetitive body movements or other behaviors, such as rocking, eye-poking, hand-waving, and head-rolling. While not necessarily harmful in themselves, mannerisms can place a visually impaired person at a social disadvantage, since they are conspicuous and call attention to the person as different or handicapped. It is not clearly known why many visually impaired children engage in manneristic behaviors. Tooze (1981) attributes them either to a child being under stress or having a "desire to move coupled with a fear of moving forward" (p. 29). It is generally suggested that children be kept busy and active, so that they will have less time to indulge in mannerisms. A structured behavior management program was conducted by Blasch (1978), who found that the contingent presentation of aversive stimuli and positive reinforcement for appropriate gestures were effective in reducing mannerisms in a classroom.

Sighted children typically learn a great deal about human sexuality through vision. They see people establish social and sexual relationships with each other;

they can see their own bodies and those of others. Since this avenue is largely or completely unavailable to visually impaired children, they may grow up with serious knowledge gaps or misconceptions about sex and reproduction, unless specific instruction is offered. In some European countries, live human models are used to familiarize blind students with anatomy, but this practice has not been widely adopted in North America. In addition to providing accurate biological information, instructional programs should also consider the emotional aspects of sexual experience and the possible genetic implications of a student's visual impairment.

Teachers of visually impaired students may find it necessary to teach specific skills that will enable their students to function as independently as possible. These may include shopping, money management, cooking, recreational activities, training in making decisions, and other areas. The specially trained teacher, the regular class teacher, other specialists, the parents, and the student should all be involved in planning and providing instruction that will be practical and relevant to the student's needs and future objectives.

Issues in Assessment

There is a continuing concern about the use (and possible misuse) of intelligence tests with visually impaired children. Intelligence tests, standardized on sighted children, are often based largely on visual concepts. They may include such questions as, "Why do people have hedges around their homes?" or "What should you do if you see a train approaching a broken track?" The results of these tests may well give an inaccurate picture of a visually impaired child's abilities and needs. Regrettably, many blind and low vision children have been placed in inappropriate educational programs because of strict reliance on standardized test performance.

Few tests have been standardized on visually impaired children. Even if they were, the results would be of questionable value because of the heterogeneity and small size of the population. Scholl and Schnur (1976) offer a comprehensive review of over 180 psychological, educational, and vocational tests and provide information about their appropriateness for visually impaired subjects. A number of instruments, while not specifically designed for the visually impaired, may be useful in assessing specific aspects of a child's performance.

In gathering information that will be helpful in developing educational goals for a visually impaired child, a variety of formal and informal assessment procedures should be drawn upon. Davis (1975) advises that testing not begin until a child has had at least 6 months to adjust to the school program. He also recommends that "one should not feel constricted by time limits," as the primary intent of any diagnostic procedure is to determine how much the student is currently capable of performing.

As Chapman (1978) suggests, the results of developmental or intelligence tests should always be supplemented by careful observations of the child's behavior in school and play situations. Teachers and parents are usually in the best position to observe the child's communication, exploration, and social interaction over an extended period. Their contributions should play a major part in planning a visually impaired child's educational program.

Orientation and Mobility

The educational program of a visually impaired child could hardly be considered complete or appropriate if it failed to include instruction in orientation and mobility. **Orientation** is defined as the ability to establish one's position in relation to the environment through the use of the remaining senses. **Mobility** is the ability to move safely and efficiently from one point to another (Lowenfeld, 1973). For most students, more time and effort is spent in orientation training than in learning specific mobility techniques. It is extremely important that, from an early age, visually impaired children be taught basic concepts that will familiarize them with their own bodies and their surroundings. For example, they need to be taught that the place where the leg bends is called a knee, and that rooms have walls, doors, windows, corners, and ceilings.

Orientation and mobility instruction is a well-developed subspecialty in the education and rehabilitation of the visually impaired. There are many specific techniques involved in teaching visually impaired students to understand their environment and maneuver through it effectively. Training in these skills should be given by qualified orientation and mobility specialists. Until recently, formal orientation and mobility instruction was seldom given to children younger than about 12 years of age. However, the importance of the early development of travel skills and related concepts is now generally recognized; today it is not at all unusual for preschool children to benefit from the services of an orientation and mobility instructor.

The long cane is the device most widely used by visually impaired persons for independent travel. The traveler does not "tap" the cane, but "sweeps" it lightly in an arc while walking, to gain information about the path ahead. Properly used, the cane enables the traveler to detect obstacles such as curbs, stairs, doors, holes, and parking meters. Changes in the travel surface (for example, from grass to concrete or from a rug to a wooden floor) can also be detected one step in advance.

A small percentage of visually impaired people travel with the aid of guide dogs. Like the cane traveler, the guide dog user must have good orientation and mobility skills, since he or she selects the route to be taken. The dog wears a special harness and has been trained to follow several basic verbal commands, to avoid obstacles, and to insure the traveler's safety. Several weeks of intensive training are required at special guide dog agencies before the person and dog can work together effectively. Misunderstandings sometimes arise when blind people with guide dogs are refused entry into restaurants, hotels, airplanes, or other places which normally do not permit animals; state and local regulations permit guide dogs to have access to these places. Guide dogs are especially helpful in situations where a person must travel over complicated or unpredictable routes, as in large cities. They are not usually available to children under 16 years of age or to people with multiple disabilities.

Most visually impaired people occasionally find it necessary to rely on the assistance of others in mobility. The sighted guide technique is a simple method of helping a visually impaired person travel. The visually impaired student should lightly grasp the sighted person's arm just above the elbow, and walk half a step behind in a natural manner. In situations where visually impaired students attend regular classes, it may be a good idea for the student and the mobility specialist to demonstrate the sighted guide technique for classmates.

Several recently developed technological devices promise to facilitate orientation and mobility for the visually impaired. These include a laser beam cane, which emits a sound to signal objects in the path of a traveler, as well as hazards overhead and drop-offs below. Other devices use SONAR, sending out sound waves to bounce off objects and give the trained traveler information about the environment. Mobility aids like these, in modified versions, are increasingly being used with blind and visually impaired infants and young children. They appear to have much potential for enhancing children's independence and early learning, by allowing them to explore the environment more thoroughly.

Whatever the preferred method of travel, most visually impaired students can generally learn to negotiate familiar places, such as school and home, on their own without special devices. Good orientation and mobility skills have many positive effects. The visually impaired child who can travel independently is likely to develop more physical and social skills and more self-confidence than the child who must continually depend on other people to get around. Good travel skills also expand the student's opportunities for employment and independent living in the community.

EDUCATIONAL ALTERNATIVES FOR VISUALLY IMPAIRED STUDENTS

Public Schools

In the past, most children with severe visual impairments were educated at residential schools for blind children. Today, however, most impaired children attend regular public school classes with their normally sighted peers. Supportive help is usually given by itinerant teacher-consultants, sometimes called *vision specialists*. These specially trained teachers may be employed by a school district, a regional education agency, a state or province, or even a residential school. Their roles and caseloads vary widely from program to program. In general, however, the itinerant teacher-consultant may be expected to assume some or all of the following responsibilities:

☐ Instruct the visually impaired student directly (within the classroom and/or individually)

☐ Obtain or prepare specialized learning materials

HELP WANTED!

Today, most visually impaired children are educated in regular public schools. Since the visually impaired population is small and widely scattered, their teachers are often itinerant—traveling from school district to school district, providing supportive services to students who attend regular classes, and to their parents and teachers as well. From the following job description, you can get an idea of the responsibilities assumed by the itinerant teacher of the visually impaired in the schools today.

The High Plains Special Education Cooperative, providing services in 19 rural southwest Kansas school districts, has a vacancy for an itinerant teacher of the visually impaired. We feel that salary and fringe benefits are excellent.

The new teacher would be based in Ulysses, a town of approximately 4,000. He/she would be responsible for providing services to both braille and print reading students of all grade levels in our co-op.

The student requiring the most direct service is a very bright braille reading student in Ulysses. He is just completing first grade. He has useful vision and does math and some reading workbook assignments with an electronic visual aid in his classroom. He is near the top of his class. Also in Ulysses, we have recently become aware of a 9-month-old with several handicaps, including visual impairment. Information is sketchy at this time. We would hope the teacher would be willing to serve as a resource person, and to do some work with the parents and child.

In Liberal, a town of 20,000, located 60 miles southeast of Ulysses, is an albino girl, just completing second grade. She is a large print reader. She does well, but needs assistance in math and fine motor skills.

There is a sixth grade boy in Elkhart, 60 miles southwest of Ulysses, who needs to be checked on periodically. His main difficulty is in the area of social relationships. He will be using regular print materials for the coming year.

We have just received word that a student currently attending the State School for the Visually Handicapped will be entering public school in Johnson this fall. Johnson is 20 miles from Ulysses. This seventh grade girl is also a print reader.

In Copeland, there is a high school student who uses all the regular school materials. He has not required any direct services for 2 years.

We have an Optacon and several other electronic aids. We contract with an orientation/mobility instructor for services in that area.

Ability to work cooperatively with classroom teachers, and a willingness to drive perhaps 100 miles per day is essential. Travel expenses are reimbursed. The teacher is given a lot of freedom in setting up his/her schedule and program. Most teachers, parents, administrators, and students are enjoyable to work with.

Send inquiries to High Plains Special Education Co-op, Garden City, Kansas 67846.

- ☐ Put reading assignments into braille, large print, or tape-recorded form, or arrange for readers
- ☐ Interpret information on the child's visual impairment and visual functioning to other educators and parents
- ☐ Suggest classroom and program modifications which may be advisable because of the child's vision
- ☐ Help plan the child's educational goals, initiate and maintain contact with various agencies, keep records of services provided
- ☐ Consult with the child's parents and other teachers

The itinerant teacher-consultant may or may not provide instruction in orientation and mobility. Some programs—particularly in rural areas—employ "dually certified" teachers who are also orientation and mobility specialists. Other programs may employ one teacher for educational support, and another for orientation and mobility training.

Some public school programs have special resource rooms for visually impaired students. In contrast to the itinerant teacher-consultant, who travels from school to school, the resource room teacher remains in one location that is equipped to serve visually impaired students for part of the school day. Resource rooms for visually impaired students are usually found in large school districts.

The amount of time that the itinerant or resource room teacher spends with a visually impaired student who attends regular classes varies considerably. Some students may be seen every day, as they require a great deal of specialized assistance. Others may be seen weekly, monthly, or even less frequently, as they are able to function well in the regular class with less support.

Residential Schools

Residential schools continue to meet the needs of a sizable number of visually impaired children. There are 52 such schools operating in the United States today. The current population of residential schools consists largely of visually impaired children with additional disabilities, such as mental retardation, hearing impairment, behavior disorders, and cerebral palsy. Some parents are not able to care for their children adequately at home, and others prefer the greater concentration of specialized personnel, facilities, and services that the residential school usually offers.

See chapter 10 for more information on multiple handicaps.

A child's placement in a residential school program need not be regarded as permanent. Many visually impaired children move from residential schools into public schools (or vice versa) as their needs change. Some students who reside in residential schools attend nearby public schools for all or part of the school day. Most residential schools encourage parent involvement and have recreational programs that bring visually impaired students into contact with nonhandicapped peers. Independent living skills and vocational training are important parts of the student's program at most residential schools.

In several states and provinces, there is close cooperation between public school and residential school programs that serve visually impaired children. Thurman (1978), for example, reports that in Canada's Atlantic provinces, the residential school employs a network of itinerant teacher-consultants who provide instruction, materials, and assistance to visually impaired children who attend regular public schools. They offer regular consultation to the various teachers who work with them. In this region, it is expected that most visually impaired children will gradually be integrated into their local public schools and that the residential school will mainly serve multihandicapped students and young visually impaired children who require training in basic skills.

Residential schools have long played an important role in the training of teachers of visually impaired children, both on a preservice and an in-service basis. The residential school is usually well equipped to serve as a resource center for instructional materials and as a place where visually impaired students can receive specialized evaluation services. An increasing number of residential schools now offer short-term training to visually impaired students who attend regular public schools. An example might be a summer workshop emphasizing braille, mobility, and vocational training.

CURRENT ISSUES/FUTURE TRENDS

As we have noted, visually impaired children constitute a very small portion of the school-age population, but they have many unique needs. While the current trend toward greater integration of visually impaired children into regular public school classes is generally welcomed, some educators caution against the wholesale placement of visually impaired children into regular schools without adequate support. Most "vision" professionals tend to resist noncategorical special education programs, at least for visually impaired students. It is unrealistic, they argue, to expect regular teachers, or teachers trained in other areas of special education, to be competent in such specialized techniques as braille, mobility, and visual efficiency.

Although financial restrictions may require some public school and residential school programs for visually impaired children to close down or consolidate with programs for children with other disabilities, there is strong support for the continuation of highly specialized services. Both public and residential programs for visually impaired children will continue to operate well into the future, occasionally challenging each other for the privilege of serving the relatively small number of available students. The result of this competition may well prove favorable, if both types of schools are encouraged to improve the quality of educational services.

There will be increased emphasis on early intervention programs for visually impaired infants and preschool children and on training for independent employment and living skills for older students. Low vision children will receive more special attention than they have in the past, not just in the area of vision utilization, but in many other aspects of their education and adjustment. There is some evidence to suggest that low vision children may have a more difficult time than blind children in being socially accepted by sighted children in public schools (Spenciner, 1972); few "mainstreaming" programs have specifically addressed the needs of low vision children, although they constitute a much larger population than blind children.

New technological and biomedical developments will continue to aid visually impaired students as they become available, particularly in the areas of mobility, communication, and use of low vision. In the not too distant future, it may even be possible to provide a form of "artificial sight" to certain totally blind people, by implanting electrodes into the brain and connecting them to a miniature television camera built into an artificial eye. Research in artificial sight is in the early experimental stages at present, but appears to have much promise (Dobelle, 1977; Marbach, 1982).

Like other groups of disabled individuals, visually impaired people are becoming increasingly aware of their rights as citizens and consumers and are beginning to fight discrimination based on their disability. As Willoughby (1980) observes, many people—some of whom work with the visually impaired—tend to underestimate the capacities of their students and deny them a full range of occupational and personal choices. The future will probably bring a gradual shift away from some of the vocational settings in which visually impaired people have traditionally worked, such as piano tuning, sheltered workshops, and rehabilitation counseling, in favor of a more varied range of employment opportunities. These and other trends will be appropriately reflected in future programs of education and training for visually impaired children.

LOW VISION

What does a child with *low vision* see? It is difficult for us to know. We may try to obtain some idea of total blindness by wearing a blindfold—but the majority of visually impaired chilren are not totally blind. Even if two children share the same cause of visual impairment, it is unlikely that they see things in exactly the same way. And the same child may see things differently at different times.

We asked a few people with low vision to describe how they see, and here is what they told us:

Have you ever been out camping in a strange place? When it's dark and you're trying to find your way from the tent to the bathroom, and you can't wear glasses or contact lenses—that's like the way I see.

I'm pretty much nearsighted. I can *see* a far object, I mean I know the image is there, but I can't *distinguish* it. I can see a house. It is just a white blob out there. I couldn't tell you what color is the roof trim, or where the windows are. (Heward & Orlansky, 1981)

Put on a pair of sunglasses. Then rub vaseline all around the central part of each lens. Now try reading a book. Or crossing a street.

I never see blackness. . . . If I am looking at a picture, it's not like I see a hole in the middle. I fill something in there, but it wouldn't necessarily be what is really there. That's how I describe it to people—take a newspaper, hold it up, and look straight ahead. Now describe what you see here, off to the side . . . that's what I see all the time. (Heward & Orlansky, 1981)

The following suggestions for teachers of students with low vision were made by the Vision Team, a group of specialists in visual impairment who work with regular class teachers in 13 school districts in Hennepin County, Minnesota.

☐ Using eyes does not harm them. The more children use their eyes, the greater their efficiency will be.

☐ Holding printed material close to the eyes may be the low vision child's way of seeing best. It will not harm the eyes.

☐ Although eyes cannot be "strained" from use, a low vision child's eyes may tire more quickly. A change of focus or activity helps.

☐ Copying is often a problem for low vision children. The child may need a longer period of time to do classwork, or a shortened assignment.

☐ It will be helpful if the teacher verbalizes as much as possible while writing on the chalkboard or using the overhead projector.

☐ A few low vision children use large print books, but most do not. As the child learns to use vision, it becomes more efficient and the student can generally read smaller print.

☐ Dittoes can be difficult for the low vision child to read. Giving her one of the first copies, or the original from which the ditto was made, can be helpful.

☐ The term "legally blind" does not mean "educationally blind." Most children who are legally blind function educationally as sighted children.

☐ Contrast, print style, and spacing can be more important than the size of the print.

☐ One of the most important things a low vision child will learn in school is to accept the responsibility of seeking help when it is needed—rather than waiting for someone to offer help.

☐ In evaluating the quality of work and in applying discipline, the teacher best helps the low vision child by using the same standards that are used with other children.

Perhaps most important of all, an attitude of understanding and acceptance can help the student with low vision succeed in the regular classroom.

List of suggestions used by permission of Glenda Martin, special education coordinator, Hennepin County, Minnesota.

1. Vision is a critical tool that children use in obtaining information about the world in which they live. Without it, they need special materials and attention if they are to learn and develop to their full potential.

2. There are both legal and educational definitions of visual impairment.
   a. A person whose visual acuity is 20/200 or less in the better eye after correction is legally blind.
   b. A person whose field of vision is 20 degrees or less is also legally blind.
   c. An educational definition considers the extent to which a visual impairment makes special educational materials or methods necessary.
   d. To educators, blind children have so little vision that they learn primarily through their other senses. Most blind children read braille.
   e. To educators, low vision children can learn through the visual channel and usually can learn to read print.
   f. Besides impairments in visual acuity and field of vision, a child may have problems with ocular motility or visual accommodation, photophobia, or defective color vision.
   g. Whether a visual impairment is congenital or adventitious, the age of onset may affect the child's educational and emotional needs.

3. The eye collects light reflected from objects, focuses the objects' image on the retina, and transmits the image to the brain. Difficulty with any part of this process can cause vision problems. Common types of visual impairment include:
   a. Myopia, nearsightedness;
   b. Hyperopia, farsightedness;
   c. Astigmatism, blurred vision caused by irregularities in the cornea or the other eye surfaces;
   d. Cataract, blurred or distorted vision caused by cloudiness in the lens;
   e. Glaucoma, loss of vision caused by high pressure within the eye;
   f. Diabetic retinopathy, retinitis pigmentosa, macular degeneration, and retinal detachment, all caused by problems with the retina;
   g. Retrolental fibroplasia, caused by administration and withdrawal of high doses of oxygen to premature infants in incubators.

4. Visual impairment is a low incidence handicap, affecting less than .1% of the school-age population.

5. Educating blind students is one of the oldest fields of special education, perhaps because blindness is readily apparent and provokes strong emotions.
   a. The first school for blind children was started by Hauy in Paris in 1784. By the early 19th century, many other European countries had started residential schools for blind children.
   b. The first American schools for blind children were private residential schools started around 1830. Public residential schools began to be opened soon afterwards.

c. Until recently, children with low vision were encouraged to not use their sight, in order to "conserve" it. Today they are taught to concentrate on developing and using their vision as much as possible.

d. The influx of children with blindness caused by retrolental fibroplasia led to the spread of regular public school programs for the visually impaired in the 1950s and 1960s.

e. Most parents today can choose between public day and residential schools for their visually impaired children, and either choice need not be considered permanent.

6. Teachers of visually impaired children need to have many specialized skills and to be knowledgeable, competent, and creative in working with the needs of individual children.

a. Visually impaired children need as many active, participatory experiences as possible.

b. Most blind children learn to read braille and write with a brailler and a slate and stylus. They can also learn to type and use special equipment for mathematics, social studies, and listening to or "feeling" regular print.

c. Children with low vision learn to use their residual vision as efficiently as possible. Many use optical aids and large print to read regular type. They may need special adaptations such as closed circuit television to let them benefit as much as possible from the materials and physical setting of the regular classroom.

d. All visually impaired children need to develop their listening skills.

e. Visually impaired students also may need special instruction in practical daily living skills, in dealing with other people, and in human sexuality.

f. Many visually impaired children need help to avoid developing distinctive mannerisms.

g. The teacher must use observation and a variety of informal and formal procedures in assessing visually impaired children. Standardized intelligence tests are often inappropriate.

h. For blind or severely visually impaired children, orientation and mobility instruction is a must. From an early age, these children must be made familiar and comfortable with their own bodies and their surroundings, if they are eventually to develop the skills to travel independently.

7. Today, most visually impaired children attend regular classes with their sighted peers.

a. In many districts, a specially trained itinerant vision specialist provides extra help for the student and teacher.

b. Some programs also have separate orientation and mobility instructors or separate resource rooms for visually impaired students.

c. Many visually impaired children—especially those with other handicapping conditions—attend residential schools.

8. Visually impaired children are likely to receive specialized services well into the future, in both regular and residential schools.

9. There will be increased emphasis on intervention with visually impaired infants and young children and on training for independence for older students.

10. Low vision children will receive more attention in the coming years, and all visually impaired people will benefit from new technological and biomedical developments.

11. Career and life-style opportunities for visually impaired persons should increase as they become more aware of their legal and human rights.

FOR MORE INFORMATION

Journals

Education of the Visually Handicapped. Published quarterly by the Association for Education of the Visually Handicapped. Includes practical and research articles for teachers of visually impaired students, orientation and mobility specialists, and administrators.

Journal of Visual Impairment and Blindness. Published 10 times per year by the American Foundation for the Blind. An interdisciplinary journal for practitioners and researchers concerned with the education and rehabilitation of visually impaired children and adults.

The Sight-Saving Review. Published quarterly by the National Society to Prevent Blindness. Emphasizes new developments in the treatment of visual impairments, low vision aids, eye safety, and education.

Books

Kastein, S., Spaulding, I., & Scharf, B. *Raising the young blind child: A guide for parents and educators.* New York: Human Sciences Press, 1980.

Mangold, S. (ed.). *A teacher's guide to the special educational needs of blind and visually handicapped children.* New York: American Foundation for the Blind, 1982.

Martin, G. J., & Hoben, M. *Supporting visually impaired students in the mainstream.* Reston, Va.: Council for Exceptional Children, 1977.

Miller, D. *Ophthalmology: The essentials.* Boston: Houghton Mifflin, 1979.

Orlansky, M. D. *Mainstreaming the visually impaired child: Blind and partially sighted students in the regular classroom.* Hingham, Mass.: Teaching Resources, 1979.

Tooze, D. *Independence training for visually handicapped children.* Baltimore: University Park Press, 1981.

Willoughby, D. M. *A resource guide for parents and educators of blind children.* Baltimore: National Federation of the Blind, 1980.

Organizations

American Foundation for the Blind, 15 West 16th Street, New York, NY 10011. Provides many publications and films about blindness. Distributes aids and appliances for the blind. Publishes *Journal of Visual Impairment and Blindness* and *Directory of Agencies Serving the Visually Handicapped in the United States.*

American Printing House for the Blind, 1839 Frankfort Avenue, Louisville, KY 40206. Provides books, magazines, and many other publications in braille, large print, and recorded form. Distributes educational materials and aids especially designed for the blind, and helpful publications for teachers. All legally blind U.S. children should be registered with APH, through state departments of education or residential schools.

Association for Education of the Visually Handicapped, 206 N. Washington Street, Alexandria, VA 22314. Emphasizes educational services and, in conjunction with the American Association of Workers for the Blind, orientation, mobility, and rehabilitation. Holds regional and national conferences in the U.S.A. and Canada. Publishes *Education of the Visually Handicapped.*

Canadian National Institute for the Blind, 1921 Bayview Avenue, Toronto, Ontario M4G 3E8. The central agency for information, materials, and supportive services for visually impaired people in Canada. Maintains regional and local offices in all provinces. A film, *Shelley*, effectively depicts the growth and development of a young blind child.

Division for the Visually Handicapped, Council for Exceptional Children, 1920 Association Drive, Reston, VA 22091. Presents sessions of interest to educators at international, state, and provincial conferences of the Council for Exceptional Children. Publishes a quarterly newsletter on educational topics.

National Association for Parents of the Visually Impaired, 2011 Hardy Circle, Austin, TX 78756. Provides practical information for parents. Sponsors parent groups in several areas. Holds conferences and workshops for parents and teachers.

National Federation of the Blind, 1800 Johnson Street, Baltimore, MD 21230. The largest organization of blind people in the United States, with many state and local chapters. Provides publications and films which emphasize the rights and capabilities of blind people. Seeks to involve blind people in education and employment and to avoid discrimination.

9

Physical and Health Impairments

Children with physical and health impairments are an extremely varied group; it is impossible to describe all of them with a single set of terms, even if the terms are very general. Their physical disabilities may be mild or severe. Their intellectual functioning may be below normal, normal, or above normal. They may have a single disability or a combination of impairments. They may have lived with a physical or health impairment since birth or may have suddenly acquired the condition.

The children whose special needs we will consider in this chapter have a great many individual differences; there is no "typical case" of anything. We can make general statements about some physical and health-related characteristics of children with certain conditions—such as cerebral palsy or epilepsy—but there are many variations in the degree and severity of those conditions and the way they affect a particular child.

As Neely (1982) observes, the psychological and emotional characteristics of children with physical and health impairments are as varied as those in the general population. Many students adjust to their disability reasonably well. They present no unusual behavior problems, are fully capable of learning in the regular classroom, and interact successfully with their nondisabled peers. Access to a standard educational program may be their primary need. Other students, however, find that their physical or health-related impairment has a great impact on their education and adjustment. A child who has been away from school during long periods of hospitalization, for example, may find it difficult to keep up with her academic work. A child who has unexpected seizures may find that his classmates are reluctant to accept him as a friend, and he may take medication that makes him drowsy in the classroom.

Because of their disabilities or illnesses, children with physical and health impairments may require modifications in the physical environment, in instructional techniques, in communication, or in other aspects of their educationa programs. Teachers need to understand the conditions that affect their students' behavior or performance in school. Today, children with physical and health impairments are generally included in educational programs on the basis of their particular learning needs, not according to their specific disability or disease. Therefore, teachers can expect to have more students in their classes who have specialized medical and physical management requirements (Mullins, 1979).

Physical and health problems can give rise to special needs in the school setting. In defining the population of "handicapped" children according to P.L. 94–142, the federal government emphasizes that a child's educational performance may be adversely affected by severe orthopedic impairments (including those caused by cerebral palsy, amputation of limbs, fractures, and burns) or by other serious or long-standing health problems that limit the child's strength, vitality, or alertness.

Some children with physical and health impairments are extremely restricted in their activities and intellectual functioning, while others have no major limitations on what they can do and learn. Some are entirely normal in appearance, while others have disabilities that are immediately apparent. Some children must use special devices or equipment that call attention to the disability; others display behaviors that are not under their own voluntary control. Some disabilities are always present, while others occur only from time to time. Over a long period, the degree of a child's disability may increase, decrease, or remain about the same.

In school, the special problems encountered by children with physical and health impairments also vary in kind and degree. Brian, who uses a wheelchair for mobility, is disappointed that he is not able to compete with his classmates in football, baseball, and track. Yet he participates fully in all other aspects of his high school program with no special modifications other than the addition of a few ramps in the building and a newly accessible washroom. Most of Brian's teachers and friends, in fact, do not think of him as needing "special" education at all.

A chance to try and a taller work table were all that David needed to succeed in the regular classroom.

In this chapter, we will focus upon information that will be helpful to the teacher in understanding the nature and effects of various physical and health impairments. Many conditions, after all, can affect a child's school experience in important ways. Janice, for example, becomes tired very easily and attends school for only 3 hours a day. Kenneth uses a specially designed chair to help him sit more comfortably in the classroom. It is important to emphasize, however, that special modifications or alterations should not be any more restrictive than necessary. A bright child who uses a wheelchair should not be totally removed from the regular school program and placed into a class where she can interact only with other disabled children.

With some conditions, possible complications or emergencies may arise in the classroom; it is important for the teacher to know how to manage the situation effectively and when and how to seek help from others. Thus, general information and suggested guidelines will form our basic approach to children with physical and health impairments.

TYPES AND CAUSES

Orthopedic and Neurological Impairments

An **orthopedic impairment** affects the child's bones, joints, limbs, and muscles. A **neurological impairment** affects the child's ability to use, feel, or control certain parts of his or her body. In many instances there is a close relationship between orthopedic and neurological impairments; for example, a child who is unable to use her legs because of damage to the central nervous system may develop disorders in the bones and muscles of the legs, especially if she does not receive proper therapy and equipment.

Orthopedic and neurological impairments, whatever their cause, are frequently described in terms of the parts of the body that are affected. The term *plegia* is derived from the Greek word meaning "to strike." **Quadriplegia** indicates that all four limbs (arms and legs) are affected. **Paraplegia** refers to paralysis or a motor disorder in the legs only. A child with **hemiplegia** is affected on one side of the body; for example, the left arm and left leg may be paralyzed. **Diplegia** refers to a major involvement of the legs, with a more minor involvement of the arms. Less common conditions include **monoplegia** (only one limb is affected) and **triplegia** (three limbs are affected). All of these terms are used to describe a variety of conditions caused by diseases or trauma.

Cerebral Palsy

Cerebral palsy is one of the most prevalent physical impairments. It is a long-term condition that is not a disease; the term is applied to a static malfunction of the brain that results in paralysis or a motion disorder of the limbs (Bleck, 1979). Cerebral palsy is actually a group of symptoms; as Cruickshank and Lewandowski (1979) point out, it is "an excellent example of a multiply handicapping condition" (p. 248). Cerebral palsy is not contagious. It cannot be

A static disorder gets neither better nor worse over time.

"cured," but usually the condition does not get progressively worse. It is not fatal and not inherited.

The causes of cerebral palsy are varied. It is generally attributed to injuries, accidents, or illnesses occurring **prenatally** (before birth), **perinatally** (during the process of birth), or **postnatally** (soon after birth). Lack of oxygen during the prenatal or perinatal period is thought to be one of the major causes of the brain damage that results in cerebral palsy. It is often difficult to specify the precise location of the brain damage, and two children who have sustained damage to the same part of the brain may have very different symptoms (Verhaaren & Connor, 1981).

Children with cerebral palsy have disturbances of their voluntary motor functions. These disturbances may include paralysis, extreme weakness, lack of coordination, involuntary convulsions, and other motor disorders. They may have little or no control over their arms, legs, or speech, depending on the type and degree of impairment. They may also have impaired vision or hearing and may have difficulty in perceptual processing.

Intellectual impairment *may* accompany cerebral palsy. A recent review of the literature (Verhaaren & Connor, 1981) estimated that approximately 1/3 of the children with cerebral palsy have intelligence within or above the "normal" range, while 1/3 function at the mildly mentally retarded level and 1/3 function at or below the moderately mentally retarded level. Caution should be used in interpreting these estimates, though, since current assessment procedures do not always give an accurate picture of the intellectual potential of children with multiple impairments. It is important to keep in mind that there is no clear relationship between the degree of motor impairment and the degree of intellectual impairment (if any) in children with cerebral palsy. A child with only mild motor impairment may also be severely mentally retarded, while another child with very severe motor impairment may be intellectually gifted.

Cerebral palsy has traditionallly been classified by type of motor disability. Among children, the most common types are **spasticity, athetosis,** and **ataxia. Rigidity** and **tremor** are additional, but less common, categories of cerebral palsy, and children may also have mixed cerebral palsy, consisting of more than one of these types.

Children with spastic cerebal palsy have tense, contracted muscles. Their movements may be jerky, exaggerated, and poorly coordinated. They may be unable to grasp objects with their fingers. If they try to control their movements, they may become even more jerky. If they are able to walk, it may be with a "scissors gait," standing on their toes with their knees bent and pointing inward.

Children with athetoid cerebral palsy make large, irregular, twisting movements which they cannot control. When they are at rest or asleep, there is little or no abnormal motion. An effort to pick up a pencil, however, may result in wildly waving arms, facial grimaces, and extension of the tongue. They may not be able to control the muscles of their lips, tongue, and throat, and may drool. They may seem to stumble and lurch awkwardly as they walk. At times, their muscles may be tense and rigid, while at other times they may be loose and flaccid. Extreme difficulty in expressive oral language often accompanies this form of cerebral palsy.

Children with ataxic cerebral palsy have a poor sense of balance and body position. They may appear to be dizzy while walking and fall easily if not supported. Their movements tend to be jumpy and unsteady, with exaggerated motion patterns. They seem to be constantly attempting to overcome the effect of gravity and to stabilize their bodies.

Children with the rare rigidity type of cerebral palsy display extreme stiffness in the affected limbs; they may be fixed and immobile for long periods. Tremor cerebral palsy, also rare, is marked by rhythmic, uncontrollable movements—the tremors may actually increase when the children attempt to control their actions.

It is difficult to determine precise criteria for describing the degree of motor involvement, but the terms *mild, moderate, severe,* and *very severe* are frequently used. The more severe forms of cerebral palsy are often identified in early childhood or even at birth, but identification of certain varieties may not occur until after a child has learned to walk and displays characteristic difficulties. According to Bleck (1979), about 80% of children with cerebral palsy are capable of learning to walk.

Since cerebral palsy is so complex, it is most effectively managed through the cooperation of physicians, teachers, physical therapists, occupational therapists, communication specialists, counselors, and other specialists who work with the children and their families. Regular exercise and careful positioning will help the child move as fully and comfortably as possible and will prevent or minimize progressive damage to the muscles and limbs.

It is especially important that physical therapy begin as early as possible in each child's life. Some medications, braces, and special adaptive equipment may be helpful in controlling muscle tension. Orthopedic surgery may be done to increase the child's range of motion or to avoid such complications as hip dislocations and permanent contractions of the muscles. Edginton (1976) advises that children with cerebral palsy should be made to feel physically secure at all times; they should never be seated in a precarious position. Children who use a wheelchair should change position from time to time by standing, lying down, stretching, sitting on a mat, or walking with assistance.

Spina Bifida

Spina bifida ("cleft spine") is a congenital defect in the formation of the spinal cord and the overlying bones of the vertebrae. A portion of the spinal cord and the nerves that normally control muscles and sensation in the lower portion of the body fail to develop normally. Spina bifida without serious consequence is called **spina bifida occulta.** If the covering of the spinal cord bulges through an opening in the child's back, it is called **meningocele.** If the spinal covering, spinal cord, and nerve roots all protrude, the child is said to have a **myelomen-**

Randy, who normally uses his crutches for support when walking, takes a swing in an improvised ball game.

ingocele. This is the most serious condition. With both meningocele and myelomeningocele, there is a high risk of paralysis and infection. Usually, children affected by spina bifida have good use of their arms and upper body. However, they may lack bowel and bladder control, since there is loss of feeling and muscle strength in the lower body.

Recent advances in surgical treatment now enable many children with spina bifida to be quite independent. The protruding spinal cord and nerves can be tucked back into the spinal column—preferably within 24 hours after birth—and spinal fluid can be drained to avoid accumulation in tissues surrounding the brain. If left untreated, this condition, which is known as **hydrocephaly,** can lead to mental retardation (Seligmann, 1982). Children with spina bifida usually walk with the aid of braces, crutches, or walkers, though they may use wheelchairs for longer distances. Some children need special help in dressing and toileting, while others are able to manage these tasks on their own. Most children need to use a **catheter** (tube) or bag to collect their urine, but are able to learn to regulate and schedule their own bowel movements (Bleck, 1979).

In treating hydrocephaly, spinal fluid is drained through a **shunt** surgically implanted in the child's neck.

Muscular Dystrophy

Muscular dystrophy refers to a group of long-term diseases that gradually weaken the muscles. The child is apparently normal at birth, but muscle weakness is usually evident by age 4 or 5. Slowness or clumsiness in walking is an early sign of muscular dystrophy. The child may walk with a peculiar gait, showing a protruding stomach and a hollow back. In Duchenne muscular dystrophy—which almost always affects boys—the calf muscles may appear unusually large, because the muscle tissue has degenerated and has been replaced by fatty tissue.

JON AND ABBY

There are many ways animals can be of help to disabled children and adults. Nearly everyone is familiar with "seeing eye" guide dogs, who can help blind people traveling independently. The Support Dogs for the Handicapped program represents a recent and especially promising use of animals with disabled people. We visited an 8-year-old boy named Jon and his Support Dog, a collie named Abby. Jon has muscular dystrophy, which gradually weakens and deteriorates the muscles. Abby provides important physical support. Jon attends a public school and divides his time between a resource room and a regular first grade classroom.

Each morning, Jon gets up and lets Abby go outside. Abby supports Jon on the way to school by allowing him to hold onto her leather harness and carries his books and supplies on her back in a special pouch that Jon's mother made.

In addition to supporting Jon while walking, Abby helps pull Jon up stairs and picks up objects he has dropped, such as pencils or coins. It is difficult for Jon to stand up if he falls or if he's seated on the floor. Jon says "stand," and Abby stands while Jon pulls himself up over her back. Other commands that Abby responds to include "come," "stay," "down," and "no." Other Support Dogs have been trained to pull wheelchairs and to open heavy doors for people with disabilities. Abby will learn new tasks as Jon's needs change.

Before Abby could attend school, Jon's parents had to get special permission from their local school board. Jon, his mother, the principal, and a representative of Support Dogs for the Handicapped visited classrooms with Abby, to explain that she is a working dog, not to be petted or played with. They answered questions from the children and demonstrated how Support Dogs are trained to assist people with physical disabilities.

When we visited Jon's classroom, the children were making cards for National Secretary's Week. Abby rested patiently near Jon's desk and took an occasional drink from her water dish. When the cards were finished, Abby helped Jon get up from his chair and walked with him and the other children to the school secretary's office. "You should have signed your card from Jon and Abby," said a classmate.

Jon's parents are pleased with the bond that has developed between Jon and Abby. They also see certain social advantages for Jon. He cannot perform some activities that other children in his neighborhood do—like riding a bicycle or playing soccer—but Abby is a constant source of attention, conversation, and admiration from playmates. On a few occasions, Abby has protected Jon by standing between him and an aggressive child. And Jon is learning to assume the responsibilities of caring for an animal.

For information about Support Dogs, contact: Support Dogs for the Handicapped, Inc., 5900 North High Street, Worthington, Ohio 43085.

Abby waits patiently while Jon receives individualized instruction from his resource room teacher.

Children with muscular dystrophy often have difficulty in getting to their feet after lying down or playing on the floor. They may fall easily. Some doctors and therapists recommend the early use of electrically powered wheelchairs, while others adopt a more aggressive approach to prolong walking as long as possible, with special braces and other devices. The child gradually loses the ability to walk; the small muscles of the hands and fingers are usually the last to be affected.

Unfortunately, there is no known cure at present for most cases of muscular dystrophy, and the disease is often fatal. A good deal of independence can be maintained, however, by regular physical therapy, exercise, and the use of appropriate aids and appliances. In school, a teacher should be careful not to lift a child with muscular dystrophy by the arms—even a gentle pull may cause the limbs to become dislocated. The teacher may also need to help the child deal with the gradual loss of physical abilities and the possibility of death.

Osteogenesis Imperfecta

Osteogenesis imperfecta is an inherited condition marked by bones that are extremely brittle. The skeletal system does not grow normally, and the children's bones are easily fractured. Children with osteogenesis imperfecta are literally fragile and must be protected. Wheelchairs are usually used, though the children may be able to walk for short distances with the aid of braces, crutches, and protective equipment. Like other children with orthopedic impairments, the child with osteogenesis imperfecta may have had frequent hospitalizations for treatment and surgery. Some children, understandably, are reluctant to be touched or handled. Usually the children have adequate use of their hands and can participate in most classroom activities if they receive appropriate physical support and protection. As the children mature, their bones may become less brittle, requiring less attention.

Spinal Cord Injuries

Spinal cord injuries usually arise from accidents or injuries. Injury to the spinal column is usually described by letters and numbers indicating where the damage occurred. For example, a *C5–6* injury means that the damage occurred at the level of the fifth and sixth cervical vertebrae—a flexible area of the neck susceptible to injury from whiplash and diving or trampoline accidents. A *T12* injury occurred at the twelfth thoracic (chest) vertebra and an *L3* at the third lumbar (lower back) area. In general, there is paralysis and loss of sensation below the level of the injury.

Children who have sustained spinal cord injuries usually use wheelchairs for their mobility. Motorized wheelchairs, though expensive, are recommended for those with quadriplegia, while self-propelled wheelchairs can be used by paraplegic children. Children with quadriplegia may have severe problems in breathing, since the muscles of the chest, which normally govern respiration, are affected. In most cases, the spinal-cord-injured child lacks bladder and bowel control and needs to follow a careful management program to maintain personal hygiene and avoid infection and skin irritation.

Rehabilitation programs for children and adolescents who have sustained spinal cord injuries usually involve physical therapy, the use of adaptive devices for mobility and independent living, and psychological support to help them adjust to a sudden disability. With supportive teachers and peers, the spinal-cord-injured student can participate fully in the school program. Adolescents and adults often are particularly concerned about sexual function. While most spinal cord injuries do affect sexuality, it is often possible for people to enjoy varied and satisfying sexual relationships, with positive attitudes toward themselves and understanding partners. Many counselors now specialize in addressing the sexual concerns of people who are disabled due to spinal cord injury or other conditions.

Amputations

Amputations or missing limbs affect a significant number of students. Artificial limbs are often used to facilitate balance, to enable the children to participate in a variety of tasks, and to result in a more "normal" appearance. Some students or their parents, however, prefer not to use artificial limbs. Children may become quite proficient at using their remaining limbs. Many children who are missing both arms, for example, learn to write, eat, and perform vocational tasks with their feet. They have a much greater feeling of being "in contact" with objects and people than if they use prosthetic limbs. Unless the child has other impairments in addition to the absence of limbs, he or she should be able to function in the regular classroom without major modifications.

Other Health-Related Conditions

There are many conditions that may affect a child's health, either permanently, temporarily, or intermittently. The usual—and proper—course of action is to seek medical treatment. In many instances, however, a health-related condition can significantly affect a child's performance and social acceptance in school, so it is important for the teacher to be aware of it. In general, the health-related conditions that we will briefly discuss in this section are less visible than the orthopedic and neurological impairments we just covered—but their effects on the child may be just as great.

Epilepsy

Epilepsy is a convulsive disorder that affects many children of school age. Children with epilepsy may have sudden, uncontrollable attacks, called *seizures*, during which they lose consciousness and muscular control. With proper medical treatment and with the support of parents, teachers, and peers, children with epilepsy need not be considered disabled or handicapped. Most children with epilepsy lead full and normal lives, and the condition is a "disorder" only while a seizure is actually in progress. A significant percentage of all children have seizures at some time during their lives, often due to a high fever or a severe blow to the head. Usually these episodes do not recur, but a person who has repeated seizures and abnormal brain wave patterns is said to have epilepsy (Batshaw & Perret, 1981).

Most children with epilepsy have normal intelligence. Their seizures may be largely or wholly controlled by anticonvulsant medications. Some children require such heavy doses of medication that, though their seizures are controlled, their learning and behavior may be adversely affected. Some medications have unpleasant side effects such as drowsiness, nausea, weight gain, or thickening of the gums.

The specific causes of epilepsy are not clearly known. Some cases can be traced to a specific incident that resulted in damage or irritation to the brain—for example, a fall, a tumor, or a disease that caused a very high fever. In about 70% of the cases, however, the cause cannot be identified (Zakariasen, 1979). Epilepsy can occur at any stage throughout life, but most frequently begins in childhood.

During a seizure, a dysfunction in the electrochemical activity of the brain causes the person to lose control of his or her muscles temporarily. Between seizures—that is, most of the time—the brain functions normally. Many unfortunate misconceptions about epilepsy have circulated in the past and are even prevalent today. Negative public attitudes, in fact, have probably been more harmful to people with epilepsy than the condition itself.

If a child is affected by epilepsy, it is important for teachers, the school nurse, and classmates to be aware of it, so that they may be prepared to deal with a seizure, should one occur in school. There are three common types of epileptic seizures.

The **grand mal** seizure is the most evident and serious type of epileptic seizure. A grand mal seizure can be very disturbing and frightening to someone who has never seen one. The child has little or no warning that a seizure is about to occur. The muscles become stiff; the child loses consciousness and falls to the floor. Then there is violent shaking of the entire body, as the muscles alternately contract and relax. Saliva may be forced from the mouth; legs and arms may jerk; the bladder and bowels may be emptied. After a few minutes, the contractions diminish, and the child either goes to sleep or regains consciousness in a confused or drowsy state. Grand mal seizures may occur as often as several times a day, or as seldom as once a year. They are more likely to occur during the day than at night.

The Epilepsy Foundation of America (1974) recommends that the teacher remain calm and explain to other children that the seizure is painless to the child and is not contagious. The following procedures are suggested in case a grand mal seizure occurs in the classroom:

1. Ease the child to the floor and loosen his or her collar. You cannot stop the seizure. Let it run its course and do not try to revive the child.
2. Remove hard, sharp, or hot objects which may injure the child, but do not interfere with movements.

However, many severely retarded children have epilepsy. The special problems presented by students with multiple handicaps are discussed in the next chapter.

3. Do not force anything between the child's teeth. If the child's mouth is already open, you might place a soft object, like a handkerchief, between the side teeth. Be careful not to get your fingers between the teeth.
4. Turn the head to one side for release of saliva. Place something soft under the child's head.
5. When the child regains consciousness, let him rest if he wishes.
6. If the seizure lasts beyond a few minutes or if the child seems to pass from one seizure to another without gaining consciousness, call the school nurse or doctor for instructions and notify the parents. This rarely happens, but should be treated immediately.

Petit mal seizures are much less severe than grand mal, but may occur much more frequently—as often as 100 times per day in some children. In a petit mal seizure, the child loses consciousness, usually for less than half a minute. The child may stare blankly, blink her eyes, grow pale, or drop a pencil she is holding. She may appear to be "daydreaming." No special first aid is necessary; the teacher should explain it to the child's classmates.

A **psychomotor** seizure may appear as a brief period of inappropriate or purposeless activity. The child may smack his lips, walk around aimlessly, or shout. He may appear to be conscious, but is not actually aware of his abnormal behavior. Psychomotor seizures usually last for a few minutes, but in some cases go on as long as several hours. The teacher should keep dangerous objects out of the child's way, and except in emergencies, should not try to physically restrain him. Some children may respond to spoken directions during a psychomotor seizure.

In some children, petit mal and psychomotor seizures go undetected for long periods. In many cases, observant teachers are instrumental in detecting the presence of a seizure disorder and in referring the child for appropriate medical help.

Today, the majority of children with epilepsy can be helped with medication. Drugs can sharply reduce or even eliminate seizures in many cases. All children with epilepsy will benefit from a realistic understanding of their condition and from accepting attitudes on the part of teachers and classmates.

Diabetes

Juvenile diabetes mellitus is a disorder of metabolism; that is, it affects the way in which the body absorbs and breaks down the sugars and starches in foods. Without proper medical management, the diabetic child's system is not able to obtain and retain adequate energy from food. Not only will the child lack energy, but many important parts of the body—particularly the eyes and the kidneys—can be affected by untreated diabetes. Early symptoms of diabetes in children include thirst, headaches, loss of weight (despite a good appetite), frequent urination, and cuts that are slow to heal.

Children with diabetes have insufficient insulin, a hormone normally produced by the pancreas, needed for the proper metabolism and digestion of foods. Insulin must be injected daily under the skin to regulate the condition.

Most children with diabetes learn to inject their own insulin, which in some cases may be necessary as frequently as four times per day, and to determine the amount of insulin they need by testing the level of sugar and other substances in their urine. It is also important that these children follow a specific and regular diet, prescribed by a physician or nutrition specialist. A regular exercise program is also usually suggested.

Teachers should be aware of the symptoms of insulin reaction, also called *diabetic shock*. It can result from taking too much insulin, from unusually strenuous exercise, or from a missed or delayed meal (the blood sugar level is lowered by insulin and exercise and raised by food). The symptoms of insulin reaction may include faintness, dizziness, blurred vision, drowsiness, and nausea. The child may appear irritable or have a marked personality change. In most cases, giving the child some form of concentrated sugar, such as a sugar cube, glass of fruit juice, or candy bar, will end the insulin reaction within a few minutes. The child's doctor or parents should inform the teacher and school health personnel of the appropriate foods to give in case of insulin reaction.

A *diabetic coma* is more serious. It indicates that too little insulin is present; that is, the diabetes is not under control. Its onset is gradual, rather than sudden. The symptoms of diabetic coma may include fatigue; thirst; dry, hot skin; deep, labored breathing; excessive urination; and "fruity smelling" breath. A doctor or nurse should be contacted if a child displays symptoms of diabetic coma.

Cystic Fibrosis

Cystic fibrosis is a serious chronic disease of children and adolescents. A thick mucus is secreted by the exocrine glands of the body; it can block the lungs and parts of the digestive system. Children with cystic fibrosis may have difficulty breathing and are susceptible to coughs and respiratory infections. They may also have large and frequent bowel movements, since food passes through the system only partially digested.

Medications prescribed for children with cystic fibrosis include enzymes to facilitate digestion and solutions to thin and loosen the mucus in the lungs. Some children may need help from teachers, aides, or classmates in vigorous physical exercises to help clear the lungs and air passages.

Research has not clearly established the cause of cystic fibrosis. It appears to be hereditary and is found mainly among Caucasian children, both male and female. The symptoms may be due to a missing chemical or substance in the body. Unfortunately, no reliable cure for cystic fibrosis has yet been found, but many children and young adults with this condition are able to lead active lives. With continued research and treatment techniques, the long-range outlook for children affected by cystic fibrosis is improving.

Hemophilia

In **hemophilia,** the blood does not clot as quickly as it should. Its most serious consequences are usually internal, rather than external bleeding; contrary to popular opinion, minor cuts and scrapes do not usually pose a serious problem. Internal bleeding can cause swelling, pain, and permanent damage to a child's joints, tissues, and internal organs and may necessitate hospitalization for blood transfusions. It is thought that emotional stress may intensify episodes of bleeding (Verhaaren & Connor, 1981). A child with hemophilia may need to be excused from some physical activities and may use a wheelchair during periods of susceptibility. However—as with most children who have health-related impairments—good physical condition is important for the child's development and well-being, so the restrictions on activities should not be any greater than necessary.

Burns

Severe burns may cause disfigurement and the loss of body parts or functions. Burns on the face, in addition to being physically painful, can affect a child's self-image, especially if teachers and peers react negatively. Some children with very severe burns wear sterilized silicone masks over their faces to protect the skin and to facilitate healing. The recovery period may be lengthy, requiring frequent surgery.

Other Health Problems

There are, of course, many other significant physical and health-related conditions that can influence a child's behavior at school. Heart disease, asthma, anemia, cancer, and juvenile rheumatoid arthritis are conditions that generally do not require the use of special teaching techniques or adaptive equipment, but may cause variations in the child's performance due to the effects of the condition itself, or because of frequent absences, medication, fatigue, pain, or concerns about the future. Further information about these and other conditions may be obtained from the student's family or physician, from the student, or from one of the references listed at the end of this chapter. A teacher's familiarity with a physical or health impairment can do much to improve the child's experience in school.

IMPORTANT VARIABLES TO CONSIDER

In assessing the effects of a physical or health impairment upon a child's behavior and development, many factors must be taken into consideration. Important among these variables are the severity and the visibility of the impairment and the age at which the disabling condition was first acquired.

Severity

Most children learn by exploring their surroundings, interacting with other people, and having a wide variety of experiences in their home, neighborhood, school, and community. A minor or transient physical or health impairment is

Students with physical impairments should be encouraged to participate as independently as possible in all aspects of the school program.

not likely to have lasting effects, but a severe, long-standing impairment can greatly limit a child's range of experiences. Many disabling conditions seriously restrict a child's mobility and independence, much as a severe visual or hearing impairment would. The child may not be able to travel alone at all and may have few opportunities to explore the environment by seeing, hearing, touching, smelling, or tasting things. He or she may spend most of the time at home or in a hospital. Some children are virtually in constant pain or become tired after any sort of physical exertion. Some take medications that decrease their alertness and responsiveness. They may be physically fragile and afraid of injury or death.

Visibility

Some physical impairments are highly visible and conspicuous. The way children think about themselves and the degree to which they are accepted by others often are affected by the visibility of the condition. Some children need to rely on a variety of special orthopedic appliances, such as wheelchairs, braces, crutches, and adaptive tables. They may ride a specially equipped bus or van to school, with other disabled children. In school, they may need assistance in using the toilet and may wear prominent helmets. While such special devices and adaptations do help children meet important needs, they often have the unfortunate side effect of increasing the visibility of the physical impairment and making the child look even more different from nondisabled children. Many disabled people report that their "hardware"—wheelchairs, artificial limbs, communication devices, and other apparatus—creates a great deal of curiosity and leads to frequent, repetitive questions from strangers. For many children, learning to

EXCEPTIONAL CHILDREN

explain their disabilities and respond to questions is an appropriate component of the educational program.

Age at Acquisition

As with virtually all exceptionalities, it is important for the teacher to consider the age of the child at the time the physical or health impairment was first acquired. A child who has not had the use of his or her legs since birth may have missed out on some important experiences during the early stages of development. In contrast, an adolescent who suddenly loses the use of the legs at age 15 will likely have had a normal range of experiences in early childhood, but may need both practical training and emotional support in making a successful adaptation to life as a disabled person.

Since there are many physical and health impairments and since there is no universally accepted definition of this population, it is difficult to obtain accurate and meaningful statistics on prevalence. Grove (1982) estimates that about 250,000 children are born with "significant birth defects" every year. Many of these are treatable by surgery or other medical means, to the extent that the children are not considered disabled or in need of special education by the time they reach school age. Most children with health-related problems are probably counted among the general school population, unless the severity of their condition makes full-time special education necessary.

A survey of handicapped children (age 3 through 21) served in special education programs during the 1981–82 school year placed the number of "orthopedically impaired" children at 48,958, and the number of "other health impaired" children at 76,174 (U.S. Department of Education, 1982c). Together, these categories would represent about 3% of all children receiving special education services. It is not known how many children with physical and health impairments are included under other special education categories, such as multihandicapped, speech impaired, or mentally retarded.

Children with cerebral palsy probably comprise the largest single group of students who are enrolled in special education programs for the physically and health impaired. The National Institutes of Health note that approximately one in every 200 infants is affected by this condition. In some educational programs, half or more of the students who are considered physically impaired may be those with cerebral palsy.

Current Incidence Trends

The causes of physical disabilities have changed somewhat over the years. Recently, medical detection and vaccination programs have significantly reduced the incidence of diseases such as polio and tuberculosis, once widespread afflictions of children. It is now also possible to correct or control a variety of orthopedic defects and health conditions—through surgery, physical therapy, artificial implantation of bones and joints, and medication—to the point where many conditions once regarded as disabling or disfiguring are no longer so.

On the other hand, more infants with severe physical and health impairments are surviving because of improved medical care; they may have multiple and severe disabilities. It is also apparent that a growing number of children suffer physical disability as the result of accidents, particularly those involving automobiles and motorcycles. In a recent year, it was estimated that over 50,000 children in the United States were permanently disabled by accidents and that more than half of these children were under 5 years old (Telford & Sawrey, 1977). There has also been an alarming increase in the number of children who are being treated for physical injuries resulting from child abuse and neglect (Best, 1978). These include severe burns, bone fractures, and other injuries that may necessitate temporary or permanent placement of the child into a special program. Emotional injuries are also a concern in the case of a child who has been subjected to abuse or neglect.

HISTORICAL BACKGROUND

Perhaps because there are so many different types of physical and health impairments, it is difficult to trace the development of services for this population with any precision. Before there were public school educational opportunities, which began around the turn of this century, most children with severely disabling conditions were kept at home, in hospitals, or in institutions. If local public schools were willing to accept them and to make any necessary modifications, some physically disabled children probably attended regular classes, especially if their handicaps were less severe and if their intellectual functioning was not impaired.

The first special public school class for physically handicapped children in the United States was established in Chicago around 1900. Two American physicians, Winthrop Phelps and Earl Carlson, made noteworthy contributions to the understanding and acceptance of physically disabled children. Phelps demonstrated that children could be helped through physical therapy and the effective use of braces, while Carlson (who himself had cerebral palsy) was a strong advocate of developing the intellectual potential of physically disabled children through appropriate education (Hewett & Forness, 1977).

The educational needs of physically and health impaired children were gradually recognized as the century progressed, and educational programs became available, in addition to the medical treatment that was already being provided. Classes for the physically and health impaired were established in hospitals, rehabilitation centers, and other institutions. Children who were kept at home for reasons of health began to receive services from "homebound" teachers, who traveled from place to place. Special self-contained classes for the physically disabled were set up in many regular public schools. Large school districts frequently established special schools solely for children with physical impairments. These special classes or schools typically had such modifications as ramps, adapted toilets, and space for wheelchairs in school cafeterias.

Many special classes and schools still exist. Today, however, there is a trend toward increased integration of physically and health impaired children into regular public school classes. Recent laws—most notably P.L. 94–142 and Section 504 of the Rehabilitation Act of 1973—that require architectural accessibility and education of the child in the least restrictive appropriate environment and forbid discrimination against the handicapped have been instrumental in this integration. A child may no longer be denied the right to attend the local public school only because there is a flight of stairs at the entrance, or because bathroom facilities are "not suitable," or because school buses are not equipped to carry wheelchairs. The school now has the obligation of doing whatever is necessary to meet the needs of the child. Today, many thousands of children with physical and health impairments are successfully attending regular classes.

EDUCATIONAL IMPLICATIONS

Alternative Settings

Early intervention programs are important for all exceptional children, and especially for those with physical and health impairments. Programs for infants and preschool children are increasingly available through school districts, hospitals, and specialized agencies (such as United Cerebral Palsy). They may focus exclusively on the special needs of disabled children or may include nondisabled children as well. Usually, early intervention programs emphasize assessment of the child's functioning in many areas and work on the systematic development of motor skills, self-help, communication, and information and support to the child's parents. A good infant or preschool program can be of immeasurable value to the child and the family in promoting development and independence.

See the list of agencies at the end of this chapter.

Special classes for physically disabled children are found in public and private schools. Some districts have entire schools designed especially for the physically disabled, while in others special classrooms are housed within regular school buildings. Special classes often provide smaller class size, more highly specialized equipment, and easier access to the services of important professionals (such as physicians, physical and occupational therapists, and communication disorders specialists) than may be possible in regular classes—particularly if the child needs constant medical and physical attention or cannot communicate easily. Some parents and educators feel that it is desirable for physically disabled children to associate with other disabled children and with teachers who are familiar with their special needs.

Other parents and educators prefer regular classes in which disabled children are educated with nondisabled children. The amount of supportive help required to enable the disabled student to function effectively varies greatly, according to the child's condition, needs, and level of functioning. Some children require relatively minor modifications—such as ramps and special seating ar-

ACCESS FOR ALL

Try spending a day in a wheelchair, or on crutches, and see which facilities in your area are truly accessible. Don't forget to use elevators, toilets, telephones, restaurants, and public transportation. After all, you not only have to get *into* buildings; you also have to get *to* them in the first place. Creating a barrier-free environment goes well beyond entrance ramps and curb cuts. These illustrations show just a few of the many architectural considerations that go into barrier-free design.

While these drawings show adaptations for wheelchairs, it is also important that buildings be accessible to people with braces and crutches. This can mean redesigning stairs and handrails, for instance, so that users will not trip on them.

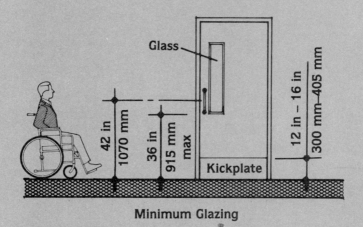

Minimum Glazing

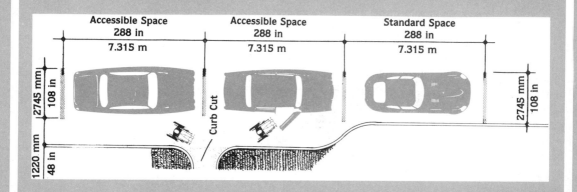

Illustrations from E. A. Aino & R. D. Loversidge. *Access for all: An illustrated handbook of barrier-free design.* Columbus, Ohio: Special Press, 1979. Copyright © 1977, 1978 by the Ohio Governor's Committee on Employment of the Handicapped and Schooley Cornelius Associates. Reprinted with permission.

rangements for students in wheelchairs—while others require special equipment and assistance in mobility, eating, using the toilet, and other activities. An integrated school setting can encourage independence and communication and can make nondisabled students more aware of their classmates with disabilities.

Some children with especially severe physical and health impairments receive education in hospitals and institutions, where they have access to the constant medical care they need. A child whose medical condition necessitates lengthy hospitalization or a child who must remain at home for long periods is still entitled to receive a free and appropriate program of education. Most large hospitals operate or have access to educational programs for children who are absent from school for more than a few weeks; cooperation with the child's home school district is usually arranged. Itinerant teachers—generally employed by local school districts—visit homebound children. In some hospital and homebound educational programs, special counseling is available to help children and their families deal with the problems of long-term or terminal illness.

The Interdisciplinary Approach

Children with physical and health impairments usually come into contact with a great many teachers, physicians, therapists, and other specialists, both in and out of school. It is important that both regular and special educators make informed decisions about the child's needs, in cooperation with parents and other professionals. There are many opportunities for members of the interdisciplinary team to share information about the child, from their own vantage points. The team approach has special relevance to the child with a physical or

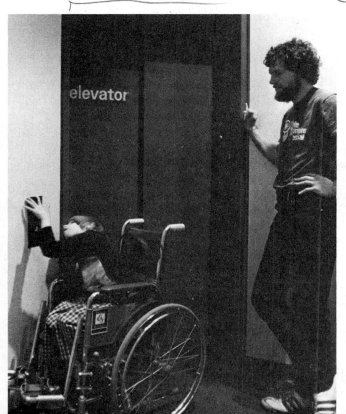

Independent travel is an important learning objective for many children with physical and health impairments.

health impairment. Medical, educational, recreational, vocational, and social needs are all important, and often complex. Sirvis (1982) suggests that the interdisciplinary team should work toward the fulfillment of four general goals in planning the educational program of a child with a physical or health impairment:

1. Physical independence, including mastery of daily living skills;
2. Self-awareness and social maturation;
3. Academic growth; and
4. Career education, including constructive leisure activities.

Two specialists of particular importance to many children with physical and health impairments are the **physical therapist** and the **occupational therapist.** Each of these specialists must complete a specialized training program and must meet rigorous professional standards. Their work frequently takes them into contact with physically and health impaired children. They are often called upon to provide practical suggestions and training to teachers and parents.

Physical therapists use specialized knowledge to plan and oversee a child's program in making correct and useful movements. They may prescribe specific exercises to help a child increase the degree of control over the muscles of the body and to use specialized equipment, such as braces, effectively. Massage and prescriptive exercises are perhaps the most frequently applied procedures, but physical therapy may also include swimming, heat treatment, special positioning for feeding and toileting, and other methods. Physical therapists encourage children to be as motorically independent as possible, help develop muscular function, and reduce pain, discomfort, or long-term physical damage. They may also suggest "do's and don't's" for sitting positions and activities in the classroom and may suggest exercise or play programs that a disabled child can enjoy along with other children.

Occupational therapists are concerned with a child's participation in activities, especially those which will be useful in self-help, employment, recreation,

Mike is determined to do one more than yesterday.

316

communication, and creativity. They may work with a child in such diverse activities as learning to drink from a modified cup, buttoning clothes, tying shoes, pouring liquids, cooking, and typewriting. These and other activities can enhance the child's physical development, independence, vocational potential, and self-concept. Occupational therapists also conduct assessments and make recommendations to parents and teachers regarding the use of appliances, materials, and activities at home and school. Many occupational therapists help students explore possible vocational and independent living settings for the postschool years.

Special Devices and Appliances

Many physically disabled children use special orthopedic devices to increase their mobility and to help the bones, joints, and muscles develop as well as possible. These devices may include canes, leg or hip braces, walkers, and wheelchairs. A specialist in the prescription and use of such aids is called an *orthopedist;* he or she usually works in cooperation with the child's physician and physical therapist. **Prostheses** are artificial devices to replace missing body parts—most frequently arms, legs, and eyes. A *prosthetist* specializes in fitting, adjusting, and evaluating artificial parts.

Teachers of children who use orthopedic and prosthetic devices should be familiar with them. Although the teacher is seldom involved in prescribing or fitting the appliances, he or she is in a good position to observe the ways in which a child uses and cares for them and can encourage the child to function as independently as possible while in school. The teacher can also advise parents of any problems or malfunctions that may come up, including discomfort that may be caused by poorly fitting devices.

A helpful series of checklists for teachers to use in evaluating orthopedic and prosthetic devices is provided by Venn, Morganstern, and Dykes (1979). They point out, for example, that braces are used for *control* in cerebral palsy and for *support* in spina bifida; support braces are generally smaller and lighter than control braces.

See pages 322–323.

Wheelchairs have many parts and specialized functions, and children are generally instructed in their use and maintenance by an orthopedist or physical therapist. Students who spend most or all of the school day in a wheelchair are susceptible to skin ulcers, muscular atrophy, and postural problems—particularly if they are not able to feel the lower portion of the body. A working knowledge of techniques associated with wheelchair use can be helpful to the teacher. Orelove and Hanley (1979) offer a school accessibility survey, which may be useful to teachers in making practical adaptations in the classroom and school for students who use wheelchairs and other orthopedic devices.

Physically disabled children also use **adaptive devices** in many everyday activities. Special eating utensils, such as forks and spoons with special handles

Where a prosthesis replaces a missing body part, an adaptive device modifies or replaces a missing or ineffective body function.

or straps, may enable children to feed themselves more independently. Communication aids are increasingly used with children whose physical impairments prevent them from speaking clearly. They allow these students to communicate both expressively and receptively, to carry out nonvocal "conversations."

Positioning and Safety Concerns

A working knowledge of positioning techniques can be helpful to the teacher of children with physical impairments. As Utley, Holvoet, and Barnes (1977) point out, the ways in which students are positioned and handled throughout the school day should be consistent, in order to increase muscle tone, develop skills such as head and arm control, and promote relaxation and comfort. If children are allowed to lie or sit in the same position for long periods or if materials are presented to them incorrectly, their muscles and joints may be damaged. The children's positions should be changed frequently.

A general guideline is that any sitting, standing, or other positioning device should provide adequate support, without locking the child into a static position. The child should be able to maintain the recommended posture while still having the opportunity to move (Kasari & Filler, 1981). Physical therapists can assist in prescribing, maintaining, and evaluating devices such as adaptive chairs, standing tables, wedges, and inflatable support equipment.

The positioning of a physically disabled child can also have significant effects on how the child is perceived and accepted by other people. A recent study (Brown, 1982) found that postural adjustment had a major influence on teachers' attitudes toward physically disabled children; "well-positioned" children were rated more positively than "poorly positioned" children. Simple adjustments in posture may greatly improve the appearance and acceptance of children with physical disabilities.

Students who use wheelchairs should learn to operate them safely and efficiently. Techniques involved in wheelchair operation include using footrests, handbrakes, and rims; turning safely; traveling over rugs, doorways, curbs, and mud; and transferring from the wheelchair to a chair, car, or toilet. Propelling a wheelchair takes up to five times more energy than normal walking (Mullins,

Sharon's wheelchair has been fitted with a special "desk top," giving her a comfortable work space for academic activities.

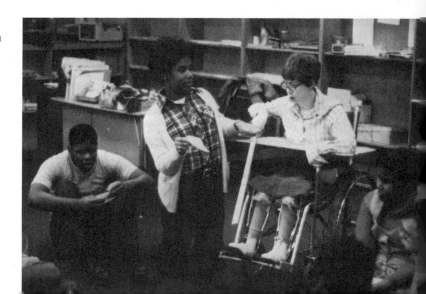

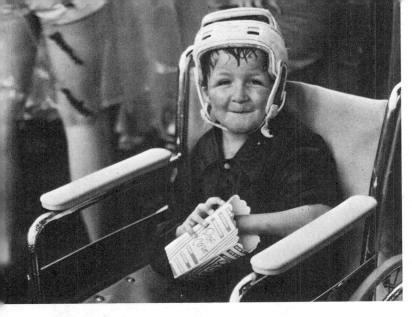

Talk about a positive outlook!

1979); some wheelchairs are motorized, which reduces the effort involved, but adds a substantial amount of additional weight. Swack (1969) observes that there are two basic causes of accidents involving wheelchairs in the classroom: (1) classmates pushing a wheelchair too rapidly and (2) wheelchairs rolling away when left unlocked. Strict enforcement of "no speeding" rules and locking the brakes on wheelchairs when not in motion should reduce classroom mishaps.

Attitudes

The ways in which parents, teachers, classmates, and others react to a child with physical disabilities are *at least as important* as the disability itself. Many disabled children suffer from excessive pity, sympathy, and overprotection, while others are cruelly rejected, stared at, teased, and excluded from participation in activities with nondisabled children. All children—disabled or not—need to develop respect for themselves and to feel that they have a rightful place in the family, school, and community.

The child with physical disabilities should be given the chance to participate in many activities and to experience success and accomplishment. Effective parents and teachers are able to accept the child as a worthwhile individual, rather than as a "case of disability." They encourage children to develop a positive, realistic view of themselves and their physical conditions. They expect children to meet reasonable standards of performance and behavior. They help them cope with the disability wherever possible, and realize that, aside from having a physical impairment, they have many other qualities that make them unique.

As Allsop (1980) points out, many nondisabled people tend to feel uncomfortable in the presence of a person with a visible disability and react with tension and withdrawal. This is probably attributable to a lack of previous contact with disabled individuals; people may fear that they will say or do the "wrong" thing. A study by Belgrave and Mills (1981) found that when disabled people specifically mentioned their disabilities in connection with a request for help ("Would you mind sharpening my pencil for me? There are just some things you can't do from a wheelchair."), they were perceived more favorably than when no mention was made of the disability.

The classroom can be a useful place to discuss disabilities and to encourage understanding and acceptance of the child with a physical or health impairment. Some teachers find that simulation or role-playing activities are useful. Nondisabled children may, for example, have the opportunity to use wheelchairs, braces, crutches, or other adaptive devices, to increase their awareness of some obstacles faced by their disabled classmate. Factual information can also be helpful in fostering a general understanding of the child's disabling condition. Classmates should learn to use appropriate terminology and to offer the correct kind of assistance when needed.

CURRENT ISSUES/FUTURE TRENDS

There is currently an increasing trend toward integrating physically disabled children into regular education programs. For many years, it was felt that regular schools were simply not an appropriate environment for children with severe physical limitations. Indeed, the architectural design of most school buildings made it difficult, if not impossible, for many capable disabled students to be included in the regular school program. It is unfortunate that some children are still excluded from public schools solely because of architectural barriers.

The educational pattern of the future will likely be one in which disabled children are served in regular classes as much as possible. Therapists and other support personnel will come into the classroom to assist the teacher, child, and classmates. This appears to be a more effective and economical use of professional time and skill than removing a disabled child from the classroom and providing services in an isolated setting.

Recent developments in technology and biomedical engineering hold exciting implications for many children with physical disabilities. People with paralysis due to spinal cord injury and other causes are already benefiting from sophisticated microcomputers able to stimulate paralyzed muscles by "bypassing" damaged nerves. In 1982, Nan Davis became the first human being ever to walk with permanently paralyzed muscles; she is able to control a computer with her brain and transmit impulses to sensors placed on her paralyzed muscles. Such systems are likely to become more efficient and widespread in the future, helping many people with certain kinds of physical impairments. Improved medical treatment will also alleviate some physical and health-related conditions.

Children with physical limitations should be encouraged to develop as much independence as their condition permits. Often, well-meaning teachers, classmates, and parents tend to do too much for the disabled child. It may be difficult, frustrating, and time-consuming for the child to learn to care for his or her own needs, but the confidence and skill gained from independent functioning will be well worth it in the long run. Most physically disabled persons need to rely on others for assistance at certain times, in certain situations. Effective teachers can help them cope with their disabilities, set realistic expectations, and accept help gracefully when it is needed.

Although a good deal of progress has been made, there are still several areas that need improvement. While physical education is an important need of most disabled people—and is specifically required to be included in the educational program of every handicapped child, according to P.L. 94–142—many schools do not provide adapted physical education programs for their disabled students, thus excluding them from any participation in most athletic and recreational activities.

A comprehensive guide to special adaptations in physical education for disabled students is provided by French and Jansma (1982).

Employment is one of the most critical aspects in any adult's life; many studies have shown that successful and remunerative work is among the most important variables in enabling disabled people to lead satisfying, productive, and independent lives. Yet negative attitudes persist on the part of many employers. Vocational and professional opportunities must be expanded to include disabled individuals more adequately. While the children are in school, their education should help them investigate practical avenues of future employment, and there should be ongoing contact between educators and vocational rehabilitation specialists.

There is also a need for improved programs of education and counseling in cases where students have terminal illnesses. These programs should give realistic support to the child and family in dealing with death and in making the best possible use of the time available to them. When a child dies, the teachers and classmates may also be seriously affected, and their needs should also be considered and talked about.

Many "self-help" groups of disabled people now exist. They can be very helpful in providing information and support to children affected by similar disabilities. It is usually encouraging for a child and parent to see capable, independent adults with severe disabilities, and worthwhile helping relationships can be established. Some groups operate centers for independent living, which emphasize adaptive devices, financial benefits, access to jobs, and provision of personal care attendents. Others are active as advocates for social change, countering instances in which disabled people are excluded from meaningful participation in society.

There is every indication that the years ahead will find children and adults with physical and health impairments participating more fully in schools, colleges, and virtually all other facets of everyday community life. However, we still need better physical access to public buildings, improved public attitudes, and greater support to parents early in the lives of their disabled children. As these needs are met, the opportunities open to people with physical and health impairments will be greatly expanded.

CHECKLISTS FOR THE CLASSROOM

John Venn, Linda Morganstern, and Mary K. Dykes have prepared information and checklists which may be useful to the teacher who works with children who use braces, protheses, and wheelchairs in the classroom. Here is a portion of the material on wheelchairs.

Wheelchairs

Wheelchair locomotion is prescribed by a physician for individuals who are unable to ambulate or for those whose ambulation is unsteady, unsafe, or too strenuous. A wheelchair may also be needed by those who can ambulate but cannot rise unassisted from sitting to standing. Those who need crutches to ambulate but have to carry things from one place to another may also require the use of a wheelchair (Hirschberg, Lewis, & Thomas, 1964).

The most commonly used type of wheelchair is made of metal and upholstery and has four wheels. The two back wheels are large and have a separate rim that can be grasped to propel the chair while the two small front wheels are casters that pivot freely. The casters are attached to the wheelchair by a fork and stem assembly that allows them to pivot 360°. Since wheelchairs are fitted to individuals, and not individuals to wheelchairs, the special parts and features are numerous. Such special features include detachable armrests, which are fitted with a locking device to secure them in place; footrests, which often have nylon heel loops to hold the foot on the footrest; leg rest panels to support the leg in proper position; and a folding device that allows the wheelchair to be folded for easier storage (Ellwood, 1971). After it has been decided that a wheelchair is needed, the wheelchair dealer, often in conjunction with a physical therapist, measures the child to insure an individual prescription that will properly fit the child. The dealer also provides instruction in the use and care of the wheelchair.

Recent wheelchair developments include increasing use of lightweight, adaptive wheelchairs as well as motorized wheelchairs. The

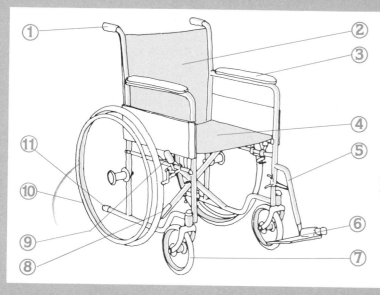

1. handgrips/push handles
2. back upholstery
3. armrests
4. seat upholstery
5. front rigging
6. footplate
7. casters
8. crossbraces
9. wheel locks
10. wheel and handrim
11. tipping lever

lightweight chairs are primarily designed for children. Features include such things as a travel chair with a unique folding mechanism that allows it to double as a stroller and a car seat. Accessories include adjustable velcro fasteners for lap belts, pads, attachable trays, and head restraints. In addition, motorized wheelchairs of various designs may be prescribed for individuals unable to propel themselves independently. Wheelchair transporters such as modified golf carts are available for relatively long driving ranges (Peizer, 1975).

The Role of the Teacher

The primary role of the teacher regarding ambulation devices is daily observation of the student's use and care of his or her equipment. Teachers should keep parents apprised of special problems and needs when they arise. The teacher, along with other special education support personnel, is responsible for designing a barrier-free classroom and also for obtaining the special equipment and materials that will allow the student to participate in classroom activities. In conjunction with the physical therapist and the family, the teacher should develop a program to encourage maximum use of ambulation devices in the classroom, the school, the home, and the community. Therefore, the teacher's role extends beyond the school's boundaries and into the home and the community.

Use of the Checklists

A checklist for use in the classroom is provided to enable the teacher to monitor the condition and function of wheelchairs. The items on each checklist are marked with "yes" and "no" answers. If the device is in proper working condition and fitted correctly, all items should be marked in the "yes" column. "No" answers indicate problems with the device that require attention. A section for comments about specific needs is provided for each item.

The classroom teacher may use these checklists for preliminary evaluations, but should refer the child to a physical therapist for reassessment or request that parents seek physical therapist assistance/reassessment before assuming that his or her (the teacher's) evaluation is correct or referring the child to a specialist.

	No	Yes	Comments		No	Yes	Comments

With the student out of the wheelchair
A. Arms
  1. Are the armrests and side panels secure and free of sharp edges and cracks?
  2. Do the armlocks function properly?
				3. When the chair is folded fully are the front post slides straight and round?
				D. Wheel locks
				  1. Do the wheel locks securely engage the tire surfaces and prevent the wheels from turning?			

B. Backs
  1. Is the upholstery free of rips and tears?
  2. Is the back taut from top to bottom?
  3. Is the safety belt attached tightly and not frayed?
				E. Large wheels
				  1. Are the wheels free from wobble or sideplay when spun?
				  2. Are the spokes equally tight and without any missing spokes?
				  3. Are the tires free from excessive wear and gaps at the joined section?			

C. Seat and frame
  1. Is the upholstery free of rips and tears?
  2. Does the chair fold easily without sticking?							

Source: (Wheelchair Prescriptions, 1968, 1976)

From Checklists for evaluating the fit and function of orthoses, protheses, and wheelchairs in the classroom by J. Venn, L. Morganstern, & M. K. Dykes, *Teaching Exceptional Children, 11*, 1979, 51–56. Copyright 1979 by The Council for Exceptional Children. Reprinted with permission. Drawing courtesy of Everest and Jennings.

SUMMARY

1. Children with physical and health impairments may need special instruction, communication techniques, physical equipment, and other modifications. They are a widely varied group—some are extremely restricted in their activities, and others are not limited at all.

2. There are many types of physical and health conditions that may make some sort of special education services necessary.

   a. Cerebral palsy, which includes any paralysis or motor disorder caused by brain malfunction, may occur in several forms and may range from mild to very severe. While it cannot be cured, it does not get progressively worse.

      (1) Cerebral palsy is caused by problems before, during, or soon after birth.

      (2) Children with cerebral palsy may have above normal, normal, or below normal intelligence. It is often, but not always, accompanied by other handicapping conditions.

      (3) The most common types of cerebral palsy are spasticity, athetosis, and ataxia. Other types are rigidity and tremor.

      (4) Cerebral palsy should be managed by a team of professionals.

   b. Spina bifida is a congenital condition that may cause loss of sensation and severe muscle weakness in the lower part of the body. However, children with spina bifida can usually participate in most classroom activities.

   c. Muscular dystrophy is a group of long-term diseases that weaken muscle tissue.

   d. Other orthopedic and neurological conditions that may affect a child's classroom performance include osteogenesis imperfecta, spinal cord injuries, and amputations or missing limbs.

   e. Epilepsy is a convulsive disorder that presents a problem only during an actual seizure.

      (1) Epilepsy can usually be controlled with medication, although certain drugs have unpleasant side effects.

      (2) There are three common types of seizures: grand mal, petit mal, and psychomotor.

      (3) Teachers and classmates of children with epilepsy need to be familiar with the disease and with procedures to use during a seizure. Their understanding and acceptance is very important to the child with epilepsy.

   f. Diabetes is a disorder of metabolism that can often be controlled with injections of insulin.

      (1) Most students learn to inject their own insulin.

      (2) Teachers must learn to recognize the symptoms of insulin reaction and diabetic coma and to deal with both problems.

g. Children with cystic fibrosis, hemophilia, severe burns, or other conditions such as heart disease and asthma may need modified activities or special education services and counseling.

3. The severity of the impairment, its visibility to other people, and the age of onset should all be considered in dealing with a physically or health impaired child.

4. Because there is no universally agreed-upon definition for this population, prevalence statistics may not be accurate.

    a. It is believed that about 3% of the children receiving special education have physical and health impairments.
    b. About 1 in every 200 infants has cerebral palsy, the largest single group of physically impaired children.
    c. While disease-related physical disabilities are decreasing and more orthopedic defects are being corrected, more multiply handicapped children are surviving infancy and more children are developing physical disabilities as a result of accidents.

5. Public school programs for physically disabled children began around the turn of the 20th century. Before that, most severely disabled children were kept at home or in institutions.

    a. The first American public school classes for physically handicapped children began around 1900.
    b. Two physicians, Phelps and Carlson, were particularly influential advocates for the acceptance and education of physically handicapped children.
    c. As the century progressed, educational programs for physically and health impaired children were brought into hospitals, other institutions, private homes, and finally special classrooms in public schools.
    d. Today, more physically and health impaired children are being successfully educated in regular classrooms, with physical modifications to the schools where necessary.

6. There are many different factors to consider in developing an educational program for a physically or health impaired child.

    a. Early intervention is especially important for the physically and health impaired.
    b. Special classes for the physically disabled offer the advantage of specialized individual attention and equipment.
    c. However, many disabled students can get along well in regular classes, where they are encouraged to be as independent and fully integrated as possible.
    d. Because some especially severe physical and health impairments require constant medical care, some children are educated in hospitals and other institutions.
    e. The interdisciplinary team for a physically or health impaired child usually includes at least the teacher, a physical therapist, and an occupational therapist.

f. Many physically disabled children need braces, wheelchairs, prostheses, or special adaptive devices.

g. The ways in which students are positioned and handled throughout the day should be carefully considered. Positions should provide support without preventing movement.

h. Students should be taught to operate wheelchairs safely and efficiently.

i. Just like everyone else, children with physical disabilities and health disorders need to develop self-respect and to be successful in many different activities. They should learn to deal with nondisabled people. The classroom is a good place to discuss disabilities and encourage the acceptance of disabled children.

7. The current trend is toward educating disabled children in regular classes as much as possible, with support personnel coming into the classroom.

8. Recent technological and biomedical advances hold great promise for many children with physical disabilities.

9. Physically and health impaired children need to develop as much independence as possible, while learning to have realistic expectations and accept help when they need it.

10. Physical education and vocational preparation are important parts of the educational program of children with physical and health impairments.

11. Independent living centers and advocacy groups can help improve the outlook for physically disabled people.

12. Public attitudes, physical access to public buildings, and services for parents of young physically disabled children still need to improve.

FOR MORE INFORMATION

Journals

Accent on Living (P.O. Box 700, Bloomington, IL 61701). A quarterly journal of practical information, with articles on a wide variety of topics. Primarily written by and about people with physical disabilities. An extensive catalog of assistive aids and devices is also published.

Disabled U.S.A. (President's Committee on Employment of the Handicapped, Washington, DC 20210). This quarterly publication emphasizes recent and innovative developments in rehabilitation, employment, and independent living for people with disabilities.

Journal of Rehabilitation (National Rehabilitation Association, 1522 K Street, N.W., Washington, DC 20036). Published bimonthly, this journal focuses on articles of interest to rehabilitation workers, counselors, physical therapists, social workers, and other professionals. New approaches to employment and adjustment are highlighted.

Rehabilitation Literature (National Easter Seal Society, 2023 West Ogden Avenue, Chicago, IL 60612). An interdisciplinary monthly publication containing abstracts of current research and practice, especially in services to children and adults with orthopedic, neurological, and other physical and health related disabilities. Extensive book reviews are a regular feature.

Books

Batshaw, M. L., & Perret, Y. M. *Children with handicaps: A medical primer.* Baltimore: Paul H. Brookes, 1981.

Bigge, J. L. *Teaching individuals with physical and multiple disabilities,* 2d ed. Columbus, Ohio: Charles E. Merrill, 1982.

Kleinberg, S. B. *Educating the chronically ill child.* Rockville, Md.: Aspen Systems, 1982.

Mullins, J. B. *A teacher's guide to management of physically handicapped students.* Springfield, Ill.: Charles C. Thomas, 1979.

Umbreit, J. (Ed.). *Physical disabilities and health impairments: An introduction.* Columbus, Ohio: Charles E. Merrill, 1983.

Organizations

A large number of agencies and organizations provide information, educational programs, and community services to children and adults with specific physical and health impairments. Many have national, state, and local chapters. A few of the largest organizations which disseminate publications and encourage research into the causes and treatment of physical and health impairments are listed below:

Epilepsy Foundation of America. 1828 L Street, N.W., Washington, DC 20036.

Muscular Dystrophy Association. 810 Seventh Avenue, New York, NY 10019.

National Easter Seal Society. 2023 West Ogden Avenue, Chicago, IL 60612.

Spina Bifida Association of America. 343 South Dearborn Street, Suite 319, Chicago, IL 60604.

United Cerebral Palsy Association. 66 East 34th Street, New York, NY 10016.

10
Severe Handicaps

Severely handicapped individuals have been called "the most seriously impaired of all disabled people" (Haring & Smith, 1978). Because of their great physical, intellectual, and behavioral disabilities, severely handicapped children grow, learn, and develop much more slowly than any other group of children (including other children who are considered handicapped or disabled). Indeed, without intensive training, many severely handicapped children would probably not be able to perform the most basic tasks necessary for human survival, such as eating, toileting, traveling, and communicating.

Despite the severity and multiplicity of their disabilities, however, it has been shown conclusively that severely handicapped students *can* and *do learn.* This realization has come about only recently. In the past, severely handicapped children were a neglected population, and it was widely felt that they were incapable of learning meaningful skills. They were often placed in institutions as infants and were considered to be beyond the responsibility of our public education system. They generally received no education at all and were given only the most basic care required to sustain life.

While *exclusion* of severely handicapped students from educational programs—and from "normal" society in general—was widely practiced in the past, a philosophy of *inclusion* now prevails, supported by law and by a growing body of evidence indicating that severely handicapped students can be successfully served in public school and community settings. As Sternberg (1982) points out, we are "in the midst of a shift toward increased emphasis on providing education for more severely disabled students" (p. 3), and this shift has greatly increased the need for information by teachers and others who provide services to severely handicapped students.

Who are severely handicapped children? We will review several different approaches to their description and definition. Because the field is so young and because it focuses on people with such a wide variety of characteristics, no one universally accepted definition of the severely handicapped has yet emerged. In examining definitions, we must keep in mind that severely handicapped children constitute a heterogeneous group. They differ from nonhandicapped children "in degree, not in kind" (Sontag, Smith, & Sailor, 1977). There is great diversity in the behaviors and abilities of children who are considered severely handicapped; the differences among severely handicapped students, according to Guess & Mulligan (1982), are "greater than their similarities."

Severely handicapped students often have intense and complex combinations of disabilities. These may include extreme deficits in intellectual functioning, motor development, speech and language, visual and auditory functioning, and adaptive behavior. Many have medical problems and physical abnormalities. Thus the severely handicapped population usually is said to include the severely and profoundly mentally retarded, the severely behavior disordered, and mentally retarded students who also have physical or sensory impairments.

The U.S. Department of Education determines eligibility for services by defining *severely handicapped children* as those who:

> because of the intensity of their physical, mental, or emotional problems or a combination of such problems, need educational, social, psychological, and medical services beyond those which are traditionally offered by regular and special education programs, in order to maximize their full potential for useful and meaningful participation in society and for self-fulfillment. (21 U.S. Code 1407[7]; 45 Code of Federal Regulations 121.1)

Some educators prefer to take a *developmental* approach to the definition of severe handicaps. Justen (1976), for example, proposes that "those individuals age 21 and younger who are functioning at a general developmental level

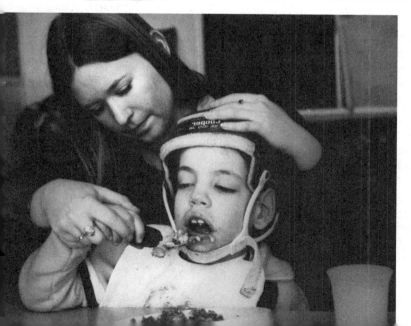

Teaching programs for severely handicapped children often include such basic skills as learning to feed oneself.

329

of half or less than the level which would be expected on the basis of chronological age" (p. 5) be considered severely handicapped. Others maintain that developmental levels have little relevance to this population and instead emphasize that the severely handicapped student—regardless of age—is one who "requires instruction in basic skills," such as getting from place to place independently, communicating with others, controlling their bowel and bladder functions, and feeding themselves (Sontag, Smith, & Sailor, 1977). Most children without disabilities are able to acquire these basic skills in the first 5 years of life, but the severely handicapped student needs special instruction in order to do so. The basic skills definition implies that traditional academic education is not appropriate for severely handicapped children.

Caution should always be exercised in defining children's abilities and limitations. As York and Edgar (1979) point out, there are "few, if any, absolute truths" in the education of severely handicapped students; the "knowledge gap in our field is tremendous" (p. 1). Marc Gold, who was a leading educator of severely handicapped individuals, suggested that a student's failure to perform certain tasks may be largely due to our present imperfect methods of testing and teaching:

> A lack of learning in any particular situation should first be interpreted as an inappropriate or insufficient use of teaching strategy, rather than an inability on the part of the learner. (1980b, p. 3)

Traditional methods of intelligence testing are virtually useless with most severely handicapped children. If tested, they tend to be assigned IQs at the extreme lower end of the continuum. Knowing that a particular student has, let us say, an IQ of 25 is of little value in designing an appropriate educational program. Educators of severely handicapped students tend to focus on the specific skills that a child needs to perform, rather than on his or her intellectual level. As Bricker and Campbell (1980) point out, the distinction between "severe and profound mental retardation" and "severe and profound handicaps" has little relevance in assessment and education. Some children who are not mentally retarded may nevertheless need instruction in basic skills, perhaps because of physical impairments, behavior disorders, or their previous lack of appropriate training. Such children should rightfully be included among the severely handicapped, as long as they need instruction in basic skills.

More important to the teacher than the student's IQ or the precise cause of the handicapping condition is an accurate understanding of the student's behavior (or, in many cases, *lack* of behavior). Because of their severe and multiple impairments, severely handicapped children often look noticeably "different" from nonhandicapped children, and their behavior may be considered deviant or extreme, particularly by people who are not familiar with them.

No specific set of behaviors is common to all severely handicapped children; each child has a different set of physical, intellectual, and social characteristics, and each has lived in a different environment. Educators of severely handicapped children generally agree, however, that the following behaviors are

Imagine the difficulty of giving an IQ test to a 5-year-old who cannot hold his head up straight or point, let alone talk.

EXCEPTIONAL CHILDREN

frequently observed (Abt Associates, 1974; Guess & Mulligan, 1982; Haring, 1978; Tawney, 1977):

1. Little or no communication. Almost all severely handicapped children are greatly limited in their ability to express themselves and to understand others. Many cannot talk or gesture meaningfully; they do not respond when communication is attempted. Of course, this makes education and social interaction extremely difficult. The children may not be able to follow even the simplest commands.

2. Delayed physical and motor development. Most severely handicapped children have limited physical mobility. Many cannot walk or even sit up by themselves. They are slow to perform such basic tasks as rolling over, grasping objects, or holding their heads up. Physical deformities are common and may be worsened by lack of therapy and lengthy stays in bed.

3. Frequent inappropriate behavior. Many severely handicapped children do things that appear to have no constructive purpose. These activities have been described as "ritualistic" (such as rocking back and forth, waving fingers in front of the face, twirling the body), "self-stimulatory" (masturbating, grinding the teeth, patting the body), and "self-injurious" (head banging, hair pulling, eye poking, hitting, scratching, or biting oneself). While many of these may not be considered "abnormal" in and of themselves, the high frequency with which some children perform these activities is a serious concern, since these behaviors interfere with teaching and with social acceptance.

4. Deficits in self-help skills. Severely handicapped children are often not able to care for their most basic needs, such as dressing, eating, exercising bowel and bladder control, and maintaining personal hygiene. They usually require special training to learn these basic skills.

5. Infrequent constructive behavior and interaction. Normal children and those whose handicaps are less severe typically play with other children, interact with adults, and seek out information about their surroundings. Most severely handicapped children do not. They may appear to be completely out of touch with reality and may not show "normal" human emotions. It may be very difficult to capture a severely handicapped child's attention or to evoke any observable response.

Multiple Handicaps

Most severely handicapped students have more than one disability. Even with the best available methods of diagnosis and assessment, it is often difficult to identify the nature and intensity of a child's multiple handicaps or to determine the ways in which combinations of disabilities affect a child's behavior. For example, many severely handicapped children do not respond to visual stimuli, such as bright lights or moving objects, in any way we can observe. Is the child blind because of eye damage, or is she able to see yet unable to respond because

SO MUCH TO LEARN

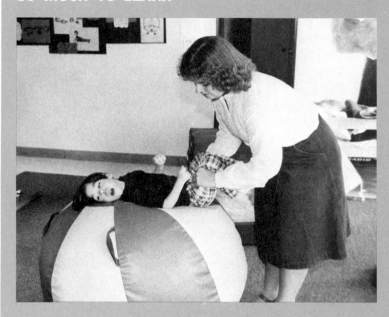

Kathi helps Mike recognize the sensations of various motions.

The St. Joseph Sensory Motor School, located outside Cincinnati, Ohio, is a residential program which serves 30 children, most of whom are preschoolers. All of the children are both nonambulatory and severely or profoundly retarded. In addition, many have other handicapping conditions, such as cerebral palsy and vision and/or hearing impairments. Kathi Mack, the school's head teacher, talked to us about their program.

The first emphasis of our program is sensory learning. If you think of a normal infant, the inputs he's getting all involve sensory stimulation—the nurturing, the holding, the talking, the stroking, the feeding. A lot of our kids need that kind of learning. The blindness, the deafness, the inability to ex-

plore your own body, to reach out and explore things in your environment, the medication some kids take to control the seizures—all isolate them and keep them from experiencing sensory learning. You need to learn that you have a body before you can learn to do anything purposeful with it. Many of our kids would never see their feet or their hands if we didn't hold them up in front of them and make them learn to do things with them. So the first emphasis in school is to provide that in a developmentally sound manner.

That gets us to our second emphasis, gross motor activity. First we must maintain and manage the children, to keep them from developing more deformities. For example, with our children who are severely involved with cerebral palsy, their muscles might be too stiff or too erratic for purposeful movement; if they're not on a continuous program of exercises and physical therapy, their muscles become even less useful.

The second aspect of the gross motor program is to try to push the child ahead. So we work on skills such as turning your head from side to side, holding your head up, learning to roll, to get your arms in front of you, to crawl around the room.

But the two—sensory learning and gross motor learning—are very much related.

Learning to recognize a sound is sensory, but to localize that sound, you have to turn your head, and that's gross motor. In addition, we have social, communication, and self-help objectives for different children. Every child's program is completely tailored to him.

I am very excited about what I'm doing. In this field, we're learning more all the time. You could work at it for years and still not know all the things you should know. There's so much to learn.

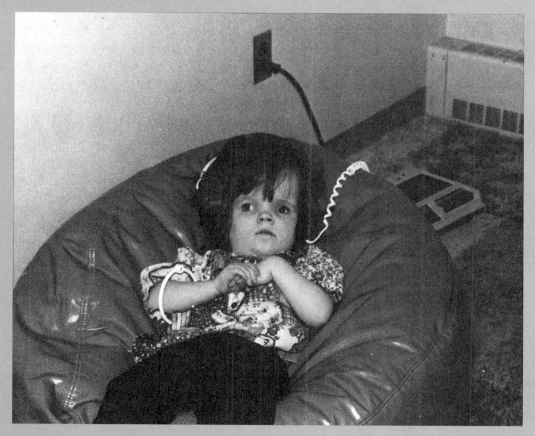

Experiencing different sounds is a first step in learning to listen.

of damage to the brain? If a child is both deaf and mentally retarded, what are the most appropriate ways to teach language and appropriate behavior? Similar questions arise in planning the educational programs for many severely handicapped students.

Severely handicapped children often have combinations of obvious and not-so-obvious disabilities which require special additions or adaptations in their education. But the fact that a child is considered "severely handicapped" does not necessarily mean that his or her achievements will be limited. As we will see, many severely handicapped students are today learning useful skills and are able to live and work in their home communities. Appropriate education and training can enable severely handicapped students to accomplish a wide variety of important and worthwhile activities.

PREVALENCE

Since there is no universally accepted definition of the severely handicapped population, there are no accurate and uniform figures on prevalence. If we accept the widely quoted prevalence of "profound mental retardation" as about 1 in every 1,000 school-age children, we would conclude that approximately 55,000 children in the United States fall into this category and would be considered among the severely handicapped. In addition, while many children with moderate and severe mental retardation and with multiple disabilities are considered severely handicapped for educational placement purposes, they may be counted among other categories of exceptionality. In 1976, the National Association for Retarded Citizens estimated that there were perhaps 300,000 severely handicapped children who were not receiving adequate educational services.

Although the existing prevalence figures are not wholly reliable, they do indicate the current uncertainties surrounding the definition and classification of severely handicapped students. The available information suggests that this is neither a small nor an isolated population—in fact, the severely handicapped population consists of several different subgroups of students, whose needs are not always the same. Today, most school districts have some children with severe and multiple handicaps among their population.

BACKGROUND OF THE FIELD

Little is known about the treatment of severely handicapped individuals throughout most of history. Since severe handicaps so often occur in conjunction with medical and physical disabilities, many of these children probably did not live past infancy. In many earlier societies—and in some parts of the world today—a philosophy of "survival of the fittest" prevailed. The abandonment or deliberate killing of children with severe impairments is thought to have been a common practice (Anderson, Greer, & Rich, 1982).

To say that humane treatment and education of children with severe handicaps did not begin until this century would be an oversimplification. During the 19th century, important efforts were made to teach systematically some children who today would be considered severely handicapped. Jean Itard, Eduard Seguin, and Samuel Gridley Howe were physicians who achieved notable advances in teaching communication and other skills to severely handicapped children. However, their efforts were isolated cases.

During the second half of the 19th century, hundreds of state-operated residential institutions for the confinement and custodial care of severely handicapped children and adults were established in the United States. An optimistic philosophy—strongly influenced by the efforts of the pioneering physicians—prevailed at the outset, and some severely handicapped individuals were, in fact, successfully educated and returned to their home communities (Wolfensberger, 1976).

At first, many institutional programs were called "asylums for the feeble-minded." Later they came to be called "hospitals," "state schools," and "training centers." But despite these titles, education and training usually were not provided to the more severely handicapped residents of these institutions. Many observers have commented on the bleak, unstimulating environments, the lack of adequate care, and the prevailing attitudes of pessimism found in most large residential institutions. Once placed in an institutional program, it was unlikely that a severely handicapped child would ever leave it. Unless parents were able to provide care and training at home or to afford an expensive private school education, there were virtually no opportunities for severely handicapped children to learn useful skills or to lead satisfying lives.

Until quite recently, society's response to severely handicapped children was to exclude them from the demands and rewards of everyday life.

See the discussion in chapter 2.

In the last 15 years or so, several judicial decisions and new laws have had important effects upon the development of educational services for severely handicapped children. Particularly significant to this population was the case of *Pennsylvania Association for Retarded Children* v. *Commonwealth of Pennsylvania* (1972). Before the PARC case, many states had laws allowing public schools to deny educational services to so-called "ineducable" severely handicapped children. The court decided against such exclusion and noted in its decision that education could be useful to severely handicapped individuals:

> Without exception, expert opinion indicates that all mentally retarded persons are capable of benefitting from a program of education. . . . The vast majority are capable of achieving self-sufficiency and the remaining few, with such education and training, are capable of achieving some degree of self-care; that the earlier such education and training begins, the more thoroughly and more efficiently a mentally retarded person will benefit from it and, whether begun early or not, that a mentally retarded person can benefit at any point in his life and development from a program of education. (*PARC v. Commonwealth of Pennsylvania*, 1972)

Many other cases, including *Wyatt* v. *Stickney,* have since upheld the right of severely handicapped students to receive a free, appropriate program of education at public expense. The provisions of P.L. 94–142 apply to severely handicapped children; they must have access to an educational program in the least restrictive setting possible, and their parents or guardians must be involved in the development and implementation of an appropriate IEP. In addition, the law gave priority to identifying and serving children who had been unserved and underserved; this provision clearly applies to the severely handicapped population. These legal and judicial developments, coupled with an increasing awareness of the potential of severely handicapped students, are bringing about a dramatic expansion of educational programs in public schools, vocational facilities, and other community-based settings. Many severely handicapped children continue to be served in institutions; they, too, are entitled to have a free and appropriate educational program.

Today, education of the severely handicapped is one of the most exciting, fastest-growing fields in special education. Its growth is illustrated by the history of The Association for the Severely Handicapped (TASH), an organization of educators, parents, and other concerned individuals. Started in 1975 by a few dozen special educators, TASH now has a membership of more than 5,000.

CAUSES

Severe handicaps can be caused by a wide variety of conditions, largely biological, which may occur before, during, or after birth. In most cases, the brain is damaged. A significant percentage of severely handicapped children are born with chromosomal abnormalities, such as Down syndrome, or with genetic or metabolic disorders that can cause serious problems in a child's physical or intellectual development. Complications of pregnancy, including prematurity, Rh incompatibility, and infectious diseases contracted by the mother, can contribute. It is also believed that women who are poorly nourished during pregnancy or who consume excessive amounts of alcohol or drugs may give birth to children who are severely handicapped. In general, children with severe handicaps are more frequently identified at or shortly after birth than are children with milder disabilities, since their impairments tend to be more extreme and more readily observable.

The birth process itself involves certain hazards and complications; infants are particularly vulnerable to oxygen deprivation and brain injury during delivery. Severe handicapping conditions can also develop later in life from accidents, ingestion of poisonous substances, malnutrition, abuse, neglect, and certain diseases (such as meningitis and encephalitis) that affect the brain.

Although hundreds of medically related causes of severe handicaps have been identified, there are many cases in which the cause of a child's disabilities cannot be clearly determined. Severe handicaps are usually considered to be less closely associated with socioeconomic status than are milder handicaps (Snell & Renzaglia, 1982). However, a child's access to good medical care, early identification of disabling conditions, education, and a stimulating home environment may be influenced by his or her family's level of education, income, and other socioeconomic factors.

Deaf-Blind Children

A particularly challenging group of children with multiple disabilities, who usually are considered severely handicapped, are the several thousand children in the United States and Canada who are classified as *deaf-blind*. Many of these children were born with visual, hearing, and other impairments after an epidemic of rubella (German measles) affected thousands of pregnant women in the mid-1960s. The U.S. federal government established a special network of regional and state centers in 1968 and allocated several million dollars for the education of deaf-blind children, thus making this the first group of exceptional children to receive special education under federal mandate and with substantial federal financial assistance. Several years later, when P.L. 94–142 was passed, it included a section on deaf-blind children, defined as those who have:

> both auditory and visual handicaps, the combination of which causes such severe communication and other developmental and educational problems that they cannot properly be accommodated in special education programs solely for the hearing handicapped child or for the visually handicapped child.

As the definition points out, deaf-blind children must have a combination of sight and hearing impairments, but are not necessarily totally blind or profoundly deaf. An educational program for deaf children is often inappropriate

Note, however, that many children with Down syndrome are *not* severely handicapped, though they may be moderately retarded. Some Down syndrome children even attend regular classrooms (see page 84).

for a child who also has limited vision, since many methods of instruction and communication rely heavily on the use of sight. Programs for visually impaired students, on the other hand, usually require students to have good hearing, since much instruction is auditory. Most students who are classified as deaf-blind do have some residual vision or hearing. However, they frequently have other physical, intellectual, and behavioral disabilities along with their impaired sight and hearing.

The intellectual level of deaf-blind students ranges from the gifted (as in the famous case of Helen Keller, who lost her sight and hearing at about 16 months of age), to the severely mentally retarded. Most children who are deaf-blind from birth have severe difficulties in acquiring communication skills, motor skills, mobility, and in learning appropriate behavior. A vivid description of the importance of sight and hearing in a child's learning and development is offered by Robert Smithdas, a deaf-blind man:

> The senses of sight and hearing are unquestionably the two primary avenues by which information and knowledge are absorbed by an individual, providing a direct access to the world in which he lives. . . . When these senses are lost or severely limited, the individual is drastically limited to a very small area of concepts, most of which must come to him through his secondary senses or through indirect information supplied by others. The world literally shrinks; it is only as large as he can reach with his fingertips or by using his severely limited sight and hearing, and it is only when he learns to use his remaining secondary senses of touch, taste, smell, and kinesthetic awareness that he can broaden his field of information and gain additional knowledge. (1981, p. 38)

Educational programs for deaf-blind children who require instruction in basic skills are often similar to those for other severely handicapped children. There is likely to be a strong emphasis on communication—most often involving some form of sign language or gestures, but including speech and tactual speech-reading for some students. Since the deaf-blind students affected by the rubella epidemics of the mid-1960s are now young adults, many efforts are currently directed toward teaching vocational skills and self-help skills which will enable them to live and work as independently as possible. It is also important to help students effectively use any residual vision or hearing they may have.

Before 1968, there were very few educational programs for deaf-blind children, and virtually all were located at residential schools for blind children. Today, deaf-blind children are being educated at hundreds of different programs, some of which are located at schools for the deaf, institutions for mentally retarded children, early childhood developmental centers, and regular public schools. Deaf-blind students who progress to the high school and postsecondary education usually are integrated into programs for students with other disabilities or into programs for nonhandicapped students, with supportive assistance provided by interpreters and tutors.

General Principles of Educational Programming

Care and concern for the welfare of severely handicapped students and giving them access to educational programs are critical. By themselves, however, they are not enough. Severely handicapped children need *more* than love, care, and classroom placement if they are to learn and develop effectively. They are not

> You will observe on the wall to the right of you a positioning chart. From this chart you can select a position that is therapeutically sound for the child. Please remember that good positioning is essential for the child and will enable him or her to better attend to and enjoy the activity.
>
> Now, you find the childs color group, you select several appropriate activities for the child from the different areas, and you find an appropriate position. You'll find the materials around you in the room. If you have questions just ask one of the teachers.
>
> P.S. If a child can't perform an activity, we try to encourage and physically assist him through the activity.

This wall chart was constructed by a physical therapist to show classroom aides and volunteers how to position each of the children correctly.

able to blossom on their own or to acquire skills solely through imitation and observation.

In the not-too-distant past, educators tended to focus largely on the "mental ages" of their students. As Bellamy and Wilcox (1982) point out, this approach contributed to the image of severely handicapped people as eternal children, and detracted from the provision of appropriate services for students with severe instructional and behavioral problems. Today, most educators of severely handicapped students feel that it is important for teachers to be familiar with the "normal" sequences and processes of child development, but that severely handicapped students often do not acquire skills in the same way as nonhandicapped students and that developmental guides should not be the only basis for determining teaching procedures. For example, a severely handicapped 20-year-old student who is just learning to communicate and to care for her own needs should not be taught in exactly the same way, or with the same materials, as a nonhandicapped 2-year-old child who is just learning to communicate and to care for her own needs. The past experiences, the present environments, and the future prospects of these two individuals are, of course, quite different, even though their ability to perform certain skills may be similar. A thoughtful critique of the developmental sequencing strategy is offered by Freagon:

> When the developmental curricular strategy is employed, severely handicapped students have considerable impediments to achieving a postschool adult life-style that is similar to those of nonhandicapped persons. In the first place, when instructional activities are based on mental, language and social, and gross and fine motor ages, severely handicapped students rarely, if ever, gain more than 1 or 2 developmental years over the entire course of their educational experience. Therefore, 18-year-old students are relegated to performing infant or preschool or elementary nonhandicapped student activities. They are never seen as ready to engage in 18-year-old activities. In the second place, little, if any, empirical evidence exists to support the notion that severely handicapped students need to learn and grow along the same lines and growth patterns as do nonhandicapped students in order to achieve the same goal of education. (1982, p. 10)

The following principles have been suggested as important in designing and carrying out instructional activities for severely handicapped students (Baumgart, Brown, Pumpian, Nisbet, Ford, Sweet, Messina, & Schroeder, 1982; Bellamy & Wilcox, 1982; Freagon, 1982).

Functionality

A functional skill is one that is frequently demanded in a student's natural environment. It should employ real materials and enhance the student's ability to perform as independently as possible. Placing pegs into a pegboard would not be considered functional, since this task is seldom required in the natural environment of most people. Learning to ride a public bus and learning to purchase items from coin-operated vending machines are examples of more functional skills.

Chronological Age-Appropriateness 2/

Wherever possible, severely handicapped students should participate in activities that are appropriate and acceptable to nonhandicapped students of their own chronological age. Severely handicapped adolescents need not use the same materials as young nonhandicapped children—in fact, when handicapped teenagers are seen doing things like sitting on the floor playing "clap-your-hands" games or cutting and pasting large snowmen, their differences are highlighted and integration is discouraged. It would be more appropriate to teach such recreational skills as bowling and tape-recorder operation or to engage in holiday projects like printing greeting cards.

Interaction with Nonhandicapped People 3/

Contact with nonhandicapped students should be scheduled as a regular part of severely handicapped students' programs. This contact may occur in the classroom with "peer tutoring," in the lunchroom, or in recreational activities. These interactions will encourage handicapped students to learn socially acceptable behaviors that will eventually help them move into vocational and residential settings in their communities and will also encourage nonhandicapped students to develop more awareness and acceptance of people with disabilities.

Directed Toward the Community 4/

A long-range goal should be to assist the severely handicapped student in living and working as independently as possible in the community. It is often necessary for teachers to identify very specific skills that are required in the community and then to proceed to teach those skills. For example, to buy a carton of milk, the student must be able to (1) arrive at the supermarket, (2) locate the area where milk is kept, (3) select the desired size and type of milk, (4) transport the milk to the check-out counter, (5) pay for the milk with the correct amount of money (usually receiving some change), and (6) take the milk home. Some students will be able to learn all these steps, while others will need to rely on certain adaptations—such as carrying a picture of the milk and requesting the assistance of store personnel or using a backpack to carry the milk home. Such "partial participation" (Baumgart et al., 1982) will enable the severely handicapped student to take part in a much wider variety of productive activities and will increase his or her chances of moving into a satisfying community-based setting, even if some "extra help" continues to be required.

Structure and Precision in Assessment and Teaching

The learning and behavior problems of severely handicapped children are so extreme and so significant that they require extensive structure in learning situations if these children's educational needs are to be adequately met (Justen, 1976). Indeed, *structure* and *precision* are essential—the teacher must know *what* skill to teach the student, *why* it is important for this skill to be taught, *how* he will attempt to teach the skill to the student, and *when* he will know that the skill has been achieved or performed by the student.

For more on task analysis see pages 106–107.

An effective teacher of severely handicapped children learns to use task analysis. Skills are broken down into a series of small, specific steps, and the student's progress at each step is carefully observed and evaluated. Table 10.1 provides an example of how one basic skill—eating with a spoon—can be broken down into precise steps. Some students might require more specific steps than the 17 illustrated here, while others might need fewer steps.

Before any instruction begins, the teacher must accurately assess the student's performance of the task. One student might be able to perform all the steps up to #13, inserting the spoon into the mouth, while another student might not even demonstrate step #1, looking at the food. This helps the teacher determine where to begin instruction. He or she can gradually teach each required step in order until the students can accomplish the entire task independently. Without this sort of structure and precision in teaching, a great deal of time is likely to be wasted.

Most educational programs for severely handicapped students are not held in conventional classrooms. Instead, the room may have mats for physical therapy, special tables and chairs to provide adequate support, clothes for teaching dressing skills, and interesting items for the students to see, hear, smell, and taste. Wherever possible, the teacher should see that skills are taught in natural settings. Getting dressed and undressed, for example, usually does not take place in the classroom, but is appropriate in a child's home or dormitory. Com-

TABLE 10.1
Steps essential to independent self-feeding

1. Orienting to food by looking at it
2. Looking at the spoon
3. Reaching for the spoon
4. Touching the spoon
5. Grasping the spoon
6. Lifting the spoon
7. Delivering the spoon to the bowl
8. Lowering the spoon into the food
9. Scooping food onto the spoon
10. Lifting the spoon
11. Delivering the spoon to the mouth
12. Opening the mouth
13. Inserting the spoon into the mouth
14. Moving the tongue and mouth to receive food
15. Closing the lips
16. Swallowing the food
17. Returning the spoon to the bowl

Source: From Erickson, M. *Assessment and management of developmental changes in children.* St. Louis: C.V. Mosby, 1976. Used by permission.

EXCEPTIONAL CHILDREN

munication and cooperation with the child's parents (or residential staff members, if the child lives in an institution) is essential to ensure that skills are being taught and practiced consistently. Again, severely handicapped children need to be taught many basic skills that most nonhandicapped children perform long before they enter school for the first time.

Successful education of severely handicapped students most often requires a behavioral approach. Careful attention should be given to the following components of a student's instructional program.

1. The student's current level of performance must be precisely assessed. Is Karen able to hold her head up without support? For how many seconds? Under what conditions? In response to what verbal or physical signal? Unlike traditional assessment procedures, which may rely heavily on standardized scores and developmental levels, assessment of the severely handicapped child emphasizes the learner's ability to perform specific, observable behaviors. Figure 10.1 presents an example of some assessment items that might be used in determining a severely handicapped student's instructional needs. Assessment should not be a "one-shot" procedure, but rather should take place at different times, in different settings, and with different persons. The fact that a severely handicapped student does not demonstrate a skill on one particular assessment does not mean that he or she is incapable of demonstrating that skill. Precise assessment of current performance is of great value in determining which skills are to be taught and at what level the instruction can start.

2. The skill to be taught must be defined clearly. "Ian will feed himself" is too broad a goal for many severely handicapped children. A more appropriate statement might be: "When applesauce is applied to Ian's right index finger, he will move the finger to his mouth within 10 seconds." A clear statement like this would enable the teacher and other observers to determine whether or not Ian has attained this goal. If, after repeated trials, he has not, it would be advisable to try a different method of instruction.

3. The skills must be ordered in an appropriate sequence. The teacher must be able to arrange "a relationship between the student and his environment which results in positive experiences for the student and small positive changes in skill acquisition" (Sailor & Haring, 1977, p. 73). This does not imply that severely handicapped students will always acquire skills in exactly the same order as nonhandicapped students, but it is useful to consider that some skills logically come before others, and some groups of skills are naturally taught at the same time.

A carefully sequenced procedure for teaching a severely handicapped child to walk was described by Meyerson, Kerr, and Michael (1967). First, the child was required to stand for 5 to 10 seconds, without support. Then she learned to pull herself up to a standing position, using chairs which were supported by adults. The child was then taught to move from one chair to another, taking several unaided steps as the distance between the chairs was

Social/Self Help Record Sheet

Items in CAPS with a blank following require number correct entered.

Circle around category key indicates a basic skill.

Testing Date ___/___/___ ___/___/___ ___/___/___ ___/___/___
Tester

	IEP	+/− note	+/− note	+/− note	+/− note

Feeding

RF 1. ⊙ suck liquid from bottle
    2. ⊙ self-feed cracker
    3. ⊙ drink from cup
    4. O hold cup and drink
    5. ⊙ bring spoon to mouth
    6. ⊙ eat solid food with spoon
    7. ⊙ turn faucet on/off
    8. ⊙ carry ¾ filled cup
    9. ⊙ pour liquid from pitcher to cup
    10. ⊙ spread with knife
    # additional IEP objectives
    Set — Mastered — Mastered — Mastered — Mastered

Dressing

    11. ⊙ cooperate while being dressed
    12. ⊙ self-remove sock
    13.   remove coat
        ⊙ a. with help
        ⊙ b. without help
    14. ⊙ pull down pants
    15. ⊙ pull up pants
    16. ⊙ put coat on
    17. ⊙ unzip
    18. ⊙ pull on shoe
    19. ⊙ pull on pullover shirt
    20. ⊙ button and unbutton
    21. ⊙ snap and unsnap
    22. ⊙ zip including thread zipper
    # additional IEP objectives
    Set — Mastered — Mastered — Mastered — Mastered

Toileting

    23. ⊙ sit on toilet
    24. ⊙ use toilet 50%
    25. ⊙ indicate must use toilet
    26. ⊙ use toilet independently
    # additional IEP objectives
    Set — Mastered — Mastered — Mastered — Mastered

Washing, Grooming

    27. ⊙ wash, dry hands
    28. ⊙ wash, dry face
    29. ⊙ brush teeth
    30. ⊙ brush, comb hair
    # additional IEP objectives
    Set — Mastered — Mastered — Mastered — Mastered

FIGURE 10.1
One page of the UPAS Record Form.

Note Key

N = Not Applicable   A = General Adaptation
S = Support   U = Upgraded Task
P = Prosthetic Device   X = No Chance/No Test

Category Key

S = Sensory
M = Motor
C = Cognitive
O = Outcome

Testing Date   / /   / /   / /   / /
Tester

	IEP	+/− note	+/− note	+/− note	+/− note

Play

31   interact appropriately with materials
   (O) a. in group activities
   (O) b. in 1:1 or small group
   (O) c. during free choice

32   interact with peers
   (O) a. low social behavior
   (O) b. high social behavior

33   claim and defend possessions
   (O) a. physically
   (O) b. verbally

34   O   independent play 20 minutes
35   (O) take turns and share
36   C   use "props" in dramatic play
37   C   dress up and pretend
38   O   play organized games
39   O   has preferred playmate

additional IEP objectives

Set | Mastered | Mastered | Mastered | Mastered

Personal Information

40   (C) tell age
41   (O) tell first, last name
42   (O) tell address
43   (O) tell phone number

additional IEP objectives

Set | Mastered | Mastered | Mastered | Mastered

Classroom Work Skills

44. (O) follow group directions
45. O work independently on paper and pencil task

additional IEP objectives

Set | Mastered | Mastered | Mastered | Mastered

$$\text{Total Nonadapted \%} = \frac{100 \times \text{①}}{45} \quad . \quad = \frac{}{45} \quad = \quad \%$$

$$\text{Total Adapted \%} = \frac{100 \times (\text{①} + \text{②} + \text{④})}{45 - \text{③}} \quad = \frac{}{} \quad = \quad \%$$

Source: N. G. Haring, O. R. White, E. B. Edgar, J. Q. Affleck, and A. H. Hayden, *Uniform performance assessment system: Record form,* R. G. Munson & M. Bendersky, eds. Columbus, Ohio: Charles E. Merrill, 1981. Used with permission.

gradually increased. After that she learned to walk holding an adult's hand. Finally, the child was able to walk across the room unsupported.

4. The teacher must provide a clear cue or instruction to the child. It is very important for the child to know what action or response is expected of her. A cue may be verbal, as when the teacher says, "Bev, say *apple*," to indicate what Bev must do before she will receive an apple. Or a cue may be physical, as when the teacher points to a light switch, to indicate that Bev should turn the light on. It may also be necessary for the teacher to demonstrate an activity many times and to guide the child physically through some or all of the tasks required in the activity.

5. The child must receive feedback and reinforcement from the teacher. Severely handicapped students must receive clear information about their performance, and they are more likely to repeat an action if it is immediately followed by a reinforcing consequence. Unfortunately, it can be quite difficult and time-consuming to determine what items or events a noncommunicative child finds rewarding. Many teachers devote extensive efforts to "reinforcer sampling"; that is, they attempt to find out which items and activities are reinforcing to a particular child and keep careful records of what is and is not effective. Striefel worked with a severely handicapped child for more than 2 years in order to find an effective reinforcer he could use in an instructional program. The items Striefel tried are listed in Table 10.2 (Spradlin & Spradlin, 1976).

6. The teacher should include strategies to encourage generalization of learning. It is well known and documented that severely handicapped students often have difficulty **generalizing** the skills they have learned. As Wilcox explains, "What is learned in one environment with one set of instructional materials does not automatically appear when the setting changes, when the materials differ, or when there are other seemingly minor changes in task demands" (1982, p. 2). An effective teacher has students perform tasks in several different settings, with different cues, and with different materials, before concluding with confidence that the student has acquired and generalized the skill. Principles and guidelines for encouraging generalization are provided by Baer (1981) and Stokes and Baer (1977).

7. The child's performance must be carefully measured and evaluated. Since severely handicapped students typically make progress in very small steps, it is important to measure their performance precisely. Careful measurement helps the teacher plan instruction that will be appropriate to the child's needs and evaluate the program's effectiveness. Change in performance is shown most clearly when data on the child's efforts are collected every day. When working on dressing skills, for example, a teacher might measure the number of seconds it takes a child to remove a sock from her right foot when given the cue, "Donna, take off your sock." Over a period of time, Donna should perform the task more rapidly. If she does not, some aspect of the instructional program may have to be changed. Accurate information about

TABLE 10.2
Items used in an attempt to find an effective reinforcer for a severely handicapped child

A. **Social**
1. Praise
2. Pat on knee
3. Hug
4. Hand-squeeze
5. Tickling ribs
6. Stroking face
7. Verbal comments such as "good girl," "that's the way," "great"
8. Another child who gets reinforced for correct responses

B. **Liquids**
1. Tang (orange and grape)
2. Lemonade
3. Koolaid (variety of flavors)
4. Soda (variety of flavors)
5. Water

C. **Edibles**
1. Ice cream (variety of flavors)
2. Candy
3. Marshmallows
4. M & M's
5. Mints
6. Cheetos
7. Pretzels
8. Candy corn
9. Peanuts
10. Butterscotch candy
11. Corn chips
12. Potato chips (plain and barbecue)
13. Dry cereals (variety)
14. Sweet and sour candy
15. Pudding (chocolate and butterscotch)

16. Chocolate-covered peanuts
17. Lollipops
18. Dried fruits (variety)
19. Cookies (variety)

D. **Toys**
1. Magazines
2. Picture books
3. The Farmer Says (talking toy)
4. Music box
5. Noisemaker
6. Horns
7. Teddy bear
8. Barking-walking dog
9. Balls
10. Toy adding machine
11. Santa Claus
12. Dolls
13. Helicopter
14. Wind-up monkey
15. Chatter telephone
16. Cars
17. Trucks
18. Scissors and paper
19. Play dough

E. **Tokens (backups included)**
1. Wide variety of nickel candy
2. Wide variety of penny candy
3. Wide variety of carnival-type toys

F. **Other**
1. Mirror
2. Tape-recorded music (wide variety)
3. Video tapes (children's programs, commercials, feedback of self)

Source: From Spradlin, J. E., & Spradlin, R. R. Developing necessary skills for entry into classroom teaching arrangements. In N. G. Haring & R. L. Schiefelbusch (eds.), *Teaching special children.* New York: McGraw-Hill, 1976, p. 241. Used by permission.

a child's performance increases the teacher's ability to design an appropriate educational program. In some programs, videotaped records are kept on severely handicapped students' performance on specific tasks. This can provide an extremely powerful dimension to documenting behavior changes over extended periods.

Communication Skills

There has recently been a good deal of interest in specialized methods of teaching communication skills to severely handicapped children. Many students are able to learn to understand and produce spoken language. For students who can attain it, this is always a desirable goal since speech is the way most people communicate with each other. A severely handicapped student who can communicate verbally is likely to have a wider range of educational, employment, residential, and recreational opportunities open to him than a student who cannot. A widely used curriculum is Functional Speech and Language Training for the Severely Handicapped (Guess, Sailor, & Baer, 1976). This program provides a step-by-step approach to teaching such expressive and receptive concepts as labeling, possession, color, size, and relationships of objects to each other. Precise guidelines for the trainer and criteria for student responses are furnished.

However, some severely handicapped students, because of their sensory, physical, intellectual, or behavioral limitations, may not learn to speak, even with extensive training. Sign language, as originally intended for use by deaf people, is now widely used by severely handicapped students. Sign language has several advantages, since teachers can readily mold children's hands into the appropriate signs, and for many signs, there is an observable relationship between the sign and the object or action it represents (Bonvillian & Nelson, 1976). Sign language is not as widely used in the general community as speech is, of course, but it can be learned by a child's teachers, peers, parents, and employers. After learning sign language, some severely handicapped students are later able to acquire speech skills. Factors to be considered in selecting the types of signs and procedures to be followed in working with severely handicapped students are discussed by Dennis, Reichle, Williams, and Vogelsberg (1982) and Kohl (1980).

Other special methods of communication that have been used with severely handicapped students include communication boards, in which a student points to or otherwise indicates a desired picture, symbol, or object. Some severely handicapped individuals carry pictures around with them, to let them communicate with others.

Vocational Training

An especially important curriculum area for most students who are severely handicapped is learning skills that will enable them to work in sheltered workshops, in special activity centers, or in competitive employment in the community. In the past few years, there has been a greatly increased effort to provide appropriate vocational training opportunities for severely handicapped students. As Rusch and Mithaug (1980) observe, much has been recently learned about methods of training complex vocational skills and about effective procedures to manage inappropriate behaviors. It is now widely believed that even the most severely handicapped person "has an untapped vocational potential that can be translated into productive and independent work" (p. xv).

Given appropriate training and supervision, many severely handicapped individuals can perform productive, meaningful work.

Precise methods of teaching vocational skills to severely handicapped individuals have largely evolved from the task analytic approach of Gold (1980) and his colleagues. Careful attention is given to the physical arrangement of the work setting, the cues provided by the trainer, and the gradual attainment of acceptable rates of production and accuracy.

Teachers and others who are involved in designing vocational programs for severely handicapped students should first investigate what specific skills and behaviors are required in settings where their students might realistically be employed. Since job requirements change from time to time and from place to place, it may be advisable to survey potential employers and workshops to determine what skills are necessary for employment or for acceptance into a more advanced vocational training program. For example, in a survey of activity centers and sheltered workshops, Mithaug and Hagmeier (1978) found that a great majority of workshop supervisors considered it important or necessary for a client to "be able to communicate basic needs" (such as hunger, pain, and toileting), and to "move safely about the shop." On the other hand, relatively few supervisors required their clients to be able to "use the telephone book to look up names and numbers" or to "have basic arithmetic skills." Assessment of current job prerequisites is thus the first step in designing a program of vocational instruction.

With each passing month, more evidence is available documenting that severely handicapped children and adults are capable of performing useful and remunerative work in a wide variety of settings. Some teachers combine classroom instruction and practical experience in the community, with children of school age. Winkler, Armstrong, Moehlis, Nietupski, and Whalen-Carrell (1982) describe a successful program in which severely handicapped students prepared and delivered classified advertising guides in their community. Most students improved in their ability to attend to tasks such as folding, collating, and packing, and many students learned money management skills with their earnings from the project. Wehman, Hill, Goodall, Cleveland, Brooke, and Pentecost (1982) offer a detailed report on a project in which severely handicapped adults were placed in community employment—mostly in "utility" jobs, such as wiping tables in restaurants or sweeping floors. After a three-year period, 67% of the clients were still employed. Their absenteeism and tardiness rates were generally as good as those of nonhandicapped workers, and the predominant attitude of co-workers toward the handicapped workers was one of "indifference as long as the client performs his/her job acceptably" (p. 12). The wages and benefits earned by the handicapped workers were substantially greater than those they would have earned in sheltered workshops. Rather than being dependent on public financial assistance, these workers were earning money and paying local, state, and federal taxes.

See Chapter 15 for more on employment of handicapped adults.

Recreational and Leisure Skills

Most children develop the ability to play, to occupy themselves constructively and pleasurably during their free time. But severely handicapped children may not learn appropriate and satisfying recreational skills unless they are specifically taught. As Voeltz and Apffel observe, a severely handicapped person is "much more likely to experience significant blocks of unstructured time throughout the lifespan" (1981, p. 83) than is a nonhandicapped person. Thus a variety of programs to teach recreational and leisure skills have recently been developed, and this is generally acknowledged to be an important part of the curriculum for most severely handicapped students.

Horst, Wehman, Hill, and Bailey (1981) describe how several severely handicapped students, ages 10 through 21, were taught age-appropriate leisure skills. The particular activities to be taught were selected "largely on the basis that many nonhandicapped peers regularly engage in these types of activities" (p. 11). Precise teaching procedures were followed in the assessment and teaching of (1) throwing and catching a frisbee, (2) operating a cassette tape recorder, and (3) playing an electronic bowling game. All students were able to increase their skills at these activities. Teaching appropriate leisure and recreational skills will help severely handicapped individuals interact socially, maintain their physical skills, and become more involved in community activities.

Teacher Competencies and Qualities

Teaching severely handicapped children is difficult and demanding. The teacher must be consistent, firm, and well organized. He or she must manage a complex educational operation, which usually involves the supervision of paraprofessional aides, student teachers, and volunteers, to attain the individualized instruction that severely handicapped students need. The teacher must be able to cooperate with other professionals, such as physicians, psychologists, physical therapists, social workers, and language specialists. He or she must maintain accurate records and must constantly be planning for the future needs of the students. Effective communication with parents (or residential staff), school administrators, vocational rehabilitation personnel, and community agencies is also important.

Severely handicapped children sometimes show little or no apparent response, so the teacher must be sensitive to small changes in the student's behavior. As Foxx (1982) points out, behavior problems are often "inherited" by teachers. if a child's previous teachers were inconsistent in dealing with the behavior. Hence the effective teacher must be tenacious and must follow through in designing and implementing strategies to improve the student's learning and behavior.

Some people would consider it undesirable to work with severely handicapped students because of their extreme disabilities and frequently inappropriate or undesirable behavior. Yet this field can offer many highly rewarding teaching experiences—such as the opportunity to teach a child to toilet himself independently or to help an adolescent move from an institution into a group home in the community. The challenge of teaching severely handicapped students is great.

Individual or Group Instruction?

Visitors to most educational programs for severely handicapped children are likely to find that instruction is largely or wholly individualized; that is, a teacher

Several recent studies have shown that for certain skills group instruction with severely handicapped learners may be more effective and cost-efficient than one-to-one teaching.

TRAINING IN ONE INSTITUTION

Robert Shrewsberry

Dr. Robert D. Shrewsberry is director of Southeastern Virginia Training Center in Chesapeake, Virginia, an institution serving 200 severely and profoundly mentally retarded persons age 6 to 65. He was previously associated with a "huge" state institution of over 2,200 retarded residents, making the delivery of educational and other services in a normalized, effective fashion virtually impossible. Dr. Shrewsberry talked about how educational programming is carried out at the Southeastern Training Center, a smaller, regionally based institution.

First of all, we try to keep people out. We've got an Institutional Prevention program that works with families in an effort to find alternatives to institutional placement. Before a person is admitted, a group consisting of community agency people, representatives of this Training Center, and the individual's family must meet. This admissions team must specify just what it is that is keeping this individual from staying in the community. We require that the person's problems be specified as behavioral deficits or excesses. A contract is then written indicating that we will provide educational programming directed at solving those problems, and that when those problems are corrected, the individual will return to the community. I sign it, the community agency signs it, the family signs it. In other words, we don't accept a new resident without a clearcut plan for his or her discharge.

A total of 8 to 10 behavioral objectives are developed from the goals agreed on by the admissions team. Each of these in turn is represented by a short-term training objective. This is where we go to work. We only have two jobs—to make some behaviors happen more often, to make others go away.

Each of our 21 cottages provides a homelike environment for 8 to 10 residents. Educational programming in each cottage is provided by seven to eight developmental aids supervised by a team leader. We keep a graph of the results of every training program for every resident. If a dressing program is conducted each day, the person's chart shows the daily progress, or lack of it. If progress isn't being made, we change some component of the program. When a team leader indicates that an objective has been met, we arrange for an independent mastery test. Someone who doesn't have a vested interest in the program, like a team leader from another cottage, conducts the mastery test. "Okay, Phil. Let's see you get dressed by yourself." If Phil can't dress himself, it's back to work.

Applied behavior analysis is the primary mode of treatment. After all, changing behavior is our business. The data we collect on each program direct our instructional decisions. The system works. Since the center opened its doors in 1975, its population has turned over 3½ times, a discharge rate of 30 to 35% per year. But we need to follow up on our "graduates." Our Transitional Training Team follows every resident who leaves our institution, to his family's home, a group home, or supervised apartment. When a problem arises, the Transitional Team works with the family or group home staff to correct it so that the person does not end up readmitted to the institution and can stay in the community where he or she rightfully belongs.

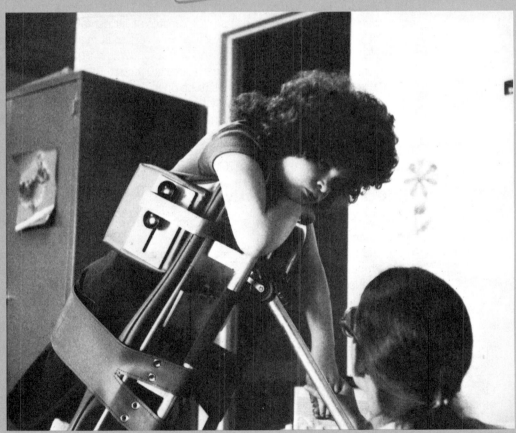

"We had a busy day, didn't we?"

works with one student at a time. In a review of professional literature, Favell, Favell, and McGimsey (1978) found that about 90% of the articles about teaching or modifying the behavior of severely handicapped students described a one-to-one approach. Some professionals, in fact, may argue that individualized training is the *only* effective method for producing changes in the behavior of the severely handicapped.

Recently, however, a number of researchers have begun to investigate the effectiveness of educating severely handicapped students in small groups. The results of some of these studies are encouraging. For example, Mansdorf (1977) found that group training was effective in teaching the severely handicapped how to use a token system. Storm and Willis (1978) found that severely handicapped students could learn to imitate motor tasks as well in groups of four as they could in individualized settings. Curran (1983) and Orelove (1982) found that severely handicapped students were capable of incidental learning of vocabulary. That is, when words were presented to a certain student in a small group, other students in the group could also learn to understand them.

Group training of severely handicapped students thus appears to be promising, though much research remains to be done. Group instruction allows teachers to use their time more effectively than one-to-one instruction, gives students the benefit of increased training time, and encourages the children to socialize. Should research continue to find group instruction effective, future programs of education and training for severely handicapped learners will most likely include a combination of group and individualized instructional techniques.

Educational Alternatives

What is the least restrictive and most appropriate educational setting for severely handicapped students? This question is the subject of much current debate and discussion. As we have said, in the past, the majority of severely handicapped individuals were placed in large residential institutions. Many educators have argued for the abolition or curtailment of these placements, on the basis that institutions do not provide a natural or effective environment in which to learn. At the present time, a sizable number of severely handicapped students continue to be served in institutional settings. Fortunately, the educational programs within many institutions are increasing in number and in quality. In most states, there is a trend toward reducing the size of institutions, providing individualized education programs for residents, increasing parent and community involvement, and developing plans for some residents to move into community-based settings. Residential institutions need not necessarily be bleak and inhuman.

The public schools, which until recently excluded most severely handicapped children, are now beginning to provide educational opportunities for them on a large scale. The most prevalent model of public school programming is the self-contained special class for severely handicapped students. Particularly when a self-contained class is located in a regular public school, this approach is seen as much more desirable, and less restrictive, than institutional placement

(Guess & Mulligan, 1982). Although their highly specialized needs make placement in a regular classroom unlikely, severely handicapped students who are educated in public schools have opportunities to come into contact with their nonhandicapped peers—for example, on the school bus, in the corridors, or in selected activities in school. It is widely assumed that these interactions will result in improved social relationships between handicapped and nonhandicapped children, but as Peck and Semmel (1982) report, this assumption has not yet been conclusively supported by research. Merely placing a severely handicapped student in a public school class does not ensure that he or she is receiving the most appropriate education possible. As Tawney and Smith observe, "Classrooms are not necessarily instructional environments. It is time to attend to the quantity and quality of instruction in these classes" (1981, p. 15).

Educational, vocational, and residential programs for severely handicapped individuals in their home communities are also expanding rapidly. This trend is strongly supported by many; in Larsen's view, "There is no service or program that can be provided in a large institution that cannot be provided better, and possibly for less money, in a community setting" (1976, p. 129). It is especially critical for education to begin as early as possible in a child's life. A severely handicapped child who receives no formal training until age 5 or 6 will surely be at a great disadvantage and may well have developed a repertoire of inappropriate behaviors that will be very difficult to deal with. Thus it is extremely important for a severely handicapped child's family to receive information and supportive services that will help them to encourage their child's development and maintain as normal a family life as possible. Any successful community program for a severely handicapped child must also serve that child's family.

See chapter 14 for a detailed discussion of the critical importance of early intervention.

CURRENT ISSUES/FUTURE TRENDS

The current extension of public education and community-based services to severely handicapped children is a tremendously important and challenging development. Those people who are providing instruction to severely handicapped students can rightfully be called "pioneers" on an exciting new frontier of special education. As Orelove suggests, professionals involved in the education of severely handicapped children "can look back with pride, and even awe, at the advances they have made. In a relatively brief period, educators, psychologists and other professionals have advocated vigorously for additional legislation and funds, extended the service delivery model into the public schools and community, and developed a training technology" (1984, p. 271).

Future research will increase our understanding of the ways in which severely handicapped children acquire, maintain, and generalize functional skills. Better techniques of measuring and changing behavior are constantly being developed. Computers, telecommunication, and other forms of educational technology are currently being successfully used with severely handicapped children (Tawney, Aeschleman, Deaton, & Donaldson, 1979) and are sure to find even wider applications in the future.

See chapter 15 for more on residential and work settings for handicapped adults.

As more and more severely handicapped people leave large residential institutions, it is especially important that adequate care and supportive services be provided in the community. There is currently a pressing need for good, well-staffed group homes, or small community residences that can accommodate severely handicapped individuals. As a study by Pratt, Luszcz, and Brown (1980) concluded, group homes can vary considerably in the quality of care they provide, and objective evaluations of their services are needed. Employment settings with appropriate tasks, good working conditions, fair wages, and adequate supervision must be further developed. Finally, we must make much better efforts at encouraging awareness and acceptance of severely handicapped individuals by the general public and must help our students become as self-sufficient and socially acceptable as possible.

Are All Children Educable?

The commitment to expanded educational opportunities for severely handicapped children is not, however, universal. Some educators, other professionals, and citizens question the wisdom of spending large amounts of money, time, and human resources attempting to train severely handicapped children, many of whom have such serious disabilities that they may never be able to function independently. Some people would prefer to see our resources spent on children who have higher apparent potential—especially when economic conditions limit the availability of educational services for all children in the public schools. "Why bother with children who fail to make significant progress?" they might ask.

Kauffman and Krouse, outspoken critics of the notion of "universal educability," feel that education must be defined in terms of the "meaningfulness" of behavior change.

> Accelerating a response rate may indeed be a worthy first goal in an educational program if there is reasonable hope of shaping the response into a meaningful skill. Nevertheless, after concerted and appropriate effort by highly trained behavior therapists, for a reasonable period of time, a child's failure to make significant progress toward acquisition of a meaningful skill could reasonably be taken as an indication that the child is ineducable. . . . Granted, all children probably are educable if education is defined as acceleration of any operant response. But such a definition trivializes the meaning of the term education and, even without consideration of benefit, moots the question of educability. Formulating consensual definitions of *education, meaningful skill,* and *significant progress* will be difficult, but it is a task we can not avoid. . . . We suggest that public response to the questions, "What is education?", "What skills are meaningful?", "What rate of progress is significant?", and "What cost/benefit ratios are acceptable?", sampled with sufficient care, could be invaluable in deciding who is educable and who is not. (1981, pp. 55–56)

Hawkins, a special educator and the parent of a severely retarded daughter, disagrees.

EXCEPTIONAL CHILDREN

. . . if anyone were to be the judge of whether a particular behavior change is "meaningful," it should certainly not be only the general taxpayer, who has no idea how rewarding it is to see your retarded 19-year-old acquire the skill of toilet flushing on command or pointing to food when she wants a second helping. I suspect that the average taxpayer would not consider it "meaningful" to *him* or *her* for Karrie to acquire such skills. But in truth, it is "meaningful" to that taxpayer whether he recognizes it or not, in the sense that it is saving him or her the cost of Karrie's being institutionalized, which she certainly would have been by now if she never showed any progress; thus it is functional for the taxpayer even though his or her answer to the question "Is this meaningful?" might well be "No" or "Not enough to pay for." And, although we cannot readily say how much Karrie's being able to flush the toilet enhances her reinforcement/ punishment ratio, I can testify that it enhances mine as a parent.

The complexity, cost, and hopelessness of evaluating fairly the "meaningfulness" of various behavior changes leads me to conclude that no one should be denied an education. I would not rule out enrichment programs or stimulation programming as a substantial *part* of this education. I know that the great majority of a severely retarded student's time in education already consists of nothing more than enrichment, and I would support continuation of some of this (though less than is currently typical). But I would be very resistant to the idea that we should now, at this infant stage of the science and technology of education for severely retarded students, give up intensive skill training for anyone. (1984, p. 285)

In many ways, our knowledge of the learning and developmental processes of severely handicapped children is still primitive and incomplete. We do know, however, that severely handicapped children are capable of benefiting significantly from appropriate and carefully implemented educational programs. Even in cases where little or no progress has been observed, we cannot conclude that the student is incapable of learning. It may instead be that our teaching methods are imperfect and that the future will bring improved methods and materials to enable the student to learn useful skills. Children, even if severely impaired, have the right to the best possible public education and training that we can offer them.

Virtually every parent of a severely handicapped child has heard a host of negative predictions from educators, doctors, and concerned friends and family. The parents are often offered such discouraging forecasts as "Your child will never talk" or "Your child will never be toilet-trained." And unfortunately, some professionals still advise parents to put their severely handicapped children in institutions and "forget" them. Given such advice, it is not surprising that some parents gradually tend to lose interest in their children. Yet in many instances, the gains of those severely handicapped children who *are* taught far exceed the original predictions of the professionals. Despite predictions to the contrary, many children *have* learned to walk, talk, toilet themselves, and perform other "impossible" tasks.

Important discussion and thoughtful commentary on both sides of the "educability debate" can be found in Heward, Heron, Hill, and Trap-Porter (1984), Kauffman (1981b), and Noonen, Brown, Mulligan, and Rettig (1982).

There are still many unanswered questions in the education of severely handicapped children. While their opportunities for education and training are rapidly expanding, nobody really knows their true learning potential, or the extent to which they can be successfully integrated into the nondisabled population. What we do know is that they will go no farther than we let them; it is up to us to open doors and raise our sights, instead of creating additional barriers. In sum, we agree with Baer, who says:

> Some of us have ignored both the thesis that all retarded persons are educable and the thesis that some retarded persons are ineducable, and instead have experimented with ways to teach some previously unteachable people. Over a few centuries, those experiments have steadily reduced the size of the apparently ineducable group relative to the obviously educable group. Clearly, we have not finished that adventure. Why predict its outcome, when we could simply pursue it, and just as well without prediction? Why not pursue it to see if there comes a day when there is such a small class of apparently ineducable persons left that it consists of one elderly institution resident who is put forward as ineducable? If it comes, that will be a very nice day, and the next day will be even better. (1984, p. 299)

INSTITUTION IS NOT A DIRTY WORD

Deinstitutionalization has become widely practiced across the nation. Yet, like every social movement, its effects are not necessarily 100% positive. Here, then, is a different perspective—one parent's story.

I watched Phil Donahue recently. He had on mothers of handicapped children who talked about the pain and blessing of having a "special" child. As the mother of a severely handicapped six-year-old boy who cannot sit, who cannot walk, who will be in diapers all of his days, I understand the pain. The blessing part continues to elude me—notwithstanding the kind and caring people we've met through this tragedy.

What really makes my jaws clench, though, is the use of the word "special." The idea that our damaged children are "special," and that we as parents were somehow picked for the role, is one of the myths that come with the territory. It's reinforced by the popular media, which present us with heartwarming images of retarded people who marry, of quadriplegics who fly airplanes, of those fortunate few who struggle out of comas to teach us about the meaning of courage and love. I like these stories myself. But, of course, inspirational tales are only one side of the story. The other side deals with the daily care of a family member who might need more than many normal families can give.

Stoicism

Parents who endure with silent stoicism or chin-up good humor are greeted with kudos and applause. "I don't know how you do it," the well-wishers say, not realizing, of course, that no one has a choice in this matter. No one would consciously choose to have a child anything less than healthy and normal. The other truth is not spoken aloud: "Thank God, it's not me."

One mother on the Donahue show talked about how difficult it was to care for her severely brain-damaged daughter, but in the end, she said serenely, "She gives much more than she takes from our family." And no, she would never institutionalize her child. She would never "put her away." For "she is my child," the woman firmly concluded as the audience clapped in approval. "I would never give her up."

Everyone always says how awful the institutions are. Don't they have bars on the windows and children lying neglected in crowded wards? Aren't all the workers sadists, taking direction from the legendary Big Nurse? Indeed, isn't institutionalizing a child tantamount to locking him away? Signing him out of your life forever? Isn't it proof of your failure as a parent—one who couldn't quite measure up and love your child, no matter what?

No, to all of the above. And love is beside the point.

Our child Zachariah has not lived at home for almost four years. I knew when we placed him, sorry as I was, that this was the right decision, for his care precluded any semblance of normal family life for the rest of us. I do not think that we "gave him up," although he is cared for daily by nurses, caseworkers, teachers and therapists, rather than by his mother and father. When we come to visit him at his "residential facility," a place housing 50 severely physically and mentally handicapped youngsters, we usually see him being held and rocked by a foster grandma who has spent the better part of the afternoon singing him nursery rhymes. I do not feel that we have "put him away."

Perhaps it is just a question of language. I told another mother who was going through the difficult decision regarding placement for her retarded child, "Think of it as going to boarding school rather than institutionalization." Maybe euphemisms help ease the pain a little bit. But I've also seen enough to know that institution need not be a dirty word.

The media still relish those institution horror stories: a page-one photo of a retarded girl who was repeatedly molested by the janitor on night duty. Oh, the newspapers have a field day with something like that. And that is how it should be, I suppose. To protect against institutional abuse we need critical reporters with sharpened pencils and a keen investigative eye. But there are other scenes from the institution as well. I've seen a young caseworker talk lovingly as she changed the diapers of a teen-age boy. I've watched as an aide put red ribbons into the ponytail of a cerebral-palsied woman, wipe away the drool and kiss her on the cheek. When we bring Zach back to his facility after a visit home, the workers welcome him with hugs and notice if we gave him a haircut or a new shirt.

The reporters don't make news out of that simple stuff. It doesn't mesh with the anti-institutional bias prevalent in the last few years, or the tendency to canonize the handicapped and their accomplishments.

Survival

This anti-institutional trend has some very frightening ramifications. We force mental patients out into the real world of cheap welfare hotels and call it "community place-ment." We parole youthful offenders because "jails are such dangerous places to be," making our city streets dangerous places for the law-abiding. We heap enormous guilt on the families that need, for their own survival, to put their no-longer-competent elderly in that dreaded last stop: the nursing home.

Another danger is that in a time of economic distress for all of us, funds could be cut for human-service programs under the guise of anti-institutionalization. We must make sure, before we close the doors of those "awful" institutions, that we have alternative facilities to care for the clientele. The humanitarians who tell us how terrible institutions are should be wary lest they become unwilling bedfellows to conservative politicians who want to walk a tight fiscal line. It takes a lot of money to run institutions. No politician is going to say he's against the handicapped, but he can talk in sanctimonious terms about efforts to preserve the family unit, about families remaining independent and self-sufficient. Translated, this means, "You got your troubles, I got mine."

Most retarded people do not belong in institutions any more than most people over 65 belong in nursing homes. What we need are options and alternatives for a heterogeneous population. We need group homes and halfway houses and government subsidies to families who choose to care for dependent members at home. We need accessible housing for independent handicapped people; we need to pay enough to foster-care families to show that a good home is worth paying for. We need institutions. And it shouldn't have to be a dirty word.

From Fern Kupfer, My turn, *Newsweek*, December 13, 1982, p. 17. Reprinted with permission.

1. Despite their limitations, children with severe handicaps can and do learn.

2. There is no universally agreed upon definition of *severely handicapped children.*

   a. The severely handicapped child needs instruction in self-help, motor, perceptual, social, cognitive, and communication skills.

   b. Traditional intelligence tests are useless in assessing the severely handicapped; instead, the teacher needs to observe the unique abilities and limitations of each child.

   c. Severely and profoundly handicapped children usually have some or all of the following characteristics:

   (1) Little or no communication
   (2) Delayed physical and motor development
   (3) Frequent inappropriate behavior
   (4) Deficits in self-help skills
   (5) Infrequent constructive behavior and interaction.

   d. These children almost always have multiple disabilities, including physical problems. They usually look and act markedly different from normal children.

3. While prevalence figures are not precise because the definitions of the severely handicapped vary so widely, we do know that this population is neither small nor isolated. Most communities include some severely, profoundly, or multiply handicapped children.

4. Education of the severely handicapped is a very recent innovation.

   a. Throughout most of history, these children probably died in infancy.

   b. During the 19th century, hundreds of state-run custodial "asylums" were established. They offered very little or nothing in the way of education and training for their residents.

   c. Within the last 15 years, court cases and laws have mandated public education for these children for the first time, recognizing that *all* children—regardless of disabilities—can benefit from education.

5. Severe and profound handicaps most often have physical causes, including chromosomal abnormalities, genetic and metabolic disorders, complications of pregnancy and prenatal care, birth trauma, and later brain damage.

   a. However, in many cases the cause is unknown.

   b. A rubella epidemic caused many cases of deaf-blindness in children born during the mid-1960s. The Deaf-blind children, regardless of intellectual functioning, have too little hearing to benefit from programs for blind students (which rely on auditory instruction) and too little sight to benefit from programs for deaf students (which rely on visual instruction).

6. Severely handicapped students should be taught skills that are functional, age appropriate, and directed toward the community. They should have regular interaction with nonhandicapped people.

7. In teaching severely handicapped children, structure and precision are needed.
   a. Skills to be taught must be broken down into small steps.
   b. Special equipment, furniture, and materials may be needed.
   c. The child's current performance must be precisely assessed, and the target skill stated very clearly.
   d. The skills must be taught in an appropriate sequence.
   e. The child needs a clear cue from the teacher before performing the skill and immediate feedback and reinforcement afterwards.
   f. The teacher must program for generalization of learning.
   g. The child's progress must be carefully measured and evaluated regularly.

8. Students who can learn speech should do so. Sign language and other forms of nonverbal communication are appropriate options for those who have not learned speech after training.

9. With training, most severely handicapped students can learn to perform useful vocational skills.

10. Severely handicapped students should also be taught age-appropriate recreation and leisure skills.

11. Teachers of severely handicapped children must be highly competent, able to work with many different kinds of people, and well organized.

12. While most severely handicapped children are taught in one-on-one settings, there is now evidence that small group training may be effective on some tasks.

13. Although many severely handicapped children are still in residential institutions, where they are receiving more and better education than in the past, community-based programs are expanding.
   a. Education for severely handicapped children should begin in infancy if possible.
   b. More and more severely handicapped children are being educated in self-contained classrooms within the regular school, so that they have the opportunity to have contact with their normal and mildly handicapped peers.
   c. Some severely handicapped children and adults are able to live in group homes or small community residences and work in supervised settings.

14. As more severely handicapped children and adults leave institutions, we must be careful to provide adequate residential facilities, educational programs, and employment opportunities to meet their needs. We also need to increase public understanding and acceptance of this group of exceptional people.

15. We still do not know very much about how severely handicapped children learn and develop. We do know, however, that the achievements of these

children often surpass the predictions of the professionals. Thus we must be optimistic and open doors for them, instead of setting limited goals.

16. While current programs for the severely handicapped are expanding rapidly, some people remain skeptical about the wisdom of this trend. However, we believe that all children are educable; it is up to us to find ways to teach them.

FOR MORE INFORMATION

Journals

Analysis and Intervention in Developmental Disabilities. Published quarterly by Pergamon Press. Includes articles on theory and behavioral research related to people "who suffer from severe and pervasive developmental disabilities."

Journal of the Association for the Severely Handicapped. Published quarterly by The Association for the Severely Handicapped. Publishes articles dealing with useful information regarding how to develop, implement, and evaluate educational programs for severely handicapped persons, including policy statements and research.

Books

Donlon, E. T., & Burton, L. F. *The severely and profoundly handicapped: A practical approach to teaching.* New York: Grune & Stratton, 1967.

Fredericks, H. D., et al. *The teaching research curriculum for moderately and severely handicapped.* Springfield, Ill.: Charles C. Thomas, 1976.

Snell, M. E. (ed.). *Systematic instruction of the moderately and severely handicapped,* 2nd ed. Columbus, Ohio: Charles E. Merrill, 1983.

Sontag, E., Smith, J., & Certo, N. (eds.). *Educational programming for the severely and profoundly handicapped.* Reston, Va.: Division on Mental Retardation, Council for Exceptional Children, 1977.

Thomas, M. A. (ed.). *Developing skills in severely and profoundly handicapped children.* Reston, Va.: Council for Exceptional Children, 1977.

Organizations

The Association for the Severely Handicapped, 7010 Roosevelt Way, N.E., Seattle, WA 98115. Possibly the most rapidly growing professional organization in special education, TASH disseminates a wide variety of useful information to teachers, parents, administrators, and others. Its annual convention provides the major professional forum for the exchange of new developments relating to the education of severely and profoundly handicapped individuals.

Department of Specialized Educational Services, Madison Metropolitan School District, 545 West Dayton Street, Madison, WI 53703. The Madison, Wisconsin, schools, in cooperation with the Department of Studies in Behavioral Disabilities at the University of Wisconsin, have been especially active in developing programs of instruction for severely handicapped children and in seeking to facilitate integration with nondisabled individuals. A number of curriculum guides and other materials are available for purchase.

Marc Gold and Associates, P. O. Box 5100, Austin, TX 78763. Dr. Gold and his colleagues have developed many task analyses, precise descriptions of how to instruct severely handicapped persons in the areas of daily living skills and vocational tasks. A film series, "Try Another Way," is also distributed by this program.

State of Oregon, Mental Health Division, MR/DD Program Office, 2575 Bittern Street, N.E., Salem, OR 97310. The Student Progress Record illustrated in Figure 10.1 may be purchased, along with other materials designed for the assessment, teaching, and IEP planning of severely handicapped students.

11
Gifted and Talented Children

Raymond H. Swassing

The Ohio State University

O ur study of exceptional children thus far has focused on children with intellectual or physical disabilities, children who require special methods and materials in order to derive maximum benefit from their educational programs. Gifted and talented children, however, may also find that a traditional curriculum is inappropriate; it may not provide the advanced and unique challenges they require to learn most effectively. Gifted and talented children represent the other extreme on the continuum of academic, artistic, social, and scientific abilities. They, too, need very special educational opportunities if they are to reach their potential.

While the regular classroom is viewed as the least restrictive environment for many exceptional children with handicaps, the standard curriculum and usual school activities are often highly inappropriate and restrictive for gifted children. When the school year begins in September, intellectually gifted students may already have all of the skills their grade-level peers are supposed to learn during the year. Thus, a school program that does not allow gifted children to explore areas of individual interest or to learn things beyond the basic curriculum would be "restrictive." Similarly, children with special talents should be given opportunities to develop those abilities further. An appropriate education for gifted and talented children must include special curriculum and instruction.

While the Education for All Handicapped Children Act does not specifically apply to gifted and talented children, they do resemble other exceptional children in one critical way: to reach their potential, to "succeed" fully in school, gifted and talented students need special instructional techniques, materials, classroom arrangements, and teachers. Individual programs tailored to their unique needs are beneficial to *all* exceptional children.

EXAMINE YOUR BELIEFS

These questions allow you to look at your beliefs regarding gifted and talented children. Before each statement place the number that most closely describes how you react to each one. Be as open as you can.

1—I strongly agree   4—I disagree
2—I agree   5—I strongly disagree
3—I have no opinion

_____ 1. The term *gifted* can mean different things to different people and often causes much confusion and miscommunication.

_____ 2. Intelligence can be developed and must be nurtured if giftedness is to occur.

_____ 3. We seldom find very highly gifted children or children we could call *geniuses;* therefore, we know comparatively little about them.

_____ 4. Thinking of, or speaking of, gifted children as superior people is inaccurate and misleading.

_____ 5. Gifted children, while interested in many things, usually are not gifted in everything.

_____ 6. Difficulty conforming to group tasks is often the result of the unusually varied interests and curiosity of a gifted child.

_____ 7. Because gifted children have the ability to think in diverse ways, teachers often see them as challenging their authority, disrespectful, and disruptive.

_____ 8. Some gifted children have been found to use their high level of verbal skill to avoid difficult thinking tasks.

_____ 9. The demand for products or meeting of deadlines can inhibit the development of a gifted child's ability to integrate new ideas.

_____ 10. Work that is too easy or boring frustrates a gifted child just as work that is too difficult frustrates an average learner.

_____ 11. Most gifted children in our present school system are underachievers.

_____ 12. Commonly used sequences of learning are often inappropriate and can be damaging to gifted learners.

_____ 13. Gifted children, often very critical of themselves, tend to hold lower than average self-concepts.

_____ 14. Gifted children often expect others to live up to standards they have set for themselves, with resulting problems in interpersonal relations.

_____ 15. The ability of gifted learners to generalize, synthesize, solve problems, and engage in abstract thinking most commonly differentiates gifted from average learners. Therefore, programs for gifted children should stress utilization of these abilities.

_____ 16. The persistent goal-directed behavior of gifted children can result in others perceiving them as stubborn, willful, and uncooperative.

_____ 17. If not challenged, gifted children can waste their ability and become mediocre, average learners.

_____ 18. Gifted children often express their idealism and sense of justice at a very early age.

_____ 19. Not all gifted children show creativity, leadership, or physical expertise.

_____ 20. People who work with, study, and try to understand gifted children have more success educating the gifted than those who have limited contact and have not educated themselves as to the unique needs of these children.

_____ 21. I would be pleased to be considered gifted, and I enjoy people who are.

The questionnaire you have just completed should give you some indication of opinions of gifted children that are supportive to their educational growth. The more "1—I strongly agree" answers you were able to give, the more closely your opinions match those who have devoted their energy to understanding gifted children.

From B. Clark, *Growing up gifted,* 2d ed. Columbus, Ohio: Charles E. Merrill Publishing Company, 1983, pp. 4–5. Reprinted by permission.

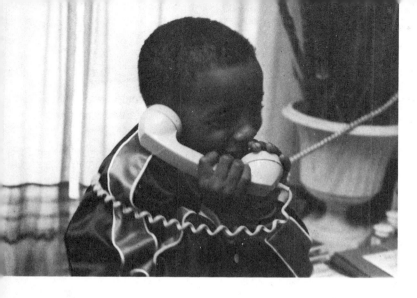

High verbal ability is a common characteristic of intellectually gifted children.

DEFINITION AND PREVALENCE OF GIFTED AND TALENTED CHILDREN

Numerous definitions of gifted and talented children have been proposed and debated over the years. Terman (1925), one of the pioneers of the field, defined the gifted as those who score in the top 2% on standardized tests of intelligence. Witty (1940), recognizing the value of including special skills and talents, described gifted and talented children as those "whose performance is consistently remarkable in any potentially valuable area" (p. 516). Both viewpoints—intellectual ability and special talents—are included within the definitions of gifted and talented children most widely used today.

Recent federal legislation defines gifted and talented children as:

> Children who give evidence of high performance capability in areas such as intellectual, creative, artistic, leadership capacity, or specific academic fields, and who require services or activities not ordinarily provided by the school in order to fully develop such capabilities." (Sec. 582, P.L. 97-35)

The areas in which children can show outstanding performance or unusual potential in order to be considered *gifted and talented* cover almost the full range of human endeavor. Overall intellectual ability and specific academic aptitude are only two areas. *General intellectual ability* refers to overall performance on intelligence or achievement tests. Children who meet this criterion usually do, or can, perform well in all academic areas. Children with *specific academic aptitude* have outstanding ability in one or two areas. For example, Reggie, who has specific academic aptitudes, may perform extremely well in science. While his work in science-related activities is truly notable, his work in social studies or English is no better than that of most of his age peers.

Leadership ability has been included in the definition of giftedness only recently. The ability to demonstrate leadership had not been recognized in most previous definitions of gifted and talented. The framers of the current definition were aware of society's need to develop leadership potential. The problems of pollution, population control, nutrition, and peace keeping require the efforts not only of scientists and economists, but also of those people who can bring groups of people together and lead them toward common goals. Answers to pressing problems may be provided by scientists. The source of the resources can be suggested by economists. But if we have no leaders to implement the scientists' and economists' solutions, the problems remain as critical, or perhaps even worse, as when first identified.

The federal definition, essentially unchanged for several years, has received widespread acceptance (Zettel, 1979). Renzulli, however, has offered an alternative definition that has gained considerable attention:

Renzuli

> Giftedness consists of an interaction among three basic clusters of human traits—these clusters being above average general abilities, high levels of task commitment, and high levels of creativity. Gifted and talented children are those possessing or capable of developing this composite set of traits and applying them to any potentially valuable area of human performance. Children who manifest or are capable of developing an interaction among the three clusters require a wide variety of educational opportunities and services that are not ordinarily provided through regular instructional programs. (1978, p. 184)

Renzulli's definition brings together the three features of ability (actual or potential), task commitment (that is, drive or perseverance), and creative expression. To be gifted and talented by this definition requires that all three traits—ability, drive, and creativity—are jointly applied to a valuable area of human endeavor. Like the federal definition, Renzulli's provides a great deal of freedom about who may be considered gifted and talented, depending on the interpretation of "valuable human performance."

Prevalence

The identification of gifted children requires a comparison with normative standards. To be considered gifted or talented for special education programs, a student will often be identified as performing in the top 3% to 5% of the school-age population (Marland, 1971). Outstanding ability is based upon the performance of the individual compared to the usual performance of age-mates on a given task or skill.

Given the estimates that gifted children comprise 3% to 5% of the school-age population, there would be between approximately 1,450,000 and 2,415,000 children in the nation's schools who meet the federal criteria. In fact, in fiscal year 1981, the 50 states and District of Columbia served approximately 909,437 students in gifted and talented programs (Mitchell, 1981, pp. 6–7) making gifted and talented students the third largest subgroup of exceptional children served by the schools. Only 17 states mandated these programs.

CHARACTERISTICS OF GIFTED AND TALENTED CHILDREN

Physically, gifted children do not differ substantially from other children their age. The widely held stereotype of the gifted child—a little adult in horn-rimmed glasses, arms laden with volumes of Homer, Plato, Descartes, and Einstein—does not hold. Any one gifted child may be taller or shorter than his or her age-mates. The child may weigh more, about the same, or less than his or her peers. On a class picnic, the gifted and talented child would not be easily identifiable.

Giftedness is a complex concept covering a wide range of abilities and traits. Some children have special talents. They may not be outstanding in academics, but they may have very special abilities in music, literature, or leadership. Other children may have intellectual abilities found only in one child in a thousand, or one child in ten thousand.

If intelligence alone does not distinguish gifted from normal children, what behaviors or characteristics do describe what gifted children are like? This section will discuss some of the distinguishing features of gifted children. However, the list reflects the group and not any single individual. You may meet a gifted child who does not fit neatly with the items listed. It is by their very giftedness that these children are unique, and this uniqueness defies any attempts to categorize them into neat, well-ordered compartments. We must also realize that many lists portray gifted children as having all virtues and no flaws (Gallagher 1975b). As Gallagher (1975b) points out, few teachers, if any, would be willing to assume the educational responsibilities for such model children.

Gallagher (1976) has summarized some of the major characteristics of the gifted child.

1. Many gifted persons have a better-than-average home life and socioeconomic background, though giftedness can be found, and should be looked for, in all populations (Hollingsworth, 1975).
2. Gifted children tend to be equal to, or slightly better than, their average age-mates in physical stature and health.
3. Gifted children tend to be more capable of handling personal problems and are more emotionally stable than their average peers.
4. The gifted child is usually popular and socially accepted.
5. Gifted children are, as a group, more successful on achievement tests than children of average ability.

This list, however, does not tell the whole story about gifted children. Their "halo" is not shiny at all times. In fact, the "halo" may sometimes be left at home on the bedpost. The very attributes by which we know them can cause some problems. High verbal ability can, for example, give gifted children the ability to talk themselves out of troublesome situations or to dominate class

Gallagher

discussions. High curiosity can give children the appearance of being aggressive or just "snoopy," as they try to find out about anything that may come to their attention (for example, papers on a teacher's or another child's desk).

This approach was first taken by Seagoe (1974).

The two lists presented in Table 11.1 describe both positive and not-so-positive aspects of intellectual giftedness. List A describes the positive side; List B, some of the problems that may occur as a result of these positive traits.

Awareness of individual differences is important in understanding the gifted. Like other children, gifted children show both **interindividual** and **intra-individual** differences. For example, if three children were given the same reading achievement test and each of the youngsters obtained a different score, we could speak of interindividual differences in reading achievement. Or a child who obtains a high reading achievement score may score much lower on an arithmetic achievement test. The child with a high reading score and a lower arith-

TABLE 11.1

Two sides to the behavior of gifted and talented students

List A	List B
1. Expresses ideas and feelings well	1. May be glib, making fluent statements based on little or no knowledge or understanding
2. Can move at a rapid pace	
3. Works conscientiously	
4. Wants to learn, explore, and seek more information	2. May dominate discussions
5. Develops broad knowledge and an extensive store of vicarious experiences	3. May be impatient to proceed to next level or task
	4. May be considered nosy
6. Is sensitive to the feelings and rights of others	5. May choose reading at the expense of active participation in social, creative, or physical activities
7. Makes steady progress	
8. Makes original and stimulating contributions to discussions	
9. Sees relationships easily	6. May struggle against rules, regulations, and standardized procedures
10. Learns material quickly	
11. Is able to use reading skills to obtain new information	7. May lead discussions "off the track"
12. Contributes to enjoyment of life for self and others	8. May be frustrated by the apparent absence of logic in activities and daily events
13. Completes assigned tasks	
14. Requires little drill for learning	9. May become bored by repetitions
	10. May use humor to manipulate
	11. May resist a schedule based on time rather than task
	12. May lose interest quickly

These lists were developed with the assistance of graduate students at The Ohio State University.

EXCEPTIONAL CHILDREN

metic score has an intraindividual difference across the two areas of performance. This child performs differently on two different measures.

A graph of any child's abilities would reveal some high points and some lower points. Scores would not be the same across all of the dimensions measured, but instead the graph would show peaks in some areas and low points in others. However, the gifted child's average level of performance on the graph may be well above the average for that grade and/or age. See Figure 11.1.

Characteristics that relate to curriculum frequently focus on learning and intellectual skills. According to Gallagher (1981), gifted children possess a "rich supply" of the following abilities:

1. The ability to relate one idea to another
2. The ability to make sound judgments

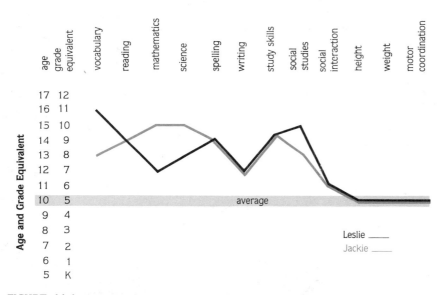

FIGURE 11.1

Profiles of two gifted 10-year-olds. Leslie and Jackie are both 10 years old and in the fifth grade. For their age and grade placement, they are performing well above what might be expected of average 10-year-old fifth graders. Only in social interactions, height, weight, and physical coordination are the two students similar to their average 10-year-old peers.

The overall abilities of Leslie and Jackie are similar. Leslie, however, performs higher in vocabulary and social studies than Jackie does, and Jackie shows higher performance in science and mathematics than Leslie. These are interindividual differences.

Each student also has intraindividual differences in scores. For example, Leslie has a vocabulary of an eleventh grader but only scores at a seventh grade equivalent in mathematics, a four-year difference. Jackie earned grade equivalents of tenth grade in science and mathematics and seventh grade in writing.

GIFTED AND TALENTED CHILDREN

3. The ability to see the operation of larger systems of knowledge than is seen by the ordinary citizen
4. The ability to acquire and manipulate symbol systems.

While the most common symbol system is language, there are, however, numerous other symbol systems, such as scientific notation, music and dance notation, mathematics, and engineering symbols. These systems can be incorporated into creative endeavors as well as academic and intellectual arenas.

Creativity

Creativity has been called "the highest expression of giftedness" (Clark, 1983, p. 30). There is, however, no universally accepted definition of *creativity*. The many possible approaches to creativity reflect the complex nature of the concept. Because creativity is one of the more intriguing aspects of human behavior, it has been studied from several points of view. Gowan (1972) lists five different approaches to creativity, including (1) cognitive, rational, and problem-solving aspects; (2) personality traits, family, and environmental origins; (3) mental health, psychological openness, and self-actualization; (4) a Freudian view; and (5) existential, psychedelic, and irrational aspects. In addition, we can add the behavior analysis approach to creativity (Goetz & Baer, 1973; Glover & Gary, 1976; Vargas & Moxley, 1979; Goetz, 1982) and Clark's (1983) integrated model, which represents a holistic view of creativity.

Guilford, in his much-cited work *Traits of Creativity* (1959), described four dimensions of creative behavior:

1. *Fluency*—many words, associations, phrases and/or sentences, and ideas are produced.
2. *Flexibility*—a wide variety of ideas, unusual ideas, and alternative solutions are offered.

"Now that's a move I haven't seen before."

372

3. *Originality*—low probability, unique words, and responses are used.
4. *Elaboration*—the ability to provide details.

Another type of creativity is sensitivity, the awareness that a problem exists (Carin & Sund, 1978). Motivation and temperament, including the willingness to work and persevere, are personality traits of many creative people. Thus, we could identify creative children as those who can identify problems, come up with a wide variety of ideas and possible solutions, some of them original, can examine those ideas, fill out the most likely one(s) with the necessary details, and then follow through on the most promising.

To be creative, a child must have some knowledge, examine it in a variety of ways, critically analyze the outcomes, *and* be able to communicate his or her ideas (Keating, 1980). There are numerous ways to communicate, such as literature, mathematics, music, poetry, dance—but the communication skills must be adequate for the idea.

IDENTIFICATION

In recent years, many educators of gifted and talented children have been critical of the intelligence testing movement, especially because it led to a one-dimensional concept of giftedness which emphasized intellectual performance exclusively. However, it is important to remember that Binet and Simon made a significant contribution to the education of gifted children by developing the first instrument that could predict school success. For gifted students, this has meant that some standardized objective measure, however crude, is available for identifying children with above-average academic potential. Intelligence tests offered the first means for locating "bright" children, and plans for meeting their special needs could then be developed.

The contributions of Binet, Simon, and other pioneers are discussed in the next section.

The use of the IQ as the sole criterion for giftedness has been out of favor with some professionals for many years (Witty, 1940). Following Terman's (1925) first report, educators and psychologists raised serious doubts about the ability of an IQ test taken during childhood to predict success, or the lack of it, in adult life. Far more than IQ is involved in defining gifted performance. Furthermore, intelligence tests do not always identify gifted persons in certain socioeconomic and culturally diverse groups. IQ measures tend to identify giftedness more readily in middle- and upper-middle-class, urban, white populations. During the 1960s, it was recognized that the usual intelligence measures were inappropriate for any child who is not representative of the normative population, including culturally diverse and handicapped children (Maker, 1977; Torrance, 1977).

Measures of intelligence may be part of the identification process, but no single index or procedure will identify all gifted and talented children. Identification usually involves a combination of procedures, including:

☐ Intelligence scores
☐ Creativity measures

☐ Achievement measures
☐ Teacher nomination
☐ Parent nomination
☐ Self-nomination
☐ Peer nomination.

The measures and procedures used for identification should be determined by the definition of *giftedness* developed for each program. Knowing what to look for will help determine where to look and how it will be recognized. Test instruments, checklists, observations forms, and other means, and how they will be used to identify gifted children are ultimately tied to the definition of giftedness being used by a given program (Frazier, 1980; Hagen, 1980).

Stephens and Wolf (1978) suggest that identification of gifted students be linked directly to the goals of the program in which they will be placed. Their approach involves five steps:

1. Establish program goals.
2. Develop objectives.
3. Specify requisite student characteristics.
4. Locate students.
5. Assign students.

Linking identification to program goals by following these steps helps increase the chances of a good student-to-program match. Students can be assigned to special programs that have objectives consistent with their individual interests and abilities. However, with this approach giftedness is limited to those who meet the program's goals. Other gifted and talented children may not be identified and adequately served.

Special talents can sometimes be identified at an early age.

One alternative to identification by goals is to develop a comprehensive definition of *giftedness* and try to identify all the children who are gifted and talented. The school would then try to offer a complete and comprehensive program meeting the needs of all of the children identified. Identification by goals does allow for systematic program growth; one set of goals and its respective program can be developed, then another, then another (Swassing, in press). But until all program goals are developed, some children will go unidentified and unserved. Comprehensive identification, on the other hand, locates all children who show special abilities or talents (or the potential) and then relies on the school, given whatever resources are available, to develop a comprehensive program serving all of the identified gifted and talented students.

In any case, identification procedures should not be used to *exclude* youngsters from programs for the gifted and talented. That is, any one measure may identify some number of children to be placed in a certain program, but it should not be used to keep everyone else out. A second measure, a third, and so on, should be used to *include* other children in special programs. School districts that provide only one or two programs may not be providing all the children in the system with the appropriate educational experiences. Gifted and talented students who do not have the specific requisite characteristics will be kept from having appropriate educational opportunities. This is not consistent with the concept of equal educational opportunities for all children. For this reason, program planners need to know about their entire school population before they establish hard and fast program goals.

HISTORICAL PERSPECTIVE

Historically, the concept of giftedness has been neither as broad nor as inclusive as the definitions we currently use. Early 19th-century works, including a classic study by Sir Francis Galton (1869), focused on the concept of "genius." Galton was the first to offer a definition of genius that used observable characteristics or outcomes. His study was based on famous adults, however, and contributed little to the identification and nurturing of potential in children. Furthermore, Galton felt that genius was genetically determined. Although Galton's work has been heavily criticized, his book *Hereditary Genius* is recognized as a major contribution to the better understanding of people of genius.

In the United States, special education for gifted and talented children can be traced back as far as 1867. In that year, the St. Louis public schools initiated a plan of *flexible promotion*. For the next 30 years, schools instituted various plans for promoting high achieving students at various rates. Around 1900, *rapid advancement* classes were established, in which children could complete two years' worth of academic work in one year, or three years' work in two.

One of the earliest *enrichment* programs for gifted children began in the early 1920s in Cleveland, Ohio (Goddard, 1928). In 1922, a group of "publicly spirited" women organized to promote classes for gifted students. H. H. Goddard, their advisor, published a description of the program in a 1928 textbook.

The Cleveland program remains today as one of the longest-running, continuous programs for gifted children in the United States.

To separate individuals into groups according to intellectual abilities, educators needed effective measuring devices. During the last quarter of the 19th century, several instruments designed to measure intellectual ability were developed. In 1905 in Paris, two French psychologists, Alfred Binet and Theophile Simon, published a graduated series of tests they called a "Measuring Scale of Intelligence." Their system was intended to classify children according to their intellectual abilities in order to facilitate their education. The Binet-Simon scale was transported to the United States, where several translations were made. The translation by Terman (1916) at Stanford University became the edition that dominated the field. The Terman translation, known as the Stanford-Binet Intelligence Scale, was published in 1916 and most recently revised in 1973 (Terman & Merrill, 1973). It has become the scale against which all other measures of intelligence have been compared.

Lewis Terman, in addition to translating the Stanford-Binet test, conducted a famous long-term study that contributed greatly to our knowledge of the characteristics of gifted individuals. From 1925 through 1959, five volumes of the *Genetic Studies of Genius* (the periodic reports of a study of approximately 1,500 gifted individuals from childhood into midlife) were published. In addition, numerous articles and papers have been developed by Terman's colleagues and students. The latest of the reports was on the life satisfaction of one group of the original male subjects (Sears, 1977).

To be included in the Terman study, a child had to have an intelligence quotient (IQ) of 140 or above, as measured by the 1916 Stanford-Binet. Measures were taken in a number of areas, including social and physical development, achievement, character traits, books read, and play interests. This long-term study refuted certain myths about the gifted, including "early ripe, early rot," "genius and insanity go hand in hand," and the stereotype of the gifted child as a little adult.

Another important contribution was made by Leta S. Hollingsworth, an educational psychologist who tested a child who earned a score of above 180 on the Stanford-Binet. This was the beginning of a series of case studies Hollingsworth conducted with children of extremely high intelligence. In her book *Children Above IQ 180* (1975), Hollingsworth reported the case histories of 12 such children from the New York City area. The school histories of these children varied considerably. One factor that differentiated the successful from the unsuccessful in school was early recognition of their superior talents and the willingness of parents and school personnel to act on that awareness. Some of the case studies revealed that the highly gifted children were frustrated and felt stifled by regular school procedures. Early identification, guidance, personal interest in the child, and special programs contributed to helping these youngsters adjust and accept learning as a rewarding challenge (Hollingsworth, 1975).

While certain myths were dispelled by the early studies, problems were also evident. A very narrow view of giftedness dominated by the IQ score prevailed for many years. It is probable that many children with special gifts and talents were not recognized and given the opportunity to develop them fully.

The IQ score came to be relied on far too heavily as an identification tool and as a predictor of success in life (Witty, 1930, 1962). Giftedness was restricted to high IQ scores and came to be associated only with the white, urban, middle- and upper-class segments of society (Witty, 1940). In the early 1950s, Guilford, a psychologist noted for his work in the area of analyzing and categorizing mental processes, challenged the field to look beyond traditional conceptions of intelligence and to view the IQ score as a small sample of mental abilities (Guilford, 1956). Since that challenge, the concept of giftedness has developed in several directions to involve many forms of intellectual activities.

During the 1960s, attention was turned to creativity and other alternatives to the traditional IQ score for identification of gifted and talented children (Frierson, 1969). Some efforts were initiated to identify and develop talent among the culturally diverse; this movement continued to expand during the 1970s (Torrance, 1977). Also, during the 1970s, the gifted and talented among girls and women and handicapped students came to be more widely recognized (Fox, 1977; Maker, 1977).

Current definitions grew out of our awareness that IQ alone does not define all of the possible areas of giftedness. We have realized that some people have advanced talents in socially valued endeavors that cannot be measured by intelligence tests; that intelligence tests are, as Guilford suggested, only a small sample of intellectual activity in limited areas of human endeavor. The concept of giftedness has, therefore, expanded to include many talents that contribute substantially to the quality of life—for both the individual and the society.

EDUCATIONAL APPROACHES

The overall goal of educational programs for gifted and talented students should be the fullest possible development of every child's actual and potential abilities. In the broadest terms, the goals of education for these youngsters are no different from the goals of education for all children. Feelings of self-worth, self-sufficiency, civic responsibility, and vocational and avocational competence are important for everyone, including gifted children. In addition, there are some specific educational outcomes that are desirable for gifted and talented students.

Gallagher (1981) has classified the educational objectives of programs for gifted students into two areas: mastering the knowledge structure of disciplines and heuristic skills. Mastering knowledge structures would include both basic principles and systems of knowledge. Heuristic skills include problem solving, creativity, and use of the scientific method. That is, gifted students need both content knowledge and the abilities to use and develop that knowledge effectively.

Feldhusen and Sokol (1982) refer to the cognitive, affective, and generative needs of gifted students. They believe important cognitive skills for gifted students include basic thinking skills, a broad store of knowledge, disciplined and in-depth inquiry, methods of research and analysis, and organizational theories and ideas. In affective terms, gifted students need stimulation through association with peers, interaction with adult models, a strong self-concept, social learning skills, and acceptance of their own abilities. Gifted students also need certain generative characteristics, including an acceptance of their roles as producers of knowledge and creative products, motivation and habits of inquiry and research, creative activity, early and continuous experience in research, and independence in investigation (pp. 51–52).

Of course, these cognitive and affective skills are appropriate for all students to some degree. The generative skills, however, emphasize the special roles that those with gifts and talents can play. Not only are gifted and talented students consumers of artistic, scientific, and creative products; they are potential *creators* of these products, which enrich the lives of all of us. Generative skills require high levels of motivation and may lead to life-styles that differ markedly from those of most other people. A glacier geologist may spend months at a time studying ice formations in remote Arctic areas; a cultural anthropologist may spend years living among the inhabitants of remote islands; and a concert pianist may spend most of his or her waking hours practicing for those few hours that are not spent practicing—the performance.

There are some who would say that the skills of reading, writing, and arithmetic need not be taught, that gifted youngsters will learn them when they need them. In fact, however, no one will be called upon to use these skills more than the gifted child, so it is essential that these children master the basic tool skills.

Questions about teaching basic skills appear to be misdirected. The question is not whether to teach the skills; it is a matter of determining the appropriate time and emphasis. If one gifted child does not have a particular skill, that skill should be taught. That does not mean, however, that all gifted children should be taught the same skills at the same time, nor does it mean that a child should be required to sit through a lesson on a skill if he or she has already mastered it. After all, some gifted youngsters enter school with many basic skills. It is unreasonable to expect them to review that learning for 3 or 4 years or even more. Then again, some gifted children enter school having acquired few, if any, of the basic skills. For these children, teaching the basic skills is most important. Through direct assessment, teachers can determine which skills to teach and which skills have been mastered.

In sum, basic skills need to be taught—not over and over, but until mastered. For some youngsters this means a 30-second lesson to explain the concept or principle. For other children, it means a sequenced set of instructional activities to develop and practice a particular skill.

For the gifted and talented student, the three R's alone do not comprise the "basics." A fourth R, *research skills*, should also be systematically taught as part of the curriculum. The skills of systematic investigation are fundamental abilities that gifted students will use throughout a lifetime of learning. These skills include use of references, use of the library, information (data) gathering, and reporting findings in a variety of ways. The skills may ultimately be used in such diverse settings as law and medical libraries, museums, chemical and electrical laboratories, theatrical archives, national parks, agribusiness, and computer science.

Curriculum Organization—Enrichment and Acceleration

The processes of goal setting and identification mean little if the children in programs for the gifted do not receive unique learning opportunities. These experiences can be considered *differentiated education*. Curricula that incorporate higher cognitive concepts should be presented by specifically prepared teachers, using strategies that accommodate the learning styles of the students. Group arrangements may include special classes, honors classes, seminars, resource rooms, and other flexible approaches to grouping and scheduling. Two widely used approaches to educational programming for gifted students are enrichment and acceleration.

Enrichment

Enrichment experiences are those that let each youngster investigate topics of interest in much greater detail than is ordinarily possible with the standard school curriculum. Topics of investigation may be based on the ongoing activities

Enrichment activities enable gifted students to investigate topics of interest in greater detail than possible in the standard curriculum.

A SPECIAL SCHOOL

For one week each summer, 60 high school students from across the state of Ohio participate in a special program sponsored by the Ohio Department of Education. One student for each 10,000 enrolled is nominated by each school district in the state. The actual participants are then selected by the degree of scholarship, leadership, and creativity demonstrated in an essay each student nominee must write. Begun in 1976, since 1977 the school has been known as the Martin W. Essex School for the Gifted.

During the program, the high school students live in a dormitory on the Ohio State University campus. The week's activities are built around the theme "Investing in Futures," with daily themes focusing upon government, science, art, environment, and people in the future.

The program brings in legislators, community workers, university faculty, and state Department of Education staff members.

There are lectures, workshops, museum and field visits, and question-and-answer sessions with experts. Parties, a picnic, theatre, and swimming round out the students' week.

During the week, the students write and publish a newspaper. With the help of a local composer, a school song is written, along with other songs that reflect the week as the students experience it.

The most frequent comment from the students at the end of the week is that they could finally talk with others who think like they do, sharing ideas with others who are interested in the same things. Many strong friendships are established. Some students leave with new ideas about future careers. Many of the students learn that they do not have to be afraid or ashamed of their special talent, and leave the school determined to make the most of their giftedness, both for themselves and for society.

Mathematical modeling—estimating the effects of the sun on a solar pond.

of the classroom; yet, the youngsters can go beyond the limits of the day-by-day instructional offerings.

Enrichment is not a "do your own thing" approach where there is no structure or guidance. Freedom of choice within a basic framework that defines limits and sets outcomes is necessary. Children involved in enrichment experiences should not be released to do a random, haphazard (and thus, inefficient) project. Their projects should have purpose, direction, and specified outcomes. The teacher should provide guidance where necessary—but no more than necessary—to keep the youngsters efficient (Renzulli, 1977).

Several approaches may be taken to implement enrichment programs. These include:

- [ ] Special experiences within the regular classroom
- [ ] Special grouping in the regular classroom
- [ ] Special classes
- [ ] Resource rooms
- [ ] Field trips and special camps
- [ ] Hobby clubs
- [ ] Extra-school programs
- [ ] Summer camps and programs
- [ ] Guest instructors
- [ ] Individual mentors (tutors)

There is little evidence yet to suggest which of the alternatives, if any, is best. The decision rests with the resources and needs of the local school, the community, and the children involved.

Acceleration

Acceleration means providing a child with learning experiences that are usually given to older children. It means speeding up the usual presentation of content without modifying that content or method of presentation. Approaches to acceleration include:

- [ ] Early admission to school
- [ ] Grade skipping
- [ ] Concurrent enrollment in both high school and college
- [ ] Advanced placement tests
- [ ] Early admission to college
- [ ] Content acceleration (giving youngsters the opportunity to move through a particular curricular sequence at their own rates)

One noted educator of gifted children, Sidney Pressey, has long advocated acceleration because it allows the child to reduce the time spent in training and gives more years of productivity. In this way both society and the individual benefit (Pressey, 1962). Research suggests that wisely practiced acceleration does not cause the problems of social and emotional adjustment often attributed to it (Gallagher, 1975a).

The study of mathematically precocious youth (Stanley, Keating, & Fox, 1974) at Johns Hopkins University has demonstrated the effectiveness of acceleration in mathematics. The project identified seventh and eighth grade students with exceptional ability in mathematical reasoning and accelerated their mathematics experiences. Some even took college courses during the first or second years in high school.

Neither enrichment nor acceleration will have particular merit if the experiences provided are not appropriate for the gifted and talented children served in the program.

Teaching-Learning Models

Several teaching-learning models (Maker, 1982) typically are used to guide development of differentiated education for gifted and talented students. We will describe five of those models. A given program may be based on any one of these approaches, or a combination of two or more.

Bloom's Taxonomy of Educational Objectives

Bloom (1956) developed his *Taxonomy of Educational Objectives* to provide a hierarchy for writing and classifying learning objectives in any area for testing purposes. The taxonomy breaks learning down into two major areas: the cognitive and the affective domains. The cognitive domain is further divided into two parts. Part I addresses knowledge, while part II focuses on intellectual skills and abilities. Following are the six levels of objectives within the cognitive domain along with examples of items that might be used to test each level.

1. Knowledge
   - "Name the continents."
   - "Distinguish between a cross section and a longitudinal section."
   - "Place these seven objects in their proper categories."
   - "Name the systems of the human body."
2. Comprehension
   - "Repeat the story."
   - "Tell me in your own words."
3. Application
   - "How could you measure this room with 15th-century measuring devices?"
   - "Write a short story."
4. Analysis
   - "What are the parts to this problem?"
   - "How do the cardiovascular and lymphatic systems relate?"

5. Synthesis
    - "What are some solutions to this problem?"
    - "Prepare an article to explain the issues to your readers."
6. Evaluation
    - "Will this new product (for example, a new work shoe) meet the requirements established for judging its effectiveness?"
    - "Tell us about the qualities of this poem which may make it a classic."

Thus, a particular student may be functioning at the level of application in arithmetic but at the level of synthesis in social studies.

Bloom's emphasis on a range of learning beyond the reiteration of facts and figures has been the basis of the taxonomy's use in enrichment programs. For example, the taxonomy has been used effectively in developing learning centers. Some of the learning center activities would be appropriate and required for all children in the class, and others would be for selected students only. Children of varying interests and abilities would be asked to do individually specified tasks. In some instances, the tasks within the categories will vary according to interests and abilities. In other instances, gifted students might be asked to do only those tasks at the higher levels of the taxonomy.

A classroom learning center on outer space travel might include activities from all six levels of the taxonomy. All children would be required to read the directions and a preliminary information sheet and to view a slide-tape presentation. Some students would then be asked to answer a series of posttest questions (knowledge level). Others would be asked to write a newspaper article (synthesis). Still others might be required to read about the Bernoulli Principle (regarding objects moving through fluids) and to demonstrate that principle in an experiment (analysis).

The next activity in the learning center might be to examine human energy requirements and nourishment in space. Again, all students would get the preliminary information, in this case via a NASA video cassette. Some students would be asked to develop a display of the basic food groups (comprehension). Some would design a new food capsule for prolonged space exploration (synthesis). Still other students would design meals based on color, texture, and nutritional requirements (evaluation). Thus, using the taxonomy allows the teacher to provide one set of materials, but still organize instruction at various levels with tasks appropriate for the differing ability levels of students in the class.

Guilford's Structure of Intellect Model

The Structure of Intellect (S.O.I.) is a three-dimensional model (Guilford, 1956). The three major dimensions of the S.O.I. model are content, operations, and products. In other words, there is some content or material upon which an individual performs an operation; the outcome of that operation is a product. Guilford used this model (see Figure 11.2) to describe human intelligence. He

FIGURE 11.2

Guilford's Structure of Intellect Model.

Source: J. P. Guilford, *The nature of human intelligence.* New York: McGraw-Hill, 1967. Reprinted by permission.

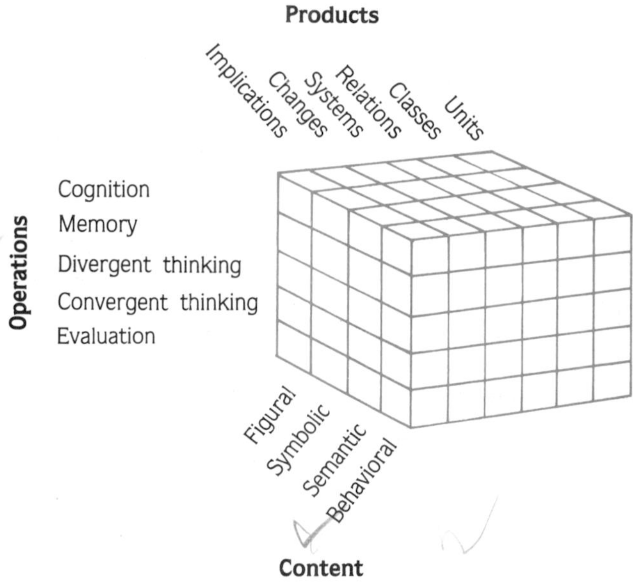

further identified four subcategories of content (figural, symbolic, semantic, and behavioral), five subcategories of operations (cognition, memory, divergent thinking, convergent thinking, and evaluation), and six subcategories of products (units, classes, relations, systems, changes, and implications). Thus, using Guilford's model, a given task can be described as the intersection of three points on the model—for instance, evaluating a semantic relationship, as in comparing.

The S.O.I. model has had its greatest impact on programs to identify and nurture creativity in children (Karnes, Shwedel, & Williams, 1983; Khatena, 1976). However, diagnostic-prescriptive instructional activities have also been developed from the model (Gurcsick, 1981; Meeker, 1969). In addition, Navarre (1983) has used the S.O.I. model in an attempt to identify careers that capitalize on an individual's strongest intellectual abilities as described by the model. For example, a person with exemplary skills in "cognition of figural units" may take special advantage of those talents in photography or graphic design. "Divergent production of figural units" emphasizes creativity with objects and shapes, which are useful for printing and layout illustrators, designers, and architects.

See the description of the University of Illinois Preschool Gifted Program, pages 391–392.

Williams' Cognitive-Affective Model

The cognitive-affective model of Williams (1970) combines (1) curriculum or subject matter, (2) pupil behaviors, both cognitive and affective, and (3) teaching strategies into a comprehensive approach to teaching and learning. The affective domain has been built into the model as an integral instructional sphere.

Williams gives several examples of how this model is used for instruction. To encourage "original thinking and imagination" in social studies using "provocative questions and visualization skills," children were asked to list everything they might see if they flew through the air on a kite string. In addition, they were asked to identify ways to return to the ground (1970, p. 23). In another example designed to encourage "fluent and original thinking" in language arts using an "organized random search and creative writing skill," the children took a field trip to a dairy and then were asked to make a "treasure chest" of all the descriptive phrases that might be used to refer to their trip. Later they were to write a story using those phrases (1970, p. 270).

Renzulli's Enrichment Triad Model

Renzulli (1977, 1982) developed the Enrichment Triad Model (ETM) to guide the planning of enrichment activities for gifted and talented children. It is based on three levels, or types, of enrichment. *General exploratory activities* (Type I) are those activities that let students survey a variety of topics and give them ideas for further study. Students are introduced to a subject and its components, in search of areas of interest. *Group training activities* (Type II) involve students in exercises designed to provide the skills, knowledge, and attitudes necessary for future, in-depth study; that is, to "learn how to learn" within the subject or content area of interest. Type III enrichment activities consist of *individual and small-group investigations of real problems.* Students are to assume the posture

This gifted high school student is about to launch an individual research project investigating the possibility of manufacturing synthetic chemical compounds in the weightlessness of outer space.

of a "real" investigator in the process of adding to the knowledge base in the selected area of interest. It is considered important that, as true investigators, students address real problems. "Real" problems are those that are not imposed by the teacher and that have meaning to the children in light of the subject matter and the circumstances in which the problems have been defined. The teacher should explain to the students, however, that as fledgling investigators they may not be at the forefront of the given area of study, though, as Renzulli (1977) points out, they may be.

Reis and Cellerino (1983), two teachers of gifted students, use a "revolving door identification model" (Renzulli, Reis, & Smith, 1981) that allows all children in their resource room program to participate in Type I and Type II enrichment activities. Only those students who show serious interest in a specific topic "revolve" into Type III investigations. Students are not compelled to begin Type III investigations; it is their option.

When a student does indicate a particular area of interest, the teacher must determine if the student's interest is serious enough to warrant launching an in-depth investigation or if it is only a temporary, superficial interest. Reis and Cellerino conducted an interview with Michael, a second grade student in their gifted program who, as a result of Type I and Type II activities, expressed a strong interest in Tchaikovsky.

1. Michael, will you tell me a little about Tchaikovsky and how you became interested in knowing more about him?
2. Have you read any books about him and his music?
3. How long have you been interested in studying about Tchaikovsky?
4. Do you like looking in different books to find information?
5. Do you have any ideas about what you would like to do with the information you find? (1983, p. 137)

Michael's responses during the interview showed his interest in Tchaikovsky to be genuine. After specifying objectives for his research, Michael's teachers helped him set up a "management plan" for his investigation. Potential sources of information were identified and a timeline developed. Then Michael was encouraged to come up with a specific idea for a product of his investigation and to consider an audience for his product. Michael's product, a "talking children's book" consisting of 30 typed pages and an audio-taped version that plays selections of Tchaikovsky's music, is now part of both his school's and his local public library's collection. On the first page of his "book," Michael wrote:

> Some of you may wonder why a second grader would want to write a book about Tchaikovsky. People get interested in different things for different reasons. For example, I got interested in Tchaikovsky because I like his music. I play the piano and have a whole book of his music. At Christmas I saw the ballet of the Nutcracker Suite. His music can be both cheerful and sad at the same time. I wondered how music can be both happy and sad at the same time so I decided to learn about Tchaikovsky's life.

I wondered if when he was sad he wrote sad music, and if when he was happy he wrote happy music. In this book you will get to know a little bit more about Tchaikovsky, how he lived and about the music he wrote. (Reis & Cellerino, 1983, p. 139).

Maker's Integrated Curriculum Model

Maker (1982) analyzed the major contributions of the various teaching-learning models and integrated what she felt were the best components of each. Her model involves a four-dimensional approach to curriculum modification for gifted and talented students: content, process, product, and environment. To provide enrichment, a teacher can modify any one or more of the four dimensions.

Content modifications emphasize complex, abstract, and varied organization of the "ideas, concepts, and facts presented" (p. 19). Process modifications address the method of presentation of the material, emphasizing the higher levels of thinking. Product modifications are aimed at what might be expected of gifted and talented children. The product will vary according to the process used to arrive at the product and the audience for whom it is intended. Environmental modifications focus on the conditions under which learning is to take place, the role of the teacher in the activities, and individual student's learning styles. The teacher as facilitator, complex activities, and open, independent learning environments are emphasized. Maker's integrated model incorporates many variables into a comprehensive approach to educational programming for gifted and talented students.

In science, for example, a lesson for the entire class might involve a basic understanding of rain forests, their levels, flora, and fauna. Content modification for the gifted students might require them to study the interactions of plants and animals and symbiosis and to draw parallels between plant, animal, and human behavior in a rain-forest environment. The learning process might be independent study or inquiry lessons. The products would be real. They might include a slide-tape presentation for the school and/or local library, a newspaper account, a videotaped report, or a presentation to the entire science class. The final modification would be in the learning environment. It must be open, so the students are free to divert from usual procedures. The teacher must be willing to remain in the background, available when needed, ready to encourage and praise an insight, but seldom directive.

Teachers of the Gifted

No instructional theory of approach is better than the teacher who implements it. One of the first questions asked about teachers is "Does the teacher have to be gifted in order to teach gifted children effectively"? The answer is "Not necessarily—in the sense of giftedness used in this chapter." All teachers should be gifted, regardless of whom they teach. Teachers should be gifted in different ways to teach different children. Teachers of gifted children do need to have some particular qualities, however. They should:

1. Be willing to accept unusual and diverse questions, answers, and projects.
2. Be intellectually curious.
3. Be systematic and businesslike.
4. Have a variety of interests.
5. Appreciate achievement (Bishop, 1968).
6. Be well prepared in instructional techniques.
7. Be well prepared in content area.
8. Want to teach gifted students (Gallagher, 1975b).
9. Be aware that they may not know as much about some specific topics as do the children, and be comfortable with that situation.

CURRENT ISSUES/FUTURE TRENDS

Many questions remain in the education of gifted and talented children. We need much research in a variety of areas, including the nature of intelligence, learning, creativity, the role of parents and families, cultural diversity, sex roles, and the impact of high technology on the education and lives of gifted and talented people. An examination of future trends suggested by *Megatrends* (Naisbitt, 1982) provides much food for thought. The new society sketched by Naisbitt has considerable implications for education in general; several points have special meaning for gifted and talented children.

We are rapidly moving from an industrial society to an information-processing, high-technology society. We can no longer remain isolated and self-sufficient as individuals or as a nation. Long-range social goals and instantaneous information based on informal human networks rather than complex political systems are an aspect of social change, personally and politically. Clearly, as Naisbitt points out, the future will call for the very best human resources available.

In this vein, we must capitalize on the resources found in special populations—women, those who are handicapped, individuals from culturally diverse groups, and those not achieving up to the potential their gifts and talents would indicate. The first major issue affecting these groups is the ability of educational planners to identify gifted and talented individuals. The usual testing procedures are often inappropriate or incomplete (Bruch, 1975; Callahan, 1979; Fox, 1977; Maker, 1977). The instruments commonly used (intelligence and achievement tests) seem to penalize anyone who is not like the group used to develop the tests' norms. We say that a test or instrument is *culturally biased* if different groups have different opportunities to learn the skills it measures. For example, do boys and girls have the same opportunities to learn vocabulary? Do children who are handicapped have the same opportunities to engage in sequential motor skills or experiences as do nonhandicapped children? If the answer is no, then the test is culturally biased and individuals from such "special" populations may be at a disadvantage when taking the test.

If society is to benefit from the contributions of the very best human resources available, every effort must be made to identify gifted and talented children, particulary in groups often overlooked in the past—women, handicapped children, and individuals from culturally diverse groups.

The question of cultural bias in commonly used intelligence tests has led to much study. While the evidence of bias is not as substantial as first expected (Sattler, 1982), the fact remains that for a given child being tested, the effects of any bias may be enough to preclude that child from being considered for a gifted and talented program.

Callahan (1979) has summarized the literature on gifted and talented women. In comparisons of gifted males and females, the literature is generally inconclusive except in mathematics, where there is a greater proportion of males identified as gifted. Cultural barriers, test and social biases, and organizational reward systems are all impediments to the advancement of gifted and talented women. These are sound reasons to emphasize special education for gifted girls, as well as sound guidance and counseling practices.

Maker (1977) raised a particularly salient point about looking for giftedness among handicapped students, which challenges the seeming dichotomy between the concepts of "handicapped" and "gifted." When all handicapped children are viewed as below average, those who are also gifted are cast into a stereotype that disavows their true abilities. A loss of mobility, for example, does not imply reduced intellectual functioning, nor does deafness reduce one's artistic abilities. Recognition of intraindividual differences emphasizing skills rather than deficits is important. Maker (1977) suggests using checklists and Meeker's (1969) approaches to testing for the identification of the gifted handicapped.

We have known for some time that there are gifted and talented persons among culturally diverse groups (Frierson, 1965; Torrance, 1977; Witty & Jenkins, 1934). But until recent years, the identification and development of gifts and talents within racially and linguistically different populations has received little attention. One notable exception is the work of Torrance (1977). Work in this important area, however, is increasing dramatically (Baldwin, Gear, & Lucita, 1978; Malone, 1978). Baldwin (1978) has listed some descriptors of culturally diverse, gifted children:

1. Depend on controls from their environment rather than control from "within"
2. Loyal to peer group
3. Able to "rebound" from environmental hardships
4. Verbally persuasive; humor rich with symbolism; language rich in imagery
5. Logical reasoning and problem-solving ability
6. Socially intelligent and active regarding justice
7. Sensitive and alert to movement. (p. 47)

The underachieving gifted represent another complex problem. Delisle (1982) has described the phenomenom of "learning to underachieve." Some gifted and talented children learn to perform below their potential because:

☐ It is socially safe, that is, teachers and peers do not single the child out;

☐ There is nothing to learn that is interesting or challenging;

☐ Peer and parent relationships are not based on expectations of superior achievement.

Whitmore (1980) has described underachievement as mild to moderate and moderate to severe. She also discusses the "unknown underachiever"; that is, the child who is performing "normally" so no one knows of the child's exceptional abilities because they are hidden. High aptitude scores with low grades or high standardized achievement scores with low grades may indicate two other kinds of underachievement (p. 169). Effective remediation involves increasing the child's motivation, working on self-perceptions, and modifying classroom instruction, environment, and curriculum. Guidance and counseling are integral to improved self-concept and self-esteem (VanTassel-Baska, 1983).

Finally, as we have seen with other groups of exceptional children, to improve the future for gifted and talented children, we must improve society's attitudes toward them. The stereotype of the gifted child as a socially ineffectual "brain," hidden indoors behind a huge stack of books, is not only inaccurate; it can be destructive and stultifying. Furthermore, many people—including some educators—feel that gifted children, by their very nature, do not need special education; they can make it on their own. This attitude can be seen from the local level to the federal government, which no longer monitors programs for gifted and talented children. In fact, gifted and talented children *do* need special education if they are to reach their potential. Too many gifted children are bored and frustrated in school; some even drop out altogether, and even more are made to settle for less than the best.

ACTIVITIES FOR PRESCHOOLERS

These activities were developed to demonstrate a method by which creative and productive thinking for gifted preschool children can be integrated into an informal setting such as the open classroom. The activities are designed to be freely chosen by individual children; after receiving instructions from a teacher, the child should be able to complete the activity independently, with minimal teacher supervision. All the activities encourage children to engage in divergent thinking—that is, creative and original thinking—as defined in Guilford's S.O.I. model.

Mark Williams, Polly Kemp, Michael Marks, and Rebecca Hansen of the University of Illinois preschool program for the gifted created these activities.

 SPACE OBJECTS

Materials: five numbered pictures of "space objects"; cassette recorder and blank tape

Directions:

Pretend that you are the captain of a spaceship which is exploring outer space. You are close to a planet which you think has some sort of people on it, so you send down a scouting party to see what they can find.

When they return to the ship, the scouting crew members report that they couldn't find any people on the planet, but that they did find all kinds of strange objects. They didn't want to disturb these objects because they didn't know what they were, so they took pictures of them with their cameras and brought back the pictures to show to you. What do you think these strange objects could be? Look at each picture, and record on the tape recorder all the ideas you have of what it might be. Don't forget to say the number of the picture before you give your ideas so everyone will know which picture you are talking about. Think of as many ideas as you can for each picture.

To Make Materials:

On a separate piece of white heavy card-stock paper, draw each of the following "space objects" as shown. Be sure to number each prominently so that the child can record the number of the object he or she is thinking about. Cover each card with clear contact paper.

From M. B. Karnes, A. M. Shwedel, & M. Williams, Combining instructional models for young gifted children, *Teaching Exceptional Children*, 1983, *15*, 132–35. Copyright 1983 by the Council for Exceptional Children. Reprinted by permission.

RAINBOW MENU

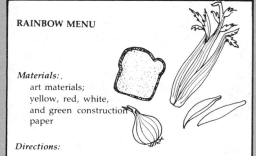

Materials:
art materials;
yellow, red, white,
and green construction
paper

Directions:

Pretend that you just became the owner of the biggest and best restaurant in the whole world. You decide that you want a new menu that is different from any other restaurant's menu, so you decide to group all of your foods according to color. Each page of your menu will be a different color and will only list foods that are that color. What are all the foods that would be on the yellow page? List all of the yellow foods you can think of, and I will write them down.

Now think of all the red foods you can. (Repeat with white foods and green foods.) Now it is time for you to make your menu. Take one sheet each of yellow paper, red paper, white paper, and green paper, and draw the foods that will be on your menu. I will remind you of foods you named if you forget.

MODERN INVENTIONS

Materials: art materials; construction materials (boxes, etc.)

Directions:

An inventor is a person who makes new things which nobody has ever made before. Inventors make new things to solve special problems, for example, garage doors that you can open without getting out of your car.

Be an inventor and make something that no one has ever made before. Use whatever material you need to make a garbage can that a dog would especially like. Before you begin, be sure to think about what a dog would like a garbage can to be like.

Substitutions:

- a trap to catch insects alive without harming them
- a mail box that does more than hold letters and packages
- a bed that is extremely convenient for a sick person
- a television set that helps with the housework

ACTIVITIES FOR A NEW CHILD

Materials: art materials

Directions:

Pretend that tomorrow morning we will be getting a new child in our classroom. She will be very different from you and all the other children, because she will be coming here from another planet somewhere in outer space. Everything here will be very new to her—the furniture, the weather, the plants, how we talk.

What activities do you think this new child would choose to do? I'm sure they would be very different from the activities that you children sign up for, because she has so much new to learn. Make an activity sheet for the new child. Give her a choice of at least six activities—be sure to try to think of things that *she* would be interested in doing.

Substitutions:

- activity sheet for a little baby
- activity sheet for an adult
- activity sheet for a new teacher
- activity sheet for a family pet

SHOE STORY

Materials none (art materials optional)

Directions:

Did you ever hear someone complaining that her feet hurt because she'd been standing or walking all day? Well, did you ever stop to think how badly that person's *shoes* must be feeling too? What if shoes could have thoughts and feelings like people? What do you suppose a shoe might think about? If a shoe could talk, what would it say?

Make up a story about a whole day in the life of a shoe, from the time it wakes up in the closet in the morning till it goes back into the closet for the night. Dictate your story to a teacher; draw pictures to go with your story if you like.

Substitutions:

- wristwatch
- wallet
- key
- pair of glasses

1. Like other exceptional children, gifted and talented students need special educational provisions to reach their full potential.

2. Gifted and talented children have unusual intellectual, creative, artistic, specific academic, or leadership ability, which requires special school services.
   a. To be considered gifted, a student must perform in the top 3 to 5% of the school-age population.
   b. Only 17 states mandated programs for gifted and talented students in fiscal year 1981.

3. While some gifted children are outstanding in many areas, others have special talents in only one or two fields. Although they are by no means perfect and their unusual talents and abilities may make them difficult to manage, many gifted children have the following characteristics:
   a. Better-than-average home life and socioeconomic background
   b. Average or slightly above-average physical stature and health
   c. Emotional health and stability
   d. Popularity and social acceptance
   e. Above-average achievement test scores.

4. Many gifted children are creative as well. Though there is no universally accepted definition of *creativity*, we know that creative children have knowledge, examine it in a variety of ways, critically analyze the outcomes, and communicate their ideas.

5. Identifying gifted and talented children usually involves several procedures, including intelligence, creativity, and achievement testing and nomination by teachers, parents, peers, and even the children themselves.
   a. It is best to match students to the goals of the programs they will be placed in.
   b. Any single identification procedure should be used only to identify certain successful students for special programs; it should not be used to keep other children from receiving special services.
   c. Most school districts will need to have more than one type of program for gifted and talented children.

6. The concept of giftedness has evolved over the years. The current concept is broader than traditional definitions.
   a. Early 19th-century works focused on "genius," which was thought to be genetically determined.
   b. Standardized intelligence tests, beginning with the Stanford-Binet, have been used during most of this century to predict school success and to identify unusually "bright" children. The reliance upon these tests tended to restrict giftedness to high IQ scores, associated with white, urban, middle- or upper-class society.

c. The research of Terman and Hollingsworth did much to increase our knowledge of the gifted and to dispel popular myths.

d. In the early 1950s, Guilford first suggested that more than IQ be considered in determining who is gifted.

e. Since then, the concept of giftedness has expanded to include creativity and other alternatives to traditional IQ scores. We have also come to recognize giftedness among the culturally diverse, among females, and among handicapped children.

7. Education of the gifted and talented should be geared toward the fullest possible development of each child's abilities.

a. Gifted students need both content knowledge and the abilities to use and develop that knowledge effectively.

b. Gifted and talented children need to know basic skills, including research skills and how to continue to learn once they leave school.

c. Two common approaches to educating the gifted are enrichment and acceleration.

d. Five models for teaching gifted students are:
   (1) Bloom's Taxonomy of Educational Objectives
   (2) Guilford's Structure of Intellect Model
   (3) Williams's Cognitive-Affective Model
   (4) Renzulli's Enrichment Triad Model
   (5) Maker's Integrated Curriculum Model

e. Teachers of the gifted must be flexible, curious, tolerant, competent, and self-confident.

8. Many questions remain in the education of gifted and talented children. We need research in a variety of areas if these children are to grow up to be leaders in our rapidly changing society.

9. The importance of identifying gifted and talented children among females, diverse cultural groups, and handicapped students is now being recognized. We need better procedures for identifying, assessing, teaching, and encouraging these children.

10. As we have seen with other exceptional children, we must improve society's attitudes toward gifted and talented children if we are to improve their futures.

FOR MORE INFORMATION

Journals

G/T/C. Published five times per year by G/T/C Publishing Company. Publishes informal ideas aimed at parents and teachers of gifted, talented, and creative youngsters.

Journal for the Education of the Gifted. Published quarterly by the Association for the Gifted, the Council for Exceptional Children. Presents theoretical, descriptive, and research articles presenting diverse ideas and different points of view on the education of gifted and talented students.

The Gifted Child Quarterly. Published four times per year by the National Association for Gifted Children. Publishes articles by both parents and teachers of gifted children.

Books

Barbe, W. B., & Renzulli, J. C. (eds.). *Psychology and education of the gifted,* 2d ed. New York: Irvington Publishers, 1975.

Clark, B. *Growing up gifted,* 2d ed. Columbus, Ohio: Charles E. Merrill, 1983.

Gallagher, J. J. *Teaching the gifted child,* 2d ed. Boston: Allyn & Bacon, 1975.

Hauck, B. B., & Freehill, M. F. (eds.). *The gifted: Case studies.* Dubuque, Iowa: Wm. C. Brown, 1972.

Kramer, A. H., Bitan, D., Butler-Por, N., Eryatar, A., & Landau, E. (eds.). *Gifted children: Challenging their potential.* New York: World Council for Gifted and Talented Children, 1981.

Newland, T. E. *The gifted in socio-educational perspective.* Englewood Cliffs, N.J.: Prentice-Hall, 1976.

Passow, H. H. (ed.). *The gifted and talented: Their education and development.* Chicago: University of Chicago Press, 1979.

Organizations

American Mensa, 1701 W. 3rd Street, Suite 1-R, Brooklyn, NY 11223. An organization made up of people who have scored in the top 2% on an intelligence test; sponsors many special interest groups and publishes a bulletin and journal.

Association for the Gifted, The Council for Exceptional Children, 1920 Association Drive, Reston, VA 22091. A growing division of CEC which includes teachers, teacher educators, administrators, and others interested in gifted and talented children.

III
Intervention

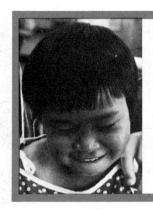

12

Multicultural Special Education

O ne of the greatest challenges facing special educators today is providing an effective, relevant education to exceptional students from culturally diverse backgrounds. Our public school system is based on a philosophy of equal educational opportunity; in the previous chapters we have emphasized the importance of assessment, educational planning, direct instruction, parent involvement, and other factors that contribute to meeting each exceptional child's needs. We hope to equip all students with the skills they need to lead satisfying and productive lives.

The Education for All Handicapped Children Act of 1975 (P.L. 94–142) is only one of many recent significant steps toward the implementation of equal educational opportunity. In addition to prohibiting discrimination in schools due to a child's intellectual or physical disability, court decisions and legislation have forbidden discrimination in education and employment on the basis of a person's race, nationality, sex, disability, or inability to speak English. Special programs now provide financial support and assistance to schools that serve refugee and migrant students and provide self-determination in education for Native Americans.

Despite these important efforts, equal opportunity for all is not yet a reality. Many exceptional students still experience discrimination or receive a less-than-adequate education because of their race, social class, or other differences from the majority. In addressing ourselves to this issue, we do not mean to imply that belonging to a cultural or linguistic group that is different from the majority culture is a handicap or disability. On the contrary, a great strength of the United States is its cultural diversity. Our society is made up of immigrants from many lands, and we have benefited from the contributions of many ethnic groups. As James Banks observes,

Ethnic diversity enriches the nation and increases the ways in which its citizens can perceive and solve personal and public problems. This diversity also enriches a society by providing all citizens with more opportunities to experience other cultures and thus to become more fulfilled as human beings. When individuals are able to participate in a variety of ethnic cultures they are more able to benefit from the total human experience. (1977, p. 7)

But while cultural diversity is a strength of our society, being a member of a cultural minority too often means discrimination and misunderstanding, closed doors, and lowered expectations. Fortunately, this situation is improving; closed doors are opening.

Currie notes that a policy of "multiculturalism" is officially pursued by the government of Canada; though English and French are the two official languages, no ethnic group takes precedence over any other. He recalls a native Canadian parent who likens multiculturalism to a bouquet that is "more beautiful because of the diversity of flowers, all of which add to the total beauty, and yet, each is beautiful in its own right. . . . It is the differences which must be recognized and accepted instead of being ignored or rejected" (1981, p. 165).

Three basic concepts of membership in cultural groups outlined by Garcia (1981) can serve as a worthwhile point of departure for our consideration of the special needs of culturally diverse exceptional students.

1. Every person needs to belong to, or have a sense of belonging to, a group. A child's ethnic or cultural group provides a system of values and behaviors and is important in developing self-concept. Group membership should be a source of strength and social sustenance rather than a source of shame or anxiety.

2. Ethnic groups have both similarities and differences. Students should be encouraged to explore the characteristics of various groups; teachers can strive for cross-cultural communication and understanding. For example, students can discuss the social implications of racial differences.

3. Segregated people develop myths, prejudices, and stereotypes about each other. Conflicts can occur when different groups first come into contact. Students may consider the consequences of separation and integration.

Stereotyping has been defined as the "arbitrary assigning of certain habits, abilities, and expectations to people solely on the basis of group membership, regardless of their attributes as individuals" (Campbell, 1979, p. 1).

As special educators, we believe strongly in the importance of interindividual and intraindividual differences, even within the context of our own widely used categories. We know, for example, that two students affected by Down syndrome may display widely different academic abilities, social behavior, and personality traits. We have seen that one blind child may read braille fluently and play the piano well, while another blind child does neither. Similarly, two members of the same racial or cultural group may function quite differently in school; we should always be objective observers of students' behavior and avoid stereotypes based on race or culture.

CULTURAL DIVERSITY IN SPECIAL EDUCATION

Recent surveys have reported that a sizable percentage of children in special education programs are members of culturally diverse groups. According to Kamp and Chinn (1982), about 1/3 of the entire population of special education students in the United States consists of students from diverse cultural groups, such as Asian Americans, Native Americans, black or Afro-Americans, and Hispanic Americans. A 1981 study by the Subcommittee on Select Education of the U. S. House of Representatives found that 38% of students in programs for educable mentally retarded children were black, though the overall percentage of black students of school age was only about 16%. Delgado (1981) described the high proportion of hearing impaired and multihandicapped students who come from non-English-speaking homes; in some programs this proportion exceeds 40% of the students.

The fact that culturally diverse children constitute a high percentage of special education students is not, in itself, a problem. Students with special needs *should* be served in special programs, whatever their ethnic background. However, the presence of large numbers of culturally diverse students raises several important concerns for special educators, including:

☐ The adequacy of assessment and placement procedures. Have students received fair and multifaceted assessments before being placed in special education programs? Is referral based upon a child's documented special needs, rather than upon value judgments about his or her background? Are there opportunities for periodic reassessment and for parent and student involvement in program planning? Are culturally diverse students and disabled students included in screenings for gifted and talented children?

☐ Provision of appropriate supportive services. Special efforts may help improve the education and adjustment of students from culturally diverse backgrounds; these services may be provided either by the school or by other agencies. Examples of special efforts that may be appropriate include (1) bilingual aides to assist non-English-speaking students in the classroom and to translate correspondence sent home, (2) in-service training for teachers, to encourage sensitivity toward different cultures and to enhance appropriate educational planning, and (3) multiethnic education for students, to increase awareness of their own and other backgrounds and to reduce the potential for conflict and misunderstanding in the classroom.

☐ Interactions between cultural background and the school. Schools generally require or expect certain behaviors of their students. For example, it is assumed that most children will learn to respond to the teacher's instructions and will be positively motivated by verbal praise. Children, however, are strongly influenced by their early contacts with family members, neighbors, and friends. If the expectations and values of their home and school environments are vastly different, the child may have serious problems. As Chan and Rueda (1979) observe, many children appear to "think, act, and be motivated appropriately in activities out of school, yet do not demonstrate these same behaviors in school. . . . many school-related problems of minority children seem to be the results of conflict between the hidden curriculum and cultural preparation" (p. 427). Such conflicts can interfere with a child's learning and behavior and are thus a legitimate concern of special educators.

TERMINOLOGY

Many terms have been applied to members of culturally diverse populations. As we have seen elsewhere in this book, it is difficult to use labels effectively. While labels serve a useful purpose in identifying certain traits, they may also have the unfortunate (and probably unintended) effect of conveying misleading or inaccurate generalizations. Nowhere is this more evident than in considering several terms that have been used to refer to children who come from different cultural backgrounds.

To refer to a child as a member of a *minority* group implies that the population of that group is small and carries some "negative connotations of being less than other groups with respect to power, status, and treatment' (Chinn & Kamp, 1982, p. 383). In many regions, however, blacks, Hispanics and Native Americans are not a minority at all, but constitute the predominant population of a particular school or locality. Members of these groups are involved as teachers, clinicians, and administrators of educational programs. A black child in Detroit, a Mexican-American child in El Paso, and a Navajo child on a reservation in Arizona could be considered a minority only with respect to the population of the nation as a whole, a comparison that would have little meaning to the child's immediate environment.

Terms such as *culturally deprived* and *culturally disadvantaged* have also been used to describe children from various backgrounds. While these labels recognize the influence of children's environment upon their education and achievement, they also make the unfortunate suggestion that, because a child s background is different from that of "majority" or more widely accepted groups, the culture of the different group is somehow inferior or lacking. A 1966 report, for example, used the terms *deprived* and *disadvantaged* in referring to a population of preschool black children in a southern town. This report also noted, however, that most of the children's families had been in the vicinity for at least three generations and that only 2 of 87 families dropped out of a 3-year-long research and demonstration project (Gray, Klaus, Miller, & Forrester, 1966, p. 1). That information strongly suggests the presence, not absence, of a stable cultural environment in the family and community. As Sue (1981) observes, it is now acknowledged that all people inherit some cultural background, and the fact that a culture may differ from white middle-class values does not mean that it is deviant, impoverished, or in need of reform.

Culturally diverse is the term we have elected to use when referring to exceptional children whose background is "different enough" to require, at times, special methods of assessment, instruction, intervention, or counseling.

The term *culturally diverse* refers to exceptional children whose background is different enough to require, at times, special methods of instruction, intervention, or counseling.

This term implies no judgment of a culture's value, and we do not mean to equate cultural diversity with disability. We view membership in a cultural group as an opportunity for an enriching experience rather than a disadvantage. We hope that this chapter's examination of issues in the education of culturally diverse exceptional children will help teachers and others to "free children from the damaging effects of premature, inaccurate, or prejudiced estimates and interpretations of their behavior that are culturally induced" (Spindler, 1974, p. 38).

ASSESSMENT OF CULTURALLY DIVERSE EXCEPTIONAL CHILDREN: PROBLEMS AND SUGGESTED SOLUTIONS

One critical concern is bias and abuse in the testing and placement of culturally diverse exceptional children. Jane Mercer's 1973 influential study of a large school district in California is often cited as evidence that race and culture may play an unfair role in determining whether a child is placed into special classes, and if so, what type of services he or she will receive. Mercer found that black and Mexican-American children were much more likely to be placed in classes for the educable mentally retarded than were Anglo-American children: only 1.8% of all Anglo-American children in the school district were enrolled in EMR classes, while 12.9% of the black children and 18.6% of the Mexican-American children were (Mercer, 1973a). These figures can be interpreted as meaning that a Mexican-American child was 10 times more likely than an Anglo-American child to receive the EMR label, which at that time led to placement in special classes for much or all of the school day. Another study of racial imbalance in special education classes, however, yielded somewhat different findings. Gottlieb, Agard, Kaufman, and Semmel (1976) reported that, while many children in a Texas school district were placed into EMR classes that were "very heavily overrepresented with children of their own race" (p. 212), this situation generally reflected the racial composition of the schools as a whole, rather than bias on the part of school officials.

The practice of placing children into special education programs for the handicapped or the gifted solely because of their performance on standardized intelligence tests is rapidly disappearing. It is widely felt that, in the past, over-reliance on IQ tests resulted in the inappropriate labeling and placement of many students from diverse cultural backgrounds; IQ tests did not present a fair or complete measure of the intelligence of culturally diverse students.

Issues in IQ testing were discussed more fully in chapter 3.

Hilliard (1975) called attention to sources of cultural bias in several widely used tests of cognitive ability. These tests appear to be based on the faulty premise that every child comes to the test with a similar background of life experiences. The following examples of potentially unfair test items are cited:

> On one test, a child must be familiar with such words as *wasp, captain, hive, casserole, shears, cobbler,* or *hydrant.* On another test, a child must know the distance from Boston to London [and] why icebergs melt. . . . The child, in order to get the answers correct, must assume that women are weak and need protection, that policemen are always nice, that labor laws are just. How is the examiner to distinguish ignorance from disagreement? (Hilliard, 1975, p. 22)

Samuda also finds an "Anglocentric" bias in many intelligence tests and contends that, when IQ scores are "interpreted with the knowledge that socio-cultural factors contaminate them" and when a child's adaptive behavior is considered, "racial imbalance in classes for the mentally retarded disappears" (1976, pp. 70–71).

It is also obvious that standardized tests in English are unlikely to give an accurate picture of a young child's abilities if the child comes from a non-English-speaking home. Thus, P.L. 94–142 specifies that assessment for the purpose of identifying handicapped children must be conducted in the child's native language, if at all possible. Unfortunately, there are not many reliable tests available in languages other than English. And there are problems inherent in translating or adapting tests. Alzate (1978) reviewed several studies of the performance of Spanish-speaking children on translated versions of American tests and concluded that translated tests are generally unreliable. DeAvila (1976) points out the great variety in language within Hispanic populations and notes that, when Mexican-American children were given a test in Spanish that was developed with a population of Puerto Rican children, they performed even more poorly than on an admittedly unfair English test. To illustrate the confusion that may result from inappropriate translations, DeAvila observes that a Spanish-speaking child may use any one of several words to describe a kite,

The law also says that notice of IEP and placement meetings and other important conferences must be given to parents in their native language.

NAVAJO CHILDREN—NOT SO DIFFERENT, AFTER ALL

Eric and Akiko Jones

Eric and Akiko Jones lived and taught on a Navajo reservation in Arizona for 4 years. Eric was a special education teacher, and Akiko (who had recently moved from Japan) taught remedial reading and a regular fourth grade class. They now live in Ohio, where Eric is an assistant professor of special education at Bowling Green State University. We asked them to recall their experiences on the reservation, and Eric shared these impressions of Navajo children with us.

When people ask me, "What is it like to teach Navajo children?" I am inclined to say it is a lot like teaching any other children. There is nothing mysterious or mystical about the principles by which Navajo children learn.

Akiko and I frequently heard the comment, "Indian children learn differently from Anglo children." Our experience leads us to believe that this is not so. You should remember, however, that Navajo children grow up under circumstances that may be radically different from those encountered by most other American children. Teachers need to be aware of at least some of these differences, especially since teacher education programs rarely prepare them to work with children from bilingual or bicultural backgrounds.

We found that most Navajo children do not speak English when they first enter school. Their language is very different from English, and only a handful of non-Navajos have mastered it. But although we find the Navajo language very hard to learn—even when we try—most Navajo children become quite proficient in English by the end of first grade. I never saw a Navajo child, even in the special ed classes, who could not speak English better than any Anglo teacher could speak Navajo. Some of us acquired quite a vocabulary, but we could easily be humbled by even the slowest learner in our classes.

The cultural differences between Navajos and Anglo-Americans are at least as great as the linguistic differences. Navajos frequently place great credence in mystical explanations for both common and uncommon events. A few examples: the *hogan*, the traditional Navajo house, always has eight sides and faces east. Misfortunes may be attributed to witchcraft or werewolves. It is considered extremely rude for a Navajo child to look directly into someone else's eyes. The extent to which Anglos thank one another and offer apologies is apt to be regarded as obsequious by Navajos. The list can go on.

Until recently, most Navajos were educated in government boarding schools. Originally, these schools attempted to "de-Indianize" the Native Americans. Children were sometimes kidnapped from their homes and forced to attend government schools. Life in the boarding schools was harshly regimented, and children reportedly were punished for speaking the Navajo language. Today there are many more public day schools, but some federal boarding schools still exist to serve children who come from remote parts of the reservation. The Navajo reservation is large, almost the size of the state of West Virginia.

It would be a mistake to be in a great rush to understand the Navajo culture, and it is probably unrealistic to expect teachers to have a *thorough* understanding of it. More reliable information will be acquired with time and patience than with direct questions. Sensitivity to the needs of individual students is perhaps the most important sensitivity of all.

For some of Eric's comments on teaching Navajo children, see page 416.

depending on the family's country of origin: *cometa, huila, volantin, papalote,* or *chiringa.* While the translation of tests and other materials into a child's native language is helpful in many instances, great caution must be taken, since the improper use of translation may actually do a disservice to the linguistically different child.

Bias or discrimination may also occur in the referral process, when children's records are reviewed and decisions are made about the type of services to be provided. In the opinion of some educators, a child's race, family background, and economic circumstances—rather than actual performance and needs—unfairly influence the label he or she is likely to receive and the degree to which the child will be removed from the regular classroom. Two children with similar performance may be treated quite differently by school personnel, because of racist attitudes.

> If a black and a white child are not learning well, the chances are that the black will be called *mentally retarded* and the white will be called *learning disabled.* The latter term has much more of a positive image, suggesting that the learning disabled white child is average but needs extra remedial help to fulfill his potential. The black child is seen as inferior and needs much less of a challenge. (Silberberg & Silberberg, 1974, p. 56)

How can bias in testing and decision making be reduced or eliminated? The current emphasis on interdisciplinary assessment of exceptional children, using a variety of formal and observational evaluation techniques and involving a team of professionals, is a healthy one that should reduce inappropriate labeling and placement. The evaluation process should concern itself with identifying a child's specific, observable skills and deficits; as Duffey, Salvia, Tucker, and Ysseldyke observe, "The problem of bias in assessment will not be resolved until educators can operationally specify the criteria to be used in decision making. Until this time, attempts to eliminate bias will be as effective as applying a bandaid to a hemorrhage" (1981, p. 433).

Mercer (1981) suggests that the observation of a child's behavior outside of school, in the family and the neighborhood, may be more valuable than formal tests in determining his or her abilities and needs and in particular may help differentiate learning disabled from mentally retarded students. If a child is "learning the skills needed to cope intelligently with the nonacademic world, then s/he may be ignorant of the skills needed to succeed in school but is not mentally retarded" (p. 101). The importance of precise descriptions of behaviors—including antecedents and consequences—is also emphasized by Dent (1976). In certain cultures and settings, "loud talking" is not always equivalent to "boisterous or aggressive behavior." "Hitting" and "name-calling" are not necessarily "hostile"—they may represent a sign of respect or affection. (pp. 89–90). Interpretations and value judgments should not be used in reporting children's behavior.

There is some interesting evidence that indicates that a child's performance in testing situations may be heavily influenced by the environment and

TRY TAKING A CULTURALLY SPECIFIC TEST

Critics have charged that most standardized intelligence and achievement tests are culturally biased. That is, because the tests are developed by and for white, primarily middle-class individuals, the items and scores discriminate against anyone from a different background. To get a feeling for what it might be like to take such a test, try to answer each of the sample items below. If they appear difficult, confusing, foreign, or unanswerable, then you are beginning to understand how test questions can be inexorably entwined with culture. (Correct answers appear at the bottom of the page.)

Examples 1 to 4 are taken from the "People Ain't Dumb—It's Them Tests!" (compiled by the editors of the Appalachian Review—West Virginia University), based on Appalachian culture.

1. Blue tick is
   a. An insect
   b. A food stamp
   c. Hound dog
   d. NRA sticker

2. Before it is fit to drink, moonshine must be
   a. Aged three months
   b. Aged three weeks
   c. Aged three days
   d. Cooled

3. The most successful method for catching catfish is
   a. Gigging
   b. Setting a trot line
   c. Dynamiting
   d. Creating electric shock with two pokers and a car battery

4. A gee-haw-whinny-diddle is a
   a. Good time
   b. Harness for a horse
   c. Toy
   d. Type of persimmon

Examples 5 to 8 are taken from "The Hana-Butta Test," based on Hawaiian culture.

5. If you were at home and someone told you to get "da kine," they could probably mean:
   a. A glass of water
   b. A towel
   c. An ash tray
   d. Dried fish
   e. Any of the above

6. "Pakalolo" is:
   a. Salted raw fish and seaweed
   b. Whiskey made from ti-root
   c. Marijuana
   d. Liquor
   e. Acid

7. If someone wanted to say dinner was delicious, he would say it was:
   a. Papa's
   b. Kukui
   c. Ewa
   D. Lola
   E. Ono

8. "Hana-butta" is known statewide as:
   a. High butterfat Hana butter
   b. Hana Dairy's margarine
   c. Toto's Snack Bar's famous peanut butter shake
   d. Mucus running from the nose of a person with a bad cold
   e. A plain ole peanut butter sandwich

Answers: (1) c; (2) d; (3) c; (4) c; (5) e; (6) c; (7) e; (8) d

From J. S. Payne and J. R. Patton, *Mental retardation*. Columbus, Ohio: Charles E. Merrill Publishing Company, 1981, pp. 180–181. Reprinted with permission.

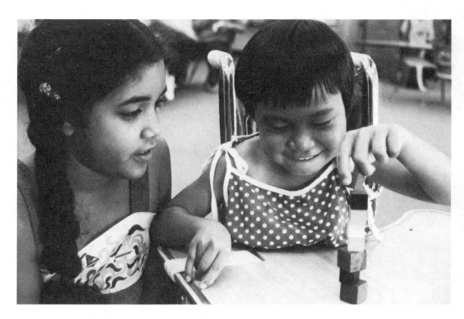

A child's sensitivity to the social environment and his or her peers should be taken into account when assessing the abilities of an exceptional child from a culturally diverse group.

the examiner. Labov (1975) presents a case study of the verbal behavior of an 8-year-old black child named Leon. When Leon was tested in school by a white interviewer who placed objects on a table and said, "Tell me everything you can about this," his response was minimal, consisting mostly of silence and one-word utterances. It appeared that Leon was functioning well below his age level and perhaps had a serious communication disorder or mental retardation. However, on another occasion, Leon was interviewed by a black examiner who took him to an apartment in a familiar neighborhood, brought along Leon's best friend and a supply of potato chips, and sat down on the floor with the child. In this situation, Leon spoke much more fluently; he had a great deal to say to the adult and to his friend. Labov has also performed a detailed linguistic analysis of the nonstandard English used by many black children and concluded that traditional classroom tests and tasks had little relevance or accuracy. "There is no reason to believe," wrote Labov, "that any nonstandard vernacular is in itself an obstacle to learning" (1975, p. 127).

Along with objective recording of behaviors, it is recommended that the child's social and cultural background be taken into account when assessing performance. What is normal and acceptable in a child's culture may be regarded as abnormal or unacceptable in school, and may result in conflict, mislabeling, or punishment. Gallimore, Boggs, and Jordan (1974) offer the example of several native Hawaiian children who sought help from other children on tests and tasks and seemed to pay little attention to the teacher. This behavior was interpreted as cheating and inattentiveness. Closer observations of the children's home and community environments, however, revealed that the Hawaiian children were typically "peer-oriented." It was normal for them to share in the responsibility for caring for each other, and they often worked cooperatively on tasks rather than following the directions of an adult.

Cox and Ramirez (1981) report that, while generalizations cannot be made about the learning styles of any group of students, it appears that many black, Hispanic, and other culturally diverse children are more group-oriented, more sensitive to the social environment, and more positively responsive to adult modeling than are white students. Students from certain cultural backgrounds may not learn effectively in highly competitive situations or on nonsocial tasks. They may be uncomfortable with trial-and-error approaches and may not be interested in the fine details of certain concepts and materials. Cox and Ramirez have designed assessment procedures that may be helpful to teachers in determining the particular learning style of a culturally diverse student. Figure 12.1 presents a behavior rating instrument that can be used to evaluate a child's preferences and orientations and then to develop teaching methods and materials that are appropriate.

Nondiscriminatory assessment requires that decisions be based on varied and accurate data. Test performance, observation of behavior, awareness of cultural differences, and consultation with parents (and with students themselves) can all play useful roles in reducing the number of culturally diverse students who are erroneously placed into special education programs. As Jones observes, "Attention to appropriate assessment of minority group children can yield approaches which will lead to the improved assessment of all children" (1976, p. 289).

SOME CONCERNS OF SPECIFIC CULTURALLY DIVERSE GROUPS

Elsie J. Smith, a counselor who specializes in working with people of diverse cultural backgrounds, finds it helpful to remember the following saying:

> Each individual is —
> like all other people,
> like some other people, and
> like no other person.
> (E. J. Smith, 1981, p. 180)

We will keep this observation in mind as we consider certain issues that have been of concern to specific cultural groups. It is not our purpose to offer generalizations; each of these cultures in reality consists of many different subcultures, and the degree to which a child inherits a distinct cultural background varies immensely. Rather, we hope to present information that may help teachers and others recognize whether their approaches and interactions with some

FIGURE 12.1

Checklist of observable
student behaviors.

Source: B. G. Cox, and M.
Ramirez, "Cognitive styles:
Implications for multiethnic
education." In J. A. Banks
(ed.), *Education in the 80's:
Multiethnic education.*
Washington, D.C.: National
Education Association, 1981,
p. 67.

Date of Observation _____

FIELD-SENSITIVE	FIELD-INDEPENDENT

RELATIONSHIP TO PEERS

1. Likes to work with others to achieve a common goal. ☐	1. Prefers to work independently. ☐
2. Likes to assist others ☐	2. Likes to compete and gain individual recognition. ☐
3. Is sensitive to feelings and opinions of others. ☐	3. Task-oriented; is inattentive to social environment when working. ☐

PERSONAL RELATIONSHIP TO TEACHER

| 1. Openly expresses positive feelings for teacher. ☐ | 1. Avoids physical contact with teacher. ☐ |
| 2. Asks questions about teacher's tastes and personal experiences; seeks to become like teacher. ☐ | 2. Formal: interactions with teacher are restricted to tasks at hand. ☐ |

INSTRUCTIONAL RELATIONSHIP TO TEACHER

1. Seeks guidance and demonstration from teacher. ☐	1. Likes to try new tasks without teacher's help. ☐
2. Seeks rewards which strengthen relationship with teacher. ☐	2. Impatient to begin tasks; likes to finish first. ☐
3. Is highly motivated when working individually with teacher. ☐	3. Seeks nonsocial rewards. ☐

THINKING STYLE

1. Functions well when objectives are carefully explained or modeled prior to activity or lesson. ☐	1. Focuses on details and parts of things. ☐
2. Deals well with concepts in humanized or story format. ☐	2. Deals well with math and science concepts. ☐
3. Functions well when curriculum content is made relevant to personal interests and experiences. ☐	3. Likes discovery or trial-and-error learning. ☐

CODE: NEVER☐   Seldom⊠   Sometimes◪   Usually■

members of diverse cultural groups are as effective as they could be. Understanding and appreciation of different cultures can do much to avoid misinterpretations of children's behavior.

Blacks/Afro-Americans

Much has been written about the unique experiences shared by Americans of African descent. Johnson (1976) states that black people have "a cultural and social distinctiveness unlike any other group in America" and contends that attitudes and labeling practices often "doubly stigmatize blacks, particularly the impaired and disabled" (pp. 164–165). Johnson expresses the view that the black exceptional child has certain special characteristics and that educators should recognize them and proceed beyond discussions of "feelings." It is most important, says Johnson, to implement instruction that will help the black exceptional child achieve important goals.

> The primary task for the black handicapped child is to master the skills of language, eliminate self-destructive behaviors, and to understand that he must become a source of knowledge which will improve his community. To do this, black educators must begin to embrace positively results-oriented techniques such as precision teaching. . . . In the case of exceptional black children the major task is to provide them with the adaptive behaviors which will permit normalization of activities of daily living, the release of latent creativity, and provide a set of technical skills which will permit maximum independence in the community. (1976, p. 170)

E. J. Smith (1981) offers a review of the distinctive cultural and historical perspectives of black Americans, which have sometimes been associated with conflict and misunderstandings in schools and other settings. According to Smith, it is the feeling of many blacks that actions speak louder than words, that "talk is cheap," and that whites beguile each other with verbal discourse. Much importance is attached to people's nonverbal behavior; blacks may spend much time observing others to "see where they are coming from."

White teachers and counselors generally place a high value on eye contact during interpersonal communication. Many blacks, says Smith, engage in conversation without making eye contact at all times. They may even take part in other activities while still paying attention to a conversation. Smith relates an incident in which a teacher reprimanded a black student for keeping her head down during a swimming lesson; the student insisted she had been paying attention. The teacher then told the student to "face her and look her squarely in the eye like the rest of the girls." "So I did," said the student. "The next thing I knew she was telling me to get out of the pool—that she didn't like the way I was looking at her" (p. 155). Communication styles may differ in other ways. Many blacks do not nod their heads, or make little "um-hmm" noises during conversation, as whites do, to indicate that they are listening to someone (Hall, 1976). Sensitivity to language and communication practices is important in working with students and parents. However, Smith cautions against "trying too hard,"

Teachers who work with students from culturally diverse groups should be sensitive to differences in language and communication practices.

noting that blacks often resent white professionals' attempts to use their slang: "Anyone who tries too hard to show you that he understands blacks doesn't understand them at all" (1981, p. 169).

The black family has been the focus of some recent study and misinterpretation. Smith contends that black families are basically intact social systems which have served as a source of strength and survival, contrary to the sometimes-held view of the black family as a decaying institution which is the source of many social problems. Smith also challenges the notion that the black family is a "matriarchy." Black families with both parents present are similar to white families in their perceptions of power and decision making within the family unit (Smith, 1981, p. 158). Many black families include extended relatives who live in or are welcome to drop in at any time; white home visitors may have different concepts of privacy and may feel uncomfortable when grandparents, cousins, siblings, and others are present when a child's needs are being discussed.

The attitudes of some black parents toward their exceptional child may seem unfamiliar to nonblack professionals. Smith notes that many black parents establish strict standards of behavior in the home, and violations of these rules are often met with physical punishment. White parents may be more inclined to discuss behavior at length with their children and perhaps to use emotional strategies (such as threatening the withdrawal of love) as a form of punishment. Black parents would likely view these strategies as inappropriate. They may also be less inclined than whites to blame or punish themselves or to feel guilty for their children's disabilities or behavior problems. Differences in approach, it should be pointed out, are related to parents' economic and educational levels, as well as cultural background.

In one of the few studies to explore racial differences in the perception of exceptionality, Schilit (1977) found that black and white college students held generally similar attitudes toward mental retardation, with two noteworthy exceptions: blacks were "more aware of the inherent dangers that persist in a low socioeconomic environment and what effect they can have on the individual in terms of development" (p. 190) and held more pessimistic views of the employment potential of mentally retarded people. With respect to the second finding, Schilit conjectured that, since the incidence of unemployment in the black community as a whole (that is, for people of normal intelligence) is high, the black students felt that mentally retarded people would have even more difficulty in finding employment. More work needs to be done on the special needs of black exceptional children and on ways of improving cross-cultural communication and parent involvement.

Hispanic Americans

One of the largest and most rapidly growing populations of culturally diverse exceptional children consists of Hispanic Americans. Although there are many social, cultural, and economic subgroups within this population, culturally relevant methods of instruction and counseling may often be called for when working with people of Hispanic background.

As in virtually all cultures, the family plays a critical role in the Hispanic-American exceptional child's early development and socialization. Rivera and Quintana Saylor offer this view of the traditional Spanish-speaking family:

> First, the family is considered as the most important social unit, and individual interests or aspirations are subordinate to those of the family. Each member has a unique and responsible role with the father being the head and responsible for providing for his family as well as for their behavior in and out of the home. He has a great degree of freedom to practice his *machismo,* which is done in a strict but gentle manner. The mother devotes herself to her husband and children with her personal interests secondary to those. She has the greatest influence in the family but exercises it in subtle ways. The children are treasured and indulged with great amounts of personal and physical affection. They are not without responsibility, however, and this may take precedence over school or personal attainment. When a disabling condition interrupts this system, it may create a serious crisis. (1977, p. 446)

The concept of *machismo* (maleness), referred to in the preceding description, has been the subject of much misinterpretation. Ruiz (1981) cautions against assumptions that Hispanic sex roles are uniform and rigid. Ruiz explains that the term *macho* (male) is used among Hispanics as a flattering term denoting "physical strength, sexual attractiveness, virtue, and potency" (p. 191). It is not meant to imply physical aggressiveness, dominance of women, sexual promiscuity, or excessive use of alcohol. "Real masculinity" among Hispanics, notes Ruiz, places a high value on "dignity in personal conduct, respect for others, love for the family, and affection for children" (p. 192).

Castaneda (1976) has described the Mexican-American family, with special implications for those who work with exceptional children. He finds that many Mexican-American children consider it selfish to strive for individual gains, since achievement for the family as a whole takes precedence over individual accomplishments. This may cause problems when parents are not involved in determining educational goals. It is suggested that teachers put the child's "characteristic preference for a cooperative mode" of achievement to good use by encouraging children to work together in group projects (Castaneda, 1976, p. 185).

Castaneda also observes that many Mexican-American children are reluctant to ask for a teacher's help, as they are accustomed to having family members respond to their nonverbal behavior in a way that avoids the "embarrassment" of requesting help. In general, he notes, children and parents are likely to turn to members of the extended family when help is needed, rather than relying on schools or agencies, which they regard as impersonal. Different value systems may also affect a child's classroom performance. Many non-Hispanic teachers adopt an objective, impartial attitude in school, in the interest of fair and equal treatment of students. However, Hispanic children may take this as a sign of rejection, feeling that the teacher does not care about them. Castaneda suggests that the teacher of Mexican-American children develop close, personalized relationships with the students and use child-centered, socially reinforcing language, such as "I am proud of you," or "You did that very well."

> The teaching style which is most characteristic in the traditional Mexican American community is *modeling*. The child learns to "do it like the teacher" and wants to become like the teacher. It is important, then, that the teacher relate personal anecdotes and be willing to interact with the child outside the classroom. The most effective rewards are those which result in a closer relationship between the child and the teacher. (Castaneda, 1976, p. 188)

Other approaches suggested for teachers who work with Hispanic American exceptional children include:

1. Use Spanish in the classroom, including some instruction in Spanish for non-Spanish-speaking students.
2. Provide instruction in English as a second language for children and parents.
3. Introduce children to books, materials, and activities that depict Hispanic people and cultures.
4. Have Spanish-speaking teachers and aides in the school, to facilitate communication with children and parents.
5. Introduce children to Hispanic disabled adults who are leading productive lives.

6. Involve members of the Hispanic community in planning school-related programs.

American Indians and Other Native Americans

Information about the prevalence of exceptionality among Native American populations is difficult to obtain. As Stewart (1977) observes, about half of all Native Americans live on recognized reservations or in culturally distinctive communities, while the other half is absorbed into the general population, mainly in urban areas. Many federal, state, tribal, and local agencies provide (and sometimes duplicate) medical, educational, and social services to Americans of Indian Eskimo, and other Native descent.

Perhaps to a greater degree than most other cultures, Native Americans often absorb handicapped or disabled children into the family and community without removing them for special services. Non-Native professionals, in fact, often have difficulty setting up programs to identify and serve exceptional children on Indian reservations or in Native Alaskan communities. There may be fear and resistance to having Native children removed from the home to be evaluated or educated in distant places. This particularly appears to happen when Native people are not involved in planning the programs.

Stewart (1977) illustrates the accepting nature of many Native American families toward a handicapped child, explaining that it is extremely hard to estimate the deaf population among certain Indian groups. Deaf children frequently become shepherds or learn to perform other useful roles in the community. They are not enrolled in schools or classes for the deaf. Among many Native groups, it is not considered negative or tragic to have a child born with a disability, since "it is assumed the child has the prenatal choice of how he wishes to be born and, if handicapped, is so by choice" (Stewart, 1977, p. 439). Indian languages also show a realistic and unemotional recognition of exceptionality. The Ute Indian term n'kvat is translated as "can't hear so can't talk," which Stewart considers much more descriptive than the archaic English term "deaf and dumb." Such attitudes of acceptance, however, may not extend to all exceptional children. Several observers have noted that Natives with obvious physical impairments and children who have seizures are often teased or regarded with alarm by their peers.

Most suggestions for improving the lives of disabled Native Americans focus on broad issues of health, economic, and social development. Richardson (1981) has provided evidence to show that, on the average, the American Indian has a much lower income and shorter life expectancy than other Americans and that there is an extremely high incidence of unemployment, alcoholism, incarceration, and suicide among Native groups. These problems, of course, merit the attention of the concerned teacher. On a more personal level, some advice has been offered for improving interpersonal communication and classroom instruction with Native students and their families (Pepper, 1976; Richardson, 1981):

1. Show children expected behavior by modeling and having them observe, rather than by verbally instructing them.

TEACHING NAVAJO CHILDREN

Here are some further comments by Eric Jones about his experiences teaching on a Navajo reservation (see pages 404–405). As Eric says, teaching Navajo students "is a lot like teaching any other children." In fact, you could probably substitute any other bilingual group for "Navajo" throughout these comments.

It was not always clear to me why the Navajo students in my special education classes had failed to achieve in the regular class programs. Some had behavioral and learning handicaps. For others, lack of proficiency in English appeared to have been the main reason for placing them into special education programs. We all felt that these students should not have been placed into special ed—but there were no other programs to meet their educational needs.

I found that the principles of applied behavior analysis and systematic instruction were among the most effective in meeting my students' needs. I remember one boy who was painfully shy, extremely reluctant to use English, and not very proficient at it. Despite his problems in school, he seemed to be bright, perhaps even gifted. The aide in my classroom described his Navajo speech as archaic and lyrical. We tried almost everything: being warm and accepting, language experience activities, . . . but he still acted as though it would cost him a dime apiece to use English words. So we developed a token reinforcement program. Any time he spoke in English, he received a token. The tokens were later exchanged for pieces of candy. At first we reinforced the use of words; later he had to produce sentences. The results were dramatic. His use of English increased markedly, and he later let us know that the tokens were not needed. After we discontinued the token program, his proficiency in English continued to increase.

I am convinced that there will never be such a thing as a "culture-fair" or "language-free" intelligence test, and it is naive to expect this. The *real* progress in bilingual/bicultural education will come from the development of carefully structured and sequenced educational programs, not from developments in testing. New developments in testing and assessment procedures will continue to have limited impact. Students learn from better teaching, not from better testing.

As in any educational effort, parents are important. One of the best ways to become aware of the needs of individual students is to work with their parents. Without parent and community support, neither bilingual nor special education programs have much chance of succeeding. Those Navajo parents who showed interest and offered help made my job much easier and more gratifying.

Well-trained special education teachers have a great deal to offer in the education of bilingual/bicultural students. They should be skilled in developing and planning instruction and have a knowledge of behavioral principles. They should be sensitive to individual and cultural differences and be willing and able to work with parents.

2. Don't reward or reprimand a child in front of the class. Quiet, private communication is usually preferred.

3. Develop the child's self-concept with assuring statements such as "You can do it." Recognize even partial success at a task.

4. Social and academic competition between children may lead to problems; use activities in which children can share and work as teams.

5. Do not overemphasize timed tests and assignments. Many Natives have a flexible attitude toward time and rules.

6. Do not expect direct eye contact. Attention and respect may be conveyed when the Native child avoids eye contact while listening.

7. Display Native pictures or artifacts in your classroom or office; use materials that depict Native people realistically and with dignity.

8. American Indians appreciate a gentle handshake, not overly firm. When greeting people, it is considered polite to offer them something, such as a cup of coffee or a glass of water.

9. Avoid condescending statements and generalizations, such as "I have a good friend who is an Indian" or "Do you Eskimos believe in God?"

10. Acceptance and restatement of a Native person's views are recommended in counseling situations. Emphasize careful listening. Periods of silence are usually acceptable.

Asian Americans

Exceptional children of Asian descent constitute a sizable and, in many areas, growing population. Particularly in Hawaii and California, some special concerns of Asian Americans with disabilities have recently been addressed with the establishment of specialized programs of service.

Wakabayashi (1977) considers Asian Americans "the least acknowledged of the national minorities" (p. 430) in the United States, and notes that there are widespread misconceptions of Asian Americans as a monolithic group when, in reality, such cultures as the Chinese, Japanese, and Vietnamese are quite different from one another.

Members of certain Asian American populations may be reluctant to seek out special services for disabled children or adults. Sue (1981) notes that Asian parents emphasize their children's obligations to the family unit and that abnormal or deviant behaviors are handled within the family as much as possible. The suppression of public acknowledgment of disability probably means that there is a largely "invisible population" of disabled Asian Americans. In Wakabayashi's view, the traditions and experiences of many Asian Americans endow them with "values and attitudes that are often incongruent with the service delivery vehicles that exist in the public sector" (1977, p. 432). Other observers note that it is more acceptable to admit to physical problems than to behavioral or psychological difficulties. This tendency may mean that, among Asian Americans, only people with more severe emotional or behavior disorders seek help from schools, clinics, and other programs.

Little has been written about special approaches which may be helpful with handicapped Asian American students. The following perspectives have been offered by Jerry Arakawa, who grew up in an Asian American community in California. Arakawa has been blind since infancy.

> Being disabled and Asian meant having an additional personality trait that can potentially cause shame to the family. Consequently, the disabled Asian youngster has a less outgoing personality and takes risks less willingly.
>
> In Western culture, individuality is praised. In Asian culture, anything that breaks homogeneity is troubling. And the disabled Asian knows he is different.
>
> The Asian perspective is to minimize the handicap. The emphasis is on adapting and doing as little out of the ordinary as possible. This even means you avoid legal actions against discrimination. To get employment, you tough it out. If buses are inaccessible, you say it doesn't really matter.
>
> Consumerism and advocacy are very hard for a disabled Asian to understand. He or she seeks to avoid underscoring a disability and focusing public attention on it. To do otherwise is discomforting.
>
> In the last few years, attitudes about disability in the Asian community have become more Western. But the basic values remain: Be a high achiever and transcend your disability. Asians want to excel. They want to be the best. (1981, p. 1)

GUIDELINES FOR TEACHERS OF CULTURALLY DIVERSE EXCEPTIONAL CHILDREN

It would not be possible to offer a comprehensive list of teaching approaches that would apply to all children of diverse cultural backgrounds. As we have just seen, each population of culturally different exceptional children differs widely within itself and from other groups usually recognized as culturally diverse. In general, it is our view that effective instructional procedures apply to children of all cultural backgrounds. Indeed, when exceptional students have the additional "special need" of adjusting to a new or different culture or language, it is even more important for the teacher to plan individualized activities, convey expectations clearly, observe and record behavior precisely, and give the child specific, immediate reinforcement according to his or her performance. Such procedures, coupled with a helpful and friendly attitude on the part of the teacher, can help increase the culturally different exceptional child's motivation and achievement in school.

Joyce King-Stoops (1980) has compiled a brief guide for teachers of migrant children. The sons and daughters of farm workers who typically live in three or four different locations each year, migrant students are usually Hispanic, but also include blacks, whites, Asians, and Native Americans. A review of some issues in the education of migrant children, then, has interest and relevance as we conclude our discussion of the special needs of culturally diverse exceptional children.

Systematic instructional procedures coupled with a helpful and friendly attitude on the part of the teacher will help any exceptional child progress in school, regardless of cultural background.

Like other culturally diverse populations, the educational needs of migrant children have been widely neglected until recently, when they became mandated and supported by federal and state legislation (notably P.L. 93–380). As with handicapped children, procedures now exist to support the identification of migrant children and to assist them in obtaining a free, appropriate program of public education. The U.S. Department of Education operates a national computerized file of information on migrant children, known as the Migrant Student Record Transfer System, to help schools in the difficult task of maintaining data on students' health, family, and educational performance.

King-Stoops offers many helpful and practical suggestions to teachers of migrant children, which may also be applicable to teachers of culturally diverse exceptional students. One useful strategy has been to employ high school or college students with migrant backgrounds (usually bilingual) as part-time aides in classrooms for younger children. This improves the self-concept of both migrant children and aides, facilitates communication with parents, and encourages some young adults from this culture to consider teaching as a profession. Also, the money earned by the aides is generally greatly needed. King-Stoops emphasizes migrant students' need to experience acceptance and success in school, recommending the use of "short tasks that are appropriate and can be accomplished in a reasonable time" (p. 23).

The development of good language and reading patterns is prerequisite to success in school and to employment for most students. King-Stoops presents some activities designed to improve children's listening and speaking skills. Migrant children sometimes speak *pocho*, a mixture of English and Spanish. The teacher should encourage communication by listening, then by modeling standard speech patterns for the child, as in this example:

Child: It lunch time, I go *walkando.*
Teacher: It's lunch time. We'll all go walking to lunch now.   (p. 29)

The teacher of culturally diverse exceptional children should adopt a flexible teaching style and use a variety of teaching approaches to meet individual differences. With a caring attitude, continuous assessment of students, careful observations of behavior, and the use of appropriate materials, the teacher can do much to help the exceptional child from a different cultural background experience success and enjoyment in school.

FROM THE TEACHER'S NOTEBOOK

*Children with disabilities, like all children, of-
ten have unique personality traits. They may
be endearing, bizarre, exasperating . . . or
"all of the above." Their behavior may
change over a period of time. Systematic observation is important—but precise notations
of a child's performance on instructional
tasks give only a partial picture of what he
or she is really like.*

*As a teacher in a residential school for
multihandicapped children, coauthor Michael
Orlansky kept a notebook. Each day, he
wrote down brief notes on the children's behavior. The following excerpts recount his
observations of one interesting student
whose cultural background exerted a strong
influence on his school performance.*

Background. Eduardo is 14 years old. His
family has just emigrated from a Latin American country. He has never been enrolled in a
school program before. He is extremely small
and frail in stature, and has severe vision and
hearing impairments, a heart ailment, slightly
deformed fingers and toes, and a variety of
other medical problems. He speaks only a
few words of English, but communicates
rather fluently in Spanish. He walks in a "tip-
toe" fashion, with his mouth always wide
open. He tends to drool.

September 11. Eduardo seemed happy to be
in our class today. He just wants to talk
about volcanoes and earthquakes, which he
seems to be very interested in.

September 13. Eduardo wants to have my
attention exclusively, for the purpose of so-
cializing and talking in Spanish. He does not
initiate communication with the other children, but has asked some questions about
them, such as "Will he ever see again?" and
"Where does she live?" He pushes others

away roughly if they try to talk to me. He
will need to learn to be a little more tolerant
of others. His efforts to communicate seem
almost frantic.

September 15. He has a great fear of losing
his vision. Near the end of the class, he began to cry, saying, "Miguel, I don't want to
be totally blind." He seems to have gotten
the impression that we will be able to make
him see and hear perfectly well, through
"miraculous drops" that can be put into his
eyes and ears. Otherwise, he seems to be adjusting well enough. He said there is a little
girl with blond hair whom he loves, but he
does not know her name.

September 19. Eduardo is in good spirits.
He is still always talking about earthquakes
and volcanoes. He gets much information
about the news from Spanish radio stations.
He said, "I like *blond* American girls."

September 25. In our lessons, I found that
Eduardo has a considerable background of
knowledge about Latin American countries.
He knows the names of practically all the
rulers, and can discuss such things as climate,
economics, and customs. He wants to write a
letter to the president of Venezuela.

September 28. Eduardo is traveling by himself now. He has been causing some problems in the cottage by using "dirty words" in
Spanish. Today four people from his cottage
contacted me and said that something had to
be done about this. I talked to Eduardo. He
thought the whole thing was very funny. He
said that another boy had called him a "bad
name" first.

October 4. Today Eduardo told of an "earth-
quake" that had just occurred in Trenton,
New Jersey. He said it "registered 7.5 on the

Richter Scale." This would have meant a major disaster, so I checked it out and found it was not so. He has also told stories about earthquakes in Philadelphia and Toledo, Ohio. He asks many questions about earthquakes.

October 5. He had a good time at our "African Dance" this afternoon. When John and Larry made a circle around Eduardo and pretended to cook and eat him, he laughed. He said he would like nothing better than to travel around to all the countries in the world and see how people live and dress.

October 9. Eduardo needs to be reminded about grooming and self-care. He's been coming to school with his shirt completely unbuttoned, and he throws his coat down on the floor. This does not go over well at school or in the cottage.

October 13. Eduardo joined our group in a birthday party for Joyce. He wanted to stay with me the whole time and ask unrelated questions, such as how much "magma" (lava?) was in the earth beneath the school building. We are encouraging him to mix with the other children.

October 19. He is using more English. But I think sometimes he gets confused or misinformed. Like this weekend he thought he was going on a camping trip with the Boy Scouts, and was all excited. Actually, he wasn't included on the trip and was very disappointed.

October 23. Eduardo is already "counting the days" until Thanksgiving vacation. The subject of church came up. He said that on Thanksgiving he would go to church and pray for the Lord to protect him from one of the boys in the cottage. He's been getting into some scraps lately, but I cannot intervene for him all the time. I tell him to take care of himself and to act more responsibly.

October 26. Yesterday afternoon, as they were walking from school together, Eduardo apparently tried to engage in some sexual play with Lilly. Lilly was left very upset and fearful. Today I asked Eduardo about what happened. He did not want to talk about it—gazed off into space and tried to change the subject by asking questions such as "How are you?" "What will we do today?" and the like. Later, we went into a private room and talked "man-to-man," as he says. He wanted to be certain that nobody could hear us. He even asked if the room was "bugged, like Watergate." I told Eduardo that he was not being punished, but that he had frightened Lilly and that he should not do this sort of thing (i.e., pulling down girls' pants) again. He seems to be repentant. He seems to be grasping the idea of *rules.*

1. Though cultural diversity is a strength of our society, many exceptional students still experience discrimination because of their race, social class, or other differences from the majority.

2. Teachers should avoid stereotypes based on race or culture.

3. About 1/3 of the children in special education programs are members of culturally diverse groups.

   a. Students' assessment for placement in special education should be fair; referral should be based upon the child's needs rather than upon his or her background.

   b. Schools may need to provide special supportive services for culturally diverse exceptional students.

   c. Special educators should be aware of each child's cultural background in evaluating classroom behaviors.

4. We have chosen to use the term *culturally diverse* to describe exceptional children whose background is different enough to require special methods of assessment, intervention, or counseling. We do not use the terms *minority, culturally deprived,* or *culturally disadvantaged* because of their unfairly negative connotations.

5. Standardized IQ tests tend to be culturally biased.

   a. They should not be used as the sole criterion for placement in special education.

   b. Translations or adaptations of IQ tests for children from non-English-speaking homes should be used with caution, as they tend to be unreliable and may not reflect the children's home dialect.

   c. Objective, interdisciplinary assessment may help overcome some of the traditional difficulties in assessing culturally diverse children.

   d. Assessment should include observation of the child outside the school. It should consider the child's social and cultural background.

6. Teachers of exceptional black students should be aware of common cultural differences between blacks and whites in communication styles, family relationships, and parental attitudes.

7. Teachers of Hispanic children should keep in mind certain common characteristics that may affect school behavior.

   a. Hispanic families often place the interests of family above the interests of the individual person.

   b. Mexican-American children often respond well to close, personalized relationships with their teachers.

   c. Classrooms should incorporate the Spanish language and Hispanic culture to facilitate communication with children and their parents.

8. Native Americans tend to absorb handicapped children into the family and community rather than segregating them.

a. Improvements of the lives of disabled Native Americans should focus on broad issues of health and economic and social development.

b. Again, teachers should consider common values and behaviors of Native Americans when they interact with the children and their families.

9. Disabled Asian Americans are a sizable, growing population, but may be hard to identify because of their attitudes toward disability and achievement.

10. Effective instructional approaches apply to children of all cultural backgrounds.

11. Migrant children, many of whom are from culturally diverse families, are another group that may need special instructional programs.

FOR MORE INFORMATION

Books

Gollnick, D. M., & Chinn, P. C. *Multicultural education in a pluralistic society.* St. Louis: C. V. Mosby, 1982.

Kamp, S. H., & Chinn, P. C. *A multiethnic curriculum for special education students.* Reston, Va.: Council for Exceptional Children, 1982.

Omark, D. R., & Erickson, J. G. (eds.). *The bilingual exceptional child.* San Diego: College-Hill Press, 1983.

Pacheco, R., & Omark, D. R. *Special education and bilingual education: Working together.* San Diego: College-Hill Press, 1984.

Placing children in special education: A strategy for equity. Washington, D.C.: National Academy of Sciences, 1982.

Sato, I. (ed.). *Balancing the scale for the disadvantaged gifted.* Los Angeles: National/State Leadership Training Institute on the Gifted and Talented, 1981.

Organization

Council for Exceptional Children, 1920 Association Drive, Reston, VA 22091. Sponsors periodic conferences on the needs of culturally diverse exceptional children. Articles on multicultural issues frequently appear in *Exceptional Children* and *Teaching Exceptional Children.* Annotated bibliographies on bilingual and multicultural exceptional children are available. The Council for Exceptional Children maintains an Office of Minority Concerns, and several caucuses of interest to special educators who work with culturally diverse students.

13

Working with Parents

A parent is the child's first teacher, the person who is always there giving prompts, encouragement, praise, and corrective feedback. The parent is responsible for helping the young preschooler learn literally hundreds of skills. In many respects, no one ever "knows" as much about a child as parents do. And nobody else holds as much vested interest in a child. These are safe enough statements—obviously true for the vast majority of parent-child relationships. Yet only recently has the special education community begun to understand the primary role of parents. Only recently have these fundamental truths been viewed as valuable guidelines for the parent-teacher relationship.

For years parents were viewed by many educators as either "troublesome" if they asked many questions (or, worse yet, if they offered suggestions about their child's education), or "uncaring" if they did not jump to attention whenever the professional determined that the parent "needed" something (typically advice from the professional). Parents, too, have often seen professionals as adversaries. But in recent years, parent involvement in special education has received a great deal of attention. Parents and teachers are developing better ways to communicate with each other and work together for the common benefit of the exceptional child. In this chapter we will examine the history of the parent-teacher relationship—why it hasn't always been so positive in the past and examples of some of the progress that has been made. In an attempt to understand a parent's perspective better, we will look at some of the ways a child's handicap can affect the many roles a parent must play. As we describe some of the techniques and programs that are being developed to improve communication with parents and to involve them in their child's education, you will see that working with parents of exceptional children is among the most important and rewarding skills the teacher can develop.

A parent is the child's first teacher.

THE PARENT-TEACHER PARTNERSHIP

Parents and teachers who work actively and effectively with one another comprise a powerful team. Heward, Dardig, and Rossett have described the benefits of developing a parent-teacher partnership.

A productive parent-professional relationship provides professionals with:

- ☐ Greater understanding of the overall needs of the child and the needs and desires of the parent.
- ☐ Data for more meaningful selection of target behaviors that are important to the child in her world outside the school.
- ☐ Access to a wider range of social and activity reinforcers provided by parents.
- ☐ Increased opportunities to reinforce appropriate behaviors in both school and home settings.
- ☐ Feedback from parents as to changes in behavior that can be used to improve programs being implemented by professionals and parents.
- ☐ The ability to comply with legislation mandating continuing parental input to the educational process.

A productive parent-professional relationship provides parents with:

- ☐ Greater understanding of the needs of their child and the objectives of the teacher.

- ☐ Information on their rights and responsibilities as parents of an exceptional child.
- ☐ Specific information about their child's school program and how they can become involved.
- ☐ Specific ways to extend the positive effects of school programming into the home.
- ☐ Increased skills in helping their child learn functional behaviors that are appropriate for the home environment.
- ☐ Access to additional important resources (current and future) for their child.

And, of most importance, a productive parent-professional relationship provides the child with:

- ☐ Greater consistency in her two most important environments.
- ☐ Increased opportunities for learning and growth.
- ☐ Access to expanded resources and services. (1979, p. 226)

These are all important reasons for establishing a strong parent-teacher relationship. But before we describe some of the ways such a partnership can be developed and maintained, we need to explain some of the reasons why parents and teachers have not always worked well together.

Barriers to Effective Parent-Teacher Interaction

Let's face it, parents and teachers do not always cooperate; they may sometimes even seem to be on two widely different "sides" doing battle over what is "best for the child." The handicapped child, unfortunately, can never win that battle. He needs the people responsible for the two places where he spends most of his life—home and school—to work together to make those environments consistent. Both home and school must be supportive of the job of learning. Some parents and teachers have made assumptions and held attitudes toward one another that have been counterproductive. Parents have complained that professionals are negative, unavailable, or patronizing. Teachers have complained that parents are uninterested, uncooperative, or hostile.

Roos (1980), a special educator who is the father of a mentally retarded child, blames much of the negative attitudes and hostility shown by parents on what he calls "professional mishandling." Many professionals hold negative stereotypes and false assumptions of what parents of handicapped children face and what they need. These attitudes have often led to poor relationships between parents and professionals.

Sonnenschein (1981) has also described some behaviors of professionals that detract from productive relationships. She examined several assumptions or approaches that, when exhibited by professionals, create roadblocks to effective partnerships:

☐ The parent as vulnerable client. Professionals who only see parents as helpless souls in need of their assistance make a grave mistake. Teachers need parents and what they have to offer as much as parents need teachers.

☐ Professional "distance." Most professionals in the human services fields develop some degree of "professional distance" as a means of not getting "too involved" with a client—supposedly to maintain objectivity and credibility. But aloofness or coldness in the name of professionalism has hindered and terminated many a parent-teacher relationship. Parents must believe the professional really cares about them.

☐ The parent as patient. Some professionals have the faulty assumption that having a handicapped child renders the parent in need of therapy. Roos writes "I had suddenly been demoted from the role of a professional to that of the 'parent as patient,' the assumption by some professionals that parents of a retarded child are emotionally maladjusted and are prime candidates for counseling, psychotherapy or tranquilizers" (1978, p. 15).

☐ The parent as responsible for the child's condition. Some parents do feel responsible for their child's disability, and with a little encouragement from a professional, can be made to feel completely guilty. A productive parent-professional relationship focuses on remediation of problems, not on a place to lay blame.

☐ The parent as less intelligent. Too often information and suggestions provided by parents are given little recognition. Parents are considered too biased, too involved, or not skilled enough to make useful observations. Some professionals do concede that parents have access to needed information, but that parents are not able, or should not, make any decisions based on what they know. One study of school personnel found that the majority of members of IEP planning teams felt that parents are expected to provide information to the planning team, but they are not expected to participate actively in making decisions about their child's program (Yoshida, Fenton, Kaufman, & Maxwell, 1978).

☐ The parent as adversary. Some teachers expect the worst whenever they interact with parents. While that attitude can be partially explained by the fact that some teachers have been "burned" by unreasonable parents, it is at best a negative influence on new relationships.

☐ Tendency to label parents. Professionals often seem eager to "label" parents, just as they often do with children. If parents disagree with a diagnosis or seek another opinion, they are "denying"; if they refuse a suggested treatment, they are labeled "resistant"; and if parents insist that something is wrong with their child despite test "evidence" to the contrary, they are called "anxious." The professional who believes that a parent's perception may be the correct one is rare; yet parents often *do* know best.

Indeed, to the extent that teachers and other special educators believe and behave in these ways, it is understandable that parents may feel intimidated, confused, or hostile. But the factors working against positive parent-teacher relationships cannot all be attributed to professional mishandling. Some parents are, in fact, difficult to work with or unreasonable.

> The attitudes and behaviors of the parents have also contributed to negative interactions. There is no easy way to tell a mother and father that their child is substantially handicapped. Some parents want to hear the hard truth; others want to be eased into it. Professionals may carefully choose their words with the greatest sensitivity, yet still offend the parents. Sometimes parents are unforgiving and do not realize the difficult position of the professional. They may vent their anger at the professional and discuss the professional's "gross lack of sensitivity" with family and friends. Frequently, parents of handicapped children have been highly critical of the professionals with whom they and their children have worked. Professionals are sometimes totally or socially excluded from community interest groups on the grounds that it is impossible for them to understand parents' feelings and needs. Parents sometimes form tight cliques with the primary goal of ostracizing and criticizing professionals. There are situations in which parents have fought long and hard for services for their handicapped child; after the services are found and the child is receiving an appropriate education, the parents continue their intensive advocacy to the point that minor issues become the basis for major confrontation. This type of posture is likely to lead to unproductive interactions among parents and professionals. (Turnbull, 1983, p. 19)

The purpose of examining some of these "causes" of parent-teacher friction is not to place blame, but rather to understand better those factors that we can change and improve. Professionals who recognize that some of their own behaviors may decrease the potential of productive relationships with parents are in a better position to change their actions and encourage the benefits such a relationship can provide. One of the surest ways to do that is to avoid sweeping generalizations about parents of exceptional children and treat them with respect as individuals. After all, isn't this how teachers wish to be treated?

Breaking Down Barriers to Effective Parent-Teacher Interaction

Negative interactions between parents and teachers, as we have seen, can be related to a lack of awareness and understanding by both groups to the others' roles and responsibilities. During the last decade, a number of forces have come together to focus national attention on the importance of a parent-teacher partnership based on mutual respect and participation in decision making (Turnbull, 1983). While many things have contributed to increased involvement of parents in the education of their exceptional children, we can view those factors as actions on the part of three groups of people—parents, educators, and legislators.

Parents: Advocates for Change

The dictionary defines an **advocate** as someone who speaks for or pleads the case of another. Parents of exceptional children have played the role of advocates for their children for many years, but in recent history they have done so with impressive effectiveness (Cain, 1976). The first parent group organized for handicapped children was the National Society for Crippled Children, which began in 1921. The National Association for Retarded Children, organized in 1950, and the United Cerebral Palsy Association, organized in 1948, are two national parent organizations that have been largely responsible for making the public aware of their children's needs. The Association for Children with Learning Disabilities (ACLD) is another group organized by and consisting mostly of parents that has been instrumental in bringing about educational reform. As we saw in chapters 1 and 2, parents were instrumental in bringing about litigation and legislation establishing the rights of handicapped children to education.

In 1980, this organization's name was changed to the Association for Retarded Citizens.

More than any other group of people, parents themselves have been responsible for their increased involvement in special education. They have formed effective organizations that have been the impetus for much educational reform. As individuals, they are learning more about the educational needs of their children and are seeing more and more the potential benefits of an effective parent-teacher partnership.

Educators: Striving for Greater Impact

Educators have recognized the necessity of expanding the traditional role of the classroom teacher in order to meet the special needs of handicapped children. This expanded role demands that we view teaching as more than delivering the three R's. Special educators now realize that daily living, social, vocational, and leisure skills are critical to the handicapped student's successful functioning. We now attach a high priority to developing and maintaining the functional skills that will enable the handicapped child or adult to be successful in school, home, work, and community settings.

Because the implementation of this "new priority" has implications and applications outside the classroom, teachers have begun to look outside the school for assistance and support. Parents are a natural and necessary resource for expanding educational services to the home and community. At the very least, teachers benefit from information provided by parents on their child's success with specific skills outside of the classroom.

See, for example, Bronfenbrenner (1974), Cooper and Edge (1978), Ryback and Staats (1970), Schumaker, Hovell, and Sherman (1977), Shearer and Shearer (1977), and Trovato and Bucher (1980).

But parents have proven to be much more than just reporters of behavior change. They can tell us what skills the child needs to learn and, just as important, which ones their child has already acquired. Parents can work with teachers to provide needed extra practice of skills at home, and even to teach their children new skills. An impressive body of research has developed in recent years that shows conclusively that parents can play (and sometimes are needed to play) an important role in the education of their handicapped child.

INTERVENTION

In short, educators are giving up the old notions that parents should not be too involved in their child's education program or that they should not try to teach their children for fear of "doing something wrong." Teachers are realizing that parents are a powerful and necessary ally (Kroth, 1978). Only through an effective parent-teacher partnership can everyone's goals—teacher, parent, and child—be fulfilled.

Legislators: Mandates for Involvement

As we saw in previous chapters, P.L. 94–142 and corresponding state laws mandate parent involvement in the education of handicapped children. The federal law provides statutory guidelines for parent-professional interaction in terms of the provision of a free, appropriate education, referral, testing, placement, and program planning. In addition, the law provides due process procedures if parents feel their child's needs are not being met. While some educators view P.L. 94–142 as being the "parents' law" and are threatened by the new role it specifies for parents, most view it as representing sound educational practice and welcome the increased parent involvement it encourages (Kroth, 1978; Turnbull & Turnbull, 1978). As Klein and Schleiter observe, "The challenge of the 1980s for both parents and professionals will be to find ways to carry out the legislative mandates for collaborative efforts to help children" (1980, p. 3).

In sum, we can attribute special educators' increased interest in working effectively with parents of handicapped children to three related factors:

1. Many parents want to be involved,
2. Educators are recognizing that their effectiveness as teachers increases with parental assistance, and
3. The law requires it.

PARENTING THE EXCEPTIONAL CHILD

Special educators usually interact with parents of exceptional children for two primary reasons: (1) to collect information and suggestions that can help the teacher do a better job in the classroom, and (2) to provide information and assistance to parents for working with their children outside the classroom. The teacher who wants to fill the roles of both seeker and provider of assistance must be able to communicate effectively with parents. Effective communication requires an understanding and respect for the responsibilities and challenges faced by parents of exceptional children.

Parental Reactions to a Handicapped Child

A great deal has been written about parents' reactions to the birth of a handicapped child or to the discovery that their child has a learning problem or physical disability. Parents are often said to pass through "stages of adjustment" that might include shock, denial, guilt, depression, anger, defensiveness, ambivalence, shame, rejection of the child, chronic sorrow, overprotectiveness, and so on, until finally, in the last stage, parents "accept" their disabled child.

For discussion of the emotional reactions and adjustment processes that parents might experience, see Barsch (1968), Chinn, Winn, and Walters (1978), Kroth (1975), and Wolfensberger and Kurtz (1969).

There is no question that the birth of a handicapped child or the discovery that a child has a disability is an intense and traumatic event. Parents can react in widely different ways, and most do go through an adjustment process trying to work their way through. But we see two problems with promoting the idea of "stages of adjustment." First, it is easy to assume that *all* parents must pass through a similar sequence of stages and that *time* is the most important variable in adjustment. In fact, parents react to the arrival of a handicapped child in many different ways (Turnbull & Turnbull, 1978). For some parents, years may pass and they are still are not "comfortable" with their child; others report that having a handicapped child has actually strengthened their life or marriage (Schell, 1981; Weiss & Weiss, 1976). The sequence and time needed for adjustment is different for every parent. One common thread is that almost all parents can be helped during their adjustment by sensitive and supporting friends and professionals (Schlesinger & Meadow, 1976; Turnbull, 1983).

Second, the stages parents are said to pass through have a distinct psychiatric flavor; professionals may mistakenly assume parents are maladjusted. Some educators seem to assume that all parents of handicapped children need counseling. However, as Farber (1975) has pointed out, it is a mistake to think of parents of handicapped children as psychological curiosities; they are more like parents of normal children than they are different. Parenting any child is a tremendous challenge that produces "emotional responses" and requires "adjustment." Parents of handicapped children, like parents of nonhandicapped children, must sometimes operate under financial, physical, emotional, and marital stress. In addition, parents of handicapped children must deal with the additional task of securing and relating to the special services (that until recently were denied them) needed by their child (Farber, 1975).

Blackstone, himself the parent of a handicapped child, gives some examples of how parents of exceptional children are often viewed and treated differently from other parents:

The parent of the normal child skips monthly PTA meetings and his behavior is considered normal. The parent of the exceptional child skips monthly meetings, and he is said to be uncaring and hard to reach.

A couple with normal children divorce. They are said to be incompatible. The couple with an exceptional child divorce, and it is said that the child ruined the marriage.

The parents of a normal child are told that because their child is having reading difficulties, it would be "nice" if they could work with her at home. The parents of the exceptional child are told that if they do not work with their child, she will not learn! (1981, pp. 29–30)

The Many Roles of the Exceptional Parent

Parenthood is an awesome responsibility. And parents of handicapped children face even more responsibilities. Educators who are not parents of a handicapped child can never know the 24-hour reality of what it is like to be an exceptional parent. But they should nonetheless try to be aware of the varied and demanding roles such parents must fulfill. Heward, Dardig, and Rossett (1979) have described seven major challenges to parents of exceptional children.

1. Teaching. While all parents are their child's first teachers, most nonhandicapped children acquire a great many skills without their parents trying to teach them. This is often not true with handicapped children, who, unless their parents use systematic teaching strategies, do not learn many important skills as early or as easily as they could (Karnes, Teska, Hodgins, & Badger, 1970; Tjossem, 1976). In addition to systematic teaching techniques, some parents of exceptional children must learn to use, or teach their child to use, special equipment such as hearing aids, braces, wheelchairs, and adapted eating utensils.

2. Counseling. All parents are counselors in the sense that they deal with the changing emotions, feelings, and attitudes of their children as they develop. But in addition to all of the normal joys and pains of helping a child grow up, parents of a handicapped child must deal with the feelings their child has as a result of his or her particular disability. "Will I still be deaf when I grow up?" "I'm not playing outside any more. They always tease me." "Why can't

Parenting any child is a tremendous responsibility, but the parent of an exceptional child faces additional challenges.

RESPITE CARE: SUPPORT FOR FAMILIES

"We were really getting worn down. For the first 4 years of Ben's life we averaged 4 hours of sleep a night. We were wearing ourselves out; I have no doubt we would have completely fallen apart," said Ben's mother, Rebecca Arnett. Ben was born with a neurological condition that produces frequent seizures and extreme hyperactivity. "My husband Roger used his vacations for sleeping in. The respite program came along just in time for us.

"It was hard at first. There's an overwhelming guilt that you shouldn't leave your child. We didn't feel like anyone else could understand Ben's problems. But we had to get away. Our church had given us some money with orders to take a vacation. It was the first time Roger and I and our 12-year-old daughter Stacy had really been together since Ben was born. I was upset at first, calling twice a day to see if everthing was all right. But it was wonderful, for everybody.

"Cleo Baker, the respite care worker who stayed with Ben that first time and many times since, is something else. She takes him to McDonald's, shopping, all over. When Ben

Cleo and Ben

knows she's coming, he runs for his jacket. He loves her. We've had five or six different respite workers stay with Ben during the year we've used the program and he likes them all.

"Once parents get over that initial period of letting go, they realize that it's okay to have a life of your own apart from your handicapped child. For us it was a real life-saver."

Chris Trussell, director of the respite care program for Franklin County, Ohio, said, "Respite gives families a chance for a more natural life-style. Some of the families we serve have gone years without a real break of any kind. Once they try our program and find that a responsible, trained adult can care for their child, it's like a new lease on life.

"At present we have 11 workers serving about 100 families. Each worker completes a 40-hour training program covering feeding techniques, first aid, use of adaptive equipment, leisure-time activities, and so on. I conduct an initial home visit to explain the program and determine the family's special needs. Our workers can be scheduled from 4 hours to up to 2 weeks of continuous care. Our respite care is conducted in the family's home. A sliding fee scale determines the hourly cost according to income and family size."

Respite care can benefit the handicapped family member as well. Susan Clark told of the time that she stayed with Stephanie, a 25-year-old mentally retarded woman, so her mother, who had not had a vacation since her daughter's birth, could go to Florida. "Stephanie and I went everywhere, to the movies, the county fair, out to eat. She did things she had never done in her life. That week was a vacation for her, too."

Another parent, Jean Williams, described the program this way. "Our son Tom's autism has meant a lot of restrictions in our family life for the past 25 years, bringing with it many problems and much resentment. At last we have been given a no-strings-attached, low-cost way to loosen some of those restrictions. Funny thing is, our Tom is such a nice guy—it's sure good to be able to get far enough away every so often to be able to see that."

I go swimming like the other kids?" Parents play an important role in determining how the handicapped child comes to feel about himself. They can help develop an active, outgoing child who confidently tries many new things or a withdrawn child with negative attitudes toward himself and others.

3. Managing behavior. While all children act out from time to time, the range and severity of maladaptive behaviors of some handicapped children demand more systematic, specialized treatment. Some parents must learn to be "behavior therapists" in order to have a good relationship with their handicapped child (Allen, 1978; Cooper & Edge, 1978).

4. Parenting nonhandicapped siblings. The presence of a handicapped child affects all members of the family (Beckman-Bell, 1981; Turnbull & Turnbull, 1978). The brothers and sisters of a handicapped child often have concerns related to their sibling's disability: what caused the handicap, will it affect them, reactions of their friends, a feeling of being "left out" or of being required to do too much for the handicapped child (Cansler, Martin, & Valand, 1975).

For more about the siblings of handicapped children, see pages 448–449.

5. Maintaining the parent-to-parent relationship. Having a handicapped child often puts certain stresses on the relationship between husband and wife (Schell, 1981). Those stresses can range from arguing over whose "fault" the child's disability is, to disagreeing over what expectations should be made on the child's behavior, to spending so much time, money, and energy on the handicapped child that little is left for one another.

6. Educating significant others. Grandparents, aunts and uncles, neighbors, even the school bus driver can all have an important effect on the handicapped child's development. While the parents of a nonhandicapped child can reasonably expect certain kinds of treatment of their child by significant others, parents of handicapped children know they cannot simply rely on appropriate interactions. Parents of a handicapped child must try to make sure that, as much as possible, other people interact with their child in a way that facilitates the acquisition and maintenance of adaptive behaviors. Schulz (1978) described her response to people who stare at her Down syndrome son. She looks the person squarely in the eye and says, "You seem interested in my son. Would you like to meet him?" This usually ends the staring and often creates an opportunity to provide information or make a friend.

7. Relating to the school and community. As we have seen, P.L. 94–142 describes certain rights (and implies certain responsibilities) of parents of handicapped children in regard to their child's education. While some degree of involvement in the educational process is desirable for all parents, it is a must for the exceptional parent. As a result, parents need to acquire special knowledge (e.g., "What is a criterion-referenced test?") and learn special skills (participating effectively in an IEP planning meeting). Parents of handicapped children often have other concerns over and above those expressed by most parents. For example, while all parents might be concerned about

INTERVENTION

having adequate playgrounds, exceptional parents may also have to work to make those playgrounds accessible to children who use wheelchairs.

We could correctly say that these seven areas comprise a list of things all parents must deal with. But we think looking at these "requirements of parenting" is useful for at least two reasons. First, it shows that exceptional parents are, in fact, more like other parents than they are different from them. Second, it highlights critical aspects of the job of parenting that can be significantly affected by having a handicapped child. This analysis starts us on our way to understanding the responsibilities faced by parents of handicapped children and begins to pinpoint specific areas where teachers and other professionals might provide useful services to parents.

PARENT-TEACHER COMMUNICATION

Regular two-way communication with parents is the foundation of an effective parent-teacher partnership (Kroth, 1975). Without open, honest communication between teacher and parent, many of the positive outcomes listed earlier cannot be achieved. Let's briefly examine the three most-used methods of communication between parents and teachers—conferences, written messages, and the telephone.

Parent-Teacher Conferences

Although parent-teacher conferences are as common to schools as recess and homework and have been with us for just about as long, conferences are not

A parent-teacher conference is a good time to review a child's specific accomplishments.

always the effective vehicle for parent-teacher communication that they should be. Too often, parent conferences turn out to be stiff, formal affairs, with teachers anxious and parents wondering what bad news they'll hear this time. Fortunately, given the increased recognition of the critical role parents play in their child's education and the increased parent participation in the schools as a result of IEP planning meetings, more and more emphasis is being placed on the importance of parent-teacher communication skills. Parents and teachers are learning to talk with one another in more productive ways.

In a face-to-face meeting, parents and teachers can exchange information and coordinate their efforts to assist the exceptional child at both home and school. Conferences should not just be limited to the beginning and end of the school year, but regularly scheduled to maintain a meaningful parent-teacher partnership. More and more educators are viewing the parent-teacher conference as a method for planning and evaluating joint parent-teacher-initiated teaching programs (Heward et al., 1979; Kroth & Simpson, 1977).

Preparation is the key to effective parent-teacher conferences. Stephens, Blackhurst, and Magliocca (1982) recommend establishing specific objectives for the conference, reviewing the student's cumulative progress, preparing some examples of the student's work along with a graph or chart showing specific performance, and preparing an agenda for the meeting. Figure 13.1 shows an outline that can be used to prepare a parent-teacher conference agenda.

Conducting the Conference

Bennett and Hensen (1977) suggest that teachers should hold parent-teacher conferences in their classroom because (1) the teacher feels comfortable in familiar surroundings, (2) the teacher has ready access to student files and instructional materials, (3) the classroom itself serves as a reminder to the teacher of things the child has done, and (4) the classroom, with its desk, chairs, and teaching materials, reminds the teacher and parents that the purpose of the conference is their mutual concern for improving the child's education. However, when conducting parent conferences in their classrooms, teachers should not make the mistakes of hiding behind their desks, creating a "barrier" between themselves and the parents, or of seating parents in undersized students' chairs.

Stephens and Wolf (1980) recommend a four-step sequence for parent-teacher conferences.

1. Rapport building. Establishing a feeling of mutual trust and the belief that the teacher really cares about the student is important to a good parent-teacher conference. Before getting into the "meat" of the conference, a few minutes should be devoted to relevant small talk. Hochman (1979) suggests that beginning with something positive about the child or family ("Teddy's getting along well with his classmates;" "Jenny tells me you're moving into a new house") is much better than superficial openings like "Nice weather we're having, isn't it?"

Conference Outline

Date_____   Time _____

Student's Name _____

Parent's Name(s) _____

Teacher's Name _____

Other Staff Present _____

Objectives for Conference:

Student's Strengths:

Area(s) Where Improvement Is Needed:

Questions to Ask Parents:

Parent's Responses/Comments:

Examples of Student's Work/Interactions:

Current Programs and Strategies Used by Teacher:

Suggestions for Parents:

Suggestions from Parents:

Follow-up Activities:
  Parents:

  Teacher:

Date Called for Follow-up and Outcome:

FIGURE 13.1

Parent-teacher conference outline.

Source: W. L. Heward, J. C. Dardig, and A. Rossett, *Working with parents of handicapped children.* Columbus, Ohio: Charles E. Merrill Publishing Company, 1979, p. 233. Used with permission.

2. Obtaining information. Parents can provide teachers with important information for improving instruction. Begin by asking open-ended questions that cannot be answered with a simple "yes" or "no." For example, "Which activities in school has Felix mentioned lately?" is better than "Has Felix told you what we are now doing in school?" The first question encourages the parent to provide more information—the teacher tries to build conversation, not preside over a question-and-answer session.

3. Providing information. Give parents concrete information about their child in jargon-free language. Show examples of schoolwork and data on student performance—what has been learned and what needs to be learned next. When the student's progress has not been as great as hoped for, use specific information to look together for ways to improve it.

4. Summarizing and follow-up activities. End the conference with a summary of what was said. Review any strategies agreed upon during the conference, and indicate the follow-up activities either party will do to help carry out those strategies. Some teachers use carbon paper and make a duplicate copy of their notes during the conference so the parents will also have a record of what was said or agreed upon.

Written Messages

While much can be accomplished in a parent-teacher conference, the amount of time required means that conferences should not be the sole means of maintaining parent-teacher communication. Some teachers use frequent written messages to communicate with parents. Although the report card that most schools send parents every grading period is a written message, its infrequency and standard format limit its usefulness as a means of communication.

Hochman (1979) regularly sends "happy grams" home with her elementary resource room students. These notes specify positive things accomplished by students, giving parents an opportunity to praise their children at home and stay abreast with activities in the classroom.

A two-way parent-teacher communication system can be built around a reporting form carried between home and school by the child. The form should be simple to use and read, with space to circle, check, or write short notes. Such an interactive reporting system can be used on either a daily or weekly basis, depending on the behaviors involved. Several studies have shown that these two-way communication programs can improve both school and home performance (Dickerson, Spellman, Larsen, & Tyler, 1973; Imber, Imber, & Rothstein, 1979).

Schumaker, Hovell, and Sherman (1977) used a daily report card system with three junior high school boys with serious academic and behavior problems. Different teachers marked a card for each boy in each of six different classes. Parents provided privileges (e.g., snacks, television time, staying up an extra half-hour before bed) based on the teachers' ratings of their child's school performance. All three students improved in following classroom rules and academic performance.

For more detailed discussion of strategies for conducting parent-teacher conferences, see Kroth (1975), Kroth and Simpson (1977), and Stephens and Wolf (1980). Wolf and Stephens (1982) have written a booklet for parents on how to participate more effectively in conferences with teachers.

See Figure 13.2.

See Figure 13.3.

FIGURE 13.2
A "happy gram."

Janey had a grrrreat day!

R. Hochman

A somewhat similar system is the home-school contract (Heward & Dardig, 1978a). A home-school contract is a **behavioral contract** that specifies parent-delivered rewards contingent upon completion of classroom tasks (for example, for each page of the reading workbook completed, the student might earn a quarter to be used to buy a model airplane). Home-school contracts use parent-controlled rewards, build in parent recognition and praise of the child's accomplishments, and involve parents and teacher together in a positive program to support the child's learning.

The class newsletter is another method some teachers use to increase parent-teacher communication. While putting together a class newsletter requires a lot of work, in many cases it is worth the effort. Most teachers have access to a mimeo machine, and a one- to three-page monthly newsletter can give parents who don't attend meetings or open houses information that is too long or detailed to give over the telephone. A newsletter is also an excellent way to recognize those parents who participate in various activities. By making the newsletter a class project, the teacher can include student-written stories and news items and create an enjoyable learning activity for the entire class.

The Telephone

A brief, pleasant telephone conversation is one of the best ways to maintain communication with parents. Used regularly, telephone calls focusing on positive

NAME: _____

DATE: _____

TEACHER: _____

Did the student . . .

	YES	NO	
Come on time?			⎫
Bring supplies?			
Stay in seat?			
Not talk inappropriately?			
Follow directions?			
Raise his hand?			Rules Section
Not physically disturb others?			
Clean up?			
Pay attention?			
Speak courteously?			⎭
Were you pleased with his performance today?			Teacher Satisfaction Section
Points on today's classwork			Classwork Section
Grade on test assignment			Grades Section
Teacher's initials			

FIGURE 13.3

Daily report card.

Source: J. B. Schumaker, M. F. Hovell, and J. A. Sherman, "An analysis of daily report cards and parent-managed privileges in the improvement of adolescents' classroom performance," *Journal of Applied Behavior Analysis*, 1977, *10*, p. 452. Copyright 1977 by the Society for the Experimental Analysis of Behavior, Inc. Used with permission.

accomplishments of children let parents and teacher share in the child's success and recognize each other's contributions.

Heron and Axelrod (1976) found that simply telephoning parents and telling them how their children did on a daily word-recognition test resulted in increased parent tutoring of the daily word list and improved scores. Teachers should set aside time on a regular basis so that each child's parent receives a call once every 2 or 3 weeks. Of course, teachers need to find out what times are convenient for parents. Keeping a log of the calls helps maintain the schedule and reminds the teacher of any necessary follow-up.

Another way teachers can use the telephone is to organize a class "telephone tree." With this system, the teacher only calls two or three parents, each of whom calls two or three more, and so on. Telephone trees can be an efficient way to get information to all of the parents in a class. A telephone tree gives parents a way to get actively involved and perhaps to get to know some of the parents of their child's classmates.

Heward and Chapman (1981) used daily recorded telephone messages as a way to increase parent-teacher communication. The teacher of a primary learning disabilities class recorded brief messages on an automatic telephone answering machine. Parents could call 5 nights a week from 5:00 P.M. until 7:00 A.M. the next morning and hear a recorded message like this one:

> Good evening. The children worked very hard today. We are discussing transportation. They enjoyed talking about the airport and all the different kinds of airplanes. The spelling words for tomorrow are: train, t-r-a-i-n; plane, p-l-a-n-e; truck, t-r-u-c-k; automobile, a-u-t-o-m-o-b-i-l-e; and ship, s-h-i-p. Thank you for calling. (Heward & Chapman, 1981, p. 13)

Figure 13.4 shows the number of telephone calls the teacher received from parents of the six children in the class each week for the entire school year. The teacher received a total of only five calls for the 32 weeks (.16 calls per week) of the study when the recorded messages were not available, compared to 112 calls (18.7 per week) during the 6 weeks the message system was in operation. Scores on daily five-word spelling tests improved for all six students when the recorded messages were available, even though during the nonmessage portions of the study the next day's spelling list was sent home with the children each day and parents had been requested to help their children with the words.

There are many ways in which recorded telephone messages can be used to improve parent-teacher communication. The system has been used to provide school-wide and classroom-by-classroom information, good news (such as "Citizen of the Month"), and suggestions for working with children at home (Weiss, Cooke, Grossman, Ryno-Vrabel, Heron, & Heward, 1983). Parent callers can also leave messages for the teacher (for example, a question or a report on how a home-based instructional program is going), enabling the system to be used for two-way communication.

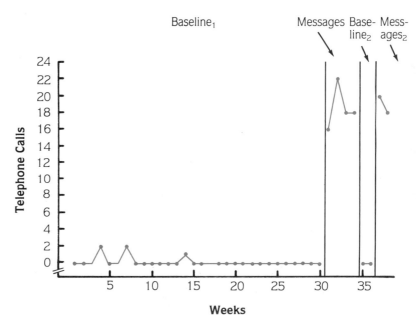

FIGURE 13.4
Graph of telephone calls with and without recorded message.

Source: W. L. Heward and J. E. Chapman, "Improving parent-teacher communication through recorded telephone messages: Systematic replication in a special education classroom," *Journal of Special Education Technology*, 1981, *4*, p. 14.

PARENT INVOLVEMENT

Parents and the Individualized Education Program

As we discussed in chapter 2, an Individualized Education Program (IEP) must be developed for every handicapped child. This is a requirement of P.L. 94–142 to ensure that each handicapped child receives educational services suited to his or her needs. Parents are required to be members of the IEP planning team, though they may waive their right to participate by signing a document stating that they do not wish to.

> The IEP meeting serves as a communication vehicle between parents and school personnel, and enables them as equal participants, to jointly decide what the child's needs are, what services will be provided to meet those needs, and what the anticipated outcomes will be. (*Federal Register*, 1981, p. 5462)

Clearly, the intention is that parents will play an active decision-making role. According to Turnbull and Turnbull, the belief that parents should share the rights and responsibilities of decision making in regard to their child's educational program is based on two assumptions, which may not be valid in all cases.

1. Parents want to be involved in education decision making and, when given the opportunity, will take advantage of it; and
2. Attending the meeting to plan their child's IEP will enable parents to be decision makers. (1982, p. 116)

However, Turnbull and Turnbull (1982) point out that surveys of what parents say they want from special educators and observations of IEP meetings do not necessarily support these assumptions. In interviews conducted with 32 mothers of preschool handicapped children, Winton and Turnbull (1981) found that, when asked to rank the characteristics of an "ideal" preschool, the parents identified parent involvement as the *least* important; the factor of most import to the mothers was competent, expert teachers. Lusthaus, Lusthaus, and Gibbs (1981) compiled questionnaire results from 98 parents of students enrolled in self-contained classrooms and resource rooms in eight elementary schools in a middle-class, suburban school district. More than half of the parents said they wanted to participate in IEP planning conferences at the level of providing information. The majority were content to let professionals make most decisions. However, when decisions were to be made about what kinds of records should be kept on their child, what medical services were to be provided, or whether their child would be transferred to another school, more parents than not wanted to have control over the decisions. Polifka (1981) concluded from a parent survey that parents do want to play an active role in IEP planning.

The research supports a belief we stated earlier. We should not rely on assumptions based on generalizations we believe to be true for *all* parents of handicapped children. We must also view this preliminary research with the understanding that most parents have for years not been asked (and in some instances have not been wanted) to participate in their child's education; then almost overnight, they are expected, or even virtually required, to do so. Thus it is not surprising that parents have a variety of feelings about how much their participation is really wanted and how much they really can or should contribute.

Studies on what actually happens during IEP meetings are more conclusive. Attendance by parents (mostly mothers) is quite high at IEP conferences, but the level of parental participation is more often passive than active (Goldstein, Strickland, Turnbull & Curry, 1980; Scanlon, Arick, & Phelps, 1981). The National Committee for Citizens in Education (1979) surveyed almost 2,300 parents from all over the United States. Slightly more than half (52%) of the parents indicated that their child's IEP had been completely written *before* the meeting. Goldstein et al. (1980) observed IEP meetings for elementary mildly handicapped students and found similar results: The average meeting lasted only 36 minutes and consisted mainly of the special education teacher explaining an already written IEP to the parent.

While these results appear discouraging, they are not necessarily so. Parents are at least being made aware of what special services their child is receiving and why, and passivity *may* mean satisfaction with the IEP (Polifka, 1981). Nevertheless, many parents do take advantage of the IEP meeting to offer significant input into their children's education programs.

> In one recent IEP conference, the mother of a moderately retarded child questioned why her son was being taught to label prehistoric animals verbally. The parent asked the teachers what type of job they expected the child to have as an adult. The teachers replied that they had never really considered job opportunities for the child, since he was only 10. To the teachers, 10 seemed young; to the parents, 10 meant that almost half of his formal education was completed. As the meeting progressed, it was clear that the parents were specifying objectives related to independence as an adult (telling time, reading survival words, sex education) that were different from the more traditional curriculum proposed by the teachers. Through sharing evaluation data, goals for the child, and special problems, all parties involved created a curriculum that met everyone's approval. (Turnbull, 1983, p. 22)

Parents and professionals are working together to increase the level of parent participation in IEP team meetings. The decision-making process developed by Dardig and Heward (1981b) is one technique for recognizing each team member's input. Turnbull, Strickland, and Brantley (1982) describe group training sessions in which parents learn what goes into an IEP and how to participate more actively in its development.

Goldstein and Turnbull (1982) investigated two strategies to increase parent participation in IEP meetings. One innovative strategy had school counselors attend the IEP conference with the parent and serve as an advocate by introducing the parent, clarifying jargon, directing questions to parents, verbally praising parents for contributing, and summarizing the decisions made at the meeting. The counselors received no formal training; they were simply given a sheet of instructions outlining their five functions. More contributions were made by parents who were accompanied by a counselor-advocate. The second strategy consisted of sending parents a list of eight questions to consider before the IEP meeting—for example, "What skills would you most like your child to learn?" "Is your child having problems at home that we could help with at school?" "What things does your child do well?" Although the advance questions did not lead to increases in parent contributions during the observed IEP meetings, they may have encouraged more fathers to attend the conference, along with the mothers.

Parents as Teachers

All parents are responsible for their children learning many skills. But most of the things children learn from their parents are not the result of parents trying to teach by using systematic procedures as a trained teacher might. Instead, children acquire many important skills as a "natural" result of the everyday

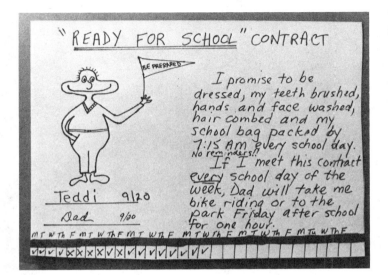

Teaching social skills: a behavioral contract between father and son.

interactions between parent and child. For some handicapped children, however, the casual routines of everyday home life may not provide enough practice and feedback to teach them important skills. Many parents have responded by systematically teaching their handicapped children needed self-help and daily living skills or by providing home tutoring sessions to supplement classroom academic instruction.

Educators do not all agree on the role parents of handicapped children should play when it comes to teaching. Barsch (1969) gives these reasons for *not* using parents to teach academic skills:

1. Parents don't have the necessary teaching skills.
2. Home tutoring sessions often end in frustration and tension for both parent and child.
3. Most parents and children would rather have academics restricted to the school day.
4. Most teachers do not have the time needed to guide and support the parents' efforts.
5. There is little "rest" for the child who is taught both at school and home.
6. Parents differ greatly in their ability as teachers.
7. Parents may feel guilty if they do not follow through regularly with home tutoring sessions.

Kronick (1969) also feels that parents should not assume the role of academic tutors because they may be so anxious for the child to succeed that both parent and child become frustrated. Referring to learning disabled children, Lerner (1976) feels that, because academic learning presents major difficulties for the child, parent tutoring puts the child in the position of constantly failing

A SISTER'S LAMENT

I moved out of my mother's apartment in August of 1980, at nearly 26 years of age. It became necessary for me to live a more separate and independent existence. Now somewhat removed from the situation, my perspectives have altered.

There never was a question of institutionalizing Douglas. From the time we first learned that he was *autistic*, we resolved to put up a good fight for him . . . not just for his sake, but for ours as well. Doug was clearly an integral part of our family . . . and nothing would change that. We hoped he would respond to a loving environment . . . and he did! Doug grew from a silent little boy into the man of 19 he is today. Handsome and taller than 6 feet, he has a distinct personality and a sense of humor. He has particular likes and dislikes. Similar to the rest of us, there are traits in his nature that are not always pleasant. He can be stubborn and when crossed, highly argumentative. And—he remains autistic, for the disability does not melt away with each passing year.

The shaping of Douglas has been well worth the battle. He has made phenomenal strides in an excellent public school "special education program." However, if the truth be told, a great deal of his progress has been highly attributable to us . . . his family. The process has been an arduous and unrelenting struggle at great emotional expense. The older Doug gets . . . the harder the fight.

As brother and sister we were always close. The public has a distorted view of the autistic child, one of an aloof and cold being. This image may apply to some of the children, but not to all and certainly not to Douglas. My brother was warm, affectionate and quick to respond to my outward displays of love. He still has an uncanny ability to read my moods, making his own jokes when I am in need of a chuckle or a hug when the time is ripe.

We went everywhere together . . . to movies, restaurants, the park. We took countless walks through the city streets, shopped in supermarkets and made joint efforts to clean up at home. We watched an endless series of Saturday morning cartoons together, long after I had outgrown them. We grew together in our different ways. We spent *too* much time together; I think that was half the problem.

I am grateful for the 7 years between us in age. Had I been younger, I do not know whether or not I could have coped with my mysterious brother. I do not know whether I would have accepted gracefully the continual sacrifices made to keep Doug home. I am not sure that I could have handled the immense responsibility that I grew so accustomed to.

There was no relief from Doug. Day in and day out, his needs had to be tended to regardless of our wants and desires. He always came first. Growing up in a household where only my mother and myself were present, the physical responsibility for Douglas was on our shoulders. Much of that burden was mine. Lessening of that responsibility was rare and came in the form of Doug spending a good part of his weekends with my father, and in the summertime when he went to sleep-away camp.

Because Douglas' presence dominated everthing, there was no real time for myself. Under these conditions, childhood takes on an uneasy dimension. A sibling is denied the fundamental right of being a child. An opportunity to have friends over does not often materialize because visits were dependent on my brother's moods and behavior. Going out was governed by my mother's need for my assistance in any way. My mother nicknamed me "the other mother" as I took my responsibility with seriousness and maturity in excess of my young years. Unfortunately, the pattern became a way of life.

In addition to the obvious task of physical care, something must be said about the mental effects on us. Throughout my youth, I was cognizant of the fact that Doug's condition was permanent. He would always be vulnerable and need protection, and he was going to live a full life span as a severely handicapped person. I cannot underestimate the impact of that knowledge, especially to a mother. My mother's frequent melancholy was warranted. Frustrated by his condition in the early days, she feared for his future. What compounded the dilemma was that we were very much alone. Some families have assorted relatives to provide respite . . . to take them out for car rides, spend holidays with, or provide emotional support when the going gets rough. Our family is small. My parents are divorced and although my father was and is emotionally and financially supportive as he could possibly be, he was not present during moments of household stress and daily crises. Who did we have? Just each other. Still, that is something. Those single parents without benefit of other children to offer help have it even tougher.

It is inevitable that one day I will lose my parents. I will inherit whatever constitutes their estates, be it money or debts, but their most important legacy will be in the form of my autistic brother. As his future guardian, I will acquire and accept the full responsibility for Douglas. As his only sister, I feel that I have already absorbed too much of this burden. I am hoping that long before my parents' demise, Doug's future will be guaranteed. The only alternative to my becoming his perpetual "other mother" is for him to be settled in a group home offering suitable living conditions.

Douglas is not the boy he was 10 years ago. He has gained many skills over the years, all of which make him a superb candidate for a group home. He is totally competent in areas of self care. One need never remind him to shower, shampoo, or shave. Actually he is rather vain. When his hair gets to an unruly stage, he will request a trip to the "hair stylist." Doug is helpful in the house as he polishes furniture, makes beds, vacuums, sets the table and cleans the dishes. He also is proficient at doing laundry.

We have not fought this hard for Douglas to be thwarted by a termination of programs. Personally, I have not given so much of myself and my life to Doug only to see his existence end in despair. Nothing can give me back the years of turbulence and prior sublimation that came out of our circumstances. It was all done for Douglas . . . and I will not see my own effort or that of my family wasted. My brother *will* have an option.

Without viable alternatives, many of us will have no choice but to remain the ever constant "keepers" . . . denied the opportunity for an independent life.

Gerri Zatlow is director of Siblings for Significant Change (823 United Nations Plaza, New York, N.Y. 10017), a national organization of people with handicapped brothers and sisters.

in front of the most important adults in his or her life. In her view, the pressures and tensions created by this academic failure will interfere with the overall parent-child relationship.

The other perspective—that parents *can* effectively serve as teachers for their children—is supported by numerous reports of research studies and parent involvement projects in which parents have successfully taught their children at home. Further, the opinions expressed by the majority of parents who have participated in home-tutoring programs indicate that they felt it was a positive experience for both the parent and the child (Fay et al., 1978; Sandler & Coren, 1981).

See Arnold, Sturgis, and Fcrehand (1977), Broden, Beasley & Hall (1978), Fay, Shapiro, and Trupin (1978), Heward, et al. (1979), Ryback and Staats (1970), Shearer (1976).

We feel that in most instances parents can and should learn to teach their children. When properly conducted, home-based parent teaching strengthens the child's educational program and is enjoyed by both the child and his parent. However, it is important for professionals to examine carefully to what extent parent tutoring is appropriate. Not all parents want to teach their child at home or have the time to learn and use the necessary teaching skills. Professionals must not interpret that situation as an indication that the parents "don't care enough" about their child (Turnbull & Turnbull, 1982).

Referring to the special problems faced by parents of severely handicapped children, Hawkins and Hawkins write:

> While we are optimistic about training parents to assess, and thus to contribute extensively to the planning of their child's education, we are less optimistic about training parents to carry out those education plans. . . .
>
> On the other hand, training and motivating parents to carry out a *small* number of teaching tasks each day does seem appropriate. These should be tasks that have most of the following characteristics: (1) they are brief, usually requiring no more than three or four minutes each; (2) the ultimate value of them to the parent is obvious (thus self-dressing, but perhaps not block-stacking); (3) they fit the daily routine almost automatically, not requiring a special, noticeable training "session" (thus self-bathing, but not basic communication-board training); (4) they are tasks that cannot be accomplished readily at school alone, either because the opportunities are infrequent or absent (getting up in the morning, toileting), or because training must occur at every opportunity if it is to achieve its objective (mealtime behaviors, walking appropriately with family). (1981, pp. 17–18)

Lovitt (1977) offers four guidelines for parents to follow when attempting to teach their children:

1. Establish a specific time each day for the tutoring sessions.
2. Keep sessions short. Brief 5- to 10-minute sessions held daily are more likely to be effective than 30- to 40-minute periods, which can produce frustration or be skipped altogether.
3. The parent's responses to the child must be consistent. Lovitt believes it is particularly important for parents to respond to the child's errors in a consistent, matter-of-fact way.

INTERVENTION

When Bryan missed a word, I simply wrote it down with little display of emotion. It is extremely important for the teacher-parent to determine what he will do when an error is made. Whatever response is chosen. it must be consistent. Some parents display a crescendo effect toward errors; they ignore the first few. then gradually respond to them with increasing concern. Finally, after a mounting number of errors have been made, panic sets in, and the parent explodes. (p. 175)

By praising the child's successful responses (materials and activities at the child's appropriate instructional level are a must) and providing a consistent, unemotional response to errors (for example, "Let's read that word again, together. Good. Now you read it again, by yourself. Great!"), parents can avoid the frustration and negative results that can occur when home tutoring is mishandled.

4. Keep a record. A parent, just like the classroom teacher, can never know the exact effects of his teaching unless a record is kept. A daily record enables both parent and child to see gradual progress that might be missed if subjective opinion is the only basis for evaluation. Most children. disabled or not, do make progress under guided instruction. A record documents that progress, perhaps providing the parent with an opportunity to see the child in a new light.

Poor parents, they are a beleaguered lot. Although they are criticized if their progeny do not develop as good citizens, they are generally discouraged from teaching them to that end. Nonsense: parents *can* teach their children. It is only necessary that they be sane and systematic about their instruction. (Lovitt, 1977 p. 182)

Mercer (1982) offers additional guidelines for parent-tutors. Numerous training manuals and materials have been developed that parents can use directly to teach academic skills (Cooper & Heron, 1978) and social behaviors (Becker, 1971; Dardig & Heward, 1981a; Patterson, 1979; Smith & Smith, 1976). Information is also available for professionals who wish to help parents implement home-based tutoring programs (Heward et al., 1979; Lillie & Trohanis, 1976).

Parent Education Groups

Education for "parenting" is not new; Kessler (1966) identified educational programs for parents dating back to the early 1800s. But as a result of the increased parent involvement in the education of handicapped children, the past decade has witnessed a literal explosion of programs being offered for and by parents. Parent education groups can serve a variety of purposes—from one-time only programs for disseminating information on a new school policy or "make-it, take-it" workshops in which parents make an instructional material (for example, a math facts practice game) to use at home to multiple-session

"courses" on participation in IEP planning or child behavior management (Heward & Dardig, 1978b).

Here is a small sample of some of the parent education programs reported in the literature. McWhirter (1976) conducted a program that provided information about learning disabilities to parents. Gordon's (1970) parent programs train parents in communication skills, called "active listening," to use with their children. Waters and Seigel (1982) conducted a successful program that trained parents of Down syndrome toddlers to increase their children's speech production. Hall and Hall (1978) have developed a "Responsive Parenting" program that teaches parents principles of behavior modification to use at home to increase desired behaviors and to decrease or eliminate maladaptive behavior. Baker and Heifetz (1976) conducted a parent training program in conjunction with a summer camp for handicapped children, and LeBuffe and LeBuffe (1982) describe the "Learning Vacation," a parent education program involving the whole family. Just a few of the many topics for which parent education groups have been conducted are listed in Table 13.1.

There is consistent agreement in the parent education literature on the importance of involving parents in the planning and, whenever possible, the actual conducting of parent groups (Kroth, 1981; Heward et al., 1979; Turnbull, 1982). Heward et al. recommend using both open and closed needs assessment procedures to determine what parents want from a parent program. An open-ended needs assessment consists of questions like these:

1. The best family time for my child is when we _____.
2. I will never forget the time that my child and I _____.
3. When I take my child to the store, I am concerned that he/she will _____.

TABLE 13.1

Possible topics for parent education groups

1. Self-help skills (dressing, brushing teeth, etc.)	22. Bicycle safety
2. Leisure-time activities	23. Interpretation of test results
3. Participation in IEP process	24. How to help your mainstreamed child adjust/succeed in the regular class
4. Summer reading program	
5. Teaching your child responsibility and organization	25. Dealing with sibling rivalry
6. Interacting with peers	26. Reading to your child at home
7. Preparing for the family vacation	27. Dealing effectively with significant others
8. Developing and implementing family rules	28. Program for grandparents
9. Safety in the home	29. Fathers only program
10. Recreation/physical education activities to do at home	30. Organizing morning activities
	31. Home fire safety and escape
11. Gardening with a handicapped child	32. Helping your handicapped child make friends
12. Adapting your home for a wheelchair	33. Setting up a parent-run resource room
13. Adapting your home for a blind child	34. Organizing a summer odd-job program for children
14. Community resources for parent of handicapped children	35. Organizing a parent-run respite care exchange system
15. Eating/mealtime behaviors	36. Acceptance and use of prosthetic equipment
16. Shopping skills	
17. How to choose/train a baby sitter	37. Preparing for your child's future
18. Making a home study carrel	38. Dealing with professionals
19. Cooking skills/activities	39. Pets for handicapped children: Selection and care
20. Speech activities/games	
21. Home-school communication systems (notes, telephone)	40. Developing a parent-to-parent support group

4. People think my child is unable to _____.
5. I'm worrying about making a decision about my child's _____.
6. Sometimes I think my child will never _____.
7. My child is especially difficult around the house when he/she _____.
8. I give my child a hug when he/she _____.
9. The hardest thing about having a special child is _____.
10. I wish I knew more about _____. (1979, p. 240)

Parents' responses to open-ended questions can provide a tremendous amount of information about what kinds of parent training programs might be needed and appreciated.

A closed needs assessment asks parents to indicate on a list of possible program topics, child behaviors, or areas of parent-child interactions those items that represent things they would like to learn more about. For example, professionals with the skills and resources to run a parent education group dealing with any of the following topics could ask parents to put one checkmark by any items that are something of a problem and two checkmarks by those areas that are of major interest.

Example of a Closed-Format Parent's Needs Assessment

_____ Bedtime behavior

_____ Eating behavior

_____ Interactions with sibling(s)

_____ Personal cleanliness (dressing, toileting)

_____ Interactions with strangers

_____ Compliance with parental requests

_____ Study habits

_____ Home chores

_____ On-task behavior

_____ Leisure-time activities

_____ Employability skills

_____ Interactions with opposite sex

_____ Making friends

_____ Other

By examining the results of needs assessment questionnaires, parents and professionals together can plan parent education groups that are responsive to the real needs of parents.

How Much Parent Involvement?

It is sometimes all too easy for professionals to get carried away with a concept, especially one like parent involvement with so much promise of positive outcomes. But teachers and everyone else involved with providing special education services to exceptional children should not take a one-sided view of parent involvement. Sometimes the time and energy parents would need to participate in home treatment programs or parent education groups causes stress among family members or guilt if the parents cannot fulfill the teacher's expectations (Doernberg, 1978; Winton & Turnbull, 1981). The time required of parents to provide additional help to their handicapped child may take too much time and attention from other family members (Kroth, 1981; Turnbull & Turnbull, 1982).

Kroth and his colleagues at the Parent Involvement Center in Albuquerque have developed a model guide for parent involvement. Kroth (1981) describes the Mirror Model for Parental Involvement as both a strength and deficit model, recognizing that parents have a great deal to offer as well as a need to receive services from special educators. The model also assumes that not all parents need everything that professionals have to offer and that all parents should not be expected to provide everything.

See figure 13.5.

The Mirror Model attempts to give parents an equal part in deciding what services they need and what services they might provide to professionals or other parents. The top half of the model assumes that professionals have certain information, knowledge, and skills that should be shared with parents to help

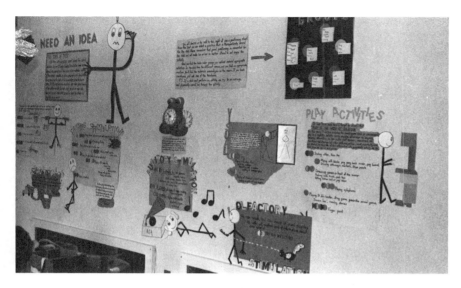

Parent volunteers in this classroom for severely handicapped preschoolers need only look at the wall for specific learning activities targeted for each child.

them with their child. The bottom half of the model assumes that parents have information, knowledge, and skills that can help professionals be more effective in helping children.

SOME GUIDELINES FOR WORKING EFFECTIVELY WITH PARENTS OF HANDICAPPED CHILDREN

The following suggestions are valuable guidelines for professionals in their interactions with parents.

1. Don't assume that you know more about the child, what he or she needs, and how those needs should be met than do the parents. If you make these assumptions, you will often be wrong, and worse, might miss opportunities to get and provide meaningful information.

2. Speak in plain, everyday language. Using "educationalese" doesn't help a professional communicate effectively with parents (or anyone else for that matter). Lovitt, a strong believer that we must "junk our jargon," gives us this example from a student's folder.

> Art shows apraxia due to a vestibular-based deficit. He has laterality, propriocep-tive, and sensorimotor dysfunction. Postural ocular deficits are present. He prefers to use right hand but his left hand is more accurate in kinesthesia and propriocep-tion. Nystagmus is depressed during vestibular stimulation. Motor planning activi-ties are difficult for him. (1982, p. 303)

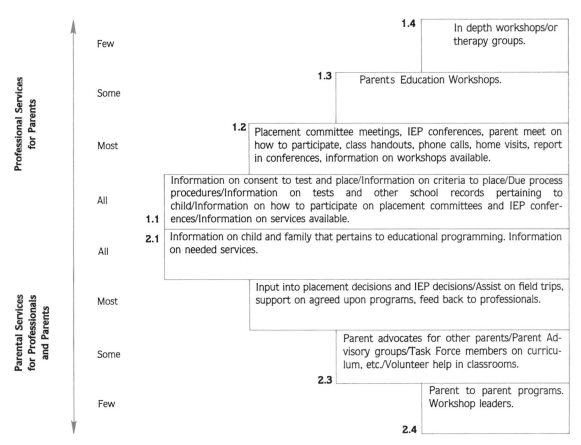

FIGURE 13.5
Mirror model for parental involvement in public schools.

Source: R. Kroth, "Involvement with parents of behaviorally disordered adolescents," in G. Brown, R. L. McDowell, and J. Smith (eds.), *Educating adolescents with behavior disorders.* Columbus, Ohio: Charles E. Merrill, 1981, p. 129. Used with permission.

Wouldn't it be better to state clearly what things Art can do now, so that specific things he needs to learn to be able to do could be identified?

3. Don't let generalization about how parents of handicapped children "feel" or what they "need" guide your efforts. If you are genuinely interested in what a father or mother feels or needs, ask him or her. Don't assume a parent is in the "x, y, or z stage" and therefore needs "a, b, or c."

4. Don't be defensive or intimidated by parents. No, you can't really "know what it's like" to be the parent of a handicapped child unless you are one. But as a trained teacher, you do know a great deal about how to help handicapped children learn; you do it every day, with lots of children. Offer the knowledge and skills you have without apology, and welcome parents' input.

5. Your primary concern is the child. If you are a child's teacher, you interact with parents in an effort to improve the child's education program. In that professional role you are not a marriage counselor or therapist. Offer to refer parents to professionals who are trained and qualified to provide non-special-education services if a parent indicates the need.

6. Help parents strive for "realistic optimism." Handicapped children and their parents benefit little from professionals who are either "doom and gloom" types or who minimize the significance of a disability. Professionals should help parents analyze and prepare for their child's future.

7. Start with something parents can be successful with. For many parents, involvement in the child's education program is a new experience. Don't punish parents who show an interest in helping their child at home by setting them up to fail, by giving them complicated materials, instructions, and a heavy schedule of nightly tutoring. Begin with something simple that is likely to be rewarding to the parent.

8. Don't be afraid to say "I don't know." Sometimes parents will ask educational questions or need services that you can't answer or provide. It's okay to say "I don't know." The mark of a real professional is knowing when you need help. Parents will think more highly of you.

See Heward, Dardig, and Rossett (1979) for a discussion of working with parents for the child's future.

CONCLUSIONS/FUTURE TRENDS

Special educators and parents will continue to develop better ways of working together for the benefit of handicapped children. In the future, more home-based interventions will probably focus not just on the parent-child relationship but on the interrelationships of all family members. Members of the extended family, such as grandparents, will receive more attention (Harris & Kotsch, 1981), and parent involvement will be viewed more and more as "family involvement" (Foster, Berger, & McLean, 1981; LeBluffe & LeBluffe, 1982). We are also beginning to see parents themselves assume a more active role in running parent involvement programs. In some programs, such as the Regional Intervention Program at George Peabody College, parents are the primary teachers of their handicapped children, train other parents in the teaching techniques, and run the program's daily operation (Timm & Rule, 1981).

Parents are the most important adults in a child's life. A good teacher should be the next most important adult in a child's life. Working together, parents and teachers can make a big difference.

THE TELEPHONE: AN OVERLOOKED METHOD OF HOME-SCHOOL COMMUNICATION?

The importance of regular communication between home and school is a topic on which virtually all parents and educators agree. How to manage parent-teacher communication most effectively is the question. A well-conducted conference can accomplish much, but parent-teacher conferences demand a great deal of time from both parties and, realistically, can only be held from time to time. Written notes from the teacher; daily, two-way home-school report card systems (see pages 440–441); and class newsletters can all be excellent means of communication. Unfortunately, the time required to prepare and reproduce daily notes or a class newsletter, with the uncertainty of student delivery, makes written communications a labor-intensive and unreliable method of parent-teacher communication—at least in terms of communicating with a number of parents on a regular, sustained basis.

Somewhat surprisingly in this burgeoning era of "high technology," the telephone—"everyday" technology that has been with us for decades—has been a relatively unexploited means of parent-teacher communication. Of course, if used in typical fashion, the time required to call and speak individually to the parents of all 15 students enrolled in a resource room program, for example, would place the telephone in the same category as conferences and written messages for regular, sustained communication; a call once a week, if you're lucky, but daily communication would most likely be out of the question. Recently, however, teachers have begun to use the telephone in a different way. By recording daily messages on a telephone-answering machine, teachers can provide a great deal of information to parents at relatively little cost. Parents, on the other hand, can call the given number and listen at their convenience, literally 24 hours a day. Parents can also leave messages on the recorder, posing a question, offering a suggestion, etc.

In addition to information exchange, some studies have begun to explore ways in which teachers can use recorded messages to help parents carry out home-based instruction. One junior high learning disabilities teacher used a telephone-answering machine to manage a summer writing program. Parents of several of her students had indicated their desire to try to help their children maintain or extend some of their academic skills over the summer months. Each day during the 9-week program, the teacher recorded instructions for the session and a "story starter" idea. For example, one story starter went like this:

"Danger on Shore"

You are going up the river in a boat. You feel safe because the unfriendly natives are on the far shore. Suddenly you notice a leak. . . .

Parent and student called together, the student wrote for 10 minutes on that day's topic, and the parent scored the student's writing according to criteria provided by the teacher. The parents rewarded their children for progress and reported the results after the next day's message. Every few days parents mailed the stories to the teacher.

For an idea of the results of the program, compare the following stories. Story #8 was written by James before his parents started the program to help him write more action words and adjectives. Story #33 was the sixth story, written after his parents began to reward adjectives!

#8

July 7, 1982   James D

First I would go to candy, always thinking of my self. Later I would go to the meat department. After the meat department I woul go to wine department

Aug 12 #33 Talking with a Star   James D
I look up from my salad, thick chocolate milk shake, hot golden crisp french fries, and delicious Big Mac with extra pickles.
I glance through shiney, clear glass and see a small, brown creature with a glowing red chest, short legs, long arms, and a large head with big greenish-blue eyes and a smashed-in nose.
I grab a white napkin and rush up to him. With the tip of his glowing right index finger he writes...   E.T.

Drawn from M. E. Hasset, C. Engler, N. L. Cooke, D. W. Test, A. B. Weiss, W. L. Heward, & T. E. Heron, A telephone-managed, home-based summer writing program for LD adolescents. In W. L. Heward, T. E. Heron, D. S. Hill, & J. Trap-Porter (Eds.), *Focus on behavior analysis in education.* Columbus, Ohio: Charles E. Merrill Publishing Co., 1984.

SUMMARY

1. Parents and education professionals are developing better ways to work together for the benefit of handicapped children.

   a. Both parents and professionals have contributed to unproductive relationships in the past. Negative attitudes and behaviors of professionals can create roadblocks to effective communications, and some parents are difficult to work with or unreasonable.

   b. Parents and professionals need to understand and be aware of each others' roles and responsibilities.

   c. Actions on the part of parents, concerned educators, and legislators have all helped increase the participation of parents in the special education process.

2. To work with parents effectively, teachers must understand the responsibilities and challenges faced by parents of exceptional children.

   a. All parents need to adjust to the birth of a handicapped child or the discovery that a child is disabled. However, this adjustment process is different for each parent, and educators should not make assumptions about an individual parent's "stage of adjustment."

   b. Parents face extra responsibilities in raising handicapped children, including teaching and counseling the child; managing behavior, dealing with their other nonhandicapped children and other significant people, maintaining the parent-to-parent relationship, and relating to the school and community.

3. Regular two-way communication is critical to effective parent-teacher partnerships.

   a. At carefully planned conferences, parents and teachers can review the child's work, evaluate current programs, and determine strategies for new programs.

   b. Teachers should send frequent written messages home to parents. Possible formats include happy-grams, home-school contracts, daily report cards, and class newsletters.

   c. The telephone is another useful tool for regular teacher-parent communication.

4. The extent to which individual parents participate in IEP meetings varies. Involvement ranges from attendance, in which parents at least become aware of what special services their child is receiving, to active participation in which parents help plan their child's program.

5. Most parents can and should learn to help teach their handicapped children.

6. Parents and professionals should be involved in planning and conducting parent education groups, which can cover a variety of topics.

7. Parents who neither tutor their children, become involved in parent education groups, nor are active decision makers at IEP meetings should not be condemned or regarded as uncaring.

8. Guidelines professionals should follow in their interactions with parents include:
   a. Don't assume that you know more about the child, what he or she needs, and how those needs should be met than do the parents.
   b. Speak in plain, everyday language.
   c. Don't let generalizations about how parents of handicapped children "feel" or what they "need" guide your efforts.
   d. Don't be defensive or intimidated by parents.
   e. Your primary concern is the child.
   f. Help parents strive for "realistic optimism."
   g. Start with something parents can be successful with.
   h. Don't be afraid to say "I don't know."

FOR MORE INFORMATION

Journals

The Exceptional Parent. Published six times per year by the Psy-Ed Corporation. Each issue contains articles for parents and professionals on subjects such as improving parent-professional relationships, family relationships, managing financial resources.

Books

Cooper, J. O., & Edge, D. *Parenting: Strategies and educational methods.* Columbus, Ohio: Charles E. Merrill, 1981.

Heward, W. L., Dardig, J. C., & Rossett, A. *Working with parents of handicapped children.* Columbus, Ohio: Charles E. Merrill, 1979.

Kroth, R. *Communicating with parents of exceptional children.* Denver: Love, 1975.

Lillie, D. L., & Trohanis, P. L. (eds.) *Teaching parents to teach: A guide for working with the special child.* New York: Walker & Co., 1976.

Turnbull, A. P., & Turnbull, H. R. *Parents speak out: Views from the other side of the two-way mirror.* Columbus, Ohio: Charles E. Merrill, 1978.

Organizations

Closer Look, 1201 16th Street NW, Washington, D.C. 20036

National Network of Parent Centers, 9451 Broadview Drive, Bay Harbor, FL 33154

National Parent CHAIN, 515 W. Giles Lane, Peoria, IL 61614. A volunteer organization whose purpose is to establish a national information and education network for handicapped citizens and their families.

Pacer (Parent Advocacy Coalition for Educational Rights) Center, 4701 Chicago Avenue South, Minneapolis, MN 55407

PEP (Parents Educating Parents) Project. Ga. Assn. for Retarded Citizens, 1851 Ram Runway, Suite 104, College Park, GA 30337

Parents Educational Advocacy Center, 116 W. Jones Street, Raleigh, NC 27611

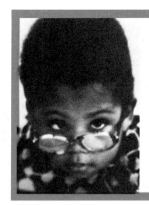

14

Early Intervention

During the critical years from birth to school age, "normal" children grow and develop in orderly, predictable ways, learning to move, to play, to communicate, to help themselves. But these are often years of missed opportunity for the handicapped child. Sadly, the early years are a time when many handicapped children fall farther and farther behind their nonhandicapped peers.

Only in recent years have we become convinced of this need to identify and intervene early. Karnes (1977) reminds us that the first federal legislation written *exclusively* for the handicapped preschooler was not passed until 1968 (The Handicapped Children's Early Childhood Assistance Act). By 1975 the Education for All Handicapped Children Act mandated services for children as young as age 3 (if the states did not already have laws limiting education for children aged 3 to 5). Since 1972, Head Start (a nationwide program begun in 1965 to provide preschool education for disadvantaged children) has been required to include 10% or more handicapped children. By 1977, 13% (a total of 36,133 children) of all children enrolled in Head Start programs across the country were handicapped ("HEW reports 13%," 1978).

See chapters 1 and 2 for more on legislation affecting exceptional children.

As we have said, the 1975 Education for All Handicapped Children Act mandated services by 1980 for handicapped children aged 3 to 5, providing that state law or practice *already* provided education for children in that age group. In the 1980–81 school year only 16 states mandated special education services for the full 3- to 5-year-old range; an additional 22 states required services for handicapped preschoolers at age 4 or 5 (U.S. Comptroller General, 1981). To stimulate other states to begin programs for handicapped preschoolers, the law includes a provision called the *Incentive Grant Program.* Incentive grants are available to any state with an approved state plan for educating handicapped children. They provide funds for establishing or improving preschool programs for handicapped children and are distributed on the basis of the number of children who have been identified in the state (Cohen, Semmes, & Guralnick, 1979).

A total of 227,612 handicapped children aged 3 to 5, or 2.6% of the total 3- to 5-year-old population, received special education services under P.L. 94–142 in school year 1981–82, compared to an estimated 8.5% of the 6- to 17-year-old school-age population (U.S. Department of Education, 1982). The difference between the percentages of the total preschool population receiving special education and the school-age population is caused by some states that do not mandate services to the preschool handicapped child and the difficulty of identifying mildly handicapped children before they enter school.

One of the most encouraging steps taken for handicapped preschoolers came late in 1978. Just before it adjourned, Congress authorized a National Institute of Handicapped Research, beginning with $50 million for 1979 projects and $100 million for 1982 and each year thereafter. The emphasis of the grants is on setting up model centers for severely handicapped children from birth to age 3. "Centers would set up services like early identification and evaluation, parent counseling, infant stimulation, physical therapy, language development and medical and psychiatric care" ("Congress Approves Program for Preschool Handicapped," 1978, p. 1C).

IMPORTANCE OF EARLY INTERVENTION

One of the most dramatic demonstrations of the critical importance of early intervention was a classic study by Skeels and Dye (1939). Two "hopeless" baby girls, age 13 and 16 months, had been transferred from an orphanage to a ward of adult women in an institution for the mentally retarded because of lack of room in "proper" facilities. "The youngsters were pitiful little creatures. They were tearful, had runny noses, and coarse, stringy, and colorless hair; they were emaciated, undersized, and lacked muscle tone or responsiveness. Sad and inactive, the two spent their days rocking and whining" (Skeels, 1966, p. 5). At the time of their transfer, the two children were classified as moderately to severely retarded with IQs estimated at 35 and 46. But after 6 months on the ward with the older women, their IQs were measured at 77 and 87, and a few months later both girls had IQs in the mid-90s. Regular intelligence testing like this was not a common procedure; but because of their unusual placement, the children were observed closely.

After learning of the girls' remarkable improvement, Skeels and Dye looked for possible causes. They found that the children had been the recipients of an unusual amount of attention and stimulation. Ward attendants had purchased toys and books for the children, and residents played and talked with them continuously. Excited by the possibilities, Skeels and Dye convinced the state authorities to permit a most unusual experiment. They selected 11 additional 1- to 2-year-old subjects; all but two of this group were classified as mentally retarded (average IQ was 64) and, by state law at the time, judged

Systematic learning experiences early in life can help reduce the negative impact of a handicap or "high risk" conditions.

unsuitable for adoption. These experimental children were removed from the nonstimulating orphanage and placed under the one-to-one care of adolescent retarded girls at the institution. Each adolescent "mother" was given training in how to care for "her" baby, learning how to hold, feed, talk to, and stimulate the child. No other direct programming or educational experiences were provided to the children.

A contrast group of 12 children under 3 years of age remained in the orphanage, receiving adequate medical and health services but no individual attention. The children in the contrast group had an average IQ of 86 at the beginning of the study; only two were classified as mentally retarded. Two years later the children in both groups were retested. The experimental group showed an average gain of 28 IQ points, high enough for 11 of the 13 children to become eligible for adoption and resulting in their placement in good homes. In two years, children in the contrast group had each lost an average of 26 IQ points.

More than 25 years later, Skeels located the subjects in the original study. The follow-up results were equally impressive (Skeels, 1966). Of the 13 experimental subjects, 11 had married, only one of the marriages had ended in divorce, and the marriages had produced nine children, all of normal intelligence. The subjects' median level of education was the twelfth grade, and four had attended college. All were either employed or homemakers, with jobs ranging from professional and business work to domestic service for the two who had not been adopted. Of the original contrast group of 12, four were still institutionalized in 1965. The median level of education for the contrast group was the third grade, and all but one of those who were employed were unskilled laborers.

While the study by Skeels and Dye (1939) can be questioned because of its lack of tight experimental method, it served as the foundation and catalyst for many subsequent intervention efforts. Skeels concluded his follow-up study by writing:

> It seems obvious that under present-day conditions there are still countless infants with sound biological constitutions and potentialities for development well within the normal range who will become retarded and noncontributing members of society unless appropriate intervention occurs. It is suggested by the findings of this study and others published in the past 20 years that sufficient knowledge is available to design programs of intervention to counteract the devastating effects of poverty, socio-cultural, and maternal deprivation. . . . The unanswered questions of this study could form the basis for many life-long research projects. If the tragic fate of the twelve contrast group children provokes even a single crucial study that will help prevent such a fate for others, their lives will not have been in vain. (1966, p. 109)

Another research study that highlighted the importance of early intervention was done by Kirk (1958). This study measured the effects of 2 years of preschool training on the social and cognitive development of mentally retarded children (IQs ranging from 40 to 85). Children in the two experimental groups—15 children living in an institution and attending a nursery school and 28 children living at home and also attending a preschool program—showed gains on tests of mental and social development. Children in the two control groups—who did not receive the preschool training—26 living at home and 12 in an institution—showed declines in performance. The differences between the groups were maintained over a period of years.

The Milwaukee Project (Garber & Heber, 1973; Heber & Garber, 1971; Strickland, 1971) is another widely cited effort at early intervention. The project was aimed at preventing mental retardation by providing a program of parent education and infant stimulation for children considered to have a high potential for retarded development because of their mother's level of intelligence and conditions of poverty. Mothers with IQs of 70 or less and their high-risk infants were chosen as subjects for the study. The mothers received training in child care and were taught how to interact with and stimulate their children. Beginning before age 6 months, the children also participated in an infant stimulation program conducted by trained teachers. By age 3½, the experimental children tested at an average of 33 IQ points higher than a control group of children who did not participate in the program.

Hailed as the "Miracle in Milwaukee" by the popular media, the study is sometimes offered as proof that a program of maternal education and early infant stimulation can reduce the incidence of cultural-familial mental retardation. However, the Milwaukee Project has been criticized for its research methods. Page (1972), for example, questioned whether bias in sampling and testing was adequately controlled. Nevertheless, Garber and Heber claim:

> Infant testing difficulties notwithstanding, the present standardized test data, when considered along with performance on learning tasks and language tests, indicate an unquestionably superior present level of cognitive development on the part of the experimental group. Also, the first wave of our children are now in public schools. None have been assigned to classes for the retarded. (1973, p. 114)

We will have to await a follow-up report to see whether the Milwaukee Project children maintain their good start. Recent studies, however, do indicate that children who received preschool training perform at higher levels during their formal school years than similar children who did not (Hayden, Morris, & Bailey, 1977; Lazar & Darlington, 1979). Virtually every special educator today recognizes the importance of early intervention for both handicapped and high-risk children. Most will also agree that the earlier intervention begins, the better. But before intervention can begin, the children must be identified.

IDENTIFYING THE YOUNG HANDICAPPED

If the first years of life are the most critical for all of us, then they are even more critical for the handicapped child. By identifying handicaps as early as possible in a child's life, we can intervene to lessen or even to prevent them. As McDaniels points out,

> These infants at risk for handicapping conditions cannot wait until age 6, or even age 3, before receiving intervention that will help them. If, as we are learning, children as young as 1 year or less can make fine discriminations, then that is the age at which programs should begin. (1977, p. 26)

We know more today about the causes and potential risks of handicaps than we have ever known. For example, we know that a history of certain handicaps in a family should make us watch for similar risks to any future children. We know that pregnancy early (before 18) or late (after age 35) means a higher risk of having a handicapped baby. We know that alcoholism in pregnant mothers often produces serious physical defects and developmental delays (called **fetal alcohol syndrome**) in their babies (Delaney & Hayden, 1977). We know that malnutrition in the mother can produce severe problems, including retardation, in her baby. We know that diseases during pregnancy, particularly rubella, can cause serious handicaps in the newborn.

We are even able to detect some kinds of handicaps during pregnancy. By withdrawing and analyzing some of the amniotic fluid which surrounds an unborn child in the mother's womb, doctors can find chromosomal abnormalities that are known to produce severe physical problems and mental retardation. Thus, in some cases, parents can be advised relatively early in the pregnancy

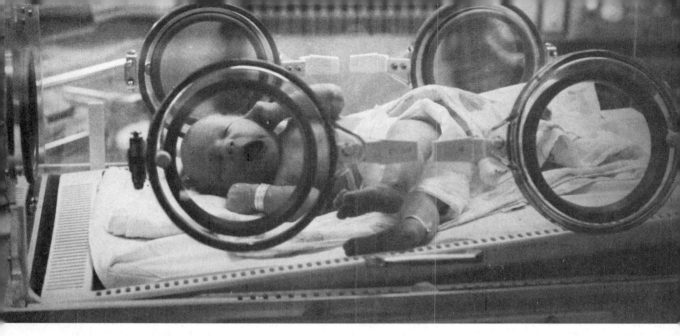

Early identification can lead to early intervention.

(and as a result of the analysis, learn their baby's sex if they wish) that the fetus is damaged, in time to decide if they want a **therapeutic abortion**.

As a general rule, the more severe the handicapping condition, the earlier in life it can be detected. In the delivery room, medical staff can identify certain handicaps, including microcephaly, cleft palate, and other physical deformities, as well as Down syndrome in most instances. Beck (1977) believes that only 6.8% of handicapped children can be identified at birth or shortly thereafter. Within a few days after birth, the analysis of a newborn's blood and urine can detect metabolic disorders that produce mental retardation if not treated within 4 to 12 weeks after birth. Within a few weeks after birth, other physical characteristics like coma, paralysis, convulsions, or rapidly increasing head size can signal possible handicapping conditions (Parmelee & Michaelis, 1971). Within the first months after birth, delays in the development of various critical behaviors can tell a trained observer that an infant is at risk of developing a handicap.

Again, the more pronounced the delay, the easier it is to identify. Some handicaps, like learning disabilities or mild retardation, do not show up until the child is in school and his or her performance in academic subjects is clearly below that of his peers. But even in these cases, if the child is enrolled in a preschool staffed by experienced professionals, it is possible to note learning problems or lags early.

Screening

As we discussed in earlier chapters, *screening* refers to a procedure in which large numbers of children are tested to identify the ones who have a greater

THE APGAR SCORE

The Apgar Evaluation Score is a screening test for newborn infants. Developed in 1952 by Dr. Virginia Apgar, an anesthesiologist, the scale measures the degree of **asphyxia** (oxygen deprivation) an infant experiences during birth. The screening is administered to virtually 100% of the babies born in American hospitals. According to Dr. Frank Bowen, director of neonatology at The Children's Hospital in Columbus, Ohio, "Every delivery should have a person whose primary interest is the newborn," and it is this person—be it nurse, nurse anesthesiologist, or pediatrician—who administers the test.

The test administrator evaluates the infant twice on five physiological measures: heart rate, respiratory effort, response to stimulation, muscle tone, and skin color. (See the figure.) On each measure, the child is given a score of 0, 1, or 2. The scoring form describes the specific characteristics of each measure so that the results are as objective as possible.

If the newborn receives a low score on the first administration of the test, which is 60 seconds after birth, the delivery room staff "takes immediate resuscitation action." Their role is to "help the infant complete the

APGAR EVALUATION SCORE

			60 sec.	5 min.
Heart rate				
	Absent	(0)		
	less than 100	(1)	1	2
	100 to 140	(2)		
Respiratory effort				
	Apneic	(0)		
	Shallow, irregular	(1)	1	1
	Lusty cry and breathing	(2)		
Response to catheter stimulation				
	No response	(0)		
	Grimace	(1)	1	2
	Cough or sneeze	(2)		
Muscle tone				
	Flaccid	(0)		
	Some flexion of extremities	(1)	1	2
	Flexion resisting extension	(2)		
Color				
	Pale, blue	(0)		
	Body pink, extremities blue	(1)	0	1
	Pink all over	(2)		
		Total	4	8

Signature of Person Rating _Dr. E. Banks_

transition" to the world outside the mother's body by establishing strong respiration. This first test measures how the baby fared during the birth process.

The scale is given again 5 minutes after birth. At that point, a total score of 0 to 3 (out of a possible 10) indicates severe asphyxia; 4 to 6, moderate asphyxia; and 7 to 10, mild asphyxia. "Some stress is assumed on all births," according to Dr. Bowen. The 5-minute score measures how successful any resuscitation efforts were. Again, a low score calls for continuing action to help the infant.

"A 5-minute score of 6 or less deserves follow up," says Dr. Bowen, "to determine what is causing the problem and what its long-term consequences will be." The Apgar has been shown to identify "high-risk" infants—those who have a greater than normal chance of developing later problems. Research has shown that oxygen deprivation at birth "contributes to neurological impairment," and the 5-minute Apgar scores correlate well with eventual neurological outcome.

While most newborns are evaluated in terms of gestational weight and age and screened for certain specific disorders, the Apgar scale is at present the only widely used screening test for high-risk infants.

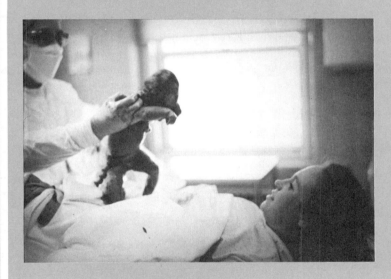

The first Apgar score is recorded when the newborn is only 1 minute old.

Early screening for developmental delays includes assessment of the infant's motor development.

likelihood of having a problem. Children identified through a screening process are then referred for more in-depth assessment.

While many measures have been developed to screen for high-risk infants and children, their use is still far from universal. One national effort is the Early and Periodic Screening, Diagnosis, and Treatment (EPSDT) provision of the Social Security Amendments of 1967. Required since 1972, EPSDT was set up to identify child health problems and developmental disabilities as early as possible. But to date EPSDT has drawn criticism, both for failing to reach more of the children it should serve and for failing to provide as much information as it could (Comptroller General, 1977; Warren, 1977). According to John Meier, former director of the Office of Child Development within the Department of Health, Education and Welfare:

> The inadequacy of available tests for predicting developmental disabilities in low income, minority group children; the necessity for assuring confidentiality and avoiding labelling; and a lack of personnel, facilities, and funds all proved to be obstacles to EPSDT. (Warren, 1977)

Even if these problems could be solved, EPSDT is empowered to screen only those children receiving Medicaid. No such program is even recommended by the federal or state governments for other children.

One screening procedure that *is* widely practiced is the analysis of newborn blood and urine samples to detect the metabolic disorder PKU, which produces mental retardation. And yet, while 48 states had PKU screening programs in 1975, only 8 states routinely screened for six other metabolic disorders which also produce retardation (Comptroller General, 1977).

INTERVENTION

Many other screening measures are available and are used fairly widely. The Apgar rating is a quick evaluation performed in almost all hospital delivery rooms, and the Brazelton Neonatal Assessment Scale (Brazelton, 1973) is a more detailed assessment of the newborn. Several other screening measures are based on the Gesell Developmental Schedules (Gesell et al., 1940; Knobloch & Pasamanick, 1974), which describe normal motor development, adaptive behavior, language, and personal-social behavior in infants and young children. The Bayley Scales of Infant Development (Bayley, 1969) which evaluate the infant's development from ages 2 and 30 months, are standardized adaptations of the Gesell schedules. The Developmental Screening Inventory (Knobloch, Pasamanick, & Sherard, 1966), also based on the Gesell scales, was designed for pediatricians to assess developmental delays in children between 1 month and 18 months old.

The Apgar rating was described on pages 468–469.

Still, none of these measures or practices adds up to any kind of truly systematic effort to screen all infants. And most state and local screening programs are aimed at older children, especially those about to start school. Even the majority of screening devices available are for older children. Wallace and McLoughlin (1979), in a survey of screening tests useful in identifying learning disabilities, note that only 2 of 24 available can be used with children under age 3. All of this means that identifying high-risk infants and young children most often depends on the experience and concern of the adults who deal with them and feel that the child may need special help. Chief among those adults are pediatricians and nurses, social workers, day-care staff, preschool teachers, and most of all, the child's parents. A recent study has shown that mothers' estimates of their preschool children's level of development correlate highly with those produced by professionals using standardized scales (Gradel, Thompson, & Sheenan, 1981).

Assessment

Not all children who are screened as high risk will necessarily have handicaps. Some grow up to live normal lives, without any special help. The goal of early screening is to identify a possible or likely handicap before it can take its full toll on the child's future. For those who are identified, screening is only the first step. The next step is a careful and detailed assessment of the child in all of the critical areas of development.

Results from the screening test(s) are used to guide an in-depth assessment, which is often conducted by professionals from various disciplines working as a team. It is important that the members of a multidisciplinary assessment team cooperate to determine their respective roles in the case of a given child before assessment begins and that the child's parents are actively involved throughout the process (Holm & McCartin, 1978; Orlando, 1981). Individuals involved in the assessment of preschool children may be from the fields of medicine, psychology, education, speech and language pathology, and social work. Rose and Logan have listed the assessment roles usually performed by

Team members and their roles are discussed in more detail later in this chapter.

See figure 14.1.

professionals from the various disciplines who are concerned with young children.

There is some intentional overlapping in the role assignments of team members. This is done in an attempt to eliminate gaps in the assessment process. It also enables the team to consider patterns of behavior in the child and the family. In this way, the team is able to develop the most comprehensive picture of the child and how that child responds to the influences and demands of the environment. (1982, p. 191)

FIGURE 14.1
Interdisciplinary team members and role descriptions

Team Member	Description
Pediatrician	1. Examines previous medical records for information that may explain etiology of developmental delays. 2. Looks into family medical history to determine if genetic or hereditary factors are involved. 3. Coordinates medical care for the child and family.
Clinical nurse	1. Provides assistance in prevention and case finding. 2. Counsels parents on child health, child rearing, and home management of selected problems. 3. Facilitates coordination, planning, and follow-up among the home, educational setting, and health care team.
Pediatric nutritionist	1. Examines conditions that may cause "failure to thrive" in the child. 2. Informs parents about dietary needs of their child. 3. Develops nutritional plan for the child and family.
Developmental therapists (occupational therapist and physical therapist)	1. Assesses gross motor skills, hand functioning, and sensory skills. 2. Develops treatment programs (as needed) that can also be used by parents and educators. 3. OT focuses on deficits in sensory integration. 4. PT emphasizes therapy in gross motor areas.
Developmental psychologist	1. Administers psychological testing in the cognitive and affective domains. 2. Considers differences between test performance and skills demonstrated in other situations. 3. Interprets test results in terms of characteristics and behavior. 4. Helps parents and educators plan programming and management.
Early childhood education specialist (ECES)	1. Helps design assessment strategies that ensure programming goals. 2. Observes and records behavior of the child in a classroom setting. 3. Suggests teaching strategies, curriculum, and behavior management for the child. 4. Works with other team members to develop an individualized education program. 5. Acts as a liaison among the child, parents, and teachers when the child leaves the preschool for another setting.

FIGURE 14.1 (continued)

Team Member	Description
Communication specialists (speech pathologist and audiologist)	1. May assess the amount of information provided by the adults in the child's environment.
	2. Determines whether articulation problems may be a function of delayed motor development or neurological impairment.
	3. Assesses auditory behaviors, receptive communication behaviors, and expressive communication behaviors.
	4. Suggests structuring of classroom environment to foster language development.
Social worker	1. Visits the family to determine the climate of the home and what feelings the parents and siblings have about one member's handicap.
	2. Surveys the expectations and values of the parents to help design an intervention program.
	3. Establishes the best process for sharing information and results of assessments between parents and other team members.
	4. Helps set up a home program and feedback process between parents and team.

Source: E. Rose and D. R. Logan, "Educational and life/career programs for the mildly mentally retarded," in P. T. Cegelka and H. J. Prehm (eds.), *Mental retardation: From categories to people.* Columbus, Ohio: Charles E. Merrill, 1982, p. 194. Used with permission.

A wide variety of assessment devices are available, including both formal, standardized measures and less formal checklists and rating scales based on observations of the child. In the first instance, McGovern and Draper (1978) list more than 45 various evaluation instruments intended to identify and assess delayed or abnormal development in intellectual development, auditory perception, or affective and social development. Likewise, Jordan, Hayden, Karnes, and Wood (1977) list a total of 68 standardized tests being used by the First Chance Network of nearly 200 model programs for young handicapped children.

As more and more intervention programs for young handicapped children are started, the number of informal observation checklists, rating scales, and other assessment devices also grows. Hayden and Edgar (1977) list 24 assessment instruments which have become available only in the last few years. Most were developed by federally funded model programs or by locally sponsored centers for young handicapped children. In general, these and other similar assessment tools seek to measure the child's development in six key areas.

1. Cognitive development includes such processes as attention, perception, memory, verbal skills, and concept learning, many of which are assessed by observing the child's performances in other areas.

2. Motor development includes the child's gross motor skills (like rolling over, crawling, walking, swimming) and fine motor skills (like eye-hand coordination, reaching, touching, grasping).

3. Language development encompasses all of the communication development, including the child's ability to respond nonverbally with gestures, smiles, or actions and the acquisition of spoken language, sounds, words, phrases, sentences, and so on.
4. Self-help skills includes skills such as feeding, dressing, and using the toilet without assistance.
5. Play skills includes playing with toys, with other children, with games, and in dramatic or fantasy roles.
6. Personal-social skills includes the child's social responses to adults and to other children, as well as skills at managing his or her own behaviors when alone.

In addition, several assessment devices also have specific sections to test the child's sensory acuity (hearing and sight in particular). And many also try to measure the child's "readiness" for academic learning with specific tasks related to early reading and math skills.

Generally, these six areas are broken down into specific, observable tasks and sequenced *developmentally*, that is, in the order in which most normal children learn them. Sometimes each task is tied to a specific age at which a child should probably be able to perform it. This arrangement allows the observer to note significant delays or gaps, as well as other unusual patterns, in a high-risk child's development.

Halle and Sindelar (1982) warn that assessment of preschool children should not be limited to checklists and rating scales which, while sufficient for targeting general areas of strength and weakness, usually do not pinpoint the specific target behaviors that define those areas. They recommend a system of direct and repeated behavioral observation to pinpoint behaviors for intervention and serve as the basis for evaluating the effects of instruction.

Of course, the accuracy and usefulness of the assessment information depend not just on the kind of device or method used. The experience and training of the observer, the number of observations, the settings in which the child is observed, and the care with which the data are interpreted all affect the reliability of an assessment.

DuBose (1981) has noted the particular difficulty posed by evaluating severely handicapped children. Because there are so few reliable assessment instruments that can be used with severely impaired children, professionals often need to adapt standardized tests and devise informal assessment tasks. DuBose warns that adaptations must be made carefully and the results interpreted with care. The examiner must know why a particular test was given, what it is meant to tap, and what the child's test performances indicate.

As several professionals have noted (Kakalik, Brewer, Dougharty, Fleischauer, Genensky, & Wallen, 1974; Hayden & Edgar, 1977), there are serious dangers if errors are made in screening or assessment. Children who are handicapped but who are not identified may fail to get needed services, and their problems may get worse. Children who are not handicapped but who are assessed as such may suffer the stigma of an erroneous label.

> It is simply never too early to intervene, and . . . from the data base we now have, it seems clear that urgently needed interventions should occur long before a child is born. Once a child has arrived, the work necessarily shifts into amelioration, away from prevention—always a second choice for intervention. . . . Beginning at birth is not too soon. (Hayden & Pious, 1979, p. 273)

As we have already noted, we now know that certain conditions are relatively likely to lead to the birth of a handicapped baby. Among these are the following:

☐ The birth of a previous child who had a chromosome abnormality;

☐ Age of the mother over 35 (while women over 35 have only 7% of the babies born, they give birth to more than 33% of all Down syndrome babies);

☐ Two or more congenital malformations in the parents;

☐ The mother is mentally retarded;

☐ The mother has failed to develop secondary sex characteristics;

☐ The mother has a history of several miscarriages. (Comptroller General, 1977)

With widespread genetic counseling, plus greater public awareness of these conditions as predictors of handicaps, many parents or prospective parents could make better decisions, based on more information, about having a child. Likewise, better prenatal care could reduce the incidence of prematurity and low birth weight of the baby, both of which are also associated with an increased frequency of handicaps. In addition to urging these steps, the U.S. Government Accounting Office has recommended to the secretary of HEW that other efforts be made to prevent mental retardation. Among those are wider screening for metabolic disorders, wider vaccination for rubella and measles, more extensive testing for lead poisoning in children, better identification of women with Rh negative blood type, and greater efforts to enhance early childhood development in low-income areas (Comptroller General, 1977).

Even with all these improvements in public awareness, prenatal care, and early education, the possibility of eliminating most handicaps is not likely to be realized in this century (Hayden & Pious, 1979). And so the need for effective early intervention programs will continue to challenge us.

EARLY CHILDHOOD SPECIAL EDUCATION PROGRAMS

A *model* program evaluates the effectiveness of new procedures and techniques (or, as is often the case, a new combination of old techniques) with the hope that, if the model proves effective, it can serve as a basis for developing other similar programs.

Certainly the most noted effort to develop early intervention programs to date is the First Chance Network, begun by the Bureau of Education for the Handicapped (BEH) in 1969. Created by the passage of the Handicapped Children's Early Education Program in 1968, the First Chance Network is a series of **model** early intervention **programs** for handicapped children from birth to age 8. The HCEEP began with 21 programs funded with $1 million in 1969–70 and grew to 214 programs funded with $22 million in federal support by 1978–79 (Swan, 1980). Seven of these were considered by BEH in 1975 to be nationally validated, and BEH gave those seven additional funds to help others set up identical programs elsewhere (Karnes, 1977).

There are now First Chance Network Programs, or programs based on techniques developed by First Chance programs, in every state. Also supporting the programs' validity and level of success is the high percentage of federally funded First Chance Programs that continue to operate with local funding after the federal dollars stop. Swan (1980) found 18 of the first 21 projects funded in 1969 still operating 10 years later. In general, these and other promising early intervention programs are built on one of three models: a home-based program, a center-based program, or a program that combines home and center as settings for intervention.

Home-Based Programs

As the name suggests, a home-based program depends heavily on the training and cooperation of the child's parents. The parents assume responsibility as the primary caregivers and teachers for their handicapped child. Parent training is usually provided by a teacher or trainer who visits the home regularly, to guide the parents, act as a consultant, evaluate the success of the intervention, and make regular assessments of the child's progress. In some programs, these *home visitors* (or *home teachers* or *home advisors,* as they are often called) are specially trained paraprofessionals. They may visit as frequently as several times a week but probably no less than a few times a month. In some cases, they may carry the results of their in-home evaluations back to other professionals who make recommendations for changes in the program.

Perhaps the best known home-based program is the nationally validated Portage Project (Shearer & Shearer, 1972). Operated by a consortium of 23 school districts in south-central Wisconsin, the Portage Project has produced its own assessment materials and teaching activities, *The Portage Guide to Early Education.* The basis for the program is 450 behaviors sequenced developmentally and classified into self-help, cognition, socialization, language, and motor skills. A project teacher normally visits the home one day each week, (1) reviewing the child's progress during the previous week, (2) describing activities for the upcoming week, (3) demonstrating to the parent(s) how to carry out the activities with the child, (4) observing the parent and child interacting, offering

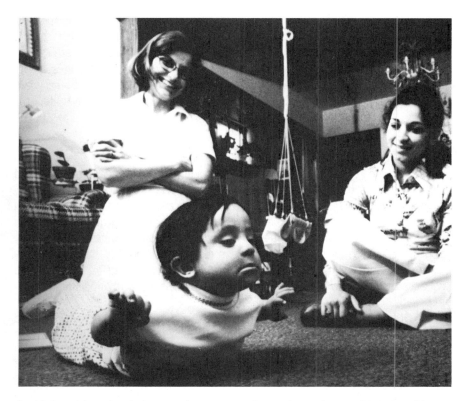

In this home-based early intervention program the teacher makes weekly home visits to evaluate the child's progress and demonstrate activities for the upcoming week.

suggestions and advice as needed, and (5) summarizing where the program stands and indicating what records should be kept during the next week. The Portage Project has now been replicated in hundred of locations around the country (Shearer & Snider, 1981).

In addition to the Portage Project, Karnes and Zehrbach (1977) offer brief descriptions of 21 other home-based programs in the First Chance Network.

An early intervention program based in the home has several advantages, especially if the home is the handicapped child's own. First of all, the home is the child's natural environment and parents are, like the parents of normal children, the child's first teachers. In addition, other family members like brothers and sisters and perhaps grandparents have more opportunity to interact with the child, both for instruction and social contact. These "significant others" in the child's life can play an important role in the child's growth and development (Heward, et al., 1979). Also, learning activities and materials conducted in the home are more likely to be natural and appropriate than artificial, contrived, or inappropriate. And it is often true that a parent can spend more time and give more attention to the child than even the most adequately staffed center or school. In addition, parents who are actively involved in helping their child learn and develop clearly have an advantage over parents who feel guilt, frustration, or defeat at their seeming inability to help their handicapped child. (Of course, this does not suggest that parents of a child in a center-based program cannot take an active role in their child's learning and growth). Finally, in sparsely populated regions, a home-based program allows a child to live at home while receiving an intensive education, without totally disrupting the family's life.

Center-Based Programs

In contrast to home-based programs, some early intervention efforts are coordinated and carried out in a special educational setting outside the home. The setting may be part of a hospital complex, a special day-care center, or preschool. In other cases, children may attend a specially designed "developmental center" or "training center" that offers a wide range of services for children with varying types and severities of handicaps. In one instance described by Jones (1977), the setting is an outdoor playground specially built on a New York City rooftop. Wherever they are located, these centers offer the combined services of many professionals and paraprofessionals, often from several different fields.

Of the 120 First Chance Network programs reviewed by Karnes and Zehrbach (1977), 31 are classified as center-based. Most of these programs encourage social interaction, and some try to integrate handicapped children with nonhandicapped children in day-care or preschool classes. In some instances, the child attends the center each weekday, sometimes for all or most of the day. In other instances, the child may come less frequently, though most centers expect to see the child at least once per week. Sometimes parents are given roles as classroom aides or are encouraged to act as the primary teacher of their child. In a few programs, parents may spend time with other professionals or take training while their child is somewhere else in the center. Virtually all of the First Chance programs, and most other effective programs for young handicapped children, recognize the critical need to involve the parents, and they welcome parents in every aspect of the program.

One of the more successful center programs is the Model Preschool Center for Handicapped Children at the University of Washington in Seattle. Here, children with a variety of handicaps come to participate in one of several highly specialized programs: an infant learning program, a communication disorders classroom, a preschool where handicapped children are integrated with normal children, a program for Down syndrome children, and a program for severely handicapped preschoolers. While all of the programs stress parent involvement, most of the *direct* instruction with the children takes place at the center. Instruction consists of rigorously applied behavior analysis—careful screening and initial assessment, pinpointing target behaviors for instruction, precise instructional planning, and daily assessments of progress. Like most centers, the curriculum focuses on key areas of development: gross and fine motor, communication, self-help, social behavior, and preacademic skills. Because of its size and its location at a major university, the center's staff is large and can offer the services of many different specialists in teaching, language and communication disorders, psychology, and medicine.

Center-based programs generally offer a number of advantages not easily built into home-based efforts. One important benefit is the opportunity for a team of specialists from different fields—medicine, education, physical and occupational therapy, speech and language pathology, and others—to observe the child and cooperate in intervention and continued assessment. For example, many centers hold regular meetings (perhaps once a month) at which all those involved with the child sit down to discuss his progress, or lack of it, his response to the strategies used, and new or revised objectives for him. In addition, the opportunity for contact with handicapped and nonhandicapped peers makes center programs especially appealing for some children. In addition, parents involved in center programs no doubt feel some relief at the support they get from professionals working with their child, and in some cases, from other parents with children at the same center.

Combined Home-Center Programs

Perhaps the most commonly used intervention model is the one which offers both center-based activities and home visitation. Few center programs take children for more than a few hours a day, for perhaps 5 days a week; but for young handicapped children intervention must be more than a matter of only a few hours a day. Thus, many programs combine the intensive help from a variety of professionals in a center with the continuous attention and sensitive care from parents at home. This effort to establish intervention that carries over from center to home clearly offers many of the advantages of the two types of programs.

A good example of a home/center program is the PEECH (Precise Early Education of Children with Handicaps) Project at the University of Illinois. Designed for children aged 3 or older with mild to moderate handicaps, PEECH combines classroom instruction for up to 10 handicapped and 5 normal children. A team approach to intervention and parental involvement includes a classroom teacher and a paraprofessional aide, a psychologist, a speech-language pathologist, and a social worker. Children spend 2 or 3 hours in class each day with some time in large and small groups and in individualized activities. The curriculum is based in part on the Illinois Test of Psycholinguistic Abilities (Kirk, et al., 1968) because, according to Karnes and Zehrbach (1977), a large percentage of the children in the project have language deficits. Parents are included in all stages of the intervention, including policy making. The project even offers a lending library and toy library for parents to use, as well as a parent newsletter. The ultimate goal of the project is to integrate handicapped youngsters successfully into regular classes whenever possible.

For more information on PEECH and 37 other center/home programs in the First Chance Network, see Karnes and Zehrbach (1977).

It is probably best to view these choices—home, center, or combined programs—as more alike than different. In fact, they do seem to have more in common than not: developmental curricula, strong parent involvement, explicit goals and frequent assessment of progress, integration of handicapped and nonhandicapped children whenever possible, and staff teams that consist of specialists in several fields.

THE DEVELOPMENTAL CURRICULUM

In a survey of 103 First Chance Network early childhood programs, the directors of every program indicated their curriculum was "developmentally based" (Stramiello, 1978). That is, the typical gains made by nonhandicapped children in sensorimotor development, language, social skills, academic readiness, and so forth are used as a basis for sequencing instructional objectives and evaluating child progress.

According to Wood and Hurley (1977), the curricula in the First Chance Network point to five different ways of organizing what we teach young children with special needs:

1. Remediating, that is, making up for delays or gaps in a child's development, whether in language, motor skills, self-help, or other areas.
2. Teaching basic "processes" like attention, perception, sensorimotor, language, social skills, and memory.
3. Teaching developmental tasks, which are skills in a range of areas (motor, language, self-help, social) in sequences that most closely match the order in which normal children learn them.
4. Teaching psychological constructs like self-concept, creativity, motivation, and cognition, assuming that this training will lead to increased learning later.
5. Teaching preacademic skills in prereading, early math, nature studies, art, dance, and so on.

Caution—young artists at work!

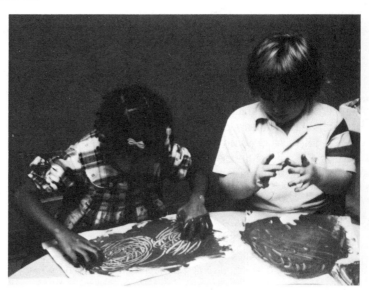

These approaches are not mutually exclusive, of course. All of them use normal development as a yardstick against which to measure each child's individual needs and progress. In other words, a curriculum may try to give a handicapped child instruction in all the "processes" or skills that a normal child might develop without specifically being taught them. Or it might try to measure all of the skills the child has already learned and then teach only those that are missing. But in both instances the ultimate goal is to help the child develop as many of the behaviors of a normal child of the same age as possible. A visit to even a few programs for young handicapped children will show that, regardless of the approach to structuring the curriculum, the children in each program are learning new skills in gross and fine motor coordination, language, self-help, social interaction, play, and perhaps preacademic subjects.

Of course, sometimes physical or sensory impairments make it unreasonable to expect a child to perform some skills. In that case, the goal must be different. Thus, it may be to teach different skills, like signing or speechreading to a deaf child or orientation and mobility skills to a blind child. It may mean teaching a child to use adaptive equipment (like a wheelchair) or a prosthetic device, if physical handicaps prevent her from using some part of her body.

Wood and Hurley (1977) also note that early intervention programs often combine one or more of the five rationales they list. Especially common are programs that combine remediation with basic skill or process training and programs that merge basic skill or process training with developmental sequences. Almost *no* programs rely exclusively on psychological constructs (such as ego development) as a structure for what to teach young children (Wood & Hurley, 1977).

Two curriculum concerns that are important to every early intervention program are promoting language development and scheduling activities to be instructionally effective.

Developing Language in Handicapped Preschoolers

A major developmental task of children is to learn the language of their native community. As we mentioned in chapter 6, most children learn to speak and communicate effectively with little or no formal teaching. By the time they enter school most children have essentially mastered their native tongue. But handicapped children often do not acquire language in the spontaneous, seemingly effortless manner of their nonhandicapped peers. As handicapped children slip farther and farther behind their peers, their language deficits make social and academic development even more difficult. Handicapped preschoolers need opportunities and activities directed at language use and development throughout the day.

> The tendency is to schedule a time during the day as "language time." Having done that, we begin to think that the children have been taught language. I don't believe children learn language in this way; language permeates everything we do. (Rieke, quoted by Magliocca, 1980, p. 14)

Eileen Allen and Jane Rieke are two language specialists who, like most of their colleagues, believe teachers of preschool children must use strategies to help children develop language skills all day long, throughout the total program. They also believe that the basic measure of how successful language intervention is should be *how much* the child talks. Research has shown that the more a child talks, the better the child talks (Hart & Risley, 1975; Rieke, Lynch, & Soltman, 1977). Allen states that good teachers do three things to ensure that effective intervention is provided for language-delayed children.

1. They arrange the environment in ways demonstrated to be conducive to promoting language: (a) by providing several interesting learning centers (blocks, housekeeping and dramatic play, creative and manipulative materials); (b) by organizing a balance of activities in terms of child-initiated and teacher-structured; and (c) by presenting materials and activities that children enjoy.

2. They manage their own interactions with children so as to maximize effective communication on the part of each language-impaired child, and use every opportunity to teach "on the fly" (White, 1975).

3. They monitor, on a regular basis, the appropriateness of (a) environmental arrangements; (b) their own behavior; and (c) that of the children, in order to validate child progress and thus program effectiveness. (1980a, p. 8)

Two models or approaches teachers can use for systematically encouraging and developing language use throughout the school day are the *incidental teaching model* (Hart & Risley, 1975) and the *communicative interaction model* (Rieke, et al., 1977) The essential feature of the incidental teaching model is that the child *wants* something from the teacher—help, approval, information, food, or drink—and the teacher uses these opportunities to promote language use. Whenever the child initiates an interaction with the teacher, the teacher uses that opportunity to get the best possible language from the child. Allen (1980b) offers the following example of an incidental teaching episode described by Hart:

A four-year-old girl with delayed language stands in front of the teacher with a paint apron in her hand. The teacher says, "What do you need?" (Teacher does *not* anticipate the child's need by putting the apron on the child at the moment.)
    If the child does not answer, the teacher tells her and gives her a prompt: "It's an apron. Can you say 'apron'?" If the child says "apron" the teacher ties it while giving descriptive praise, "You said it right. It *is* an apron. I am tying your apron on you." The teacher's last sentence models the next verbal behavior, "Tie my apron," that the teacher will expect once the child has learned to say "apron."
    If the child does not say "apron," the teacher ties the apron. No further comments are made at this time. The teacher must not coax, nag or pressure the child. If each episode is kept brief and pleasant, the child will contact the teacher frequently. Thus, the teacher will have many opportunities for incidental teaching. If the teacher pressures the child, such incidental learning opportunities will be

lost. Some children may learn to avoid the teacher—they will simply do without; other children may learn inappropriate ways, such as whining and crying, to get what they want.

Through repeated interactions of this type children learn that language is important; it can get them what they want, and teachers listen when they speak and want to hear more about things of interest to them. An important guideline in incidental teaching is to keep interactions brief and pleasant, so there will be many more opportunities. The child should never be interrogated or put "on the spot" (Allen, 1980a).

In the communicative interaction model, the teacher is in the role of facilitator, always seeking to make things happen by saying or doing things that encourage the child to use language. Rieke and her colleagues (1977) recommend that teachers of young children avoid the two-unit, question-and-answer pattern of interaction often typical of adult-child communications. Those interactions do not encourage the child to continue talking and may lead the child to avoid the interrogating adult. Instead, the teacher-facilitator uses a three-unit format for dialogues that may be initiated either by teacher or child.

Child:	points
Teacher:	"You want the car? Say 'car'."
Child:	nods and makes sound approximating "car."
Child:	"Look at my painting."
Teacher:	"You used red, blue and _____?"
Child:	"and green and yellow and some more red."
Child:	"What you doing?"
Teacher:	"Watch me and see if you can tell *me* what I am doing."
Child:	"play dough—me help?"
Teacher:	(to nonverbal child): "Where did you park your trike?"
Child:	points to shed.
Teacher:	"In the *shed;* you remembered!"
Teacher:	"What a pretty new dress!"
Child:	"my birthday"
Teacher:	"Your birthday dress! What else did you get for your birthday?"
Teacher:	"You have a new baby at your house! Is it a boy or a girl?"
Child:	"boy"
Teacher:	"A new boy baby! What's his name?" (Allen, 1980a, pp. 9–10)

Both models of assisting children in developing language skills have much in common. Both view the teacher as (1) an astute and systematic observer and recorder of children's language, (2) a sensitive and willing listener, and (3) a systematic responder who helps the child "say it better" through differential feedback (Allen, 1980a).

Developing a Preschool Activity Schedule

Teachers in preschool programs for handicapped children face the challenge of organizing the 2 to 3 hours of the day that the children spend in the program into a schedule that meets each child's individual learning needs. The schedule should include both one-to-one and group instruction, provide children with many learning opportunities throughout the day, allow easy transition from activity to activity—in short, the schedule should provide a framework for maximizing instruction while at the same time remaining manageable and flexible.

Lund and Bos (1981) suggest that teachers begin planning a preschool schedule by determining the basic activities or time blocks. Figure 14.2 shows the components that are common to many preschool programs. The next steps in constructing the schedule are filling in the approximate amount of time to be spent on each activity each day, sequencing the components, scheduling children for individual and group instruction, and assigning staff (teachers, aides, and volunteers).

FIGURE 14.2

Considerations in planning a schedule

Approx. Amount of Time	Components
	Circle—opening exercises that vary in content from day to day or week to week.
	Interactive Play—a play area where students interact with peers using teacher-structured materials and activities, e.g., dramatic play centered around a theme, woodworking, kitchen, block building..
	Movement—gross motor activities in either an indoor or outdoor setting; may also include physical/occupational therapy exercises.
	Snack—fruit juices (natural sugars only), milk, popcorn, dried fruit, granola, etc.
	Bathroom—as scheduled with group or according to individual toileting schedule.
	Activity Table—students work at one or several activity tables; activities generally focus on fine motor and preacademic tasks.
	Small Groups—students work in small groups on individual and group programs; content of activities varies but usually focuses on communication and preacademic tasks.
	Story—simple picture books, flannel board, hand puppets/finger puppets.
	Music—action songs, finger plays, rhythm band.
	Rest/Relax—low lights, mats, listening to soft music, relaxing exercises.
	Flex Time—a time when any of the above activities or special experiences (field trips, special guests, etc.) can be planned; activities vary from day to day.
	Special Needs Therapy—speech/language therapy, occupational therapy, physical therapy, adaptive physical education.

Source: K. A. Lund & C. S. Bos, "Orchestrating the preschool classroom: The daily schedule," *Teaching exceptional children*, 1981, *14*, 120–125. Copyright 1981 by the Council for Exceptional Children. Used with permission.

The physical arrangement of the classroom itself must support the planned activities. Lund and Bos offer the following suggestions for setting up a preschool classroom:

See figure 14.3.

- ☐ Place individual work areas and quiet activities together, away from avenues of traffic. This should encourage attending behavior.
- ☐ Provide a stable area such as an activity table and rug where a variety of group programs can be conducted.
- ☐ Place the activity table within easy access to storage so that materials can be quickly retrieved when working with students.
- ☐ Place materials used most often close together for accessibility, e.g., clipboard, individual program materials.
- ☐ Label or color code all storage areas so the aide and volunteer can easily find the needed materials.
- ☐ Arrange equipment and group areas so that the students may move easily from one activity to another. Picture or color codes can be applied to various work areas.
- ☐ Provide lockers or cubbies for students so they know where their belongings can be found. Again, picture cues can be added to help the students identify their own lockers.*

WHO CAN HELP?

The success of efforts to prevent handicaps in children, and to identify, assess, and intervene with special needs children as early as possible, requires the training and experience of a wide range of professionals. Those discussed below are the most important.

No other professional has as great an opportunity to prevent certain handicaps as the obstetrician. Since he or she knows many of the conditions that predict possible handicaps, the doctor can examine the family history and recommend genetic counseling if there appears to be a significant risk. Since he sees an expectant mother several times during pregnancy, he can monitor any possible problems that appear, perform or refer her for amniocentesis if necessary, and generally insure the kind of prenatal care that reduces the risk of problems at birth. In the delivery room, the doctor's concern for possible birth trauma can contribute to preventing or identifying problems early.

In the same way, the pediatrician (or perhaps the family doctor) has the chance to see the infant after birth and regularly during the first months afterwards. His or her attention to the Apgar ratings and immediate postnatal ex-

*From "Orchestrating the preschool classroom" by K. A. Lund and C. S. Bos, *Teaching exceptional children*, 1981, *14*, 123. Copyright © 1981 by The Council for Exceptional Children. Reprinted with permission.

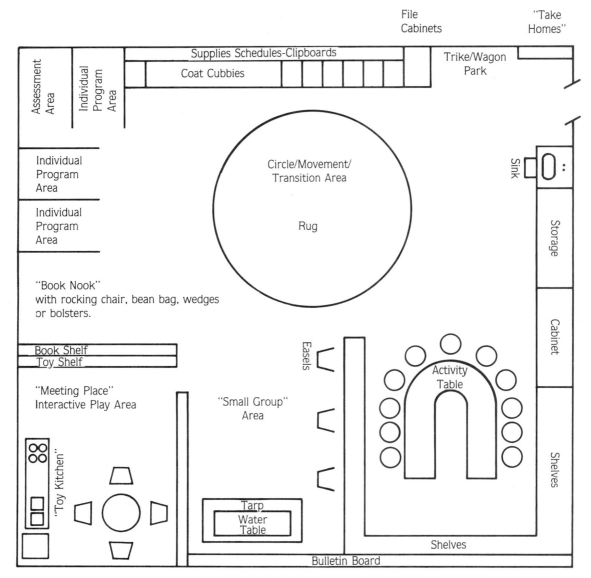

FIGURE 14.3
One arrangement for a preschool classroom

Source: K. A. Lund and C. S. Bos, "Orchestrating the preschool classroom: The daily schedule, *Teaching exceptional children*, 1981, *14*, 120–25. Copyright 1981 by The Council for Exceptional Children. Used with permission.

amination of the infant can help prevent problems or identify high-risk infants. Since most moderate handicaps and sensory impairments will be recognizable at birth or soon afterwards, the doctor's role is critical. Besides these handicaps, other conditions like parental neglect or abuse may be evident to the attentive physican. For the same reasons, nurses and nurse practitioners can be of enormous help in noting and questioning possible handicaps or conditions in the home that might lead to a handicap.

Other health professionals contribute to identification, assessment, or treatment of specific problems that can cause handicaps. The ophthamologist can detect early vision problems, and he or an optometrist can fit a child with corrective lenses. The audiologist can make a careful assessment of a child's hearing, so that a hearing aid or other treatment can be prescribed if there is a loss.

In many programs, a psychologist assists in the evaluation of the child's social-emotional skills and cognitive development. Psychologists often participate in the initial assessments of a child by giving standardized tests. Finally, staff psychologists often participate in team planning for a child.

Because so large a portion of mild handicaps are based in social and cultural factors, the social worker can be instrumental in helping children receive services. It is often the social worker who has admittance to many homes in low socioeconomic areas, which are correlated with higher incidences of mild retardation and learning problems. The case worker can take note of young children whose behavior suggests future problems and can refer them for assessment and possible placement. Afterward, the social worker may help explain, monitor, or evaluate the progress of a home-based intervention.

See chapter 3's discussion of cultural-familial retardation.

Because acquiring language is so critical in the development of all children, a speech-language pathologist is an important part of almost every intervention team. Speech and language specialists usually assess every child referred for services, and they participate in the intervention plans for many children. In fact, over half of the handicapped children enrolled in Head Start programs in 1977 were speech-impaired, and nearly 5% more were deaf or hearing impaired ("HEW reports 13%," 1978). For all these children, intervention must include a specialist in language acquisition and speech disorders.

For children who have physical or multiple handicaps, a physical therapist can help. Physical therapy can help prevent further deterioration of muscles; it can also be applied to teaching the child gross and fine motor coordination. Likewise, the occupational therapist contributes to the intervention program for children with physical, multiple, or other severe impairments. He or she provides instruction in movement, self-help skills, and the use of adaptive equipment.

With children with mild handicaps, teachers and other staff in regular preschools and day-care centers may be the first to identify certain delays in development or other problems like mild sensory impairments, social-emotional problems, learning difficulties, or language problems. Prompt referral for special education services can often get these children the help they need, before they fall significantly behind their peers. As more and more handicapped children are integrated into regular preschools, the role of teachers and paraprofessionals in these settings will become increasingly critical.

The actual delivery of services, whether in a home or center program, most often centers on the special teacher, regardless of what title that person has. This is the person who must be most knowledgeable about the child's instructional goals and objectives, the specific strategies and activities that will accomplish them, and the day-to-day progress the child makes. The teacher must be well-trained in observing, analyzing, selecting, and sequencing learning tasks so that the child overcomes delays rather than falling farther behind. The teacher must be imaginative and willing to try new things, but patient enough to give a program a chance once it is begun. Not only must he or she be able to find what motivates and reinforces a child, but the teacher must also be able to relate to all the others involved in the child's program. In a home-based program, the home teacher or visitor must be able to train parents to take the primary responsibility for teaching their children. Even in center-based programs, a large share of the center's parent-training efforts may fall to the special teacher.

Parents—Most Important of All

Of all the people needed to make early intervention work, parents are the most important. Given enough information, parents can help to prevent many risks and causes of handicaps—before pregnancy, before birth, or at least before the infant has gone months or years without help. Given the chance (as recent laws have done), parents can become active in determining their child's educational needs and goals. Given some guidance and training, parents can teach their handicapped child in the home and even in the school.

See chapter 13 for a detailed discussion of parent involvement.

It is no wonder, then, that the most successful intervention programs for young handicapped children take great care to involve parents. Shearer and Shearer (1977) report that parents involved in early childhood programs for the handicapped have taken roles as members of advisory councils for the programs, as consumers who inform others, as staff members, primary teachers, recruiters, curriculum developers, counselors, assessment personnel, and evaluators and record keepers.

Parents are the most frequent and constant observers of their children's behavior. They usually know better than anyone else what the child needs, and they can help educators to set realistic goals based on their observations. They can report on events in the home which outsiders might never see—for instance, how the child responds to other family members. They can monitor and report on the child's progress at home, beyond the more controlled environment of the center or preschool. In short, they can contribute to their child's program at every stage—assessment, planning, classroom activities, and evaluation.

Many parents even work in classrooms as teachers, teacher aides, volunteers, or other staff members. Programs like those we examined earlier all contain strong parent involvement. At the Model Preschool Center in Seattle, a center-based program:

> one of the most distinguishing features of this program (for infants) is that parents of enrolled infants are bona fide members of the team. One of the underlying principles is that continuity of care is critical, and that continuity can best be

INTERVENTION

achieved if the parents, who spend so much more time with the infant than do the other team members, participate in assessment and remediation. (Adams, Beck, Chandler, & Livingston, 1977, p. 304)

At the PEECH Project, a combined home-center program:

The parent involvement program focuses on helping to provide home assistance to parents and on helping parents to develop a basic understanding of the school and its program. . . . In addition, a weekly workshop is held for the approximately 10 mothers who can attend. Topics during these workshops include reinforcing behaviors at home, selecting safe toys, and parent's responsibilities to the school. (Karnes & Zehrbach, 1977, p. 34)

As we have seen, a number of early intervention programs focus on the home as the best and most natural learning environment and on the parent as the best and most natural teacher for the handicapped child. And as the two statements above make clear, even center-based programs rely heavily on parents as teachers who carry the center program over into the home.

Shearer and Shearer (1977) believe, "based on experience in the Portage Project, which teaches parents to teach their own child, that the most effective way of remediating behavioral excesses or deficits is to teach the child's first teacher to become the child's best teacher" (p. 230). They list six techniques for getting and keeping parents involved:

1. Set goals at a level the child and parent will accomplish within a short time, for instance, a week.
2. Model for the parents. Show them, do not just tell them what to do.
3. After modeling, allow the parents to take over and work on the same activity with the child while the teacher observes.
4. Reinforce the parents. Let them know they are doing it right.
5. Remember that parents are *not* the same. It is as important to individualize for the parents based on their present behavior as it is to individualize for the child based on his.
6. Involve the parents in planning appropriate goals for the child. (p. 230)

LEARNING TOGETHER

The Early Education Program at Ohio State University's Nisonger Center is a cooperative venture between public education, the university, and the community. The program consists of four classrooms serving a total of 40 mildly, moderately, and severely developmentally delayed children between the ages of 18 months and 6 years. In addition to the 10 handicapped children in each classroom, 3 to 5 nondelayed children are enrolled. The handicapped children are referred to the preschool by the Franklin County Board of Mental Retardation and Developmental Disabilities. The nonhandicapped children come from one of three groups: siblings of enrolled handicapped children, children of Ohio State University faculty and staff, and children of parents who have responded to ads placed in local newspapers recruiting for the program.

Dr. Rosalind Williams, coordinator of early education at the center, spoke with us about the program. "We have two primary purposes for integrating handicapped and nonhandicapped children. One is to provide opportunities for the delayed child to learn through modeling, by observing his or her nondelayed peers. We'll often have a nonhandicapped child participate in an individual learning activity with a delayed child. The task chosen may be below the developmental level of the nondelayed child, one he's al-

Circle time.

ready mastered. An example would be forming simple shapes for a nondelayed 4-year-old. For his handicapped peer, making those circles and squares may be difficult. Seeing his nonhandicapped peer perform the activity is not only beneficial from a modeling viewpoint, we find it also serves as powerful motivation. Somehow watching your playmate do it is more interesting than watching the teacher.

"A second reason for integrating the children relates to the center's role as a training and research facility in addition to being a service provider. Having the nondelayed children in the classroom with the handicapped children exposes our student trainees to the full continuum of childhood development. Many professionals who have been trained only in segregated special education settings lose the perspective and important knowledge of what normal development looks like. Such knowledge is essential for planning and evaluating intervention programs for handicapped children.

"Of course, there's another benefit from integration. And that is the learning that takes place by the nonhandicapped children. One of the big cognitive tasks during early childhood is to learn what it's like from the other person's perspective, moving a bit from being totally me-centered to understanding another's point of view. Part of that is learning about differences between the child and others. A good example of what I'm talking about happened a couple weeks ago. I entered one of the classrooms with a new student, a nonhandicapped child. We walked up to the water table and another nonhandicapped child playing there asked, "Can she talk?" She showed an understanding that most 3-year-olds don't have—being aware of and considering the possibility that another child may be different and have special needs."

SUMMARY

1. It is especially important to identify and work with handicapped children as early as possible. Fortunately, the relatively new movement in early education has received government support in the form of legislative mandates and funds for preschool programs and model centers for severely handicapped babies.

2. The effectiveness of early intervention with high-risk infants has been demonstrated by numerous research studies and model programs.

3. We can use our knowledge of causes of handicapping conditions to detect certain handicapping conditions during pregnancy, in the delivery room, or soon after birth.
   a. As a rule, the more severe the handicap, the earlier it can be detected.
   b. Good preschool personnel can sometimes pick up signs of mild handicaps.

4. In spite of what we know about the advantages of early identification of handicaps, there is no universally used system to screen all infants.
   a. Most newborns do receive an Apgar rating and screening for certain metabolic disorders.
   b. Other screening tests based on normal child development are widely used, but not unless a concerned adult feels an evaluation is needed.

5. Once a child is identified as being at risk to develop a handicap, the next step is detailed assessment.
   a. This assessment is often conducted by members of an interdisciplinary team.
   b. There are many formal, standardized tests available to assess delayed or abnormal development in intellectual development, auditory perception, and affective and social development.
   c. There is also a growing number of informal checklists, rating scales, and other assessment devices as well. Most measure cognitive development, motor development, language development, self-help skills, play skills, and personal-social skills.
   d. Because of the serious effects of failing to identify a child who needs special services or labeling a child "handicapped" who is not, it is important that the person doing the assessment be experienced and well trained, able to interpret the raw data accurately.

6. As much as possible, we should use more genetic counseling, better prenatal care, wider screening for metabolic disorders, and public education to help prevent the development of handicaps.

7. Most early intervention programs are based on one of three models.
   a. In home-based programs, the child's parents act as the primary teachers, with regular training and guidance from a teacher or specially trained paraprofessional who visits the home.

b. Home-based programs offer the advantages of taking place in a natural environment with appropriate materials, involving family members, and allowing the parents to feel they are helping their child.

c. In center-based programs, the child comes to the center for direct instruction, though the parents are usually involved.

d. Center programs offer the opportunity for a team of specialists to work with the child and for the child to meet other handicapped and nonhandicapped children.

e. Many programs offer both home visits and center-based programming, thus combining the advantages of the two models.

8. There are several different approaches to organizing curricula for young children: remediating delays, teaching basic processes, teaching developmental tasks, teaching psychological constructs, and teaching preacademic skills.

a. All these approaches use normal development as a standard against which to measure each child.

b. Two important curriculum concerns are promoting language development and scheduling activities to be instructionally effective.

9. A wide range of professionals should be involved in the team which works with young handicapped children. They include:

a. Obstetricians, pediatricians, and nurses
b. Other health specialists
c. Psychologists
d. Social workers
e. Speech-language pathologists
f. Physical and occupational therapists
g. Teachers and staff in day-care centers
h. Special teachers

10. Parents are the most important people in an early intervention program. They can act as advocates, participate in educational planning, observe the child's behavior and help set realistic goals, work in the classroom, and teach the child at home.

FOR MORE INFORMATION

Journals

Day Care and Early Education. Published bimonthly by Human Sciences Press Periodicals. Directed at day-care personnel; articles focus on innovative ideas for educating preschool children.

Topics in Early Childhood Education

Young Children. Published bimonthly by the National Association for the Education of Young Children. Articles spotlight current projects, theory, and research in early childhood as well as practical teaching ideas.

Books

Fallen, N. H., with McGovern, J. E. *Young children with special needs.* Columbus, Ohio: Charles E. Merrill, 1978.

Jordan, J., Hayden, A., Karnes, M., & Wood, M. (eds.) *Early education for exceptional children: A handbook of ideas and exemplary practices.* Reston, Va.: The Council for Exceptional Children, 1977.

Tjossem, T. D. (ed.) *Intervention strategies for high risk infants and young children.* Baltimore: University Park Press, 1976.

Organization

The Division for Early Childhood, The Council for Exceptional Children, 1920 Association Drive, Reston, VA 22091.

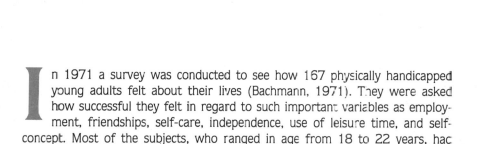

15

The Disabled Adult

I n 1971 a survey was conducted to see how 167 physically handicapped young adults felt about their lives (Bachmann, 1971). They were asked how successful they felt in regard to such important variables as employment, friendships, self-care, independence, use of leisure time, and self-concept. Most of the subjects, who ranged in age from 18 to 22 years, had graduated from "special" schools in 1964 or 1965.

The results were at least enlightening if not encouraging. All but a few of the young adults felt their lives were *un*successful in *all* areas. Most of the subjects were unemployed; only nine were competitively employed. Few had any friends, most were almost completely dependent on their parents, and all but one had a poor self-concept. And remember, these were young adults who had graduated from "special" schools, schools with curricula that were supposedly preparing them to enter the real world.

A major disability can handicap a young person in all areas of life. Fortunately, special educators are becoming more and more aware of the need to provide training and educational experiences beyond the traditional walls of the classroom. Trained personnel are needed to teach functional, daily living skills, increase personal independence, provide vocational rehabilitation, and teach recreation and leisure skills, not only to school-age handicapped children but to handicapped adults, who either never received the necessary training and services as children, who simply need continued training in order to realize their maximum independence and feeling of self-worth, or who become handicapped—either through disease or accident—as adolescents or adults. In all, about one out of eleven people between the ages of 16 and 65 are handicapped.

In this chapter we will look at three areas where special educators and other professionals are trying to improve the lives of handicapped adults—residential alternatives, employment, and recreation and leisure.

BONNIE

Bonnie Consolo

Bonnie Consolo is a 44-year-old divorced mother of two teen-age boys. She lives in a comfortable split-level house in a Midwestern suburb and supports her family with money earned from speaking engagements around the country. Most of the time, she drives to those engagements. Bonnie is also currently writing the story of her life, which doesn't sound remarkable until you realize that she was born without arms.

Because of my physical difference, my life is more interesting. I meet more people, possibly because I've been on TV [featured on CBS' "60 Minutes" as well as local programs] and in newspapers. People don't tend to shy away from me. A lot of people con-

sider their lives dull; they're in a rut. My physical difference eliminates the rut for me. Of course people have stared at me for 44½ years and probably will for the rest of my life. It used to bother me but now I realize that it's a normal human reaction to stare at things you're not used to seeing.

Being "handicapped" doesn't affect me in the community. I feel a lot of pride in my life. God uses my life and everything I do. My just going along, head held high, with a look of pride on my face, helps some people see that there have to be some problems in life to help us to grow. Every time I meet somebody I try to go away a better person. I hope the other person goes away with some kind of better understanding of the relationship, at least, no matter how brief it is.

I am sure, though, that my handicap has a big effect on the men I meet socially. I've been told by a male friend that ever since he met me he's wondered what it would be like to make love to me. This is not an emotional attraction, more a matter of curiosity. I'm sure other men have the same reaction. My personality wouldn't matter. It would take men getting to know me before they could relate to me as a woman. There are a lot of obstacles between men and me; because of the way they've grown up, it would take a bit more for them to relax and see me as a person than it would if I had the same personality but had arms. I suspect they're saying, "What would the guys think? Oh, surely, he could find someone better!" That's a likely first reaction (and possibly their reaction after they do get to know me!)

Even though it seems there are obstacles, I would like to get married again. I've never had the warm, loving relationship I've always wanted, even though I've been married twice. I don't think my handicap affected my first marriage. However, Bill was a para-plegic, so maybe that brought us closer to-gether. My second husband was a person used to getting whatever he wanted. I think he saw me as a means of achieving his goals. He was willing to "use" my handicap in a way that I, up to that point, wasn't. He pushed for a film to be made of me and got me started on my speaking career. At the time, my younger son was only 3, and I wanted to stay at home and be a wife and mother. Now I'm glad that Frank made me go ahead and do things; I'm not sorry.

When I first had kids, I was worried about what they would think of me, how they would adjust to having a mother who is "different." I didn't want them to think of me as anything but Mom, to be embarrassed. So as soon as they were old enough to talk about it, we did. We always laughed and made jokes about it. Now Mark is almost 16 and Matt is 11½. They bring their friends home just like any other teen-agers, and we all get along well.

I like what I'm doing now. I have friends all over the country. I feel that if people can cope with me, that's fine. I'm me. There's nothing I can do, or want to do, to change it. In fact, I wouldn't if I could. If people don't like me as I am, that's their problem. I'm happy.

Might later on have my own house—right in the middle of town. That way you don't have to walk your legs off. Boy, they make a lot of new houses out here. (Gollay, Freedman, Wyngarten, & Kurtz, 1978, p. 58)

Where a person lives determines a great deal about how that person lives. Where a person lives influences where he or she can work, the availability of community services and resources, who friends will be, opportunities for recreation and leisure, and, to a great extent, feelings of self and place in the community. It was not long ago that the total-care institution was the only place you could live if you were severely handicapped and could not live independently or did not live with your family. There were no other options, no such thing as residential *alternatives.* Today we are witnessing a significant increase in community-based residential alternatives and services for the adult handicapped. In fact, the principle of normalization has probably had its greatest effect in residential placement.

Chapter 3 discusses normalization and what it means for retarded students.

A variety of living arrangements for the handicapped are now available in many communities and geographical regions. Today there is a range of environments—with several alternatives between the two extremes of an institution or full independent living—from which to serve the differing needs of individual persons. Three residential alternatives that are seeing increased use are foster family homes, group homes, and apartment living.

Foster Homes

When a family opens their home to an unrelated person for an extended period of time, the term **foster home** is often used. While foster homes have been used for years in providing temporary residential services and family care for children (usually wards of the court), more and more families are beginning to share their homes with handicapped adults. In return for providing room and board to their "new" family member, foster families receive a modest financial reimbursement.

For the handicapped adult, there can be numerous advantages to life in a foster family home. The resident can participate and share in the day-to-day activities of a normal family, receive individual attention from people vitally interested in his or her continued growth and development, and develop close interpersonal relationships. As part of a family unit, the handicapped adult also has increased opportunities to interact with and be accepted by the community at large.

However, Baker, Seltzer, and Seltzer (1977) warned that, even though adults living in foster homes might be involved regularly with the new "family members," they are sometimes discouraged from getting involved with people and activities outside the home, thereby resulting in unnecessary restrictions and isolation.

Group Homes

Group homes provide "family-life" living to a group of handicapped adults, from as few as 3 or 4 to as many as 10 or 15. Most group homes operating today serve mentally retarded adults, though there are some group homes with residents with other handicaps. Group homes vary as to purpose. Some are principally residential and represent a permanent placement for their residents. In this type of group home, educational programming revolves around developing self-care and daily living skills, forming interpersonal relationships, and learning recreational skills and use of leisure time. During the day, most residents would be outside the house employed in the community or in a **sheltered workshop.**

Other group homes operate more as "halfway houses." Their primary function is to prepare the handicapped adult for a more independent living situation, such as a supervised apartment. These transitional group homes typically serve residents who have recently been discharged from institutions, bridging the gap between institutional and community living.

Two key aspects of group homes make them a much more normalized place to live than an institution: their *size* and, importantly, their *location* (Wolfensberger, 1972). Most people grow up in a typical family-sized group, where there is opportunity for personal attention, care, and privacy. Certainly, the 40-bed-to-a-ward, mass-living arrangement common to many institutions cannot be said to be "normalized," regardless of the efforts of hardworking, caring staff. By keeping the number of residents in a group home small, there is a greater chance for a family-like atmosphere. Size is also directly related to the neighborhood's ability to assimilate the members of the group home into normal, routine activities of the community, which is the key element of normalization.

Betty made her own work schedule to remind her of her household duties in the group home.

Although research on the effects of size of group homes has been inconclusive, operators of community residential programs consistently state that residential settings of three or four individuals are much more likely to be integrated into the community (Cooke, 1981). Bronston (1980) offers four arguments favoring small residential settings: (1) the group and the home do not attract undue attention by being larger than a large family; (2) the smaller the number of "different" individuals in a group home, the more likely the neighborhood will absorb them; (3) large groups tend to become self-sufficient, orienting inward and thereby resisting movement outward into the community; and (4) in groups larger than six or eight, "houseparents" and advisors can no longer relate properly to individual group members.

The location and physical characteristics of the group home itself are also vital determiners of its ability to provide a normalized life-style for its residents. Therefore, a group home must be located within the community, in a residential area, not a commercially zoned district. It must be in an area where residents have convenient access to shopping, schools, churches, public transportation, and recreational facilities. In other words, a group home must be located in a normal residential area where you or I might live. And it must *look like a home*, not be conspicuously different from any of the other family dwellings on the same street. You won't find a group home by driving down the street looking for a sign out front that reads "Elm Street Group Home for the Retarded."

Wolfensberger and Glenn (1975) have developed a method for assessing the degree to which a service setting meets the criteria of normalization. Called Program Analyses of Service Systems (PASS), the assessment produces a quantitative rating. Pieper and Cappuccilli (1980) have suggested the following set of questions, based on PASS, as a means of determining how appropriate a given residential setting may be. A group home would be considered a normalized setting if all or most of these questions can be answered "yes."

☐ Did the residents choose to live in the home?

☐ Is this type of setting usually inhabited by people in the residents' age group?

☐ Do the residents live with others their own age?

☐ Is the home located within a residential neighborhood?

☐ Does the residence look like the other dwellings around it?

☐ Can the number of people living in the residence be reasonably expected to assimilate into the community?

☐ Are community resources and facilities readily accessible from the residence?

☐ Do the residents have a chance to buy the house?

☐ Do the managers of the place act in an appropriate manner toward the residents?

☐ Are the residents encouraged to do all they can for themselves?

☐ Are the residents encouraged to have personal belongings that are appropriate to their age?

☐ Are residents encouraged to use community resources as much as possible?

☐ Are all the residents' rights acknowledged?

☐ Are the residents being given enough training and assistance to help them be growing, developing individuals?

☐ Would I want to live in the home? Here is the final test. If the residence appears good enough for you to want to live in it, it will probably be an appropriate living arrangement for persons with special needs. We should demand residential arrangements for persons with special needs that are comparable to those inhabited by most nondisabled citizens. (pp. 52–54)

Group homes have become the most widely used residential alternative to institutional placement for mentally retarded adults. New group homes are opening every day all across the country. And, as might be expected, they are generally well liked by the residents, particularly those who have lived in institutions.

However, as you also might expect, group homes have run into obstacles. The public has been slow to accept group homes into their neighborhoods. Most agencies, service groups, and individuals who have started (or attempted to start) group homes for retarded adults have run into harsh resistance. Convinced that the mentally retarded are dangerous or "crazy," that they will be bad influences on their children, or that property values will go down if a group home comes into the area, neighborhood associations have too often been effective in keeping group homes from starting. Unfortunately, this has resulted in too many group homes having to locate in poor, run-down areas of a community. Currently, a number of organizations are conducting educational campaigns in an effort to inform the general public and dispel many of the untruths and myths about mentally retarded people that hamper efforts to integrate these citizens into the mainstream of our society. One organization that is trying to combat the misconceptions, fears, guilt, and resentment many feel toward the handicapped is One-to-One. One-to-One is a nonprofit organization that helps group homes for mentally retarded adults get underway. It works with the news and entertainment media in an effort to dispel the public's misconceptions of handicapped people.

Apartment Living

Apartment living offers the handicapped adult an even greater opportunity for integration into the community than group homes do. Where, in a group home, the handicapped resident interacts primarily with other handicapped persons, in an apartment-living arrangement (assuming the apartment is in a regular apartment complex), the likelihood of interacting with more nonhandicapped persons is increased. Some professionals believe that full integration into the community will only be achieved when all handicapped persons are in private homes or apartments, that even small group homes are too "institutional." Bronston (1980) has even suggested that "apartment dwellings could suffice for all our

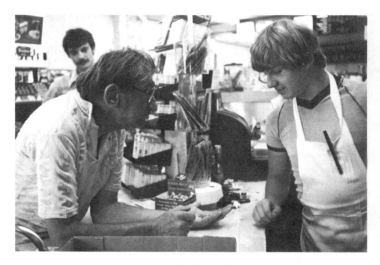

Evaluating a teaching program in money management where it really counts: making an independent purchase at the corner store.

adult service needs, except where acute medical/hospital services were needed to stabilize a person for short-term duration." Three forms of apartment living for handicapped adults are most common: the apartment cluster, the coresidence apartment, and the maximum-independence apartment.

An apartment cluster consists of a small number of apartments housing handicapped persons and another nearby apartment for a supervisory person or staff. An apartment cluster is an extremely workable arrangement because it allows for a great deal of flexibility in the amount and degree of supervision needed by residents in the various apartments. While some residents might require direct help with such things as shopping, cooking, or even getting dressed, others will need only limited assistance or suggestions and prompts. In an apartment cluster, some apartments are occupied by nonhandicapped persons, which facilitates social integration.

A coresidence apartment is shared by a handicapped and a nonhandicapped person. While this arrangement is sometimes permanent, most coresidence apartments are used as a step toward independent living. The live-in roommates are often unpaid volunteers.

Two to four handicapped adults usually co-habit maximum-independence apartments. These adults have all of the self-care and daily living skills required to take care of themselves and their apartment on a day-to-day basis. A supervisory visit is made once or twice a week to help the residents deal with any special problems they may be having.

Models of Residential Services and Staff Training

Foster homes, group homes, and apartments all represent different, community-based residential options. Although scientifically sound research is scarce, a review of the literature on residential alternatives for handicapped adults indicates that community living is better than institutional placement (Peck, Blackburn, & White-Blackburn, 1980). And at least one study has shown superior develop-

502 INTERVENTION

mental progress by mentally retarded adults living in the community as compared to matched controls living in an institution. But many problems and challenges are faced by those responsible for planning and implementing community-based residential services for handicapped adults. One kind of problem has to do with what has been called the "relocation syndrome" (Cochran, Sran, & Varano, 1977) or "transition shock" (Coffman & Harris, 1980). The person who has just left the institution needs support in the community. In the early days of the deinstitutionalization movement, too many former residents of state institutions were "dumped" into the community without the necessary skills to cope successfully in their new environment and without easy access to support and follow-up services to see that the transition was successful. A 1974 statement by the National Association of Superintendents of Public Residential Facilities for the Mentally Retarded reflected this concern.

> While the Association advocates without reservation the rights of the retarded to live in the least restrictive environment and to enjoy fully the benefits of a free and open society whenever possible, it does express concern over the manner in which this goal is being realized. First, the quality of community programs and services being offered to the mentally retarded and other developmentally disabled persons in many parts of the country is inadequate. All too often, "community back wards" and "closeting" (being shut up at home) are being substituted for institutional "warehousing." Neither community nor residential back wards or closeting are justified: the rights of the retarded must be respected wherever they reside (1974, pp. 2–3)

Fortunately, today there are fewer "horror stories" of institutional residents being released into the community and being victimized or served by the criminal justice system as a result of vagrancy, destitution, or a criminal offense. The major problem is one of providing a flexible *system* of residential options that truly meets the needs of individuals (Cooke, 1981). Most professionals agree that no one "type" of residential setting is best for all handicapped adults and that a continuum of options is needed (Bradley, 1978; Fanning, 1975; Seltzer & Seltzer, 1977). But the continuum of services approach, with residential options ranging from most restrictive to least restrictive, is not without its problems and critics. The typical continuum of residential options does not guarantee against gaps between one option and the next, nor does it recognize the possibility that there may be other, perhaps innovative, alternatives that are appropriate for some individuals (Cooke, 1981). Also, continuum of service models usually assume that a person moves into the residential service system at the more restrictive end and must "earn his way up" (Scheerenberger, 1974). The handicapped person is forced to earn the right to a least restrictive living arrangement.

This is not unlike the continuum of services model of educational placement options, described in chapter 2.

> The underlying philosophy of this model is not at all consistent with civil rights decisions in other areas. The Supreme Court ruled in the 1960s that black people had a right to ride in the front of the bus and to go to their neighborhood

JUDY AND KATHY

Judy and Kathy are two of the eight mentally retarded women who live in the St. Joseph Group Home in Westerville, Ohio. All of the women came there from Columbus Developmental Center (CDC), a large state-run institution for mentally retarded persons in Columbus, Ohio. When we visited them at the group home, Judy and Kathy talked to us about living there.

Judy, where did you live before you came here:
CDC.

Can you tell me what it is like living here compared to CDC? Which do you like better?
I like the group home best. Because you get more privileges. You get more freedom.

What kind of things can you do here that you couldn't do at CDC?
Here you can do a lot of things. Like planting a garden, working on the garden, help to do a lot of things in the house, go to work. And then they give you time to go to work.

Where do you work, Judy?
At Arcraft Workshop [a sheltered workshop].

What do you think about doing housework? Do you like it?
Yes. We get to do chores in the house every day. We get to cook our own food. We don't have to have nobody cook it for you. Each girl has a day to cook.

What do you like to cook best?
Fish, baked potatoes, and sweet potatoes, and then lime punch and lettuce salad.

What would you like to learn to cook?
Macaroni and cheese.

Can you cook it now?
No, Rose [the live-in director of the home] is teaching me.

Have you made any friends since you've come here, Judy?
One of my friends is Kathy, my roommate.

Do you two like to do things together?
Yes. We get to go outside and play, walk around. Talk to each other in our room.

Judy is specially proud of her library card.

Judy, what do you need to learn before you could have your own apartment?
I need to learn how to go shopping by myself. I will have my old man teach me.

Your old man? Do you have a boyfriend?
Yep, Phil.

Phil. Where does he live?
CDC. But he is planning to go out too, out in the community as soon as they find a place for him in a boy's apartment.

Do you ever get to see Phil?
Yep, sure do. He's coming next Tuesday when I get off work, at 3:30.

What are you going to do when he comes?
Cook his best supper for him and my best supper for all the ladies and the caseworkers.

What is his best supper?
Baked potatoes, onion rings, lima beans, meatloaf.

Kathy, how do you like living here?
I like this. This is a nicer home than CDC. We keep our house real nice and neat. And sometimes when I was at CDC, the boys walked in when I was doing something and embarrassed me.

So you have more privacy here?
Yes, it's better.

Your house is beautiful. But here you have to clean it yourself. You don't mind doing the work?
No.

Have you made any friends while you've been here?
Yes, I have. Judy. Judy is my favorite friend here.

What kinds of things do you and Judy do when you have free time?
We go up in our bedroom and talk to each other and also we clean our bedroom every Saturday. And I help her out when she's sick, and she helps me out when I'm sick.

How about seeing men? Do you have a boyfriend?
Yes, I do. His name is James.

When do you get to see James?
When I go to my boyfriend's house.

How do you get to your boyfriend's house?
Rose drives me.

How did you meet James?
From CDC.

Is he living in a group home now too?
Yes, on Dennison Road

Does he like it?
Yes, but he doesn't keep his house clean.

You'll have to tell him about that.
I did.

What did he say?
"I will, honey." Then when I went to his house last week, his house was clean.

What did you say to him?
"Congratulations!"

Tuesday is Kathy's day to clean the yellow bathroom.

schools, rights based simply on their citizenship—not rights they had to earn. But with "developmentally disabled" people we have said you must earn the right to live in an integrated setting. You must behave yourself before we'll ever give you this right. This is clearly a basic form of discrimination. (Hitzing, 1980, p. 84)

Several innovative models for residential services for handicapped adults that are based on the belief that residential placements must be adapted to the needs of clients—not vice versa—have been developed in recent years (Apolloni & Cooke, 1981; Hitzing, 1980; Provencal, 1980).

A significant problem faced by planners and administrators of any community-based residential option is securing, training, and keeping competent staff. Direct care staff in residential settings must perform a demanding role, often serving as family member, friend, counselor, and teacher to one individual all in a day's time. In many programs, there is little incentive for staff members to try to help the residents become more independent. A resident who becomes too self-sufficient moves away, replaced by a new, more dependent resident (Cooke, 1981). Lakin and Bruininks (1981) found very high rates of staff turnover in community residential programs.

The training received by residential staff members varies considerably from one program to another. The more successful residential services programs place tremendous emphasis on staff training, making it mandatory and ongoing. Most training objectives are practical as opposed to theoretical; they stress first aid, fire safely, nutrition, neighborhood relations, behavior management, teaching daily living skills, and so on (Cooke, 1981).

EMPLOYMENT

Work can be defined as using your physical and/or mental energies to accomplish something productive. Our society is based on a work ethic; we place a high value on work and people who "contribute." Besides providing for economic support, work offers opportunities for social interaction, a chance to use and further enhance skills in your chosen line of work. Work generates the respect of others, and importantly, it can be a source of pride and self-satisfaction (Terkel, 1974).

In spite of the much-heralded accomplishments of some handicapped persons, getting a job presents a major difficulty for the majority of handicapped adults. While all young adults face important questions about what to do with their lives—whether to attend college or technical school; whether to work as a brick layer or an accountant—for the nonhandicapped the difficulty lies mostly in choosing from a number of options. But the handicapped adult often has few, if any, options to choose from. Occupational choices are decreased if the handicapped person has limited skills; decreased further in most cases by the nature of the disability (for example, the blind cannot perform jobs that require vision); and needlessly decreased still further by prejudices and misconceptions about

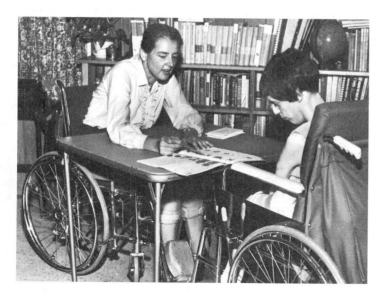

Staff in a community-based residential program must play many roles—family member, friend, counselor, teacher.

handicapped people that many employers hold. For many handicapped adults, obtaining and holding a job is *the major rehabilitation goal.*

The need for vocational rehabilitation and training is dramatically evident in the statistics produced by recent studies and surveys. The Bureau of the Census estimates that there are 12.4 million noninstitutionalized persons aged 16 to 64 with a "work disability," and 7.7 million more who are not in the labor force. Viscardi (1976) reported that, of 11 million handicapped adults who could work, only 4 million were working and most of those were underemployed. A community survey of 161 disabled adults in Columbia, Missouri, found only 46% either employed or going to school (Schoepke, 1979). When handicapped adults do find work, they typically are underemployed and underpaid. Wolfe (1980) analyzed data gathered by the Department of Labor in 1977 and found the average wage rate per hour was $2.57 for disabled workers and $4.27 for the nondisabled. Both male and female handicapped workers as a group, at every educational level, were paid less than their nonhandicapped counterparts.

Section 504 of the Rehabilitation Act forbids job discrimination on the basis of handicap, but the problem remains.

State vocational rehabilitation agencies have been, and continue to be, the major source of support for facilities and training programs that provide vocational counseling, training, and work experiences for the handicapped. Congress passed the Vocational Rehabilitation Amendments of 1954 and 1965, providing funds for development of employment services and training for mentally retarded adults. These funds have mostly been used to support sheltered workshop facilities and staff that serve only moderately retarded individuals. Federal legislation (for example, the Developmental Disabilities Services and Facilities Construction Act of 1970) has emphasized the need to provide vocational rehabilitation services to severely handicapped adults, who in the past have been judged as unsuitable for training because of the severity of their handicaps. A new law, P.L. 95–602, the Rehabilitation Comprehensive Services and Develop-

VOCATIONAL TRAINING WITH A FLAVOR

The Country Squire Restaurant in Killingworth, Connecticut, is open for dinner Tuesday through Sunday, in addition to its Monday through Friday Squire lunches. The 25 employees of the Country Squire—the cooks, bakers, waitresses, dishwashers, bartender, cashier—are all adults with handicaps such as mental retardation, autism, and cerebral palsy. Under the supervision of five trainers, they are learning the skills required for various restaurant jobs.

The Country Squire is one of a constellation of small businesses operated by SARAH, the Shoreline Association for Retarded and Handicapped Citizens, in and around Guilford, Connecticut. SARAH's progressive and very successful commitment to a nontraditional small-business model for training and employing persons with disabilities is attracting widespread recognition. Over 100 handicapped adults participate in training and employment programs throughout SARAH's varied businessess—two restaurants, a greenhouse, a landscaping service, and a nine-hole golf course, to name a few. Each of the businesses serves the public and must attract customers and achieve profitability by delivering a high-quality product.

Peter McManus, director of vocational services, indicated that SARAH (which also operates residential and recreational programs) elected not to pursue contracted benchwork,

---

THE CUP & THE BOWL

**1. BAKED ONION
   GRATINEE** 1.25   1.75

2. TODAY'S SOUP .. see blackboard
Our soups are freshly made daily.

3. THE SPINACH SALAD 3.25
   Fresh spinach with garnish of mushrooms, bacon, sliced egg, red oinion and Swiss Cheese. Tossed with a special oil and vinegar dressing. Served with freshly made bread and butter.

4. THE BURGER 3.75
   A. With melted Blue Cheese *or*
   B. With sauteed mushrooms
   Hand-pressed chuck steak burger on our own freshly baked English sytle muffin. Served with Squire Fries, lettuce, tomato and a side order of Herb Dressing.

6. **THE QUICHE** .... see blackboard
&   Quiche served with herb green beans,
7. cranberry salad mold on a bed of lettuce with tomato and Herb Dressing.

THE USUAL SANDWICH
*Presented on our own
freshly baked pumpernickel and rye
bread with Squire Fries and Demi Salad.*

8. HOT PASTRAMI 2.75

9. SHAVED HAM & SWISS ... 2.95

10. TUNA SALAD 2.95

THE UNUSUAL SANDWICH
*Served with Squire Fries
and Demi Salad.*

11. CHEESE DREAM 2.50
   Grilled cheese on whole wheat bread with tomato and herbs.

**12. TURKEY AND HAM
   MORNAY** 3.75
   Ham, white meat of turkey and fresh broccoli spears arranged on toast. Topped with cheese sauce and broiled till golden.

**13. THE ONLY SQUIRE
   IN TOWN** 3.65
   Lean hot pastrami, grilled onions, tomatoes, and melted Swiss Cheese layered on pumpernickel & rye bread.

14. THE BLUE MAX 3.75
   Ham, turkey, bacon, tomato and Blue Cheese, layered on pumpernickel and rye bread. Topped with Muenster Cheese and broiled until golden.

THE HALF & HALF

**15. SOUP & HALF
   SANDWICH** 2.50
   A cup of Onion or Today's Soup with ½ of your usual sandwich.

**16. SALAD & HALF
   SANDWICH** 2.65
   Small Spinach Salad with ½ of your usual sandwich.

THE KIDDIES CORNER
Served with Squire Fries and Pickles.

(4) HAMBURG 1.50

(9) HAM AND CHEESE 1.45

(10) TUNA SALAD 1.45

(11) GRILLED CHEESE 1.25

THE BEVERAGE

A. COFFEE .... .45

B. HOT TEA .... .40

C. SQUIRE'S ICE TEA .... .50

D. HERB TEA .... .45

E. MILK .... .40

F. SODA .... .45
a. Coke   b. Tab   c. Ginger Ale   d. Orange

THE DESSERT
See blackboard for selection.

PLEASE ORDER BY
NUMBER OR LETTER.

THANK YOU.

the traditional sheltered employment for handicapped persons. "These are jobs that the private business sector is eliminating through automation. On the other hand, there is an increasing demand for high-quality personal services."

The Country Squire seats up to 72 guests at 25 tables, keeping everyone very busy during the rush hours. The employees smile as they go about their jobs taking orders, slicing meat, removing rolls from the oven, serving food. Waitress Jane Lemley calls it her second home. "I have friends here." For 46-year-old waitress Doris Babcock, it's the first job she's ever had "I love it here." But as much as she loves and respects her employees, restaurant manager Roberta Banks hopes to see them move on to competitive employment. "Many employees now have the skills needed to work in any restaurant or kitchen."

Some people come to the restaurant out of curiosity, but they return for the food.

A real job provides an important sense of pride and self-worth.

ment Disabilities Amendments of 1978, provides a 5-year extension of comprehensive rehabilitation services for severely disabled individuals. The program focuses on providing services to handicapped persons whose disabilities are so severe that employment is not the primary goal.

Eligibility for federal and state vocational rehabilitation services is based on a physical or mental/behavioral disability that constitutes a substantial handicap to employment. The program provides all services free of charge to disabled persons who are unable to pay; the disabled person who is financially able to bear part or all of the cost must pay for some services. Humphreys (1979) outlined the basic services provided by the vocational rehabilitation program:

☐ Comprehensive evaluation;

☐ Medical, surgical, and hospital care, along with related therapy to remove or reduce disability;

☐ Prosthetic and orthotic devices;

☐ Counseling, guidance, referral, placement, and training;

☐ Use of comprehensive or specialized rehabilitation facilities;

☐ Maintenance and transportation during rehabilitation;

☐ Tools, equipment, and licenses for work on a job or in establishing a small business;

☐ Initial stock, supplies, and management assistance for small businesses, including establishment of vending facilities by the state agency;

☐ Readers for blind persons and interpreters for deaf people;

☐ Recruitment and training to provide new careers for disabled people in the field of rehabilitation and other public service areas;

☐ Construction or establishment of rehabilitation facilities;

☐ Provision of facilities and services that promise to contribute to a group of handicapped persons but do not relate directly to the rehabilitation plan of any one person;

INTERVENTION

☐ Services to families of handicapped persons when the services will contribute to the rehabilitation of the handicapped client;

☐ Follow-up to help disabled persons hold a job;

☐ Other goods and services necessary to render handicapped persons employable. (p. 235)

Bigge (1982) has identified five types of vocational training and rehabilitation services that are provided by rehabilitation centers, sheltered workshops, and other similar agencies. These are work evaluation, work adjustment, work experience, vocational skills training, and on-the-job training programs. In work evaluation programs, the client performs a variety of tasks. The staff assesses the client's current skills and helps him or her arrive at realistic employment goals. Work adjustment programs are designed to help the handicapped person acquire and learn necessary attitudes and skills that are part of any work environment. These include being on time, staying on-task, and getting along with others. Clients who have worked competitively at one time, but need a supervised work situation in order to relearn various skills before reentering the job market, might participate in a work experience program. Vocational skills training means a concentrated program designed to teach specific skills required in a given trade or for a certain job. Once the handicapped person has learned the necessary skills, he or she seeks employment in the competitive job market. If this training takes place in the place where the person is to be employed, it is called on-the-job training.

On-the-job training: the prospective employer points out for client and trainer the criteria for good work.

Figure 15.1 shows the sequence of activities and services used by one vocational program that trains severely disabled adults for competitive employment in the community (Vogelsberg, Williams, & Ashe, 1981). Each trainee passes through the four stages of evaluation, on-the-job training, placement, and maintenance and follow-up. In this program, a job opening in the community is matched with the available client most likely to learn and maintain the job successfully. Training takes place at the actual job site, with the vocational trainer at the trainee's side. Formal placement on the job begins when the trainer is only needed for weekly observations. Monthly follow-up observations are conducted until the worker is completely integrated into the work setting and no further assistance is needed.

Sheltered Workshops

The sheltered workshop is the most widely used type of vocational training facility for handicapped adults. In 1966, there were 885 certified sheltered workshops in the United States serving 47,000 clients. By 1975, the numbers had more than doubled to 2,766 workshops serving more than 117,000 clients (Victor, 1976). Sheltered workshops serve clients with a wide variety of handicapping conditions—although about half of all clients in sheltered workshops are mentally retarded—and degrees of disability. Sheltered workshops can be classified as providing one (or a combination) of three types of programs: evaluation and training for competitive employment in the community (these are commonly referred to as *transitional workshops*), extended or long-term employment, and work activities.

FIGURE 15.1
Training cycle for competitive employment

I. Evaluation	II. Intensive On-the-Job Training	III. Placement	IV. Maintenance and Follow-up
Referral	Interview	Employer, trainee and trainer agree to start fading trainer	Monthly observations
VR eligible?	Training Baseline		Monthly evaluation forms filled out by:
Initial Intake	Intensive training on	Gradual withdrawal of assistance	trainee
Individual Skill Inventory	direct work skills indirect work skills		trainer
Parent/Guardian Consent	Trainee/Trainer/Employer decisions about placement	Agreement to begin formal placement	supervisor/employer parent/guardian
Total Service Plan	Employer participation in the training	Begin weekly overt and covert observations	Gradual fading monthly telephone calls
Job Sample Assessment	Establishment of an acceptable work rate	Provide retraining as necessary for jobs changes and needs	Placement into community position without any formal follow-up services
Parent/Guardian Support	Establishment of all necessary indirect work skills	Maintenance begins	
Job Tryout			

Source: R. T. Vogelsberg, W. W. Williams, and W. Ashe, "Improving vocational services through interagency cooperation." In C. L. Hansen (ed.), *Severely handicapped persons in the community*. Seattle: University of Washington, 1981.

INTERVENTION

Many sheltered workshops offer both transitional employment and extended employment situations within the same building. Transitional workshops continually try to place their clients in competitive employment outside the workshop. Extended employment workshops are operated to provide whatever training and support services are required to enable severely handicapped clients to work productively within the sheltered environment. The Wage and Hour Division of the U.S. Department of Labor requires that clients working in an extended sheltered workshop receive at least 50% of the minimum wage. Clients may be paid an hourly wage or at a piecework rate.

All sheltered workshops have at least two elements in common. First, they offer rehabilitation, training, and (in some instances) full employment through work. Second, in order to provide meaningful work for clients, a sheltered workshop must operate as a business. Sheltered workshops, especially extended workshops that must provide steady, meaningful, paid employment for their clients, generally engage in one of three types of business ventures—*contracting, prime manufacturing,* or *reclamation.*

Contracting is the major source of work in most workshops. Contracts are agreements that a sheltered workshop will complete a specified job (for instance, assembling and packaging a company's product) within a specified time for a given price. Most sheltered workshops have one or more professional staff, called *contractors* or *contract procurement persons,* whose sole job is to obtain and negotiate contracts with business and industry in the community.

> In order to obtain these contracts, someone must sell the workshop product. This "product" can be sold to industry if the workshop representative who is assigned to talk with business knows what it is that is being sold. Workshops are not selling "poor, unfortunate, handicapped workers." They are selling a meaningful product that can benefit many businesses. The product being sold to the business is:
>
> ☐ Expanded production capacity for that business with no additional investments in personnel, equipment, or space.
> ☐ Quality work by well-trained workers.
> ☐ The elimination of additional personnel costs. The cost of hiring, recruiting, and maintaining additional workers is eliminated.
> ☐ An opportunity for the business to make an important contribution to the community and make a profit at the same time.
> ☐ There is no need for the sheltered workshop to go begging for work if it represents its product to the people in the private sector who can benefit from it. (Brolin, 1982, p. 322)

Business and industry do not award contracts to sheltered workshops as a form of charity or community service. Workshops must bid competitively for each job and therefore must carefully take into account, in addition to whatever wages are paid to workers, their equipment needs, training costs, production rate, overhead, and so on. As you can easily tell, successfully operating a sheltered workshop requires good business management.

THE DISABLED ADULT 513

This employee in a sheltered workshop self-records his own production rate.

Prime manufacturing involves the designing, producing, marketing, and shipping of a complete product. The advantage of prime manufacturing over contracting, assuming a successful product is being manufactured, is that the workshops do not have problems with down time when they are between contracts. They can plan their training and labor requirements more directly. Unfortunately, most sheltered workshops are neither staffed nor equipped to handle the more sophisticated business venture of prime manufacturing, though it is hoped that in the future more will be able to do so.

In a salvage or reclamation operation, a workshop purchases or collects salvageable material, performs the salvage or reclamation operation, and then sells the reclaimed product. Salvage and reclamation operations have proven successful for many sheltered workshops because they require a lot of labor, are low in overhead, and usually can continue indefinitely.

Another kind of sheltered work environment, usually not referred to as such, is called a **work activity center.** A work activity center offers programs of activities for handicapped clients whose disabilities are so severe as to preclude productive work. Rehabilitation and training revolves around concentration and persistence at a task. Intervals of work are often only an hour long, interspersed with other activities—training in social skills, self-help skills, household skills, community skills, and recreation. Clients at work activity centers receive a small amount of remuneration, usually less than 50% of the minimum wage, for their work.

RECREATION AND LEISURE

Many of us take our leisure and recreational activities for granted. We have enjoyed and benefited from a lifetime of learning how to play or how to enjoy a personal hobby or craft. But for many handicapped adults, appropriate recreational and leisure-time activities do not come easily; in some communities they may not even be available.

Using community recreation resources requires transportation, the physical ability or skills to "play the game," and often other willing and able friends to "play with us." Often these three variables work effectively to limit the recreation and leisure-time activities available to the handicapped adult. Transportation is not available; his disability doesn't allow him to swim, bowl, or play tennis; and he has no friends with similar skills and interests and no convenient way to make friends.

Providing age-appropriate and in other ways normalized recreation and leisure-time activities is an important facet of extending services to handicapped adults. In addition, special educators must realize the importance of including training for recreation and leisure in curricula for handicapped children. Special educators must also realize the increased importance leisure activities take on for the disabled adult who cannot function in even a sheltered work environment. Too many handicapped adults do nothing more than sit in front of a television set. These persons must be helped to find a self-satisfying life-style, and recreation and enjoyable use of leisure are primary means to that end.

Bigge (1982) describes in detail how numerous games, hobbies, crafts, and projects can be adapted to become enjoyable, worthwhile leisure-time pursuits for handicapped persons. Among some of the areas she suggests are raising guinea pigs, music appreciation and study, photography, card games, and nature study.

Horseback riding is an outdoor pursuit that is becoming popular with many physically and mentally handicapped persons. Often called *therapeutic horsemanship* or *equine therapy*, horseback riding has given many handicapped persons the excitement and thrills of the sport while at the same time improving their gross-motor functioning, social skills, and feeling of pride and improved self-concept. The National Riding for the Disabled Association, founded in England in 1967 and now with groups in many countries, has developed a training program, exercises, and a variety of adaptive equipment to enable persons with just about any kind of disability to ride a horse.

Learning appropriate leisure skills is particularly important for severely and profoundly mentally retarded adults. Most severely retarded persons have ample free time but do not use it constructively, often engaging in inappropriate behaviors such as body rocking, hand flapping, or bizarre vocalizations (Wehman & Schleien, 1981). Recently, a number of promising studies have been reported in which leisure skills that are appropriate for their age have been taught to moderately and severely retarded adults (Johnson & Bailey, 1977; Nietupski & Svoboda, 1982; Schleien, Kiernan, & Wehman, 1981). Schleien, Wehman, and Kiernan (1981) successfully taught three severely retarded, multihandicapped adults to throw darts, and Hill, Wehman, & Horst (1982) taught a group of severely retarded young adults to play pinball machines.

Therapeutic Recreation

The National Recreation and Park Association defines **therapeutic recreation** as:

> A process which utilizes recreation services for purposive intervention in some physical, emotional, and/or behavior to bring about a desired change in that behavior and to promote the growth and development of the individual.

"High-risk" activities like rappelling, which used to be considered too dangerous for handicapped individuals, are a regular part of today's therapeutic recreation programs.

Therapeutic recreators, then, are people who use recreation as a medium to assist disabled people to change certain physical, emotional, or social characteristics so they may live their leisure lifestyles as well and independently as possible. Because these individuals are functioning at different and unique levels of ability, therapeutic recreators use recreation in many ways to help them realize their potentials for leisure enjoyment.

Therapeutic recreators are concerned with eliminating or minimizing disability, but further, are concerned with the quality of the person's total existence. This includes not only the physical and emotional self, but the environment in which the individual must live. (p. 1)

Many communities have therapeutic recreation programs. For example, the Division of Therapeutic Recreation of the Cincinnati Recreation Commission offers a full schedule of recreational activities throughout the year for handicapped children and adults. Dancing, bicycling, swimming, softball, tennis, soccer, golf, fishing, camping, and hiking are just some of the activities that are offered for mentally retarded, physically handicapped, autistic, learning disabled, and emotionally disturbed citizens. The program has even begun to teach handicapped children and adults to participate in such "high-risk" activities as rappelling and canoeing. These efforts have met with great success, as Sam Brown, supervisor of the Division of Therapeutic Recreation, explains: "The increase in pride and self-confidence that a handicapped person experiences after he finds that he too can manage a canoe or get himself safely down the side of a cliff is just tremendous."

Brown defines therapeutic recreation as:

> recreation that has a secondary benefit. A benefit other than just the fun or recreational aspect—although the fun is extremely important too. The secondary benefit may be increased socialization skills, eye-hand coordination, physical development, or even cognitive or language development. It's planned intervention through recreation, with a definite purpose and goal.

One of the goals of the Cincinnati program is to help handicapped persons move into the recreational mainstream; that is, to participate in integrated activities with nonhandicapped people as much as possible. To help staff evaluate and monitor each participant's progress toward that goal, the Division of Therapeutic Recreation has developed a continuum of five levels.

Level I consists of activities for persons who require a 1:1 or 1:2 staff:participant ratio. Mat activities (such as tumbling), music, crafts, and camping are used to help participants increase their sensorimotor and self-help skills.

Level II is a program for people who have basic skills (such as running, throwing, striking) and are able to begin functioning in a group situation. Team sports such as volleyball and softball are used, but the emphasis is on group interaction rather than on specific rules or skills of the game.

In Level III, teamwork is assumed, and the emphasis shifts to learning how to play the game or perform the activity well (for example, learning to convert spares and to keep score in bowling). Skill improvement is the primary objective in Level III programs.

In Level IV, activities are held in regular community center facilities and are conducted by regular staff of those facilities instead of by therapeutic recreation specialists. However, the handicapped clients still participate as a segregated group.

Finally, in Level V, handicapped individuals participate in recreational programs and activities offered by the Cincinnati Recreation Commission for everyone in the community. Staff from the Division of Therapeutic Recreation monitor and follow up on these mainstreaming efforts, working with regular recreation staff somewhat the same way resource room teachers work with regular classroom teachers to help ease the integration of handicapped students into the regular classroom.

CURRENT ISSUES/FUTURE TRENDS

A final, continuing problem is the acceptance of handicapped citizens as full members of our society with all of the rights, privileges, and services entitled to any other person. While we have made much progress in this regard—witness the litigation and legislation in behalf of handicapped persons that we have mentioned throughout this book—we still have a tremendous way to go. Courts can decree and laws can be passed, but neither can alter the way individuals feel toward and treat disabled people.

Most disabled adults feel the biggest barriers to full integration into society are not inaccessible buildings or the actual handicaps their disabilities may impose, but the differential treatment afforded them by nondisabled people. Just as the terms *racism* and *sexism* indicate prejudiced, discriminatory treatment of racial groups and women, the term **handicapism** has been coined to denote the biased reactions toward a person with a disability. Reactions and treatment are based not on any qualities or actual performances of the individual, but on a presumption of what the disabled person "must feel," or "must be like," because of the disability. Biklen and Bogdan (1976) define handicapism as:

> a theory and set of practices that promote unequal and unjust treatment of people because of apparent or assumed physical or mental disability. It manifests itself in relations between individuals, in social policy and cultural norms, and in the helping professions as well. Handicapism pervades our lives, but the concept of handicapism can also serve as a vital tool by which anyone can scrupulously examine personal and societal behaviors toward disabilities.

Handicapism occurs at the personal, professional, and societal level. Biklen and Bogdan describe the following examples of handicapism in personal relations.

> First, there is a tendency to presume sadness on the part of the person with a disability. For example, one woman who has a physical disability and who, incidentially smiles a lot, told us of an encounter with a man who said, "It's so good that you can still smile. Lord knows, you don't have much to be happy for."
>
> Second, there is the penchant to pity. You might have heard, "It is a tragedy that it had to happen to her; she had so much going for her." Or people sometimes tell us, "It is so good of you to give up your lives to help the poor souls." Or "My, you must be so patient to work with them. I could never do it."
>
> Third, people without disabilities sometimes focus so intensely on the disability as to make it impossible to recognize that the person with the disability is also simply another person with many of the same emotions, needs, and interests as other people. This attitude is reflected in the perennial questions, "What is it like to be deaf?" "It must be hard to get around in a wheelchair," and "You must really wish you could see sometimes."
>
> Fourth, people with disabilities are often treated as children. Notice for example, that feature films about people with mental retardation and physical handicaps are so frequently titled with first names: "Joey," "Charley," "Larry," and "Walter." We communicate this same message by calling disabled adults by first names when full names and titles would be more appropriate and by talking in a tone reserved for children.
>
> Fifth is avoidance. Having a disability often means being avoided, given the cold shoulder, and stared at from a distance. The phrases "Sorry, I have to go now," "Let's get together sometime (but not now and not any specific time),"

and "I'd like to talk but I have to run" are repeated too consistently for mere coincidence.

Sixth, we all grow up amidst a rampage of handicapist humor. It must take a psychological toll. "Did you hear the one about the moron who threw the clock out the window?" "There was a dwarf with a sawed-off cane . . . ." "Two deaf brothers went into business with each other . . . and a blind man entered the store."

Seventh, people with disabilities frequently find themselves spoken for, as if they were not present or were unable to speak for themselves. In a similar vein, people without disabilities sometimes speak about people with disabilities in front of them, again as if they were objects and not people.

In terms of personal relations, then, if you are labeled "handicapped," handicapism is your biggest burden. It is a no-win situation. You are not simply an ordinary person.

Only when the disabled man or woman is allowed to simply be an ordinary person—given the opportunity to strive and sometimes succeed as well as being allowed the freedom and dignity to strive and sometimes fail—can normalization become a reality.

YES, I'M STILL LEARNING DISABLED

Elizabeth Wiig

I grew up in a time when we didn't have all the labels that we have now for disabilities. When I look at my life, I realize I had a bona fide learning disability. When I entered the third grade, I was a nonreader. My auditory memory skills had helped me so much that it was impossible to catch me before. Everybody thought I was reading from the page; but I was actually reciting, utilizing other cues such as pictures and getting my buddies to give me the key words that started the sentences. If I got the key word that started the sentence, I could rattle off the rest. But in the third grade they took the pictures away from the readers. I hadn't started to associate text and topics and sentences with page numbers up in the corner. So I was just lost. But reading was not the only problem I had.

I couldn't do math either. My problem is visual-spatial orientation; and when you put a math problem down on paper, the numbers have to be lined up properly. I knew what it meant to subtract, and to multiply and divide; and I could handle it as long as it was verbal—"7 times 7" or "6 times 3." Basically I learned the problems by heart. But once you get past the two-digit numbers and up into the hundreds, all of a sudden you have to put it down on paper. I couldn't place a number that had to be subtracted beneath the column it had to be subtracted from. Nor could I do problems where you have to carry. I couldn't put the carried-over digits in the right place; they hung all over the place. It was impossible for me to do even a simple sum. When they finally found out it was not the basic operations I had problems with, they modified their approach. I was introduced to little grids that helped me set the problems up, and that countered my visual problems just fine.

I went through all kinds of things. I was in a classroom for the mentally retarded for a while. Yet when I look back on the early years, I did not realize how different I was. When I went to nursery school, at age 5, my mother was still dressing me. I didn't know that other kids could dress themselves.

I was constantly in trouble. The teacher would come over to me and I would start singing, because it would make her so mad that I would get thrown out of the room. If I could just get the teacher to expel me from the room, I could fantasize my whole day away. If I started singing when I wasn't supposed to, by 9:15 I could be out of the room. So I had all of the nonadaptive strategies, things kids learn how to do to get out of the mess they're in. And as long as you can get out of the mess, you can have a modicum of self-esteem.

I still consider myself learning disabled because there are times when I fail because of my problems. As long as there are very specific times when you fail, you still have a learning and perceptual problem.

One example occurred when I was up for my driver's test. I forgot I had to take directions from the policeman. He used "right," and "left," and I didn't know which way to turn. He yelled and screamed at me and took me back and failed me. The second time I went, I told the policeman about my problem head on. I said, "I'm confused when people say 'right' and 'left,' and I know you'll be telling me to turn 'right' and 'left.' Can I paste these letters on my hands?" He said yes. So I stuck big letters on the backs of my hands where I could see them while holding the wheel. By facing my problem head on, I did fine.

It's almost a daily occurrence. When I have to go places, the first few times I cannot find my way. I build in an extra half hour whenever I have to go someplace new. I'm okay on the freeway; but if there's any opportunity for failure, I get lost. I still get lost on campus, because there are parts that aren't familiar to me. To hold a map, you have to know where you are and which way you're facing. I go the wrong way anyway. One time I attended a professional meeting in Las Vegas, and I couldn't find anyplace. By the time I got there, the meetings were always over. I ended up sitting in my hotel room and crying. I went home three days early.

I've learned to overcome failure by knowing where I need support systems. For example, I'm an author who cannot spell. So I have a secretary who knows what my spelling error patterns are. Without her, I cannot write.

When I travel professionally, I don't rent a car because I'd get lost. So if people want me to speak, they have to pick me up. If I must travel by car, I stay in motels right by major roads. Otherwise, who knows if I'll ever get on the road again? I could be driving in the opposite direction. It's happened often.

Support systems are absolutely essential. I make sure I earn enough to pay for my support systems. Early in my career, my payments for support systems were exorbitant in relation to my salary. But I knew I had to pay to succeed.

Anxiety attacks used to leave me exhausted, like when I got lost and had to go back. These days I say, "So what? I can't find it? They're waiting for me. I'll call and they can come and get me." It's easy in the role of success, but it's totally different for young adults on the way up. Once you've "arrived," you can ask those who want things from you to help you. You don't feel so terrible about not always being quite with it.

My self-esteem has grown with every success, but it took me until I was 40 or older until I had reconciled who was, until I no longer had anxiety attacks and nightmares. Since I reached 40, with every gain toward inner equanimity I have moved ahead. My growth has been tremendous.

Elisabeth H. Wiig is now Professor of Speech Pathology at Boston University. Dr. Wiig is the author of three textbooks, four language assessment tests, and over 50 research articles dealing with language disorders in children and adolescents. She speaks six languages fluently. We are grateful to Dr. Wiig for her willingness to share some of her experiences with us.

SUMMARY

1. Today there are a variety of residential alternatives available for handicapped adults. All of these options provide a more "normalized" life than
an institution.
    a. In a family home, a handicapped adult is part of the day-to-day activities
    of a normal family and has an increased chance to interact with the
    community at large.
    b. In a group home, a small group of handicapped adults live together with
    "houseparents." The group home may be primarily a permanent resi-
    dence or serve as a transition between institutional and community liv-
    ing.
    c. In supervised apartment living, the handicapped person may live alone,
    receiving help when needed, with a nonhandicapped roommate, or with
    several handicapped roommates. Apartment living allows the handi-
    capped person to be integrated into the community while receiving nec-
    essary support services.
    d. It is critical that handicapped adults living in the community have the
    supportive services they need to make the transition from institution to
    community or from one residence to another.
    e. A significant problem of community-based residences is securing, train-
    ing, and keeping competent staff.
2. Obtaining and holding a job can be a major problem for handicapped adults,
even though state rehabilitation agencies provide vocational counseling,
training, and work experience programs.
    a. There are five types of vocational services provided: work evaluation,
    work adjustment, work experience, vocational skills training, and on-the-
    job training programs.
    b. Many handicapped people work in sheltered workshops. Sheltered work-
    shops provide training for competitive community employment, long-
    term employment, and/or work activities.
    c. All sheltered workshops operate as a business, usually in contracting,
    prime manufacturing, or reclamation.
3. Finding appropriate recreation and leisure-time activities is not easy for
handicapped adults. There are too few community resources and recreation
training programs.
    a. Research has shown that severely retarded adults *can* learn appropriate
    leisure skills.
    b. Many communities are now developing therapeutic recreation programs
    for handicapped children and adults.
4. A continuing problem is the true acceptance of handicapped persons as full
members of our society.

INTERVENTION

Journals

Career Development for Exceptional Individuals. Published two times per year by the Division on Career Development, the Council for Exceptional Children. Focuses on education and other programs for complete life experiences, including vocational, residential, and leisure activities, of handicapped children and adults.

Books

Brolin, D. E. *Vocational preparation of persons with handicaps,* 2d ed. Columbus, Ohio: Charles E. Merrill, 1982.

Brolin, D. E. (ed.) *Life-centered career education: A competency-based approach.* Reston, Va.: The Council for Exceptional Children, 1978.

Brolin, D. E., & Kokaska, C. *Career education for handicapped children and youth.* Columbus, Ohio: Charles E. Merrill, 1979.

Wehman, P. (ed.). *Recreation programming for developmentally disabled persons.* Baltimore: University Park Press, 1978.

Organizations

Association on Handicapped Student Service Programs in Post-secondary Education, P. O. Box 21192, Columbus, OH 43221. A young association devoted to providing accessibility and equal opportunities for disabled college and university students. Includes special interest groups on deafness, learning disabilities, community colleges, and rural institutions.

Division on Career Development, The Council for Exceptional Children, 1920 Association Drive, Reston, VA 22091. A relatively new division of CEC which focuses on career and life-style education for handicapped persons.

Postscript

All introductory textbooks contain a great deal of information. In that respect our book is no different from others. You have been introduced to many things in the 15 preceding chapters—definitions, statistics, principles, and concepts. Looking back over what we have written, we feel that the book does a good job of presenting this basic information. But we hope you will come away with more than just an increased knowledge of some basic facts and information about exceptional children and special education. We hope the book has caused you to examine your own attitudes, beliefs, expectations, and relationships toward handicapped children and adults.

In chapter 1 we stated six beliefs or attitudes that we hold toward exceptional children and the field of special education. We would like to repeat them now:

1. We believe that handicapped people have the right to live and participate in settings that are as normal as possible, that they have the right to as much independence as we can help them to achieve, and that our society's current support and development of services for handicapped people ought to continue to growh.
2. We believe that education and the other helping professions must recognize the needs of all handicapped people, including the very young and the adult, as well as the school-age child.
3. We believe that effective intervention for handicapped people can progress only if efforts cut across all the disciplines in the helping professions—and into the community as well. As educators, we see our primary responsibility in improving instruction in all areas—personal, social, and vocational as well as academic. But we consider it foolish to argue over territorial rights when

we can accomplish more by working with other professionals in medicine, psychology, the social services, and vocational rehabilitation.

4. We believe that professionals have for too long ignored the needs of the parents and families of exceptional children, treating them more as patients or adversaries than as clients, consumers of services, or co-workers. We believe that we have too often given the impression that parents were there to serve professionals, when in fact the opposite is more correct. We believe that we have long neglected to recognize parents as a child's first—and in many ways best—teachers. We believe that no really successful intervention program can fail to involve parents who want to take part in their child's education.

5. We believe that teachers must demand effectiveness from their instructional approaches and that the best way to evaluate instructional effectiveness is through direct observation and measurement of each child's performance of the skills being taught.

6. Finally, we are essentially optimistic about the futures of handicapped children. That is to say, we have enough confidence in their potentials to affirm that they can succeed in building fuller and more independent lives in the community. We believe that we have only begun to discover the ways to improve teaching, to increase learning, to prevent handicapping conditions, to encourage acceptance, and to develop technology to compensate for disabilities. And while we make no predictions for the future, we are certain that we have not come as far as we can in helping exceptional individuals to help themselves.

We wrote in chapter 1 that we did not necessarily expect you to agree with us and we still don't. We've reprinted our views here because we feel that, after reading the book, you are better able to judge these statements in relation to your own beliefs. And, beyond presenting basic information in what we hope you have found to be an effective and interesting manner, our goal was to get you to take a close look at your own views regarding handicapped people. We will end by offering several considerations we feel are important as you evolve your own skills, beliefs, and attitudes concerning handicapped children and adults. These considerations differ depending upon your role—as a member of the field or as a member of the community.

AS A MEMBER OF THE FIELD

To you, the prospective special educator—whether you aspire to be a teacher or a professional in any related discipline that provides direct services to exceptional children as its primary function—we will be most specific, most direct. First, view special education as a *profession* and yourself as a *professional.* View yourself as someone with a set of skills and the knowledge to practice them wisely; you are different from people without your special training. This is not to imply that you should see yourself as the only person who can relate to and provide appropriate interventions for the exceptional child—that's just not so. But some educators have not taken their profession seriously enough, perhaps adding to the belief (unfortunately held by too many in our society) that teaching is something you do if you can't do anything else, or is something to "fall back on."

This brings us to our second point. Commitment and a desire to help exceptional children develop as fully as possible are wonderful, but they are only a first step. Too often, special education has been perceived by people considering the field for their life's work as a nice thing to do if you love children and have lots of patience. (We've all heard the one about "Oh, you must have great patience to work with *those* chidlren.") In fact, what most exceptional children probably need most is teachers who are more *im*patient—teachers who are impatient with methods and materials that don't help children learn; teachers who are patient enough to discover and make the modifications in their techniques necessary to produce learning, but who are *never* patient with lack of progress.

As we have just implied, and have stressed at every opportunity throughout this book, teaching exceptional children requires *systematic instruction.* It is demanding work. Prepare yourself for that work in the very best way you can. Demand relevant, up-to-date information and hands-on practical experiences from your teacher-training program. Put as much as you can into your preservice training program; get as much as you can out of it. As you continue your teaching career, also continue your education and training. Stay on top of your field. Talk to colleagues, read the professional journals, go to meetings where new instructional techniques and research results are being presented, and take advantage of in-service training opportunities.

We do not mean to suggest by urging commitment and hard work that special education is a grim, thankless business. Quite the opposite—special education is an exciting, dynamic field that offers a personal satisfaction and feeling of accomplishment equaled in few areas of endeavor. To those of you planning a career in special education, welcome aboard!

AS A MEMBER OF THE COMMUNITY

The degree of success that a handicapped person may enjoy in the normal routine of daily life does not depend solely on the special educator, nor even on the handicapped person alone. In large measure, integration of handicapped citizens in contemporary society rests on the attitudes and actions of people who have, in the past, had little knowledge of or experience with handicapped people. No wonder, then, that the challenge facing society is so great: how do people come to accept a group they do not know, a group they have regarded and labeled as "abnormal," a group to whom they have in both obvious and subtle ways denied some rights and opportunities?

In effect, a society can control who will enter and who will be kept out, much as a gatekeeper lets some visitors pass and refuses others. To the handicapped, society's gatekeeper might have been a doctor who declared that an infant "would always be an imbecile" and urged the parents to institutionalize and forget about their child. It might have been a teacher in a regular public school classroom—already overburdened by large classes, by mountains of paperwork, and by the social and financial problems all schools face—who resisted having any "problem kids" in her class. It may have been a school psychologist whose test scores added up an IQ below 50 and a label of "trainable mentally retarded." It might have been an employer who wanted nothing to do with hiring handicapped workers, a social worker, a school board member, or a voter, who kept the gate for society on any given occasion in the past. Perhaps saddest of all, it might even have been a parent, who concluded early in a child's life that he or she would never be able to learn what most children learn, to go places most children go, to see or hear or feel or achieve what most children can.

In other words, the ways that a society views and defines handicapped people influences the way that individual members of the community view and respond to each individual handicapped person. As we have tried to point out throughout this book, the views of society are changing—or are being changed by people who believe that our past principle of exclusion is primitive and unfair. Nowhere can we find a better example of this change than in the court cases and recent laws which have ensured that all handicapped children, regardless of the kind or severity of their handicap, are fully entitled to an education.

Thus, all the categories and labels, all the research and experience, and all the theories and practices we have presented in this book must translate into personal terms for those of you who will not choose careers in direct service to handicapped children or adults. Not only has all this information been collected to show you how handicapped people are *different* from nonhandicapped people; it has been put together to show you that handicapped people are still more *like* nonhandicapped people than not. And the conclusion we hope you have come to is this: regardless of your relationship to handicapped people, it is critical to view and respond to each handicapped child and adult as an individual, not as a member of a category or a labeled group.

IN SUM

Viewing every handicapped individual as a person first, and as a handicapped person second, may be the most important step in integrating him or her into the mainstream of community life. But this change in attitude will not diminish the person's handicap, will not make it go away—whether it be a physical or sensory impairment, a delay in development, or a learning or behavior problem.

What it will do is give us a new outlook—more objective as well as more positive—on his handicap. It will allow us to begin to see a handicap as a set of *special needs* this person has that most others do not have. And viewing handicapped people in this way—as individuals with special needs—tells us much about how to respond to them. And that way of responding, whether it occurs in a special class or in the larger community, is the essence of special education.

REFERENCES

Abt Associates. *Assessment of selected resources for severely handicapped children and youth* (Vol. 1). Cambridge, Mass.: Abt Associates, 1974.

Accreditation Council for Facilities for the Mentally Retarded. *Standards for residential facilities for the mentally retarded.* Chicago: Joint Commission on Accreditation of Hospitals, 1971.

Achenbach, T. M. *Developmental psychopathology.* New York: Ronald Press, 1974.

Adams, G., Beck, R., Chandler, L., & Livingston, S. S. The need for adjunctive services in the management of severely and profoundly handicapped individuals; Part II. The infant diagnostic classroom—A community resource. In N .G. Haring & L. J. Brown (Eds.), *Teaching the severely handicapped,* (Vol. II). New York: Grune & Stratton, 1977.

Adler, S. Behavior management: A nutritional approach to the behaviorally disordered and learning disabled child. *Journal of Learning Disabilities.* 1978, *11,* 651–56.

Aiello, B. Up from the basement: A teacher's story. *New York Times,* April 25, 1976 *12:* 14.

Alber, M. B. *Listening: A curriculum guide for teachers of visually impaired students.* Springfield: Illinois Office of Education, 1974.

Alberto, P., & Troutman, A. *Applied behavior analysis for teachers: Influencing student performance.* Columbus, Ohio: Charles E. Merrill, 1982.

Algozzine, B. The disturbing child: A matter of opinion. *Behavioral Disorders,* 1980, *5,* 112–15.

Algozzine, B., & Ysseldyke, J. Special education services for normal children: Better safe than sorry? *Exceptional Children,* 1981, *48,* 238–43.

Allen, K. E. The teacher therapist: Teaching parents to help their children through systematic contingency management. *Journal of Special Education Technology,* 1978, *2,* 47–55.

Allen, K. E. The language impaired child in the preschool: The role of the teacher. *The Directive Teacher,* 1980, *2*(3), 6–10. (a)

Allen, K. E. *Mainstreaming in early childhood education.* Albany, N.Y.: Delmar, 1980. (b)

Alley, G., & Deschler, D. *Teaching the learning disabled adolescent: Strategies and methods.* Denver: Love, 1979.

Allsop, J. Mainstreaming physically handicapped students. *Journal of Research and Development in Education,* 1980, *13*(4), 37–44.

Alzate, G. Analysis of testing problems in Spanish speaking children. In A. H. Fink (Ed.), *International perspectives on future special education.* Reston, Va.: Council for Exceptional Children, 1978.

American Association for the Study of the Feeble-minded. 1924, *29*, 58–70.

American Council on Science and Health. *Diet and hyperactivity: Is there a relationship?* New York: Author, May 1979.

American Psychiatric Association. *Diagnostic and statistical manual of mental disorders* (3rd. ed., DSM-III). Washington, D.C.: Author, 1980.

Ames, L. B. Learning disabilities: Time to check our roadmaps? *Journal of Learning Disabilities,* 1977, *10*, 328–30.

Anderson, L. E. (Ed.). *Helping the adolescent with the hidden handicap.* Los Angeles: California Association for Neurologically Handicapped Children, 1970.

Anderson, R. M., Greer, J. G., & Rich, H. L. An introduction to severely and multiply handicapped persons. In J. G. Greer, R. M. Anderson, & S. J. Odle (Eds.), *Strategies for helping severely and multiply handicapped citizens.* Baltimore: University Park Press, 1982.

Anthony, D. *Seeing essential English.* Anaheim, Calif.: Anaheim School District, 1971.

Apolloni, T., & Cooke, T. P. (Eds.). *California housing resources for persons with special developmental needs.* Unpublished manuscript, California Institute on Human Services at Sonoma State University, 1981.

Arakawa, J. Minority voices: Neither part of a double disability is the whole person. *Disabled USA.,* 1981, *4*(8), 1.

Arnold, S., Sturgis, E., & Forehand, R. Training a parent to teach communication skills: A case study. *Behavior Modification,* 1977, *1*(2), 259–76.

ASHA, Committee on the Mid-Century White House Conference. *Journal of Speech and Hearing Disorders,* 1952, *17*(1), 129–37.

Atkins, C. P., & Cartwright, L. R. National survey: Preferred language elicitation procedures used in five age categories. *Journal of the American Speech and Hearing Association,* 1982, *24*, 321–23.

Bachmann, W. *Influence of selected variables upon economic adaption of orthepedially handicapped and other health impaired.* Unpublished doctoral dissertation, University of the Pacific, 1971.

Baer, D. M. *How to plan for generalization.* Lawrence, Kans.: H. & H Enterprises, 1981.

Baer, D. M. We already have multiple jeopardy; why try for unending jeopardy? In W. L. Heward, T. E. Heron, D. S. Hill & J. Trap-Porter (Eds.), *Focus on behavior analysis in education.* Columbus, Ohio: Charles E. Merrill, 1984.

Baer, D. M., Wolf, M. M., & Risley, T. R. Some current dimensions of applied behavior analysis. *Journal of Applied Behavior Analysis,* 1968, *1*, 91–97.

Baker, B. L. & Heifetz, L. J. The Read Project: Teaching manuals for parents of retarded children. In T. D. Tjossem (Ed.), *Intervention strategies for high risk infants and young children.* Baltimore, Md.: University Park Press, 1976.

Baker, B. L., Seltzer, G. B., & Seltzer, M. M. *As close as possible: Community residences for retarded adults.* Boston: Little, Brown, 1977.

Baldwin, A. Y. Curriculum and methods: What is the difference? In A. Y. Baldwin, Gear, G. H., & L. J. Lucita (Eds.), *Educational planning for the gifted: Overcoming cultural, geographic, and socioeconomic barriers.* Reston, Va.: Council for Exceptional Children, 1978.

Baldwin, A. Y., Gear, G. H., & Lucita, L. J. (Eds.). *Educational planning for the gifted: Overcoming cultural, geographic, and socioeconomic barriers.* Reston, Va.: Council for Exceptional Children, 1978.

Balow, I. H., Farr, R., Hogan, T. P., & Prescott, G. A. Metropolitan Achievement Tests: 1978 Edition. New York: Psychological Corporation, 1978.

Banks, J. A. *Multiethnic education: Practices and promises.* Bloomington, Ind.: Phi Delta Kappa Educational Foundation, 1977.

Bankson, N. W. The speech and language impaired. In E. L. Meyen (Ed.), *Exceptional children and youth* (2nd ed.). Denver: Love, 1982.

Baroff, G. S. Predicting the prevalence of mental retardation in individual catchment areas. *Mental Retardation,* 1982, *20,* 133–35.

Barr, M. W. *Mental defectives: Their history, treatment, and training.* Philadelphia: Blakiston Co., 1913.

Barraga, N. C. *Increased visual behavior in low vision children.* New York: American Foundation for the Blind, 1964.

Barraga, N. C. *Teacher's guide for development of visual learning abilities and utilization of low vision.* Louisville: American Printing House for the Blind, 1970.

Barraga, N. C. *Visual handicaps and learning: A developmental approach.* Belmont, Calif.: Wadsworth, 1976.

Barraga, N. C. *Source book on low vision.* Louisville:, American Printing House for the Blind, 1980.

Barsh, R. H. *The parent of the handicapped child: The study of child rearing practices.* Springfield, Ill.: Charles C Thomas, 1968.

Barsch, R. H. *The parent-teacher partnership.* Arlington, Va.: Council for Exceptional Children, 1969.

Batshaw, M. L., & Perret, Y. M. *Children with handicaps: A medical primer.* Baltimore: Paul H. Brookes, 1981.

Baumgart, D., Brown, L., Pumpian, I., Nisbet, J., Ford, A., Sweet, M., Messina, R., & Schroeder, J. Principle of partial participation and individualized adaptations in educational programs for severely handicapped students. *Journal of the Association for the Severely Handicapped,* 1982, *7*(2), 17–27.

Bayley, N. *Bayley's Scales of Infant Development.* New York: Psychological Corporation, 1969.

Beatty, L., Madden, R., & Gardner, E. Stanford Diagnostic Arithmetic Test. New York: Harcourt Brace Jovanovich, 1966.

Beck, R. The need for adjunctive services in the management of severely and profoundly handicapped individuals: A view from primary care. In N. G. Haring & L. Brown (Eds.), *Teaching the severely handicapped* (Vol. 2). New York: Grune & Stratton, 1977.

Becker, W. C. Consequences of different kinds of parental discipline. In M. L. Hoffman & L. W. Hoffman (Eds.), *Review of child development research* (Vol. 1). New York: Russell Sage Foundation, 1964.

Becker, W. C. *Parents are teachers.* Champaign, Ill.: Research Press, 1971.

Becker, W. C., Engelmann, S., & Thomas, D. R. *Teaching: A course in applied psychology.* Chicago: Science Research Associates, 1971.

Becker, W. C., & Engelmann, S. E. *Technical report 1976–1.* Eugene: University of Oregon, 1976.

Beckman-Bell, P. Child-related stress in families of handicapped children. *Topics in Early Childhood Special Education,* 1981, *1,* 45–53.

Belgrave, F. Z., & Mills, J. Effect upon desire for social interaction with a physically disabled person of mentioning the disability in different contexts. *Journal of Applied Social Psychology,* 1981, *11,* 44–57.

Bellamy, G. T., & Wilcox, B. Secondary education for severely handicapped students: Guidelines for quality services. In K. P. Lynch, W. E. Kiernan, & J. A. Stark (Eds.), *Prevocational and vocational education for special needs youth: A blueprint for the 1980s.* Baltimore: Paul H. Brookes, 1982.

Bennett, L. M., & Hansen, F.O. *Keeping in touch with parents: The teacher's best friend.* Hingham, Mass: Teaching Resources, 1977.

Bensberg, G. J., & Sigelman, C. K. Definitions and prevalence. In L. L. Lloyd (Ed.), *Communication assessment and intervention strategies.* Baltimore: University Park Press, 1976.

Berman, J. L., & Ford, R. Intelligence quotients and intelligence loss in patients with phenylketonuria and some variant states. *Journal of Pediatrics,* 1970, *77,* 764–70.

Best, G. A. *Individuals with physical disabilities: An introduction for educators.* St. Louis: C. V. Mosby, 1978.

Bierly, K. Public Law 94–142: Answers to the questions you're asking. *Instructor,* 1978, *87*(9), 63–67.

Bigge, J. L. *Teaching individuals with physical and multiple disabilities.* (2nd ed.). Columbus, Ohio: Charles E. Merrill, 1982.

Bijou, S. W. A functional analysis of retarded development. In N. R. Ellis (Ed.), *International review of research in mental retardation* (Vol. 1). New York: Academic Press, 1966.

Bijou, S. W., & Dunitz-Johnson, E. Interbehavior analysis of developmental disabilities. *Psychological Record,* 1981, *31,* 305–29.

Biklen, D., & Bogdan, R. Handicapism in America. *WIN,* 1976.

Bishop, M. E. (Ed.). *Mainstreaming: Practical ideas for educating hearing-impaired students.* Washington, D.C.: Alexander Graham Bell Association for the Deaf, 1979.

Bishop, W. Successful teachers of the gifted. *Exceptional Children,* 1968, *39,* 317–25.

Blackstone, M. How parents can affect communitization, or, what do you mean I'm a troublemaker? In C. H. Hansen (Ed.), *Severely handicapped persons in the community.* Seattle: University of Washington, PDAS, 1981.

Blasch, B. B. Blindisms: Treatment by punishment and reward in laboratory and natural settings. *Journal of Visual Impairment & Blindness,* 1978, *72,* 215–30.

Blatt, B. *Revolt of the idiots: A story.* Glen Ridge, N.J.: Exceptional Press, 1976.

Blatt, B., & Kaplan, F. *Christmas in purgatory: A photographic essay on mental retardation.* Boston: Allyn & Bacon, 1966.

Bleck, E. E. Integrating the physically handicapped child. *Journal of School Health,* 1979, *49,* 141–46.

Bloom, E. S. (Ed.). *Taxonomy of educational objectives, handbook I: Cognitive domain.* New York: David McKay, 1956.

Bloom, L., & Lahey, M. *Language development and language disorders.* New York: John Wiley, 1978.

Bonvillian, J. D., & Nelson, K. E. Sign language acquisition in a mute autistic boy. *Journal of Speech and Hearing Disorders.* 1976, *41*, 339–47.

Bonvillian, J. D., Orlansky, M. D., & Novack, L. L. Sign language acquisition and early cognitive and motor development. *Child Development,* 1983, *54*(6), 1435–45.

Boone, D. R. Our profession: Where are we? *Journal of the American Speech and Hearing Association,* 1977, *19,* 3–6.

Bornstein, H. Signed English: A manual approach to English language development. *Journal of Speech and Hearing Disorders,* 1974, *3,* 330–43.

Boshes, B., & Myklebust, H. R. A neurological and behavioral study of children with learning disorders. *Neurology,* 1964, *14,* 7–12.

Bostow, D. E., & Bailey, J. Modification of severe disruptive and aggressive behavior using brief time-out and reinforcement procedures. *Journal of Applied Behavior Analysis,* 1969, *2,* 31–37.

Bower, E. M. *Early identification of emotionally handicapped children in school* (2nd ed.). Springfield, Ill.: Charles C Thomas, 1969.

Bower, E. M., & Lambert, N. M. *A process for in-school screening of children with emotional handicaps.* Princeton, N.J.: Educational Testing Service, 1962.

Bradley, V. *Deinstitutionalization of developmentally disabled persons: A conceptual analysis and guide.* Baltimore: Unviersity Park Press, 1978.

Brazelton, T. B. *Neonatal assessment scale.* Philadelphia: J. B. Lippincott, 1973.

Bricker, W. A., & Campbell, P. H. Interdisciplinary assessment and programming for multihandicapped students. In W. Sailor, B. Wilcox, & L. Brown (Eds.), *Methods of instruction for severely handicapped students.* Baltimore: Paul H. Brookes, 1980.

Broden, M., Beasley, A., & Hall, R. V. In-class spelling performance: Effects of home tutoring by a parent. *Behavior Modification,* 1978, *2*(4), 511–30.

Brolin, D. E. *Vocational preparation of persons with handicaps* (2nd ed.). Columbus, Ohio: Charles E. Merrill, 1982.

Bronfenbrenner, U. *A report on longitudinal evaluations of preschool programs: Is early intervention effective?* (Vol. 2). Washington, D.C.: U.S. Department of Health, Education and Welfare, 1974.

Bronston, W. Matters of design. In T. Apolloni, J. Cappuccilli, & T. P. Cooke (Eds), *Achievements in residential services for persons with disabilities: Toward excellence.* Baltimore: University Park Press, 1980.

Brown, B. E. The influence of postural adjustment of physically handicapped children on teachers' perceptions (Doctoral dissertation, Teachers College of Columbia University, 1981). *Dissertation Abstracts International,* 1982, *42,* 4393A. (University Microfilms No. 8207305).

Brown, N.P. CAMEO: Computer-assisted management of educational objectives. *Exceptional Children,* 1982, *49,* 151–53.

Bruch, C. B. Assessment of creativity in culturally different children, *The Gifted Child Quarterly,* 1975, *19,* 164–74.

Bruening, S. E., & Davis, V. J. Reinforcement effects on the intelligence test performance of institutional retarded adults: Behavioral analysis, directional control, and implications for habilitation. *Applied Research on Mental Retardation,* 1981, *2,* 307–21.

Bryan, W. H., & Jeffrey, D. L. Education of visually handicapped students in the regular classroom. *Texas Tech Journal of Education,* 1982, *9,* 125–31.

Bryant, J. E. *Helping your child speak correctly* (pamphlet). New York: Public Affairs Committee, Inc., 1970.

Bryant, N. D. Subject variables: Definition, incidence, characteristics, and correlates. In N. D. Bryant & C. E. Kass (Eds.), *Leadership training institute in learning disabilities* (Vol. 1). Washington, D.C.: Bureau of Education for the Handicapped, 1972.

Burchard, J. D., & Harig, P. T. Behavior modification and juvenile delinquency. In H. Leitenberg (Ed.), *Handbook of behavior modification and behavior therapy.* Englewood Cliffs, N.J.: Prentice-Hall, 1976.

Buros, O. K. *The eighth mental measurement yearbook.* Highland Park, N.J.: Gryphon, 1978.

Buss, A. H. *Psychopathology.* New York: John Wiley, 1966.

Cain, L. F. Parent groups: Their role in a better life for the handicapped. *Exceptional Children,* 1976, *42,* 432–37.

Callahan, C. M. The gifted and talented woman. In H. H. Passow, (Ed.), *The gifted and talented: Their education and development.* Chicago: University of Chicago Press, 1979.

Campbell, P. B. *Diagnosing the problem: Sex stereotyping in special education.* Newton, Mass.: Education Development, 1979

Cansler, D. P., Martin, G. H., & Valand, M. C. *Working with families.* Winston-Salem, N.C.: Kaplan Press, 1975.

Carin, A., & Sund, R. B. *Creative questioning and sensitive listening techniques: A self-concept approach* (2nd ed.). Columbus, Ohio: Charles E. Merrill, 1978.

Carrow, E. Carrow Elicited Language Inventory. Austin, Tex.: Author, 1974.

Castaneda, A. Cultural democracy and the educational needs of Mexican American children. In R. L. Jones (Ed.), *Mainstreaming and the minority child.* Reston, Va.: Council for Exceptional Children, 1976.

Cavan, R. S., & Ferdinand, T. N. Juvenile delinquency (3rd ed.). New York: J. B. Lippincott, 1975.

Cawley, J. F. & Webster, R. E. Reading and behavior disorders. In G. Brown, R. L. McDowell, & J. Smith (Eds.), *Educating adolescents with behavior disorders.* Columbus, Ohio: Charles E. Merrill, 1981.

Center for Residential and Community Services. *1982 National Survey of Residential Facilities.* Minneapolis: University of Minnesota, 1983.

Chan, K. S., & Rueda, R. Poverty and culture in education: Separate but equal. *Exceptional Children,* 1979, *45,* 421–28.

Chaney, C., & Frodyma, D. A noncategorical program for preschool language development. *TEACHING Exceptional Children,* 1982, *14,* 152–55.

Chapman, E. K. *Visually handicapped children and young people.* London: Routledge & Kegan Paul, 1978.

Childs, R. E. Perceptions of mainstreaming by regular classroom teachers who teach mainstreamed educable mentally retarded students in the public schools. *Education and Training of the Mentally Retarded,* 1981, *16,* 225–227.

REFERENCES

Chinn, P. C., & Kamp, S. H. Cultural diversity and exceptionality. In N. G. Haring (Ed.), *Exceptional children and youth* (3rd ed.). Columbus, Ohio: Charles E. Merrill, 1982.

Chinn, P. C., Winn, J., & Walters, R. *Two-way talking with parents of special children.* St. Louis: C. V. Mosby, 1978.

Clark, B. *Growing up gifted* (2nd ed.). Columbus, Ohio: Charles E. Merrill, 1983.

Clarke, B., & Leslie, P. Environmental alternatives for the hearing handicapped. In J. W. Schifani, R. M. Anderson, & S. J. Odle (Eds.), *Implementing learning in the least restrictive environment: Handicapped children in the mainstream.* Baltimore: University Park Press, 1980.

Classification of AAMD from the Committee on Definition and Terminology of CEC-MR. *Education and Training of the Mentally Retarded,* 1979, *14,* 74–76.

Clausen, J. A. Mental deficiency: Development of a concept. *American Journal of Mental Deficiency,* 1967, *71,* 727–45.

Clearinghouse for Offender Literacy Programs. *Literacy: Problems and solutions: A handbook for correctional educators.* Washington, D.C.: American Bar Association, 1975.

Clements, S. D. *Minimal brain dysfunction in children.* (NINDS Monograph No. 3, Public Health Service Bulletin No. 1415). Washington, D.C.: U.S. Department of Health, Education and Welfare, 1966.

Cochran, W. E., Sran, P. K., & Varano, G. A. The relocation syndrome in mentally retarded individuals. *Mental Retardation,* 1977, *15,* 10–12.

Coffman, T. L., & Harris, M. C. Transition shock and adjustments of mentally retarded persons. *Mental Retardation,* 1980, *18,* 28–32.

Cohen, H. L. Behavior modification and socially deviant youth. In C. E. Thoresen (Ed.), *Behavior modification in education.* Chicago: University of Chicago Press, 1973.

Cohen, S., Semmes, M., & Guralnick, M. J. Public Law 94–142 and the education of preschool handicapped children. *Exceptional Children,* 1979, *4,* 279–85.

Comptroller General of the United States. *Preventing mental retardation—More can be done.* Report to the Congress, October 3, 1977.

Congress approves program for preschool handicapped. *Report on Preschool Education,* 1978, *22*(10), 10.

Congressional Record, October 10, 1978, H-12179.

Connolly, A., Natchman, W., & Prichett, E. *Key Math Diagnostic Arithmetic Test.* Circle Pines, Minn.: American Guidance Service, 1973.

Connor, L. E. Reflections on the year 2000. *Exceptional Children,* 1968, *34*(10).

Connors, C. K., Goyette, C., Southwick, D., Lees, J., & Andrulonis P. Food additives and hyperkinesis: A controlled double blind study. *Pediatrics,* 1976, *58,* 154–66.

Conroy, J. W. Trends in deinstitutionalization of the mentally retarded. *Mental Retardation,* 1977, *15*(4), 44–66.

Cook, P. S., & Woodhill, J. M. The Feingold dietary treatment of the hyperkenetic syndrome. *Medical Journal of Australia,* 1976, *2,* 85–90.

Cooke, N. L., Heron, T. E., & Heward, W. L. *Peer tutoring: Implementing classwide programs in the primary grades.* Columbus, Ohio: Special Press, 1983.

Cooke, N. L., Heron, T. E., Heward, W. L., & Test, D. W. Integrating a Down syndrome student into a classwide peer tutoring system. *Mental Retardation,* 1982, *20,* 22–25.

Cooke, T. P. Your place or mine? Residential options for people with developmental

disabilities. In C. L. Hansen (Ed.), *Severely handicapped persons in the community.* Seattle: University of Washington PDAS, 1981.

Cooper, J. O. Measuring behavior (2nd ed.). Columbus, Ohio: Charles E. Merrill, 1981.

Cooper, J. O., & Edge, D. *Parenting: Strategies and educational methods.* Columbus,
Ohio: Charles E. Merrill, 1978.

Cooper, J. O., & Heron, T. E. Educational materials and strategies for home use. In D.
Edge, B. J. Strenecky, & S. I. Mour (Eds.), *Parenting learning-problem children:
The professional educator's perspective.* Columbus: Ohio State University, Na-
tional Center for Educational Materials and Media for the Handicapped, 1978.

Cooper, J. O., & Johnson, J. Guildelines for direct and continuous measurement of academic behavior. *The Directive Teacher,* 1979, *1,* 10–11, 21.

Cornett, R. O. What is cued speech? *Gallaudet Today,* 1974, *5*(2), 3–5.

Cott, A. Megavitamins: The orthomolecular approach to behavioral disorders and learning disabilities. *Academic Therapy,* 1972, *7,* 245–58.

Cox, B. G., & Ramirez, M., III. Cognitive styles: Implications for multiethnic education. In
J. A. Banks (Ed.), *Education in the 80's: Multiethnic education.* Washington, D.C.:
National Education Association, 1981.

Cruickshank, W. M., & Lewandowski, L. J. Cerebral palsy. In W. C. Morse (Ed.), *Humanistic teaching for exceptional children.* Syracuse, N.Y.: Syracuse University Press,
1979.

Curran, B. E. *Effects of one-to-one and small-group instruction on incidental learning by
moderately/severely handicapped adults.* Unpublished master's thesis, The Ohio
State University, Columbus, Ohio, 1983.

Curran, J. J. & Algozzine, B. Ecological disturbance: A test of the matching hypothesis.
Behavioral Disorders, 1980, *5,* 159–74.

Currie, W. Teacher preparation for a pluralistic society. In J. A. Banks (Ed.), *Education
in the 80's: Multiethnic education.* Washington, D.C.: National Education Association, 1981.

Cuvo, A. J., Veitch, V. D., Trace, M. W., & Konke, J. L. Teaching change computation to
the mentally retarded. *Behavior Modification,* 1978, *2,* 531–48.

D'Angelo, K. Wordless picture books and the young language-disabled child. *Teaching
Exceptional Children,* 1981, *14,* 34–37.

Dardig, J. C., & Heward, W. L. *Sign here: A contracting book for children and their
parents* (2nd ed.) Bridgewater, N.J.: F. Fournies, 1981. (a)

Dardig, J. C., & Heward, W. L. A systematic procedure for prioritizing IEP goals. *The
Directive Teacher,* 1981, *3,* 6–8. (b)

Davis, C. J. Personal communication, May 15, 1975.

Davis, H., & Silverman, S. R. (Eds.). *Hearing and deafness* (3rd ed.). New York: Holt,
Rinehart & Winston, 1970.

DeAvila, E. Mainstreaming ethnically and linguistically different children: An exercise in
paradox or a new approach? In R. I. Jones (Ed.), *Mainstreaming and the minority
child.* Reston, Va.: Council for Exceptional Children, 1976.

Delaney, S., & Hayden, A. Fetal alcohol syndrome: A review. *AAESPH Review,* 1977,
2(3), 164–68.

Delgado, G. L. Hearing-impaired children from non-native language homes. *American
Annals of the Deaf,* 1981, *126,* 118–21.

Delisle, J. Learning to underachieve. *Roeper Review*, 1982, *4*, 16–18.

Dennis. R., Reichle, J., Williams, W., & Vogelsberg, R. T. Motoric factors influencing the selection of vocabulary for sign procuction programs. *Journal of the Association for the Severely Handicapped*, 1982. *7*(1), 20–32.

Dent, N. E. Assessing black children for mainstream placement. In R. L. Jones (Ed.), *Mainstreaming and the minority child*. Reston, Va.: Council for Exceptional Children, 1976.

Denton, D. M. *A philosophical foundation for total communication*. Paper presented at the Indiana School for the Deaf, Preschool Parent Conference, Indianapolis, August 18, 1972.

Deschler, D. D. Lowrey, N., & Alley, G. R. Programming alternatives for learning disabled adolescents: A nationwide survey. *Academic Therapy*. 1979. *14*(4).

Dickerson, D., Spellman, C. R., Larsen, S. C., & Tyler, L. Let the cards do the talking: A teacher-parent communication program. *Teaching Exceptional Children*, 1973, *5*, 170–78.

Dickson, S. (Ed.). *Communication disorders: Remedial principles and practices*. Glenview, Ill.: Scott, Foresman, 1974.

Divoky, D. Can diet cure the LD child? *Learning*, 1978, *3*, 56–57.

Dobelle, W. H. Current status of research on providing sight to the blind by electrical stimulation of the brain. *Journal of Visual Impairment and Blindness*, 1977, *71*, 290–97.

Doernberg, N. L. Some negative effects on family integration of health and educational services for young handicapped children. *Rehabilitation Literature*, 1978, *39*, 107–10.

Doll, E. A. The essentials of an inclusive concept of mental deficiency. *American Journal of Mental Deficiency*, 1941, *46*, 214–19.

Doll, E. A. Vineland Social Maturity Scale. Circle Pines, Minn.: American Guidance Service, 1965.

Drabman, R. S., Spitalnik, R., & O'Leary, K. D. Teaching self-control to disruptive children. *Journal of Abnormal Psychology*, 1973, *82*, 10–16.

DuBose, R. F. Assessment of severely impaired young children: Problems and recommendations. *Topics in Early Childhood Special Education*, 1981, *1*, 9–12.

Duffin, S. In M. D. Orlansky & W. L. Heward, *Voices: Interviews with handicapped people*. Columbus, Ohio: Charles E. Merrill, 1981.

Duffey, J. D., Salvia, J., Tucker, J., & Ysseldyke, J. Nonbiased assessment: A need for operationalism. *Exceptional Children*. 1981, *47*, 427–434.

Dunlap, G., & Koegel, R. L. Motivating autistic children through stimulus variation. *Journal of Applied Behavior Analysis*, 1980, *13*, 619–27.

Dunn, L. B. Peabody Picture Vocabulary Test. Circle Pines, Minn.: American Guidance Service, 1965.

Dunn, L. M. Special education for the mildly retarded—Is much of it justifiable? *Exceptional Children*, 1968, *35*, 5–24.

Dunn, L. M., & Markwardt, F. C. The Peabody Individual Achievement Test. 1970.

Dunn, L. M. Children with mild general learning disabilities. In L. M. Dunn (Ed.), *Exceptional children in the schools* (2nd ed.). New York: Holt, Rinehart, and Winston, 1973.

Durrell, D. D. Durrell Analysis of Reading Difficulty. New York: Harcourt Brace Jovanovich, 1955.

Edgerton, R. B., & Bercovici, S. M. The cloak of competence: Years later. *American Journal of Mental Deficiency*, 1976, *80*, 485–97.

Edginton, D. *The physically handicapped child in your classroom: A handbook for teachers*. Springfield, Ill.: Charles C Thomas, 1976.

Egel, A. L. Reinforcer variation: Implications for motivating developmentally disabled children. *Journal of Applied Behavior Analysis*, 1981, *14*, 3–12.

Ellwood, P. Prescription of wheelchairs. In F. Krussen, F. Kottke, & P. Ellwood. *Handbook of physical medicine and rehabilitation* (2nd ed.). Philadelphia: W. B. Saunders, 1971.

Engelmann, S. E. Sequencing cognitive and academic tasks. In R. D. Kneedler & S. G. Tarver (Eds.), *Changing perspectives in special education*. Columbus, Ohio: Charles E. Merrill, 1977.

Epilepsy Foundation of America. *Epilepsy school alert*. Washington, D.C.: Author, 1974.

Fanning, J. W. *A common sense approach to community living arrangement for the mentally retarded*. Springfield, Ill.: Charles C Thomas, 1975.

Farber, B. Family adaptations to severely mentally retarded children. In M. Begab & S. A. Richardson (Eds.), *The mentally retarded and society: A social science perspective*. Baltimore: University Park Press, 1975.

Favell, J. E., Favell, J. E., & McGimsey, J. F. Relative effectiveness and efficiency of group vs. individual training of severely retarded persons. *American Journal of Mental Deficiency*, 1978, *83*, 104–9.

Fay, G., Shapiro, S., & Trupin, E. Should parents teach reading to their children? Further evidence that they should. In D. Edge, B. J. Strenecky, & S. I. Mour (Eds.), *Parenting learning-problem children: The professional educator's perspective*. Columbus: Ohio State University, National Center for Educational Materials and Media for the Handicapped, 1978.

Federal Register. Washington, D.C.: U.S. Government Printing Office, August 23, 1977.

Federal Register. Washington, D.C.: U.S. Government Printing Office, January 19, 1981.

Fein, D. J. The prevalence of speech and language impairments. *ASHA*, 1983, *25*, 37.

Feingold, B. F. Hyperkinesis and learning disabilities linked to artificial food flavors and colors. *American Journal of Nursing*, 1975, *75*, 797–803. (a)

Feingold, B. F. *Why your child is hyperactive*. New York: Random House, 1975. (b)

Feingold, B. F. Hyperkinesis and learning disabilities linked to ingestion of artificial food colors and flavorings. *Journal of Learning Disabilities*, 1976, *9*, 551–59.

Feldhusen, J., & Sokol, L. Extra school programming to meet the needs of gifted youth: Super-Saturday. *Gifted Child Quarterly*, 1982, *26*, 51–56.

Fernald, G. M. *Remedial techniques in basic school subjects*. New York: McGraw-Hill, 1943.

Ferrari, M., & Harris, S. L. The limits and motivating potential of sensory stimuli as reinforcers for autistic children. *Journal of Applied Behavior Analysis*, 1981, *14*, 339–43.

Fiske, E. B. Special education is now a matter of civil rights. *New York Times*, April 25, 1976, *12*(1), 14.

Fitzgerald, E. *Straight language for the deaf*. Washington, D.C.: Alexander Graham Bell Association for the Deaf, 1929.

Flexer, R. W., & Martin, A. S. Sheltered workshops and vocational training settings. In

M. E. Snell (Ed.), *Systematic instruction of the moderately and severely handi-capped*. Columbus, Ohio: Charles E. Merrill, 1978.

Flygare, T. J. De jure: Supreme court holds that P.L. 94-142 does not require sign-language interpreter for deaf student. *Phi Delta Kappan*, 1982, *64*, 62–63.

Foster, M., Berger, M., & McLean, M. Rethinking a good idea: A reassessment of parent involvement. *Topics in Early Childhood Special Education*, 1981, *1*, 55–65.

Fox, L. H. Sex differences: Implications for program planning for the academically gifted. In J. C. Stanley, W. C. George, & C. H. Solano (Eds.), *The gifted and crea-tive: A fifty-year perspective*. Baltimore: Johns Hopkins, 1977.

Foxx, R. M. *Variables in setting up programs for severely handicapped students*. Paper presented at the Fifth Canadian Congress of the Council for Exceptional Children, London, Ontario, November 5, 1982.

Frank, A. R. Breaking down learning tasks: a sequence approach. *Teaching Exceptional Children*, *1973, 6*, 16–19.

Freagon, S. Present and projected services to meet the needs of severely handicapped children: Keynote address. In *Proceedings of the National Parent Conference on Children Requiring Extensive Special Education Programming*. Washington, D.C.: U.S. Department of Education, Special Education Programs, 1982.

French, R. W., & Jansma, P. *Special physical education*. Columbus, Ohio: Charles E. Mer-rill, 1982.

Friedman, P. R. *The rights of mentally retarded persons*. New York: Avon, 1976.

Friedman, P. R. Human and legal rights of mentally retarded persons. *International Journal of Mental Health*, 1977, *6*, 50–72.

Frierson, E. C. Upper and lower status children: A study of differences. *Exceptional Chil-dren*, 1965, *32*, 83–90.

Frierson, E. C. The gifted. *Review of Educational Research*, 1969, *39*, 25–37.

Froehlinger, V. J. (Ed.). *Today's hearing impaired child: Into the mainstream of educa-tion*. Washington, D.C.: Alexander Graham Bell Association for the Deaf, 1981.

Frostig, M., & Horne, D. The Frostig program for the development of visual perception (Rev. ed.). Chicago: Follett, 1973.

Frostig, M., Lefever, D. W., & Whittlesey, J. R. B. The Marianne Frostig Development Test of Visual Perception. Palo Alto, Calif.: Consulting Psychology Press, 1964.

Fusfeld, I. S. How the deaf communicate: Written language. *American Annals of the Deaf*, 1958, *103*, 255–63.

Furth, H. G. *Deafness and learning: a psychosocial approach*. Belmont, Calif: Wadsworth, 1973.

Gallagher, J. J. Characteristics of gifted children: A research summary. In W. B. Barbe & J. S. Renzulli (Eds.), *Psychology and education of the gifted* (2nd ed.). New York: Irvington, 1975. (a)

Gallagher, J. J. *Teaching the gifted* (2nd ed.). Boston: Allyn & Bacon, 1975. (b)

Gallagher, J. J. The gifted child in elementary school. In W. Dennis & M. W. Dennis (Eds.), *The intellectually gifted: An overview*. New York: Grune & Stratton, 1976.

Gallagher, J. J. Differential curriculum for the gifted. In A. H. Kramer, D. Bitan, N. Butler-Por, A. Eryatar, & E. Landau (Eds.), *Gifted children: Challenging their po-tential*. New York: World Council for Gifted and Talented Children, 1981.

Gallimore, R., Boggs, J., & Jordan, C. *Culture, behavior, and education*. Beverly Hills, Calif.: Sage, 1974.

Galton, F. Genius as inherited. From *Hereditary genius: An inquiry into its laws and consequences*. London: Macmillan, 1869. Reprinted in A. Rothenberg & C. R. Hausman (Eds.), *The creativity question*. Durham, N.C.: Duke University, 1936.

Garber, H. C. *Prevention of mental retardation: The Milwaukee project*. Portland, Ore.: American Association on Mental Deficiency, May 1975.

Garber, H., & Heber, R. *The Milwaukee Project: Early intervention as a technique to prevent mental retardation*. (Technical Paper) Storrs: The University of Connecticut, 1973.

Garcia, R. L. *Education for cultural pluralism: Global roots stew*. Bloomington, Ind.: Phi Delta Kappa Educational Foundation, 1981.

Gates, A. T., & McKillop, A. S. Gates-McKillop Reading Diagnostic Test. New York: Columbia University, Teachers College, Bureau of Publication, 1962.

Gearheart, B. R., & Litton, F. W. *The trainable retarded: A foundations approach*. St. Louis: C. V. Mosby, 1975.

Gelof, M. Comparisons of systems of classification relating degrees of retardation to measured intelligence. *American Journal of Mental Deficiency*, 1963, *68*, 297–317.

Gesell, A., & Associates. Gesell Developmental Schedules, 1940 Series. New York: Psychological Corporation, 1940.

Gilhool, T. K. Changing public policies: Roots and forces. *Minnesota Education*, 1976, *2*(2), 8.

Glavin, J. P., & Annesley, F. R. Reading and arithmetic correlates of conduct-problem and withdrawn children. *Journal of Special Education*, 1971, *5*, 213–19.

Glover, J., & Gary, A. L. Procedures to increase some aspects of creativity. *Journal of Applied Behavior Analysis*, 1976, *9*, 79–84.

Goddard, H. H. *School training of gifted children*. New York: World Book, 1928.

Goetz, E. M. A review of functional analyses of preschool children's creative behaviors. *Education and Treatment of Children*, 1982, *5*, 157–77.

Goetz, E. M., & Baer, D. M. Social control of form diversity and the emergence of new forms in children's blockbuilding. *Journal of Applied Behavior Analysis*, 1973, *6*, 209–18.

Gold, M. W. Task analysis of a complex assembly task by the retarded blind. *Exceptional Children*, 1976, *43*, 73–85.

Gold M. W. An alternative definition of mental retardation. In M. C. Gold (Ed.), *"Did I say that?" Articles and commentary on the Try Another Way System*. Champaign, Ill.: Research Press, 1980. (a)

Gold, M. W. *Try another way: Training manual*. Champaign, Ill.: Research Press, 1980. (b)

Goldstein, S., Stickland, B., Turnbull, A. P., & Curry, L. An observational analysis of the IEP conference. *Exceptional Children*, 1980, *46*(4), 278–86.

Goldstein, S., & Turnbull, A. P. The use of two strategies to increase parent participation in the IEP conference. *Exceptional Children*, 1982, *48*, 360–61.

Gollay, E., Freedman, R., Wyngarten, M., & Kurtz, N. R. *Coming back: The community experiences of deinstitutionalized mentally retarded people*. Cambridge, Mass.: Abt Books, 1978.

Gonzales, R. Mainstreaming your hearing impaired child in 1980: Still an oversimplification. *Journal of Research and Development in Education*, 1980, *13*(4), 14–21.

Goodenough, F. L., & Harris, D. B. *The Goodenough-Harris Drawing Test.* New York: Harcourt Brace Jovanovich, 1963.

Goodman, L. V. A bill of rights for the handicapped. *American Education,* 1976, *12*(6), 6–8.

Gordon, T. *Parent effectiveness training.* New York: Peter H. Wyden, 1970.

Gottlieb, J. Mainstreaming: Fulfilling the promise? *American Journal of Mental Deficiency,* 1981, *86,* 115–26.

Gottlieb, J., Agard, J. A., Kaufman, M. J., & Semmel, M. I. Retarded children mainstreamed: Practices as they affect minority group children. In R. L. Jones (Ed.), *Mainstreaming and the minority child.* Reston, Va.: Council for Exceptional Children, 1976.

Gottlieb, J., & Leyser, Y. Facilitating the social mainstreaming of retarded children. *Exceptional Education Quarterly,* 1981, *1,* 57–69.

Gowan, J. C. *Development of the creative individual.* San Diego: Robert R. Knapp, 1972.

Gradel, K., Thompson, M. S., & Sheehan, R. Parental and professional agreement in early childhood assessment. *Topics in Early Childhood Special Education,* 1981, *1,* 31–39.

Gray, S. W., Klaus, R. A., Miller, J. O., & Forrester, D. J. *Before first grade: The early training project for culturally disadvantaged children.* New York: Teachers College Press, 1966.

Gray, W. S. *Gray Oral Reading Tests.* Indianapolis: Bobbs-Merrill, 1963.

Gresham, F. M. Misguided mainstreaming: The case for social skills training with handicapped children. *Exceptional Children,* 1982, *48,* 422–33.

Groht, M. A. *Natural language for deaf children.* Washington, D.C.: Alexander Graham Bell Association for the Deaf, 1958.

Grossman, H. J. (Ed.). *Manual on terminology and classification in mental retardation* (1973 rev.) Washington, D.C.: American Association on Mental Deficiency, 1973.

Grossman H. J. (Ed.). *Manual on terminology and classification in mental retardation.* (1977 rev.). Washington, D.C.: American Association on Mental Deficiency, 1977.

Grossman, H. J. (Ed.). *Classification in mental retardation.* Washington, D.C.: American Association on Mental Deficiency, 1983.

Grove, N. M. Conditions resulting in physical disabilities. In J. L. Bigge (Ed.), *Teaching individuals with physical and multiple disabilities* (2nd ed.). Columbus, Ohio: Charles E. Merrill, 1982.

Guess, P. D., & Mulligan, M. The severely and profoundly handicapped. In E. L. Meyen (Ed.), *Exceptional children and youth: An introduction* (2nd ed.). Denver: Love, 1982.

Guess, P. D., Sailor, W., & Bear, D. M. *Functional speech and language training for the severely handicapped.* Lawrence, Kans.: H. & H Enterprises, 1976.

Guilford, J. P. The structure of intellect. *Psychological Bulletin,* 1956, *53*(4), 276–93.

Guilford, J. P. Traits of creativity, In H. H. Anderson (Ed.), *Creativity and its cultivation.* New York: Harper & Brothers, 1959.

Gurcsick, B. Justifying your program with a diagnostic-prescriptive approach. *G-C-T,* 1981, *19,* 12–13.

Gustason, G., Pfetzing, D., & Zawolkow, E. *Signing exact English.* Los Alamitos, Calif.: Modern Signs Press, 1980.

Hall, E. T. How cultures collide. *Psychology Today,* 1976, *10*(2), 66–74, 97.

Hall, M. C., & Hall, R. V. *Responsive parenting manual.* Lawrence, Kans.: H. & H Enterprises, 1978.

Hallahan, D. P. & Cruickshank, W. M. *Psychoeducational foundations of learning disabilities.* Englewood Cliffs, N.J.: Prentice-Hall, 1973.

Hallahan, D. P., & Kauffman, J. M. *Exceptional children: Introduction to special education.* Englewood Cliffs, N.J.: Prentice-Hall, 1978.

Hallahan, D. P., & Kauffman, J. M. *Introduction to learning disabilities: A psychoeducational approach.* Englewood Cliffs, N.J.: Prentice-Hall, 1976.

Hallahan, D. P., & Kauffman, J. M. Labels, categories, behaviors: ED, LD, and EMR reconsidered. *The Journal of Special Education,* 1977, *11,* 139–49.

Halle, J. W., & Sindelar, P. T. Behavioral observation methodologies for early childhood education. *Topics in Early Childhood Special Education,* 1982, *2,* 43–54.

Hammer, E. K. *Issues in assessment.* Paper presented at the National Conference on Innovation in Education for Deaf-Blind Children and Youth, Alexandria, Virginia, December 13, 1978.

Hammill, D. D. Defining learning disabilities for programmatic purposes. *Academic Therapy,* 1976, *12,* 29–37.

Hammill, D. D. The field of learning disabilities: A futuristic perspective. *Learning Disability Quarterly,* 1980, *3,* 2–9.

Hammill, D. D., Goodman, L., & Wiederholt, J. T. Visual-motor processes: Can we train them? *Reading Teacher,* 1974, *27,* 469–78.

Hammill, D. D. & Larsen, S. The effectiveness of psycholinguistic training. *Exceptional Children,* 1974, *41,* 5–15.

Hammill, D. D., & Larsen, S. The effectiveness of psycholinguistic training: A reaffirmation of position. *Exceptional Children,* 1978, *44,* 402–17.

Hammill, D. D., Leigh, J. E., McNutt, G., & Larsen, S. C. A new definition of learning disabilities. *Learning Disability Quarterly,* 1981, *4,* 336–42.

Haring, N. G. The severely handicapped. In N. G. Haring (Ed.), *Behavior of exceptional children* (2nd ed.). Columbus, Ohio: Charles E. Merrill, 1978.

Haring, N. G., Bateman, B., & Carnine, D. Direct instruction—DISTAR. In N. G. Haring & B. Bateman (Eds.), *Teaching the learning disabled child.* Englewood Cliffs, N.J.: Prentice-Hall, 1977.

Haring, N. G., Lovitt, T. C., Eaton, M. D., & Hansen, C. L. *The fourth R: Research in the classroom.* Columbus, Ohio: Charles E. Merrill, 1978.

Haring, N. G., & Schiefelbusch, R. L. (Eds.). *Teaching special children.* New York: McGraw-Hill, 1976.

Haring, N. G., & Smith, J. The profoundly handicapped. In N. G. Haring (Ed.), *Behavior of exceptional children* (2nd ed.). Columbus, Ohio: Charles E. Merrill, 1978.

Harris, G., & Kotsch, L. S. Extended families and young handicapped children. *Topics in Early Childhood Special Education,* 1981, *1,* 29–35.

Hart, B., & Risley, T. R. Incidental teaching of language in the preschool. *Journal of Applied Behavior Analysis,* 1975, *8,* 411–20.

Hatlen, P. H. Priorities in education programs for visually handicapped children and youth. *Division for the Visually Handicapped Newsletter,* Winter 1976, 8–11.

Hatlen, P. H. The role of the teacher of the visually impaired: A self definition. *Division for the Visually Handicapped Newsletter,* Fall 1978, 5.

Hatten, J. T., & Hatten, P. W. *Natural language*. Tucson: Communication Skill Builders, 1975.

Hawkins, R. P. What is "meaningful" behavior change in a severely/profoundly retarded learner? The view of a behavior analytic parent. In W. L. Heward, T. E. Heron, D. S. Hill, & J. Trap-Porter (Eds.), *Focus on behavior analysis in education*. Columbus, Ohio: Charles E. Merrill, 1984.

Hawkins, R. P., & Hawkins, K. K. Parental observations on the education of severely retarded children: Can it be done in the classroom? *Analysis and Intervention in Development Disabilities*, 1981, *1*, 13–22.

Haycock, G. S. *The teaching of speech*. Stoke-on-Trent, Eng.: Hill & Ainsworth, 1933.

Hayden, A. H., & Edgar, E. B. Identification, screening, and assessment. In J. B. Jordan, A. H. Hayden, M. B. Karnes, & M. M. Woods (Eds.), *Early childhood education for exceptional children: A handbook of ideas and exemplary practices*. Reston, Va.: Council for Exceptional Children, 1977.

Hayden, A. H., & Edgar, E. Developing individualized education programs for young handicapped children. *Teaching Exceptional Children*, 1978, *10*, 67–70.

Hayden, A., Morris, K., & Bailey, D. *The effects of early education*. Seattle: University of Washington, Model Preschool Center for Handicapped Children, 1977.

Hayden, A. H., & Pious, C. G. The case for early intervention. In R. York & E. Edgar (Eds.), *Teaching the severely handicapped* (Vol. 4). Seattle: American Association for the Education of the Severely/Profoundly Handicapped, 1979.

Haywood, H. C. What happened to mild and moderate mental retardation? *American Journal of Mental Deficiency*, 1979, *83*, 427–31.

Heber, R. F. A manual on terminology and classification in mental retardation (rev. ed.). *Monograph Supplement American Journal of Mental Deficiency*, 1961, *64*.

Heber, R. F., & Garber, H. An experiment in prevention of cultural-familial mental retardation. In D. A. Primrose (Ed.), *Proceedings of the Second Congress of the International Association for the Scientific Study of Mental Deficiency*. Warsaw: Polish Medical Publishers, 1971.

Hechinger, F. M. Bringing the handicapped into the mainstream. *New York Times*, April 25, 1976, 12:15.

Heim, K. M., et al. Juvenile detention: Another boundary issue for physicians. *Pediatrics*, 1980, *66*, 239–45.

Hemming, H., Lavender, T., & Pill, R. Quality of life of mentally retarded adults transferred from large institutions to new small units. *American Journal of Mental Deficiency*, 1981, *86*, 157–69.

Heron, T. E. Maintaining the mainstreamed child in the regular classroom: The decision-making process. *Journal of Learning Disabilities*, 1978, *11*, 210–16.

Heron, T. E., & Axelrod, S. Effectiveness of feedback to mothers concerning their children's word-recognition performance. *Reading Improvement*, 1976, *13*, 74–81.

Heron, T. E., & Harris, K. C. *The educational consultant: Helping professionals, parents, and mainstreamed students*. Boston: Allyn & Bacon, 1982.

Heron, T. E., & Skinner, M. E. Criteria for defining the regular classroom as the least restrictive environment for LD students. *Learning Disability Quarterly*, 1981, *4*, 115–21.

Heston, L. L. The genetics of schizophrenic and schizoid disease. *Science*, 1970, *167*, 249–56.

HEW reports 13 percent of Head Start children are handicapped. *Report on Preschool Education,* 1978, 10.

Heward, W. L. Visual Repsonse System: A mediated resource room for children with learning problems. *Journal of Special Education Technology,* 1978, *2,* 40–46.

Heward, W. L. Teaching students to control their own behavior: A critical skill. *Exceptional Teacher.* 1979, *1,* 3–5, 11.

Heward, W. L., & Chapman, J. E. Improving parent-teacher communication through recorded telephone messages: Systematic replication in a special education classroom. *Journal of Special Education Technology,* 1981, *4,* 11–19.

Heward, W. L., Heron, T. E., & Cooke, N. L. Tutor huddle: Key element in a classwide peer tutoring system. *The Elementary School Journal,* 1982, *83,* 115–123.

Heward, W. L., & Dardig. J. C. Improving the parent-teacher relationship through contingency contracting. In D. Edge, B. J. Strenecky, & S. I. Mour (Eds.), *Parenting learning-problem children: The professional educator's perspective.* Columbus: The Ohio State University, National Center for Educational Materials and Media for the Handicapped, 1978. (a)

Heward, W. L., & Dardig, J. C. Inservice for parents of special needs children. *Viewpoints in Teaching and Learning,* 1978, *54,* 127–37. (b)

Heward, W. L., Dardig, J. C., & Rossett, A. *Working with parents of handicapped children.* Columbus, Ohio: Charles E. Merrill, 1979.

Heward, W. L., Eachus, H. T., & Christopher, J. *Establishment of talking in an elective mute.* Unpublished manuscript, University of Massachusetts, 1974.

Heward, W. L., Heron, T. E., Hill, D. S., & Trap-Porter, J. (Eds.). *Focus on behavior analysis in education.* Columbus, Ohio: Charles E. Merrill, 1984.

Hewett, F. M. A hierarchy of educational tasks for children with learning disorders. *Exceptional Children,* 1964, *31,* 207–14.

Hewett, F. M. *The emotionally disturbed child in the classroom.* Boston: Allyn & Bacon, 1968.

Hewett, F. M. & Forness, S. R. *Education of exceptional learners* (2nd ed.). Boston: Allyn & Bacons, 1977.

Hewett, F. M., & Taylor, F. D. *The emotionally disturbed child in the classroom: The orchestration of success.* Boston: Allyn & Bacon, 1980.

Hieronymous, A. N., & Lindquist, E. F. Iowa Tests of Basic Skills. Boston: Houghton Mifflin, 1978.

Hill, J. W., Wehman, P., & Horst, G. Toward generalization of appropriate leisure and social behavior in severely handicapped youth: Pinball machine use. *Journal of The Association for the Severely Handicapped,* 1982, *6*(4), 38–44.

Hilliard, A. G., III. The strengths and weaknesses of cognitive tests for young children. In J. D. Andrews (Ed.), *One child indivisible.* Washington, D.C.: National Association for the Education of Young Children, 1975.

Hingtgen, J. N., & Bryson, C. Q. Recent developments in the study of early childhood psychoses: Infantile autism, childhood schizophrenia, and related disorders. *Schizophrenia Bulletin,* 1972, No. 5, 8–54.

Hirschberg, G., Lewis, C., & Thomas, D. *Rehabilitation.* Philadelphia: Lippincott, 1964.

Hitzing, W. ENCOR and beyond. In T. Apolloni, J. Cappuccilli, & T. P. Cooke (Eds.), *Achievements in residential services for persons with disabilities: Toward excellence.* Baltimore: University Park Press, 1980.

Hobbs, N. *The futures of children.* San Francisco: Jossey-Bass, 1975.

Hobbs, N. (Ed.). *Issues in the classification of children* (Vol. 1). San Francisco: Jossey-Bass, 1976. (a)

Hobbs, N. (Ed.). *Issues in the classification of children* (Vol. II). San Francisco: Jossey-Bass, 1976. (b)

Hobbs, N. *The troubled and troubling child.* San Francisco: Jossey-Boss, 1982.

Hochman, R. Communicating with parents about the classroom. *Exceptional Teacher,* 1979, *1*(3), 6–7.

Hoemann, H. W., & Briga, J. I. Hearing impairments. In J. M. Kauffman and D. P. Hallahan (Eds.), *Handbook of special education.* Englewood Cliffs, N.J.: Prentice-Hall, 1981.

Holland, A. L., & Reinmuth, O. M. Aphasia in adults. In G. H. Shames & E. H. Wiig (Eds.), *Human communication disorders: An introduction.* Columbus, Ohio: Charles E. Merrill, 1982.

Hollingsworth, L. S. *Children above 180 I.Q.: Stanford Binet: Origin and development* (Reprint ed.). New York: Arno Press, 1975.

Holm, V., & McCartin, R. Interdisciplinary child development team: Team issues and training in interdisciplinaries. In K. E. Allen, V. A. Holm, & R. I Schiefelbusch (Eds.), *Early intervention: A team approach.* Baltimore: University Park Press, 1978.

Hops, H., Beickel, S., & Walker, H. M. *CLASS (Contingencies for Learning Academic and Social Skills): Manual for Consultants.* Eugene: University of Oregon, Center at Oregon for Research in Behavioral Education of the Handicapped, 1976.

Horst, G., Wehman, P., Hill, J. W., & Bailey, C. Developing age-appropriate leisure skills in severely handicapped adolescents. *Teaching Exceptional Children,* 1981, *14,* 11–16.

Howell, K. W., Kaplan, J. S., & O'Connell, C. Y. *Evaluating exceptional children: A task analysis approach.* Columbus, Ohio: Charles E. Merrill, 1979.

Hull, F. M., Mielke, P. W., Willeford, J. A., & Timmons, R. J. *National speech and hearing survey.* Final report. Project No. 50978. Grant No. OE-32-15-0050-5010 (607). Washington, D.C.: U.S. Department of Health, Education, and Welfare, 1976. (Cited in Fein, 1983).

Humphreys, R. P. The federal-state vocational rehabilitation program. *Amicus,* 1979, *4,* 235–36.

Imber, S. C., Imber, R. B., & Rothstein, C. Modifying independent work habits: An effective parent-teacher communication program. *Exceptional Children,* 1979, *46,* 218–21.

Ireland, W. W. *The mental affections of children: Idiocy, imbecility, and insanity.* Philadelphia: Blakiston, 1900.

Iscoe, I., & Payne, S. Development of a revised scale for the functional classification of exceptional children. In E. P. Trapp & P. Himelstein (Eds.), *Readings on the exceptional child.* New York: Appleton-Century-Crofts, 1972.

Itard, J. M. G. [*The wild boy of Aveyron*] (G. Humphrey & M. Humphrey, Eds. and trans.). New York: Appleton-Century-Crofts, 1962. (Originally published 1894.)

Jastak, J. F., & Jastak, S. R. *The Wide Range Achievement Test* (rev. ed.). Wilmington, Del.: Guidance Associates, 1965.

Johnson, D., & Myklebust, H. *Learning disabilities: Educational principles and practices.* New York: Grune & Stratton, 1967.

Johnson, J. L. Special education and the inner city: A challenge for the future or another means of cooling the mark out? *Journal of Special Education*, 1969, *3*, 241–51.

Johnson, J. L. Mainstreaming black children. In R. L. Jones (Ed.), *Mainstreaming and the minority child*. Reston, Va.: Council for Exceptional Children, 1976.

Johnson, M., & Bailey, J. The modification of leisure behavior in a halfway house for retarded women. *Journal of Applied Behavior Analysis*, 1977, *10*, 273–82.

Joiner, L. M., & Sabatino, D. A. A policy study of P. L. 94–142. *Exceptional Children*, 1981, *46*, 24–32.

Jonas, G. *Stuttering: The disorder of many theories*. New York: Farrar, Straus & Giroux, 1976.

Jones, M. H. Physical facilities and environments. In J. B. Jordan, A. H. Hayden, M. B. Karnes, & M. M. Wood (Eds.), *Early childhood education for exceptional children: A handbook of ideas and exemplary practices*. Reston, Va.: Council for Exceptional Children, 1977.

Jones, R. L. (Ed.). *Mainstreaming and the minority child*. Reston, Va.: Council for Exceptional Children, 1976.

Jordan, J. B., Hayden, A. H., Karnes, M. B., & Wood, M. M. (Eds.). *Early childhood education for exceptional children: A handbook of ideas and exemplary practices*. Reston, Va.: Council for Exceptional Children, 1977.

Journal of Applied Behavior Analysis. Lawrence, Kansas: Society for the Experimental Analysis of Behavior, 1968–1983.

Justen, J. E. Who are the severely handicapped? A problem in definition. *AAESPH Review*, 1976, *1*(2), 1–12.

Kakalik, J. S., Brewer, G. D., Dougharty, L. A., Fleischauer, P. D., Genensky, S. M., & Wallen, L. M. *Improving services to handicapped children*. Sants Monica, Calif.: Rand Corporation, 1974.

Kamp, S. H., & Chinn, P. C. *A multiethnic curriculum for special education students*. Reston, Va.: Council for Exceptional Children, 1982.

Karnes, M. B. Exemplary early education programs for handicapped children: Characteristics in common. *Educational Horizons*, 1977, *56*(1), 47–54.

Karnes, M. B., Shwedel, A. M., & Williams, M. Combining instructional models for young gifted children. *Teaching Exceptional Children*, 1983, *15*, 128–35.

Karnes, M. B., Teska, J. A., Hodgins, A. S., & Badger, E. D. Educational intervention at home by mothers of disadvantaged infants. *Child Development*, 1970, *41*, 925–35.

Karnes, M. B., & Zehrback, R. R. Alternative modes for delivering services to young handicapped children. In J. B. Jordan, A. H. Hayden, M. B. Karnes, & M. M. Woods (Eds.), *Early childhood education for exceptional children: A handbook of ideas and exemplary practices*. Reston, Va.: Council for Exceptional Children, 1977.

Kasari, C., & Filler, J. W. Using inflatables with severely motorically involved infants and preschoolers. *TEACHING Exceptional Children*, 1981, *14*(1), 22–26.

Kass, C. R. Final report, Advanced institute for Leadership Personnel in Learning Disabilities. U.S. Office of Education, Bureau of Education for the Handicapped 1970.

Katz, L., Mathis, S. L., & Merrill, E. C. *The deaf child in the public schools* (2nd ed.). Danville, Ill.: Interstate printers & Publishers, 1978.

Kauffman, J. M. *Characteristics of children's behavior disorders.* Columbus, Ohio: Charles E. Merrill, 1977.

Kauffman, J. M. Where special education for disturbed children is going: A personal view. *Exceptional children,* 1980, *48,* 522–27.

Kauffman, J. M. *Characteristics of children's behavior disorders* (2nd ed.). Columbus, Ohio: Charles E. Merrill, 1981. (a)

Kauffman, J. M. (Ed.). Special issue: Are all children educable. *Analysis and Intervention in Developmental Disabilities,* 1981, *1*(1) (b) (entire issue)

Kauffman, J. M., & Krouse, J. The cult of educability: Searching for the substance of things hoped for; the evidence of things not seen. *Analysis and Intervention in Developmental Disabilities,* 1981, *1*(1), 53–61.

Kavale, K. Functions of the Illinois Test of Psycholinguistic Abilities (ITPA): Are they trainable? *Exceptional Children,* 1981, *47,* 496–510.

Kavale, K., & Mattison, P. D. "One jumped off the balance beam": Meta-analysis of perceptual-motor training. *Journal of Learning Disabilities,* 1983, *16,* 165–73.

Kazdin, A. E. Behavior modification in retardation. In J. T. Neisworth & R. M. Smith (Eds.), *Retardation: Issues, assessment and intervention.* New York: McGraw-Hill, 1978.

Keating, D. P. Four faces of creativity: The continuing plight of the intellectually underserved. *Gifted Child Quarterly,* 1980, *24,* 56–61.

Keller, W. D., & Bundy, R. S. Effects of unilateral hearing loss upon educational achievement. *Child Care, Health & Development,* 1980, *6,* 93–100.

Kelly, M. Parent's almanac: Early stutterers. *Washington Post,* July 15, 1982, D5.

Kelly, T. J., Bullock, L. M., & Dykes, M. K. Behavioral disorders: Teacher's perceptions. *Exceptional Children,* 1977, *43,* 316–18.

Kenowitz, L. A., Zweibel, S., & Edgar, E. Determining the least restrictive educational opportunity for the severely and profoundly handicapped. In N. Haring & D. Bricker (Eds.), *Teaching the severely handicapped* (Vol. 3). Seattle: American Association for the Education of the Severely/Profoundly Handicapped, 1978.

Kephart, N. C. *The slow learner in the classroom* (2nd ed.). Columbus, Ohio: Charles E. Merrill, 1971.

Kershner, J., Hawks, W., & Grekin, R. *Megavitamins and learning disorders: A controlled double-blind experiment.* Unpublished manuscript, Ontario Institute for Studies in Education. 1977.

Kessler, J. W. *Psychopathology of childhood.* Englewood Cliffs, N.J.: Prentice-Hall, 1966.

Khatena, J. Major directions in creativity research. *The Gifted Child Quarterly,* 1976, *20*(3), 336–49.

Kidd, J. W. An open letter to the Committee on Technology and Classification of AAMD from the Committee on Definition and Terminology of CEC-MR. *Education and Training of the Mentally Retarded,* 1979, *14,* 74–76.

King-Stoops, J. *Migrant education: Teaching the wandering ones.* Bloomington, Ind.: Phi Delta Kappa Educational Foundation, 1980.

Kirk, S. A. *Early education of the mentally retarded: An experimental study.* Urbana: University of Illinois, 1958.

Kirk, S. A. Behavioral diagnosis and remediation of learning disabilities. In *Proceedings of the conference on exploration into the problems of the perceptually handicapped child.* Chicago: Perceptually Handicapped Children, 1963.

Kirk, S. A. Foreword. In D. F. Moores, *Educating the deaf: Psychology, principles, and practices.* Boston: Houghton Mifflin, 1978. (a)

Kirk, S. A. An interview with Samuel Kirk. *Academic Therapy*, 1978, *13*, 617–20. (b)

Kirk, S. A. Foreword to the first edition. In D. F. Moores, *Educating the deaf: Psychology, principles, and practices* (2nd ed.). Boston: Houghton Mifflin, 1981.

Kirk, S. A., & Gallagher, J. J. *Educating exceptional children* (4th ed.). Boston: Houghton Mifflin, 1983.

Kirk, S. A., McCarthy, J. J., & Kirk, W. D. Illinois Test of Psycholinguistic Abilities (rev. ed.). Urbana: University of Illinois Press, 1968.

Klein, S. D., & Schleifer, M. J. The challenge for the 1980s: Parent-professional collaboration. *The Exceptional Parent*, 1980, *10*(1), 2–3.

Klima, E., & Bellugi, U. *The signs of language.* Cambridge, Mass.: Harvard University Press, 1979.

Klinghammer, H. D. Social perception of the deaf and of the blind by their voices and their speech. In *Report of the proceedings of the international congress on the education of the deaf and of the 41st meeting of the Convention of American Instructors of the Deaf.* Washington, D.C.: U.S. Government Printing Office, 1964.

Knobloch, H., & Pasamanick, B. *Gesell's and Amatruda's developmental diagnosis: The evaluation and management of normal and abnormal neuropsychologic development in infancy and early childhood.* Hagerstown, Md.: Harper & Row, 1974.

Knobloch, H., Pasamanick, B., & Sherard, E. S., Jr. Developmental Screening Inventory. New York: Psychological Corporation, 1966.

Knoblock, P. *Teaching and mainstreaming autistic children.* Denver: Love, 1982.

Koestler, F. *The unseen minority: A social history of blindness in the United States.* New York: David McKay, 1976.

Kohl, F. Effects of motoric requirements on the acquisition of manual sign responses by severely handicapped students. *American Journal of Mental Deficiency*, 1980, *85*, 396–403.

Kolstoe, O. P. *Mental retardation: An educational viewpoint.* New York: Holt, Rinehart, Winston, 1972.

Kolstoe, O. P., & Frey, R. *A high school work-study program for mentally subnormal students.* Carbondale: Southern Illinois Press, 1965.

Krim, M. Scientific research and mental retardation. *President's Committee on Mental Retardation Message* (No. 16). Washington, D.C.: U.S. Government Printing Office, 1969.

Kronick, D. *They too can succeed: A practical guide for parents of learning-disabled children.* San Rafael, Calif.: Academic Therapy, 1969.

Kroth, R. L. *Communicating with parents of exceptional children.* Denver: Love, 1975.

Kroth, R. L. Parents: Powerful and necessary allies. *Teaching Exceptional Children*, 1978, *10*, 88–90.

Kroth, R. L. Involvement with parents of behaviorially disordered adolescents. In G. Brown, R. L. McDowell, & J. Smith (Eds.), *Educating adolescents with behavior disorders.* Columbus, Ohio: Charles E. Merrill, 1981.

Kroth, R. L., & Simpson, R. *Parent conferences as a teaching strategy.* Denver: Love, 1977.

Kugel, R. B., & Wolfensberger, W. (Eds.). *Changing patterns in residential services for the mentally retarded.* Washington, D.C.: Superintendent of Documents, 1969.

REFERENCES

Kuhlman, F. Mental deficiency, feeble-mindedness, and defective delinquency. *American Association for the study of the Feeble-Minded*, 1924, *29*, 58–70.

Labov, W. The logic of nonstandard English. In P. Stoller (Ed.), *Black American English: Its background and its usage in the schools and in literature.* New York: Dell, 1975.

Lakin, K. & Bruininks, R. *Occupational stability of direct-care staff or residential facilities for mentally retarded people.* Developmental Disabilities Project on Residential Services and Community Adjustment, Project Report No. 14. Minneapolis: University of Minnesota, Department of Psychoeducational Studies, 1981.

Lambert, N., Windmiller, M., Cole L., & Figueroa, R. AAMD Adaptive Behavior Scale, Public School Version (1974 rev.). Washington, D.C.: American Association on Mental Deficiency, 1975.

Lancaster, J. *Improvement in education.* London: Collins & Perkins, 1806.

LaPorta, R. A., McGee, D. I., Simmons-Martin, A., Voce, E., von Hippel, C. S., & Conovan, J. *Mainstreaming preschoolers: Children with hearing impairment.* Washington, D.C.: U.S. Government Printing Office, 1978. (Stock number 017-092-00032-4)

Larsen, L. A. Deinstitutionalization. In M. A. Thomas (Ed.), *Hey, don't forget about me! Education's investment in the severely, profoundly, and multiple handicapped.* Reston, Va.: Council for Exceptional Children, 1976.

Larsen, S. C. Learning disabilities and the professional educator. *Learning Disability Quarterly*, 1978, *1*, 5–12.

LaVor, M. L. Federal legislation for exceptional persons: A history. In F. J. Weintraub, A. Abeson, J. Ballard, & M. L. LaVor (Eds.), *Public policy and education of exceptional children.* Reston, Va.: The Council for Exceptional Children, 1976.

Lazar, D., & Darlington, R. *Lasting effects after preschool: A report by the central staff of the consortium for longitudinal studies.* Washington, D.C.: U.S. Department of Health, Education, and Welfare, DHEW Publication No. (OHDS) 80-30179, October 1979.

LeBuffe, L. A., & LeBuffe, J. R. The learning vacation: A formula for parent education. *Teaching Exceptional Children*, 1982, *14*, 182–95.

Leff, R. B. *How to use the telephone.* Paoli, Pa.: Instructo Corporation, 1975.

Leonard, L. B. Early language development and language disorders. In G. H. Shames & E. H. Wiig (Eds.), *Human communication disorders: An introduction.* Columbus, Ohio: Charles E. Merrill, 1982.

Leone, P., Lovitt, T. C., & Hansen, C. A descriptive follow up study of learning disabled boys. *Learning Disability Quarterly*, 1981, *4*, 152–62.

Lerner, J. *Children with learning disabilities* (2nd ed.). Boston: Houghton Mifflin, 1976.

Levitt, E. E. The results of psychotherapy with children: An evaluation. *Journal of Consulting Psychology*, 1957, *21*, 189–96.

Levitt, E. E. Psychotherapy with children: a further evaluation. *Behavior Research and Therapy*, 1963, *1*, 45–51.

Liebergott, J., Favors, A., von Hippel, C. S., & Needleman, H. L. *Mainstreaming preschoolers: Children with speech and language impairments.* Washington, D.C.: U.S. Government Printing Office, 1978. (Stock number 017-092-00033-2)

Lillie, D. L., and Trohanis, P. L. (eds.) *Teaching parents to teach.* New York: Walker and Company, 1976.

Lindman, F. T., & McIntyre, J. M. *The mentally disabled and the law.* Chicago: University of Chicago Press, 1961.

Lingwell, J. Remarks quoted in M. Kelly, Parent's almanac: Early stutterers. *Washington Post,* July 15, 1982, D5.

Lloyd, J., Sabatino, D., Miller, T., & Miller, S. Proposed federal guidelines: Some open questions. *Journal of Learning Disabilities,* 1977, *10,* 69–71.

Lotter, V. Epidemiology of autistic conditions in young children—Part 1: Prevalence. *Social Psychiatry,* 1966, *1*(3), 124–37.

Lovaas, O. I., Koegel, R. L., Simmons, J. Q., & Long, J. S. Some generalization and follow-up measures on autistic children in behavior therapy. *Journal of Applied Behavior Analysis,* 1973, *6,* 131–66.

Lovaas, O. I., & Newsom, C. D. Behavior modification with psychotic children. In H. Leitenberg (Ed.), *Handbook of behavior modification and behavior therapy.* Englewood Cliffs, N.J.: Prentice-Hall, 1976.

Lovitt, T. C. Applied behavior analysis and learning disabilities—Part I: Characteristics of ABA, general recommendations and suggestions for practitioners. *Journal of Learning Disabilities,* 1975, *8,* 432–43. (a)

Lovitt, T. C. Applied behavior analysis and learning disabilities—Part II: Specific research recommendations and suggestions for practitioners. *Journal of Learning Disabilities,* 1975, *8,* 504–18. (b)

Lovitt, T. C. *In spite of my resistance . . . I've learned from children.* Columbus, Ohio: Charles E. Merrill, 1977.

Lovitt, T. C. The learning disabled. In N. G. Haring (Ed.), *Behavior of exceptional children* (2nd ed.). Columbus, Ohio: Charles E. Merrill, 1978.

Lovitt, T. C. *Because of my persistence . . . I've learned from children.* Columbus, Ohio: Charles E. Merrill, 1982.

Lowell, E. L., & Pollack, D. B. Remedial practices with the hearing impaired. In S. Dickson (Ed.), *Communication disorders: Remedial principles and practices.* Glenview, Ill.: Scott, Foresman, 1974.

Lowenfeld, B. (Ed.). *The visually handicapped child in school.* New York: John Day, 1973.

Lowenthal, B. Effect of small-group instruction on language-delayed preschoolers. *Exceptional Children,* 1981, *48,* 178–79.

Lund, K. A., & Bos, C. S. Orchestrating the preschool classroom: The daily schedule. *TEACHING Exceptional Children,* 1981, *14,* 120–25.

Lund, K. A., Foster, G. E., & McCall-Perez, F. C. The effectiveness of psycholinguistic training: A reevaluation. *Exceptional Children,* 1978, *44,* 310–319.

Lusthaus, C. S., Lusthaus, E. W., & Gibbs, H. Parents' role in the decision process. *Exceptional Children,* 1981, *48,* 256–57.

MacMillan, D. L. *Mental retardation in school and society* (2nd ed.). Boston: Little, Brown, 1982.

Madle, R. A. Alternative residential placements. In J. J. Neisworth & R. M. Smith (Eds.), *Retardation: Issues, assessment, and intervention.* New York: McGraw-Hill, 1978.

Maestas y Moores, J., & Moores, D. F. Language training with the young deaf child. In D. Bricker (Ed.), *Early language intervention with handicapped children.* San Francisco: Jossey-Bass, 1980.

Mager, R. F. *Goal Analysis,* Belmont, Calif.: Fearon, 1972.

Magliocca, L. A. Interview with Jane Rieke, *The Directive Teacher*. 1980, *2*(3), 14.

Maker, J. C. *Providing programs for the gifted handicapped*. Reston, Va.: The Council for Exceptional Children, 1977.

Maker, C. J. Teaching models in education of the gifted. Rockville, Md.: Aspen, 1982.

Malone, C. (Ed.). Disadvantaged and gifted handicapped. *The Gifted Child Quarterly*, 1978, *22*.

Mansdorf, I. J. Rapid token training of an institution ward using modeling. *Mental Retardation*, 1977, *15*(4), 37–39.

Marbach, W. D. Building the bionic man. *Newsweek*, July 12, 1982, 78–79.

Marland, S. P. *Education of the gifted and talented*. Washington, D.C.: U.S. Office of Education, 1971.

Marsh, G. E., Gearheart, C. K., & Gearheart, B. R. *The learning disabled adolescent: Program alternatives in the secondary school*. St. Louis: C. V. Mosby, 1978.

Marshall, A. E., & Heward, W. L. Teaching self-management to incarcerated youth. *Behavioral Disorders*, 1979, *4*, 215–26.

Martin, B. Parent-child relations. In F. D. Horowitz (Ed.), *Review of child development research* (Vol. 4). Chicago: University of Chicago Press, 1975.

Martin, G., & Pear, J. *Behavior modification: What it is and how to do it* (2nd ed.). Englewood Cliffs, N.J.: Prentice-Hall, 1983.

Matthews, J. The professions of speech-language pathology and auciology. In G. H. Shames & E. H. Wiig (Eds.), *Human communication disorders: An introduction*. Columbus, Ohio: Charles E. Merrill, 1982.

Mayhall, W., & Jenkins, J. Scheduling daily or less-than-daily instruction: Implications for resource programs. *Journal of Learning Disabilities*, 1977, *10*, 150–63.

Mayo, L. W. *A proposed program for national action to combat mental retardation*. Report of the Presidents' Committee on Mental Retardation. Washington, D.C.: U.S Government Printing Office, 1962.

McDaniels, G. Successful programs for young handicapped children. *Educational Horizons*, 1977, *56*(1), 26–27, 30–33.

McGovern, J. E., & Draper, D. Identification, assessment, and intervention. In N. H. Fallen with J. E. McGovern (Eds.), *Young children with special needs*. Columbus, Ohio: Charles E. Merrill, 1978.

McKinney, J. D., McClure, S., & Feagans, L. Classroom behavior of learning disabled children. *Learning Disability Quarterly*, 1982, *5*, 45–52.

McLoughlin, J. A., & Kelly, D. Issues facing the resource teacher. *Learning Disability Quarterly*, 1982, *5*, 58–64.

McLoughlin, J. A., & Netick, A. Defining learning disabilities: A new and cooperative direction. *Journal of Learning Disabilities*, 1983, *16*, 21–23.

McNutt, G., & Heller, G. Services for the learning disabled adolescent: A survey. *Learning Disability Quarterly*, 1978, *1*, 101–3.

McWhirter, J. J. A parent education group in learning disabilities. *Journal of Learning Disabilities*, 1976, *9*, 16–20.

Meadow, K. P. *Deafness and child development*. Berkeley: University of California Press, 1980.

Meehl, P. Schizotoxia, schizotypy, schizophrenia. In A. Buss (Ed.), *Theories of schizophrenia*. New York: Atherton, 1969.

Meeker, M. N. *The structure of intellect: Its interpretation and uses*. Columbus, Ohio: Charles E. Merrill, 1969.

Menolascino, F. L. *Challenges in mental retardation: Progressive ideology and sources.* New York: Human Services Press, 1977.

Menolascino, F. J., & Eyde, D. R. Biophysical bases of autism. *Behavioral Disorders,* 1979, *5,* 41–47.

Mercer, J. R. *Labelling the mentally retarded.* Berkeley: University of California Press, 1973. (a)

Mercer, J. R. The myth of 3% prevalence. In R. K. Eymon, C. E. Meyers, & G. Tarjon (Eds.), *Sociobehavioral studies in mental retardation.* Monographs of the American Association on Mental Deficiency, 1973 (No. 1). (b)

Mercer, J. R. Testing and assessment practices in multiethnic education. In J. A. Banks (Ed.), *Education in the 80's: Multiethnic education.* Washington, D. C.: National Education Association, 1981.

Meyen, E. L. (Ed.). *Exceptional children and youth: An introduction.* Denver: Love, 1978.

Meyerson, L., Kerry, N., & Michael, J. L. Behavior modification in rehabilitation. In S. W. Bijou & D. M. Baer (Eds.), *Child development: Readings in experimental analysis.* New York: Appleton-Century-Crofts, 1967.

Miller, D. *Ophthalmology: The essentials.* Boston: Houghton Mifflin, 1979.

Minskoff, E. Research on psycholinguistic training; Critique and guidelines. *Exceptional Children,* 1975, *42,* 136–144.

Mitchell, P. B. (ed.) *A policymaker's guide to issues in gifted and talented education.* Washington, D.C.: National Association of State Boards of Education, 1981.

Mithaug, D. E., & Hagmeier, L. D. The development of procedures to assess prevocational competencies of severely handicapped young adults. *AAESPH Review,* 1978, *3,* 94–115.

Mollick, L. B., & Etra, K. S. Poor learning ability . . . or poor hearing? *Teacher,* 1981, *98*(7), 42–43.

Montgomery, P. A., & Van Fleet, D. Evaluation of behavioral and academic change through the Re-Ed process. *Behavioral Disorders,* 1978, *3,* 136–146.

Moore, P. Voice disorders. In G. H. Shames & E. H. Wiig (Eds.). *Human communication disorders: An introduction.* Columbus, Ohio: Charles E. Merrill, 1982.

Moores, D. F. *Educating the deaf: Psychology, principles and practices* (2nd ed.). Boston: Houghton Mifflin, 1981.

Moores, D. F., & Maestas y Moores, J. Special adaptations necessitated by hearing impairments. In J. M. Kauffman & D. P. Hallahan (eds.), *Handbook of special education.* Englewood Cliffs, N.J.: Prentice-Hall, 1981.

Morse, W. C. The education of socially maladjusted and emotionally disturbed children. In W. M. Cruickshank & G. O. Johnson (Eds.), *Education of exceptional children and youth* (3rd ed.). Englewood Cliffs, N.J.: Prentice-Hall, 1975.

Morse, W. C. Worksheet on life-space interviewing for teachers. In N. Long, W. Morse, & R. Newman (Eds.), *Conflict in the classroom.* Belmont, Calif.: Wadsworth, 1976.

Morse, W. C., Cutler, R. L., & Fink, A. H. *Public school classes for the emotionally handicapped: A research analysis.* Washington, D.C.: Council for Exceptional Children, 1964.

Mow, S. How do you dance without music? In D. Watson (Ed.), *Readings on deafness.* New York: New York University School of Education, Deafness Research and Training Center, 1973.

Moyer, J. R., & Dardig, J. C. Practical task analysis for special educators. *TEACHING Exceptional Children*, 1978, 1–16.

Mullins, J. B. *A teacher's guide to management of physically handicapped students.* Springfield, Ill.: Charles C Thomas, 1979.

Murray, C. A. *The link between learning disabilities and juvenile delinquency: Current theory and knowledge.* Washington, D.C.: American Institute for Research, 1976.

Myers, P. I., & Hammill, D. D. *Methods for learning disorders* (2nd ed.). New York: John Wiley, 1976.

Myers, P. I., & Hammill, D. D. *Learning disabilities: Basic concepts, assessment practices, and instructional strategies.* Austin, Tex.: Pro-Ed, 1982.

Naisbett, J. *Megatrends: Ten new directions transforming our lives.* New York: Warner Books, 1982.

Napierkowski, H. The role of language in the intellectual development of the deaf child. *TEACHING Exceptional Children*, 1981, *14*, 106–9.

National Association for Retarded Citizens. *Educating the twenty-four hour retarded child.* Arlington, Tex.: Author, 1976.

National Association for Superintendents of Public Residential Facilities for the Mentally Retarded. *Contemporary issues in residential programming.* Washington, D.C.: President's Committee on Mental Retardation, 1974.

National Center for Health Statistics. *Prevalence of selected impairments: United States—1971.* Washington, D.C.: Department of Health, Education and Welfare Publication No. (HRA) 75–1526, 1975. (Cited in Fein, 1983.)

National Center for Health Statistics. *Prevalence of selected impairments: United States—1977.* Washington, D.C.: Department of Health, Education and Welfare Publication No. (PHS) 82–1562, 1981. (Cited in Fein, 1983.)

National Committee for Citizens in Education. Unpublished manuscript serving as basis for congressional testimony, 1979.

National Joint Committee on Learning Disabilities. *Learning disabilities: Issues on definition.* Unpublished manuscript, 1981.

National Society for Autistic Children. A short definition of autism. *Newsletter*, September 1977.

Navarre, J. How the teacher of the gifted can use the S.O.I. *G/C/T*, 1983, *26*, 17–18.

Neely, M. A. *Counseling and guidance practices with special education students.* Homewood, Ill.: Dorsey Press, 1982.

Neisworth, J. T., & Smith, R. M. (Eds.). *Retardation: Issues, assessment, and intervention.* New York: McGraw-Hill, 1978.

Nelson, C. M. Techniques for screening conduct-disturbed children. *Exceptional Children*, 1971, *37*, 501–7.

Nelson, C. M. (Ed.). *Field-based teacher training: Application in special education.* Minneapolis: University of Minnesota, Department of Psychoeducational Studies, 1978.

Nietupski, J., & Svoboda, R. Teaching a cooperative leisure skill to severely handicapped adults. *Education and Training of the Mentally Retarded*, 1981, *17*, 38–43.

Nihira, K., Foster, R., Shellhaas, M., & Leland, H. AAMD Adaptive Behavior Scale (1974 rev.). Washington, D.C.: American Association on Mental Deficiency, 1974.

Nolan, C. Y. The visually impaired. In E. L. Meyen (Ed.). *Exceptional children and youth: An introduction* (2nd ed.). Denver: Love, 1982.

Noonan, M. J., Brown, F., Mulligan, M., & Rettig, M. A. Educability of severely handicapped persons: Both sides of the issue. *Journal of the Association for the Severely Handicapped,* 1982, *7*(1), 3–12.

Norman, C. A. & Zigmond, N. Characteristics of children labeled and served as learning
disabled in school systems affiliated with child service demonstration centers.
Journal of Learning Disabilities, 1980, *13,* 542–47.

Norris, C. (Ed.). *Letters from deaf students.* Eureka, Calif.: Alinda Press, 1975.

Northcott, W. H., & Erickson, L. C. *The UNISTAPS Project.* St. Paul: Minnesota Department of Education, 1977.

Northern, J. L., & Lemme, M. Hearing and auditory disorders. In G. H. Shames & E. H.
Wiig (Eds.), *Human communication disorders: An introduction.* Columbus, Ohio:
Charles E. Merrill, 1982.

Oakland, T. An evaluation of the ABIE, pluristic norms, and estimated learning potential.
Journal of School Psychology, 1980, *18,* 3–11.

O'Brien, J. How we detect mental retardation before birth. *Medical Times,* 1971, *99,*
103.

O'Leary, S. G., & Dubey, D. R. Applications of self-control procedures by children: A
review. *Journal of Applied Behavior Analysis,* 1979, *12,* 449–65.

Oliver, L. I. *Behavior patterns in school and youth 12–17 years.* (National Health Survey, Series 11, No. 139, U.S. Department of Health, Education and Welfare).
Washington, D.C.: U.S. Government Printing Office, 1974.

Olson, J., Algozzine, B., & Schmid, R.E. Mild, moderate, and severe EH: An empty distinction? *Behavioral Disorders,* 1980, *5,* 96–101.

Orelove, F. P. Acquisition of incidental learning in moderately and severely handicapped
adults. *Education and Training of the Mentally Retarded,* 1982, *17,* 131–36.

Orelove, F. P. *Educating all handicapped persons: How can we get there from here?*
Paper presented at the Conference on Behavior Analysis in Education, Ohio State
University, Columbus, September 1982.

Orelove, F. P., & Hanley, C. D. Modifying school buildings for the severely handicapped:
A school accessibility survey. *AAESPH Review,* 1979, *4,* 219–36.

Orlando, C. Multidisciplinary team approaches in the assessment of handicapped preschool children. *Topics in Early Childhood Special Education,* 1981, *1,* 23–30.

Orlansky, J. Z. *Mainstreaming the hearing impaired child.* Hingham, Mass.: Teaching Resources, 1979.

Page, E. B. Miracle in Milwaukee: Raising the IQ. *Educational Researcher,* 1972, *15,*
8–16.

Parmelee, A. H., & Michaelis, R. Neurological examination of the newborn. In J. Hell-
muth (Ed.), *Exceptional infant* (Vol. 2). New York: Brunner/Mazel, 1971.

Patterson, G. R. *Living with children: New methods for parents and teachers.* (rev. ed.)
Champaign, Ill.: Research Press, 1979.

Patterson, G. R., Cobb, J. A., & Ray, R. S. Direct intervention in the classroom: A set of
procedures for the aggressive child. In F. W. Clark, D. R. Evans, & L. A. Hammer-
lynch (Eds.), *Implementing behavioral programs in schools and clinics.* Champaign, Ill.: Research Press, 1972.

Patterson, G. R., Reid, J. B., Jones, R. R., & Conger, R. E. *A social learning approach to
family intervention; Vol. 1: Families with aggressive children.* Eugene, Ore.: Cas-
talia, 1975.

Patton, J. R. Historical perspectives. In J. S. Payne & J. R. Patton, *Mental retardation*, Columbus, Ohio: Charles E. Merrill, 1981.

Payne, J. S., & Patton, J. R. *Mental retardation*. Columbus, Ohio: Charles E. Merrill, 1981.

Peck, C. A., Blackburn, T., & White-Blackburn, G. Making it work: A review of the empirical literature on community living arrangements. In T. Apolloni, J. Cappuccilli, & T. P. Cooke (Eds.), *Achievements in residential services for persons with disabilities: Toward excellence*. Baltimore: University Park Press, 1980.

Peck, C. A., & Semmel, M. I. Identifying the least restrictive environment (LRE) for children with severe handicaps: Toward an empirical analysis. *Journal of the Association for the Severely Handicapped*, 1982, 7(1), 56–63.

Peizer, E. Wheelchairs. In *Atlas of orthotics*. St. Louis: C. V. Mosby, 1975.

Pepper, F. C. Teaching the American Indian child in mainstream settings. In R. L. Jones (Ed.), *Mainstreaming and the minority child*. Reston, Va.: Council for Exceptional Children, 1976.

Perkins, W. H. *Speech pathology*. St. Louis: C.V. Mosby, 1977.

Pfeiffer, S. I. The superiority of team decision making. *Exceptional Children*, 1982, 49, 68–69.

Pieper, B., & Cappuccilli, J. Beyond the family and the institution: The sanctity of liberty. In T. Apolloni, J. Cappuccilli, & T. P. Cooke (Eds.), *Achievements in residential services for persons with disabilities: Toward excellence*. Baltimore: University Park Press, 1980.

Pihl, R. O., & Parke, M. Hair element content in learning disabled children. *Science*, 1978, 198, 204–6.

Polifka, J. C. Compliance with Public Law 94–142 and consumer satisfaction. *Exceptional Children*, 1981, 48, 250–53.

Pratt, M. W., Luszcz, M. A., & Brown, M. E. Measuring dimensions of the quality of care in small community residences. *American Journal of Mental Deficiency*, 1980, 85, 188–94.

President's Committee on Mental Retardation. *The six-hour retarded child*. Washington, D.C.: U.S. Department of Health, Education and Welfare, 1969.

Pressey, S. L. Educational acceleration: Occasional procedure or major issue? *Personnel and Guidance Journal*, 1962, 12–17.

Prinz, P. M., & Prinz, E. A. Simultaneous acquisition of ASL and spoken English in a hearing child of a deaf mother and hearing father. *Sign Language Studies*, 1979, 25, 283–96.

Provencal, G. The Macomb-Oakland regional center. In T. Apolloni, J. Cappuccilli, & T. P. Cooke (Eds.), *Achievements in residential services for persons with disabilities: Toward excellence*. Baltimore: University Park Press, 1980.

Quay, H. C. The facets of educational exceptionality: Conceptual framework for assessment, grouping, and instruction. *Exceptional Children*, 1968, 35, 25–31.

Quay, H. C. Patterns of aggression, withdrawal and immaturity. In H. C. Quay & J. S. Werry (Eds.), *Psychopathological disorders of childhood*. New York: John Wiley, 1972.

Quay, H. C. Classification in the treatment of delinquency and antisocial behavior. In N. Hobbs (Ed.), *Issues in the classification of children* (Vol. 1). San Francisco: Jossey-Bass, 1975.

Reger, R. What does "mainstreaming" mean? *Journal of Learning Disabilities*, 1974, *7*, 513–515.

Reis, S. M., & Cellerino, M. Guiding gifted students through independent study. *Teaching Exceptional Children*, 1983, *15*, 136–39.

Renfrew, C. E. *Speech disorders in children*. Oxford, Eng.: Pergamon Press, 1972.

Renzulli, J. S. *The enrichment triad model: A guide for developing defensible programs for the gifted and talented*. Weathersfield, Conn.: Creative Learning Press, 1977.

Renzulli, J. S. What makes giftedness?: Reexamining a definition. *Phi Delta Kappan*, 1978, *261*, 180–84.

Renzulli, J. S. What makes a problem real: Stalking the illusive meaning of qualitative differences in gifted education, *Gifted Child Quarterly*, 1982, *26*, 147–56.

Renzulli, J. S., Reis, S. M., & Smith, L. H. *The revolving door identification model*. Mansfield Center, Conn.: Creative Learning Press, 1981.

Repp, A. C., & Barton, L. E. Naturalistic observations of institutionalized retarded persons: A comparison of licensure decisions and behavioral observations. *Journal of Applied Behavior Analysis*, 1980, *13*, 333–41.

Reynolds, M. C., & Birch, J. W. *Teaching exceptional children in all America's schools* (2nd ed.). Reston, Va.: Council for Exceptional Children, 1982.

Reynolds, M. C., & Rosen, S. W. Special education: Past, present, and future. *Educational Forum*, 1976, *40*, 551–62.

Rhodes, W. C., & Tracy, M. L. (Eds.). *A study of child variance, Vol. I: Theories*. Ann Arbor, Michigan: University of Michigan, 1972. (a)

Rhodes, W. C., & Tracy, M. L. (Eds.). *A study of child variance, Vol. II: Interventions*. Ann Arbor, Michigan: University of Michigan, 1972. (b)

Rhodes, W. C., & Head, S. (Eds.). *A study of child variance, Vol. III: Service delivery systems*. Ann Arbor, Michigan: University of Michigan, 1974.

Rhyne, J. M. Comprehension of synthetic speech by blind children. *Journal of Visual Impairment & Blindness*, 1982, *76*, 313–16.

Richardson, E. H. Cultural and historical perspectives in counseling American Indians. In D. W. Sue, *Counseling the culturally different: Theory and practice*. New York: John Wiley, 1981.

Richardson, S. A. Careers of mentally retarded young persons: Services, jobs, and interpersonal relations. *American Journal of Mental Deficiency*, 1978, *82*, 349–58.

Rieke, J. A., Lynch, L. L., & Soltman, S. F. *Teaching strategies for language development*. New York: Grune & Stratton, 1977.

Rimland, B. *Infantile autism*. New York: Appleton-Century-Crofts, 1964.

Rimland, B. The differentiation of childhood psychoses: An analysis of checklists for 2,218 psychotic children. *Journal of Autism and Childhood Schizophrenia*, 1971, *1*, 161–74.

Rincover, A., Cook, R., Peoples, A., & Packard, D. Sensory extinction and sensory reinforcement principles for programming multiple adaptive behavior change. *Journal of Applied Behavior Analysis*, 1979, *12*, 221–33.

Rivera, O. A., & Quintana Saylor, L. Unique problems of handicapped individuals with Spanish surnames. In *The White House Conference on Handicapped Individuals* (Vol. 1). Washington, D.C.: U.S. Government Printing Office, 1977.

Robbins, L. *Deviant children grown up*. Baltimore: Williams & Wilkins, 1966.

Robinson, D. The IEP: Meaningful individualized education in Utah. *Phi Delta Kappan*, 1982, *64*, 205–6.

Robinson, N. M., & Robinson, H. B. *The mentally retarded child: A psychological approach* (2nd ed.). New York: McGraw-Hill, 1976.

Rooney, T. E. Signing vs. speech: What's a parent to do? *SEE What's Happening*, 1982, *1*(1), 6–8.

Roos, P. Parents of mentally retarded children—misunderstood and mistreated. In A. P. Turnbull & H. R. Turnbull (Eds.), *Parents speak out: views from the other side of the two-way mirror*. Columbus, Ohio: Charles E. Merrill, 1978.

Roos, P. The handling and mishandling of parents of mentally retarded persons. In F. Menolascino (Ed.), *Bridging the gap*. New York: John Wiley, 1980.

Rorschach, H. *Rorschach psychodiagnostic plates*. New York: The Psychological Corporation, 1942.

Rose, E., & Logan, D. R. Educational and life/career programs for the mildly mentally retarded. In P. T. Cegelka & H. J. Prehm (Eds.), *Mental retardation: From categories to people*. Columbus, Ohio: Charles E. Merrill, 1982.

Rose, T. L. The functional relationship between artificial food colors and hyperactivity. *Journal of Applied Behavior Analysis*, 1978, *11*, 439–46.

Rosenbaum, M. S., & Drabman, R. S. Self-control training in the classroom: A review and critique. *Journal of Applied Behavior Analysis*, 1979, *12*, 467–85.

Ross, A. O. *Psychological disorders of children*. New York: McGraw-Hill, 1974.

Ross, M. Review, overview, and other educational considerations. In M. Ross & L. W. Nober (Eds.), *Educating hard of hearing children*. Reston. Va.: Council for Exceptional Children, 1981.

Ross, M., & Nober, L. W. *Educating hard of hearing children*. Reston, Va.: Council for Exceptional Children, 1981.

Rothman, E. P. *Troubled teachers*. New York: David McKay, 1977.

Rubin, R. A., & Balow, B. E. Prevalence of teacher identified behavior problems: A longitudinal study. *Exceptional Children*, 1978, *45*, 102–11.

Ruiz, R. A. Cultural and historical perspectives in counseling Hispanics. In D. W. Sue, *Counseling the culturally different: Theory and practice*. New York: John Wiley, 1981.

Rules for the education of handicapped children (effective July 1, 1982). Columbus, Ohio: Ohio Department of Education, 1982.

Rusch, F. R., & Mithaug, D. E. *Vocational training for mentally retarded adults: A behavior analytic approach*. Champaign, Ill.: Research Press, 1980.

Russo, D. C., & Koegel, R. L. A method for integrating an autistic child in a normal public-school classroom. *Journal of Applied Behavior Analysis*, 1977, *10*, 579–90.

Rutter, M. Medical aspects of the education of psychotic (autistic) children. In P.T.B. Western (Ed.), *Some approaches to teaching autistic children*. Oxford, Eng.: Pergamon Press, 1965.

Ryback, D., & Staats, A. Parents as behavior therapy technicians in treating reading deficits (dyslexia). *Journal of Behavior Therapy and Experimental Psychiatry*, 1970, *1*, 109–19.

Sailor, W., & Haring, N. G. Some current directions in education of the severely/multiply handicapped. *AAESPH Review*, 1977, *2*, 67–87.

Salvia, J. Perspectives on the nature of retardation. In J. T. Neisworth & R. M. Smith (Eds.), *Retardation: Issues, assessment, and intervention*. New York: McGraw-Hill, 1978.

Sameroff, A. J., & Chandler, M. J. Reproductive risk and the continuum of caretaking casualty. In F. D. Horowitz (Ed.), *Review of child development research* (Vol. 4). Chicago: University of Chicago Press, 1975.

Samuda, R. J. Problems and issues in assessment of minority group children. In R. L. Jones (Ed.), *Mainstreaming and the minority child.* Reston, Va.: Council for Exceptional Children, 1976.

Sandler, A., & Coren, A. Integrated instruction at home and school: Parents' perspective. *Education and Training of the Mentally Retarded,* 1981, *16*(3), 183–87.

Sapon-Shevin, M. Another look at mainstreaming: Exceptionality, normality, and the nature of difference. *Phi Delta Kappan,* 1978, *60,* 119–21.

Sattler, J. M. *Assessment of children's intelligence and special abilities.* (2nd ed.). Boston: Allyn & Bacon, 1982.

Scanlon, C. A., Arick, J., & Phelps, N. Participation in the development of the IEP: Parents' perspective. *Exceptional Children,* 1981, *47,* 373–74.

Schalock, R. L., Harper, R. S., & Carver, G. Independent living placement: Five years later. *American Journal of Mental Deficiency,* 1981, *86,* 170–77.

Scharr, K. Community core ordered for D.C. mental patients. *APA Monitor,* February 1976, *7*(2), 1.

Scheerenberger, R. C. A model for deinstitutionalization. *Mental Retardation,* 1974, *12,* 3–7.

Scheerenberger, R. C. Treatment from ancient times to the present. In P. T. Cegelka & H. J. Prehm (Eds.), *Mental retardation: From categories to people.* Columbus, Ohio: Charles E. Merrill, 1982.

Schell, G. C. The young handicapped child: A family perspective. *Topics in Early Childhood Special Education,* 1981, *1,* 21–27.

Schiefelbusch, R. L., & McCormick, L. Language and speech disorders. In J. M. Kauffman & D. P. Hallahan (Eds.), *Handbook of special education.* Englewood Cliffs, N.J.: Prentice-Hall, 1981.

Schilit, J. Black versus white perception of mental retardation. *Exceptional Children,* 1977, *44,* 189–90.

Schleien, S. J., Kiernan, J., & Wehman, P. Evaluation of an age-appropriate leisure skills program for moderately retarded adults. *Education and Training of the Mentally Retarded,* 1981, *16,* 13–19.

Schleien, S. J., Wehman, P., & Kiernan, J. Teaching leisure skills to severely handicapped adults: An age-appropriate darts game. *Journal of Applied Behavior Analysis,* 1981, *14,* 513–19.

Schlesinger, H. S., & Meadow, K. P. Emotional support for parents. In D. L. Lillie & P. L. Trohanis (Eds.), *Teaching parents to teach.* New York: Walker, 1976.

Schmid, R. E. Historical perspective. In C. D. Mercer, *Children and adolescents with learning disabilities.* Columbus, Ohio: Charles E. Merrill, 1979.

Schoepke, J. M. *Lifelong career development needs assessment study.* Working paper No. 3. Columbia: University of Missouri, July 1979.

Scholl, G. T. Vision problems. In W. C. Morse (Ed.), *Humanistic teaching for exceptional children.* Syracuse, N.Y.: Syracuse University Press, 1979.

Scholl, G., & Schnur, R. *Measures of psychological, vocational, and educational functioning in the blind and visually handicapped.* New York: American Foundation for the Blind, 1976.

Schulz, J. B. The parent-professional conflict. In A. P. Turnbull & H. R. Turnbull (Eds.), *Parents speak out: Views from the other side of the two-way mirror.* Columbus, Ohio: Charles E. Merrill, 1978.

Schumaker, J. B., Hovell, M. F., & Sherman, J. A. An analysis of daily report cards and parent-managed privileges in the improvement of adolescents' classroom performance. *Journal of Applied Behavior Analysis,* 1977, *10,* 449–64.

Scranton, T., & Downs, M. Elementary and secondary learning disabilities programs in the U.S.: A survey. *Journal of Learning Disabilities,* 1975, *8,* 394–99.

Seagoe, M. V. Some characteristics of gifted children. In R. A. Martinson (Ed.), *The identification of the gifted and talented.* Ventura, Calif.: Office of the Ventura County Superintendent of Schools, 1974.

Sears, R. R. Sources of life satisfaction of the Terman gifted men. *American Psychologist,* 1977, *32*(2), 119–28.

Secord, W. Test of Minimal Articulation Competence. Columbus, Ohio: Charles E. Merrill, 1981.

Seligmann, J. Saving spina bifida babies. *Newsweek,* November 15, 1982, 110.

Seltzer, M. M., & Seltzer, G. B. Community living: Accommodations and vocations. In P. Mittler (Ed.), *Research to practice in mental retardation* (Vol. 1). Baltimore: University Park Press, 1977.

Semel, E. M., & Wiig, E. H. *Clinical Evaluation of Language Functions.* Columbus, Ohio: Charles E. Merrill, 1980.

Shames, G. H., & Florence, C. L. *Stutter-free speech: A goal for therapy.* Columbus, Ohio: Charles E. Merrill, 1980.

Shearer, D. E., & Snider, R. S. On providing a practical approach to the early education of children. *Child Behavior Therapy,* 1981, *3,* 78–80.

Shearer, M. S. A home-based parent-training model. In D. Lillie & P. Trohanis (Eds.), *Teaching parents to teach.* New York: Walker, 1976.

Shearer, M. S. & Shearer, D. E. The Portage project: A model for early childhood education. *Exceptional Children,* 1972, *39,* 210–17.

Shearer, M. S. & Shearer, D. E. Parent involvement. In J. B. Jordan, A. H. Hayden, M. B. Karnes, & M. M. Wood (Eds.), *Early childhood education for exceptional children: A handbook of ideas and exemplary practices.* Reston, Va: Council for Exceptional Children, 1977.

Silberberg, N. E., & Silberberg, M. C. *Who speaks for the child?* Springfield, Ill.: Charles C Thomas, 1974.

Simpson, R. L. Screening and assessment strategies for behaviorally disordered adolescents. In G. Brown, R. L. McDowell, & J. Smith (Eds.), *Educating adolescents with behavior disorders.* Columbus, Ohio: Charles E. Merrill, 1981.

Sirvis, B. The physically disabled. In E. L. Meyen (Ed.), *Exceptional children and youth: An introduction* (2nd ed.). Denver: Love, 1982.

Sisk, D. A. Education of the gifted and talented: A national perspective. *Journal for the Education of the Gifted,* 1978, *1,* 5–24.

Skeels, H. M. Adult status of children with contrasting early life experiences. *Monographs of the Society for Research in Child Development,* 1966, *31* (No. 3).

Skeels, H. M., & Dye, H. B. A study of the effects of differential stimulation on mentally retarded children. *Convention Proceedings American Association on Mental Deficiency,* 1939, *44,* 114–36.

Slingerland, B. H. *A multi-sensory approach to language arts for specific language disability children: A guide for primary teachers.* Cambridge, Mass.: Educators Publishing Service, 1971.

Smith, D. D. *Teaching the learning disabled.* New York: Prentice-Hall, 1981.

Smith, E. J. Cultural and historical perspectives in counseling blacks. In D. W. Sue, *Counseling the culturally different: Theory and practice.* New York: John Wiley, 1981.

Smith, J. M., & Smith, D. E. *Child management: A program for parents and teachers.* Champaign, Ill.: Research Press, 1976.

Smith, R. M. *An introduction to mental retardation.* New York: McGraw-Hill, 1971.

Smith, R. M. & Neisworth, J. T. *The exceptional child: A functional approach* (2nd ed.). New York: McGraw-Hill, 1975.

Smith, R. M., Neisworth, J. T., & Hunt, F. M. *The exceptional child: A functional approach.* (2nd ed.). New York: McGraw-Hill, 1983.

Smithdas, R. Psychological aspects of deaf-blindness. In S. R. Walsh & R. Holzberg (Eds.), *Understanding and educating the deaf-blind/severely and profoundly handicapped: An international perspective.* Springfield, Ill.: Charles C Thomas, 1981.

Snell, M. E., & Renzaglia, A. M. Moderate, severe, and profound handicaps. In N. G. Haring (Ed.), *Exceptional children and youth* (3rd ed.). Columbus, Ohio: Charles E. Merrill, 1982.

Sonnenschein, P. Parents and professionals: An uneasy relationship. *TEACHING Exceptional Children,* 1981, *14,* 62–65.

Sontag, E., Smith J., & Sailor, W. The severely and profoundly handicapped: Who are they? Where are we? *Journal of Special Education,* 1977, *11,* 5–11.

Sowell, V., Packer, R., Poplin, M., & Larsen, S. The effects of psycholinguistic training on improving psycholinguistic skills. *Learning Disability Quarterly,* 1979, *2,* 69–77.

Spache, G. D. Diagnostic Reading Scales. Monterey: California Test Bureau, 1963.

Spenciner, L. J. Differences between blind and partially sighted children in rejection by sighted peers in integrated classrooms, grades 2–8. In B. W. Tuckman (Ed.), *Conducting educational research.* New York: Harcourt Brace Jovanovich, 1972.

Spindler, G. D. *Education and cultural process.* New York: Holt, Rinehart & Winston, 1974.

Spradlin, J. E., & Spradlin, R. R. Developing necessary skills for entry into classroom teaching arrangements. In N. G. Haring & R. L. Schiefelbusch (Eds.), *Teaching special children.* New York: McGraw-Hill, 1976.

Spring, C., & Sandoval, J. Food additives and hyperkinesis: A critical evaluation of the evidence. *Journal of Learning Disabilities,* 1976, *9,* 560–69.

Stainback, W., Stainback, S., Raschke, D., & Anderson, R. J. Three methods for encouraging interactions between severely retarded and nonhandicapped students. *Education and Training of the Mentally Retarded,* 1981, *16,* 188–92.

Stanley, J. C., Keating, D. P., & Fox, L. H. *Mathematical talent: Discovery, description, and development.* Baltimore: Johns Hopkins, 1974.

Stephens, T. M. *CRC: Criterion-Referenced Curriculum.* Columbus, Ohio: Charles E. Merrill, 1982.

Stephens, T. M. *Teaching skills to children with learning and behavior disorders.* Columbus, Ohio: Charles E. Merrill, 1977.

Stephens, T. M., Blackhurst, A. E., & Magliocca, L. A. *Teaching mainstreamed students.* New York: John Wiley, 1982.

Stephens, T. M., & Wolf, J. S. The gifted child. In N. G. Haring (Ed.), *Behavior of exceptional children: An introduction to special education* (2nd ed.). Columbus, Ohio: Charles E. Merrill, 1978.

Stephens, T. M., & Wolf, J. S. *Effective skills in parent/teacher conferencing.* Columbus: Ohio State University, National Center for Educational Materials and Media for the Handicapped, 1980.

Sternberg, L. Perspectives on educating severely and profoundly handicapped students. In L. Sternberg & G. L. Adams, *Educating severely and profoundly handicapped students.* Rockville, Md.: Aspen, 1982.

Stewart, J. L. Unique problems of handicapped Native Americans. In *The White House Conference on Handicapped Individuals* (Vol. 1). Washington, D.C.: U.S. Government Printing Office, 1977.

Stevens, G. D. *Taxonomy in special education for children with body disorder: The problem and a proposal.* Pittsburgh: University of Pittsburgh, Department of Special Education and Rehabilitation, 1962 (mimeo).

Stocker, C. S. *Listening for the visually impaired: A teaching manual.* Springfield, Ill.: Charles C Thomas, 1973.

Stokes, T. F., & Baer, D. M. An implicit technology of generalization. *Journal of Applied Behavior Analysis,* 1977, *10,* 349–67.

Storm, R. H., & Willis, J. H. Small-group training as an alternative to individual programs for profoundly retarded persons. *American Journal of Mental Deficiency,* 1978, *83,* 283–88.

Stowell, L. J., & Terry, C. Mainstreaming: Present shock. *Illinois Libraries,* 1977, *59,* 475–77.

Stramiello, A. *A descriptive study of selected features of handicapped children's early education programs.* Greeley: University of Northern Colorado, 1978.

Strickland, S. P. Can slum children learn? *American Education,* 1971, *7*(6), 3–7.

Sue, D. W. *Counseling the culturally different: Theory and practice.* New York: John Wiley, 1981.

Sulzer-Azaroff, B., & Mayer, G. R. *Applying behavior analysis procedures with children and youth.* New York: Holt, Rinehart & Winston, 1977.

Suran, B. G., & Rizzo, J. V. *Special children: An integrative approach.* Glenview, Ill.: Scott, Foresman, 1979.

Swack, M. J. Therapeutic role of the teacher of physically handicapped children. *Exceptional Children,* 1969, *35,* 371–74.

Swallow, R. M. *Cognitive development.* Paper presented at the North American Conference on Visually Handicapped Infants and Preschool Children, Minneapolis, May 1978.

Swan, W. W. The handicapped children's early education program. *Exceptional Children,* 1980, *47,* 12–16.

Swassing, R. The fourth R for the gifted and talented. *Ohio Media Spectrum,* 1978, *30*(3), 59–61.

Swassing, R. The multiple component alternative. *The Gifted Child Quarterly,* in press.

Tarjan, G., Wright, S. W., Eyman, R. K., & Keeran, C. V. Natural history of mental retardation: Some aspects of epidemiology. *American Journal of Mental Deficiency*, 1973, *77*, 369–79.

Tarver, S., & Hallahan, D. P. Children with learning disabilities: An overview. In J. M. Kauffman & D. P. Hallahan (Eds.), *Teaching children with learning disabilities: Personal perspectives.* Columbus, Ohio: Charles E. Merrill, 1976.

Tawney, J. W. New considerations for the severely and profoundly handicapped. In R. D. Kneedler & S. G. Tarver (Eds.), *Changing perspectives in special education.* Columbus, Ohio: Charles E. Merrill, 1977.

Tawney, J. W., Aeschleman, S. R., Deaton, S. L., & Donaldson, R. M. Using telecommunications technology to instruct rural severely handicapped children. *Exceptional Children*, 1979, *46*, 118–25.

Tawney, J. W., & Smith, J. An analysis of the forum: Issues in education of the severely and profoundly retarded. *Exceptional Children*, 1981, *48*, 5–18.

Telford, C. W., & Sawrey, J. M. *The exceptional individual* (3rd ed.). Englewood Cliffs, N.J.: Prentice-Hall, 1977.

Templin, M.C. Templin Speech Sound Discrimination Test. In M. C. Templin, *Certain language skills in children.* Minneapolis: University of Minnesota Press, 1957.

Templin, M. C., & Darley, F. L. The Templin-Darley Test of Articulation (2nd ed.). Iowa City: University of Iowa, Bureau of Educational Research and Service, Division of Extension and University Services, 1969.

Terkel, S. *Working: People talk about what they do all day and how they feel about what they do.* New York: Pantheon, 1974.

Terman, L. M. *The measurement of intelligence.* Boston: Houghton Mifflin, 1916.

Terman, L. M., & Merrill, M. A. Stanford-Binet Intelligence Scale: Manual for the third revision, Form L-M. Boston: Houghton Mifflin, 1973.

Terman, L. M. et al. *The mental and physical traits of a thousand gifted children.* Stanford, Calif.: Stanford University Press, 1925.

Test, D. W., and Heward, W. L. Teaching road signs and traffic laws to learning disabled students. *Learning Disability Quarterly*, 1983, *6*, 80–83.

Thomas, A., Chess, S., & Birch, H. G. *Temperament and behavior disorders in children.* New York: New York University Press, 1968.

Thomas, D. R., Becker, W. C., & Armstrong, M. Production and elimination of disruptive classroom behavior by systematically varying teacher's behavior. *Journal of Applied Behavior Analysis*, 1968, *1*, 35–45.

Thurman, D. Mainstreaming and the visually impaired: A report from Atlantic Canada. *Education of the Visually Handicapped*, 1978, *10*, 35–37.

Timm, M. A., & Rule, S. RIP: A cost-effective parent-implemented program for handicapped children. *Early Childhood Development and Care*, 1981, *7*, 147–63.

Tjossem, T. D. (Ed.). *Intervention strategies for high risk infants and young children.* Baltimore: University Park Press, 1976.

Tooze, D. *Independence training for visually handicapped children.* Baltimore: University Park Press, 1981.

Torrance, E. P. *Discovery and nurturance of giftedness in the culturally different.* Reston, Va.: Council for Exceptional Children, 1977.

Tredgold, A. F. *A textbook on mental deficiency.* Baltimore: Wood, 1937.

Trovato, J., & Bucher, B. Peer tutoring with or without home-based reinforcement, for reading comprehension. *Journal of Applied Behavior Analysis*, 1980, *13*, 129–41.

Turnbull, A. P. Parent-professional interactions. In M. E. Snell (Ed.), *Systematic instruction of the moderately and severely handicapped* (2nd ed.). Columbus, Ohio: Charles E. Merrill, 1983.

Turnbull, A. P., Strickland, B., & Brantley, J. C. *Developing and implementing Individualized Education Programs* (2nd ed.). Columbus, Ohio: Charles E. Merrill, 1982.

Turnbull, A. P., & Turnbull, H. R. *Parents speak out: Views from the other side of the two-way mirror.* Columbus, Ohio: Charles E. Merrill, 1978.

Turnbull, A. P., & Turnbull, H. R. Parent involvement in the education of handicapped children: A critique. *Mental Retardation,* 1982, *20,* 115–22.

U.S. Comptroller General. *Disparities still exist in who gets special education.* Report to the Chairman, Subcommittee on Select Education, Committee on Education and Labor, House of Representatives of the United States, September 30, 1981.

U.S. Department of Education. Education Department reports steady progress on mainstreaming handicapped students. In *Programs for the Handicapped,* Spring, 1982, 1–2. (a)

U.S. Department of Education. Sources for statistics on disability. In *Programs for the Handicapped,* 1982, No. 4, 9–13. (b)

U.S. Department of Education. Report of handicapped children receiving special education and related services (internal report). Special Education Programs, June 22, 1982. (c)

U.S. Department of Justice, Federal Bureau of Investigation. *Uniform Crime Reports for the United States, 1981.* Washington, D.C.: Author, 1981.

Utley, B., Holvoet, J., & Barnes, K. Handling, positioning, and feeding the physically handicapped. In E. Sontag, J. Smith, & N. Certo (Eds.), *Educational programming for the severely and profoundly handicapped.* Reston, Va.: Council for Exceptional Children, 1977.

van den Pol, R. A., Iwata, B. A., Ivanic, M. T., Page, T. J., Neef, N. A., & Whitely, F. P. Teaching the handicapped to eat in public places: Acquisition, generalization, and maintenance of restaurant skills. *Journal of Applied Behavior Analysis,* 1981, *14,* 61–69.

Van Houten, R. Social validation: The evolution of standards of competency for target behaviors. *Journal of Applied Behavior Analysis,* 1979, *12,* 581–91.

Van Riper, C. *Speech correction: Principles and methods* (6th ed.). Englewood Cliffs, N.J.: Prentice-Hall, 1978.

VanTassel-Baska, J. The teacher as counselor for the gifted. *TEACHING Exceptional Children,* 1983, *15,* 144–50.

Vargas, J. G., & Moxley, R. A. Teaching for thinking and creativity: The radical behaviorist's view. In A. E. Lawson (Ed.), *The psychology of teaching for thinking and creativity, 1980 AETS Yearbook.* Columbus: The Ohio State University, 1979.

Venn, J., Morganstern, L., & Dykes, M. K. Checklists for evaluating the fit and function of orthoses, prostheses, and wheelchairs in the classroom. *TEACHING Exceptional Children,* 1979, *11,* 51–56.

Verhaaren, P. R., & Connor, F. P. Physical disabilities. In J. M. Kauffman & D. P. Hallahan (Eds.), *Handbook of special education.* Englewood Cliffs, N.J.: Prentice-Hall, 1981.

Victor, J. Some selected findings from the Greenleigh Associates study of sheltered workshops. In *The Auburn conference on the Greenleigh study of sheltered workshops.* Auburn, Ala.: Auburn University, Rehabilitation Services Education Department, April 1976.

Viscardi, H. Speech presented at the President's Committee on Employment of the Handicapped annual meeting. Washington, D.C., April 29, 1976.

Voeltz, L. M., & Apffel, J. A. A leisure activities curricular component for severely handicapped youth: Why and how. *Viewpoints in Teaching and Learning,* 1981, *57,* 82–93.

Vogelsberg, R. T., Williams, W. W., & Ashe, W. Improving vocational services through interagency cooperation. In C. L. Hansen (Ed.), *Severely handicapped persons in the community.* Seattle: University of Washington PDAS, 1981.

Vorrath, H. H., & Brendtro, L. K. *Positive peer culture.* Chicago: Aldine Publishing Company, 1974.

Wakabayashi, R. Unique problems of handicapped Asian Americans. In *The White House Conference on Handicapped Individuals* (Vol. 1). Washington, D.C.: U.S. Government Printing Office, 1977.

Walker, H. M. *The acting-out child: Coping with classroom disruption.* Boston: Allyn & Bacon, 1979.

Walker, H. M., & Buckley, N. K. Teacher attention to appropriate and inappropriate classroom behavior: An individual case study. *Focus on Exceptional Children,* 1973, *5,* 5–11.

Walker, H. M., & Hops, H. Use of normative peer data as a standard for evaluating classroom treatment effects. *Journal of Applied Behavior Analysis,* 1976, *9,* 159–68.

Wallace, G., & McLoughlin, J. A. Learning disabilities: Concepts and characteristics (2nd ed.). Columbus, Ohio: Charles E. Merrill, 1979.

Ward, M. E. Children with visual impairments. In M. S. Lilly (Ed.), *Children with exceptional needs: A survey of special education.* New York: Holt, Rinehart & Winston, 1979.

Warren, J. Early and periodic screening, diagnosis, and treatment. *Educational Researcher,* 1977, 14–15, 20.

Waters, J. M. & Siegel, L. V. Parent recording of speech production of developmentally delayed toddlers. *Education and Treatment of Children,* 1982, *5,* 109–20.

Wechsler, D. *Manual for the Wechsler Intelligence Scale for Children—Revised.* New York: Psychological Corporation, 1974.

Wehman, P., Hill, M., Goodall, P., Cleveland, P., Brooke, V., & Pentecost, J. H. Job placement and follow-up of moderately and severely handicapped individuals after three years. *Journal of the Association for the Severely Handicapped,* 1982, *7*(2), 5–16.

Wehman, P., & Schleien, S. J. *Leisure programs for handicapped persons: Adaptations, techniques, and curriculum.* Baltimore: University Park Press, 1981.

Weintraub, F. J., & Abeson, A. New education policies for the handicapped: The quiet revolution. *Phi Delta Kappan,* 1974, *55,* 526–29, 569.

Weiss, A., Cooke, N. L., Grossman, M. A., Ryno-Vrabel, M., & Hassett, M. E. *Home-school communication: Setting up a telephone-managed program.* Columbus, Ohio: Special Press, 1983.

Weiss, C. E., & Lillywhite, H. S. *Communicative disorders: A handbook for prevention and early intervention.* St. Louis: C. V. Mosby, 1976.

Weiss, H. G., & Weiss, M. S. *Home is a learning place: A parents' guide to learning disabilities.* Boston: Little, Brown, 1976.

Wepman, J. M. *Wepman Auditory Discrimination Test.* Chicago: Language Research Associates, 1958.

Whelan, R. J. Prologue. In G. Brown, R. L. McDowell, & J. Smith (Eds.). *Educating adolescents with behavior disorders.* Columbus, Ohio: Charles E. Merrill, 1981.

White, B. L. *The first three years of life.* Englewood Cliffs, N.J.: Prentice-Hall, 1975.

White, O. R., & Haring, N. G. *Exceptional teaching* (2nd ed.). Columbus, Ohio: Charles E. Merrill, 1980.

Whitmore, J. R. *Giftedness, conflict, and underachievement.* Boston: Allyn & Bacon, 1980.

Wiederholt, J. L. Historical perspectives on the education of the learning disabled. In L. Mann & D. Sabatino (Eds.). *The second review of special education.* Philadelphia: JSE Press, 1974. (a)

Wiederholt, J. L. Planning resource rooms for the mildly handicapped. *Focus on Exceptional Children,* 1974, *6,* 1–10.

Wiederholt, J. L., Hammill, D. D., & Brown, V. *The resource teacher: A guide to effective practice.* Boston: Allyn & Bacon, 1978.

Wilcox, B. Forum: Mastering prerequisite skills: The "readiness" logic. *Newsletter of the Association for the Severely Handicapped,* 1982, *8*(7), 1–2.

Williams, F. E. *Classroom ideas for encouraging thinking and feeling.* Buffalo, New York: D.O.K., 1970.

Williams, J. The impact and implication of litigation. In G. Markel (Ed.), *Proceedings of the University of Michigan Institute on the Impact and Implications of State and Federal Legislation Affecting Handicapped Individuals.* Ann Arbor: University of Michigan, School of Education, 1977.

Williamson, G. G. The Individualized Education Program: An interdisciplinary endeavor. In B. Sirvis, J. W. Baken, & G. G. Williamson (Eds.), *Unique aspects of the IEP for the physically handicapped, homebound, and hospitalized.* Reston, Va.: Council for Exceptional Children, 1978.

Willoughby, D. M. *A resource guide for parents and educators of blind children.* Baltimore: National Federation of the Blind, 1980.

Winer, M. A course on resources for the newly blind. *Journal of Visual Impairment & Blindness,* 1978, *72,* 311–15.

Winitz, H. Articulation disorders: From prescription to description. *Journal of Speech and Hearing Disorders,* 1977, *42,* 143–47.

Winkler, B., Armstrong, K., Moehlis, J., Nietupski, J., & Whalen-Carrell, B. Ad guide preparation and delivery for severely handicapped students. *Teaching Exceptional Children,* 1982, *15,* 29–33.

Winton, P., & Turnbull, A. P. Parent involvement as viewed by parents of preschool handicapped children. *Topics in Early Childhood Special Education,* 1981, *1,* 11–19.

Witty, P. A. *A study of one hundred gifted children.* Lawrence: University of Kansas, Bulletin of Education, 1930, *2*(7).

Witty, P. A. Contributions to the IQ controversy from the study of superior deviates. *School and Society,* 1940, *51,* 503–8.

Witty, P. A. A decade of progress in the study of the gifted and creative pupil. In W. B. Barbe & T. M. Stephens (Eds.), *Attention to the gifted a decade later.* Columbus: Ohio Department of Education, 1962.

Witty, P. A., & Jenkins, M. D. The educational achievement of a group of gifted Negro children. *Journal of Educational Psychology,* 1934, *25,* 585–97.

Wolf, J. S., & Stephens, T. M. *Effective skills in parent/teacher conferencing: The parents' perspective.* Columbus: Ohio State University, National Center for Educational Materials and Media for the Handicapped, 1982.

Wolf, M. M. Social validity: The case for subjective measurement, or how applied behavior analysis is finding its heart. *Journal of Applied Behavior Analysis,* 1978, *11,* 203–14.

Wolfe, B. *Monthly Labor Review,* September, 1980.

Wolfensberger, W. The origin and nature of our institutional models. In R. B. Kugel & W. Wolfensberger (Eds.), *Changing patterns in residential services for the mentally retarded.* Washington, D.C.: President's Committee on Mental Retardation, 1969.

Wolfensberger, W. *Normalization: The principal of normalization in human services.* Toronto, Can.: National Institute on Mental Retardation, 1972.

Wolfensberger, W. The origin and nature of our institutional models. In R. B. Kugel & A. Shearer (Eds.), *Changing patterns in residential services for the mentally retarded.* Washington, D.C.: President's Committee on Mental Retardation, 1976.

Wolfensberger, W., & Glenn, L. *Program analysis of service systems.* Toronto, Can.: National Institute on Mental Retardation, 1975.

Wolfensberger, W., & Kurtz, R. A. (Eds.). *Management of the family of the mentally retarded.* Chicago: Follett, 1969.

Wood, F. W., & Zabel, R. H. *Making sense of reports on the incidence of behavior disorders/emotional disturbance in school populations.* Minneapolis: University of Minnesota, 1978.

Wood, M. M., & Hurley, O. L. Curriculum and instruction. In J. B. Jordan, A. H. Hayden, M. B. Karnes, & M. M. Wood (Eds.), *Early childhood education for exceptional children: A handbook of ideas and exemplary practices.* Reston, Va: Council for Exceptional Children, 1977.

Woodcock, R. Woodcock Reading Mastery Tests. Circle Pines, Minn.: American Guidance Services, 1974.

Wyatt v. Stickney, 344 F. Supp. 387, 344 F. Supp. 373 (M.D. Ala. 1972), 334 F. Supp. 1341, 325 F. Supp. 781 (M.D. Ala. 1971), *aff'd sub nom. Wyatt v. Aderholt,* 503 F. 2d 1305 (5th Cir. 1974).

Ysseldyke, J., Algozzine, B., Richey, L., & Graden, J. Declaring students eligible for learning disability services: Why bother with the data? *Learning Disability Quarterly,* 1982, *5,* 37–44.

Ysseldyke, J. E., & Salvia, J. Diagnostic-prescriptive teaching: Two models. *Exceptional Children,* 1974, *41,* 181–86.

York, R., & Edgar, E. *Teaching the severely handicapped* (Vol. 4). Seattle: American Association for the Education of the Severely/Profoundly Handicapped, 1979.

Yoshida, R., Fenton, K., Kaufman, M. J., & Maxwell, J. P. Parental involvement in the special education pupil planning process: The school's perspective. *Exceptional Children,* 1978, *44,* 531–33.

Zakariasen, H. Is there a child with epilepsy in the classroom? *Education Unlimited,* 1979, *1,* 14–16.

Zettel, J. J. Gifted and talented education over half a decade of change. *Journal for the Education of the Gifted,* 1979, *3,* 14–37.

GLOSSARY

acceleration An educational approach that involves providing a child with learning experiences usually given to older children. Most often used with gifted and talented children.

adaptive device Any piece of equipment designed to extend the function of a body part. Examples include standing tables and special spoons that can be used by people with weak hands or poor muscle control.

adventitious handicap A handicap that develops at any time after birth, from disease, trauma, or any other cause; most frequently used with sensory or physical impairments. Contrasts with *congenital* handicap.

advocate Anyone who pleads the cause of a handicapped person or group of handicapped people, especially in legal or adminsitrative proceedings or public forums.

albinism A congenital condition marked by deficiency in, or total lack of, pigmentation. People with albinism have pale skin; white hair, eyebrows, and eyelashes; and eyes with pink or pale blue pupils.

amblyopia Dimness of sight without apparent change in the eye's structures; can lead to blindness in the affected eye if not corrected.

amniocentesis The insertion of a hollow needle through the abdomen into the uterus of a pregnant woman. Used to obtain amniotic fluid in order to determine chromosomal abnormality. The sex of the fetus can also be determined.

anoxia Lack of oxygen severe enough to cause tissue damage; can cause permanent brain damage and retardation.

aphasia Loss of speech functions; often, but not always, used to refer to inability to speak due to brain lesions.

applied behavior analysis A scientific approach to studying and modifying behavior that employs direct and daily measurement of the target behavior of individual students. Environmental variables (e.g., teacher praise, instructional cues, etc.) are systematically manipulated in an attempt to demonstrate experimentally functional relationships between the target behavior and those variables.

aqueous humor Fluid which occupies the space between the lens and the cornea of the eye.

articulation   The production of distinct language sounds by the vocal organs.

asphyxia   A lack of oxygen usually caused by interruption of respiration; can cause unconsciousness and/or brain damage.

astigmatism   A defect of vision usually caused by irregularities in the cornea; results in blurred vision and difficulties in focusing. Can usually be corrected by lenses.

ataxia   Poor sense of balance and body position and lack of coordination of the voluntary muscles, characteristic of one type of cerebral palsy.

athetosis   A type of cerebral palsy characterized by large, irregular, uncontrollable twisting motions. The muscles may be tense and rigid or loose and flaccid. Often accompanied by difficulty with oral language.

audiogram   A graph of the faintest level of sound a person can hear at least 50% of the time at each of several frequencies, including the entire frequency range of normal speech.

audiology   The science of hearing.

audiometer   A device which generates sounds at specific frequencies and intensities; used to examine hearing.

auditory training   A program to teach hearing impaired persons to make as much use as possible of their residual hearing by working on listening skills.

autism   A severe behavior disorder usually characterized by extreme withdrawal and lack of language and communication skills. Lack of affect, self-stimulation, self-abuse, and aggressive behavior are also common in autistic children.

baseline   A measure of the level or amount of behavior prior to implementation of an instructional procedure to be evaluated. Baseline data are used as an objective measure against which to compare and evaluate the results obtained during the proposed instruction.

behavior modification   The systematic application of procedures derived from the principles of behavior (e.g., reinforcement) in order to achieve desired changes in behavior.

behavioral contract   An agreement between two parties in which one agrees to complete a specified task (e.g., a child agrees to complete a homework assignment by tomorrow morning). In return, the other party agrees to provide a specific reward (e.g., a teacher allows a child to have 10 minutes free time) upon completion of the task.

binocular vision   Vision using both eyes working together to perceive a single image.

blind, educationally   Totally without sight or having so little sight that all learning must depend upon senses other than vision.

blind, legally   Visual acuity of 20/200 or less in the better eye after the best possible correction with glasses or contact lenses, or vision restricted to a field of 20 degrees or less. Acuity of 20/200 means the eye can see clearly at 20 feet what the normal eye can see at 200 feet.

braille   A system of writing letters, numbers, and other language symbols by a combination of six raised dots. Blind persons can be taught to read the dots with their fingertips.

cataract   A reduction or loss of vision that occurs when the crystalline lens of the eye becomes cloudy or opaque.

catheter   A tube inserted into a body to permit injections or withdrawal of fluids or to keep a passageway open; often refers to a tube inserted into the bladder to remove urine from a person who does not have effective bladder control.

cerebral palsy   Motor impairment caused by brain damage, which is usually inflicted during the prenatal period or during the birth process. Can involve a wide variety of symptoms (see *ataxia, athetosis, rigidity, spasticity,* and *tremor*) and range from mild to severe. Neither curable nor progressive.

cleft palate   A congenital split in the palate that results in an excessive nasal quality of the voice. Can often be repaired by surgery or dental appliance.

communication   The process by which individuals interact to, transmit, and receive messages by any means, including sounds, symbols, gestures, and others.

conduct disorder   A group of behavior disorders including disobedience, disruptiveness, fighting, and tantrums, as identified by Quay (1975).

conductive hearing loss   Hearing loss caused by obstructions in the outer or middle ear or malformations that interfere with the conduction of sound waves to the inner ear. Can often be corrected surgically or medically.

congenital   Any condition which is present at birth. Contrasts with *adventitious* handicap.

cornea   The transparent part of the eyeball that admits light to the interior.

cultural-familial mental retardation   Any case of mental retardation for which an organic cause cannot be found; suggests that retardation can be caused by a poor social and cultural environment.

cystic fibrosis   An inherited disorder that causes a dysfunction of the pancreas, mucus, salivary, and sweat glands. Cystic fibrosis causes severe, long-term respiratory difficulties. No cure is currently available.

deafness   A condition of being unable to use hearing to understand speech, even with a hearing aid.

decibel   The unit used to describe the relative intensity of sound on a scale beginning at zero. Zero decibels refer to the faintest sound a person with normal hearing can detect.

deinstitutionalization   The entire social movement to return handicapped persons, especially mentally retarded individuals, from large institutions to smaller, community-based residences and work settings.

diabetes   See *juvenile diabetes mellitus.*

diabetic retinopathy   Type of vision impairment caused by hemorrhages on the retina and other disorders of blood circulation in people with diabetes.

dialect   A variety within a specific language; can involve variation in pronunciation, word choice, word order, and inflected forms.

differential reinforcement of other behavior (DRO)   A behavior modification technique in which any behavior the student does except the targeted maladaptive response is reinforced; results in a reduction of the inappropriate behavior. DRO is used to strengthen any other responses that are incompatible (that is, cannot be performed at the same time) with the target behavior. For example, DRO might be used with a child who exhibits a very high rate of head banging; any response other than head banging would be reinforced.

diplegia   Paralysis that affects either both arms or both legs.

disability   A physical problem that limits a person's ability to perform certain tasks.

Down syndrome   A chromosomal anomaly that often causes moderate to severe mental retardation, along with certain physical characteristics such as a large tongue, heart problems, poor muscle tone, and broad, flat bridge of the nose. Formerly called *mongolism,* it occurs in all racial groups.

due process   Set of legal steps and proceedings carried out according to established rules and principles; designed to protect an individual's constitutional and legal rights.

duration (of behavior)   Measure of how long a person engages in a given activity (e.g., the duration of Susan's tantrum was 12 minutes).

dyslexia   A disturbance in the ability to read or learn to read.

echolalia   The repetition of what other people say as if echoing them; characteristic of some children with delayed development, severe behavior disorders, and communication disorders.

electroencephalograph (EEG)   Device which detects and records brain wave patterns.

enrichment   Educational approach that involves providing a child with extra learning experiences which the standard curriculum would not normally include. Most often used with gifted and talented children.

epilepsy   Convulsive disorder that causes sudden seizures (see *grand mal seizure, psychomotor seizure,* and *petit mal seizure*); can usually be controlled with medication, though the drugs may have undesirable side effects; may be temporary or life-long.

etiology   The cause(s) of an abnormal condition or disease. Includes genetic, physiological, and environmental or psychological factors.

evoked-response audiometry   A method of testing hearing by measuring the electrical activity generated by the auditory nerve, in response to auditory stimulation. Often used to measure the hearing of infants and children who are considered difficult to test.

exceptional children   Children whose performance deviates from the norm, either below or above, to the extent that special educational programming is needed.

extinction   Behavior modification procedure in which reinforcement for a previously reinforced behavior is withheld. For example, a teacher now ignores a child's disruptive behavior instead of "scolding." If the actual reinforcers that are maintaining the behavior are identified and withheld, the behavior will gradually decrease in rate until it no longer, or seldom, occurs.

fetal alcohol syndrome   A condition sometimes found in the infants of alcoholic mothers; can involve low birth weight, severe retardation, and cardiac, limb, and other physical defects.

field of vision   The expanse of space visible with both eyes while looking straight ahead; measured in degrees; 180° is considered normal.

fluency   The rate and smoothness with which a movement is made. In communication, the rate and ease of speech; the most common speech fluency disorder is stuttering.

foster home   A living arrangement where a family opens up their home to a person who is not a relative. Long used with children who for some reason cannot temporarily live with their parents, foster homes are now being used with retarded adults as well.

generalization   Performing a behavior under conditions other than the conditions under which the behavior was originally learned. Stimulus generalization occurs when a person performs a behavior in the presence of relevant stimuli (people, settings, instructional materials) other than the stimuli which were present originally. For instance, stimulus generalization occurs when a child who has learned to label baseballs and beach balls as "ball" identifies a basketball as a "ball." Response generalization occurs when a person performs relevant behaviors that were never directly trained but are similar to the original trained behavior. For example, a child is taught to say "Hello, how are you?" and "Hi, nice to see you" as greetings. If the child combines the two to say "Hi, how are you?" response generalization has taken place.

genetic counseling   A discussion between a specially trained medical counselor and people who are considering having a child, about the chances of having a handicapped child, based on the parents' genetic backgrounds.

glaucoma   An eye disease characterized by abnormally high pressure inside the eyeball. If left untreated, it can cause total blindness, but most cases detected early enough can be arrested.

grand mal seizure   The most severe type of epileptic seizure, in which the individual has violent convulsions, loses consciousness, and becomes rigid.

group home   A residential arrangement for handicapped adults, especially the mentally retarded, where several residents live together in a house with nonhandicapped supervisors. The residents usually have outside jobs.

handicap   The problems a person encounters because of a physical disability or behavioral characteristics considered unusual by society.

handicapism   Prejudice or discrimination against people solely on the basis of their disability, rather than their individual characteristics.

hard of hearing   Describes hearing loss that makes it difficult, though not impossible, to comprehend speech through the sense of hearing alone.

hearing impaired   Anyone who has a hearing loss significant enough to require special education, training, and/or adaptations; includes both deaf and hard-of-hearing.

hemiplegia   Paralysis of both the arm and the leg on the same side of the body (e.g., right arm and right leg are affected).

hemophilia   An inherited deficiency in blood-clotting ability which can cause serious internal bleeding.

hertz (Hz)   A unit of sound frequency equal to one cycle per second; used to measure pitch.

homophonous   Two or more words that sound different but look alike on the lips, making distinguishing them through speech reading difficult.

hydrocephalus   Condition present at birth or developing soon afterwards; involves an enlarged head caused by cerebral spinal fluid accumulated in the cranial cavity; often causes brain damage and severe retardation.

hyperactive behavior   Excessive motor activity or restlessness.

hyperopia   Farsightedness; condition in which the image comes to a focus behind the retina instead of on it, causing difficulty with seeing near objects.

immaturity   Group of behavior disorders, including short attention span, extreme passivity, daydreaming, preference for younger playmates, and clumsiness, as identified by Quay (1975).

incidence   The percentage of people who, at some time in their lives, will be identified as having a specific condition. Sometimes reported as the number of births per 1,000 with a given condition.

individualized education program (IEP) Written document required by federal law to detail the year's plan for every handicapped child; includes statements of present performance, annual goals, short-term instructional objectives, specific educational services needed, relevant dates, regular education program participation, and evaluation procedures; must be signed by parents as well as educational personnel.

inflection Change in pitch or loudness of the voice to indicate mood or emphasis.

inservice training Any educational program designed to provide practicing professionals (such as teachers, administrators, or physical therapists) with additional knowledge and skills.

interindividual difference Differences between two or more people on one skill or set of skills.

intervention All the efforts made on behalf of handicapped children and adults; may be preventive, remedial, or compensatory.

intraindividual difference Differences within one individual on two or more measures of performance.

iris The opaque, colored portion of the eye that contracts and expands to change the size of the pupil.

juvenile diabetes mellitus A children's disease characterized by inadequate secretion or use of insulin and the resulting excessive sugar in the blood and urine. Controlled with diet and/or medication, but can be difficult to control. Can cause coma and eventually death if left untreated or treated improperly. Can also lead to visual impairments and limb amputation. Not curable at the present time.

language A system of vocal symbols (sounds) that give a group of people who understand the language a way to communicate. Nonverbal languages, such as American Sign Language, use movements and physical symbols instead of sounds.

least restrictive environment For any child, the educational setting in which he or she can succeed which is most like the regular classroom.

lens The clear part of the eye that focuses rays of light upon the retina.

locomotion The act of moving from place to place.

longitudinal study A research study that follows one subject or a group of subjects over an extended period of time, usually for several years.

low incidence disability A disability that occurs relatively infrequently in the general population; in particular, used to refer to vision and haring impairments, severe mental retardation, severe behavior disorders such as autism, and multiple handicaps.

low-vision (child) A child with vision so limited that special educational services are required, but who is able to learn through the visual channel.

macular degeneration A deterioration of the central part of the retina, which causes difficulty in seeing details clearly.

magnitude (of behavior) The force with which a response is emitted.

mainstreaming Refers to the return to the regular classroom, for all or part of the school day, of exceptional children previously educated exclusively in segregated (self-contained) settings.

meningitis An inflammation of the membranes covering the brain and spinal cord; can cause problems with sight and hearing and/or mental retardation.

meningocele Type of spina bifida in which the covering of the spinal cord protrudes through an opening in the vertebrae, but the cord itself and the nerve roots are enclosed.

mental retardation Refers to significantly subaverage general intellectual functioning existing concurrently with deficits in adaptive behavior, and manifested during the developmental period (Grossman, 1973, p. 5).

microcephalus A condition characterized by an abnormally small skull with resulting brain damage and mental retardation.

minimal brain dysfunction A once-popular term used to refer to learning disabled children with no actual (clinical) evidence of brain damage.

mobility The ability to move safely and efficiently from one point to another.

model program A program which implements and evaluates new procedures or techniques in order to serve as a basis for developing other similar programs.

monoplegia Paralysis affecting one limb.

morpheme The smallest element of a language that carries meaning.

multifactored testing Assessment and evaluation of a handicapped child with a variety of test instruments and observation procedures; required by P.L. 94–142 when assessment is for purposes of educational placement of a child who is to receive special education services; helps prevent the possibility of misdiagnosing and misplacing a student as the result of only one test score.

muscular dystrophy A group of diseases that gradually weaken muscle tissue, usually becoming evident by age 4 or 5.

myelomeningocele A protrusion on the back of a child with spina bifida, consisting of a sac of nerve tissue bulging through a cleft in the spine.

myopia Nearsightedness; results when light is focused on a point in front of the retina, resulting in a blurred image for distance objects.

neurological impairment Any physical disability caused by damage to the central nervous system (brain, spinal cord, ganglia, and nerves).

normal curve A mathematically derived curve depicting the probability or distribution of a given variable (such as a physical trait or test score) in the general population. Indicates that approximately 68.26% of the population will fall within one standard deviation above and below the mean; approximately 13.59% will fall between one and two standard deviations above the mean and another 13.59% between one and two standard deviations below the mean; and less than 3% will achieve more extreme scores of more than two standard deviations in each direction.

normalization The principle of allowing each handicapped person's life to be as "normal" as possible in all aspects, including residence, schooling, or work, recreational activities, and overall independence. Similarities between handicapped and nonhandicapped people of the same age are emphasized.

nystagmus A rapid, involuntary, rhythmic movement of the eyes that may cause difficulty in reading or fixating any objects.

occupational therapist A professional who programs and/or delivers instructional activities and materials to help handicapped children and adults learn to participate in useful activities.

ocular motility The eye's ability to move.

operant audiometry Method of measuring hearing by conditioning the subject to make an observable response to sound. For example, a child may be taught to drop a block into a box each time she hears a tone from the audiometer. Once this response is conditioned, the volume and pitch of the tone can gradually be decreased. When the child no longer drops the block into the box, the audiologist knows the child cannot hear the tone. The procedure is used to test the hearing of nonverbal children and adults.

optic nerve   The nerve which carries impulses from the eye to the brain.

oral (approach to education of deaf children)   An approach to education of deaf children which stresses learning to speak as the essential element to integration into the "hearing world."

orientation   The ability to establish one's position in relation to the environment.

orthopedic impairment   Any disability caused by disorders to the musculoskeletal system.

ostenogenesis imperfecta   A hereditary condition in which the bones do not grow normally and break easily; sometimes called "brittle bones."

otitis media   An infection or inflammation of the middle ear which can cause a conductive hearing loss.

overcorrection   A behavior modification procedure in which the learner is made to make restitution, or repair, the effects of his or her undesirable behavior, then leave the environment in even better shape. For example, the child who doesn't put away his art supplies must clean up the entire art area. Used to decrease the rate of undesirable behaviors.

paraplegia   Paralysis of the lower part of the body, including both legs; usually results from injury to or disease of the spinal cord.

paraprofessionals (in education)   Trained classroom aides who assist teachers; may include parents.

perceptual handicap   Term formerly used to describe some conditions now included under *learning disability;* usually used with problems with no known physical cause.

perinatal   Occurring at or immediately after birth.

peripheral vision   Vision at the outer limits of the field of vision.

personality disorder   A group of behavior disorders, including social withdrawal, anxiety, depression, feelings of inferiority, guilt, shyness, and unhappiness, as identified by Quay (1975).

petit mal seizure   A type of epileptic seizure in which the individual loses consciousness, usually for less than half a minute; may occur very frequently in some children.

phenylketonuria (PKU)   An inherited metabolic disease which can cause severe retardation; can now be detected at birth and the detrimental effects prevented with a special diet.

phonemes   The smallest unit of sound that can be identified in a spoken language. There are 36 phonemes, or sound families, in the English language.

photophobia   Extreme sensitivity of the eyes to light; occurs most notably in albino children.

physical therapist   A professional trained to help handicapped persons maintain and develop muscular and orthopedic capability and to make correct and useful movements.

positive reinforcement   Any stimulus or event which occurs after a behavior has been emitted that has the effect of increasing the occurrence of that behavior in the future.

postlingual   Occurring after the development of language; usually used to classify hearing losses that begin after the person has learned to speak.

postlingual hearing impairment   A hearing impairment that develops after a person has developed speech and language.

postnatal   Occurring after birth.

precision teaching   An approach to instruction involving pinpointing the behaviors to be changed; measuring the initial frequency of those behaviors; setting an "aim," or goal, for the child's improvement; direct, daily measurement of progress made under an instructional program; graphing results of those measurements; and changing the program if the child is not progressing toward his aim.

prelingual hearing impairment   A hearing impairment that develops before a child has developed speech and language.

prenatal   Occurring before birth.

prevalence   The number of people who have a certain condition at any given time.

projective tests   Psychological tests which require a person to respond to a standardized task or set of stimuli (e.g., draw a picture or interpret an ink blot); those responses are thought to be a "projection" of the test-taker's personality and are scored according to the given test's scoring manual to produce a personality profile.

prosthesis   Any device used to replace a missing body part.

psychomotor seizure   A type of epileptic seizure in which the individual goes through a period of inappropriate activity of which he is not aware.

psychotic   A severely behavior disordered person.

pupil   The circular hole in the center of the iris of the eye, which contracts and expands to let light through.

quadriplegia   Paralysis of all four limbs.

rate (of behavior)   A measure of how often a particular action is performed; usually reported as the average number of responses per minute."

refraction   The "bending" or deflection of light rays from a straight path as they pass from one medium (e.g., air) into another (e.g., the eye). Used by eye specialists in assessing and correcting vision.

rehabilitation   A social service program designed to teach a newly handicapped person basic skills needed for independence.

reinforcement   See *positive reinforcement.*

remediation   An educational program designed to teach a person to overcome a handicap through training and education.

residual hearing   The remaining hearing, however slight, of a hearing impaired person.

resource room   Classroom in which certain students spend part of the school day and receive individualized special education services.

retina   A sheet of nerve tissue at the back of the eye on which the image is focused.

retinitis pigmentosa   An eye disease in which the retina gradually degenerates and atrophies, causing the field of vision to get progressively narrower.

retrolental fibroplasia (RLF)   A condition characterized by abnormally dense growth of blood vessels and scar tissue in the eye, often causing total blindness.

rigidity   Type of cerebral palsy characterized by increased muscle tone, minimal muscle elasticity, and little or no stretch reflex.

rubella German measles; when contracted by a woman during the first trimester of pregnancy, may cause visual impairments, hearing impairments, mental retardation, and/or other birth defects, in her child.

schizophrenic A severe behavior disorder characterized by loss of contact with one's surroundings and inappropriate affect and actions.

screening A procedure where groups of children are examined and/or tested in an effort to identify "high-risk" children; identified children are then referred for more intensive examination and evaluation.

self-contained class Special classroom, usually located within regular public school building, which includes only exceptional children.

semantics The study of meaning in language.

sensorineural hearing loss A hearing loss caused by damage to the auditory nerve or the inner ear.

sheltered workshop A work environment in which handicapped persons who cannot, or who are preparing for, work in a competitive setting can perform meaningful, productive work and receive payment; may be transitional (preparing handicapped workers for competitive employment in the community) and/or long term. Most sheltered workshops also provide training programs for job-related skills, e.g., budgeting and being on time.

shunt Tube inserted in the body to drain fluid from one body part to another; often implanted in people with hydrocephalus to remove extra cerebrospinal fluid from the head and send it directly into the heart or intestines.

social validity Desirable characteristic of the objectives, procedures, and results of instruction. For example, the goal of riding a bus independently would have social validity for learners residing in most cities, but not for those in small towns or rural areas.

socialized delinquency A group of behavior disorders, including truancy, gang membership, theft, and delinquency, as identified by Quay (1975)

spasticity A type of cerebral palsy characterized by tense, contracted muscles.

special education The individually planned and systematically monitored arrangement of physical settings, special equipment and materials, teaching procedures, and other interventions designed to help exceptional children achieve the greatest possible personal self-sufficiency and academic success.

speech A system of using breath and muscles to create specific sounds for communicating.

spina bifida A congenital malformation of the spine in which the vertebrae that normally protect the spine do not develop fully; may involve loss of sensation and severe muscle weakness in the lower part of the body.

spina bifida occulta Type of spina bifida which usually does not cause serious disability. Although the vertebrae do not close, there is no protrusion of the spinal cord and membranes.

standard deviation A unit used to measure the amount by which a particular score varies from the mean with respect to all the scores in the norm sample.

stereotype An overgeneralized or inaccurate attitude held toward all members of a particular group, on the basis of common characteristics such as age, sex, race, or disability.

stereotypic behavior Repetitive and nonfunctional movements (e.g., hand flapping, rocking), characteristic of autism.

stuttering A complex disorder of fluency of speech, affecting the smooth flow of words; may involve repetition of sounds or words, prolonged sounds, facial grimaces, muscle tension, and other physical behaviors.

strabismus Condition in which one eye cannot attain binocular vision with the other eye because of imbalanced muscles.

syntax The system of rules governing the meaningful arrangement of words in a language.

therapeutic abortion Deliberate termination of a pregnancy because the fetus is known or suspected to be defective or because of a threat to the mother's life.

therapeutic recreation A process which utilizes recreation services for purposive intervention in some physical, emotional, and/or social behavior to bring about a desired change in that behavior and to promote the growth and development of the individual.

time-out A behavior management technique which involves removing the opportunity for the child to be reinforced for a specific period of time following an inappropriate behavior; results in a reduction of the inappropriate behavior.

token economy System of reinforcing various behaviors by delivering tokens (e.g., stars, points, poker chips) when the specified behaviors are emitted. Tokens are accumulated and turned in for the child's choice of items on a "menu" of back-up reinforcers (e.g., a sticker, hall monitor for a day).

topography (of behavior) The physical shape or form of a response.

total communication An approach to education of deaf students which combines oral speech, sign language, and finger spelling.

tremor Type of cerebral palsy characterized by regular, strong, uncontrolled movements. May cause less overall difficulty in movement than other cerebral palsy types.

triplegia Paralysis of any three limbs (e.g., two arms and one leg); relatively rare.

Usher's syndrome An inherited combination of visual and hearing impairments. Usually, the person is born with a profound hearing loss and loses vision gradually in adulthood because of retinitis pigmentosa (which affects the visual field).

visual acuity The ability to clearly distinguish forms or discriminate details at a specified distance.

vitreous humor The jelly-like fluid which fills most of the interior of the eyeball.

vocational rehabilitation A program designed to help the handicapped adult obtain and hold a job.

work activity center A sheltered work and activity program for severely disabled persons where they are taught concentration and persistence, along with basic life skills, for a small amount of pay.

NAME INDEX

Fitzgerald, E., 254
Fleischauer, P. D., 474
Flexer, R. W., 14
Florance, C. L., 216, 227
Flygare, T. J., 40
Ford, A., 340, 341
Ford, G. R., 57
Ford, R., 102
Forehand, R., 450
Forness, S. R., 8, 66, 157, 211, 240, 312
Forrester, D. J., 401
Foster, G. E., 134
Foster, M., 457
Foster, R., 77, 79
Fox, L. H., 382, 388
Foxx, R. M., 351, 377
Frank, A. R., 106
Frazier, 374
Freagon, S., 340
Fredericks, H. D., 363
Freedman, R., 498
Freehill, M. F., 395
Freeman, G. G., 226
French, R. W., 321
Frey, R., 67
Friedman, P. R., 100
Frierson, E. C., 377, 389
Frodyma, D., 210, 217
Froehlinger, V. J., 256
Frostig, M., 127, 128, 133
Furth, H. G., 228
Fusfeld, I. S., 248

Gallagher, J. J., 114, 205, 369, 371, 377, 382, 388, 395
Gallimore, R., 408
Galton, F., 375
Garber, H., 465, 466
Garcia, R. L., 399
Gardner, E., 126
Gardner, W. I., 63
Gary, A. L., 372
Gates, A. T., 126
Gear, G. H., 390
Gearheart, B. R., 67, 118, 141, 149
Gearheart, C. K., 118, 141, 149
Gelof, M., 81
Genensky, S. M., 474
Gibbs, H., 445
Gilhool, T. K., 35
Glavin, J. P., 164
Glenn, L., 500
Glover, J., 372
Goddard, H. H., 375
Goetz, E. M., 372
Gold, M., 80, 81, 95, 330, 349
Goldstein, S., 445, 446
Gollay, E., 498
Gollnick, D. M., 424

Gonzales, R., 238
Goodall, P., 350
Goodenough, F. L., 182
Goodman, L., 133
Goodman, L. V., 35, 57
Gordon, T., 452
Gottlieb, J., 93, 403
Gowan, J. C., 372
Goyette, C., 123
Gradel, R., 471
Graden, J., 143
Gray, S. W., 401
Gray, W. S., 126
Greer, J. G., 334
Grekin, R., 123
Gresham, F. M., 43
Griffin, B. F., 264
Groht, M. A., 254
Grossman, H. J., 70, 76, 77, 78, 443
Grove, N. M., 311
Guess, P. D., 329, 331, 348, 355
Guilford, J. P., 372, 377, 383, 384
Guralnick, M. J., 463
Gurcsick, B., 384
Gustason, G., 253

Haase, B., 117
Hagen, 374
Hagmeier, L. D., 349
Hall, E. T., 411
Hall, M. C., 452
Hall, R. V., 450, 452
Hallahan, D. P., 113, 119, 149
Halle, J. W., 474
Hammer, E. K., 50
Hammill, D. D., 116, 118, 119, 125, 128, 133, 134, 138, 143, 149
Hanley, C. D., 317
Hansen, C. L., 132, 139, 512
Hansen, F. O., 438
Hansen, R., 391
Harig, P. T., 185
Haring, N. G., 63, 131, 132, 136, 328, 331, 343, 345, 347
Harper, R. S., 92
Harris, D. B., 182
Harris, G., 137, 457
Harris, M. C., 503
Harris, S. L., 173
Hart, B., 482
Hasset, M. E., 459
Hatlen, P. H., 284
Hatten, J. T., 219
Hatten, P. W., 219
Hauck, B. B., 395
Hauy, V., 275
Hawkins, K. K., 450
Hawkins, R. P., 356, 450
Hawks, W., 123
Hawthorne, N. Y., 169

Haycock, G. S., 206
Hayden, A. H., 14, 52, 345, 466, 473, 474, 475, 494
Haywood, H. C., 86
Head, S., 184
Heber, R., 465, 466
Hechinger, F. M., 58
Heifetz, L. J., 452
Heim, K. M., 161
Heller, G., 141
Hemming, H., 89
Heron, T. E., 43, 45, 46, 47, 61, 93, 137, 357, 443, 451, 459
Heston, L. L., 179
Heward, W. L., 23, 49, 61, 93, 145, 146, 163, 170, 180, 185, 186, 187, 357, 426, 433, 438, 439, 441, 443, 444, 446, 450, 451, 452, 457, 459, 461, 477
Hewett, F. M., 8, 66, 152, 153, 155, 157, 158, 160, 195, 211, 240, 312
Hieronymus, A. N., 126
Hill, D. S., 357, 459
Hill, J. W., 350
Hill, M., 350
Hilliard, A. G., III, 403
Hingtgen, J. N., 160
Hirschberg, G., 322
Hitzing, W., 506
Hoagland, C., 145
Hobbs, N., 10, 185, 190, 191, 195
Hoben, M., 295
Hochman, R., 137, 140, 438, 440
Hodgins, A. S., 433
Hoemann, H. W., 229, 233, 237, 249
Hogan, T. P., 135
Holland, A. L., 211
Hollingsworth, L. S., 369, 376
Holm, V., 471
Holvoet, J., 318
Hops, H., 164, 183, 184
Horne, D., 133
Horst, G., 350
Hovell, M. F., 430, 440, 442
Howe, S. G., 67, 68, 335
Howell, K., 63, 129
Hubbard, M., 241
Hull, F. M., 205
Humphreys, R. P., 510
Hunt, F. M., 10
Hurley, O. L., 480, 481

Imber, R. B., 440
Imber, S. C., 440
Ireland, W. W., 69
Iscoe, I., 11
Itard, J. M. G., 67, 68, 94, 335
Ivancic, M. T., 95, 97, 98, 99
Iwata, B. A., 95, 97, 98, 99

SUBJECT INDEX

Association for Retarded Citizens, 111, 430
Association for the Gifted, 395
Association for the Severely Handicapped, The (TASH), 85, 336, 363
Association on Handicapped Student Service Programs in Post-secondary Education, 523
Astigmatism, 271
Ataxia, 300, 301
Athetosis, 300–301
Attention, disorders of, 120
Audiograms, 234, 236, 237, 238, 239
Audiologists, 473, 487
Audiology, 233, 234
Auditory training, 245–247
Augmentative communication systems, 221–223
Autism, 153, 179
Autistic children, 153, 159, 160, 161, 172–176, 177, 178

Barnes v. *Converse College*, 257
Baseline, 176, 177, 178, 186, 187
Bayley Scales of Infant Development, 471
BEH (*see* Bureau of Education for the Handicapped)
Behavior disordered adults, 168
Behavior disordered children
    behavior changes in, 183, 184, 189–190
    characteristics of, 161, 164–173, 176
    educational approaches for, 183–185, 190–192
    home behavior change programs for, 162–163
    self-management skills of, 185–188
    standardized intelligence test scores of, 164–165
    teaching skills for, 188–190
Behavior disorders
    acting-out behavior, 164–165
    aggressive behavior, 165–168
    autism, 153, 159, 160, 161, 172–176, 177, 178
    causes of, 176, 179–181
    classification of, 155–159
    clustering of, 155, 156
    definitions of, 151–155
    duration of, 154–155
    elective mutism, 170–172
    identification and assessment of, 181–183, 184
    magnitude of, 154, 155
    prevalence of, 159–161
    prevention of, 180–181
    rate of, 154

topography of, 154, 155
    withdrawn behavior, 168–172
Behavior modification (*see* Applied behavior analysis)
Behavior shaping, 218
Behavioral contracts, 441
Behavioral observation, 214
Bilingual instruction, 414
Binocular vision, 268
Biochemical imbalances, 122–124
Biomedical impairments, 80
Black children, 411–413
Blindness, 266–267 (*see also* Visual impairments)
Bloom's Taxonomy of Educational Objectives, 382–383
Boy Scouts of America, 13
Braille, 267, 277–279
Brain damage, 113, 114, 118, 119, 120–121, 299–302, 304–305, 306 (*see also* Learning disabilities)
Brain dysfunctions, 113, 114, 118, 121, 306 (*see also* Brain damage)
Brazelton Neonatal Assessment Scale, 471
Brown v. *Board of Education of Topeka*, 27, 28
Bureau of Education for the Handicapped (BEH, 28, 476–480
Burns, 309

CA (*see* Chronological age)
Canadian National Institute for the Blind, 283, 296
Carrow Elicited Language Inventory, 214
Cataracts, 271–272
CEC (*see* Council for Exceptional Children)
Center-based programs, 478–479
Central nervous system dysfunctions, 118, 119 (*see also* Brain damage)
Central York District v. *Commonwealth of Pennsylvania Department of Education*, 28
Cerebral palsy, 205, 240, 299–301, 311
Chronological age (CA), 115
Civil Rights Act of *1964*, 41
Civil rights movement, 12, 27
Civil rights of exceptional children, 12, 26, 100–101
    court cases regarding, 28, 33, 35
    due process, 29–30, 33, 34
    equal protection, 27, 29
    legislation regarding, 11–12, 28–29, 35–42
Classroom environments, 189
CLD (*see* Council for Learning

Disabilities)
Cleft palate, 205
Clinical Evaluation of Language Functions, 214
Closed circuit television systems, 282
Closer Look, 34, 461
Cognitive-affective model, 384–385
Cognitive development, 473
Communication, definition of, 197
Communications disorders
    articulation disorders, 204–205, 206–208, 213, 215
    assessment and evaluation of, 212, 214
    environmental influences on, 210
    fluency disorders, 208–210, 216
    history of, 211–212
    language disorders, 203–204, 210–211, 216–218
    prevalence of, 204–205
    specialists working with, 211, 218–220, 473
    speech impairments, 6, 202–203
    stuttering, 201, 205, 209–210, 216
    technological aids for, 220, 221–223
    treatment and remediation of, 214–219
    types and causes, 205–211
    voice disorders, 205, 208, 215–216
Communicative interaction model, 482, 483
Community attitudes toward the handicapped, 526–527
Computer-based communications systems, 220, 221–223
Congenital disorders, 211
Consultant teachers, 136–137
Coordination deficits, 120
Council for Children with Behavior Disorders, 196
Council for Exceptional Children, 23, 113, 424
    Division for Children with Communication Disorders (DCCD), 118, 227
    Division for Children with Learning Disabilities (DCLD), 150
    Division for Early Childhood (DEC), 494
    Division for the Visually Handicapped (DVH), 296
    Division on Career Development (DCD), 523
    Division on Mental Retardation (DMR), 111
Council for Learning Disabilities (CLD), 113, 118
Cranmer Abacus, 279
Creativity, 372–373
Criterion-referenced tests, 75, 128, 129

THE AUTHORS

William Lee Heward *(right)* grew up in Three Oaks, Michigan. He earned a bachelor's degree in psychology and sociology at Western Michigan University and a doctorate in special education at the University of Massachusetts.

Bill has had a variety of experiences as a teacher and administrator in educational programs serving children with learning and behavior disorders. He is currently a professor in the Department of Human Services Education at The Ohio State University. His current research interests include the design and analysis of systems for group instruction and working with parents and families of exceptional children.

In addition to his publications in many professional journals, Bill has co-authored the textbook *Working with Parents of Handi-*

capped Children (Merrill, 1979), and *Sign Here: A Contracting Book for Children and Their Parents,* and has served as co-editor of *Focus on Behavior Analysis in Education* (Merrill, 1984). Bill has also written for the trade market. His popular book *Some Are Called Clowns* chronicled his five summers as a pitcher with the Indianapolis Clowns, the last of the "barnstorming" baseball teams. Bill keeps up his interest in baseball by serving as pitching coach for a nearby college team.

Michael Dean Orlansky *(left)* was born in Philadelphia and raised in New York City. He received a bachelor's degree from Yale University and a master of education degree from Boston College, specializing in the education of deaf-blind and multihandicapped children. At the University of Idaho, Mike's doctoral dissertation research concerned the effects of different instructional techniques on the achievement and attitudes of college students in an introductory special educational course.

Mike taught severely handicapped children for several years and later was involved in coordinating educational, diagnostic, and in-service training programs. He served as an education and training specialist in the U.S. Air Force. He was a faculty member at the University of Virginia for 5 years, and is now an associate professor in the Department of Human Services Education at The Ohio State University. Mike was recently a Fulbright Scholar in special education at the University of Zagreb, Yugoslavia.

Mike's current research interests include communicative development, attitudes, cultural diversity, and multiple disabilities. Among his publications are two other books, *Mainstreaming the Visually Impaired Child* and *Voices: Interviews with Handicapped People* (Merrill, 1981), co-authored with Bill Heward.